Early Christianity
and the Roman Empire

Professor T. D. Barnes

T. D. Barnes

Early Christianity
and the Roman Empire

VARIORUM REPRINTS
London 1984

Copyright © 1984 by   Variorum Reprints

Published in Great Britain by   **VARIORUM**
                                 Ashgate Publishing Limited
                                 Gower House
                                 Croft Road,
                                 Aldershot, Hampshire GU11 3HR

                                 Ashgate Publishing Company
                                 Old Post Road
                                 Brookfield, Vermont 05036
                                 U S A

                                 Reprinted 1998

British Library CIP Data   Barnes, Timothy D.
                                   Early Christianity and the Roman Empire
                                   —(Collected studies series; CS270)
                                   1. Church history—Primitive and early
                                   church, ca 30-600   2. Rome —History—
                                   Empire, 30 B.C. – 476 A.D.
                                   I. Title
                                   270.1   BR170

                                 ISBN 0-86078-155-0

                                 This book is printed on acid free paper

Printed in Great Britain by   Biddles Short Run Books
                                 King's Lynn

                                 VARIORUM REPRINT CS207

CONTENTS

viii

This volume contains a total of 314 pages.

PREFACE

I began research into the history of the Roman Empire in the second and third centuries in 1964, wrote my first article in 1966 and saw it published in 1967. Since then I have probably occupied more than my fair share of the space available in learned journals consecrated to the study of Greek and Roman antiquity, besides writing four books. It might be asked, therefore, whether the present collection of reprinted articles is needed. In answer, I am tempted to quote the dictum of a Toronto colleague, unfortunately now deceased: "Students only believe what they read in books, not what they read in articles." The present volume will be useful (I hope) in collecting together studies intimately connected with the composition of *Tertullian. A Historical and Literary Study* (1971), *The Sources of the Historia Augusta* (1978), *Constantine and Eusebius* (1981), and *The New Empire of Diocletian and Constantine* (1982). It contains articles which are used in, but not superseded by, those books, and excludes articles whose material is there reworked afresh. Hence a volume devoted to the two topics which were the twin foci of my research between 1964 and 1979 — Christianity in the pagan Roman Empire, and the history and culture of that empire from Trajan to Constantine.

Two negative criteria have also guided the selection of articles reprinted. Very short pieces are omitted, and I have excluded articles where too much now strikes me as imperfect to justify republication in full. Their exclusion also removes any temptation to attempt to bring articles written many years ago up to date, or to remove obvious flaws by means of addenda and corrigenda. A certain number of misprints have been corrected, but otherwise the original texts are reproduced without alteration.

For kind permission to reproduce the twenty articles reprinted in the present volume, I am most grateful to the following: Oxford University Press (I, III, VIII, XIX); the Society for the Promotion of Roman Studies (II, VI, IX); Dr. Rudolf Habelt GmbH (IV, V); the Classical Association of Canada (VII, XII);

the Johns Hopkins University Press (X); Duke University Press (XI, XVI, XVII, XX); the University of Chicago Press (XIII, XV); Akademie-Verlag, Berlin (XIV); and Professor Ernst Badian (XVIII).

T. D. BARNES

Oxford
13 March 1984

PUBLISHER'S NOTE

The articles in this volume, as in all others in the Collected Studies Series, have not been given a new, continuous pagination. In order to avoid confusion, and to facilitate their use where these same studies have been referred to elsewhere, the original pagination has been maintained wherever possible.

Each article has been given a Roman number in order of appearance, as listed in the Contents. This number is repeated on each page and quoted in the index entries.

PRE-DECIAN *ACTA MARTYRUM*[1]

THE legal basis of the persecutions of the Christians in the Roman Empire before 250 has long been debated without any universal agreement on fundamentals. Yet the problems are perhaps soluble if the status and reliability of all the relevant evidence is clearly defined.[2] Since an important part of the evidence consists of accounts of how Christians were actually tried, a preliminary study is requisite: how far are these accounts, the *acta martyrum*, to be regarded as either contemporary or accurate records? Of the vast mass of hagiographical literature preserved from late antiquity the greater part has no relevance to the realities of early Christian history. Comparison of the *Acta Sanctorum* and the Bollandist *Bibliotheca Hagiographica* with the successive prunings in T. Ruinart's *Acta Primorum Martyrum Sincera et Selecta* (first published in 1689) and in any modern collection will show how much has rightly been discarded.[3] But has the process of rejection gone far enough? It is the purpose of this survey to consider the date of composition and the reliability of those nine pre-Decian *acta martyrum* which are commonly assumed to be wholly accurate or wholly contemporary reports.

Many other *acta* may contain something of value or be based on historical fact.[4] But no more than nine from the period before Decius have been accepted as wholly authentic by competent scholars of the present century. These nine appear in the collection of R. Knopf and G. Krüger, *Ausgewählte Märtyrerakten* (3rd ed., 1929; 4th ed.—a photographic reprint of the 3rd, with corrections, additions, and a supplementary bibliography—by G. Ruhbach, 1965), are admitted by B. Altaner and A. Stuiber, *Patrologie*[7] (1966), pp. 91 f., and were (with one exception) championed by H. Delehaye, *Les Passions des martyrs et les*

[1] I am grateful for discussion with Professors H. Chadwick and G. D. Kilpatrick, Dr. F. G. B. Millar, and Mr. G. E. M. de Ste Croix, all of whom have made very helpful suggestions.

[2] T. D. Barnes, 'Legislation against the Christians', to appear in *J.R.S.* lviii (1968).

[3] Contrast E. Le Blant, 'Les actes des martyrs (supplément aux *Acta sincera* de Dom Ruinart)', *Mém. de l'Inst. de France* (*Acad. des Inscr.*), xxx. 2 (1883), p. 57. His attempt to reverse the process stands, however, in virtual isolation.

[4] See, e.g., K. J. Neumann, *Der römische Staat und die allgemeine Kirche bis auf Diocletian*, i (1890), pp. 274 ff.; K. Bihlmeyer, *Die 'syrischen' Kaiser zu Rom (211–35) und das Christentum* (1916), pp. 157 ff.; H. Delehaye, 'Les actes de saint Timothée', *Anatolian Studies presented to W. H. Buckler* (1939), p. 77, reprinted in *Mélanges d'hagiographie grecque et latine* (*Subsidia Hagiographica*, xlii, 1966), p. 408.

genres littéraires (1921, reprinted 1966). Slightly shorter lists are given by O. von Gebhardt, *Ausgewählte Märtyreracten* (1902), H. Lietzmann, *P–W*, xiv (1930), col. 2048, and G. Lazzati, *Gli sviluppi della letteratura sui martiri nei primi quattro secoli* (1956); but that is only because they deny that two out of the nine (nos. III and IX) may properly be styled *acta martyrum*.[1] The collection of Knopf–Krüger will, therefore, be taken as a standard for comparison in the following pages.

1. *Martyrdom of Polycarp*

No compelling argument has yet been advanced to demonstrate that chaps. 1–20 cannot be what they purport to be—a contemporary letter from the Christians of Smyrna to the church of Philomelium. If genuine, therefore, the *Martyrdom* dates from no more than a few weeks after the death of Polycarp. For it was written in response to a request for a detailed account from the Christians of Philomelium, who seem to have heard vague rumours of what had happened in Smyrna (20. 1). The manuscripts present three appendices to the letter: a chapter giving a date (21), a pious paragraph which probably dates from the fourth century (22. 1),[2] and a description of the transmission of the text (22. 2/3, with an expanded version in the Moscow manuscript). The last appendix contains one very suspicious feature: 'Pionius' rediscovered the text of the *Martyrdom* after Polycarp showed it to him in a vision. That is not too dissimilar to the accounts of their transmission which preface such *pseudepigrapha* as the *Ephemeris Belli Troiani* of Dictys the Cretan or the *De Excidio Troiae* of Dares the Phrygian.[3] Nevertheless, chaps. 1–20 are not necessarily thereby discredited,[4] and even the writer of chap. 21 knew that Philippus the Asiarch came from Tralles and could furnish a name for the proconsul who condemned Polycarp.[5]

H. von Campenhausen has attempted to show that the original letter has been considerably worked over and interpolated.[6] Proof, he claims, is provided by the differences between the manuscript text of the *Martyrdom* and the report of it by Eusebius.[7] This is Campenhausen's

---

[1] Compare also the lists tabulated by H. Leclercq, *Dict. d'arch. chrét.* i (1903), cols. 409/10.

[2] P. T. Camelot, *Ignace d'Antioche*[3]: *Sources chrétiennes*, 10bis (1958), p. 240.

[3] Cf. R. Syme, *Ammianus and the Historia Augusta* (1968), p. 124.

[4] Compare the story of the finding of the last thirteen cantos of the *Divina Commedia* in Boccaccio's *Vita di Dante*.

[5] *P.I.R.*[2] J 460 (incorporating errors, cf. *J.T.S.*, N.S. xviii (1967), pp. 434, 437).

[6] 'Bearbeitungen und Interpolationen des Polykarpmartyriums', *Sitzungsber. der Heidelberger Akad., Phil.-hist. Kl.* 1957, Abhand. 3, reprinted in *Aus der Frühzeit des Christentums* (1963), p. 253.

[7] *H.E.* iv. 15. 1–46. The discussion of the variant readings by E. Schwartz, *De Pionio et Polycarpo* (1905), is still valuable.

central argument. But, although it has found favour,[1] it rests on a mistaken estimate of Eusebius, whose inaccuracy even in direct quotation can be abundantly documented.[2] In the present case, moreover, there appear to be wide divergences only where Eusebius is paraphrasing: where he is professedly quoting verbatim the differences are comparatively trivial.[3] (Perhaps the only significant difference here is Eusebius' omission of περιστερὰ καὶ at 16. 1: either the words are a later interpolation or Eusebius deliberately left them out as implausible.) The correct conclusion to be drawn from these facts is that Eusebius has produced an inaccurate paraphrase of the *Martyrdom* in order to heighten its rhetorical effect.[4]

Nor are Campenhausen's supporting arguments any stronger. If the truth has been distorted—e.g. by the 'imitatio Christi' motif, which impels Campenhausen to the hypothesis of an 'Evangelion-Redaktor'[5] —nothing so far adduced proves that the distortion cannot have been made by a contemporary.[6] Even the episode of Quintus may be a genuine happening of the 150s, and surely belongs to the original letter: the words "οὗτος δὲ ἦν ὁ παραβιασάμενος ἑαυτόν . . ." (4) imply that the Philomelians already knew of Quintus' action, but not the name of its perpetrator.[7] Modern treatment of this chapter has tended to be arbitrary. Campenhausen, who puts the date of Polycarp's death *c.* 167,[8] pronounces the episode an anti-Montanist interpolation into the original text.[9] H. Grégoire uses it to buttress his date of 177 for the martyrdom by maintaining that it was penned after the Montanist heresy had arisen in the early 170s.[10] M. Simonetti, in contrast, cites it as evidence that

[1] W. H. C. Frend, *J.T.S.*, N.S. ix (1958), p. 371.

[2] H. J. Lawlor and J. E. L. Oulton, *Eusebius*, ii (1928), pp. 19 ff.

[3] H.-I. Marrou, *Theologische Literaturzeitung*, lxxxiv (1959), col. 362.

[4] G. Lazzati, 'Nota su Eusebio epitomatore di Atti dei Martiri', *Studi in onore di A. Calderini e R. Paribeni*, i (1956), p. 377.

[5] Accepted by Frend, op. cit., pp. 371 f. The theory is not new: it was forcefully argued by M. Joel, *Blicke in die Religionsgeschichte*, ii (1883), pp. 156 ff., that the part played by the Jews was interpolated by one who was intent on assimilating Polycarp more closely to Jesus.

[6] Cf. O. Perler, 'Das vierte Makkabaeerbuch, Ignatius von Antiochien und die ältesten Märtyrerberichte', *Riv. arch. crist.* xxv (1949), p. 47; M. Pellegrino, 'L'imitation du Christ dans les actes des martyrs', *La Vie spirituelle*, xcviii (1958), p. 38.

[7] A. Wifstrand, Εἰκότα IV, p. 6 = *Bull. Soc. Roy. des Lettres de Lund* 1938–1939, p. 14.

[8] Following W. Telfer, *J.T.S.*, N.S. iii (1952), pp. 79 ff.; H.-I. Marrou, *Anal. Boll.* lxxi (1953), pp. 5 ff. For comment on this dating, see E. Griffe, *Bull. litt. eccl.* liv/lxxiii (1953), pp. 178 ff.   [9] Op. cit., pp. 21 ff.

[10] 'La véritable date du martyre de S. Polycarpe (23 février 177) et le "Corpus Polycarpianum" ', *Anal. Boll.* lxix (1951), p. 1, at pp. 21 f. Grégoire's date was refuted by E. Griffe, *Bull. litt. eccl.* lii/lxxi (1951), pp. 170 ff.

512

Montanism began in the 150s, not after 170.[1] But all three views share a common error: there is no necessity to imagine any allusion whatever to Montanism.[2]

The precise date of Polycarp's death is not easy to determine, although some degree of certainty is attainable if the correct method of inquiry is followed.[3] First, Eusebius must be disregarded.[4] Although he assigns Polycarp's death to the reign of Marcus Aurelius,[5] it is unlikely that he possessed any reliable evidence,[6] since he also dates the Decian *Passion of Pionius* to the same period.[7] Secondly, chap. 21 of the *Martyrdom* must be assessed. It gives two contradictory statements for the year: that Philippus of Tralles was high-priest and that Statius Quadratus was proconsul of Asia. Philippus was high-priest of Asia no later than 149/50, while no conceivable argument could put Quadratus' proconsulate earlier than 153/4.[8] But the notice about Philippus may easily be a mistaken inference from 12. 2.[9] Hence the posing of a dilemma points to a definite year. Either the Christians of Smyrna forgot the name of the proconsul who condemned Polycarp, or he was L. Statius Quadratus (*consul ordinarius* in 142).[10] If the former is the case, it becomes difficult to credit any Christian tradition, however early. If the latter, an argument is available from the known careers of Roman senators. In the Antonine age, no man is attested holding one of the senior proconsulates (Asia and Africa) a mere twelve years after his consulate: an interval of thirteen years is very rare, while fourteen appears to be the normal minimum and fifteen and sixteen are common.[11] In the present state of our evidence, therefore, 154/5 is excluded for the proconsular year of Polycarp's death, while 155/6 is possible, and 156/7 perhaps the most probable, Quadratus having been *consul ordinarius*; but there is nothing against 157/8 or even 158/9.

[1] *Giorn. ital. di filol.* ix (1956), pp. 332 ff.
[2] So J. B. Lightfoot, *The Apostolic Fathers Part II. S. Ignatius. S. Polycarp*, i² (1889), pp. 619 f., 677. Later discussions add very little.
[3] Cf. T. D. Barnes, 'A Note on Polycarp', *J.T.S.*, N.S. xviii (1967), p. 433.
[4] There is a precise parallel. The era of Caesarea Philippi was still used for dating in the fifth century A.D., and yet Eusebius misplaces Philip the tetrarch's refoundation of the city by twenty-seven years (*J.T.S.*, N.S. xix (1968), p. 206).
[5] *H.E.* iv. 15. 1; *G.C.S.* xx, p. 222; xlvii, p. 205.
[6] Barnes, op. cit., p. 436.
[7] *H.E.* iv. 15. 46/7, cf. *G.C.S.* xlvii, p. 205.
[8] Barnes, op. cit., pp. 434 ff.
[9] Ibid., p. 437.
[10] Attested as proconsul of Asia by *I.G.R.R.* iv. 1339 (Magnesia ad Sipylum): a tomb inscription laying down that if the tomb is alienated a fine is to be paid εἰς τὸν Καίσαρος φίσκον.
[11] Barnes, op. cit., p. 436, following R. Syme, *Rev. ét. anc.* lxi (1959), p. 311; lxvii (1965), pp. 351 f.

The day of Polycarp's death is given by chap. 21 as

$$\mu\eta\nu\grave{o}\varsigma\ \Xi\alpha\nu\theta\iota\kappa o\hat{v}\ \delta\epsilon\upsilon\tau\acute{\epsilon}\rho\underline{a}\ \acute{\iota}\sigma\tau\alpha\mu\acute{\epsilon}\nu o\upsilon,\ \pi\rho\grave{o}\ \acute{\epsilon}\pi\tau\grave{a}$$
$$\kappa\alpha\lambda\alpha\nu\delta\hat{\omega}\nu\ M\alpha\rho\tau\acute{\iota}\omega\nu,\ \sigma\alpha\beta\beta\acute{a}\tau\omega\ \mu\epsilon\gamma\acute{a}\lambda\omega.^1$$

According to the body of the letter, Polycarp was arrested on a Friday in the evening (7. 1) and met his death in Smyrna on a 'great sabbath' (8. 1). The Smyrnaeans were not unconcerned about accuracy in such matters, since they declare their intention of celebrating the anniversary of the martyrdom (18. 3).

From this some argue that the year is 155,[2] others that it is 156,[3] while those who wrongly put their trust in Eusebius can claim to find here evidence for 166[4] or for 177,[5] and one scholar reduces the problem to a straight choice between 155 and 166.[6] But caution is necessary. Is enough known about the Asian or the Christian or (if it is relevant) the Jewish calendar in the second century to permit completely secure deductions from these data? At the very least, it is doubtful if anyone has yet adequately explained how a Saturday in late February can be a 'great sabbath'.[7] Perhaps it is something peculiar to the Christians of Smyrna.

The name of the proconsul, then, tells in favour of February 157. None the less, the argument for 156 may carry more conviction. If the Asian date be regarded as the primary fact, the Julian equivalent for the second day of the month Xanthicus in a leap-year such as 156 is 22 (not 23) February,[8] and in 156 22 February fell on a Saturday.[9] There

---

[1] Cf. *Pass. Pion.* 2. 1.

[2] The classic statement of this view is by Lightfoot, op. cit., pp. 677 ff. It has recently been reiterated by M. Sordi, *Rivista di storia della Chiesa in Italia*, xv (1961), pp. 277 ff. She, however, fails to take account of the serious difficulty which had already been stated clearly by Syme in 1959.

[3] C. H. Turner, 'The Day and Year of St. Polycarp's Martyrdom', *Studia Biblica*, ii (1890), p. 105; E. Schwartz, 'Christliche und jüdische Ostertafeln', *Abhand. der königl. Gesellsch. zu Göttingen*, N.F. viii (1905), Nr. 6, pp. 125 ff.

[4] W. Schmid, *Rhein. Mus.*, N.F. xlviii (1893), p. 80.

[5] Grégoire, op. cit., p. 28.

[6] E. Griffe, *Bull. litt. eccl.* liv/lxxiii (1953), p. 179.

[7] H.-I. Marrou, *Theologische Literaturzeitung*, lxxxiv (1959), col. 363, rejects the phrase ὄντος σαββάτου μεγάλου in chap. 8. 1: 'l'expression ne pourrait signifier que le "Samedi-Saint" et cette date est incompatible avec [celle] du 23 Février, assurée par la tradition liturgique.' But the same equation appears at *Pass. Pion.* 2. 1.

[8] The clearest exposition is by H. Dessau, 'Zum Kalender der Provinz Asien', *Hermes*, xxxv (1900), p. 332, citing *O.G.I.S.* 458 and ll. 447 ff. of the long inscription of A.D. 104 later republished in *Forschungen in Ephesos*, ii (1912), pp. 127 ff., no. 27.

[9] Computed from the table in E. J. Bickermann, *La cronologia nel mondo antico* (1963), p. 98; *Chronology of the Ancient World* (1968), p. 60.

514

is, however, a difficulty. In ordinary years the first day of Xanthicus was called Σεβαστή, the second πρώτη, the third δευτέρα, and so on.[1] In leap-years, Xanthicus being the intercalary month, the names of the days ran πρώτη Σεβαστή, δευτέρα Σεβαστή, πρώτη, δευτέρα, etc.[2] In 156, therefore, the Asian equivalent of 22 February in the Julian calendar was not μηνὸς Ξανθικοῦ δευτέρα (as in the *Martyrdom*), but μηνὸς Ξανθικοῦ δευτέρα Σεβαστή, the anniversary of which should be celebrated on μηνὸς Ξανθικοῦ Σεβαστή.[3]

II. *Acts of Carpus, Papylus, and Agathonice*[4]

Both the date and the original form of these *acta* are uncertain.[5] Neither the Greek nor the Latin can, as extant, reproduce the original without additions. Each contains words, phrases, and whole sections not in the other. The Latin version, moreover, seems to have been revised in the interests of orthodoxy: it depicts Agathonice as formally condemned to death by the proconsul of Asia, whereas the Greek describes a voluntary self-immolation without trial, a veritable suicide.[6] The date assigned to these *acta* has been either the 160s (with Eusebius)[7] or the persecution of Decius (as in the Latin version).[8] But, while the proponents of each date easily expose the flimsiness of the arguments for the other, they can offer nothing better to support the date which they espouse. There is no decisive evidence. The voluntary martyrdom of Agathonice, which some cite as proof of the second-century date,[9] could equally well belong to the third century.[10] The mentions of Decius and of the proconsul 'Optimus' in the Latin version are not found in

---

[1] The references to the day Σεβαστή are collected by M. P. Nilsson, 'Die Entstehung und religiöse Bedeutung des griechischen Kalenders', *Kungl. Hum. Vetens. i Lund, Scripta Minora 1960–1961*, i (1962), p. 67.

[2] Dessau, op. cit., p. 334.

[3] W. Kubitschek, 'Die Kalenderbücher von Florenz, Rom und Leyden', *Denkschr. der Kaiserl. Akad. in Wien*, lvii. 3 (1915), p. 90.

[4] For a bibliography see now F. Halkin in *Mullus: Festschrift Th. Klauser* (1964), pp. 150 ff.

[5] H. Lietzmann, 'Die älteste Gestalt der Passio SS. Carpi, Papylae et Agathonices', *Festgabe für K. Müller* (1922), p. 46, reprinted in *Kleine Schriften*, i (*Texte u. Unters.* lxvii, 1958), p. 239; H. Delehaye, 'Les actes des martyrs de Pergame', *Anal. Boll.* lviii (1940), p. 142.

[6] § 6 Latin ~ §§ 42–7 Greek; cf. M. Simonetti, *Studi agiografici* (1955), pp. 101 ff.

[7] A. Harnack, *Texte u. Unters.* iii. 4 (1888), pp. 435 ff.; Lietzmann, op. cit.; W. H. C. Frend, *Martyrdom and Persecution in the Early Church* (1965), pp. 289, 296, n. 32.

[8] J. de Guibert, *Rev. quest. hist.* lxxxiii (1908), pp. 5 ff.; H. Leclercq, *Dict. d'arch. chrét.* viii (1929), cols. 680 ff.

[9] Lietzmann, *Kleine Schriften*, i, p. 250; Frend, op. cit., p. 296, n. 32.

[10] Cf. G. E. M. de Ste Croix, *Past and Present*, xxvi (1963), pp. 21 ff.

the Greek, and are therefore probably later accretions to the original text.[1] Eusebius, though setting the deaths of Carpus, Papylus, and Agathonice in the joint reign of Marcus and Lucius, appears to be dependent on a collection of *acta* to all of which he assigns the same date.[2] But this included both the *Martyrdom of Polycarp* (?157) and the undoubtedly Decian *Passion of Pionius*.[3] None the less, a sentence occurs in both versions which may offer a clue towards the correct date:

> 3: et dixit ad eum: principalis es?
>
> 24: ὁ ἀνθύπατος ἐπὶ τὸν Παπύλον ἐτρέπετο λέγων αὐτῷ· βουλευτὴς εἶ;

Although its author wisely refuses to commit himself on the date of the *Acts of Carpus*, a recent study of the development of the curial class seems to indicate that the question was more likely to be asked in the third century than in the second.[4]

III. *Martyrdom of Ptolemaeus and Lucius*

The story of these two martyrs is told by their contemporary Justin:[5] they were tried and condemned to death in Rome by the city prefect Q. Lollius Urbicus in the early 150s.[6] That Justin is contemporary does not of itself prove his account perfectly trustworthy. Such a manifest fiction as the letter of Marcus Aurelius testifying to the 'Thundering Legion' found ready and almost contemporary acceptance from Tertullian.[7] In this case, however, nothing is known to contradict Justin, whose information surely comes from an eye-witness: Lucius was a spectator of the trial of Ptolemaeus, and his presence in the prefect's court implies the presence of other bystanders.[8] One may, nevertheless, still ask how far Justin has refashioned the story for literary ends.[9]

IV. *Acts of Justin and his Companions*

The text printed in the third edition of Knopf–Krüger cannot be the original version of these *acta*, since this, or at least a closer approximation

---

[1] Lietzmann, op. cit., pp. 241 ff., 250.

[2] *H.E.* iv. 14. 10–15. 1; 15. 46–8.

[3] On which see the appendix below, pp. 529 ff.

[4] P. D. A. Garnsey, *Social Status and Legal Privilege in the Second and Third Centuries of the Roman Empire with special reference to the Curial Class* (unpub. Oxford D.Phil. thesis, 1967), esp. pp. 328, 574. The earliest certain reference to 'principales' as a legal category is *Dig.* xlviii. 19. 27. 1 (Callistratus).

[5] *Apol.* ii. 2.   [6] W. Hüttl, *Antoninus Pius*, ii (1933), pp. 191 f.

[7] *Apol.* 5. 6; *Scap.* 4. 7; cf. Apollinaris in Eusebius, *H.E.* v. 5. 4.

[8] For the prefect's court see G. Vitucci, *Ricerche sulla Praefectura Urbi in età imperiale* (1956), pp. 43 ff.

[9] Cf. P. Keresztes, 'The "So-called" Second Apology of Justin', *Latomus*, xxiv (1965), p. 858.

to it, is extant.¹ The readings of the *Codex Parisinus Graecus* 1470 were published in 1902 by P. Franchi de' Cavalieri,² who later recognized their excellence.³ In 1953, however, G. Lazzati demonstrated that this manuscript preserves not just a series of superior readings, but a distinct recension of the *acta* which is simpler and more primitive than is otherwise attested.⁴ A single passage will suffice to show the extent and nature of the divergences. In the most ancient version the account of the trial opens:

Ὧν εἰσαχθέντων ὁ ἔπαρχος Ἰουστίνῳ εἶπεν· τίνα βίον βιοῖς; Ἰουστῖνος εἶπεν· ἄμεμπτον καὶ ἀκατάγνωστον πᾶσιν ἀνθρώποις.

The corresponding section in the commonly accepted redaction reads:

Ὧν εἰσαχθέντων πρὸ τοῦ βήματος Ῥούστικος ἔπαρχος εἶπεν πρὸς Ἰουστῖνον· πρῶτον πείσθητι τοῖς θεοῖς καὶ ὑπάκουσον τοῖς βασιλεῦσιν. Ἰουστῖνος εἶπεν· ἄμεμπτον καὶ ἀκατάγνωστον τὸ πείθεσθαι τοῖς προσταχθεῖσιν ὑπὸ τοῦ σωτῆρος ἡμῶν Ἰησοῦ Χριστοῦ.

Yet it is the longer, unhistorical version which some still use as a verbally accurate report of the trial of Justin and his companions.⁵

Even in the short recension there is a peculiarity: the opening question of the city prefect, Q. Junius Rusticus,⁶ is unexpected. When he interrogates Chariton, Euelpistus, Hierax, and Liberianus, he properly begins by putting the charge and asking each one in turn whether he is a Christian (4). But his first question to Justin is τίνα βίον βιοῖς; This may simply be a generalized variant of the precise question 'Are you a Christian?' On the other hand, it could indicate that Rusticus deliberately gave Justin an opportunity to avoid incriminating himself by claiming to be a philosopher.⁷ The circumstances of Justin's arrest are

¹ The short, medium, and long versions can be found together in G. Lazzati, *Gli sviluppi della letteratura sui martiri nei primi quattro secoli* (1956), pp. 119 ff.; and now appear in Knopf–Krüger–Ruhbach, *Ausgewählte Märtyrerakten⁴* (1965), pp. 15 ff. (the medium version—with a few readings from the short), 125 ff. 'The Oldest MS. of St. Justin's Martyrdom' (F. C. Burkitt, *J.T.S.* xi (1909–10), pp. 61 ff.) preserves the medium version.

² 'Note agiografiche II', *Studi e Testi*, viii (1902), pp. 25 ff.

³ 'Note agiografiche VI', *Studi e Testi*, xxxiii (1920), pp. 5 ff.

⁴ 'Gli atti di S. Giustino Martire', *Aevum*, xxvii (1953), p. 473.

⁵ Frend, op. cit., pp. 253 f.; A. Birley, *Marcus Aurelius* (1966), pp. 206 ff.; *P.I.R.*² J 871.

⁶ *P.I.R.*² J 814; perhaps prefect from 162 until 167. The standard date of 165 depends on *Chronicon Paschale*, p. 482 Bonn, alone, and is therefore uncertain. Eusebius' *Chronicon* characteristically records Justin's martyrdom in the previous decade (*G.C.S.* xx, p. 221; xlvii, p. 203).

⁷ Contrast Frend, op. cit., p. 269: 'The influence, too, of his (sc. Marcus') closest advisers Cornelius Fronto and Junius Rusticus was anti-Christian. Both were now old men and hated and feared the revolutionary tendencies they saw in the Christians'.

unfortunately unclear. Eusebius misreports Tatian to prove that Justin's
death was encompassed by the machinations of the Cynic Crescens:[1]
Tatian merely says that Crescens plotted against both Justin and himself.[2] But if Justin really was accused by Crescens, the question put by
Rusticus appears in a new light.

v. *The Martyrs of Lugdunum*[3]

That the letter of the Christians of Vienna and Lugdunum preserved
by Eusebius[4] is the contemporary record of an outbreak of persecution
in Gaul in the reign of Marcus Aurelius has gone almost unchallenged
apart from two wholly implausible theories.[5] The one dated the persecution a century later, in the reign of Aurelian, almost entirely on the
grounds that Marcus was not a 'persecuting emperor'.[6] The other trans-
fers the scene of the persecution to Galatia.[7] But it perverts the sense of
a valuable notice in the *Historia Augusta*,[8] and ignores J. A. Robinson's
acute observation that the letter seems to have been written by one
familiar with a Latin translation of the Bible.[9] Yet, though both theories
accuse Eusebius of gross error, neither has impugned the document
itself, which, despite some fantastic details,[10] clearly preserves the testimony of eye-witnesses.

P. Nautin has claimed that the letter is the work of none other than
Irenaeus.[11] He argues that it ought to come from the head of the Christian
community in Gaul, that it is addressed to the churches in Asia and
Phrygia because Irenaeus was playing an active part in the controversies
which were at the time dividing the Asian churches, and that it exhibits
certain turns of phrase which recur in Irenaeus' *Adversus Haereses*.
There seems to be no possibility of conclusive proof or disproof. All
that is certain is that whoever wrote the letter wrote in the name of the
Christians of Vienna and Lugdunum.

[1] *H.E.* iv. 16. 7–9; cf. Lawler–Oulton, op. cit., pp. 137 f.
[2] *Oratio ad Graecos*, 19. See the note of J. K. T. Otto, *Corpus Apologetarum*,
vi (1851), p. 85.
[3] For full historical commentary, U. Kahrstedt, 'Die Märtyrerakten von
Lugdunum 177', *Rhein. Mus.*, N.F. lxviii (1913), p. 395; Frend, op. cit., pp. 1 ff.
[4] *H.E.* v. 1–3.
[5] Note, however, C. Guignebert, *Tertullien: Étude sur ses sentiments à l'égard
de l'Empire et de la société civile* (1901), pp. 100 ff.
[6] J. W. Thompson, *Amer. J. Theol.* xvi (1912), pp. 359 ff., xvii (1913), pp. 249 ff.
[7] J. Colin, *L'Empire des Antonins et les martyrs gaulois de 177* (1964).
[8] Viz. *Comm.* 7. 1. For an elucidation see T. D. Barnes, 'In Attali gratiam',
to appear in *Historia*.   [9] *Texts and Studies*, i. 2 (1891), pp. 97 ff.
[10] Note especially *H.E.* v. 1. 24, which prompted J. Geffcken, *Hermes*, xlv
(1910), p. 488, to style the letter 'diesem aus Wahrheit und Phantasie gemischten
Documente'.
[11] *Lettres et écrivains des IIe et IIIe siècles* (1961), pp. 54 ff., cf. pp. 38 f.

518

The date of 177 comes near to universal and unquestioning acceptance.[1] It depends, however, on Eusebius' *Ecclesiastical History* alone.[2] The *Chronicon* puts the martyrdoms in Gaul a decade earlier.[3] A decision between Eusebius' two dates cannot be made: that the governor wrote to the (single) emperor (44; 47) need not exclude the joint reign of Marcus and Lucius.[4] Still less is it possible to establish a third precise date as the correct one.[5] One ought instead to ask whether Eusebius possessed any reliable evidence,[6] and what criteria avail to assign the pogrom in Gaul to the reign of Marcus rather than to any other.

The precise occasion of the martyrdoms also raises a problem. The letter describes how many of the martyrs perished

τῆς ἐνθάδε πανηγύρεως (ἔστι δὲ αὕτη πολυάνθρωπος ἐκ πάντων τῶν ἐθνῶν συνερχομένων εἰς αὐτήν) ἀρχομένης συνεστάναι (47).

Identification of this festival with the annual commemoration of Drusus' dedication of the altar of Rome and Augustus at Lugdunum on 1 August 12 B.C. can hardly be denied.[7] Yet the *Martyrologium Hieronymianum* puts the celebration of the Gallic martyrs on 2 June.[8] The easiest solution of the difficulty is to suppose that confusions have led to error in the *Martyrologium*, which in its present form scarcely antedates 600.[9]

The background to the persecution is illuminated by the *senatus consultum de sumptibus ludorum gladiatorum minuendis* (of 177/8).[10] It has

[1] Thus, in three years alone, J. Deininger, *Die Provinziallandtage der römischen Kaiserzeit* (1965), p. 104; M. Sordi, *Il cristianesimo e Roma* (1965), p. 181, etc.; Frend, op. cit., p. 1, etc.; Birley, op. cit., p. 329; P. Keresztes, *Historia*, xvi (1967), pp. 75 ff.; H. Bengtson, *Grundriß der römischen Geschichte*, i (1967), p. 358; T. D. Barnes, *J.T.S.*, N.S. xviii (1967), p. 436 (by implication); H. Chadwick, *The Early Church* (1967), p. 29; F. Millar, *The Roman Empire and its Neighbours* (1967), p. 154. Doubts had already been expressed by P. Meinhold, *P–W*, xxi (1952), cols. 1679 f.   [2] *H.E.* v. pr.
[3] *G.C.S.* xx, p. 222; xlvii, p. 205—dating it to the reign of Marcus and Lucius rather than to 167 precisely.
[4] Marcus alone was in Rome from 162 to 166, while Lucius was in the east: see, most recently, T. D. Barnes, *J.R.S.* lvii (1967), pp. 70 ff.
[5] Nautin, op. cit., pp. 62 ff., contrives to ignore Eusebius' earlier date and proposes 175 on the grounds that the *Ecclesiastical History* synchronizes the persecution with the accession of Eleutherus as bishop of Rome (v. pr.).
[6] Compare the firm statement of Meinhold, loc. cit.
[7] Deininger, op. cit., pp. 104 f., cf. pp. 21 ff.
[8] *Acta Sanctorum*, Nov. ii. 2, pp. 292 f., 297 f.
[9] H. Quentin, *Anal. Boll.* xxxix (1921), p. 129. But for other possible solutions see Frend, op. cit., p. 24, n. 39.
[10] *I.L.S.* 5163 = Bruns, *Fontes iuris Romani*[7], no. 63 = *F.I.R.A.*[2] i, no. 49; re-edited by J. H. Oliver and R. E. A. Palmer, 'Minutes of an Act of the Roman Senate', *Hesperia*, xxiv (1955), p. 320. The date is to be deduced from the apparent presence in the Senate of both Marcus and Commodus and from *HA, Marcus*, 27. 4–6: see *P.I.R.*[2] i, p. 302.

been contended that the pogrom occurred in 177 because the emperor had just created a special privilege which enabled the priests of the imperial cult in the Three Gauls to purchase condemned prisoners cheaply for use as gladiators.[1] Some go further still and suppose that the year 177 saw the first general persecution of the Christians throughout the empire with imperial connivance.[2] Unfortunately for these theorists, the letter of the Gallic churches depicts the Christians as being executed by the governor alone (8/9;10; 14; 17; 21; 31; 44; 46/7; 50; 57) and does not so much as mention the priests of the imperial cult. In addition, the theories simply assume a date which has been challenged above. There need, in fact, be no connection at all between the outbreak of persecution and the *senatus consultum*. But if there is, the connection is surely that the pogrom was partly the result of the shortage of gladiators which the *senatus consultum* set out to alleviate. Hence no temporal relationship between the two can be established.

VI. *Acts of the Scillitan Martyrs*[3]

O. Seeck has been alone in rejecting these *acta* outright on specific grounds: he alleged that no trial 'in secretario' (1) is known before 303.[4] This is a very dubious argument from silence, especially since rooms identifiable as *secretaria* existed even in the first century.[5] None the less, the *acta* present difficulties. They open with the proconsul, Vigellius Saturninus,[6] urging the Christians to change their minds: the accusation or putting of the charge is absent. At the end, six Christians are sentenced to death in addition to the six whose trial has been described (16). Moreover, while the herald's public announcement of the proconsul's verdict specifies twelve names (16), the verdict itself contains six of the names (the same six who appear earlier in the *acta*) and the

---

[1] Oliver–Palmer, op. cit., p. 325. They are followed by H. Grégoire, *La Nouvelle Clio*, vii–ix (1955–7), p. 301; J. Vogt, 'Zur Religiosität der Christenverfolger im römischen Reich', *Sitzungsber. der Heidelberger Akad., Phil.-hist. Kl.* 1962, Abhand. 1, p. 14; Frend, op. cit., pp. 8 ff.

[2] P. Orgels, *La Nouvelle Clio*, vii–ix (1955–7), p. 303.

[3] For the similarities of these *acta* with other trials of Christians one may consult L. Alfonsi, 'Sugli "Atti dei martiri scillitani" ', *Convivium*, xxv (1957), p. 732—although he implausibly conjectures derivation from Pliny, *Epp.* x. 96.

[4] *P–W*, iiA (1923), cols. 979 ff., s.v. 'secretarium'. S. Lieberman, *Jew. Q. Rev.* xxxv (1944), pp. 18 f., on similar grounds, argues that the words 'in secretario' are a late addition to the *acta*. If so, it is hard to account for their presence in the most primitive extant redactions and absence from the later versions. (For the different forms of the *acta* see Robinson, op. cit., pp. 106 ff.)

[5] R. Hanslik, '*Secretarium* und *Tribunal* in den *Acta Martyrum Scillitanorum*', in *Mélanges offerts à Mlle Chr. Mohrmann* (1963), p. 165.

[6] On whom see B. E. Thomasson, *Die Statthalter der römischen Provinzen Nordafrikas von Augustus bis Diocletianus*, ii (1960), p. 87; *Ann. Ép.* 1966. 470.

520

words 'et ceteros' (14). This phrase in particular has been judged to be extremely suspicious.[1] Accordingly, the six extra names and the words 'et ceteros' might be explained away as an interpolation.[2] But perhaps the difficulty at the end is explicable in the same way as that at the beginning: by supposing that the *Acts* are an incomplete record of the trial in Carthage on 17 July 180.[3] Either part of the trial of that day has been omitted or else the whole of an earlier hearing, possibly before municipal magistrates.[4] One may compare the *Acts of Phileas*. The Latin version begins abruptly:

Imposito Philea super ambonem, Culcianus praeses dixit illi: potes iam sobrius effici?[5]

The recently published Greek version makes it clear that Phileas had appeared in court before:

Ἀπολογία Φιλέου ἐπισκόπου Θμούεως . . . πέμπτον προσαχθέντος, etc.[6]

The parallel with the *Acts of the Scillitan Martyrs* is far from remote.

VII. *Acts of Apollonius*

The extant Greek and Armenian texts of these *acta* exhibit wide divergences,[7] and the version known to Eusebius differed greatly from both.[8] For example, according to Eusebius' report, the accuser was executed by having his legs broken and Apollonius by beheading.[9] There is no mention at all of the accuser in the extant *acta*; and, while the Armenian version has Apollonius beheaded, in the Greek the martyr is sentenced to *crurifragium*.[10] Since the salient differences so often concern legal technicalities, their extent and significance can best be considered together with the other evidence for the legal position of

---

[1] M. Hoffmann, *Der Dialog bei den christlichen Schriftstellern der ersten vier Jahrhunderte* (*Texte u. Unters.* xcvi, 1966), pp. 43, 49.

[2] F. Corsaro, *Nuovo Didaskaleion* (1956), pp. 32 ff.; M. Simonetti, *Rev. ét. aug.* ii (1956), pp. 43 f.; H. Karpp, 'Die Zahl der scilitanischen Märtyrer', *Vig. Chr.* xv (1961), p. 165.

[3] Cf. H. Niedermeyer, *Über antike Protokoll-Literatur* (1918), pp. 57 f.

[4] For examples of cases referred to the governor by local officials see, e.g., Tertullian, *Scap.* 4. 4; *Pass. Pion.* 3 ff., esp. 9. 1; 19. 1 ff. The evidence relating to the town Scilli (?) is collected in *P–W*, iiA, cols. 819 f.

[5] Knopf–Krüger, p. 113.

[6] *P. Bodmer*, xx. The Greek text, together with the only critical edition of the Latin, is also to be found in F. Halkin, 'L' "Apologie" du martyr Philéas de Thmuis (Papyrus Bodmer XX) et les actes latins de Philéas et Philoromus', *Anal. Boll.* lxxxi (1963), p. 5.

[7] F. C. Conybeare, *Monuments of Early Christianity* (1894), pp. 35 ff., and O. von Gebhardt, *Ausgewählte Märtyreracten* (1902), pp. 44 ff., provide, respectively, an English and a German translation of the Armenian text.

[8] *H.E.* v. 21.   [9] Ibid. 21. 3/4.   [10] § 45.

Christians.[1] It must suffice here to state dogmatically a conclusion argued elsewhere: §§ 1–10 alone may consist of or be based upon an accurate account of the trial of Apollonius before Perennis, the praetorian prefect. The rest either derives from Apollonius' *Apology* or is a free composition drawing largely on apologetic commonplaces.[2]

VIII. *Passion of Perpetua and Felicitas*

Besides the Latin text of the *Passion of Perpetua* printed by Knopf–Krüger there is extant a Greek version.[3] Since some have drawn deductions from the supposed independence of the latter,[4] it is of some importance to decide the relationship between the two. Detailed philological investigation now seems to have settled the question: the Greek is a translation (not necessarily from a text exactly identical with the extant Latin), and the *Passion* was originally composed in Latin alone.[5] There are, in addition, some *Acts of Perpetua*; but these must be dismissed as deriving from the *Passion*.[6]

The *Passion* comprises several sections. After an introduction and a statement that Perpetua and her companions were arrested (1/2), there is a long account of Perpetua's trial and experiences in prison (3–10) taken from a manuscript which she wrote herself:

haec ordinem totum martyrii sui iam hinc ipsa narravit, sicut conscriptum manu sua et suo sensu reliquit (2).

Then comes the vision of Saturus (11–13), again reproduced from an account written by the martyr's own hand (11. 1; cf. 14). The *Passion* ends with a description of further happenings in prison (14–17) and the martyrs' death in the amphitheatre (18–21. 4), followed by a brief epilogue (21. 5). That chaps. 3–10 and 11–13 do genuinely come from the hands of Perpetua and Saturus appears to be confirmed by their style: each section differs markedly both from the other and from the rest of the *Passion*.[7]

---

[1] A discussion of the *Acts of Apollonius* will appear in my 'Legislation against the Christians', *J.R.S.* lviii (1968).

[2] Simonetti, op. cit. (1956), pp. 42 f., attempts to prove that §§ 39/40 imitate Clement, *Stromateis*, v. 14. 108.

[3] See the edition of C. J. M. J. van Beek, *Passio Sanctarum Perpetuae et Felicitatis*, i (1936).

[4] Viz. that the author was Tertullian: e.g. C. J. M. J. van Beek, *Florilegium Patristicum*, xliii (1938), p. 3.

[5] E. Rupprecht, 'Bermerkungen zur Passio SS. Perpetuae et Felicitatis', *Rhein. Mus.*, N.F. xc (1941), p. 177; V. Reichmann, *Römische Literatur in griechischer Übersetzung* (*Philologus*, Suppl. xxxiv. 3, 1943), pp. 100 ff.; J. Campos, 'El autor de la "Passio SS. Perpetuae et Felicitatis"', *Helmántica*, x (1959), p. 357, esp. pp. 362 ff.   [6] See Beek, op. cit. (1936), pp. 98* ff.

[7] W. H. Shewring, *J.T.S.* xxx (1928–9), pp. 56 f.; *Rev. bénéd.* xliii (1931), pp. 15 ff.

522

The vision of Perpetua, if not the extant passion, was known to Tertullian when he wrote his treatise *De Anima c.* 210.[1] Moreover, as the work shows traces of Montanist influence but no hostility towards the church (1. 2–1. 4), Africa of the very early third century is an entirely appropriate milieu for its composition. Some go further and claim Tertullian as the author, or at least the editor.[2] But there is no argument of any real weight in favour. The style of the *Passion* has, it is true, affinities with Tertullian's writings.[3] But the striking similarities occur almost entirely in the exordium and the epilogue (1; 21. 5).[4] The dissimilarities of style elsewhere surely indicate the authorship not of Tertullian, but of a contemporary, perhaps a friend or disciple.[5] No Christian who was writing in Africa soon after 200 could have escaped the overwhelming influence of his forceful rhetoric.

The extremely early date of the *Passion* is guaranteed by one decisive fact: it constitutes the only genuine explicit evidence for the birthday of Septimius Severus' younger son. Perpetua was martyred on the Nones of March 203: though the year might be doubted, the day is beyond question.[6] According to the *Passion*, the day of the martyrdom coincided with the 'natale Getae Caesaris' (7. 4). The meaning of the phrase has not always been conceded: it signifies the birthday of Geta,[7] not the anniversary of his accession,[8] nor the anniversary of his proclamation as Caesar,[9] nor again that of the Senate's confirmation of the title 'Caesar

---

[1] *An.* 55. 4, on which see the commentary of J. Waszink (1947), pp. 561 f.

[2] Beek, op. cit., pp. 92* ff.; J. Quasten, *Patrology*, i (1950), pp. 181 f. (with full bibliographies); A. G. Amatucci, *Studi in onore di A. Calderini e R. Paribeni*, i (1956), p. 367.

[3] P. de Labriolle, *Bull. d'anc. litt. et d'arch. chr.* iii (1913), pp. 126 ff., *La Crise montaniste* (1913), pp. 345 ff.; Campos, op. cit., pp. 377 ff.

[4] A. Harnack, *Die Chronologie der altchristlichen Litteratur bis Eusebius*, ii (1904), p. 322.

[5] R. Braun, *Rev. ét. lat.* xxxiii (1955), pp. 79 ff.; Campos, op. cit., p. 381, both suggest that the author is the deacon Pomponius (mentioned at *Pass. Perp.* 3. 4; 10. 1). That cannot be proved; but no one will quarrel with Campos's final verdict: 'si la Passio no es de Tertuliano, arguye pertenecer a un discípulo muy aprovechado en ideas y en estilo literario del gran maestro africano.'

[6] N. Bonwetsch, *Die Schriften Tertullians nach der Zeit ihrer Abfassung* (1878), pp. 76 f. Beek, op. cit., pp. 162* ff., gives the evidence: for the day the earliest is the Chronographer of 354, for the year the *Fasti Vindobonenses*. W. H. C. Frend, who fails anywhere to refer to the work of Beek, paradoxically has no doubts about the year but questions the day (*The Donatist Church* (1952), p. 118; op. cit., pp. 321, 363).

[7] So Neumann, op. cit. (p. 509, n. 4), pp. 171, 174; A. Pieper, *Christentum, römisches Kaisertum und heidnischer Staat* (1907), p. 2.

[8] A. Audollent, *Carthage romaine* (1901), p. 455.

[9] Harnack, op. cit., pp. 323 f.

nobilissimus'.[1] Now the evidence for Geta's birthday does, notwithstanding apparent contradictions, point to early March.

The *Historia Augusta* asserts that Geta was born

Severo et Vitellio conss. Mediolanii, etsi aliter alii prodiderunt, VI. kal. Iunias (*Geta* 3. 1).

That Geta was born in Milan is false,[2] and the *Vita Getae* is not based on a reliable source—indeed, it consists mainly of fiction.[3] Its statement that Geta was born on 27 May can, therefore, cheerfully be set aside as a fabrication[4]—and with it goes the deduction that he died at the end of February 212.[5]

Xiphilinus' epitome of Cassius Dio states that Geta lived twenty-two years and nine months.[6] Hence, although there is no authentic testimony apart from the *Passion of Perpetua*, his birthday can be computed (within certain limits) from the date of his death. For this the Chronographer of 354 appears to provide the necessary evidence when he gives the length of Geta's reign as 'm.X d.XII'.[7] But, as Septimius Severus died on 4 February 211,[8] either Dio was mistaken in reporting that Caracalla tried to murder his brother during the Saturnalia (which began on 17 December),[9] or else one or both of the Chronographer's figures are wrong. The former possibility must be excluded: Dio was almost certainly in Rome.[10]

The necessary evidence is, however, provided by the *Historia Augusta*. Behind the *Vita Caracallae*, despite abbreviation and confusion, there lies an excellent biography of Caracalla from the early third century.[11] According to this *vita*, after the death of Geta, the emperor

[1] V. Fluss, *P–W*, iiA (1923), cols. 1566 f. The theory advanced by E. Buonaiuti, *Il cristianesimo nell'Africa romana* (1928), p. 15, is even more intricate and implausible.

[2] Contrast *Sev.* 4. 2: suscepitque Romae alterum filium. The *Severus* is based on a good source: T. D. Barnes, *Historia*, xvi (1967), pp. 87 ff.; *J.R.S.* lvii (1967), p. 74, n. 36.

[3] J. Hasebroek, *Die Fälschung der Vita Nigri und Vita Albini in den Scriptores Historiae Augustae* (1916), pp. 73 ff.; T. D. Barnes, *J.R.S.* lvii (1967), p. 74, n. 39.   [4] Syme, op. cit. (p. 510, n. 3), p. 123.

[5] Thus, among many others, S. N. Miller, *C.A.H.* xii (1939), p. 43; F. Millar, *Journ. Eg. Arch.* xlviii (1962), p. 126.   [6] Dio, lxxviii (lxvii). 2. 5.

[7] *Mon. Germ. Hist.*, *Auct. Ant.* ix, p. 147; *Chronica Minora*, i (Teubner, 1892), p. 118.

[8] Dio, lxxvii (lxxvi). 15. 2; cf. *Feriale Duranum*, col. i, l. 17.

[9] Dio, lxxviii (lxxvii). 2. 1. The coins of Geta's fourth *tribunicia potestas* (*Br. Mus. Cat., Roman Empire*, v, p. 429) prove, at the most, that he lived beyond 10 December 211.

[10] F. Millar, *A Study of Cassius Dio* (1964), pp. 18 f., 150.

[11] So Syme, op. cit., pp. 34, 92; cf. W. Reusch, *Der historische Wert der Caracallavita in den Scriptores Historiae Augustae* (*Klio*, Beiheft xxiv, 1931).

filium etiam Papiniani, qui ante triduum quaestor opulentum munus
ediderat, interemit. isdem diebus occisi sunt innumeri, qui fratris partibus faverant (*Carac.* 4. 2/3).

The latter sentence implies that Papinian's son was killed no more than
a few days after Geta. Furthermore, the quaestors gave their games in
December,[1] and the calendar of Philocalus has the entry 'MUNUS' against
ten days between 2 December and 24 December.[2] Hence the unfortunate
quaestor was executed between the fifth and the twenty-seventh day of
December 211. For Geta, consequently, a ready conclusion commends
itself. He was killed on 26 December 211[3] (the text of the Chronographer
of 354 being emended to 'm.X d.XXII') and born between 27 February
and 26 March. Cassius Dio undoubtedly gave the length of his life to the
day, but Xiphilinus has omitted the days. Elsewhere his epitome leaves
out the days for Nero and Vespasian,[4] rounds off the length of Hadrian's
reign to a complete number of months by adding a day,[5] and omits the
length of Caligula's life altogether.[6]

The evidence of papyri lends support. U. Wilcken long ago argued
that news from Rome took about fifty days to reach Thebes in Upper
Egypt,[7] and his estimate has never been seriously disputed.[8] Admittedly,
the elder Pliny records voyages from the straits of Messina and Puteoli
to Alexandria which were completed in five and eight days respectively.[9]
But those were record runs in fast ships. The journey from Rome to
Alexandria would normally last from twenty to twenty-five days;[10] and
from Alexandria news travelled slowly up the Nile.[11]

Three Egyptian documents of 212 bear the names of Caracalla and
Geta as joint emperors: they were written at Hibeh (3 January), at
Oxyrhynchus (9 January), and at Soknopaiou Nesos (30 January).[12] But
a series of contracts made in Antinoopolis[13] (which is almost two hundred

---

[1] T. Mommsen, *Römisches Staatsrecht*, ii³ (1887), p. 534; *C.I.L.* i², p. 336.
[2] *C.I.L.* i², p. 278.
[3] Stated as a fact by A. von Domaszewski, 'Die Personennamen bei den
Scriptores Historiae Augustae', *Sitzungsber. der Heidelberger Akad., Phil.-hist.
Kl.* 1918, Abhand. 13, pp. 63 f.   [4] Dio, lxiii. 29. 3; lxvi. 17. 3.
[5] Dio, lxix. 23. 1; cf. *P.I.R.*² A 184.   [6] Dio, lix. 30. 1.
[7] *Griechische Ostraka*, i (1899), pp. 800 ff.
[8] It is accepted by C. Préaux, *Mélanges G. Smets* (1952), pp. 573 f.; G. Chalon,
L'Édit de Tiberius Julius Alexander (1964), pp. 91 f. One may compare the times
taken for official communications to be sent from Hermopolis to Panopolis (120
miles) which are given by T. C. Skeat, *Papyri from Panopolis* (1964), pp. xxiii ff.
[9] *Nat. Hist.* xix. 3.
[10] L. Casson, *Trans. Amer. Phil. Ass.* lxxxi (1950), p. 51.
[11] Some startling examples are collected by Wilcken, loc. cit.
[12] *P. Hibeh*, 216; *P.S.I.* 1358; *Corp. Pap. Rain.* 239.
[13] *P. Lond.* 1164 (published in 1907).

miles north of Thebes) in Pharmouthi recognize Caracalla as sole emperor. Since the earliest of these is dated 2 Pharmouthi, i.e. 28 March,[1] the death of Geta must fall no later than the middle of February.[2]

The independent evidence, therefore, though it does not suffice for formal proof that Geta's birthday fell precisely on the Nones of March, nevertheless renders that date a strong possibility. If the *Passion of Perpetua* alone has preserved the exact day, can its author be other than a contemporary? After Geta's death all traces of his existence were assiduously eradicated, even in the remotest corners of the Roman world.[3] His birthday could be remembered only because Caracalla made an annual expiatory sacrifice to the *manes* of his dead brother.[4] Hence Geta's birthday rapidly fell into oblivion. It is not recorded in the *Feriale Duranum* or in any known calendar.[5] It was eclipsed by a happier imperial anniversary: the Nones of March long continued to be celebrated as the *dies imperii* of Marcus and Lucius.[6]

ix. *Martyrdom of Potamiaena and Basilides*

The story of the martyrdoms of Potamiaena and Basilides is narrated by Eusebius,[7] who is perhaps reporting not simply an oral tradition from Alexandria, but the content of a hymn or a tale in verse:

τὴν περιβόητον Ποταμίαιναν . . . περὶ ἧς πολὺς ὁ λόγος εἰς ἔτι νῦν παρὰ τοῖς ἐπιχωρίοις ᾄδεται (*H.E.* vi. 5. 1).

Even if nothing calls into question the basic facts, it is uncertain how far the narrative has been altered in retelling through the third century or remoulded for commemoration in verse.[8] One thing might arouse deep suspicion. Boiling pitch is said to have been poured over Potamiaena. This particular punishment is not attested in any *acta martyrum* which are in the least likely to be historical. It is not, however, thereby proved fictitious. One must weigh the predilection of hagiographical fiction for

---

[1] Ibid., l. 19. Although most of the other dates in the file have been added later, this one seems to belong to the original document.

[2] *Contra* Wilcken, op. cit., p. 805. But the earliest attestation in Upper Egypt of Caracalla alone known to him was of 7 Epeiphi, i.e. 1 July (A. H. Sayce, *Rev. ét. gr.* iv (1891), p. 47 = *I.G.R.R.* i. 1269).

[3] See S. Sauneron, 'Les querelles impériales vues à travers les scènes du temple d'Esné', *Bull. inst. fr. d'arch. orient.* li (1952), p. 111.

[4] Dio, lxxviii (lxxvii). 12. 6.

[5] Yet the birthday of Aelius Caesar was still remembered in the fourth century: *C.I.L.* i², p. 255.

[6] W. F. Snyder, *Yale Class. Stud.* vii (1940), pp. 251 f.

[7] *H.E.* vi. 5. 1–5. 6.

[8] See the critical discussion by F. Augar, *Die Frau im römischen Christenprocess* (*Texte u. Unters.*, N.F., xiii. 4, 1905), pp. 16 ff.

526

refined tortures[1] against the Roman addiction to cruelty.[2] Tertullian credited contemporary executioners with 'omne ingenium in tormentis';[3] and Dionysius, the bishop of Alexandria during the Decian persecution, described how two martyrs of his own day were covered with quicklime and thus painfully dissolved away.[4] Moreover, two factors make extreme cruelty in this case all the more credible. Potamiaena was perhaps a slave,[5] and she was certainly provocative.

The date deserves a brief mention. Potamiaena came before Aquila,[6] i.e. Subatianus Aquila, whom dated papyri certify as prefect of Egypt from October/November 206 until the Egyptian year 210/11.[7] Many have argued that Aquila became prefect as early as 203[8] or even 202.[9] For they falsely assumed that there was a sudden, widespread, and short-lived persecution of Christians throughout the empire in 202/3 stimulated by an imperial edict.[10] But the edict is demonstrably fictitious and 'the Severan persecution of 202/3' a myth.[11] For Egypt at least, the truth, dimly perceived in 1910 but then disregarded,[12] is now established beyond all possible doubt. A papyrus published in 1957 shows Claudius Julianus as prefect between 198 and 211;[13] another, published only

[1] e.g. Jerome, *Vita Pauli*, 3 (*P.L.* xxiii, col. 19): a young man was covered in honey and then exposed to flies under the hot Egyptian sun. On the character of the *Vita*, which some still accept as basically historical, see Syme, op. cit., pp. 80, 83.

[2] H. Delehaye, *Les Passions des martyrs et les genres littéraires*[2] (1966), pp. 197 ff.   [3] *Mart.* 4. 2.

[4] Eusebius, *H.E.* vi. 41. 15; cf. G. Zuntz, *Vig. Chr.* v (1951), pp. 50 ff.

[5] As alleged by Palladius, *Hist. Laus.* 3 (ed. C. Butler, *Texts and Studies*, vi. 2 (1904), pp. 18 f.), who, however, dates the episode in the reign of either Maximin or Maximianus.   [6] *H.E.* vi. 5. 2.

[7] *P. Oxy.* 1100 (206); *P. Leit.* 12 (210/11). This paragraph owes much to Dr. J. Rea, who kindly allowed me to consult his article 'The date of the prefecture of Claudius Julianus', *La Parola del Passato*, xxii/cxii (1967), p. 48, while it was still in typescript.

[8] Thus A. Stein, *Die Präfekten von Ägypten* (1950), pp. 111 ff.; O. W. Reinmuth, *P–W*, xxii (1954), col. 2374.

[9] So Frend, op. cit., p. 342, n. 149, despite the fact that Q. Maecius Laetus has long been known to have been in office as late as 25 February 203 (*P.S.I.* 199).

[10] So, most recently, Frend, op. cit., pp. 320 ff.; H. Chadwick, *The Early Church* (1967), p. 100.

[11] K. H. Schwarte, *Historia*, xii (1963), pp. 185 ff.; T. D. Barnes, *J.R.S.* lviii (1968).

[12] F. Zucker, *Sitzungsber. der preuß. Akad., Berlin*, 1910, pp. 710 ff., argued from *P. Berol.* 11532 = *Sammelbuch* 4639 that Claudius Julianus was prefect in 204, with Aquila as prefect both before and after him. So far as it concerned Julianus, Zucker's view was long assumed to be disproved by A. Stein, *Archiv für Papyrusforschung*, v (1913), pp. 418 ff.

[13] M. Vandoni, *Acme*, x (1957), pp. 161 f. = *Sammelbuch* 9393 = *P. Mil. Vogl.* 237.

recently, shows him in office in 204.[1] The other evidence concerning Claudius Julianus falls into place:[2] he probably became prefect of Egypt before the end of August 203[3] and remained until the late summer of 205, if not longer.[4]

There is a corollary of some interest and importance. Eusebius wrote of Origen

ἔτος δ' ἦγεν ὀκτωκαιδέκατον καθ' ὃ τοῦ τῆς κατηχήσεως προέστη διδα-σκαλείου· ἐν ᾧ καὶ προκόπτει ἐπὶ τῶν κατὰ Ἀκύλαν τῆς Ἀλεξανδρείας ἡγούμενον διωγμῶν, ὅτε καὶ μάλιστα διαβόητον ἐκτήσατο παρὰ πᾶσιν τοῖς ἀπὸ τῆς πίστεως ὁρμωμένοις ὄνομα (*H.E.* vi. 3. 3).

Since he also implies that Origen was sixteen in the tenth year of Severus' reign (202/3),[5] he thus stands convicted of yet another chrono-logical error.

Not all of the pre-Decian *acta martyrum* discussed can be regarded as accurate reports of the trials of Christians. The *Acts of Apollonius* (no. VII) must be rejected, except possibly §§ 1–10. The *Acts of Carpus, Papylus, and Agathonice* (no. II), even if they are based on a genuine substratum, are inadmissible in their extant recensions,[6] and perhaps belong to the Decian persecution rather than to the second century. The stories of Ptolemaeus and Lucius (no. III) and of Potamiaena and Basilides (no. IX) may have been refashioned for literary genres. The accuracy of the *Acts of the Scillitan Martyrs* (no. VI) has been defended,[7] as has that of the short recension of the *Acts of Justin and his Companions* (no. IV). The *Martyrdom of Polycarp* (no. I), *The Martyrs of Lugdunum* (no. V), and the *Passion of Perpetua and Felicitas* (no. VIII)[8] have all been argued to be contemporary with the events they describe. The *acta* are of different types.[9] The *Passion of Perpetua* was clearly

[1] *Berl. griech. Urk.* xi. 1 (1966), no. 2024, with commentary by H. Maehler.
[2] *P.I.R.*[2] C 898/9 need drastic revision.
[3] *P. Giess.* 48 = *Chrestomathie* 171, which may, however, belong instead to the regnal year 203/4 (Rea, op. cit., p. 50).
[4] *P. Marmarica* = *P. Vat. Gr.* 11 recto: see Rea, op. cit., pp. 50 ff., on this puzzling document. If this be rejected as uncertain evidence, the latest attesta-tion of Julianus is about December 204 (*Sammelbuch* 4639).
[5] *H.E.* vi. 2. 2; 2. 12. But see Rea, op. cit., p. 53.
[6] M. Simonetti, *Studi agiografici* (1955), pp. 101, 105 ff.
[7] But note the doubts of Corsaro, op. cit., pp. 25 ff., and others.
[8] Which is, as even J. Geffcken, *Hermes*, xlv (1910), p. 484, readily conceded, 'die Perle dieser Litteratur . . . zum Teil auf Aufzeichnungen der Perpetua selbst beruhend'.
[9] Cf. M. Simonetti, 'Qualche osservazione a proposito dell'origine degli Atti dei martiri', *Rev. ét. aug.* ii (1956), p. 39.

designed to be read aloud in church (1. 1; 1. 5; 21. 5).[1] The *Martyrdom of Polycarp* and *The Martyrs of Lugdunum* are both letters written in the first instance to definite recipients by Christian communities which had suffered persecution. The *Martyrdom of Ptolemaeus and Lucius* is an edifying tale told by the apologist Justin. All four accounts, however, are alike in either being, or being written from, the reports of eye-witnesses. By contrast, the *Acts of Justin* and the *Acts of the Scillitan Martyrs* are both in the form of court records.[2] Yet, as with the *Acta Alexandrinorum*, that need not imply that they were originally copied from the official records of the trials.[3] Official records could be copied, and the majority of protocols on papyri are private copies made from official archives.[4] But were *acta martyrum* normally based on official documents?[5] The only ones which explicitly claim to be derived from the official transcript of a trial (the *Acts of Tarachus*, of 304)[6] contain some very suspicious features indeed.[7] None the less, the Scillitani were tried 'in secretario': hence, if the *acta* are not pure fiction, they ought to derive from an official record.[8]

In the present state of the evidence, therefore, the historian is justified in supposing that the earliest known versions of six pre-Decian *acta* (nos. I, III, IV, V, VI, VIII) preserve as accurate a report of what happened as may be expected from a contemporary. Yet the *Acts of Justin* provoke

---

[1] Cf. G. D. Kilpatrick, *The Origins of the Gospel according to Saint Matthew* (1946), pp. 64 f.

[2] For which, in general, see T. Mommsen, *Römisches Strafrecht* (1899), pp. 512 ff.; A. Steinwenter, *Beiträge zum öffentlichen Urkundenwesen der Römer* (1915); R. A. Coles, *Reports of Proceedings in Papyri* (*Papyrologica Bruxellensia*, iv, 1966).

[3] Delehaye, op. cit., p. 130; H. A. Musurillo, *The Acts of the Pagan Martyrs* (1954), pp. 249 ff. [4] Coles, op. cit., p. 16.

[5] The thesis of E. Le Blant, 'Les *Acta Martyrum* et leurs sources', *Nouv. rev. hist. de droit*, iii (1879), p. 463. For a balanced discussion of the problem see Delehaye, op. cit., pp. 125 ff.

[6] T. Ruinart, *Acta Primorum Martyrum Sincera et Selecta²* (1713), pp. 422 ff.; whence *Acta Sanctorum*, Oct. v, pp. 566 ff. F. Halkin, *Inédits byzantins d'Ochrida, Candie et Moscou* (*Subsidia Hagiographica*, xxxviii, 1963), pp. 20 ff., 211 ff., has published a new recension of the whole Greek text including the prefatory letter which was previously known only in Latin. Although 'Valerius', the author of the *Acts of Pontius* (*Acta Sanctorum*, Mai. iii, pp. 274 ff.), claims to have bought 'gesta martyris ab exceptoribus' (3. 17), his account of Pontius' trial is allegedly drawn from what he saw with his own eyes (1. 1).

[7] J. Geffcken, 'Die Stenographie in den Akten der Märtyrer', *Archiv für Stenographie*, lvii (1906), p. 81, therefore denied that any writer of martyr-literature ever consulted official records.

[8] Against, Geffcken, op. cit., p. 89: 'So ist denn auch m. E. die Passio Scilitanorum kein Aktenstück aus stenographischer Feder, sondern entstammt der Erinnerung, worauf auch ihre Kürze führt.' Similarly Hoffmann, op. cit. (p. 520, n. 1), p. 51. But from whose recollection?

a melancholy reflection. Neither before nor after the short recension was known did anyone challenge the only version printed in the third edition of Knopf–Krüger on specific historical grounds. That implies that the critical tools of modern scholarship are not, and perhaps never can be, sharp enough always to root out the later elements which may still lie buried in those *acta* which the historian must perforce accept as wholly authentic.

This survey has mainly addressed itself to two closely related problems: how many pre-Decian *acta martyrum* are wholly authentic even in details? and how many are contemporary documents? Even if finality of judgement is unattainable, the lines between the genuine and the spurious have (it is hoped) been drawn more clearly than before.

Appendix. The Date of the Passion of Pionius[1]

Eusebius seems to have possessed and used a collection of documents relating to Asian martyrs—Polycarp, Metrodorus, and Pionius at Smyrna and Carpus, Papylus, and Agathonice at Pergamum—all of whose deaths he dates to the joint reign of Marcus and Lucius (March 161 to December 168).[2] It has been argued above that Eusebius' dates for the *Martyrdom of Polycarp* and the *Acts of Carpus, Papylus and Agathonice* are erroneous, partly on the grounds that, since he has misdated the *Passion of Pionius* by more than eighty years, he may also have misdated the other documents in the same collection.[3] The premiss of that argument must now be substantiated.

The *Passion* sets Pionius' martyrdom in the Decian persecution (2. 1), contains an incidental reference to the emperor Gordian, who ruled from 238 to 244 (9. 4), and carries a full date:

ταῦτα ἐπράχθη ἐπὶ ἀνθυπάτου τῆς Ἀσίας Ἰουλίου Πρόκλου Κυντιλλιανοῦ, ὑπατευόντων αὐτοκράτορος Γ. Μεσίου Κύντου Τραιανοῦ Δεκίου Σεβαστοῦ τὸ δεύτερον καὶ Οὐεττίου Γράτου, πρὸ τεσσάρων εἰδῶν Μαρτίων κατὰ Ῥωμαίους, κατὰ δὲ Ἀσιανοὺς μηνὸς ἕκτου ἐννεακαιδεκάτῃ (23).[4]

H. Grégoire–P. Orgels–J. Moreau, however, argue that the correct date is 177: they rely on Eusebius and what they suppose to be historical plausibility, but, though they dismiss the dates at the beginning and end

---

[1] A critical edition with full commentary has been promised by L. Robert, *Hellenica*, xi/xii (1960), p. 262; *Rev. ét. anc.* lxii (1960), p. 319. He will argue that the *Passion* reflects life in Smyrna under Decius, not under Marcus Aurelius.

[2] *H.E.* iv 14. 10–15. 1; 15. 46–8; cf. 26. 1. For the date of Lucius' death see now T. D. Barnes, *J.R.S.* lvii (1967), p. 73.

[3] pp. 512, 515.

[4] Whence *Chronicon Paschale*, p. 504 Bonn. The proconsul is called Quintillianus alone at 19. 2, 20. 6.

of the *Passion*, they overlook the reference to Gordian.[1] M. Simonetti is both forthright and consistent: this passage is 'un elemento introdotto in un secondo tempo, di pari passo con la datazione del martirio all'epoca della persecuzione di Decio'.[2]

There is apparent confirmation in an Armenian version of the *Passion* which is assigned to the years 436 to 439.[3] This omits the passage which mentions Gordian. But an examination of the context will show how little probative force there is in the omission. Its editor's German translation of chap. 9 of the Armenian version reads:

Und dann fragte er (sc. Polemon) den Namen eines jeden und womit sie beschäftigt seien und was für ein Amt sie inne hätten, und befahl, sie zum Gefängnis zu führen. Aber die Menge häufte sich sehr, so daß sie den ganzen Marktplatz einnahm, und einige sprachen über Pionius: Wie rot ist jetzt sein Antlitz, das immer blaß war. Und Sabina hielt sich an Pionius fest wegen des Gedränges der großen Menge, und einige sprachen: Sie fürchtet, daß sie von ihm getrennt werde.[4]

Comparison with Knopf–Krüger reveals the writer's method. He summarizes his Greek exemplar in one short sentence, and then turns to the next chapter. Thus he mentions Sabina, but leaves out many of the genuine details about her in the Greek *Passion*, including the reference to Gordian.

The sentence mentioning Gordian is also omitted by the Latin version which Ruinart considered to be the most primitive recension then known.[5] But without that sentence the text hardly makes sense, and the whole version is characterized by a systematic omission of those touches of local colour, found in the Greek, Armenian, and another, longer, Latin text, which make the *Passion* such a valuable document for the topography and institutions of ancient Smyrna.[6]

There is, therefore, no valid reason to imagine that those passages which indicate that Pionius met his death in the Decian persecution are interpolated. On the contrary, two good reasons prove that the date of 250 must be correct. First, the date at the end of the *Passion* (23) contains full and authentic details of nomenclature, in contrast with those *acta martyrum* which really do bear a fictitious Decian date.[7] Whereas in the *fasti* of chronographers the consuls of 250 appear simply as 'Decio (with or without the sign of iteration) et Grato',[8] the *Passion* not only states the

---

[1] 'Les martyres de Pionios et de Polycarpe', *Bull. Acad. Roy. de Belg.*, *Cl. des Lettres*[5], xlvii (1961), p. 72. For a discussion of the various versions of the *Passion* see L. Wohleb, *Röm. Quartalschr.* xxxvii (1929), pp. 173 ff.

[2] Op. cit. (1955), p. 24.

[3] Published by M. Srapian, 'Das Martyrium des hl. Pionius', *Vienna Oriental Journal*, xxviii (1914), p. 376. [4] Ibid., p. 398.

[5] Op. cit., pp. 139 ff. [6] Wohleb, op. cit., pp. 174 ff.

[7] Note the *Acts of Saturninus* (Ruinart, op. cit., p. 130), and the occurrences in *acta* of 'sub Decio imperatore et Optimo proconsule' (or very similar words) which are discussed by Lietzmann, *Kleine Schriften*, i, pp. 242 ff.

[8] e.g. *Mon. Germ. Hist.*, *Auct. Ant.* ix, pp. 59, 227, 288, 439. For the simplicity of these consular dates compare the fragment of a Greek chronicle (*P. Berol.* 13296) discussed by Lietzmann, op. cit., pp. 420 ff.

emperor's name in full and correctly, but also, allowing for corruption in the manuscripts,[1] gives the *gentilicium* of Gratus.[2] The latter is nowhere else explicitly attested, although a single contemporary inscription from Rome has Decius' colleague as ']ττιο GRATO'.[3] The name of the proconsul of Asia lacks only the *praenomen*:[4] Julius Proculus Quintillianus.[5] Quintillianus seems to appear on two inscriptions from Eleusis which purely epigraphical criteria assign to the third century:

$$Κοι[ντιλλιανῷ]$$
$$[ἀν]θυπάτῳ Ἀσίας$$
$$[Εὐ]μολπίδῃ \qquad\qquad (I.G. \text{ ii/iii}^2. 4219);$$

$$μύστην ἀνθύπατον σε[μνὸν Πρόκλον, φάος ἱρῇ]$$
$$Εὐμο[λπ]ου γενεῇ [ὄν, ξένε, τῇδ' ἐσο]ρᾷ⟨ς⟩$$
$$(\text{Ibid. } 4218, \text{ ll. } 1/2).$$

Secondly, the historical situation envisaged in the narrative of the *Passion* never arose before 250. When Pionius and his companions were praying

ἐπέστη αὐτοῖς Πολέμων ὁ νεωκόρος καὶ οἱ σὺν αὐτῷ τεταγμένοι ἀναζητεῖν καὶ ἕλκειν τοὺς Χριστιανοὺς ἐπιθύειν καὶ μιαροφαγεῖν. καί φησιν ὁ νεωκόρος· οἴδατε πάντως τὸ διάταγμα τοῦ αὐτοκράτορος ὡς κελεύει ὑμᾶς ἐπιθύειν τοῖς θεοῖς (3. 1/2).

Decius was the first emperor to promulgate such an edict,[6] and to impose the responsibility for enforcing it on local officials.[7]

Thus, even if all the explicit indications that the date is the middle of the third century were disregarded as interpolations, the circumstances of Pionius' arrest would still furnish adequate proof of the Decian date.

---

[1] See Lightfoot, op. cit. (p. 512, n. 2), pp. 717 ff.; O. von Gebhardt, *Archiv für slavische Philologie*, xviii (1896), p. 171.

[2] *P.I.R.*[1] V 328; G. Barbieri, *L'albo senatorio da Settimio Severo a Carino (193–285)* (1952), no. 1750; E. Sattmann, *P–W*, viiiA (1958), col. 1859.

[3] *C.I.L.* vi. 31849. In contrast, *I.L.S.* 2190; 7049; *Ann. Ép.* 1898. 62; 1933. 113 all have merely 'Grato'.

[4] 'Γ.' has perhaps dropped out in transmission, since the Armenian version calls the proconsul simply Gaius (Srapian, op. cit., p. 405).

[5] Barbieri, op. cit., no. 1611; *P.I.R.*[2] J 502.

[6] For earlier legislation against the Christians see T. D. Barnes, *J.R.S.* lviii (1968). This argument was rightly adduced by M. Sordi, *Rivista di storia della Chiesa in Italia*, xv (1961), p. 284—but inconsistently, since she also believes that Marcus and Lucius had issued a similar edict in the 160s (*Studi romani*, ix (1961), pp. 365 ff.).

[7] H. Wittig, *P–W*, xv (1932), col. 1282; K. Gross, *R.A.C.* iii (1957), col. 625. E. Liesering, *Untersuchungen zur Christenverfolgung des Kaisers Decius* (1933), pp. 13 ff., quotes most of the evidence in full.

II

LEGISLATION AGAINST THE CHRISTIANS *

The modern bibliography on the subject of the juridical basis of the persecutions of the Christians in the Roman Empire before 250 is vast, contentious—and in large part worthless.[1] For no-one has yet attempted to gather together in a small compass and to scrutinize without preconceptions all the primary evidence for specific actions or legal enactments of the Senate or of emperors before Decius which directly concerned the Christians, or which were directly rendered necessary by them. Ulpian collected the imperial rescripts relating to the punishment of Christians in the seventh book of his *De Officio Proconsulis*.[2] This chapter has left no discernible trace in the *Digest* commissioned by the Christian emperor Justinian. The evidence which remains, therefore, is scattered and often difficult to evaluate. What follows is an attempt to present clearly the primary evidence for the legal basis of the condemnation of Christians before 250 without the accretions of later hagiography or of modern interpretations.

THE LITERARY EVIDENCE FOR SPECIFIC ENACTMENTS [3]

In each case only the earliest item of evidence will be cited, or else all the evidence up to and including Eusebius. Everything demonstrably later than Sulpicius Severus will be ignored. No writer of the fifth or any subsequent century can be shown to have drawn on reliable evidence for the period before 250 which had been omitted by Eusebius ; and what Sulpicius Severus himself says is conclusive proof that he possessed none.[4]

(1) Tiberius : Tertullian, *Apol.* 5, 2 ; cf. 21, 24 ; Eusebius, *Chronicon, GCS* xx, 214 ; cf. XLVII, 176 f.; *HE* II, 2.

Tertullian alleges that Tiberius referred to the Senate a report from Palestine which revealed the divinity of the Christ. This he did ' cum praerogativa suffragii sui '. Although the Senate rejected his proposal, Tiberius threatened accusers of the Christians with punishment. The utter implausibility of the story ought to need no argument ; but, since it has found recent defenders,[5] a short discussion cannot be avoided.

First, the status of the evidence must be assessed. It all derives from Tertullian ; and there is no warrant for supposing that he took the story from the *Apology* of Apollonius, who in turn had obtained his information from the *acta senatus* of the reign of Tiberius.[6] Eusebius, in both the *Chronicon* and the *Ecclesiastical History*, quotes Tertullian by name and has nothing which does not come from Tertullian. Jerome's edition of the *Chronicon* and the *Chronicon Paschale* repeat the citation of Tertullian, doubtless taking it from Eusebius.[7] When later writers give the same story without naming Tertullian as the ultimate source, it does not follow that they are independent of Tertullian and Eusebius, only that

* Many have helped in the composition of this paper. Lack of space prevents me from acknowledging by name all of those to whom I am grateful, but I must single out for mention Professor H. Chadwick, Professor R. Syme, Mr. G. E. M. de Ste Croix and Dr. F. G. B. Millar. To the last-named in particular both form and content owe much.

[1] For the main lines of the controversy see A. N. Sherwin-White, ' The Early Persecutions and Roman Law Again ', *JTS*, N.S. III (1952), 199 ff., reprinted with slight additions at *The Letters of Pliny* (1966), 772 ff.; A. Wlosok, ' Die Rechtsgrundlagen der Christenverfolgungen der ersten zwei Jahrhunderte ', *Gymnasium* LXVI (1959), 14 ff. The clearest exposition of the problems is that of G. E. M. de Ste Croix, ' Why were the early Christians persecuted ? ', *Past and Present* XXVI (1963), 6 ff.

[2] Lactantius, *Div. Inst.* v, 11, 19 : ' Domitius de officio proconsulis libro septimo rescripta principum nefaria collegit, ut doceret quibus poenis adfici oporteret eos qui se cultores dei confiterentur '.

[3] Vague references to a ' νόμος/lex ' against the Christians (such as Athenagoras, *Legatio* 7 ; Tertul-

lian, *Apol.* 4, 4 ff.) will be disregarded : they show merely that Christianity was illegal, not how it came to be so.

[4] Below, p. 35.

[5] E. Volterra, ' Di una decisione del Senato Romano ricordata di Tertulliano ', *Scritti in onore di C. Ferrini pubblicati in occasione della sua beatificazione* I (1947), 471 ff.; C. Cecchelli, ' Un tentato riconoscimento imperiale del Cristo ', *Studi in onore di A. Calderini e R. Paribeni* I (1956), 351 ff.; M. Sordi, ' I primi rapporti fra lo Stato Romano e il Cristianesimo ', *Rendiconti Acc. Naz. Lincei*[8] XII (1957), 58 ff.; ' Sui primi rapporti dell' autorità romana con il Cristianesimo ', *Studi Romani* VIII (1960), 393 ff.; *Il Cristianesimo e Roma* (1965), 26, *et al.*

[6] So M. Sordi, *Il Cristianesimo e Roma* (1965), 418 ; cf. ' Un senatore cristiano dell' età di Commodo ', *Epigraphica* XVII (1955), 104 ff.; ' L'apologia del martire romano Apollonio ', *Rivista di Storia della Chiesa in Italia* XVIII (1964), 169 ff.

[7] *GCS* XLVII, 176 f.; *Chronicon Paschale* p. 430 f. Bonn.

they have not named their authorities.[8] And when the *Doctrina Addai* (*circa* 400) [9] produces additional details—viz. an exchange of letters between Abgar of Edessa and Tiberius,[10] that proves, not that it drew on any early and reliable tradition,[11] but that Eusebius has been embroidered with the use of legendary and fictitious material.[12] The historical reliability of late tradition is revealed all too plainly in the ' Preaching of Peter ' known from an Arabic manuscript dated 799, but no doubt composed much earlier : it describes how Peter baptized Nero, his son and the whole imperial court.[13]

Tertullian alone, therefore, needs to be considered. The next question is obvious and simple : what does he say ? In effect, that the Senate refused an imperial request to make Jesus a God of the Roman Pantheon. There is no hint of a *senatusconsultum* to make Christianity illegal, and the passage which immediately follows implies that there was none : there it is Nero who is ' dedicator damnationis nostrae '.[14]

It is consequently irrelevant to argue that Pilate may plausibly be assumed to have sent Tiberius a report about the Christians as a result of disturbances in Judaea in 35/6,[15] or that the *Acta Apollonii* show that a *senatusconsultum* was the legal basis for the condemnation of a Christian in the reign of Commodus.[16] The evidence of these *acta* will be discussed below—and discounted.[17] As for the report of Pilate, Tertullian, who on this point provides the primary evidence from which all else derives, implies unmistakably that it was not followed by any legal enactment against the Christians. Moreover, the *Acts of the Apostles* provides confirmation. Gallio, the proconsul of Achaea in 51/2,[18] brusquely dismissed a complaint against the teaching of Paul by the leading Jews of Corinth. Had it been a case of wrongdoing or dishonesty, he said, he would have listened : but he had no desire to be an arbiter of verbal quibbling and Jewish law.[19] Sergius Paulus, the proconsul of Cyprus,[20] so far from regarding Paul and Barnabas as criminals, had shown great interest in what they had to say, and is even alleged to have become a Christian convert after watching Paul strike a false prophet down with blindness.[21] Later still, about 60, when the enemies of Paul had instigated his arrest in Jerusalem, the tribune of the cohort stationed there sent him to Caesarea, giving his escort a letter to the governor which stated that Paul's offence was a matter of Jewish law and nothing to merit execution or imprisonment.[22] And, although their main motives seem to have been to gain a bribe or to avoid offending the Jews, neither Felix nor Festus either punished Paul or was willing to try him.[23] Indeed, Festus told Agrippa that in his opinion Paul had done nothing which deserved the death penalty.[24] In brief, no Roman official in the *Acts of the Apostles* regards Christianity as a punishable offence, still less as an offence which had been the object of recent legislation.

---

[8] For the universal dependence of later eastern writers on Eusebius see F. Haase, *Altchristliche Kirchengeschichte nach orientalischen Quellen* (1925), esp. 116 ff.
[9] I. Ortiz de Urbina, *Patrologia Syriaca* (1958), 41 f.
[10] G. Phillips, *The Doctrine of Addai, the Apostle* (1876), 36 f. (Eng. trans.).
[11] As asserted by Volterra, o.c., 478 ff. M. Sordi, *Rendiconti Acc. Naz. Lincei*[8] XII (1957), 81 f. adduces as proof of an independent tradition Moses of Chorene, *Hist. Armen.* II, 33—which is both indubitably no earlier than the ninth century (P-W, Suppl. VI, 534 ff.) and demonstrably based on the *Doctrina Addai* (R. A. Lipsius, *Die edessenische Abgar-sage kritisch untersucht* (1880), esp. 31 ff.).
[12] For the rapid development of other legends concerning Abgar see A. von Gutschmid, ' Untersuchungen über die Geschichte des Königreichs Osroëne ', *Mém. Acad. Imp. St.-Pétersbourg*[7] XXXV, I (1887), 10 ff.; E. Kirsten, *RAC* IV, 588 ff. Already in the time of Eusebius the fictitious correspondence between Jesus and King Abgar was said to be in the official archives of Edessa (*HE* I, 13, 5 ff.). The motive for these pious inventions is fully discussed by H. Koester, *HTR* LVIII (1965), 290 ff., esp. 305 f.
[13] M. D. Gibson, ' Apocrypha Sinaitica ', *Studia Sinaitica* V (1896), 52 ff., esp. 59. Another version of the same tale was published by A. S. Lewis, ' Acta Mythologica Apostolorum ', *Horae Semiticae* III

(1904) : Arabic text ; IV (1904), 210 ff.: Eng. trans.
[14] *Apol.* 5, 3. Yet W. H. C. Frend, *CR* n.s. XVII (1967), 196, following Sordi, represents the passage as saying that Tiberius' communication with the Senate ' resulted in a *senatus consultum* unfavourable to the new religion '.
[15] e.g. M. Sordi, *Studi Romani* VIII (1960), 393 ff.
[16] e.g. M. Sordi, *Il Cristianesimo e Roma* (1965), 59, etc.
[17] Pp. 46-48.
[18] *PIR*[2] J 757, after E. Groag, *Die römischen Reichsbeamten von Achaea* (1939), 34 f.
[19] *Acts* 18, 14 ff.
[20] The date can only be inferred from the disputed chronology of *Acts* : P-W II A, 1716 f.
[21] *Acts* 13, 6 ff. Whatever the implausibility of the story to the sceptical, there is hardly a conversion in *Acts* which is not occasioned by some display of supernatural powers : for the ancient writer, as for the modern believer, ' it is as one inspired by the (Holy) Spirit that Paul defeats the false prophet ' (G. W. H. Lampe, *Peake's Commentary on the Bible* (1962), 788h).
[22] *Acts* 21, 27 ff., esp 23, 26 ff. (the letter).
[23] *Acts* 23, 33 ff., esp. 24, 26 (Felix' hope of a bribe) ; 24, 27 ; 25, 9 (Festus' desire to please the Jews).
[24] *Acts* 25, 25. For Paul's so-called ' appeal ' to the emperor, see the convincing exposition of P. D. A. Garnsey, *JRS* LVI (1966), 182 ff.

34

(2) Nero : Tacitus, *Annales* XV, 44 ; Suetonius, *Nero* 16, 2 ; Tertullian, *Apol.* 5, 3 ; Eusebius, *Chronicon*, *GCS* XX, 216 ; cf. XLVII, 185 ; *HE* II, 25.

Suetonius records (among Nero's good deeds)[25] merely the fact that Christians were done to death. Tacitus is both fuller and clear in his exposition. In 64 a large part of Rome burnt, and neither imperial largesse nor religious rites could quiet the popular suspicion that the fire had been ordered by Nero. Accordingly a scapegoat was necessary. The Christians, detested as they were by the populace, were therefore accused of incendiarism. The charge, if indeed a precise charge was needed at such a time, was not that they were Christians but that they had set fire to Rome. Much difficulty has been caused to modern scholarship by the failure to see that it was Nero's policy at the time to confuse the issue by equating the confession of Christianity with an admission of arson, and that the equation found a ready acceptance from the hysterical mob.[26]

(3) Nero : Tertullian, *Nat.* I, 7, 8/9.

Pliny did not know of any law or *senatusconsultum* which outlawed the Christians, and Trajan did not enlighten his ignorance.[27] Yet many have argued from Tertullian that there was some sort of law or decree passed against them under Nero, what Tertullian himself calls the *institutum Neronianum*.[28] But a confrontation of the passage of the *Ad Nationes* which uses the phrase with two others which do not will show that the deduction so often drawn from it has no justification whatever :

Melito, at Eusebius, *HE* IV, 26, 9 :

μόνοι πάντων, ἀναπεισθέντες ὑπό τινων βασκάνων ἀνθρώπων, τὸν καθ' ἡμᾶς ἐν διαβολῇ καταστῆσαι λόγον ἠθέλησαν Νέρων καὶ Δομετιανός, ἀφ' ὧν καὶ τὸ τῆς συκοφαντίας ἀλόγῳ συνηθείᾳ περὶ τοὺς τοιούτους ῥυῆναι συμβέβηκεν ψεῦδος.

Tertullian, *Nat.* I, 7, 8/9 :

principe Augusto nomen hoc ortum est, Tiberio disciplina eius inluxit, Nerone damnatio invaluit, ut iam hinc de persona persecutoris ponderetis : si pius ille princeps, impii Christiani ; si iustus, si castus, iniusti et incesti Christiani ; si non hostis publicus, nos publici hostes : quales simus, damnator ipse demonstravit, utique aemula sibi puniens. ' et tamen permansit erasis omnibus hoc solum institutum Neronianum, iustum denique ut dissimile sui auctoris.'[29]

Tertullian, *Apol.* 5, 3/4 :

consulite commentarios vestros, illic reperietis primum Neronem in hanc sectam cum maxime Romae orientem Caesariano gladio ferocisse. tali dedicatore damnationis nostrae etiam gloriamur : qui enim scit illum, intellegere potest non nisi grande aliquod bonum a Nerone damnatum. temptaverat et Domitianus, portio Neronis de crudelitate . . . tales semper nobis insecutores, iniusti, impii, turpes, quos et ipsi damnare consuestis, a quibus damnatos restituere soliti estis.

Tertullian is surely modelling his argument on that of Melito.[30] Melito had linked Christianity to the Roman Empire by maintaining both that it began under the first emperor Augustus and that it was persecuted only by the ' bad ' emperors Nero and Domitian.[31] Both ideas were new ones, appearing for the first time in the *Apology* of Melito.[32]

---

[25] cf. *Nero* 19, 3.

[26] R. Syme, *Tacitus* (1958), 553, n. 5, justly observes that ' Tacitus reproduces the mixed character of the situation itself '. At the time of writing, the latest discussion is by E. Koestermann, ' Ein folgenschwerer Irrtum des Tacitus (*Ann.* 15, 44, 2 ff.) ? ', *Historia* XVI (1967), 456 ff.

[27] Pliny, *Epp.* x, 96/7. The opposite inference is drawn by P. Keresztes, *VChr* XVIII (1964), 204 ; but see n. 48.

[28] Indeed, Keresztes, ibid., goes so far as to claim that ' there is today an almost general agreement that the Christians, under normal circumstances, were not tried on the basis of either the *ius coercitionis* or the general criminal law, but on the basis of a special law introduced during Nero's rule, proscribing Christians as such '.

[29] The quotations of Tertullian are all taken from *Corpus Christianorum, Series Latina* I/II.

[30] E. Renan, *Marc-Aurèle* (1882), 284, quotes Melito and observes ' le système des apologistes, si chaudement soutenu par Tertullien (*Apol.* 5), d'après lequel les bons empereurs ont favorisé le christianisme et les mauvais empereurs l'ont persécuté, était déjà complètement éclos '. But he failed to see the relevance of Tertullian's two successive versions of Melito's argument for the *institutum Neronianum*. A similar blindness led J. Zeiller, *Miscellanea G. Mercati* v (*Studi e Testi* CXXV, 1946), 3 to state that the phrase also occurs in the *Apologeticum*.

[31] Eusebius, *HE* IV, 26, 7 ff.

[32] So, e.g., W. H. C. Frend, *Martyrdom and Persecution in the Early Church* (1965), 286 f.

Both reappear in the *Ad Nationes*. But Tertullian, adopting one of his favourite devices, concentrates attention on the origin of persecution. Hence, by omitting all mention of Domitian, he is able to brand persecution as an *institutum Neronianum*. When he came to revise and refine his arguments for the *Apologeticum*,[33] Tertullian discarded the first of Melito's new ideas, presumably because he realized its obvious falsity, and put in its place the story of Tiberius and the report from Pilate.[34] He also appealed to Tacitus (in the guise of ' commentarii vestri ') in order to provide proof acceptable to pagans that Nero really was the first persecutor,[35] and he generalized Melito's second argument, dropping the lame ironical comments on Nero's motive and the continuance of the *institutum*. In his earlier adaptation of Melito, he combined the two ideas of Nero as the first persecutor and persecution as inspired by an ' ἄλογος συνήθεια ' to produce the phrase *institutum Neronianum*, which in its context can denote only persecution or the habit or practice of persecution, not its juridical basis.[36] When the argument became more universal in the *Apologeticum*, the phrase had no place in it. The *institutum Neronianum*, therefore, has no relevance to the legal basis of the persecutions, since it was designed to be a tendentious description of persecution itself.

(4) Nero (and others ?) : Sulpicius Severus, *Chronica* II, 29, 3.

After describing the killing of Christians by Nero to avert from himself blame for the burning of Rome, Sulpicius Severus continues :

> hoc initio in Christianos saeviri coeptum. post etiam datis legibus religio vetabatur, palamque edictis propositis Christianum esse non licebat. tum Paulus et Petrus capitis damnati.

Severus clearly has no knowledge of any specific law or edict against the Christians. An indefinite number of laws and edicts are stated to be later than the fire of Rome (in 64) and the consequent deaths of Christians as incendiaries, while the earliest of them is implied to have preceded the execution of Peter and Paul (which Eusebius assigned to the year 68).[37] The vague plurals show that Severus has simply made an inference from the fact that Christianity was illegal. The quality of his inferences and of his historical outlook can be gauged from his statement that Trajan forbade Christians to be maltreated because he found in them nothing which merited death or even punishment.[38]

(5) Domitian : Hegesippus, at Eusebius, *HE* III, 19 f.; Melito, at Eusebius, *HE* IV, 26, 9 ;
      Tertullian, *Apol.* 5, 4 ; Eusebius, *Chronicon*, *GCS* xx, 218 ; cf. XLVII, 192 (both
      citing Bruttius).[39]

Melito, Tertullian, and Bruttius stated that Domitian persecuted the Christians. Melito and Bruttius vouchsafe no details, Tertullian only that Domitian soon changed his mind and recalled those whom he had exiled. Hegesippus makes Domitian stop the persecution after seeing and discharging members of the family of Jesus who were peasant farmers, presumably in Palestine. Eusebius alleges that Flavia Domitilla was banished for being a Christian, whereas Dio reports that her crime, and that of others, was sympathy for

---

[33] The sequence of the two works has been demonstrated beyond possible doubt by C. Becker, *Tertullians Apologeticum : Werden und Leistung* (1954).
[34] *Apol.* 5, 2 ; cf. 21, 24. Although Tertullian is the earliest evidence for Pilate's letter to Tiberius (above, pp. 32 f.) Justin (*Apol.* I, 35 ; 48) appeals to ' τὰ ἐπὶ Ποντίου Πιλάτου γενόμενα ἄκτα ' to establish the facts concerning the crucifixion of Jesus. But the public records of the province of Judaea were burnt in 66 (Josephus, *BJ* II, 427). (On the apocryphal Pilate-literature which is still extant, see G. C. O'Ceallaigh, *HTR* LVI (1963), 21 ff.).
[35] J. Moreau, *Die Christenverfolgung im römischen Reich²* (1961), 64 holds that Tertullian is citing Suetonius, and that ' das institutum Tertullians stammt also aus Sueton '. But Suetonius does not

explicitly state either that the executions occurred in Rome or that Christianity was at that time just beginning to gain a hold in the capital : both facts, however, appear in Tacitus, *Ann.* XV, 44.
[36] J. W. P. Borleffs, ' Institutum Neronianum ', *VChr* VI (1952), 129 ff.
[37] Eusebius, *Chronicon*, *GCS* xx, 216 ; *HE* II, 25, 5 assigns the deaths of Peter and Paul to the time of the first persecution, that of Nero, as does Jerome, *GCS* XLVII, 185. Both, however, put the persecution four years after the fire, an error which Sulpicius Severus was able to avoid through his knowledge of Tacitus.
[38] *Chronica* II, 31, 2.
[39] *PIR²*B 159. Perhaps the Christians are misreporting an account of the victims of Domitian by Bruttius Praesens (ib. 164).

Judaism[40] and Suetonius omits her exile altogether from his lists of Domitian's good and bad actions.[41] The temptation for later Christians to see in Flavia Domitilla a sympathy for, or adherence to, Christianity was irresistible : [42] even the executed consul Flavius Clemens eventually became a Christian.[43] Yet, even if there is some truth behind these stories (which is unlikely),[44] nowhere in them is there mention of any legal ordinance against the Christians.

(6) Trajan : rescript to Pliny, with Pliny's original letter, Pliny, *Epp.* x, 96/7 ;[45] cf. Tertullian, *Apol.* 2, 6 f., on which alone Eusebius (*Chronicon, GCS* xx, 218 f. ; xLVII, 195 ; *HE* III, 33) depends.

Christians were accused before Pliny, who states in his letter that he did not know how they were normally punished because he had never taken part in any trial concerning them. Nevertheless, he executed those who admitted to being Christians—except for those who were Roman citizens, whom he sent to Rome.[46] After the first trial (or trials), more were accused in an anonymous *libellus* and by an informer. Pliny released those who said that they were not Christians and never had been, but first he made them invoke the Gods, sacrifice before statues of the Gods and of the emperor and curse the Christ. He also made those who said that they had been Christians but were no longer do the same. But, before releasing them, he wrote to Trajan. Trajan, in reply, professed to be laying down no universal rule,[47] but declared that Christians, though they were not to be hunted out, were to be punished if openly accused and convicted. However, if a man said he was not a Christian and proved it by sacrificing to the Gods, his change of heart should earn him pardon, even if his past was not free from suspicion.

Pliny, when trying the Christians before him, had no need to rely on any law which made Christianity a capital crime : indeed he appears not even to have known whether there was one.[48] There were three categories of accused : those who confessed to being Christians ; those who denied ever being Christians ; and those who admitted having been Christians in the past, but said that they were no longer. Pliny was certain how he ought to treat the first two classes. The second he released, while the first he either executed on the spot (the non-citizens) or sent to Rome for punishment (the citizens). The third class, however, a very large one, presented a problem and caused Pliny to write to the emperor. When he executed or despatched to Rome those who confessed, he had no doubts that punishment was merited. But his investigation of the third class revealed that the Christians had committed no illegal acts like robbery or adultery : their only crime was a depraved superstition. He accordingly urged on Trajan at some length the advantages of allowing ' paenitentiae locus '.[49]

[40] Dio LXVII, 14.

[41] Domitilla is mentioned only because the murderer of Domitian was ' Stephanus, Domitillae procurator ' (*Dom.* 17, 1).

[42] The same factors lie behind the progressive exaltation of the status of the martyr Apollonius : Eusebius calls him ' ἄνδρα τῶν τότε πιστῶν ἐπὶ παιδείᾳ καὶ φιλοσοφίᾳ βεβοημένον ' (*HE* V, 21, 2) ; Jerome a ' Romanae urbis senator ' (*De Viris Illustribus* 42).

[43] Syncellus, p. 650 Bonn.

[44] See further E. M. Smallwood, ' Domitian's Attitude toward the Jews and Judaism ', *CP* LI (1956), 1 ff.

[45] For commentary on these two letters see A. N. Sherwin-White, *The Letters of Pliny* (1966), 691 ff.; R. Freudenberger, *Das Verhalten der römischen Behörden gegen die Christen im 2. Jahrhundert* (*Münchener Beiträge zur Papyrusforschung und antiken Rechtsgeschichte* LII, 1967). The date of the letters is probably autumn 110 (Sherwin-White, o.c., 80 f.; 693), not 112 (as Freudenberger, o.c. 17, implies).

[46] This was a common, perhaps the normal, procedure : F. G. B. Millar, *JRS* LVI (1966), 159 ; P. D. A. Garnsey, ibid. 181 f.

[47] cf. Freudenberger, o.c. 203 ff.

[48] *Epp.* x, 96, 1–3 : ' cognitionibus de Christianis interfui numquam : ideo nescio quid et quatenus aut

puniri soleat aut quaeri. nec mediocriter haesitavi, sitne aliquod discrimen aetatum . . . ; nomen ipsum, si flagitiis careat, an flagitia cohaerentia nomini puniantur. interim . . . hunc sum secutus modum. interrogavi ipsos an essent Christiani. confitentes iterum ac tertio interrogavi supplicium minatus : perseverantes duci iussi. neque enim dubitabam, qualecumque esset quod faterentur, pertinaciam certe et inflexibilem obstinationem debere puniri '. These words surely disprove the inference of P. Keresztes, *VChr* XVIII (1964), 204 : ' It is clear from the well-known correspondence of Pliny and Trajan that before and at the time of this correspondence there was a law proscribing Christianity as such '. Keresztes appears to rely on the assumption ' nullum crimen sine lege '—which is false for Roman law (de Ste Croix, o.c. (n. 1), 12).

[49] That this is the main point of the letter was realized by E. G. Hardy, *Plinii Epistulae ad Traianum* (1889), 65, and can be securely deduced from three facts : Pliny places his suggestion in an emphatic position, at the very end ; he constructs the argument of the letter to build up to it ; and he stresses how large a number are still in custody (9 : ' visa est enim mihi res digna consultatione, maxime propter periclitantium numerum ').

It is not clear whether Trajan, in his reply, made a change in the legal position of Christians or not. Since Pliny implies that trials of Christians were far from rare, it is hard to believe that no-one before had been accused of Christianity after ceasing to be a Christian. Governors before Pliny may have set free those who answered ' non sum ' to the putting of the charge ' Christianus es ? ', without enquiring whether they had been Christians in the past. However, whether Trajan's ruling is an innovation or the reaffirmation of a principle already established, Christianity is placed in a totally different category from all other crimes. What is illegal is being a Christian : the crime is erased by a change of heart. The function of the sacrifice is to demonstrate that, even if a man has been a Christian, his change of heart is genuine and not just a matter of words.[50]

During the second and early third centuries those accused of being Christians continued to be set free if they performed a symbolic act of sacrifice, and punished if they did not. In the language of Pliny and the apologists, condemnation was for the *nomen* ;[51] and, as Tertullian remarked, there was nothing to prevent a man from denying and regaining his liberty ' iterum Christianus '.[52] There is but one example of suspected Christians being punished even after apostasy : in the violent persecution at Lugdunum. In this case, however, there was apparent evidence of those *flagitia* which Trajan had considered irrelevant : some pagan slaves belonging to Christians were threatened with torture and denounced the Christian community for Thyestean feasts and Oedipodean incests.[53]

(7) Hadrian : rescript to Minicius Fundanus, proconsul of Asia in 122/3,[54] Justin, *Apol.* 1, 68 ; [55] Justin, at Eusebius, *HE* IV, 9 ; cf. Melito, at Eusebius, *HE* IV, 26, 10.

Hadrian's rescript states that Fundanus' predecessor as proconsul of Asia, Serennius Granianus (in fact, Q. Licinius Silvanus Granianus Quadronius Proculus[56]), had written to him. Hadrian's reply prohibits condemnation in response to mere shouting and clamour, and recommends the proconsul to deal severely with those who bring a frivolous accusation of Christianity. The rescript seems to presuppose both that there had been a public outcry similar to that which later led to the death of Polycarp in the stadium at Smyrna,[57] and that *delatores* were employing the imputation of Christianity to stir up prejudice against those whom they accused of less serious crimes.[58] The genuineness of the rescript can be defended by one important fact : despite Christian interpretations of it, the rescript itself makes no change in the legal position as defined by Trajan.[59]

(8) Pius : letters cited by Melito, at Eusebius, *HE* IV, 26, 10.

Melito asserts that, while Marcus was associated with him in the imperial power, Pius wrote to the cities ' περὶ τοῦ μηδὲν νεωτερίζειν περὶ ἡμῶν '. The letters which Melito names specifically are ones to Larisa, to Thessalonica, to Athens and to all the Greeks (by which he may well mean the letter to the κοινόν of Asia), and he explicitly states that they had the same tenor as the rescript of Hadrian to Minicius Fundanus. By ' μηδὲν νεωτερίζειν ' Melito probably means ' take no violent measures ',[60] so that the letters in effect forbade pogroms of Christians without proper trial.[61]

(9) Pius or Marcus : letter to the κοινόν of Asia, at Eusebius, *HE* IV, 13 ; *Cod. Par. Gr.* 450 (reproduced at *GCS* IX, 1, 328).

Eusebius, who cites Melito's *Apology* for corroboration, and the manuscript of Justin's

[50] de Ste Croix, o.c. 19 f.
[51] Pliny, *Epp.* x, 96, 2 ; Justin, *Apol.* 1, 4 ; etc.
[52] *Apol.* 2, 17.
[53] Eusebius, *HE* v, 1, 14 ; 1, 25 ff.; 1, 33 ff.
[54] The year is fixed by *AÉ* 1957, 17.
[55] In the MS. of Justin the original Latin has been supplanted by Eusebius' Greek translation. The Latin which stands at Rufinus, *HE* IV, 9, is no more than a retranslation of Eusebius' Greek (Schanz-Hosius, *Gesch. der röm. Litt.* III³ (1922), 250 f.).
[56] *PIR*¹ L 170 ; A. Degrassi, *Fasti Consolari* (1952), 32.
[57] *Mart. Polyc.* 3, etc.
[58] Compare the constant employment of the charge of *maiestas* against senators at Rome in the reign of Tiberius.

[59] E. Groag, P-W XIII, 462 f. ; W. Schmid, ' The Christian Re-interpretation of the Rescript of Hadrian ', *Maia* VII (1955), 5 ff.; P. Keresztes, ' The Emperor Hadrian's Rescript to Minicius Fundanus ', *Latomus* XXVI (1967), 54 ff. = *Phoenix* XXI (1967), 119 ff.; Freudenberger, o.c. 216 ff. Hadrian and the Christians had different views of what was meant by ' εἴ τις δείκνυσίν τι παρὰ τοὺς νόμους πράττοντας '. The latter took the clause to prohibit condemnation for the *nomen* alone, whereas Hadrian was in fact here mainly considering the case of those who were falsely accused of Christianity ' συκοφαντίας χάριν '.
[60] See L-S-J, s.v.
[61] Compare ' μηδὲ μόναις βοαῖς ' in Hadrian's rescript to Fundanus.

Apologies present the same alleged imperial letter, with minor variations in the text but with completely different headings. The manuscript of Justin makes it a letter of Antoninus Pius in his twenty-fourth *tribunicia potestas*, i.e. between 10th December, 160, and his death on 7th March, 161.[62] Eusebius inserts the letter among the events of Pius' reign and also explicitly ascribes it to him : but the manuscripts, without exception, give the writer as Marcus Aurelius (with the title Ἀρμένιος) in his fifteenth *tribunicia potestas* and after the start of his third consulate, i.e., since he is also styled ἀρχιερεὺς μέγιστος, between 7th March and 10th December, 161.[63] On the assumption that the letter is a fabrication, a plausible explanation can be given for this discrepancy.[64] The letter speaks of continual earthquakes, and Aelius Aristides reports violent earthquakes during the proconsulate of Albus.[65] Now L. Antonius Albus, long supposed to have been proconsul of Asia about 147/8[66] or in 151/2,[67] may without difficulty be assumed to be the proconsul for 160/1, since a date either shortly before or shortly after 160 seems to have been established by recently published inscriptions.[68] Hence it is possible, perhaps even probable, that there was a genuine imperial letter in that proconsular year, occasioned by the earthquakes or their aftermath.[69] (It may easily have mentioned Christians.[70]) The two different headings may, therefore, come from a Christian who wished to concoct proof that natural disaster had induced imperial favour to the Christians, who knew the year (proconsular or local) of the earthquakes and that an imperial letter resulted from it, but who was uncertain which emperor he should make the writer of the letter which he himself had composed. He solved his difficulty by furnishing his creation with the two extant and different headings. If this theory is correct, the letter was fabricated after 164 when Marcus took the title *Armenicus*,[71] and, if it is the same as the letter described by Melito as being from Pius to all the Greeks, before 176.[72]

However that may be, the letter purports to reaffirm the opinion of the previous emperor that Christians were to be left alone unless they were plotting against the government, and it states that Christians are not to be punished simply for being Christians.[73] But no previous affirmation of the principle is known, and the contrary principle, that Christians are *eo ipso* criminals is well attested in the years immediately after 161. It is assumed in the imperial letter concerning the Gallic Christians,[74] is attacked by Melito in his *Apology*,[75] and seems to have provided the charge upon which Justin and his companions were tried and executed between 161 and 168.[76] Hence, whatever the genesis of the variant headings, the letter is hardly genuine as it stands—and the lack of independent evidence renders it impossible to isolate the authentic elements, if there are any.[77]

[62] *PIR²* A 1513.

[63] *PIR²* A 697.

[64] A. Harnack, ' Das Edikt des Antoninus Pius ', *Texte u. Unters.* XIII, 4 (1895), 56 ff. was, however, possibly correct in maintaining that the Christian who composed the letter styled the emperor quite simply 'Ἀντωνῖνος ', and that a later hand produced what stands in Eusebius, while ' der nicht ungelehrte Redaktor B ' produced what is in *Cod.Par.Gr.* 450 to remove the discrepancy in Eusebius.

[65] XLIX, 38 ff. Keil.

[66] e.g. W. Hüttl, *Antoninus Pius* II (1933), 48 f.; Degrassi, o.c. (n. 56), 38 ; cf. *PIR²* A 810.

[67] W. M. Ramsay, *JÖAI* XXVII (1932), Beiblatt 245 ff.; followed (for the date of the earthquakes) by Frend, o.c. (n. 32), 240.

[68] G. W. Bowersock, ' The Proconsulate of Albus ', *HSCP* LXXII (1967), 289 ff., arguing from the inscriptions at *JÖAI* XLIV (1959), 143 (= *SEG* XIX, 684) ; *JÖAI* XLIV (1959), Beiblatt 257 ff.

[69] cf. Bowersock, o.c. 292 : ' the rescript has a genuine historical context, and that is why, bogus as it probably is, it can oscillate between two emperors in the year 161 '.

[70] For letters from emperors to provincial councils on the subject of criminals liable to capital punishment compare *Dig.* XLVII, 14, 1 (Hadrian to the *concilium Baeticae* : about rustlers) ; *P. Ox.* 2104, of of which *Dig.* XLIX, 1, 25 preserves the first part

(Alexander to the κοινόν of Bithynia : about appeals, some on capital charges).

[71] C. H. Dodd, *Num. Chr.*⁴ XI (1911), 209 ff.

[72] Eusebius, *HE* IV, 26, 10. Since the *Apology* is addressed to one emperor alone (ibid. 6 ff.), it was presumably composed between the death of Lucius Verus in the winter of 168/9 and Commodus' investiture as Augustus in 177.

[73] 6/7 : ὑπὲρ δὲ τῶν τοιούτων ἤδη καὶ πολλοὶ τῶν περὶ τὰς ἐπαρχίας ἡγεμόνων καὶ τῷ θειοτάτῳ ἡμῶν ἔγραψαν πατρί, οἷς καὶ ἀντέγραψεν μηδὲν ἐνοχλεῖν τοῖς τοιούτοις, εἰ μὴ ἐμφαίνοιντό τι περὶ τὴν Ῥωμαίων ἡγεμονίαν ἐγχειροῦντες. καὶ ἐμοὶ δὲ περὶ τῶν τοιούτων πολλοὶ ἐσήμαναν· οἷς δὴ καὶ ἀντέγραψα κατακολουθῶν τῇ τοῦ πατρὸς γνώμῃ. εἰ δέ τις ἐπιμένοι τινὰ τῶν τοιούτων εἰς πράγματα φέρων ὡς δὴ τοιοῦτον, ἐκεῖνος ὁ καταφερόμενος ἀπολελύσθω τοῦ ἐγκλήματος καὶ ἐὰν φαίνηται τοιοῦτος ὤν, ὁ δὲ καταφέρων ἔνοχος ἔσται δίκης.

[74] Eusebius, *HE* V, 1, 47. (On the date, *JTS* n.s. XIX (1968), 517.)

[75] ibid. IV, 26. Also by Athenagoras, *Legatio* 1 ff.

[76] *Acta Just.* 4 f. (short recension). Sentence is, however, passed in the following words : ' οἱ μὴ βουληθέντες ἐπιθῦσαι τοῖς θεοῖς, φραγελλωθέντες ἀπαχθήτωσαν τῇ τῶν νόμων ἀκολουθίᾳ ' (ibid. 5).

[77] As attempted by Harnack, o.c.; R. Freudenberger, ' Christenreskript : ein umstrittenes Reskript des Antoninus Pius ', *Zeitschr. für Kirchengesch.* LXXVIII (1967), 1 ff.

II

(10) Marcus and Lucius : *Vita Abercii* 1.

The date of the composition of the *Vita Abercii* cannot be determined with any degree of precision, but since it refers to Julian the Apostate it cannot be earlier than 361.[78] The opening sentence states that a decree went out from the emperors Marcus Antoninus and Lucius Verus to all the empire of the Romans proclaiming that sacrifices and libations to the Gods were to be performed in public. The writer of the *Vita* had some reliable information at his disposal.[79] But this decree is condemned as spurious no less by the total ignorance of it shown by all earlier writers and by the statement that one of its recipients was P. Dolabella, the governor of Phrygia Salutaris,[80] than by the parody of Luke : although its content is inevitably different, and is copied from the persecuting edicts of Decius and Diocletian,[81] the promulgation of the decree is no more than an imitation of the decree of Caesar Augustus that all the world should be taxed.[82]

(11) Marcus : Tertullian, *Apol.* 5, 6 ; whence Eusebius, *HE* v, 5, 5 ff.; cf. *Scap.* 4, 6.

Tertullian appeals to the letter which Marcus Aurelius wrote :

quibus illam Germanicam sitim Christianorum forte militum precationibus impetrato imbri discussam contestatur. sicut non palam ab eiusmodi hominibus poenam dimovit, ita alio modo palam dispersit, adiecta etiam accusatorum damnatione, et quidem taetriore.

Tertullian's statement has usually (and correctly) been dismissed as an apologetic invention.[83] Recently, however, his veracity has found a champion.[84] For the purpose of this article it will suffice to observe that, according to Tertullian, Marcus made no change in the legal position of Christianity, and that there is no valid corroborative evidence that their accusers were ever punished.[85] On the contrary, the omission of such a startling manifestation of imperial sympathy by all other apologists and even by Tertullian himself in his *Ad Nationes* is proof enough that it never occurred.

(12) Marcus : Melito, at Eusebius, *HE* IV, 26, 5 f.

Addressing Marcus in his *Apology*, Melito denounces a new happening : the Christians are being harassed by new decrees throughout Asia. Some scholars infer from this that there had recently been imperial action affecting the status of Christians.[86] But Melito asks the emperor whether the new decrees are issued at his command : therefore, they do not emanate from him directly.[87] A plausible explanation can be offered of both the complaint and the question. The innovation might be that the proconsul, in the edict normally issued by any governor on entering his province,[88] has for the first time explicitly included Christianity among the offences of which he proposes to take cognisance. That could only encourage the delation of Christians, who could now be accused with no fear that the proconsul might either acquit the defendant or round on the accuser.[89]

---

[78] *Vita* 66.

[79] e.g. that Lucius Verus returned from Syria to Ephesus to marry Marcus' daughter (*Vita* 45, cf. *JRS* LVII (1967), 72).

[80] *Vita* 1. The province of Phrygia Salutaris is certainly no older than the Diocletianic reforms, and its formation may be even later : see A. H. M. Jones, 'The Date and Value of the Verona List', *JRS* XLIV (1954), 21 ff.

[81] For the terms of these edicts see, respectively, J. R. Knipfing, 'The Libelli of the Decian Persecution', *HTR* XVI (1923), 345 ff.; G. E. M. de Ste Croix, 'Aspects of the "Great" Persecution', *HTR* XLVII (1954), 75 ff.

[82] Luke 2, 1. The decree is, nonetheless, accepted as authentic by M. Sordi, 'I "nuovi decreti" di Marco Aurelio contro i Cristiani', *Studi Romani* IX (1961), 365 ff.

[83] Perhaps most effectively by J. B. Lightfoot, *The Apostolic Fathers Part II. S. Ignatius. S. Polycarp*, I² (1889), 488 ff.

[84] M. Sordi, 'Le polemiche intorno al Cristianesimo del II secolo', *Rivista di Storia della Chiesa in Italia* XVI (1962), 19 ff.; o.c. (n. 16), 193 ff.

[85] Eusebius, *HE* v, 21, 3, it is true, states that the accuser of Apollonius was executed : but see below, pp. 46–48.

[86] So, most recently, Sordi, o.c. (n. 82) ; Frend, o.c. (n. 32), 268 f.

[87] H. Grégoire—P. Orgels, *Bull. Ac. Roy. Belg.* XXXVIII (1952), 44 f. = *Les Persécutions dans l'empire romain* ² (1964), 174 f. ; G. E. M. de Ste Croix, *JTS* n.s. XVIII (1967), 219.

[88] For an indication of the problems surrounding the provincial edict see G. Chalon, *L'Édit de Tiberius Julius Alexander* (1964), 72 ff. Sherwin-White, o.c. (n. 45) gives no annotation on Pliny's edict in Bithynia (*Epp.* x, 96, 7), merely referring to its 'routine publication' (o.c. 583).

[89] Grégoire—Orgels, l.c., argue that the decrees come from the cities of Asia. But the cities ought not (at this date) to concern themselves with a capital offence ; and the view in the text perhaps accords better with the words ' εἰ δὲ καὶ παρὰ σοῦ μὴ εἴη ἡ βουλὴ αὕτη καὶ τὸ καινὸν τοῦτο διάταγμα' (Eusebius, *HE* IV, 26, 6 fin.).

40

(13) Marcus (?) : rescript to the governor of Gallia Lugdunensis, at Eusebius, *HE* v, 1, 47.

During an outbreak of persecution at Lugdunum,[90] the governor wrote to the emperor about the punishment of those Christians who were Roman citizens. Marcus replied that Christians should be done to death (apparently prescribing decapitation for the citizens), but added that apostasy merited freedom.[91] The legal attitude which he adopts is, therefore, precisely the same as Trajan had enunciated.[92]

(14) Commodus : Eusebius, *HE* v, 21, 3.

Eusebius asserts that the servant who accused Apollonius had his legs broken[93] at the start of his master's trial, since an (apparently very recent) imperial decree did not allow informers on such points to live.[94] The implausibility of the execution of both accuser and accused ought to be obvious,[95] even though the evidence of slaves and *liberti* against their masters or *patroni* was often inadmissible in court.[96] It was undoubtedly normal to punish slaves for accusing their masters falsely,[97] and it is perhaps to this custom that Eusebius refers. Perhaps, though, Eusebius has misunderstood a reference to testimony under torture.[98] Yet the *Acta Apollonii* as extant do not so much as mention the servant.[99] Apollonius was, however, condemned to death, and for the *nomen* alone,[100] so that the alleged imperial decree can have made no alteration in the law as it affected the Christians themselves.

(15) Septimius Severus : *HA, Severus* 17, 1.

According to the *Historia Augusta*, Septimius Severus :

Iudaeos fieri vetuit. idem sanxit de Christianis.

The putting of Christians and Jews on the same level is an idea which recurs later in the *Historia Augusta* in indubitable fiction ;[101] and that alone, without supporting arguments, would be enough to bring the statement about Severus and the Christians under the gravest suspicion, even though the prohibition of Jewish proselytism may well be historical.[102] Modern scholars have often claimed that the alleged edict is genuine because it was immediately followed by a persecution directed precisely against catechumens, i.e., against recent converts.[103] But in the only contemporary account of a martyrdom of the time which is extant, the *Passio Perpetuae*, the charge is still being a Christian, not having become one.[104] There is, moreover, no close temporal connection between the alleged edict and the attested

---

[90] For the date, and the possibility that the emperor is not Marcus, see *JTS* n.s. xix (1968), 518.

[91] ἐπιστείλαντος γὰρ τοῦ Καίσαρος τοὺς μὲν ἀποτυμπανισθῆναι, εἰ δέ τινες ἀρνοῖντο, τούτους ἀπολυθῆναι . . . καὶ πάλιν ἐξήταζεν, καὶ ὅσοι μὲν ἐδόκουν πολιτείαν Ῥωμαίων ἐσχηκέναι, τούτων ἀπέτεμνε τὰς κεφαλάς, τοὺς δὲ λοιποὺς ἔπεμπεν εἰς τὰ θηρία. Cf. 50 : καὶ γὰρ καὶ τὸν Ἄτταλον (a Roman citizen) τῷ ὄχλῳ χαριζόμενος ὁ ἡγέμων ἐξέδωκε πάλιν πρὸς θηρία. 'ἀποτυμπανισθῆναι' raises a problem. It describes a particular mode of execution (D. M. Macdowell, *Athenian Homicide Law* (1963), 111 ff.). But the context here seems to require a vague word for execution in general ; and it must not be forgotten that Marcus will have written to the governor in Latin.

[92] It is not here relevant that Pliny sent the citizens to Rome whereas the governor of Lugdunensis did not : cf. Garnsey, l.c. (n. 46).

[93] For the punishment see P-W iv, 1731 ; TLL iv, 1246 f. Eusebius, l.c., and *Acta Apoll.* 45 (Greek) surely demonstrate that *crurifragium* was a form of execution.

[94] Eusebius does not identify this decree with the alleged measure of Marcus Aurelius recorded at *HE* v, 5, 6.

[95] J. Geffcken, *Hermes* xlv (1910), 486. The edict of Constantine *de accusationibus* (Bruns, *Fontes*⁷ no. 94 = *FIRA*² 1, no. 94), though adduced by Th. Mommsen, 'Der Prozess des Christen Apollonius unter Commodus', *S-B Berlin* 1894, 497 ff. = *Ges. Schr.* iii (1907), 447 ff., offers no parallel : there slaves or freedmen who accuse their master or

patrons are to be crucified ' denegata audientia '.

[96] Th. Mommsen, *Römisches Strafrecht* (1899), 414 f., who also shows that such evidence was becoming acceptable in an ever-increasing number of cases.

[97] ibid.

[98] The normal practice when hearing the evidence of slaves and freedmen : ibid. 416 ff.

[99] See further below, pp. 46–48.

[100] *Acta Apoll.* 1/2 (Greek) ; Eusebius, *HE* v, 21, 4 ; cf. below, pp. 46, 47.

[101] *Elag.* 3, 4/5 ; *Alex.* 22, 4 (both discussed below) ; *Quad. Tyr.* 8, 6 f.; cf. R. Syme, ' Ipse ille patriarcha ', *Bonner Historia-Augusta-Colloquium 1966–67* (1968), 119 ff. ; *Ammianus and the Historia Augusta* (1968), 61 ff.

[102] J. Juster, *Les Juifs dans l'Empire romain* 1 (1914), 226, 258 ; M. Avi-Yonah, *Geschichte der Juden im Zeitalter des Talmud* (1962), 45. Historical interpretation of the actions of Septimius Severus has for too long been vitiated by the assumption that he was anti-Roman (e.g. Avi-Yonah, o.c. 38) : for a refutation see *Historia* xvi (1967), 87 ff.

[103] See the long list given by K. H. Schwarte, *Historia* xii (1963), 189 ff. Since then the argument has been repeated by Frend, o.c. (n. 32), 320 ff. On the other hand, H. Grégoire, *Les Persécutions dans l'empire romain*² (1964), 36 uses the edict as evidence of Severus' favouring Christianity.

[104] *Pass. Perp.* 6.

outbreaks of persecution. Although the relevant section of the *Vita Severi* is highly condensed and slightly confused, it explicitly places the prohibition of conversion to Judaism and to Christianity after Severus' departure from Antioch, before his arrival in Alexandria and during his journey south through Palestine in 199.[105] It is improbable in the extreme that the *Historia Augusta* has transferred to the journey south through Palestine actions which its source assigned to a return journey in 201 : for the imperial house almost certainly travelled back from Alexandria to Antioch by sea.[106] Perpetua and her companions were martyred in March, 203,[107] and Eusebius dates the beginning of persecution in Alexandria to Severus' tenth year (either August, 201 to August, 202 or April, 202 to April, 203).[108] This persecution seems to have continued sporadically for some years, since some martyrs were put to death by Subatianus Aquila,[109] who is not attested as prefect of Egypt until 206.[110] To argue that there is a connexion between Severus' edict and a widespread outbreak of persecution in 202/3 is, therefore, mistaken in one minor and one major respect.[111] Persecution did not flare up and then cease at once, but dragged on for some time. It also began (so far as the evidence goes) not less than two years after the date given for the edict by the only author who asserts its existence.[112]

There is, however, a still more serious difficulty in accepting the edict as historical. If Christians are in the same position as Jews and conversion alone is illegal, then simply being a Christian from birth is not illegal and Christianity itself is no crime.[113] But there is no hint in any Christian writer that the legal position of the Christians had been thus alleviated—not even in the contemporary Tertullian, who cites examples of Severus' favours to the Christians.[114] Eusebius, on the contrary, thought that Severus stirred up persecution rather than abated its severity.[115] And, as the *Passio Perpetuae* shows, men continued, after 199 as before, to be condemned to death solely because they were Christians.

(16) Elagabalus : *HA, Elagabalus* 3, 4/5.

The *Historia Augusta* relates that Elagabalus, as soon as he arrived in Rome in 219,[116]

Heliogabalum in Palatino monte iuxta aedes imperatorias consecravit eique templum fecit, studens et Matris typum et Vestae ignem et Palladium et ancilia et omnia Romanis veneranda in illud transferre templum et id agens, ne quis Romae deus nisi Heliogabalus coleretur. dicebat praeterea Iudaeorum et Samaritanorum religiones et Christianam devotionem illuc transferendam, ut omnium culturarum secretum Heliogabali sacerdotium teneret.

If Elagabalus had given Christianity a place in his grand syncretism of the major religious cults of the Roman Empire, that would certainly imply that Christianity, being part

---

[105] See J. Hasebroek, *Untersuchungen zur Geschichte des Septimius Severus* (1921), 118 ff. For Severus' stay in Egypt, W. L. Westermann—A. A. Schiller, *Apokrimata : Decisions of Septimius Severus on Legal Matters* (1954); H. C. Youtie—A. A. Schiller, *Chronique d'Égypte* xxx (1955), 327 ff.
[106] *CIG* 5973 = *CIL* vi, 1603 ; also printed by G. J. Murphy, *The Reign of the Emperor L. Septimius Severus from the Evidence of the Inscriptions* (1945), 28 f.
[107] C.J.M.J. van Beek, *Passio Sanctarum Perpetuae et Felicitatis* 1 (1936), 162* ff.
[108] *HE* vi, 2, 2. It has not yet been proved that Eusebius always dates events in Egypt by the official Egyptian regnal years (as A. Stein, *Die Präfekten von Ägypten* (1950), 111). Nor is it by any means certain that the *Ecclesiastical History*, following the scheme of the *Chronicon*, always reckons an emperor's regnal years from September to September (as H. J. Lawlor—J. E. L. Oulton, *Eusebius* ii (1928), 37 f.). However, the length of Philip's reign is given as seven years (*HE* vi, 39, 1)—a figure which must come from Egyptian regnal years (see *PIR²* J 461).
[109] Eusebius, *HE* vi, 3, 3 ; 5, 2.
[110] The earliest evidence is *P. Ox.* 1100 (October/ November, 206). Claudius Julianus is now attested as

prefect from 203 until at least the end of 204 : see J. Rea, ' The Prefecture of Claudius Julianus ', *La Parola del Passato* xxii (1967), 48 ff. ; T. D. Barnes, *JTS* n.s. xix (1968), 526 f.
[111] Hippolytus' *Commentary on Daniel*, though often adduced, offers no support at all to the view here criticized : see below, pp. 42 f.
[112] It is worth noting that A. Wirth, *Quaestiones Severianae* (1888), 34, argued ' a. 200 verus persecutionis annus putandus est'. The difficulty which he saw is too often evaded : thus Frend, o.c. 321, blithely speaks of ' the edict of 202 '.
[113] K. H. Schwarte, ' Das angebliche Christengesetz des Septimius Severus ', *Historia* xii (1963), 185 ff. Frend, o.c. 341, n. 144, rejects Schwarte's cogent arguments with the peculiar and irrelevant observation ' the victims of the outbreak would hardly thank Dr. Schwarte for telling them that the Severan decree against the Christians was an " Erfindung " '.
[114] *Scap.* 4, 5.
[115] *HE* vi, 1, 1.
[116] O. F. Butler, ' Studies in the Life of Heliogabalus ', *Univ. of Michigan Studies, Humanistic Series* iv (1910), 1 ff., at 75 ff.

42

of the official religion of the state, was no longer illegal. The idea of such an incorporation has, however, been invented by the author of the *Historia Augusta*.[117] It was perhaps because he feared that his mendacity might become too obvious if he stated the incorporation as a fact, that he contented himself with representing it as an unfulfilled intention.[118] No other ancient writer knows of this project, and its falsity seems to follow from its illogicality. Elagabalus did transfer from their resting-places and gather together in Rome the cult objects and statues on which many cults throughout the empire centred.[119] But it is absurd to imagine that he thought of transferring to Rome the 'religiones Iudaeorum et Samaritanorum' and the 'Christiana devotio': they were incorporeal, not holy objects like the rest. What is more, the drawing of a distinction between Jews and Samaritans smacks of the last decade of the fourth century.[120]

(17) Severus Alexander : *HA, Alexander* 22, 4.

The *Vita Alexandri* is largely a historical romance,[121] and one of the actions of this ideal emperor is that he :

Iudaeis privilegia reservavit. Christianos esse passus est.

Although the approval of religious toleration which is expressed here and elsewhere cannot be the only or the main motive which prompted the composition of the *Historia Augusta* as a whole,[122] the themes of toleration and the privileges of Jews had a sharp contemporary relevance to the writer, at the very end of the fourth century.[123] No argument ought now to be necessary to demonstrate that the six references to the Christians in the *Vita Alexandri* are all the inventions of the author.[124] There is no confirmatory evidence whatsoever ; [125] and it is entirely illegitimate to maintain that there might be some truth behind them[126]—as if their motivation had always to be sought in the period about which the *Historia Augusta* writes, and never in the period at which it was written.[127]

(18) An unknown emperor of the early third century : Hippolytus, *In Dan.* 1, 20, 2/3.

Hippolytus is commenting on the story of Susanna, which, like the rest of *Daniel*, he holds to be a foreshadowing of the contemporary sufferings of Christians.[128] When he reaches the passage where the two old men who desire to seduce Susanna find her alone and say :

'ecce ostia pomarii clausa sunt et nemo nos videt, et nos in concupiscentia tui sumus ; quamobrem assentire nobis, et commiscere nobiscum : quod si nolueris, dicemus contra te testimonium, quod fuerit tecum iuvenis et ob hanc causam emiseris puellas a te ',[129]

he observes :

ἔστι δὲ καὶ καταλαβέσθαι ἀληθῶς τὸ συμβὰν ἐπὶ τῇ Σωσάννῃ. τοῦτο γὰρ νῦν καὶ ἐπὶ τῇ ἐκκλησίᾳ εὕροις πληρούμενον. ἡνίκα γὰρ οἱ δύο λαοὶ συμφωνήσουσι διαφθεῖραί τινας τῶν ἁγίων, παρατηροῦνται ἡμέραν εὐθῆ καὶ ἐπεισελθόντες εἰς τὸν οἶκον τοῦ θεοῦ προσευχομένων ἐκεῖ πάντων καὶ τὸν θεὸν ὑμνούντων, ἐπιλαβόμενοι ἕλκουσί τινας καὶ

---

[117] Nevertheless, it is still accepted as historical by many : e.g. Avi-Yonah, o.c. 41 ; Sordi, o.c. (n. 16), 238 ; and (with some hesitation) Frend, o.c. 328 ; 344, n. 207.

[118] Compare the same technique at *Alex.* 24, 4 (' habuit in animo '), where an imitation of Aurelius Victor, *Caes.* 28, 6 f. (on Philip) has been detected by A. Chastagnol, *Bonner Historia-Augusta-Colloquium 1964-1965* (1966), 55 f.

[119] G. Wissowa, *Religion und Kultus der Römer*² (1912), 366.

[120] H. Dessau, ' Die Samaritaner bei den S.H.A.', *Janus* 1 (1921), 124 ff.

[121] See the analyses by K. Hönn, *Quellenuntersuchungen zu den Viten des Heliogabalus und des Severus Alexander im Corpus der S.H.A.* (1911), 33 ff.; N. H. Baynes, *The Historia Augusta. Its date and purpose* (1926), 118 ff.

[122] A. D. Momigliano, *Journal of the Warburg and Courtauld Institutes* XVII (1954), 40 f. = *Secondo Contributo alla Storia degli Studi Classici* (1960), 129 ff. = *Studies in Historiography* (1966), 163 f.

[123] Syme, l.c. (n. 101).

[124] R. Syme, *Ammianus and the Historia Augusta* (1968), 61 ; 138.

[125] It is particularly significant that K. Bihlmeyer, *Die ' syrischen' Kaiser zu Rom* (211-235) *und das Christentum* (1916), 111 ff. could find none, though he wished to accept as many of the six as possible.

[126] As Frend, o.c. 329.

[127] No less weak, in the case of the *Historia Augusta*, is the argument from plausibility : e.g. Bihlmeyer, o.c. 101 ; Avi-Yonah, o.c. 41. But what seems plausible to the modern scholar may have been invented by the ancient romancer precisely because it seemed plausible to him too.

[128] *In Dan.* 1, 1, etc.

[129] *Dan.* 13, 1 ff. (Vulgate), esp. 13, 20/1.

κρατοῦσι λέγοντες· δεῦτε, συγκατάθεσθε ἡμῖν καὶ τοὺς θεοὺς θρησκεύσατε, ‘ εἰ δὲ μή, καταμαρτυρήσομεν ’ καθ’ ὑμῶν. τούτων δὲ μὴ βουλομένων προσάγουσιν αὐτοὺς πρὸς τὸ βῆμα καὶ κατηγοροῦσιν ὡς ἐναντία τοῦ δόγματος Καίσαρος πράσσοντας καὶ θανάτῳ κατακρίνονται.

The date at which Hippolytus wrote his *Commentary on Daniel* cannot be determined at all exactly,[130] and the assumption that it was in or shortly after 203[131] derives from a mistaken acceptance as historical of the edict of Septimius Severus invented by the *Historia Augusta*.[132] The emperor who is mentioned here cannot, therefore, be securely identified. Moreover, when Hippolytus writes ‘ ἐναντία τοῦ δόγματος Καίσαρος πράσσοντας ’, he surely means no more than ‘ acting illegally ’ : he need have no more care for pedantic, literal accuracy than is shown by Tertullian when he passes from depicting pagans as saying ‘ non licet esse vos ’ to his derision of ‘ lex tua ’ and then to discussion of the ‘ origo eiusmodi legum ’.[133] The words ‘ ἐναντία τοῦ δόγματος Καίσαρος ’ are a biblical echo : at Thessalonica the Jews complained that the Christians ‘ πάντες ἀπέναντι τῶν δογμάτων Καίσαρος πράσσουσιν ’.[134]

(19) Maximin : Eusebius, *HE* vi, 28.

Eusebius relates that out of hatred for the Christians of Alexander's household Maximin started a persecution, and ordered the leaders of the church to be put to death. He cites as evidence some passages from the writings of Origen, but these, even when taken with other evidence, hardly prove a widespread persecution.[135] Whatever the facts, however, there is no hint of any change in the law.

(20) Philip : Eusebius, *HE* vi, 34.

Eusebius reproduces a story that Philip was a Christian and that his actions showed him to be god-fearing.[136] But, even if Philip felt some sympathy for the Christians, there is no evidence that he altered their legal position. The bishop of Alexandria, Dionysius, stated in a letter that there had been an outbreak of persecution in Alexandria a full year before the persecution consequent on Decius' edict.[137] Unless Dionysius is in error, this outbreak occurred while Philip was still emperor.[138] The *libelli* attesting sacrifice in accordance with imperial command which have been found in the Fayum date from June and July, 250,[139] and Philip was still recognized as emperor in Egypt as late as September, 249.[140]

This section could not even pretend to be complete unless some omissions were justified. First, Suetonius's statement that Claudius :

Iudaeos impulsore Chresto adsidue tumultuantes Roma expulit.[141]

---

[130] The explicit internal evidence from which a date is *prima facie* to be deduced is stated succinctly by A. Bonwetsch, *GCS* I, xx : ‘ Die Abfassung liegt später als die von De Antichristo, nicht zu lange nach einer heftigen Verfolgung, während Ein Kaiser zu herrschen scheint ’. Elsewhere, however, Bonwetsch produced other reasons for putting the *In Danielem* among Hippolytus' earlier works (*Studien zu den Kommentaren Hippolyts* (1897), 81 ff.).

[131] So, e.g., A. Harnack, *Die Chronologie der altchristlichen Litteratur bis Eusebius* II (1904), 249 f.; G. Bardy, *Hippolyte : Commentaire sur Daniel* (*Sources Chrétiennes* xiv, 1947), 12 f.; M. Lefèvre, ibid., 111 ; Frend, o.c. 375 ; 387, n. 219 ; B. Altaner–A. Stuiber, *Patrologie*[7] (1966), 166 f.

[132] Above, pp. 40 f.

[133] *Apol.* 4, 4 ; 4, 5 ; 5, 1.

[134] *Acts* 17, 7. Noted by A. Bonwetsch, *GCS* I, 32.

[135] G. W. Clarke, ‘ Some Victims of the Persecution of Maximinus Thrax ’, *Historia* xv (1966), 445 ff.

[136] Hence claimed as the first Christian emperor by Grégoire, o.c. (n. 103), 9 ff. The development of Christian views of Philip is of some interest. The contemporary Dionysius refers to his sympathy (Eusebius, *HE* vi, 41, 9), and Eusebius in the *Chronicon* implies it (*GCS* xx, 226 ; cf. *HE* vi, 39, 1). In the *Ecclesiastical History*, however, Eusebius goes

further and represents Philip as a convinced Christian (vi, 34), a statement which Jerome inserts into his edition of the *Chronicon* (*GCS* xlvii, 217). Would such a story have been invented before there was a Christian emperor ? If not, his statements about Philip are relevant to the problems raised by the various versions of Eusebius' *Ecclesiastical History*. (Suspiciously similar is the story which Philostorgius, *HE* vii, 8 (*GCS* xxi, 89 f.), reports about the hostility to the Christians of either Numerian or Decius.)

[137] Eusebius, *HE* vi, 41, 1 : ὁ δὲ αὐτὸς (sc. Dionysius) ἐν ἐπιστολῇ ... τῶν κατὰ Δέκιον μαρτυρησάντων ἐν ᾿Αλεξανδρείᾳ τοὺς ἀγῶνας τοῦτον ἱστορεῖ τὸν τρόπον· οὐκ ἀπὸ τοῦ βασιλικοῦ προστάγματος ὁ διωγμὸς παρ᾿ ἡμῖν ἤρξατο, ἀλλὰ γὰρ ὅλον ἐνιαυτὸν προὔλαβεν.

[138] The year ought perhaps to be counted, not from the promulgation of the edict in Rome (winter 249/50 : P-W xv, 1281), or even in Alexandria, but rather from the date fixed in Egypt for compliance with its terms.

[139] Knipfing, o.c. (n. 81).

[140] *PIR*² J 461. Note especially the Alexandrian coins of Philip's seventh year, minted after 29th August, 249.

[141] *Claud.* 25, 4.

44

Dispute has long raged over whether or not the expulsion was the result of riots occasioned by the preaching of Christianity. If it was,[142] it follows that to the emperor a Christian was still a type of Jew. If not (the more probable view),[143] the episode is irrelevant to a consideration of the emperor's dealings with Christians.

Second, Domitian's harshness in exacting the tax of two *denarii* a head levied on all Jews.[144] The legal disputes which this policy provoked may have caused magistrates and other pagans to realize more clearly that Christians were different from Jews, but it need imply no measure directed against the new religion, and there is no evidence that Christians were condemned as a result.[145]

Next, the statement of Modestinus that :

si quis aliquid fecerit, quo leves hominum animi superstitione numinis terrentur, divus Marcus huiusmodi homines in insulam relegari rescripsit.[146]

No Christian is known to have been banished to an island for ' alarming the fickle minds of men with superstitious dread ' : indeed, execution was the Christian's normal punishment. To invoke this rescript as evidence for the legal basis of the persecutions is to evade the problem : how was it that Christians came to be put to death simply for being Christians ? The same objection tells against adducing a rule of unknown date in the *Sententiae Pauli* which declares :

qui novas sectas vel ratione incognitas religiones inducunt, ex quibus animi hominum moveantur, honestiores deportantur, humiliores capite puniuntur.[147]

Finally, the *senatusconsultum de pretiis gladiatoriis minuendis* (of 177 or 178).[148] While this *senatusconsultum* may have some bearing on the political and social background of, for example, the pogrom in Gaul which is traditionally, but on inadequate evidence, dated to 177, it can neither be brought into close connection with it,[149] nor be identified with the ' new decrees ' of which Melito complained,[150] nor explain how Christians came to be treated as criminals in the first place.[151]

THE TRIALS OF CHRISTIANS

Modern scholarship, besides unearthing purer recensions of *acta martyrum* previously known only in a late and unreliable form, has succeeded in proving that many of the transmitted *acta* or *passiones* of pre-Decian martyrs are neither contemporary nor authentic records of what actually happened. Although there may be many other *acta martyrum* which contain nuggets of fact or which are fictitious compositions based on something authentic,[152] there is a mere handful whose genuineness as a whole has not been (and perhaps never will be) successfully impugned.[153] These must, therefore, rank as primary evidence for the trials of Christians.[154] In this select class, the majority of accounts mention no law or imperial decree or legal enactment, of any kind. The emperor, if mentioned, is for the most part mentioned almost incidentally : the Christian is urged to swear by his τύχη or *genius*,[155] to sacrifice for his safety,[156] or is reprimanded for disloyalty to him,[157] or has

---

[142] So A. D. Momigliano, *Claudius*² (1961), 32 f.; 99.

[143] See now E. A. Judge—G. S. R. Thomas, ' The Origin of the Church at Rome : A New Solution ? ', *Reformed Theological Review* xxv (Melbourne, 1966), 81 ff.

[144] Suetonius, *Domit.* 12, 2.

[145] See, in general, Smallwood, o.c. (n. 44).

[146] *Dig.* XLVIII, 19, 30.

[147] *Sent. Pauli* v, 21, 2.

[148] Re-edited by J. H. Oliver—R. E. A. Palmer, ' Minutes of an Act of the Roman Senate ', *Hesperia* XXIV (1955), 320 ff.

[149] *JTS* N.S. XIX (1968), 518 f.

[150] As appears to be conjectured by A. Birley, *Marcus Aurelius* (1966), 329. But the ' new decrees ' seem to have mentioned the Christians in particular, not just criminals in general (see Eusebius, *HE* IV, 26, 5).

[151] Similarly, the theory that Christians were punished for their *contumacia* towards the magistrate who tried them (Sherwin-White, o.c. 780 ff.) fails to explain why they were haled into court to appear before him.

[152] See, e.g., K. J. Neumann, *Der römische Staat und die allgemeine Kirche bis auf Diocletian* I (1890), 274 ff.

[153] See T. D. Barnes, ' Pre-Decian *Acta Martyrum* ', *JTS* n.s. XIX (1968), 509 ff. *Acta Martyrum* are quoted here from R. Knopf—G. Krüger—G. Ruhbach, *Ausgewählte Martyrerakten*⁴ (1965), except where otherwise stated.

[154] The importance of this type of evidence is rightly emphasized by S. Lieberman, ' Roman Legal Institutions in Early Rabbinics and in the Acta Martyrum ', *JQR* xxxv (1944–1945), 1 ff.

[155] *Mart. Polyc.* 10, 1 ; *Acta Scill.* 3 ; 5 ; also *Acta Apoll.* 3.

[156] *Acta Scill.* 3 ; *Pass. Perp.* 6, 2 ; cf. Pliny, *Epp.* x, 96, 6.

[157] *Acta Scill.* 2 ff.; cf. *Acta Apoll.* 6 ; 8 f. (Apollonius tries to rebut the suspicion of disloyalty).

explained to him the possibility of his pardon.[158] In the descriptions of three trials, however, there occur more substantial references to the emperor, and in one to a law or *senatus consultum*, which require examination.

In the *acta* of Carpus, Papylus and Agathonice there are several mentions of the decrees of either a single emperor or plural emperors.[159] But only one occurs in both the Greek and the Latin versions :

(11) ὁ ἀνθύπατος εἶπεν· θῦσαί σε δεῖ· οὕτως γὰρ ἐκέλευσεν ὁ αὐτοκράτωρ

(2) Proconsul dixit : Sacrificate ; ita enim iussit imperator.

This reference to the emperor is the only one which may be authentic : what stands in one version alone must be presumed not to have stood in the exemplar from which both independently derive.[160] It does not, however, follow that what stands in both is necessarily original.[161] Moreover, the historical value of these *acta* is largely vitiated by the impossibility of deciding conclusively whether the martyrdoms described belong to the middle of the second century or to the time of Decius.[162] For, although Eusebius assigns the deaths of Carpus, Papylus and Agathonice to the same period as that of Polycarp, he is dependent on a document containing a collection of *acta martyrum* ;[163] and this included the undoubtedly Decian *Passio Pionii*, which Eusebius also assigns to the middle of the second century.[164]

The recension of the *acta* of Justin and his companions which is commonly accepted as a genuine record of their trial has the following passages mentioning the emperor(s) :

(1) ἐν τῷ καιρῷ τῶν ἀνόμων ὑπερμάχων εἰδωλολατρείας προστάγματα ἀσεβῆ κατὰ τῶν εὐσεβούντων Χριστιανῶν κατὰ πόλιν καὶ χώραν ἐξετίθετο, ὥστε αὐτοὺς ἀναγκάζεσθαι σπένδειν τοῖς ματαίοις εἰδώλοις. συλληφθέντες οὖν οἱ μνημονευθέντες ἅγιοι εἰσήχθησαν πρὸς τὸν τῆς Ῥώμης ἔπαρχον ὀνόματι Ῥούστικον.

(2, 1) ὧν εἰσαχθέντων πρὸ τοῦ βήματος Ῥούστικος ὁ ἔπαρχος Ἰουστίνῳ εἶπεν· πρῶτον πείσθητι τοῖς θεοῖς καὶ ὑπάκουσον τοῖς βασιλεῦσιν.

(5, 8) Ῥούστικος ἔπαρχος ἀπεφήνατο λέγων· οἱ μὴ βουληθέντες θῦσαι τοῖς θεοῖς καὶ εἶξαι τῷ τοῦ αὐτοκράτορος προστάγματι, φραγελλωθέντες ἀπαχθήτωσαν, κεφαλικὴν ἀποτιννύντες δίκην κατὰ τὴν τῶν νόμων ἀκολουθίαν.

The first and third passages ought to have aroused suspicions long ago. The first speaks of a persecuting edict of a type which other evidence appears to indicate that Decius was the earliest to promulgate ;[165] while in the third the *praefectus urbi*, Q. Junius Rusticus, should speak of the joint emperors Marcus and Lucius.[166] There are, however, two other redactions of these *acta*.[167] The longest and most rhetorical of the three may be left out of account : it has ' Antoninus the impious ' as the single reigning emperor throughout. The shortest version omits both the references to the emperor(s) which occur in the second and third of the passages quoted ; and in place of the first passage it has :

ἐν τῷ καιρῷ τῶν ἀνόμων προσταγμάτων τῆς εἰδωλολατρείας συλληφθέντες οἱ μνημονευθέντες ἅγιοι . . .

Thus a comparison of the three recensions eliminates all references to the emperors as later than the earliest discoverable stage of the tradition, and the *Acta Justini* do not mention an imperial command at all. ' ἐν τῷ καιρῷ τῶν ἀνόμων προσταγμάτων τῆς εἰδωλολατρείας ' merely signifies that Christianity is illegal.

---

[158] *Acta Scill.* 1.

[159] 2 (Latin) ; 4 ; 11 ; 45 (Greek).

[160] H. Lietzmann, ' Die älteste Gestalt der Passio SS. Carpi, Papylae et Agathonikes ', *Festgabe für K. Müller* (1922), 46 ff. = *Kl. Schr.* 1 (*Texte u. Unters.* LXVII, 1958), 239 ff.

[161] M. Simonetti, *Studi agiografici* (1955), 105 ff.

[162] *JTS* n.s. XIX (1968), 514 f., arguing from the question ' principalis es ?/βουλευτὴς εἶ ;' that the Decian date is the more probable of the two.

[163] *HE* IV, 15, 48 : ἑξῆς δὲ καὶ ἄλλων ἐν Περγάμῳ πόλει τῆς Ἀσίας ὑπομνήματα μεμαρτυρηκότων φέρεται, Κάρπου. . . .

[164] ibid. 47 : τῶν γε μὴν τότε περιβόητος μάρτυς εἰς τις ἐγνωρίζετο Πιόνιος. On the date of Pionius' martyrdom, see now *JTS* n.s. XIX (1968), 529 ff.

[165] So, e.g., H. Lietzmann, *CAH* XII (1939), 521 : ' there began under the emperor Decius the first systematic Christian persecution, organized for the whole empire by imperial command '.

[166] *PIR²* J 814 gives the evidence relevant to the date.

[167] All three are to be found together at G. Lazzati, *Gli sviluppi della letteratura sui martiri nei primi quattro secoli* (1956), 119 ff.

46

The *Acta Apollonii* present intricate and perhaps insoluble problems. The passages in which a legal justification appears for Apollonius' condemnation are several : in each case both the Greek version and an English translation of the Armenian must be given.[168]

1/2 οὗ προσαχθέντος, Περέννιος ὁ ἀνθύπατος εἶπεν· 'Απολλώ, Χριστιανὸς εἶ ; 'Απολλὼς εἶπεν· ναί, Χριστιανός εἰμι.

1/2 The prefect Terentius had him brought before the Senate and said to him : ' Apollonius, why do you resist the invincible laws and decree of the emperors and refuse to sacrifice to the gods ? ' Apollonius said : ' Because I am a Christian'.

3 Περέννιος ὁ ἀνθύπατος εἶπεν· μετανόησον, πεισθείς μοι, 'Απολλώ, καὶ ὄμοσον τὴν τύχην τοῦ κυρίου ἡμῶν Κομόδου τοῦ αὐτοκράτορος.

3 The prefect said : ' But you ought to repent because of the edicts of the emperors and swear by the fortune of the emperor Commodus'.

13/14 Περέννιος ὁ ἀνθύπατος εἶπεν· διὰ τὸ δόγμα τῆς συγκλήτου συμβουλεύω σοι μετανοῆσαι καὶ σέβειν καὶ προσκυνεῖν τοὺς θεούς . . . 'Απολλὼς εἶπεν· ἐγὼ μὲν τὸ δόγμα τῆς συγκλήτου γινώσκω, Περέννιε· ἐγενόμην δὲ θεοσεβής . . .

13/14 The prefect answered : ' Because of the decree of the Senate I advise you to repent and to sacrifice to the gods . . . I think you are not unaware of the decree of the Senate'. Apollonius said : ' I know the decree of almighty God . . . '

23/24 Περέννιος ὁ ἀνθύπατος εἶπεν· 'Απολλώ, τὸ δόγμα τῆς συγκλήτου ἐστὶν Χριστιανοὺς μὴ εἶναι. 'Απολλὼς δέ, ὁ καὶ Σακκέας, εἶπεν· ἀλλ' οὐ δύναται νικηθῆναι τὸ δόγμα τοῦ θεοῦ ὑπὸ δόγματος ἀνθρωπίνου.

23/24 The prefect said : ' You have philosophized enough and filled us with admiration, but do you not know, Apollonius, that it is the decree of the Senate that no-one at all anywhere shall be called a Christian ? ' Apollonius answered : ' Yes, but it is not possible for a human decree of the Senate to prevail over the decree of God'.

45 Περέννιος ὁ ἀνθύπατος εἶπεν· θέλω σε ἀπολῦσαι, 'Απολλώ, κωλύομαι δὲ ὑπὸ τοῦ δόγματος Κομόδου τοῦ αὐτοκράτορος· πλὴν φιλανθρώπως χρήσομαί σοι ἐν τῷ θανάτῳ. καὶ ἔδωκεν σίγνον κατ' αὐτοῦ κατεαγῆναι τοῦ μάρτυρος τὰ σκέλη.

45 The magistrate said : ' I wish to set you free, but I cannot because of the decree of the Senate ; yet I shall pronounce a kind sentence'. And he ordered him to be beheaded with a sword.

47 And the executioners led him away at once and beheaded him.

The Armenian version is in some ways by far the superior. Though it perverts Perennis' name to ' Terentius ', it correctly styles him ' prefect '. (He was *praefectus praetorio* from 180 or 182 to 185.[169]) The Greek version erroneously makes him proconsul of Asia. Moreover, it seems to turn Apollonius into a combination of the Apollos of the *Acts of the Apostles*[170] and the Ammonius Saccas who taught Plotinus and Origen.[171] The evidence of Eusebius complicates the matter still further. He relates that the servant who delated Apollonius had his legs broken (the Greek *acta* make this the punishment of Apollonius himself), while the martyr was interrogated by Perennis, delivered a speech before the Senate, and was then sentenced by the Senate to be beheaded (the punishment in the Armenian *acta*) because that was the penalty prescribed by an ancient law for Christians who would not renounce their beliefs.[172] Those who wish to read all that Apollonius said at his trial, his replies to Perennis and the speech he made before the Senate in defence of

---

[168] The translation given here is a rendering into modern English of that by F. C. Conybeare, *Monuments of Early Christianity* (1894), 35 ff. O. von Gebhardt, *Ausgewählte Märtyreracten* (1902), 44 ff. conveniently prints a German translation of the Armenian beneath the Greek text.
[169] See F. Grosso, *La lotta politica al tempo di Commodo* (1964), 139 ff.; 190 ff.

[170] *Acts* 18, 24 f.: 'Ιουδαῖος δέ τις 'Απολλῶς ὀνόματι, 'Αλεξανδρεὺς τῷ γένει, ἀνὴρ λόγιος > *Acta Apoll.* pref. (Greek): 'Απολλῶς δὲ ὁ ἀπόστολος, ἀνὴρ ὢν εὐλαβής, 'Αλεξανδρεὺς τῷ γένει.
[171] P-W I, 1863.
[172] *HE* v, 21, 4 ; cf. above, p. 40.

Christianity, are referred by Eusebius to the collection of passions which he himself had made.[173]

The extent and nature of the legal problems raised by the procedure at the trial have often been discussed.[174] But the fundamental question has sometimes gone unnoticed, or at least unasked. Are the *Acta Apollonii* a coherent whole or the conflation of the record of Apollonius' trial with an apology which he had previously composed and published ? It has recently been suggested that Eusebius reveals that he had in front of him not one document but two.[175] Perhaps that is not an inescapable deduction from Eusebius' words. Nonetheless, it seems to be a necessary hypothesis that the extant *acta* reproduce in an abbreviated form the historical record of Apollonius' trial and his literary defence of Christianity, wrongly combined.[176] It is not far-fetched to suggest that there has been such a conflation : Eusebius makes a similar mistake when he deduces from Tertullian's *Apologeticum* that its author was an eminent man at Rome.[177] Once the same assumption was made for Apollonius' *Apology*, it only remained to find a suitable occasion for its delivery, and his trial was the obvious choice. The second part of the extant *acta* has two suspicious features. First, Apollonius, besides defending Christianity, indulges in a polemic against paganism which includes several stock *exempla* of second century apologetics.[178] Secondly, the presence of senators at the trial is implausible on historical grounds : the members of a body so conscious of its status and ancient privileges would hardly flock *en masse* to serve on the *consilium* of the pretorian prefect or to be mere spectators of a trial conducted by him.[179] Their presence is also an irrelevance : according to the *acta* Perennis conducts the whole trial alone and passes sentence alone. When Eusebius reports that it was the Senate which condemned Apollonius, he is, perhaps unawares, evading a real difficulty.[180]

If the theory of conflation be admitted, the references to the *senatusconsultum*, being in the section ultimately derived from Apollonius' *Apology*, do not belong to the record of his trial. Even if the theory is not admitted, however, the *acta* can hardly be used as if they were an accurate record of what happened until some explanation is given for certain important discrepancies. In the Armenian *acta* Apollonius is accused of flouting 'the invincible laws and decree of the emperors' ; in the corresponding Greek the charge is 'Χριστιανὸς εἶ ;'.[181] Again, the Armenian version sets the whole of the trial before the Senate, the Greek the second hearing alone.[182] In the latter part of the trial, the Armenian text consistently represents the basis of Apollonius' condemnation as a *senatusconsultum*, while the Greek wavers between that and a decree of Commodus.[183] But Eusebius thought that the basis was an ancient law,[184] while Rufinus alleges that a *senatusconsultum* was passed in accordance with an already existing law for the express purpose of sentencing Apollonius to death.[185] The discrepancies are easily explicable if all these statements are

---

[173] ibid. 5.

[174] See Knopf—Krüger—Ruhbach, o.c. 35.

[175] E. Gabba, ' Il processo di Apollonio ', *Mélanges offerts à J. Carcopino* (1966), 397 ff. Cf. Rufinus, *HE* V, 21, 4 : ' tum deinde exoratur beatus Apollonius martyr, uti defensionem pro fide sua, quam audiente senatu atque omni populo luculenter et splendide habuerat, ederet scriptam '.

[176] Yet A. Harnack, *Deutsche Literaturzeitung* XXV (1904), 2464 ff. had no difficulty in showing that the argument from apologetic motifs is not by itself sufficient.

[177] *HE* II, 2, 4 ; cf. v, 5, 5.

[178] J. Geffcken, ' Die Acta Apollonii ', *Gött. Gel. Nachr., Phil.-hist. Kl.* 1904, 262 ff.; *Zwei Griechische Apologeten* (1907), 246 ff.; *Hermes* XLV (1910), 486 ff.

[179] Note the attitude of Dio, which is doubtless typical : F. Millar, *A Study of Cassius Dio* (1964), 115 f. Significantly, Mommsen, o.c. (n. 95), 499 = 449 felt compelled to conjecture that Apollonius was actually brought before the Senate, not by Perennis, but by the consuls.

[180] Modern scholars often evade the difficulty and improve on Eusebius, who did not consider Apollonius to be a senator (above, n. 42). Thus L. L.

Howe, *The Pretorian Prefect from Commodus to Diocletian* (A.D. 180–305) (1942), 96 f. cites the trial as ' an illustration of the procedure which must generally have been followed in trying Senators ' ; and J. Beaujeu, *La religion romaine à l'apogée de l'Empire* I (1955), 393 states ' à Rome même, un personnage de rang sénatorial nommé Apollonius fut jugé et condamné à la décapitation par le Sénat '.

[181] *Acta Apoll.* 1/2.

[182] ibid. 1 ; 11 ff.

[183] E. Griffe, ' Les Actes du martyr Apollonius et le problème de la base juridique des persécutions ', *Bull. litt. eccl.* LIII/LXXII (1952), 65 ff. is surely mistaken in translating ' τὸ δόγμα τῆς συγκλήτου ' as merely ' la volonté du sénat '. J. Zeiller, *Mélanges J. Lebreton* II (*Rech. sci. rel.* XL, 1952), 155 f. takes the wavering as proof that Christianity was originally outlawed by the joint action of emperor and Senate.

[184] *HE* V, 21, 4 : κεφαλικῇ κολάσει ὡς ἂν ἀπὸ δόγματος συγκλήτου τελειοῦται, μηδ' ἄλλως ἀφεῖσθαι τοὺς ἅπαξ εἰς δικαστήριον παριόντας καὶ μηδαμῶς τῆς προθέσεως μεταβαλλομένους ἀρχαίου παρ' αὐτοῖς νόμου κεκρατηκότος.

[185] *HE* V, 21, 5 : ' et post hoc secundum senatus consultum capite plexus est. ita namque a prioribus lex iniquissima promulgata censebat '.

later attempts to provide a legal basis for the condemnation, and are nothing more than rationalizations from the fact that Christianity was illegal.[186] On the other hand, if they are not, there is no valid criterion for deciding which of them is historically correct. The earliest attested version of the martyrdom—Eusebius'—has at least one major implausibility which is absent from the two known later versions : the execution of Apollonius' accuser.[187]

The tradition, therefore, varied, but the details of its development cannot be traced. Hence it is impossible to decide which elements in it (if any) are original and historical.

It would be begging the question to argue that the references to imperial or senatorial ordinances in these three passions must be later additions and therefore false or anachronistic. But other reasons have been adduced for concluding that they are not original. The only one not completely eliminated is the exhortation to sacrifice in accordance with the emperor's command in the *acta* of Carpus, Papylus, and Agathonice. Yet, even if this document does not belong to the Decian persecution but to the mid-second century, what does the vague phrase prove ? It surely implies no more than the continuance of the legal position of the Christians as defined by Trajan. In the other genuine records no mention can be discovered of any legal enactment whatever : hence, either the legal basis for the condemnation of Carpus and Papylus should be held to be different from the basis in all other documented cases, or else it was never disobedience to the emperor's command. The order to sacrifice because the emperor has commanded it is scarcely more than another mode of urging a return to Roman ways.[188] And, in a sense, the emperor had commanded sacrifice : for he had ordained that an accused Christian who sacrificed should be set free.

CONCLUSIONS

What, therefore, does the primary evidence reveal about the juridical basis of the persecutions ? The central fact is Trajan's rescript to Pliny. The legal position of Christians continues exactly as Trajan defined it until Decius. After Trajan's rescript, if not already before, Christianity was a crime in a special category : whereas all other criminals, once convicted, were punished for what they had done in the past, the Christian was punished for what he was in the present, and up to the last moment could gain pardon by apostasy. There is no evidence to prove earlier legislation by the Senate or the emperor. Indeed, the exchange of letters between Pliny and Trajan implies that there was none. Given the normally passive nature of Roman administration,[189] the earliest trial and condemnation of Christians for their religion should be supposed to have occurred because the matter came to the notice of a provincial governor in the same way as it was later brought to the attention of Pliny. (There is no justification for assuming either that this must have happened first in Rome or that it had any connection with the fire of Rome in 64 or that the emperor was consulted.[190]) When Pliny was making his tour of Pontus,[191] Christians were denounced before him by accusers. The earliest magistrate to condemn Christians presumably had as little hesitation as Pliny in sentencing them to death—and as little knowledge of the nature of their crime.[192]

The date when this occurred cannot be determined at all precisely. But there is a foreshadowing of what was to come in the *Acts of the Apostles*. At Thessalonica the Jews stirred up trouble for Paul and Silas by alleging that the Christians were acting illegally because they proclaimed Jesus as their king.[193] At Philippi, after Paul had cast a spirit out of a slave-girl, her owners denounced Paul and Silas to the local magistrates for disturbing the city and advocating practices which it was not lawful for Romans to admit or perform.[194]

[186] Compare the *senatus consultum* in the Talmudic *Deut. Rabba* 2, 24 (quoted by Y. Baer, *Scripta Hierosolymitana* VII (1961), 84, n. 14).
[187] Above, p. 40.
[188] Cf. *Acta Scill.* 14 : ' Speratum . . . et ceteros ritu Christiano se vivere confessos, quoniam oblata sibi facultate ad Romanorum morem redeundi obstinanter perseveraverunt, gladio animadverti placet '.
[189] F. G. B. Millar, *JRS* LVI (1966), 166.
[190] Contrast J. A. Crook, *Law and Life of Rome*

(1967), 279 : ' The equation " Christian = man to be punished " can only have been established by government directive '.
[191] *Epp.* x, 92 is written from Amisus, 98 from Amastris. Cf. Sherwin-White, o.c. 693 f.
[192] Note Pliny's words, *Epp.* x, 96, 3 : ' perseverantes duci iussi. neque enim dubitabam, qualecumque esset quod faterentur, pertinaciam certe et inflexibilem obstinationem debere puniri '.
[193] *Acts* 17, 5 ff.
[194] *Acts* 16, 16 ff.

Since the two apostles were also denounced as Jews, the accusation might be one of proselytism combined with magic. The latter (if of the wrong sort) was always an illegal practice ;[195] the former, if not strictly illegal, was widely felt to be improper[196] and so might at any time turn into a charge upon which magistrates were prepared to punish a man. But the gravamen of the charges at Philippi was surely a breach of the peace : that would explain the punishment of Paul and Silas—a moderately severe beating and a single night's imprisonment, followed by expulsion from the city.[197] In these two episodes the enemies of Paul approach the municipal magistrates. But there are already present the conditions necessary for a Roman magistrate or governor to regard Christians as *eo ipso* malefactors. The new religion could be viewed (as at Philippi) as something intrinsically alien to Roman ways. When the teaching of it caused rioting, someone might allege (as at Thessalonica) that a revolutionary political doctrine was being preached.[198] A governor might well decide (like Pliny) that, whatever the true nature of Christianity, Christians merited exemplary punishment. They were, after all, troublemakers who disturbed the ' quies provinciae ', the preservation of which was his paramount duty.[199]

The *Acts of the Apostles*, moreover, exhibits persecution on purely religious grounds in the Greek cities of the East. Paul and Barnabas were forced to leave Pisidian Antioch, Iconium, and Lystra. At Antioch Jews approached the leading men of the city.[200] At Iconium the populace was bitterly divided over the teaching and miracles of the two apostles.[201] At Lystra Paul and Barnabas were at first greeted as Gods. Then Jews so turned the crowds against them that Paul was attacked, stoned, and left for dead.[202] Later, in Athens, Paul was seized (this time without any intervention by Jews) and taken before the Areopagus.[203] Accused of introducing a new religion, he acquitted himself by claiming that his was not a new God but one who already possessed an altar in the city.[204] At Ephesus, though there was no trial, a riot ensued when the Ephesians suspected that the cult of Artemis was being menaced. Even if the instigators of the trouble were themselves moved by pecuniary considerations, the slogan shouted by the mob was ' μεγάλη ἡ ῎Αρτεμις ᾿Εφεσίων '. The disturbance was quelled when a magistrate stated that the Goddess was not being desecrated or blasphemed, but that the riot had been provoked by men with a private grudge.[205]

The future is implicit in these episodes. For what would have happened at Ephesus if the magistrate, as well as the crowd, had considered the Christians to be threatening the cult of Artemis ? Once it was realized that theirs was a new religion which entailed the abandonment of the established cults, the Christians could expect little sympathy or protection. The religious sentiments of the pagan world, if of a different type, were no less real and powerful than those of the Christians.[206]

Rulers united with the ruled in a common prejudice. Although it was only in 250 that an emperor decreed that all the inhabitants of the empire should openly sacrifice to the Gods,[207] the same concern for ancestral religion can be discerned far earlier. Vigellius

[195] Mommsen, o.c. (n. 96), 639 ff.; R. MacMullen, *Enemies of the Roman Order* (1966), 124 ff.

[196] Momigliano, o.c. (n. 142), 29 ff.

[197] A. N. Sherwin-White, *Roman Society and Roman Law in the New Testament* (1963), 82 f. comments ' had the case not been abandoned, the next step would have been the dispatch and arraignment of the prisoner before the proconsul, either at the capital of the province, or at the nearest assize city '.

[198] For the social and economic background see B. Baldwin, ' Lucian as Social Satirist ', *CQ* n.s. xi (1961), 199 ff.

[199] Compare, for a later period, Ulpian, *Dig.* 1, 18, 13 : ' congruit bono et gravi praesidi curare, ut pacata atque quieta provincia sit quam regit '.

[200] *Acts* 13, 50.

[201] *Acts* 14, 3 ff.

[202] *Acts* 14, 8 ff.

[203] I hope to justify the interpretation advanced here in *JTS* n.s. xx (1969).

[204] *Acts* 17, 16 ff. The episode receives no mention

whatever from Sherwin-White, o.c., in his chapter entitled ' Paul and the Cities '.

[205] *Acts* 19, 23 ff., esp. 27 f.; 34 ; 37. Sentence of death for a religious offence happens to be attested at Ephesus at an earlier period : F. Sokolowski, *HTR* LVIII (1965), 427 ff.

[206] A. D. Nock, ' The Augustan Restoration ', *CR* xxxix (1925), 60 ff.; *CAH* x (1934), 465 ff.; H. W. Pleket, *HTR* LVIII (1965), 331 ff.

[207] For the traditional character of Decius' requirement see E. Liesering, *Untersuchungen zur Christenverfolgung des Kaisers Decius* (1933), 33 ff.; R. Andreotti, ' Religione ufficiale e culto dell' Imperatore nei " libelli " di Decio ', *Studi in onore di A. Calderini e R. Paribeni* I (1956), 369 ff. There is no proof that the edict applied only to Roman citizens, even though one of the Egyptian *libelli* which seemed to constitute a *prima facie* proof that it did not (Knipfing, o.c. (n. 81), 385, no. 35) has been re-read (see H. C. Youtie, ' The Textual Criticism of Documentary Papyri : Prolegomena ', *Bull. Lond. Inst. Cl. St.*, Supp. vi (1958), 16 f.).

Saturninus, as proconsul of Africa in 180, refused to allow a Christian to expound his faith : ' I shall not listen if you speak evil of what is sacred to us '.[208] When Pliny urged Trajan to pardon Christians who renounced their beliefs, his main argument was that this would restore the temples and cults of town and countryside to their former condition.[209] Whatever the private attitude of Pliny, the significant fact is his belief that the emperor was concerned for the cults of northern Asia Minor. There seems to be a line of continuity here which has not yet been fully explored, and which might be traceable far back into the days of the Republic.[210]

It would be a mistake to assume that there was a single Roman policy towards foreign cults which was unambiguous and unchanging[211]—or even that Roman law provided unequivocal guidance on the subject.[212] The famous Black Stone of Pessinus was brought to Rome in 204 B.C. and the cult of the Magna Mater became part of the officially recognized religion of the Roman state.[213] Yet there was also a strong feeling that only ancestral Gods ought to be worshipped, and in the traditional way.[214] The feeling could even acquire the force of law. In A.D. 57 A. Plautius was allowed by the Senate to gather a *consilium* of his friends and to sit as *paterfamilias* in judgement on his wife, Pomponia Graecina :   the crime alleged was ' superstitio externa ', and the charge was capital.[215]

The relevance of these facts to the problem of the legal basis of the condemnation of Christians ought to be clear. A provincial governor was predisposed to punish those who attacked the established religions, and would do so without waiting for a legal enactment by the Senate or the emperor. *Mos maiorum* was the most important source of Roman law, and it was precisely *mos maiorum* in all its aspects that Christians urged men to repudiate. The theory of ' national apostasy ' [216] fails as an explanation of the legal basis of the condemnation of Christians ; but it comes close to the truth if it is applied, not to the law, but to the attitudes of men. It is in the minds of men, not in the demands of Roman law, that the roots of the persecution of the Christians in the Roman Empire are to be sought.

The Queen's College, Oxford

[208] *Acta Scill.* 5 : ' initianti tibi mala de sacris nostris aures non praebebo '.

[209] *Epp.* x, 96, 9/10.

[210] E. Le Blant, *Les Persécuteurs et les martyrs* (1893), 67 ff. For example, the instructions to the consuls in 186 B.C. imply a religious as well as a moral objection to the Bacchic rites : these are to be rooted out ' exstrad quam sei quid ibei sacri est ' (*SC de Bacchanalibus*, line 28)/' extra quam si qua ibi vetusta ara aut signum consecratum esset ' (Livy xxxix, 18, 7). Permission for Bacchanalia can only be given to those who claim a prior religious obligation to celebrate them (*SC*, line 4 ; Livy xxxix, 18, 8).

[211] As H. Last, ' The Study of the Persecutions ', *JRS* xxvii (1937), 80 ff.

[212] As Mommsen, o.c. (n. 96), 567 ff.

[213] Wissowa, o.c. (n. 119), 317 ff.

[214] See Cicero, *Leg.* ii, 18 ff. One of the laws of

Cicero's ideal state is : ' separatim nemo habessit deos neve novos neve advenas nisi publice adscitos ; privatim colunto, quos rite a patribus < cultos acceperint > ' (19). The context implies that this proposal was not regarded as a break with tradition. The enunciation of the religious laws of the ideal state is greeted with the comment ' non multum discrepat ista constitutio religionum a legibus Numae nostrisque moribus ' (23). Unfortunately, the full justification advanced for the specific proposal just quoted is probably lost in a lacuna (25 f.). But the same attitude was later expressed by Dio (LII, 36), and seems to lie behind the actions of Decius (Andreotti, o.c. 376).

[215] Tacitus, *Ann.* xiii, 32.

[216] Th. Mommsen, ' Der Religionsfrevel nach römischem Recht ', *Hist. Zeitschr.* LXIV (1890), 389 ff. = *Ges. Schr.* iii (1907), 389 ff.

III

AN APOSTLE ON TRIAL[1]

ANOTHER article on Paul in Athens might appear otiose. The bibliography compiled by A. J. and M. B. Mattill (which goes down to 1961) catalogues more than 150 studies devoted to Acts 17: 16–34 alone, excluding all discussions of the passage in works of wider compass.[2] Nor does the growth of exegetical literature show any obvious sign of ceasing.[3] Yet one may detect a certain imbalance in 'the history of the question'. Scholars have tended to concentrate their attention on Paul's speech (*vv.* 22–31). Its purpose, character, and theology, the sources of its inspiration, its similarity to or differences from what the historical Paul either actually said or would have said— these are the constant topics of debate.[4] The context of the speech and the historical background tend simply to be assumed, and often misrepresented. Thus the words '(ὁ) Ἄρειος πάγος' (so many allege) must denote either the council of the Areopagus or the hill of the Areopagus, but not both together, not the council sitting on the hill. Hence, when Paul speaks after being taken 'ἐπὶ τὸν Ἄρειον πάγον' (*v.* 19), there is said to be a choice of three possibilities. Either he delivers a missionary sermon to the populace of Athens on the hill;[5] or he addresses the council (or one of its organs) somewhere else;[6] or perhaps the author of

---

[1] I am grateful to Professor Sparks, to Martin Hughes and Peter Levi, to Michael Reeve and Peter Rhodes for many improvements and refinements in an earlier draft of this article: the errors and inconcinnities which remain are my own.

[2] A. J. and M. B. Mattill, *A Classified Bibliography of Literature on the Acts of the Apostles* (*New Testament Tools and Studies*, vii [1966]), pp. 430–9, nos. 6029–6179. It would be pedantic to complain at the omission of the lucid summary of no. 6041 given at *Berliner philologische Wochenschrift*, xiv (1894), cols. 444–5.

[3] Note, for example, E. des Places, *Studiorum Paulinorum Congressus Internationalis Catholicus 1961* (*Analecta Biblica*, xvii/xviii [1963]), ii, pp. 183 ff.; G. Turbessi, ibid., pp. 383 ff.; H. Conzelmann, *Studies in Luke-Acts: Essays in honor of Paul Schubert* (1966), pp. 217 ff.; R. E. Wycherley, *J.T.S.*, N.S. xix (1968), pp. 619 ff.

[4] For the progress of the long controversy, cf. E. Beurlier, *Rev. d'hist. et de litt. rel.* i (1896), pp. 344 ff.; B. Gärtner, *The Areopagus Speech and Natural Revelation* (*Acta Seminarii Neotestamentici Upsaliensis*, xxi [1955]), pp. 37 ff.; H. Hommel, *Zeitschr. für neut. Wiss.* xlvi (1955), pp. 145 ff.

[5] A. Harnack, *Texte u. Unters.* xxxix. 1 (1913), p. 7; E. Norden, *Agnostos Theos* (1913), pp. 3 ff.; E. Meyer, *Ursprung und Anfänge des Christentums*, iii (1923), pp. 89 ff.; M. Dibelius, *Sitzungsber. der Akad. der Wiss. Heidelberg*, Phil.-hist. Kl. 1939, Abhand. 2, reprinted and translated in *Studies in the Acts of the Apostles* (1956), pp. 26 ff.

[6] K. Lake and H. J. Cadbury, *The Beginnings of Christianity* (ed. F. Jackson and K. Lake), iv (1933), pp. 212 f.; G. W. H. Lampe, *Peake's Commentary on the Bible*[2] (1962), § 794 l.

408

Acts simply failed to realize the ambiguity of his words and did not consciously distinguish between the first two possibilities.[1] Few, however,—not even those whose primary interest lies in Roman history[2]— seem disposed to seek out and state clearly on what scanty and irrelevant evidence they base their distinction between the two senses of '(ὁ) Ἄρειος πάγος'.

Progress can therefore be made by attempting to segregate attested fact from dubious hypothesis. Discussions of Paul in Athens too often present the latter as if it were the former, and all too often the un-suspecting reader is deceived. If this article does no more than prevent such deception in future, the author will fully have achieved his purpose in writing.

I. IRRELEVANT EVIDENCE

In Athens, Paul was taken 'ἐπὶ τὸν Ἄρειον πάγον' (Acts 17: 19), and delivered a speech 'ἐν μέσῳ τοῦ Ἀρείου πάγου' (17: 22). The significance of this episode can hardly be understood without investigating the powers and functions of the Areopagus. First, however, two common hypotheses must be discarded. One is that, since the council of the Areopagus always met in the Stoa Basileios, Paul must have been taken either before the council there or to the hill of the Areopagus (where the council no longer assembled).[3] The other is that Paul appeared before a permanent educational commission of the Areopagus.[4]

What is the evidence that the Areopagus met in the Stoa Basileios? A single passage of the first speech against Aristogeiton (commonly designated [Demosthenes] xxv).[5] The date and authorship of this oration are disputed. Some hold it to be genuine Demosthenes;[6] others a real speech delivered in Athens in 325 or 324 B.C. by someone

---

[1] A. D. Nock, *Gnomon*, xxv (1953), p. 506.

[2] Cf. W. M. Ramsay, *St. Paul the Traveller and the Roman Citizen* (1895), pp. 243 ff.; A. N. Sherwin-White, *Roman Society and Roman Law in the New Testament* (1963), p. 175.

[3] e.g. J. H. Lipsius, *Das attische Recht*, i (1905), pp. 365 f.; H. J. Cadbury, *The Book of Acts in History* (1955), pp. 51 f.

[4] e.g. Gärtner, op. cit., p. 57: 'there was, for example, an education com-mission, whose task was to supervise instruction. . . . This commission for the education of the young people was still in existence in 61 A.D.'

[5] Cf. G. Mathieu, *Démosthène: Plaidoyers politiques*, iv (Collection Budé, 1947), p. 148, n. 3. E. Curtius, *Die Stadtgeschichte von Athen* (1891), pp. 262 f., also adduced Plato's *Euthyphro*. But that contains nothing relevant to the Areopagus, only to the *archon basileus* (cf. *Ath. Pol.* 57. 3/4).

[6] F. Blass, *Die attische Beredsamkeit*², iii. 1 (1893), pp. 409 ff.; C. H. Kramer, *De priore Demosthenis adversus Aristogitonem oratione* (Diss. Leipzig, 1930); Mathieu, op. cit., p. 138.

else;[1] others again a rhetorical exercise by an Alexandrian scholar of the third century.[2] Or might it perhaps be a conflation of two fourth-century documents, a speech and a philosophical disquisition?[3] In any event, therefore, it is evidence for Athenian practice nearly four centuries before Paul. Furthermore the exact words of the speech have sometimes been forgotten:

ἔρανος γάρ ἐστι πολιτικὸς καὶ κοινὸς πάνθ' ὅσα, ταξάντων τῶν νόμων, ἕκαστος ἡμῶν ποιεῖ. . . . ὧν ἐν ᾗ δύ' ἐρῶ παραδείγματος ἕνεκα, τὰ γνωριμώτατα. . . . τὸ τὴν ἐξ Ἀρείου πάγου βουλήν, ὅταν ἐν τῇ βασιλείῳ στοᾷ καθεζομένη περισχοινίσηται, κατὰ πολλὴν ἡσυχίαν ἐφ' ἑαυτῆς εἶναι, καὶ ἅπαντας ἐκποδὼν ἀποχωρεῖν ([Demosthenes] xxv. 22/3).

Is this proof that the Areopagus always met in the Stoa Basileios? By no means: the writer merely states that when it meets there and is roped off no-one else is admitted.[4] Although the precise location is regrettably so far unknown,[5] the council of the Areopagus still normally assembled somewhere on the hill. Proof of that is provided by three other documents of the fourth century: a speech delivered c. 340, a law of 337/6, and the Ἀθηναίων Πολιτεία—in that section which describes the working of the Athenian constitution in the 320s.[6]

Nowhere is there any hint that the council ever ceased to meet on the hill.[7] Indeed, the contrary is asserted by three authors who lived in the century after Paul: namely, Aelius Aristides, Pausanias, and Lucian.[8] To be sure '(ὁ) Ἄρειος πάγος' may denote either the council or the hill[9]—it

---

[1] P. Treves, Athenaeum, N.S. xiv (1936), pp. 252 ff.

[2] A. Schaefer, Demosthenes und seine Zeit, iii. 2 (1858), pp. 113 ff.; R. Sealey, Essays in Greek Politics (n.d., publ. 1967), p. 186.

[3] M. Pohlenz, 'Anonymus περὶ νόμων', Gött. Gel. Nach. 1924, pp. 19 ff.

[4] Cf. R. E. Wycherley, The Athenian Agora, iii: Literary and Epigraphical Testimonia (1957), p. 21: 'the Areopagus sometimes sat in the stoa.'

[5] For divergent views, cf. B. D. Meritt, Hesperia, xxi (1952), p. 358; H. A. Thompson, Hesperia, xxii (1953), p. 52; B. D. Meritt, ibid., p. 129; R. E. Wycherley, J.H.S. lxxv (1955), pp. 118 ff.

[6] [Demosthenes] lix. 80–3; Supp. epig. Graec. xii. 87 = J. Pouilloux, Choix d'inscriptions grecques (1960), no. 32; Ath. Pol. 57. 3/4; 60. 2/3.

[7] E. Renan, Saint Paul (Histoire des origines du christianisme, iii [1869]), p. 194, attempted to interpret Vitruvius, De Architectura, II. i. 5 in this sense. But the ancient hut to which Vitruvius refers is clearly irrelevant to the council of the Areopagus, cf. W. Judeich, Topographie von Athen (1905), p. 269.

[8] Aristides, Panathenaicus 43 Oliver = vol. i, p. 171 Dindorf; Pausanias, I. xxviii. 5, cf. xxviii. 8; Lucian, Bis accusatus 4; 12. For comment, see J. H. Oliver, The Civilising Power (Trans. Amer. Phil. Soc. N.S. lviii. 1 [1968]), p. 105; J. G. Frazer, Pausanias's Description of Greece, ii (1898), pp. 362 ff.; J. Delz, Lukians Kenntnis der athenischen Antiquitäten (Diss. Basle, 1950), pp. 153 ff.

[9] Even this has been denied, as by F. Blass, Acta Apostolorum: Editio philologica (1895), p. 190: 'non dicitur Ἄρειος πάγος nisi de loco.'

410

carries the same ambiguity as the phrase 'the House of Commons' (which can denote an assembly, a debating-chamber, or the larger part of a certain building). Pedantic accuracy might require that the council be designated 'ἡ ἐξ Ἀρείου πάγου βουλή': that is the customary formula of official decrees in Roman Athens.[1] But even in official documents strict protocol was not always observed.[2] The corollary is clear. If the council of the Areopagus still normally met on the hill of that name, there is no need to introduce an artificial distinction between two senses of '(ὁ) Ἄρειος πάγος' when discussing Paul. The obvious meaning of the words in Acts should be accepted: Paul was taken before the Areopagus, i.e. before the council sitting on the hill.[3]

As for the alleged educational commission, again there is a solitary item of evidence.[4] It is a passage from the pseudo-Platonic *Axiochus*:

ἐπειδὰν δὲ εἰς τοὺς ἐφήβους ἐγγραφῇ, κοσμητὴς καὶ φόβος χειρῶν, ἔπειτα Λύκειον καὶ Ἀκαδήμεια καὶ γυμνασιαρχία καὶ ῥάβδοι καὶ κακῶν ἀμετρίαι· καὶ πᾶς ὁ τοῦ μειρακίσκου πόνος ἐστὶν ὑπὸ σωφρονιστὰς καὶ τὴν ἐπὶ τοὺς νέους αἵρεσιν τῆς ἐξ Ἀρείου πάγου βουλῆς (366e–367a).

How is this relevant to Paul? Although the *Axiochus* may have been composed *c.* 50 B.C.,[5] its view of the Areopagus is romantic and unhistorical: the close supervision over the ephebes which it ascribes to the council seems nowhere else to be explicitly attested, except in the anachronistic and equally romantic theorizing of Isocrates.[6] Perhaps, therefore, 'αἵρεσις ἐπὶ τοὺς νέους' means no more than 'control over the young'. For there seems to be no close parallel for the word in the sense of 'permanent educational commission'.[7] However, even if such a com-

---

[1] D. J. Geagan, *The Athenian Constitution after Sulla* (*Hesperia*, Supp. xii [1967]), p. 32.

[2] *Sylloge*³ 796 B = *I.G.* iv². 83: Ἄρειος πάγος ἐν Ἐλευσῖνι.

[3] Cf. W. A. McDonald, *The Political Meeting Places of the Greeks* (1943), p. 130: 'there is no evidence for this period (i.e. the first century A.D.) to show that the council was not continuing to meet regularly on the Areopagus itself, and the chances are that such a time-honored custom would persist.'

[4] Cf. E. Haenchen, *Die Apostelgeschichte* (*Kritisch-exegetischer Kommentar über das Neue Testament*, iii¹³ [1961]), p. 456, n. 7. On Plutarch, *Cicero*, 24. 5 and Quintilian, *Inst. Orat.* v. ix. 13, which are sometimes adduced, see below, p. 413.

[5] J. Souilhé, *Platon*, xiii. 3 (Collection Budé, 1962), pp. 123 ff. O. Immisch, *Philologische Studien zu Plato*, i (1896), pp. 14 f., preferred to date it to the late fourth century.

[6] *Areopagiticus*, 37 ff.

[7] L.S.J.⁹, s.v. III. 2, correctly cites *I.G.* iv². 83 (to which may be added *I.G.* xii. 3. 330, l. 249) for 'αἵρεσις' as 'embassy'. But that might tend rather to support Souilhé's interpretation: 'les précepteurs que l'Aréopage choisit pour la jeunesse' (op. cit., p. 141).

mission did exist,[1] the plain statement of Acts cannot simply be disregarded: Paul came 'ἐπὶ τὸν Ἄρειον πάγον', not before a committee.

II. THE POWERS OF THE AREOPAGUS

'The Areopagus was the predominant corporation of Roman Athens': that is the clear and unimpeachable verdict of a recent investigation of the Athenian constitution after its reorganization by Sulla in 86 B.C.[2] Discussions of Paul in Athens, however, have not always acknowledged this cardinal fact.[3] The evidence, therefore, ought to be allowed to speak for itself.

Cicero assumes the dominant position of the Areopagus when making a philosophical point:

sed id praecise dicitur: ut, si quis dicat Atheniensium rempublicam consilio regi, desit illud 'Areopagi', sic cum dicimus providentia mundum administrari deesse arbitrato 'deorum' (*De Natura Deorum*, ii. 74).

Two centuries later, Aelius Aristides made the same assumption when praising the constitution of Athens: the Areopagus there corresponds to 'τὰ ἑτέρωθί που κύρια καὶ ἡγούμενα'.[4] Inscriptions confirm. When a Roman emperor wrote to the city, he normally addressed 'the *boule* of the Areopagus, the *boule* of the Six (later, Five) Hundred and the *demos* of the Athenians':[5] that was the correct order, and the order which corresponded to political reality. Accordingly, when the whole city paraded on a ceremonial occasion, the Areopagus preceded the other *boule*, which itself preceded the *demos*.[6] The standing of the Areopagus was reflected in the enhanced dignity of its herald: he now appears in the official archon-list,[7] and has in his possession the seal of the city.[8]

[1] For the evidence relevant to possible commissions of the Areopagus, see B. Keil, *Beiträge zur Geschichte des Areopags* (*Berichte über die Verhand. der Sächs. Akad. der Wiss. zu Leipzig*, Phil.-hist. Kl. lxxi. 8 [1920]), pp. 72 ff.
[2] Geagan, op. cit., p. 41. Cf. also J. Touloumakos, *Der Einfluß Roms auf die Staatsform der griechischen Stadtstaaten des Festlandes und der Inseln im ersten und zweiten Jhdt. v. Chr.* (Diss. Göttingen, 1967), pp. 77 ff., esp. 94 ff. The predominance of the Areopagus antedates direct Roman influence, cf. W. S. Ferguson, *Hellenistic Athens* (1911), pp. 419 ff.
[3] Note Sherwin-White, op. cit., p. 175: in Acts 'even at Athens there is no word of the council which administered the city'. He appeals to P. Graindor, *Athènes de Tibère à Trajan* (1931), pp. 62 ff., 117 ff. The truth had already been stated succinctly by Keil, op. cit., p. 95.
[4] *Panathenaicus*, 262 ff. Oliver.   [5] Geagan, op. cit., p. 32.
[6] *I.G.* ii/iii². 3606, ll. 24 ff. (the return of Herodes Atticus from Sirmium c. 172, cf. Philostratus, *Vit. soph.* II. i. 11).
[7] Geagan, op. cit., pp. xii f., 57 ff.
[8] *I.G.* iv². 83. Cf. Keil, op. cit., pp. 54 ff.

412

The Areopagus was also the chief court of imperial Athens, apparently retaining its judicial functions until very late antiquity, despite political impotence.[1] The evidence for the early empire, both epigraphic and literary, is meagre but decisive.[2] Journeying to his province in A.D. 18, the governor of Syria, Cn. Calpurnius Piso, failed to secure a pardon for his friend Theophilus, whom the Areopagus had condemned for forgery.[3] In the second century, various essays of Lucian assume that the contemporary Areopagus has jurisdiction in cases of kidnapping and assault, and Pausanias implies that it still conducted trials for murder.[4] As for the penalties which the Areopagus could exact, an inscription attests exile[5] and Lucian implies capital punishment.[6] Although it is difficult to segregate contemporary description from traditional elements in Lucian's writings,[7] that is not incredible. The widespread modern belief that, in any province of the Roman Empire, the law permitted the Roman governor alone to execute criminals, requires a critical reappraisal.[8]

The Areopagus possessed religious prestige and a reputation for sagacity, as is evident from a story recorded by Valerius Maximus. A woman of Smyrna killed her second husband and their son because they had murdered her son by a previous marriage. She was denounced before the proconsul of Asia, P. Cornelius Dolabella,[9] who sent the case to the Areopagus (so at least the story runs).

[1] See the scholiast on Aristides, *Panathenaicus* 266 Oliver (vol. iii, p. 335, ll. 18 ff. Dindorf). On the intricate (and largely unresolved) problem of the historical value of such scholia, cf. F. Lenz, *Untersuchungen zu den Aristeides-scholien* (*Problemata*, viii [1934]); *Philologus*, cvii (1963), pp. 278 ff.

[2] Cf. Geagan, op. cit., p. 48: 'there is ample testimony for its expanded judicial competence'. However, *I.G.* ii/iii². 1100 shows some fiscal cases going either to the other *boule* or before the *demos*.   [3] Tacitus, *Ann.* ii. 55.

[4] Lucian, *Bis accusatus* 12; 15 ff.; *Timon* 46; *Vit. auct.* 7; Pausanias, I. xxviii. 5.
[5] Keil, op. cit., pp. 52 f.   [6] Delz, op. cit., pp. 108 f., 151 ff.

[7] J. H. Oliver, *Amer. Journ. Phil.* lxxii (1951), p. 217; R. J. Hopper, *Class. Rev.* lxvi (1952), p. 47.

[8] Sherwin-White, op. cit., pp. 3 ff., argues from Ulpian's statement that a governor cannot delegate *gladii potestas* to anyone else (*Dig.* I. xvi. 6). There are two flaws in his argument. First, the inference backwards from the theories of Severan jurists to the first century is very hazardous: cf., in different contexts, M. W. Frederiksen, *J.R.S.* liv (1964), p. 132; P. Garnsey, *J.R.S.* lviii (1968), pp. 58 f. Second, and even more serious, Ulpian's statement does not formally exclude the possibility that others in the province might have possessed *gladii potestas* besides the governor: compare the analogous case of *emancipatio* (Ulpian at *Dig.* I. xvi. 3; a law of 290 at *Cod. Just.* VIII. xlviii. 1). Moreover, when discussing Judaea, Sherwin-White misinterprets Josephus, *Antiquities*, xx. 202 (op. cit., pp. 38 f., 54); on the meaning of which, see G. D. Kilpatrick, *The Trial of Jesus* (1953), pp. 8 f., 18.

[9] The date is 68 B.C.: T. R. S. Broughton, *The Magistrates of the Roman Republic*, ii (1952), pp. 139, 142.

quia ipse neque liberare duabus caedibus contaminatam neque punire tam iusto dolore impulsam sustinebat (*Facta et dicta memorabilia*, viii. 1, Amb. 2).

The council prudently ordered that the trial be adjourned for a hundred years. Religious considerations might also be invoked to explain something curious in Quintilian:

nec mihi videntur Ariopagitae, cum damnaverint puerum coturnicum oculos eruentem, aliud iudicasse, quam id signum esse perniciosissimae mentis multisque malo futurae, si adolevisset (*Inst. orat.* v. ix. 13).[1]

But the beastly boy may easily be a stock *exemplum* and fictitious, invented centuries before Quintilian.

In short, therefore, the Areopagus seems to be the effective government of Roman Athens and its chief court. As such, like the imperial Senate in Rome, it could interfere in any aspect of corporate life— education, philosophical lectures, public morality, foreign cults. It is not necessary to invent any special powers for the Areopagus in order to explain particular actions. For example, when Cicero persuaded the Areopagus to ask the philosopher Cratippus to stay to teach in Athens,[2] the reason was not that the Areopagus had any special control over the lectures of philosophers,[3] but that Cicero considered an invitation from the Areopagus the most likely to influence Cratippus. Hence there is no need to suppose that the Areopagus had special 'surveillance over the introduction of foreign divinities' in order to interest itself in Paul.[4] Its general constitutional position enabled it to control religion no less than any other part of the life of Athens.

Even granted that Paul was taken before the Areopagus, was he in any sense put on trial? The possibility is often excluded on the grounds that there is no formal accusation and no formal verdict.[5] That argument, however, appears to presuppose an anachronistic notion of what constitutes a criminal trial. The almost uniform practice of the Roman world was an informal process, with hardly any rules to circumscribe

---

[1] On quails in the ancient world, cf. O. Keller, *Die antike Tierwelt*, ii (1913), pp. 161 ff.; D'A. W. Thompson, *A Glossary of Greek Birds* (1936), pp. 215 ff.

[2] Plutarch, *Cicero*, 24. 5.

[3] So Ramsay, op. cit., pp. 246 ff. But, for the comparatively great independence enjoyed by ancient universities, see A. Cameron, *Cahiers d'histoire mondiale*, x (1967), pp. 653 ff.

[4] As appears to be implied by Geagan, op. cit., p. 50.

[5] e.g. Gärtner, op. cit., p. 53: 'there is nothing to indicate judicial proceedings —neither prosecutor, nor accusation, nor anything in the speech itself, which is addressed to Athenians generally.' Cf. further below, pp. 417–18.

either procedure or penalties or the nature of the charge.[1] The confusion which could on occasion ensue in the Roman Senate is plain in the pages of Tacitus and Pliny.[2] Why imagine the Areopagus in Roman Athens to be any more shackled by rules of procedure?

Examination of the powers and functions of the Areopagus, therefore, fails to reveal any implausibility in the view that Paul was put on trial accused of introducing a new religion.

III. The Persecution of Paul

Paul encountered violent hostility and active opposition throughout Asia Minor and Greece.[3] Sometimes the opposition was fanned by Jews (Pisidian Antioch, Iconium, Lystra, Thessalonica, Corinth). On other occasions Paul's persecutors were pagans (Philippi, Ephesus). Sometimes the apostles were forced to flee a city after a riot (Antioch, Iconium, Lystra, Ephesus). Sometimes there was a formal accusation before the local magistrates (Philippi, Thessalonica), and in Corinth Paul was hauled before the Roman governor.[4] On other occasions the legal process (if any) is unclear, even when local magistrates intervene (Antioch, Ephesus).[5] All these episodes, however, share one important feature: the authorities, local or imperial, only appear because the Christians are being attacked for their missionary activities.

Athens is surely no exception.[6] As at Philippi, Thessalonica, and Corinth, Paul is seized by force: 'ἐπιλαβόμενοι δὲ αὐτοῦ ἐπὶ τὸν Ἄρειον πάγον ἤγαγον' (v. 19). The meaning of the Greek is undeniable: in Luke and Acts 'ἐπιλαμβάνεσθαι' always signifies 'to take hold of', and in this context that is hard to interpret as a friendly action.[7] For, if Paul went before the Areopagus 'by special invitation',[8] what need was there of physical constraint? In Philippi and Thessalonica, there had been

[1] P. Garnsey, Past and Present, xli (1968), pp. 11 ff.
[2] e.g. Tacitus, Ann. iii. 49–51; Pliny, Epp. viii. 14.
[3] Acts 13: 13 ff.; 16: 6ff.; 19: 23 ff. On the historical background, cf. Sherwin-White, op. cit., pp. 71 ff.; W. H. C. Frend, Martyrdom and Persecution in the Early Church (1965), pp. 151 ff.; T. D. Barnes, J.R.S. lviii (1968), pp. 33, 48 ff.
[4] L. Junius Gallio Annaeanus, proconsul of Achaea in 51/2 (P.I.R.² J 757).
[5] For comment, cf. Sherwin-White, op. cit., pp. 83 ff., 97 f.
[6] But note N. B. Stonehouse, Paul before the Areopagus and other New Testament Studies (1957), p. 5: 'Paul . . . was taking a brief holiday in Athens.'
[7] Luke 9: 47; 14: 4; 23: 26; Acts 9: 27; 16: 19; 18: 17; 21: 30, 33; 23: 19. Luke also uses the word twice metaphorically, with 'λόγου' and 'ῥήματος' (20: 20, 26). In Acts four of its six occurrences (apart from Acts 17: 19) connote violence: the arrest of Paul and Silas at Philippi, the beating of Sosthenes in Corinth, Paul's seizure by the crowd in Jerusalem, and his subsequent binding in chains by the tribune. [8] A. D. Nock, Conversion (1933), p. 191.

denunciation before the local magistrates: at Athens, a much larger town and a *civitas libera*,[1] the Areopagus was the chief court and the effective government.[2] At Corinth, the Jews charged Paul with teaching men to worship God illegally; in Athens too those who seized Paul maintained that he was introducing a new religion (*vv.* 19/20).[3] Although the form of words is politer than at Corinth, why should it not be construed as an accusation?

IV. PAUL IN ATHENS

The argument so far has assumed that the narrative of Acts may be used as historical evidence for Paul's visit to Athens. This assumption now requires some justification. For E. Norden, M. Dibelius, and A. D. Nock have all denied the historicity of Acts' story of Paul's adventures in Athens. Norden argued, largely from the vocabulary of 17: 18, 21, that the episode was lifted from a biography of Apollonius of Tyana written in fine Attic Greek.[4] Dibelius simply stigmatized the description of Athens as stylized.[5] Nock's reasoning was avowedly more subjective: 'brilliant as is the picture of Athens, it makes on me the impression of being based on literature, which was easy to find, rather than on personal observation.'[6] Perhaps that is to attribute excessive erudition to the author.[7] More important, what does Acts actually say?

17: 16   Waiting for Timothy and Silas in Athens, Paul was annoyed at the idolatry of the city.

17: 17   Paul talked in the synagogue to the Jews and *sebomenoi*, and in the *agora* to passers-by.

---

[1] Strabo, ix, p. 398. On the status and privileges of such cities, cf. A. H. M. Jones, *Anatolian Studies presented to W. H. Buckler* (1939), pp. 103 ff.

[2] Above, pp. 411–13.

[3] For hostility to religious innovators, see the brief hints at *J.R.S.* lviii (1968), pp. 49 f.

[4] Norden, *Agnostos Theos*, pp. 52 ff., 333 ff. F. C. Burkitt, *J.T.S.* xv (1913/14), pp. 455 ff., provided a genial demolition.

[5] *Studies*, pp. 64 ff.

[6] *Gnomon*, xxv (1953), p. 506.

[7] The 'erudition' of Minucius Felix stands as a warning. J. P. Waltzing, in his edition of the *Octavius* with full commentary in 1903, professed to have discovered very numerous allusions to classical authors, and his high estimate of Minucius' learning can still be quoted with approval (G. W. Clarke, *Journal of Religious History*, iii (1965), p. 205). But strong doubts are in place. For Waltzing alleged no less than eleven allusions to Juvenal—which would be a startling phenomenon, cf. A. D. E. Cameron, *Hermes*, xcii (1964), pp. 367 ff. In fact, the eleven allusions all turn out to be commonplaces (G. Highet, *Juvenal the Satirist* (1954), pp. 296 f.). I suspect that a candid appraisal would lead to the same result for most of the other allusions detected by Waltzing.

416

17: 18   Some Epicurean and Stoic philosophers confronted him. Some said 'What is this prater saying?', others 'He is introducing new Gods.' Explanation of the author.

17: 19/20   They took hold of him and led him to the Areopagus, saying 'May we know what this new doctrine of yours is?'

17: 21   Comment of the author on the Athenians' intellectual curiosity.

17: 22 ff.   Paul's speech.

Verse 21 is clearly parenthetical: any argument based on its language is therefore irrelevant to what precedes and follows. As for the rest of the passage, where is the 'brilliant picture' of Athens, or the stylized description? The truth, as often, seems obvious and unpretentious: the writer is simply recounting what happened to Paul in Athens.[1]

Another line of argument is less immediately vulnerable. Perhaps the whole of Acts (not just 17: 16–34) is unhistorical, perhaps it is all a mere literary elaboration based on a bare itinerary of Paul's journeys.[2] At first sight, such a theory appears inexpugnable. For there exists no independent evidence to provide specific confirmation or disproof of the detailed narrative of Acts. But doubts quickly arise. Even if it were the author of Acts who has himself elaborated a bare list of place-names, it still needs to be proved that the material which he added is unhistorical and cannot derive from an independent and authentic tradition.[3] It is not reassuring to read Dibelius's verdict on Acts' account of Paul's shipwreck: 'Truly literary criticism will lead us to suppose that the nautical description is taken from the numerous accounts of sea-voyages in literature and not from experience.'[4] Why? Even Nock, though well disposed to Dibelius's technique, found this hard to swallow.[5] If an author expresses himself in clichés or allusively, that does not of itself demonstrate that events did not occur as he describes them. As for the 'numerous accounts of sea-voyages in literature', it is unfortunate that neither Dibelius nor the scholars to whom he appeals for proof of his assertions[6] offer any precise references. For an important distinction

---

[1] For a modification of this view, cf. below, pp. 418–19.

[2] M. Dibelius, *Studies*, pp. 73 ff., 104 ff.

[3] Contrast the criticisms of E. Haenchen, *Zeitschr. für Theol. und Kirche*, lviii (1961), pp. 329 ff., reprinted in *Gesammelte Aufsätze*, i: *Gott und Mensch* (1965), pp. 227 ff.

[4] *Studies*, p. 107.

[5] *Gnomon*, xxv (1953), p. 499.

[6] Viz. P. Wendland, *Die urchristlichen Literaturformen* (*Handbuch zum Neuen Testament*, i. 2[2, 3] [1912]), p. 324; J. Wellhausen, *Kritische Analyse der Apostelgeschichte* (*Abhand. Göttingen*, Phil.-hist. Kl., N. F. xv. 2 [1914]), pp. 53 ff.

needs to be drawn. Ancient writers often did retail fictitious sea-voyages. But these tended to possess certain definable characteristics: they tended to be mythical voyages, with figures of legend (like Circe and Polyphemus in the *Odyssey*), or to have a close connection with ethnography, or else to be the thrilling adventures of an ancient novelist.[1] In sharp contrast stand certain historical voyages, and shipwrecks, like that of the Jewish historian Josephus.[2] There ought to be no dispute to which category the sea-voyage in Acts must be assigned.

In brief, the form-critics have failed to realize the limitations of their chosen method. Although form-criticism is indispensable if one wishes to segregate the various strata in Acts or the Gospels, the question of the historicity of the primitive elements in a complicated narrative can only be decided by an appeal (open or covert) to historical criteria.[3]

V. THE SPEECH

Paul's speech (Acts 17: 22–31) is conventionally interpreted as a missionary sermon,[4] the chief dispute being how much is Pauline and how much not. Another view is at least arguable. The speech can be construed as an effective answer to the charge of introducing a new religion.[5] As follows:

17: 22   Paul begins with an ambiguous comment on the Athenians' religiosity: the connotations of 'δεισιδαιμονεστέρους' depend on the prejudices of the hearer.[6]

         'ἄνδρες Ἀθηναῖοι' is often taken for proof that Paul is not addressing the Areopagus alone, but a gathering of the populace of Athens.[7] But this form of address is here logically

---

[1] Cf. R. Reitzenstein, *Hellenistische Wundererzählungen* (1906), p. 12; E. Rohde, *Der griechische Roman und seine Vorläufer*[3] (1914), pp. 178 ff. And note that the sea-voyage in Acts contains no identifiable reminiscences of pagan literature.

[2] *Vita*, 14 f., especially the revealing remark: 'φθάσαντες τοὺς ἄλλους ἐγώ τε καί τινες ἕτεροι περὶ ὀγδοήκοντα σύμπαντες ἀνελήφθημεν εἰς τὸ πλοῖον.'

[3] Observe Dibelius's treatment of the conversion of Cornelius (Acts 10: 1–11: 8): after isolating the original 'straightforward legend of a conversion' (*Studies*, pp. 109–21), he concedes that such stories 'reproduced historical events, expressed, of course, in the style of "legend" ' (p. 121), and then passes on to the events' real historical context (pp. 121–2).

[4] As still by U. Wilckens, *Die Missionsreden der Apostelgeschichte*[2] (1963), pp. 87 ff.

[5] For this view, cf. K. Bornhäuser, *Studien zur Apostelgeschichte* (1934), pp. 136 ff.; J. Dupont, *Les Actes des apôtres* (1953), pp. 154 ff. For a detailed linguistic commentary, E. Haenchen, *Kritisch-exegetischer Kommentar über das Neue Testament*, iii[13] (1961), pp. 458 ff.

[6] L.S.J.[9], s.v. δεισιδαίμων.   [7] e.g. Sherwin-White, op. cit., p. 175.

418

necessary. Accused of introducing a religion alien to Athens, Paul replies that his audience already acknowledges his God. Since the evidence he quotes is relevant only to the Athenians as a whole, he must avoid the possible objection that the cult of the unknown God need not have the approval of the Areopagus.

17: 23 Altars dedicated 'ἀγνώστοις θεοῖς' existed, and are attested at Olympia, Pergamum, and Phalerum (near Athens).[1] None is otherwise known with the dedication 'ἀγνώστῳ θεῷ'. Paul is therefore (on this view of the speech) using the sophistical trick of slightly misrepresenting the evidence in his own favour—as Jerome, who understood the technique only too well, clearly perceived.[2] Paul thus claims that the Athenians already have altars to the God whom he is proclaiming: how then can he be introducing a new religion?

17: 24–9 Paul cleverly brings out some affinities between his religion and Stoic metaphysics,[3] capping them with a quotation from 'one of your poets'[4]—an appeal to an authority acknowledged by the audience.

17: 30–1 Having refuted the charge, Paul now passes on to purely Christian ideas.

17: 32–3 The meeting of the Areopagus breaks up.

17: 34 Some converts are made.

Verses 32–4 pose a real difficulty for the interpretation here propounded. The author evidently does not intend his readers to understand the outcome of Paul's speech as an acquittal after trial.[5] The difficulty, however, is not necessarily insuperable. All will concede that Acts has an apologetic tendency. Why, therefore, may it not be supposed that the author has deliberately presented Paul's trial by the Areopagus as something other than it really was? Dibelius and Nock defined the aim of Acts 17: 16–34 as the presentation of Christianity in the cultural capital of the world, and from this they wished to deduce that the whole episode was composed by the author of Acts, i.e. that it is fiction.[6] Is it not more probable that the writer has merely recast genuine facts

[1] Norden, op. cit., pp. 53 ff.; M. P. Nilsson, *Geschichte der griechischen Religion*, ii[2] (1961), pp. 338, 355, 357.   [2] *Ad Titum*, i. 12 (*P.L.* xxvi. 572).
[3] Cf. M. Pohlenz, *Zeitschr. für neut. Wiss.* xlii (1949), pp. 69 ff.
[4] On the attribution of the quotation, see M. Dibelius, *Studies*, pp. 51 ff., 187 f.
[5] G. W. H. Lampe, *Peake's Commentary*,[2] § 795 g: 'any idea of a trial seems to have disappeared at this stage.'
[6] Dibelius, *Studies*, pp. 64 ff.; Nock, *Gnomon*, xxv (1953), pp. 504, 506.

to suit his apologetic purposes? That would explain why he has left so many traces of what is here contended to have been the true course of events.

VI. CONCLUSION

Too much must not be claimed for the arguments formulated above. They are not intended to perform the clearly impossible task of providing positive proof that Paul was put on trial in Athens. Rather, a more modest aim has been pursued. The first two sections sought to destroy the twofold basis of most previous claims to the contrary: viz. the hypothesis that 'ἐπὶ τὸν Ἄρειον πάγον' need not mean 'before the *boule* of the Areopagus' (§ I), and a misapprehension of the Areopagus' true constitutional position in Roman Athens (§ II). Next, it was argued that the view that Paul was on trial posesses intrinsic plausibility (§ III). It was then contended, against the form-critics, that Acts should be regarded as valid historical evidence (§ IV), and that Paul's speech could be interpreted as a speech of defence to the charge of introducing a new religion to Athens (§ V). Hence the conclusion which emerges is a negative one: the possibility that Paul was actually tried by the Areopagus has not yet encountered adequate refutation. It is a further step (but a justifiable one) to assert that the possibility should be treated as a probability.[1]

'Perhaps no passage in the whole of the Acts has suffered more from hazy and ill-considered interpretation than that dealing with the visit of St. Paul to Athens.'[2] That verdict, delivered almost seventy-five years ago, also applies to most subsequent work on the subject. The present writer hopes to have inaugurated an improvement: however ill-considered his views, he has attempted to avoid the accusation of haziness.

[1] Cf. *J.R.S.* lviii (1968), p. 49.
[2] A. F. Findlay, *Annual of the British School at Athens*, i (1894–5), p. 78.

IV

THE LOST KAISERGESCHICHTE AND THE LATIN HISTORICAL TRADITION

Quellenforschung is an indispensable tool of scholarship. Much of the historical writing which survives from antiquity is decades or even centuries removed from the events which it describes. No modern historian of the ancient world, therefore, can for ever shun the task of enquiring whence the authors still extant derived their information. In the recent past, however, Quellenforschung too often induced addiction—and a healthy reaction has set in[1]. For too many have regarded the discovery of his sources as the central or even the only problem when they were discussing a Greek or Roman historian[2]. Such preoccupation with the search for sources has not only diverted attention from the real historical importance of the extant authors, it has engendered some bizarre fantasies. One scholar held that Herodotus drew most of his knowledge of Xerxes' invasion of Greece from a written source also used by Ephorus[3]. Other scholars forgot that Cassius Dio resided in or near Rome for most of the half century after the death of Marcus Aurelius[4]. One argued that both Dio and Herodian took most of their facts from a lost source which ended in 218 and was written in Latin[5]. Another alleged that Dio's narrative of the reign of Commodus was largely cribbed from Marius Maximus[6]. These theories belong to the curiosities of classical scholarship. Nevertheless, even some professedly contemporary historians do pose the question of written sources. Herodian claims to be a contemporary witness, sometimes even an eye-witness, of the events he retails[7]. Yet his narrative has an opaque

---

[1] Note the protest of F. MILLAR, A Study of Cassius Dio (1964), viii; 34 ff.

[2] The paradigm case is R. LAQUEUR, Eusebius als Historiker seiner Zeit (1929), who concentrated exclusively on the sources and successive rewritings of Hist. Eccl. VII—IX.

[3] Viz. from Dionysius of Miletus (FGrH 687): E. OBST, Klio, Beiheft XII (1913), 27 ff.

[4] Dio LXXII. 4. 2; LXXX. 1. 2—2. 1; cf. LXXII. 7. 2.

[5] E. BAAZ, De Herodiani fontibus et auctoritate (Diss. Berlin, 1909), 61 f.

[6] J. C. P. SMITS, Die Vita Commodi und Cassius Dio (1914), 29 ff.

[7] I. 1. 3; 15. 4; III. 8. 10.

quality, with much of the vagueness and timelessness of a fairy-tale[8]. Perhaps a thorough comparison of Herodian with his literary models in every genre will both reveal the explanation and finally determine his status as historical evidence[9].

On these grounds alone a discussion of the lost K a i s e r g e -
s c h i c h t e (henceforward KG) could be justified—as a contribution to the history of Latin literature in the fourth century, and as an investigation of the value of fourth century authors as evidence for the first three centuries of imperial history. But there is something else, even more important. Through almost eighty years of bitter controversy, the true relevance of the KG to the H i s t o r i a A u g u s t a has passed virtually unnoticed.

• •

•

ALEXANDER ENMANN published his theory in June 1883[10]: he argued that the main source of the C a e s a r e s of Aurelius Victor, of Eutropius' B r e v i a r i u m VII—IX and of parts of the HA was 'eine verlorene Geschichte der römischen Kaiser' whose nature and extent he attempted to define[11]. Although it was ENMANN who proved and illustrated it in its fullness, the idea was not novel. In 1873 V. PIROGOFF had declared that Victor, Eutropius and the HA drew on a common source[12]. But he simply enunciated a thesis for future discussion, and the proof which he promised seems never to have been published[13]. In 1884 but independently of ENMANN, A. COHN argued that, for the period 31 B. C. to 96 A. D., Victor, Eutropius and the anonymous E p i t o m e d e C a e s a r i b u s all used a common source, a 'Suetonius auctus'—that is, an epitome of Suetonius with additional material from other sources[14]. This work had already been postulated

---

[8] E. HOHL, Sb. Berlin, Kl. f. Ges. 1954, Nr. 1; Sb. Berlin, Kl. f. Phil. 1956, Nr. 2; D. TIMPE, Hermes XCV (1967), 470 ff.

[9] Note E. NORDEN, Die antike Kunstprosa ²(1909), 397 f. (use of Xenophon's Cyropaedeia); A. G. Roos, JRS V (1915), 191 ff. (peculiar use of Dio). The arguments of NORDEN and Roos tend to be ignored, as by K. MUENSCHER, Xenophon in der griechisch-römischen Literatur (Philologus, Supp. XIII. 2, 1920), 136; F. CASSOLA, 'Erodiano e le sue fonti', Rendiconti Acc. di Arch., Lett. e Belle Arti, N. S. XXXII (1957), 165.

[10] See the notice of its publication at Deutsche Literaturzeitung IV (1883), 861.

[11] Philologus, Supp. IV (1884), 335 ff.

[12] De Eutropii Breviarii ab U. C. indole ac fontibus I (Diss. Berlin, 1873), 3.

[13] So far as I can discover, PIROGOFF published only one other work: Studies in Roman History mainly in the sphere of the Third Decade of Livy (St. Petersburg, 1878 — in Russian).

[14] Quibus ex fontibus Sex. Aurelii Victoris et libri de Caesaribus et Epitomes undecim capita priora fluxerint (1884). COHN's main purpose (successfully achieved) was to refute the hypothesis advanced by TH. OPITZ, Acta Soc.

by P. EBELING as a source for Eutropius[15], and was identified by ENMANN
with the early chapters of the KG[16].

Since 1883 few have failed to concede existence of a lost KG. Because ENMANN's hypothesis is necessary to explain the resemblances
between Victor and Eutropius, the controversy over the HA is irrelevant to its existence[17]. Consequently, the hypothesis is admitted
by almost all: by H. DESSAU and O. SEECK no less than by H. PETER and
TH. MOMMSEN, by E. HOHL, A. VON DOMASZEWSKI and N. H. BAYNES no
less than by F. LEO and CH. LÉCRIVAIN, and by R. SYME no less than by
A. MOMIGLIANO[18]. Some have added the gratuitous conjecture that the
KG (clearly a Latin work) was either translated from Greek or wholly
dependent on Greek sources[19]. On one fundamental fact, however, almost all seem agreed: Victor and Eutropius employed a common
source. It is on four further questions that opinions continue to differ:
when was the KG composed? which authors besides Victor and Eutropius used it? what was its precise nature and scope? and what was
its own derivation?

·   ·

·

For ENMANN not only were all the resemblances between Victor,
Eutropius and the HA due to the independent use of the KG by all
three, but the HA was composed in the reigns of Diocletian, Constantius and Constantine. Therefore, since 'Flavius Vopiscus' was
already using the KG in 305/6 (Aur. 44, 5), while 'Iulius Capitolinus',

---

Phil. Lipsiensis II (1872), 199 ff. by L. JEEP, Riv. fil. I (1873), 505 ff. (who asserted
it only of the Epitome), and by E. WOELFFLIN, Rh. Mus. N. F. XXIX (1874), 282 ff.,
Bursians Jahresber. III (1874), 787 ff., that the extant Caesares and the Epitome
were independent abbreviations of Victor's lost original history in the grand
style. Nonetheless, the hypothesis still received not unfavourable treatment
from SCHANZ-HOSIUS, Gesch. d. röm. Litt. IV. 1² (1914), 76.

[15] Quaestiones Eutropianae (Diss. Halle, 1881).
[16] o. c. 407 ff., esp. 431 f.
[17] Cf. E. HOHL, Bursians Jahresber. CCLVI (1937), 147: ‚Selbst wenn man
die HA ganz aus dem Spiele läßt, ergibt sich die Unentbehrlichkeit der These
ENMANNS schon aus den Berührungen zwischen Aurelius Victor, Eutrop und
der Epitome, die sich befriedigend nur durch eine gemeinsame Quelle, wie
ENMANN sie erschlossen hat, erklären lassen'.
[18] H. DESSAU, Hermes XXIV (1889), 361; TH. MOMMSEN, Hermes XXV (1890),
273 f. = Ges. Schr. VII (1909), 344 f.; O. SEECK, Jahrb. f. class. Phil. CXLI (1890),
638; H. PETER, Die geschichtliche Litteratur über die römische Kaiserzeit bis
Theodosius I und ihre Quellen II (1897), 137 ff.; F. LEO, Die griechisch-römische
Biographie (1901), 304 f.; CH. LÉCRIVAIN, Études sur l'Histoire Auguste (1904),
423 ff.; E. HOHL, Klio XI (1911), 192 ff.; A. VON DOMASZEWSKI, Sb. Heidelberg,
Phil.-hist. Kl. 1918, Abh. 13, 3; N. H. BAYNES, The Historia Augusta. Its date
and purpose (1926), 48; A. MOMIGLIANO, Secondo Contributo alla Storia degli
Studi Classici (1960), 117 f.; R. SYME, Ammianus and the Historia Augusta
(1968), 105 f.
[19] F. GRAEBNER, Byz. Zeitschr. XIV (1905), 87 ff.; DOMASZEWSKI, o. c. 109 f.

'Aelius Spartianus' and 'Trebellius Pollio' employed it before 305 (Marcus 16, 3 ff.; Sev. 17, 5 ff.; Claud., passim), he concluded that the KG ended either with or soon after the accession of Diocletian[20]. C. WAGENER, soon to be followed by PETER, attempted to define the terminus precisely: the KG came to an end in 305, was written in that year and used by 'Vopiscus' in 305/6[21].

The resemblances between Victor and Eutropius, however, so far from ceasing about 284 or in 305, clearly persist far into the fourth century. ENMANN accordingly felt forced to posit a continuation of the KG down to the battle of Strassburg in 357[22]. His argument was soon demolished: in 1889 DESSAU perceived that the HA was written not near the beginning but near the end of the fourth century[23]. Whatever its precise date (it does not matter here), the HA draws material for some v i t a e from Aurelius Victor: hence it was composed after 360[24]. What need, then, to postulate an original KG which the HA used c. 300 and a later continuation? On the facts so far adduced, it could legitimately be assumed that in the only form in which it ever existed the KG went down to 357[25].

One suspicious fact ought to have excited more attention. As Septimius Severus advanced on Rome in the early summer of 193, Didius Julianus was gradually deserted by his generals and soldiers. Severus was thus established as emperor in Rome with hardly any fighting, and Julianus was murdered in the imperial palace[26]. Victor and Eutropius correctly give Julianus' death *in Palatio;* but in addition they insert a fictitious defeat *apud Mulvium pontem* (Caes. 19. 4; Brev. VIII. 17)[27]. The defeat, therefore, was registered in the KG. There was only one famous historical battle at the Milvian bridge—when Constantine fought Maxentius in 312. The invented battle surely comes after the real one[28]—and the KG was written later than 312[29].

---

[20] o. c. 432 ff.

[21] C. WAGENER, Philologus XLV (1886), 544 f.; PETER, o. c. 141.

[22] o. c. 443 ff. Accepted, at least in principle, by E. HOHL, Neue Jahrb. XXXIII (1914), 704; SYME, o. c. 104.

[23] Hermes XXIV (1889), 337 ff. There is no point here in retailing the long controversy.

[24] DESSAU, o. c. 361 ff.; A. CHASTAGNOL, Rev. phil.³ XLI (1967), 85 ff., reprinted in a slightly different form at Bonner Historia-Augusta-Colloquium 1966/67 (1968), 53 ff.

[25] So W. H. FISHER, JRS XIX (1929), 126.

[26] Dio LXXIV (LXXIII). 16. 1 ff.; HA, Did. Jul. 5. 1 ff.; Herodian II. 11. 7 ff.

[27] Also Jerome's edition of Eusebius' Chronicon (GCS XLVII. 210)—but not in Eusebius, who omits Julianus altogether (GCS XX. 223; Hist. Eccl. V. 26). Though the distinction is important, some carelessly ascribe the fictitious battle at the Milvian bridge to Eusebius himself: e. g. VON WOTAWA, P—W V. 423 f.; M. BESNIER, Histoire Romaine IV. 1 (1937), 11; H. BENGTSON, Grundriß der römischen Geschichte I (1967), 363.

[28] E. HOHL, Phil. Wochenschr. LXII (1942), 241; BENGTSON, o. c. 363.

[29] Cf. SYME, o. c. 106.

Can the date be determined more precisely? ENMANN held that Victor and Eutropius shared a common source as far as 357[30]. That is a disturbing conclusion. For Victor was writing in 359/60, and his C a e s a r e s closes with the battle of Strassburg (42. 17)[31]. It hardly seems credible that he should consult a written source in order to compose a mere six lines on an event scarcely three years old. Another date for the end of the KG, somewhat earlier, is imposed by a detailed and cautious examination of the relevant texts.

*   *

*

Two general truths must not be neglected. One concerns the similarities between Victor and Eutropius, the other the dissimilarities. First, any pair of very brief accounts of any period of history will inevitably agree to some extent in the recording of facts. Kinship between them can only be demonstrated in three ways: from linguistic similarities, from concurrence in easily avoidable error, or from their joint possession of marked idiosyncrasies (e. g. peculiar selection of facts). Secondly, even where he is closely following a written source, a writer will often draw on personal recollection of events within living memory in order to produce corrections or additions of his own. Thus Victor, brooding sombrely on the arrogance of the low-born who rise high, cites two examples: *Marius patrum memoria*, and Diocletian (Caes. 39. 6). Later he observes that an emperor especially ought to possess literary and social accomplishments, which *memoria mea Constantinum, quamquam ceteris promptum virtutibus, adusque astra votis omnium subvexere* (40. 14). Earlier, Marcus' restoration of towns ravaged by earthquakes called to Victor's mind the destruction of Nicomedia in 358 (16. 12), and Philip's celebration of the thousandth anniversary of Rome moved him to contrast the lack of interest in the eleven hundredth: *adeo in dies cura minima Romanae urbis* (28. 2). Even Eutropius, who hardly ever adds material from his own head or reflects on the events which he chronicles, prefaces his account of Julian's campaign in Mesopotamia with the words *cui expeditioni ego quoque interfui* (Brev. X. 16. 1). Hence, when they are writing of the fourth century, wide divergences between Victor and Eutropius need not imply that they do not both depend on the same written source[32].

---

[30] o. c. 443 ff.

[31] ENMANN, o. c. 455, recognised these facts, but never doubted Victor's use of a written source.

[32] For the style and personality of Victor, see TH. OPITZ, Jahrb. f. class. Phil. CXXVII (1883), 217 ff.; COHN, o. c. 49 ff.; R. LAQUEUR, Probleme der Spätantike (1932), 25 ff.; C. G. STARR, Amer. Hist. Rev. LXI (1956), 574 ff.; for Eutropius, J. SORN, Der Sprachgebrauch des Eutropius I (Prog. Hall in Tirol, 1888), II (Prog. Laibach, 1889).

Diocletian and Constantine aroused great and differing emotions. Victor's attitude is unlike that of Eutropius; and consequently his conception and treatment of the two reigns is dissimilar. He judiciously emphasises the favourable aspects of Diocletian wherever possible, while Eutropius stresses his cruelty. And though both must needs be lavish in their praise of Constantine, Victor alone hints at his faults, particularly his ambition (Caes. 40. 2.; 40. 15; 40. 29; 41. 21).

Nonetheless, close resemblances continue to occur, which are inexplicable except on the hypothesis of a common source. For example, on the Persian victory of Galerius in 298:

Victor, C a e s. 39. 34/5

Eutropius, B r e v. IX. 25

a quis primo graviter vexatus (sc. Galerius) contracto confestim exercitu e veteranis ac tironibus per Armeniam in hostes contendit; quae ferme sola seu facilior vincendi via est. denique ibidem Narseum regem in dicionem subegit, simul liberos coniugesque et aulam regiam.

mox tamen per Illyricum Moesiamque contractis copiis rursus cum Narseo Hormisdae et Saporis avo in Armenia maiore pugnavit successu ingenti nec minore consilio, simul fortitudine, quippe qui etiam speculatoris munus cum altero aut tertio equite susceperit. pulso Narseo castra eius diripuit; uxores sorores liberos cepit, infinitam extrinsecus Persarum nobilitatem, gazam Persicam copiosissimam[33].

Even if the exact wording of the two passages seems dissimilar, both possess the same overall structure and are clearly related. But each has facts not in the other. Victor gives the status of Galerius' recruits, Eutropius their local origin. Festus, however, who was writing later than either, gives both, even if his vocabulary is anachronistic:

reparato de limitaneis Daciae exercitu (Brev. XXV)[34].

Eutropius, therefore, cannot derive entirely from Victor; and the nature of the similarities between them indicates that both Victor and Eutropius (and Festus too) have independently used a lost source, namely the KG.

The common source is still discernible in the two accounts of the pronunciamento of Maxentius and its consequences:

[33] Eutropius is quoted from the edition of H. Droysen, MGH Auct. Ant. II (1878, reprinted 1961); Victor and the Epitome from that of F. Pichlmayr (Teubner, 1911; revised 1961, 1966).
[34] Cf. JRS LVIII (1968), 264.

Caes. 40. 5—8

interim Romae vulgus turmaeque praetoriae Maxentium retractante diu patre Herculio imperatorem confirmant. quod ubi Armentarius (i. e. Galerius) accepit, Severum Caesarem, qui casu ad urbem erat, arma in hostem ferre propere iubet. is circum muros cum ageret, desertus a suis, quod praemiorum illecebris Maxentius traduxerat, fugiens obsessusque Ravennae obiit. hoc acrior Galerius ascito in consilium Iovio Licinium vetere cognitum amicitia Augustum creat.

Brev. X. 2. 3/4; 4. 1

Romae interea praetoriani excito tumultu Maxentium Herculi filium, qui haud procul ab urbe in villa publica morabatur, Augustum nuncupaverunt. quo nuntio Maximianus Herculius ad spem arrectus resumendi fastigii quod invitus amiserat Romam advolavit ... sed adversum motum praetorianorum atque Maxentii Severus Caesar Romam missus a Galerio cum exercitu venit obsidensque urbem militum suorum scelere desertus est. auctae Maxentii opes confirmatumque imperium. Severus fugiens Ravennae interfectus est ... per hoc tempus a Galerio Licinius imperator est factus Dacia oriundus notus ei antiqua consuetudine ...

Victor and Eutropius agree here not only in fact and phrasing, but in error. Although Severus fled to Ravenna after his troops deserted him and was besieged there, it seems that Maximianus enticed him out of the city, took him back towards Rome and put him to death near the capital[35]. That, at least, is the version of the O r i g o C o n s t a n t i n i I m p e r a t o r i s (10), of the E p i t o m e (40. 3) and Zosimus (II. 10), and of the Chronographer of 354 and the C o n s u l a r i a C o n s t a n t i n o p o l i t a n a[36]. Moreover, Eutropius cannot depend solely on Victor, since he supplies a fact not recorded by him: the Dacian origin of Licinius[37].

Striking similarity is still shown in the two accounts of the death of Constantine:

Caes. 41. 16

ita anno imperii tricesimo secundoque, cum totum orbem tredecim tenuisset, sexaginta natus atque amplius duo, in Persas tendens a

Brev. X. 8

bellum adversus Parthos moliens, qui iam Mesopotamiam fatigabant, uno et tricesimo anno imperii, aetatis sexto et sexagesimo,

---

[35] D. J. A. WESTERHUIS, Origo Constantini Imperatoris sive Anonymi Valesiani pars prior (Diss. Groningen, 1906), 20.

[36] MGH Auct. Ant. IX. 148; 231.

[37] Also at Origo Const. Imp. 13; Socrates, Hist. Eccl. I. 2; Zonaras XII. 34 (p. 624 Bonn).

quis bellum erumpere occeperat, | Nicomediae in villa publica obiit.
rure proximo Nicomediae, An- denuntiata mors eius est etiam
chyronam vocant, excessit, cum per crinitam stellam, quae inusi-
id taetrum sidus regnis, quod cri- tatae magnitudinis aliquamdiu ful-
nitum vocant, portendisset. sit, Graeci cometen vocant.

Constantine's exact age was always a matter for conjecture: the guesses range from sixty two to sixty six[38]. There is no obstacle, then, to inferring a common source from the verbal similarities. More important, Victor and Eutropius are almost alone in recording the comet which presaged the emperor's death. It is not in Eusebius' Vita Constantini. Nor can it be found in Jerome's edition of Eusebius' Chronicon, or in Zosimus or Orosius, or in the Epitome or Origo Constantini Imperatoris. And in the whole tradition of Greek ecclesiastical history it has left but one trace: a sentence in the Passio Artemii identified as coming from Philostorgius—and thus presumably from a Greek translation of Eutropius[39].

Victor and Eutropius inevitably produce accounts of the reign of Constantine's sons (Constans, Constantius and Constantine) which are factually similar. Writing as they were in 359/60 and 369/70, it was hard to do otherwise: both were compressing the same series of recent events into a very brief compass. But after 337 they exhibit no example of either close verbal similarity or common error or shared idiosyncrasy. The KG, therefore, finished with the death of Constantine, and was composed not long afterwards, presumably no later than 340[40].

•   •
•

The lost KG was certainly the main—and probably the only—direct source of Victor's Caesares and the imperial history in Eutropius' Breviarium. But a complete Quellenforschung of either is almost certainly not a worthwhile undertaking. This enquiry will concentrate instead on a humbler question. In which other Latin authors is use of the common source of Victor and Eutropius evident?

---

[38] WESTERHUIS, o. c. 8.
[39] Passio Artemii 7 = Philostorgius, Hist. Eccl. II. 16ᵃ (GCS XXI. 26).
[40] Cf. SEECK, o. c. 638: ‚die Übereinstimmungen zwischen Victor, Eutropius, der Epitome und Zosimos, aus welchen wir die „Kaiserchronik" reconstru- ieren, reichen, wie jeder sich leicht überzeugen kann, bis zum tode Constan- tins'. It was a mistake to bring in Zosimus and the Epitome. The former may never have used the KG (below, pp. 26 ff.), while the latter shows no sign of using it after 41. 2—3 (~ Victor, Caes. 40. 2—4; cf. below, pp. 25 ff.). None- theless, SEECK had perceived a fundamental truth about the KG.

First, Festus and Jerome[41]. It is impossible to trace all the genuine information in either Festus' B r e v i a r i u m or Jerome's edition of Eusebius' C h r o n i c o n back to extant sources. Consequently, for the periods of Roman history remote from themselves, they drew on works which are now lost. For imperial history, the chief among these (or perhaps the only source) may without difficulty be identified as the KG[42]. One passage from each author will illustrate[43].

Festus records the site of Aurelian's defeat of Zenobia: it was *apud Immas* (Brev. XXIV). That is a valuable detail. *Immae* was about thirty miles from Antioch, along the road to Beroea[44]. The place-name in Festus supplements the longer account of Zosimus, whose topography is vague (I. 50 ff.), and permits an appreciation of the strategy of Aurelian[45]. Festus' brief account of the campaign has linguistic affinities with Eutropius' (Brev. IX. 13. 2). But he is the first to name *Immae* as the site of the main battle[46]. He has, therefore, consulted the source of Eutropius, the KG[47].

For Jerome an entry under the year 248 deserves notice:

Filippus urbem nominis sui in Thracia construxit[48].

Philip did found a city of Philippopolis—but in Arabia, as Victor correctly states (Caes. 28. 1)[49]. No other text earlier than Jerome reports the foundation. Hence he cannot have taken it from Eutropius or Festus; and his error (the Thracian city was built by Philip of Macedon) implies that he did not here consult Victor, whom he had read (Epp. X. 3. 2). Both surely came across Philip's foundation of Philippopolis in the KG—with the locality not specified[50].

---

[41] See, respectively, J. W. EADIE, The Breviarium of Festus (1967), esp. 88 ff.; R. HELM, Rh. Mus., N. F. LXXVI (1927), 138 ff.; 254 ff.; and, for Jerome's additions to Eusebius in the matter of literary history, R. HELM, Philologus, Supp. XXI. 2 (1929).

[42] EADIE, o. c. 98; HELM, o. c. 304 f.

[43] For further examples see above, p. 18; below, pp. 29 f.; 36.

[44] P—W IV A. 1657 f.

[45] G. DOWNEY, Trans. Amer. Phil. Ass. LXXXI (1950), 57 ff.

[46] *Immae* reappears at Jerome, GCS XLVII. 222; Jordanes, Rom. 291; Syncellus p. 721 Bonn. EADIE, o. c. 93, suggests that Jerome and Jordanes may both have got the name from Festus, and that the former has combined Festus with Eutropius. It is simpler to believe that Jerome consulted a single source—the KG.

[47] There is a corollary: Festus' direct use of Eutropius becomes almost unprovable: see JRS LVIII (1968), 264; against, E. WOELFFLIN, Archiv f. lat. Lex. XIII (1904), 69 ff.; 173; EADIE, o. c. 98.

[48] GCS XLVII. 217 f.

[49] Cf. P—W XIX. 2263.

[50] The standard view seems to be that Jerome never consulted the KG: A. SCHOENE, Die Weltchronik des Eusebius (1900), 217; MOMMSEN, o. c. (1909), 606 ff.; SCHANZ-HOSIUS, o. c. 446; A. MOMIGLIANO, The Conflict between Paganism and Christianity in the Fourth Century (1963), 86. But note F. RUEHL, Literarisches Centralblatt 1892, 5 f.: Jerome never used Eutropius, only the common source of Eutropius and Festus.

The Epitome de Caesaribus offers a special problem. For the most part, its first eleven chapters run parallel to Victor, the later ones (as far as 38) with Eutropius[51]. Yet the Epitome has much authentic material which can come from neither[52]: e. g., the origin of Trajan *ex urbe Tudertina* (13. 1)[53], three Gordiani (26/7) where Victor and Eutropius have only two (Caes. 26/7; Brev. IX. 2), the plausible Etruscan cognomen *Perpenna* for Decius' son Hostilianus (30. 2)[54]. Perhaps derivation of mere facts from the KG cannot be proved conclusively. But for its consultation by the author of the Epitome on at least one occasion, the following pair of passages seems decisive:

Victor, Caes. 34. 3—5

proditum ex libris Sibyllinis est primum ordinis amplissimi victoriae vovendum. cumque is, qui esse videbatur, semet obtulisset, sibi potius id muneris competere ostendit, qui revera senatus atque omnium princeps erat. ita nullo exercitus detrimento fusi barbari summotique, postquam imperator vita reipublicae dono dedit.

Epitome 34. 3

Claudius vero cum ex fatalibus libris, quos inspici praeceperat, cognovisset sententiae in senatu dicendae primi morte remedium desiderari, Pomponio Basso, qui tunc erat, se offerente ipse vitam suam haud passus responsa frustrari dono reipublicae dedit, praefatus neminem tanti ordinis primas habere, quam imperatorem.

The phrasing is close, and only the later work names the *princeps senatus*[55]: Pomponius Bassus, *cos. ord.* 259, cos. II 271, and *praefectus urbi*[56]. The Epitome, it seems, depends on the source of Victor. But a complication arises. Its author was writing after 395 (48. 19/20). Hence he could, if he chose, read the recently published history of Ammianus Marcellinus[57]. One or two fourth century items in the Epitome may well derive from the extant books of Ammianus[58]. But that part

---

[51] PETER, o. c. 363; SCHANZ-HOSIUS, o. c. 76 f. But C. WACHSMUTH, Einleitung in das Studium der alten Geschichte (1895), 674, held that the sources of Epitome 12—38 could not be determined. More important, the Epitome has no clear affinity with either Victor or Eutropius after 41. 2—3 (discussed below, pp. 25 f.).

[52] See, in general, HOHL, Klio XI (1911), 192 ff.

[53] R. SYME, Tacitus (1958), 786.

[54] Cf. PIR¹V 8; P—W XV. 1248 f.; 1285 f.

[55] That is surely the man meant: TH. MOMMSEN, Römisches Staatsrecht III (1888), 976.

[56] CIL VI. 31747 = IGRR I. 137; A. DEGRASSI, Fasti Consolari (1952), 70; 72; G. BARBIERI, L'Albo senatorio (1952), no. 1698. Like that of L. Caesonius Ovinius etc. (AE 1964. 223), the prefecture of Bassus is absent from the Chronographer of 354 (cf. below, n. 61).

[57] For the date of Ammianus' work, see now SYME, o. c. (1968), 5 ff.

[58] Epitome 42. 14 ~ Ammianus XVI. 12. 63; 45. 2 ~ XXX. 7. 2. But HOHL, o. c. 227 ff. strongly denied derivation from Ammianus.

of his history which dealt with events from 96 to 353 is lost. In the circumstances, who can know how much the E p i t o m e owes to Ammianus for this period? It is not impossible that a fact like the name of Pomponius Bassus might come to the E p i t o m e only indirectly from the KG, via Ammianus. A fortiori, the E p i t o m e's use of Victor and Eutropius cannot be put beyond doubt: the intrusion of two unknowns (the lost books of Ammianus as well as the lost KG) precludes definitive proof. The most prudent course is to acknowledge that the E p i t o m e's close parallels with Victor and Eutropius may always be due to independent derivation from the KG.

For still later Latin authors, use of the KG is unlikely. Thus Orosius, writing c. 417, based his H i s t o r i a   a d v e r s u s   P a g a n o s on Justin's epitome of Pompeius Trogus, on Florus and Eutropius. He added much from many other sources, notably from Livy (or rather an epitome of Livy) for Republican, from Suetonius for early imperial, and from Jerome for Christian history[59]. With these works at his disposal, Orosius had little incentive to seek out the now antiquated KG—and he seems to have nothing which he need have derived from it directly.

Another text which might have used the KG was written before it. For use in 354, someone compiled a collection of heterogeneous documents which form a sort of illustrated almanac—hence the standard designation of 'The Chronographer of 354'[60]. Some of the documents are based on earlier calendars, and some possibly on archives: there is a calendar of 'd e p o s i t i o n e s   m a r t y r u m', and a list of 'p r a e - f e c t i   u r b i' from 254[61]. One section, the 'C h r o n i c a   U r b i s   R o m a e', has an obvious affinity with the KG. After an annotated list of kings of Latium, Alba Longa and Rome from Picus down to Tarquinius Superbus and a bare list of dictators, it gives a list of emperors. Each entry has the exact length of the reign, the size of the total largesse distributed during it, the place of the emperor's decease and notable happenings of a sensational sort. Thus the entry for Caligula reads:

> imp. ann. III m. VIII d. XII. cong. dedit * LXXIIS et de basilica Iulia sparsit aureos et argenteos, in qua rapina perierunt homines XXXII, ⟨mulieres⟩ CCXLVII et spado. occisus Palatio[62].

---

[59] B. Lacroix, Orose et ses idées (1965), 58 ff. There is a bibliography of studies of Orosius' sources by G. Fink, Revista de archivos, bibliotecas y museos LVIII (1952), 298 ff.

[60] See Th. Mommsen, Abh. d. sächs. Ges. d. Wiss. II (1850), 547 ff.; Schanz-Hosius, o. c. 62 ff.; H. Stern, Le Calendrier de 354: étude sur son texte et ses illustrations (1953), for a full description.

[61] MGH Auct. Ant. IX. 65 ff. The list of praefecti is certainly not complete before 288 (above, n. 56): presumably, therefore, for the years 254 to 287, it records only the praefecti in office on 1 January.

[62] MGH Auct. Ant. IX. 143 ff.

Surely the writer (or a predecessor) has used some sort of collection of *mirabilia*[63]. Enough evidence does not survive to render possible the identification of the Chronographer's sources. It is certain, however, that he did not use the KG. Like some other documents in the collection (e. g. the 'd e p o s i t i o e p i s c o p o r u m' and the 'l i b e r g e n e r a t i o n i s') the 'C h r o n i c a U r b i s R o m a e' was put together before the death of Constantine[64]. Moreover, it agrees with what was in the KG solely on matters of fact; and on at least two points preserves a purer historical tradition. It has Caracalla's alleged incest with Julia Domna: *hic suam matrem habuit*[65]. So had the KG— but falsifying the relationship and calling Julia his step-mother (Victor, Caes. 21.3; Eutropius, Brev. VIII. 20. 1; Epitome 21. 5). The C h r o - n i c a also knows that Severus met his end at the hands of Maximianus close to Rome: the KG stated that after fleeing to Ravenna he was killed there (Victor, Caes. 40. 7; Eutropius, Brev. X. 2. 4)[66].

The O r i g o C o n s t a n t i n i I m p e r a t o r i s (otherwise known as the first part of the A n o n y m u s V a l e s i a n u s) raises a vexed and complicated problem which cannot be discussed here: the relationship between the many accounts of the career and reign of Constantine[67]. Difficulties arise both from the contentious nature of the subject and from the status of the primary evidence. For the most important contemporary witnesses—five panegyrists, Lactantius and Eusebius' V i t a C o n s t a n t i n i—all stand outside and apart from the main historical tradition. Nevertheless, the present enquiry can proceed. Despite assertions to the contrary[68], the O r i g o never drew on the KG. Three passages are commonly adduced to prove dependence, and all three must be carefully examined.

First, the marriage of Constantius:

> *relicta enim Helena priore uxore, filiam Maximiani Theodoram*
> *duxit uxorem, ex qua postea sex liberos Constantini fratres habuit.*
> *sed de priore uxore Helena filium iam Constantinum habuit qui*
> *postea princeps potentissimus fuit* (Origo Const. Imp. 1);

---

[63] For the genre, P—W XVIII. 2. 1137 ff., s. v. Paradoxographoi; A. GIANNINI, Paradoxographorum Graecorum Reliquiae (n. d., publ. 1966).

[64] STERN, o. c. 42 ff. That, of course, does not prove two recensions of the whole work.

[65] MGH Auct. Ant. IX. 147.

[66] Above, p. 19.

[67] See, e. g., A. MADDALENA, Atti del Reale Istit. Veneto XCV. 2 (1935—36), 247 ff. (with conjectural stemma of the relationships between the various sources); T. KOTULA, Klio XL (1962), 159 ff.

[68] WAGENER, o. c. 545 ff.; O. SEECK, P—W I. 2334; J. MOREAU, Excerpta Valesiana (Teubner, 1961), vi. For WAGENER, however, the common source of the Origo and of Victor and Eutropius after 284 was not exactly a continuation of the KG, but 'eine familiengeschichte Constantins' (o. c. 546; 551).

Iulium Constantium, Galerium Maximianum, cui cognomen Armentario erat, creatos Caesares in affinitatem vocant. prior Herculii privignam, alter Diocletiano editam sortiuntur diremptis prioribus coniugiis (Victor, Caes. 39. 24/5);

atque ut eos etiam adfinitate coniungeret, Constantius privignam Herculii Theodoram accepit, ex qua postea sex liberos Constantini fratres habuit, Galerius filiam Diocletiani Valeriam, ambo uxores quas habuerant repudiare conpulsi (Eutropius, Brev. IX. 22. 1);

Constantinum et Galerium Maximianum, cognomento Armentarium, Caesares creavit, tradens Constantio Theodoram, Herculii Maximiani privignam abiecta uxore priore (Epitome 39. 2).

The O r i g o corresponds to Victor, Eutropius and the E p i t o m e in almost nothing but facts. That it shares with Eutropius (and Jerome)[69] the words *ex qua postea sex liberos Constantini fratres habuit* is hardly sufficient to prove use of a common source—especially since interpolation is a strong possibility[70]. For the O r i g o has an error which the other three all avoid. They correctly state that Theodora was the step-daughter of Maximianus, the O r i g o erroneously makes her the daughter[71].

Second, the flight of Constantine to his father:

tunc eum Galerius patri remisit. qui ut Severum per Italiam transiens vitaret, summa festinatione veredis post se truncatis Alpes transgressus ad patrem Constantium venit apud Bononiam quam Galli prius Gesoriacum vocabant. post victoriam autem Pictorum Constantius pater Eboraci mortuus est et Constantinus omnium militum consensu Caesar creatus (Origo Const. Imp. 4);

Constantinus, cuius iam tum a puero ingens potensque animus ardore imperitandi agitabatur, fugae commento, cum ad frustrandos insequentes publica iumenta, quaqua iter egerat, interficeret, in Britanniam pervenit; nam is a Galerio religionis specie ad vicem obsidis tenebatur. et forte iisdem diebus ibidem Constantium patrem vel parentem[71a] vitae ultima urgebant. quo mortuo cunctis qui aderant annitentibus imperium capit (Victor, Caes. 40. 2—4);

hic dum iuvenculus a Galerio in urbe Roma religionis specie obses teneretur, fugam arripiens atque ad frustrandos insequentes publica iumenta, quaqua iter egerat, interfecit et ad patrem in

---

[69] GCS XLVII. 226.

[70] E. KLEBS, Philologus XLVII (1889), 66.

[71] She was the daughter of Maximianus' wife Eutropia, probably by Hannibalianus: O. SEECK, P—W VI. 1519; J. VOGT, The Conflict between Paganism and Christianity in the Fourth Century (ed. A. MOMIGLIANO, 1963), 55 (a family tree).

[71a] So PICHLMAYR. A. CAMERON, CR, n. s. XV (1965), 21, argues that the words *vel parentem* were interpolated by a scribe who had read the Epitome.

Britanniam pervenit; et forte iisdem diebus ibidem Constantium
parentem fata ultima perurgebant. quo mortuo cunctis qui aderant
annitentibus, sed praecipue Croco, Alamannorum rege, auxilii
gratia Constantium comitato imperium capit (Epitome 41. 2/3);

ἔγνω τοὺς τόπους λιπεῖν, ἐν οἷς ἔτυχεν διατρίβων, ἐξορμῆσαι δὲ πρὸς τὸν
πατέρα Κωνστάντιον ἐν τοῖς ὑπὲρ τὰς ῎Αλπεις ἔθνεσιν ὄντα καὶ τῇ Βρετ-
τανίᾳ συνεχέστερον ἐνδημοῦντα. δεδιὼς δὲ μή ποτε φεύγων καταληφθείη
(περιφανὴς γὰρ ἦν ἤδη πολλοῖς ὁ κατέχων αὐτὸν ἔρως τῆς βασιλείας)
τοὺς ἐν τοῖς σταθμοῖς ἵππους, οὓς τὸ δημόσιον ἔτρεφεν, ἅμα τῷ φθάσαι
τὸν σταθμὸν κολούων καὶ ἀχρείους ἐῶν τοῖς ἑξῆς ἑστῶσιν ἐχρῆτο. καὶ
ἑξῆς τοῦτο ποιῶν τοῖς μὲν διώκουσιν ἀπέκλεισε τὴν ἐπὶ τὸ πρόσω πορείαν,
αὐτὸς δὲ προσήγγιζεν τοῖς ἔθνεσιν ἐν οἷς ἦν ὁ πατήρ. συμβὰν δὲ τὸν
αὐτοκράτορα Κωνστάντιον ἐν αὐτῷ τελευτῆσαι τῷ χρόνῳ, ... οἱ περὶ τὴν
αὐλὴν στρατιῶται ... τὴν τοῦ Καίσαρος ἀξίαν αὐτῷ (sc. Constantine)
περιέθεσαν (Zosimus II. 8. 2—9. 1).

Some hold that all four passages derive from the KG[72]. That is
unlikely. Admittedly, Victor and the E p i t o m e do here derive
independently from the same source: their phrasing is very similar,
but only the later work has Crocus (better perhaps, Erocus)[73], king
of the Alamanni. But the O r i g o diverges widely, both in its
language and on fact. The C a e s a r e s and the E p i t o m e both
state that Constantine fled from Galerius and found his father in
Britain on his deathbed. The O r i g o reports that Constantine was
sent by Galerius and that he met his father in Gaul at Bononia; it
also implies that Constantius, so far from being on the point of death,
then conducted a campaign against the Picts. The O r i g o, therefore, has a completely different story from that retailed by the KG—
and probably the true one[74]. By parity of reasoning, the O r i g o is
independent of Zosimus, who sides with Victor and the E p i t o m e.

The third passage has no direct parallel in either Victor or
Eutropius:

igitur Galerius sic ebriosus fuit, ut, cum iuberet temulentus ea
quae facienda non essent, a praefecto admonitus constituerit, ne
iussa eius aliquis post prandium faceret (Origo Const. Imp. 11);
quo ebrius quaedam corrupta mente aspera iubebat; quod cum
pigeret factum, differri quae praecepisset in tempus sobrium
ac matutinum statuit (Epitome 40. 19).

The story is basically the same, but the phrasing dissimilar and the
subject different. The story is a 'Wanderanekdote': Victor tells it of

---

[72] O. SEECK, P—W I. 2334; MOREAU, o. c. vi.
[73] E. STEIN, P—W IV. 1725; O. SEECK, P—W VI. 483.
[74] WESTERHUIS, o. c. 12. The version of the Origo is confirmed by a speech
of 310 (Pan. Lat. VI [VII]. 7). The other was, however, soon current and appears
in Lactantius, Mort. Pers. 24 and Eusebius, Vita Const. I. 21.

Trajan (Caes. 13. 10), the O r i g o of Galerius, Eusebius (Hist. Eccl. VIII. 14. 11) and the E p i t o m e of Maximinus Daia[75]. If the Epitome represents the KG here, therefore, the O r i g o appears to be independent of it for a third time[76].

Perhaps the O r i g o   C o n s t a n t i n i   I m p e r a t o r i s was written before the KG. Its language and contents are judged to put its composition long before 400[77]. Excepting the interpolations from Orosius and a possible interpolation from Eutropius or Jerome[78], may it not be the work of a contemporary? If it was composed in 337 or very soon afterwards, no written sources need be postulated—and its independence of the KG is easily explicable[79].

•   •
•

This study of the KG would gain little from discussing either Latin authors later than Orosius or any Greek author. As the fifth century progresses, the unknowns in the chain of literary derivation from the KG multiply as swiftly as the likelihood of its use diminishes. To put the matter briefly: for no writer demonstrably later than the E p i t o m e   d e   C a e s a r i b u s can direct use of the KG be proved. As for Greek writers, some assume that the emperor Julian had read the KG[80]. Others descend a century and assert that Zosimus used it, perhaps only in a Greek version[81]. But again the unknowable precludes any degree of certainty. For the major Greek writers of contemporary history in the later third and early fourth centuries are all either lost or extant only in fragments or brief summary[82]. Who can tell what Julian or Zosimus owed to the history of Dexippus, who went as far as Claudius? What to the first Eusebius, who finished

---

[75] Hohl, Klio XI (1911), 219.

[76] Westerhuis, o. c. 20 f., argues that the Origo has misattributed the anecdote either out of ignorance of eastern affairs or through misunderstanding 'Galerius Maximinus' (i. e. Maximinus Daia) in a written source.

[77] Klebs, o. c. 53 ff.; Moreau, o. c. v—vi.

[78] It was Klebs, o. c. 53 ff., who finally proved these passages to be insertions and not part of the original text.

[79] Some, however, put its composition much later: F. Goerres, Jahrb. f. class. Phil. CXI (1875), 201 ff., held the Origo to be Theodosian, E. Patzig, Byz. Zeitschr. VII (1898), 572 ff., to depend on the lost books of Ammianus. The verdict of Momigliano is justly cautious: 'all is in doubt about the first part of the Anonymus Valesianus' (o. c. [1963], 87).

[80] Chastagnol, o. c. 89; A. Alfoeldi, Bonner Historia-Augusta-Colloquium 1966/67 (1968), 1 ff. But the resemblances between Julian's Caesares and Victor, Eutropius and the Epitome which Alfoeldi there adduces are mainly factual—e. g. Trajan's propensity to excessive drinking.

[81] Seeck, o. c. (1890), 638 (quoted above, n. 40); Graebner, o. c. 87 ff.—and others.

[82] See FGrH 100; 101; FHG IV. 2 ff.

with the reign of Carus? What to the pagan Praxagoras who wrote two books on Constantine? And what of the continuator(s) of Cassius Dio? Or of minor figures? In contrast with Rome and the west, the Greek world, and especially Athens, continued to produce major works of literature[83]. Hence it is impossible to discuss the historical sources of Julian or Zosimus without first writing a detailed history of Greek literature in the third and fourth centuries. Where so many imponderables operate, even a balance of probability is unattainable.

. * *

The most important text has so far been ignored. Did the HA ever draw on the KG? J. HASEBROEK denied it in 1916, DESSAU and later W. HARTKE concurred, and the arguments against have recently been reformulated by T. DAMSHOLT[84]. DAMSHOLT argues that in certain passages the HA has demonstrably failed to consult the KG. For example, though absent from Victor and Eutropius, the usurpers Taurinus and Septimius[85] appear in the E p i t o m e , under the reigns of Severus Alexander and Aurelian respectively (24. 2; 35. 3). The E p i t o m e has surely taken the names from the KG. Now the author of the HA searched for as many usurpers as possible, especially for his T y r a n n i   T r i g i n t a , supplementing the genuine with invented characters[86]. But he includes no Taurinus or Septimius. Consequently, he has failed to consult the KG[87]. Again, the KG recorded both the sons of Gallienus, viz. Cornelius Valerianus and Saloninus[88]. Both were known to the E p i t o m e (32. 2; 33. 1) and to Polemius Silvius[89]. Eutropius does not register any children of Gallienus (Brev. IX. 7—10); Victor (Caes. 33. 3), Zosimus (I. 38. 2) and Zonaras (XII. 24) register one son. But while Victor and Zosimùs call him Saloninus, Zonaras has Gallienus. The HA too states that Gallienus had a single son, but it knows of two names:

> de huius nomine magna est ambiguitas. nam multi eum Gallienum, multi Saloninum historiae prodiderunt (Gall. 19. 2).

---

[83] K. CHRIST, Gesch. d. gr. Litt. II[6] (1924), 663 ff.
[84] J. HASEBROEK, Die Fälschung der Vita Nigri und der Vita Albini in den Scriptores Historiae Augustae (Diss. Heidelberg, 1916), 6; H. DESSAU, Wochenschrift f. klass. Phil. 1918, 392; W. HARTKE, De saeculi quarti exeuntis historiarum scriptoribus quaestione (Diss. Berlin, 1932), 56 ff.; Klio, Beiheft XLV (1940), 12 f.; T. DAMSHOLT, Class. et Med. XXV (1964), 146 ff.
[85] Or Septiminus: see BARBIERI, Albo 409.
[86] H. PETER, Abh. sächs. Ges. d. Wiss. LVII (1909), 179 ff.; BARBIERI, Albo 401 ff.
[87] DAMSHOLT, o. c. 147; cf. HARTKE, o. c. (1940), 13.
[88] PIR[1] L 123/4; BARBIERI, Albo nos. 1628/9.
[89] MGH Auct. Ant. IX. 521.

The HA, therefore, is ignorant of the other son, Valerianus, whose name stood in the KG[90].

Such an argument is easily refuted. If the HA failed to employ the KG in certain passages or for certain facts, it does not follow that it never consulted it on any occasion. A single case will suffice to show the contrary:

> contra Persas profectus nullo sibi occurrente Mesopotamiam Carus cepit et Ctesiphontem usque pervenit occupatisque Persis domestica seditione imperatoris Persici nomen emeruit (Carus 8. 1).

Carus' march into Mesopotamia in 283 appears also in Victor (Caes. 38. 2/3), Eutropius (Brev. IX. 18. 1), Festus (Brev. XXIV) and Jerome[91]. All four mention Ctesiphon, the last three also recording the capture of Coche, i. e. Seleucia[92]. Festus and the HA are alone, however, in stating the lack of serious opposition—the normal strategy of Parthian or Persian in the face of Roman invasion, practised alike against Corbulo, Trajan and L. Verus, against Septimius Severus and Julian[93]. But the HA has two genuine facts not recorded by any of the other four: that Carus attacked when the Persians were distracted by internal revolt, and his c o g n o m e n Persicus. Persian evidence confirms the revolt: the viceroy of Khorassan had forsworn his allegiance to King Varahran II (276—93) and was striving to set himself up as an autonomous ruler[94]. The c o g n o m e n Persicus is attested by two inscriptions and a small posthumous issue of coins[95]. The HA hardly discovered these facts by diligent research among the contemporary evidence. The five accounts (Victor, Eutropius, Festus, Jerome, HA) are closely parallel and obviously interrelated. But, if the HA has two genuine facts not in any of the other four, it cannot be wholly derived

[90] DAMSHOLT, o. c. 148.

[91] GCS XLVII. 224 f. See, in general, P. MELONI, Il regno di Caro, Numeriano e Carino (Annali Cagliari XV. 2, 1948), 92 ff.

[92] TLL, Onomasticon II. 519.

[93] The clearest and fullest accounts are Tacitus, Ann. XIII. 34 ff.; XIV. 23 ff.; XV. 1 ff.; Dio LXII. 19 ff. (Corbulo); Ammianus XXIII. 2. 6 ff. (Julian). But note also Dio LXVIII. 26. 4² (Trajan). If the HA and Festus are both reporting a genuine fact, it is time wasted to essay a proof that the HA modelled nullo sibi occurrente on Festus' quasi nullo obsistente (as HARTKE, o. c. (1932), 56 f.; o. c. (1940), 14 f.; J. STRAUB, Studien zur Historia Augusta [1952], 125; against, E. HOHL, Klio XXVII [1934], 159 f.).

[94] A. CHRISTENSEN, L'Iran sous les Sassanides² (1944), 227 f. The HA has hardly got the more accurate occupatis Persis domestica seditione from Eutropius' vaguer Persarum tumultu (as G. ALFOELDY, Bonner Historia-Augusta-Colloquium 1964/65 [1966], 24, maintains). Perhaps an oration delivered in 291 is also relevant: ipsos Persas ipsumque regem adscitis Sacis et Rufiis et Gelis petit frater Ormies (Pan. Lat. XI [III]. 17. 2).

[95] CIL VIII. 12 522 = ILS 600 (Carthage); IGRR I. 1144 (Antinoopolis); RIC V (2). 140. These coins, minted in Rome, have DIVO CARO PERS (ICO); others, minted at Siscia and Lugdunum, have DIVO CARO PARTHICO (ibid. 138; 147 f.).

from any combination of them. Neither did it serve as the source for all four[96]: its date precludes. Therefore, the HA has consulted the source which some or all of them used independently—it has consulted the KG.

· ·
·

The HA begins as a compilation. Down to the death of Caracalla in 217 the author possessed an excellent source: an unknown continuator of Suetonius, modest in pretensions, sober in style and with a penchant for facts[97]. Hence the inestimable value of the HA for any student of the second and early third centuries. The biographer provided most of the material for the lives of Hadrian, Pius, Marcus Aurelius, L. Verus, Commodus, Pertinax, Didius Julianus, Septimius Severus and Caracalla[98]. The HA made additions (some probably at a later stage) from Marius Maximus, from Aurelius Victor, and from other sources[99]. And it was only after composing this series of vitae, it seems, that the author began the lives of princes and pretenders: Aelius Caesar, Avidius Cassius, Pescennius Niger, Clodius Albinus and Geta[100]. These five biographies combine facts taken from the main series with long stretches of pure fiction. They foreshadow the author's mature manner—or perhaps merely display it. For there is a sign that they were composed after the Vita Alexandri[101]. However that may be, MOMMSEN summed up their historical value long ago[102].

The good source ended with the death of Caracalla[103]. For the lives of Macrinus and his son, therefore, the HA employs Herodian and fills up the space with almost unadulterated fiction[104]. The product is historically worthless[105]. The Elagabalus presents a strange contrast. Inevitably, much is said about Elagabalus' vices and perversions. But is that necessarily all free composition by the author?

---

[96] Which EADIE, o. c. 93 f., still admits as a possibility.
[97] JRS LVII (1967), 65 ff.; R. SYME, Bonner Historia-Augusta-Colloquium 1966/67 (1968), 131 ff.; Hermes XCVI (1968), 494 ff.
[98] JRS LVII (1967), 74; R. SYME, Bonner Historia-Augusta-Colloquium 1966/67 (1968), 131 ff.
[99] Maximus: G. BARBIERI, Riv. fil. XXXII (1954), 36 ff.; 262 ff.; R. SYME, Hermes XCVI (1968), 494 ff. Victor: DESSAU, o. c. 361 ff.; E. HOHL, Historia IV (1955), 220 ff. Among the others, note Ausonius: JRS LVII (1967), 70.
[100] R. SYME, Ammianus and the Historia Augusta (1968), 177; below, pp. 285 ff.
[101] Below, p. 35 f.
[102] o. c. (1909), 324: ,Nicht etwa eine getrübte Quelle, sondern eine Kloake'.
[103] JRS LVII (1967), 74.
[104] Macr. 8. 3 ff. < Herodian IV. 15. 6 ff. See K. HOENN, Quellenuntersuchungen zu den Viten des Heliogabalus und des Severus Alexander im Corpus der Scriptores Historiae Augustae (1911), 10 ff.
[105] HOENN, o. c. 11; 17, was justly severe on both the Macrinus and the Diadumenianus. But he admitted that there might be something from the KG.

No sooner was the young Syrian dead than the sophist Aelian came cut with a κατηγορία τοῦ Γύννιδος[106]. And within a few years Cassius Dio was penning his account of the reign—a violent and hysterical diatribe[107]. Whether Dio's report is fact or fiction, the HA could never have surpassed it. In fact, the comparison reveals the HA to be feeble and dull. Dio denounced the wretched youth with self-righteous indignation and a wealth of salacious detail[108]. The HA is less loathsome and a little too scholarly—as if the author's main purpose was to outdo the recherché vocabulary of Apicius' cookery-book[109]. Yet it is not obvious that even the later chapters of the E l a g a-b a l u s must be wholly the author's invention. On the contrary, much may come from a contemporary source. For the earlier sections of the v i t a contain valuable items. They give a detailed and circumstantial narrative of the attempts on Alexander's life and Elagabalus' own murder, with the telling point of the latter's retreat ad hortos Spei veteris (13—17, esp. 13. 5)[110]. There are also names—Cordius (perhaps better, Gordius: 6. 3;12. 1;15. 2), Hierocles (6. 5;15. 2), Zoticus (10. 2 ff.)[111]—and the fullest extant account of the emperor's religious innovations (3. 4;6. 6 ff.)[112]. The author undoubtedly added much of his own: e. g., the mention of Jews, Christians and Samaritans (3. 5)[113]. But whence comes the large substratum of genuine fact? Perhaps not all derives from the same source. But for the bulk of it there is a clear candidate. SYME has already conjectured that Marius Maximus is the source for several chapters (viz. 13—17)[114]. May he not be the main source for the whole v i t a[115]? That he is quoted once as if by an afterthought (11. 6) is no obstacle. If this hypothesis be admitted, the contrast between the E l a g a b a l u s and the M a c r i-n u s suggests a further conjecture: perhaps this was the first occa-

---

[106] Philostratus, Vit. soph. II. 31.

[107] Dio LXXX (LXXIX). 1. 1 ff.; cf. MILLAR, o. c. 168 ff.

[108] Note Dio LXXX (LXXIX). 16. 7 (p. 470 BOISSEVAIN): Elagabalus wished to have a doctor incise female genitalia. This story is not in the HA.

[109] Cf. SYME, o. c. 113; 187 f.

[110] Cited as a mark of genuineness by H. LAMBERTZ, P—W VIII A. 402 f. The sceptical, however, will not fail to notice that, unlike the shrine, the gardens of Spes Vetus are nowhere else attested: S. B. PLATNER-T. ASHBY, A Topographical Dictionary of Ancient Rome (1929), 272.

[111] Dio LXXX (LXXIX). 14—16; 19. 3; 21; cf. H. SOLIN, Eranos LXI (1963), 65 ff. The HA has, however, hardly taken them from Dio, of whom it never demonstrably shows knowledge: E. HOHL, Bursians Jahresber. CC (1924), 204 f.

[112] Cf. G. WISSOWA, Religion und Kultus der Römer² (1912), 89; 365 f.; K. GROSS, RAC IV. 992 ff.; A. DEGRASSI, Scritti vari di antichità (1962), 457 ff.

[113] H. DESSAU, Janus I (1921), 124 ff. Cf. now JRS LVIII (1968), 41 f.

[114] Hermes XCVI (1968), 500.

[115] This view must be carefully distinguished from two similar but erroneous views: namely, that Maximus is the main source of all the primary vitae down to the Elagabalus, and that Maximus is the main source of both Elagabalus and Alexander (LÉCRIVAIN, o. c. 201 ff.).

sion on which the HA employed Maximus, and the references to him in the earlier v i t a e were added after the E l a g a b a l u s was finished. One curious fact may indicate that the HA suddenly turned to Maximus: he is invoked no less than five times in the A l e x a n - d e r—always for what he says about earlier emperors (5. 4; 21. 4; 30. 6; 48. 6; 65. 4).

Maximus wrote the lives of the emperors from Nerva to Elaga-balus[116]. Safety and precedent (Tacitus and Suetonius) recommended the omission of the reigning sovereign, Severus Alexander. The HA was, therefore, faced with a recurrence of the old problem. The main source had again run out. What was to be done now? Again, the author made some use of Herodian[117]. And he took one striking item (perhaps) more from Victor (24. 4 < Caes. 28. 6—7).[118] But for the most part he indulged his passion for pure fiction. Consequently, his picture of Alexander bears a strong resemblance to the historical Julian. That was unavoidable for a pagan of the late fourth century who wished to romance about an emperor he admired[119]. Yet his main intent was not to glorify Julian, to state a serious political ideal, or to enter a plea for religious toleration. In his inventions the author of the HA can never long abstain from comedy[120].

Those who saluted Alexander too affably, he relates, were either forcibly expelled from his presence for adulation or, if their rank was too high for that, insulted with an enormous guffaw (17. 4—18. 1). The emperor's fondness for his mother Mammaea was excessive. It led him to build her a summer-house in the palace bearing her name, which the uneducated still call ad Mammam (26. 9). The worthy young man used to sing nobly, to paint wonderfully and to wrestle. He wrote the lives of the good emperors in verse[121]. He played the lyre, the flute, the organ and even the trumpet—which was unusual for an emperor (27. 7—9). Vulgar pleasures he despised: his greatest delight was to watch puppies playing with small piglets, partridges fighting, or jackdaws flying up and down. And he had an engaging hobby to assuage the cares of state: he was a bird-fancier. He kept an aviary in the palace, with peacocks, pheasants, cocks, ducks, partridges—and twenty thousand pigeons. And so great was his public spirit that he appointed slaves to rear them, lest they might become a charge on the annona (41. 5—7).

---

[116] JRS LVII (1967), 66. The fragments and testimonia are collected at HRR II. 121 ff.

[117] Below, pp. 35 ff.

[118] A. CHASTAGNOL, Bonner Historia-Augusta-Colloquium 1964/65 (1966), 54 ff.; Rev. phil.³ XLI (1967), 95 ff.

[119] W. OTTO, Byz. Zeitschr. XXIX (1929—30), 37 f.; R. SYME, Ammianus and the Historia Augusta (1968), 118.

[120] SYME, o. c. 203 ff.

[121] Cf. Gord. 3. 2—3.

Whatever their purpose, however, the inventions in the A l e x a n -
d e r are cast into a framework of fact which it is tempting to identify
as the KG. A brief analysis will perhaps add plausibility to the
conjecture.

*   *

*

The fictions in the Alexander must largely be ignored here. Some
are patent and all will concede their falsity: e. g., the emperor's
tutors (3. 2—3), his birthday on the anniversary of the death of
Alexander the Great (5. 2; 13. 1)[122], or his eating habits (37. 3—12).
Others have occasionally appeared more doubtful, and there have
been desperate attempts at rescue: e. g., the council of twenty lawyers
and fifty sages (16. 1)[123], the reported vilification of Alexander as
Syrus archisynagogus (28. 7)[124], or his domestic chapel (29. 2)[125]. But the
discovery of fresh evidence is continually increasing the area of
demonstrable fiction. Thus the myth of Ulpian as the wise counsellor,
guiding the young emperor in statecraft[126] or excogitating a vast mass
of constructive legislation (15. 6; 31. 2—3; 34. 6; 51. 4; 67. 2; 68. 1)[127],
is now shattered beyond repair: a papyrus proves that he was dead
before the reign was two years old[128]. It would, however, be ex-
traneous to present purposes to discuss all the passages whose status
may still be disputed. Hence, though the curious and sceptical can
fortunately be referred to the successive studies of LÉCRIVAIN,
W. THIELE, K. HOENN, A. JARDÉ and BAYNES[129], the choice of what to
present as the factual framework of the v i t a cannot but contain an
element which is personal, arbitrary and perhaps dogmatic.

[122] Severus Alexander was born on 1 October (below, p. 38); Alexander
the Great died on 10 June 323 B. C. (A. E. SAMUEL, Ptolemaic Chronology
[1962], 46 f.).
[123] J. A. CROOK, Consilium Principis (1955), 86 ff.
[124] A. MOMIGLIANO, Athenaeum XII (1934), 151 ff. Against, E. HOHL,
Bursians Jahresber. CCLVI (1937), 156; cf. H. J. LEON, The Jews of Ancient
Rome (1960), 163 ff.
[125] W. H. C. FREND, Martyrdom and Persecution in the Early Church
(1965), 329.
[126] For a long list of believers in this view see J. MODRZEJEWSKI-
T. ZAWADZKI, Rev. hist. de droit⁴ XLV (1967), 565 ff.
[127] A. M. HONORÉ, Stud. et doc. hist. et iur. XXVIII (1962), 162 ff.
HONORÉ's methods and conclusions had been anticipated sixty years earlier
by W. KALB, Commentationes Woelfflinianae (1891), 329 ff.
[128] P. Oxy. 2565. The date of his death was probably spring 223:
L. L. HOWE, The Pretorian Prefect from Commodus to Diocletian (A. D.
180—305) (1942), 100 ff.
[129] LÉCRIVAIN, o. c. 212 ff.; W. THIELE, De Severo Alexandro Imperatore
(Diss. Berlin, 1908); HOENN, o. c. (1911); A. JARDÉ, Études critiques sur la vie
et le règne de Sévère Alexandre (1925); BAYNES, o. c. (1926), 118 ff. See also
A. STEIN, PIR² A 1610.

1. 1—3   Cf. Victor, C a e s. 24. 1; Eutropius, B r e v. VIII. 23.
The place of birth is correct (Dio LXXIX (LXXVIII). 30. 3). Alexander was saluted Caesar in June 221 (Fer. Dur. II. 16/7). He was proclaimed emperor and accorded his first imperatorial salutation by the soldiers on 13 March 222: on a later day (probably 14 March) the Senate voted him the titles of Augustus, *pater patriae* and *pontifex maximus* (Fer. Dur. I. 23 ff.). Hence all the powers recorded in 1. 3 were not voted together. The constitutional niceties[130], together with the remarks on the *nomen Antoninorum* (1. 1) and the erroneous family tree (1. 2), come from the author's head.

1. 4—2. 5   Why Alexander was given all these powers at once.

3   His education.

4   His personal demeanour and physique.
At least some of this comes from the KG: *cunctis hominibus amabilis* (4. 5) corresponds to *omnibus amabilis* in Jerome (GCS XLVII. 215).

5   Why the emperor accepted the name of Alexander, but refused to be called Antoninus[131] or Magnus.

6. 1—12. 1   His speech of refusal in the Senate, with the Senate's acclamations.

12. 2—3   His return home as if in triumph.

12. 4   Why the soldiers called him Severus.

12. 5   Cf. Victor, C a e s. 24. 3; Eutropius, B r e v. VIII. 23; Jerome (GCS XLVII. 215). The severity and the dismissal of mutinous legions stood in the KG and recur at 59. 4—5. But there also seems to be petty polemic against Victor. He observed that the dismissal *in praesens gloriae, mox exitio datum est*: the HA replies *illi ingentem in praesentia reverentiam, magnam apud posteros gloriam peperit*.

13. 1—14. 6ᵃ   *Omina imperii*[132].

14. 6ᵇ—7   More personal qualities and his mother's influence (cf. 60. 2).

15. 1—24. 6   Civil reforms, comportment as emperor, concern for justice and morality. There is (to the best of my knowledge) no evidence to prove the truth of anything in this section, with the exception of the rebuilding operations in 24. 3[133]. A special issue of coins in 223

---

[130] Cf. Marcus 6. 6.
[131] Which sometimes appears: e. g., CIL XV. 7334.
[132] Cf. J. Straub, Heidnische Geschichtsapologetik in der christlichen Spätantike (1963), 125 ff.
[133] Cf. Baynes, o. c. 123 ff. But Jardé, o. c. 21 ff., has by no means been alone in attempting to rehabilitate many individual items.

features the Colosseum, i. e. the *amphitheatrum Flavium* (BMC Roman Empire VI. 54; 128 f.).

25. 1/2   Refutation of Herodian VI. 1. 7; 9. 8.

25. 3—26. 11   Buildings. There is genuine information, but more invention. Comment is given only where directly relevant evidence exists.

25. 3   Baths. Eutropius states that Nero's baths *nunc Alexandrianae appellantur* (Brev. VII. 15. 3); Jerome (GCS XLVII. 215), the Chronographer of 354 (MGH Auct. Ant. IX. 147) and P. O x y. 412, col. ii, lines 63 ff. record Alexander's construction of baths[134]. Aqueduct: B M C R o m a n E m p i r e VI. 63 f.; 146 f.; Polemius Silvius (MGH Auct. Ant. IX. 546)[135].

25. 6   Cf. E l a g. 17. 9[136].

25. 7   Modelled on E l a g. 24. 6: in the HA *primus instituit* is usually fiction.

26. 1   Coins show five *liberalitates:* B M C R o m a n E m p i r e VI. 49 etc.[137]

    Victor, C a e s. 35. 7; HA, A u r. 35. 2; E p i t o m e 35. 6 record that Aurelian began the distribution of free pork.

26. 4   Cf. M a r c u s 22. 7 (certainly true); A l e x. 25. 8; 28. 6; T a c. 9. 5 (all three surely fiction). If 25. 8 and 28. 6 are modelled on 26. 4, that might create a presumption of its genuineness.

26. 5/6   Cf. Victor, C a e s. 24. 6; Eutropius, B r e v. VIII. 23; Festus, B r e v. XXII. Elagabalus' pretorian prefects were killed with him (Dio LXXIX. 21. 1), and Ulpian was still only *praefectus annonae* on 31 March 222 (Cod. Just. VIII. 37. 4). The HA knows of two versions of Ulpian's appointment: the erroneous view presumably comes from Victor, the correct one (cf. Dio LXXX. 1. 1; Zosimus I. 11. 2) from the KG. The passage also shows a second derivation from Victor: the HA's alleged prefecture of Paulus surely comes from a hasty misreading of him[138]. Eutropius has nothing about Ulpian's prefecture (both he and Festus record him only as *magister scrinii /scriniorum*) and nothing at all about Paulus. An important consequence follows. If

---

[134] Further evidence at PLATNER-ASHBY, o. c. 531.

[135] Cf. P—W I. 1398; PLATNER-ASHBY, o. c. 20.

[136] The truth of the report is doubted by PLATNER-ASHBY, o. c. 520 f., following A. VON DOMASZEWSKI, Sb. Heidelberg, Phil.-hist. Kl. 1916, Abh. No. 7, 8.

[137] Cf. G. BARBIERI, Diz. epig. IV. 863 f.

[138] So CHASTAGNOL, o. c. (1967), 90. On Paulus, see further HOWE, o. c. 105 f.

	the prefecture of Paulus here is due to misunderstanding Victor, then A l e x. 26. 6 was written before P e s c. N i g. 7. 4. That implies that all the N e b e n - v i t e n were written after the A l e x a n d e r[139].
26. 7	Probably fiction[140]: cf. G o r d. 32. 6.
26. 9	Cf. Victor, C a e s. 24. 5; Eutropius, B r e v. VIII. 23; Jerome (GCS XLVII. 215). Though the HA has a great liking for the word *unice*[141], this occurrence surely comes from the KG. For the HA has precisely the same words as Jerome and in the same order: *in matrem Mammaeam unice pius fuit*[142]. Eutropius has *in Mammaeam matrem suam unice pius*[143]. *Ita ut Romae ... censetur* is of course the author's own.
27. 1—4	Alexander's innovations in the matter of permissible dress.
27. 5—10	His cultural attainments.
28. 1	Alexander did hold three ordinary consulates (222, 226, 229)[144]. The rest is false: he is attested as sole consul on 15 April 222 (CIL VI. 1454).
28. 2—5	Treatment of thieves.
28. 6	Cf. 26. 4.
28. 7	Alexander's wish to be a Roman and shame at being a Syrian.
29. 1—44. 9	His daily life, with numerous brief insertions on other topics. There does not appear to be one genuine item in the whole of this long section[145].
45. 1—5	Alexander's conduct *de rebus vel tacendis vel prodendis.*
45. 6—46. 5	Attitude towards appointments.
47	Habitual preparations for military expeditions.
48	The attempted usurpation of *Ovinius Camillus, senator antiquae familiae delicatissimus*[146].
49. 1—2	Appointments again.

---

[139] Cf. R. Syme, below, pp. 285 ff.

[140] Platner-Ashby, o. c. 76.

[141] Cf. JRS LVII (1967), 68.

[142] Chastagnol, o. c. 91, however, argues that the HA has copied Eutropius. He seems to have overlooked Jerome.

[143] In yet another place, therefore, Jerome has consulted the KG (see above, p. 21).

[144] Degrassi, o. c. (1952), 62 ff.

[145] Several are, however, accepted by Jardé, o. c. 21 ff.

[146] Taken for genuine by Barbieri, Albo no. 1122. The inspiration for *Camillus* is obvious (cf. Pesc. Nig. 12. 1). But why *Ovinius?* Domaszewski, o. c. (1918), 18, opined that it came from Orosius VI. 19. 20. A lost epitome of Livy may be more likely (cf. H. A. Sanders, Trans. Amer. Phil. Ass. XXXVI (1905), 5 ff.).

49. 3—5	Dexippus on Alexander's wife and his relationship to Elagabalus[147].
49. 6	Christians again: cf. 22. 4; 29. 2; 43. 6; 45. 7.
50	The behaviour of the soldiers and of Alexander on his Persian expedition.
51—54	Alexander's general demeanour and comportment again.
55	Cf. Victor, C a e s. 24. 2; Eutropius, B r e v. VIII. 23; Festus, B r e v. XXII; Jerome (GCS XLVII. 215).

55. This account of Alexander's campaign and victorious return is mostly free composition. Nevertheless, there is a genuine factual basis, which surely came from the KG. Victor has *apparatu magno* and *fuso fugatoque*, while Festus alone records the triumph[148]. Furthermore, the HA's *Artaxerxes* is nearer the truth than the *Xerxes* of the other four Latin authors. Herodian had 'Αρταξάρης, and the king's real name was Ardashir[149].

56—57	Alexander's speech in the Senate after his victory, and actions in Rome[150].
58	Military successes elsewhere and measures resulting from them[151].
59. 1—6	Cf. Victor, C a e s. 24. 2—3; Eutropius, B r e v. VIII. 23.

59. 1—6. For Alexander's German expedition, in contrast to the Persian, the HA possesses a good deal of authentic information. The difference of opinion about the place of his murder in 59. 6 indubitably betrays knowledge of Victor[152]. Again, however, most of the facts appear to come from Victor's source rather than from Victor himself: the HA avoids Victor's error of making Alexander rush direct from Persia to the Rhine.

59. 7—8	Addition from Herodian VI. 8. 2; 9. 4—6.
60. 1	Cf. Chronographer of 354 (MGH Auct. Ant. IX. 147); Victor, C a e s. 24. 7; Eutropius, B r e v. VIII. 23.

60. 1. Since Alexander's *dies imperii* was 13 March 222 (Fer. Dur. I. 23 f.), and Maximinus was coopted into several priesthoods on 25 March 222 (CIL VI. 2001), the figure

---

[147] Not necessarily a genuine or accurate quotation: HOENN, o. c. 198.

[148] Attested on coins of 233: BMC Roman Empire VI, 82 f. ;206 f.

[149] C. STAVENHAGEN, on Herodian VI. 2. 1 (Teubner, 1922; reprinted 1967); A. STEIN, PIR² A 1166.

[150] JARDÉ, o. c. 81 f.; A. STEIN, PIR² A 1610, argue that 56. 9 goes back to authentic information about Alexander's titles. But *vere Parthicus, vere Persicus* is an easy invention: cf. *Parthos et Persas Antoninus vincat* (7. 6).

[151] On the relevance of this chapter to the HA's date, see SYME, o. c. 43 ff.

[152] CHASTAGNOL, o. c. (1967), 91.

of nine days can hardly be correct, unless it be interpreted as the day on which Alexander's death became known in Rome.

For the length of Alexander's life, the E p i t o m e (24. 4) gives twenty five years, while Herodian implies that his birth fell in 209 or 210 (V. 3. 3; 7. 4). His birthday was the Kalends of October (CIL I². pp. 255; 274), and he was murdered in March 235[153]. Hence either the HA was wrong on both years and months or the manuscripts are corrupt.

60. 2	Mammaea, universally regarded as the real ruler, was killed with her son (Herodian VI. 1. 1 ff.; 9. 7)[154].
60. 3—8	*Omina mortis.*
61. 1—7	Alexander's neglect of them causes his death.
61. 8	Addition from Herodian VII. 2. 1.
62	Alexander's contempt for death.
63. 1—2	Sorrow at his murder.
63. 3	Alexander's apotheosis (which did not, of course, occur in 235 as is here implied) is attested by I L S 1315 = C I L VIII. 627 (Mactar); I G R III. 1033 = O G I S 640 (Palmyra); R I C IV (3). 132 nos. 97*, 98*; C I L I². p. 255. For neither the tomb nor the cenotaph is there any other evidence.
63. 4	No *sodalis Alexandrianus* has yet been discovered[155], nor is any festival of Alexander and his mother known. His own birthday, wrongly given at 5. 2; 13. 1, was remembered in the fourth century (CIL I². pp. 255; 274).
63. 5—6	Cause of Alexander's death as given by *amatores Maximini*[156].
64. 1—2	The struggles for the throne after Alexander.
64. 3	Criticisms of the emperor.
64. 4—5	Appeal to *Acholius* for Alexander's proclamation as Caesar by the Senate, not the soldiers[157].
65—68	Invocation of Constantine, and learned disquisition on how a young Syrian was able to become such an excellent emperor.

---

[153] A. STEIN, PIR² A 1610. P. Oxy. 912 appears to attest the recognition of Maximin as emperor in Egypt in late February 235. Something is surely wrong (cf. E. HOHL, P—W X. 866 f.)—perhaps the date is a later addition.

[154] Further, PIR² J 649.

[155] M. HAMMOND, The Antonine Monarchy (1959), 209; 231 f.

[156] JARDÉ, o. c. 91, conjectured that this might come from Dexippus.

[157] Surely directed against the view expressed by Eutropius, Brev. VIII. 23: *ab exercitu Caesar, a senatu Augustus nominatus.* CH. LÉCRIVAIN, Rev. ét. anc. I (1899), 141 f., attempted to prove the authenticity of *Acholius.*

The KG was a series of brief biographies: to call it a 'Kaiserchronik' as some did was misleading[158]. For each biography ENMANN identified the following schema:

(1) the emperor's name and origin, a remark on his previous life (not a detailed career), the place of his proclamation if he came to the throne by rebellion;

(2) wars against barbarians and pretenders;

(3) public works, striking legislation and character of the reign;

(4) the place and manner of the emperor's death, his place of burial and posthumous honours, the length of his reign.

All this was compressed into a very few lines[159]. Analysis of the V i t a A l e x a n d r i enables ENMANN's picture of the KG to be given a clearer outline. The factual framework of the v i t a consists of parts of 1. 1—2; 4. 5; 24. 3; 25. 3—26. 11; 28. 1; 55. 1—2; 59. 1—6; 60. 1—2; 63. 3. That was surely the whole of the KG's account of Alexander[160].

•   •

•

The KG was composed in or soon after 337[161]. Its author's memory, therefore, could not stretch back far beyond 280. What written sources did he press into service? For the very early empire, clearly Suetonius —supplemented from a historical tradition which has now perished. Hence the characterisation (by ENMANN and others) of the early chapters of the KG as a ' S u e t o n i u s   a u c t u s '[162]. For the century subsequent to the accession of Nerva there was Marius Maximus, and the unknown continuator of Suetonius who must be postulated as a direct source for the HA[163]. Identifiable traces of both remain in works deriving from the KG. Maximus traced the pedigree of Marcus Aurelius back to Numa on one side, and to king Sallentinus, founder of Lopiae on the other (HA, Marcus 1. 6). Both these ancestors are registered by Eutropius (Brev. VIII. 8. 1). The unknown biographer was the main source of the V i t a   V e r i[164], and described Lucius' fatal illness as *subito ... morbo, quem apoplexin vocant* (Verus 9. 11).

---

[158] E. HOHL, Klio XI (1911), 188. BAYNES, o. c. 71, repeated the error.

[159] o. c. 432 ff.

[160] W. H. FISHER, JRS XIX (1929), 129 ff., and MELONI, o. c. 173 ff., attempt to reconstruct the KG on Aurelian and Carus. Both manage to include some things which are manifestly the work of the author of the HA: e. g., the mention of *Heraclammon* at Aur. 22. 6; 23. 1 (FISHER, o. c. 131; against, SYME, o. c. 65; 172) and the verdicts on Carus at Car. 3. 8; 9. 4 (MELONI, o. c. 178; 182; cf. JRS LVII [1967], 67). P. DAMERAU, Klio, Beiheft XXXIII (1934), 1 ff., showed greater caution when discussing the Claudius.

[161] Above, p. 20.

[162] ENMANN, o. c. 407 ff., esp. 432.

[163] Above, pp. 30 ff.

[164] JRS LVII (1967), 65 ff.

The word *apoplexis* recurs, twice as a gloss, in the same context in Eutropius (Brev. VIII. 10. 3), in Jerome[165], and in the E p i t o m e (16. 5).

Another example has important implications. Victor implies and Eutropius states that Pescennius Niger was killed at Cyzicus (Caes. 20. 8; Brev. VIII. 18. 4). That is false: Niger was killed in Syria not far from Antioch[166]. The mistake is sometimes imputed to the author of the KG[167]. But it appears also in the V i t a S e v e r i :

> dein conflixit cum Nigro eumque apud Cyzicum interemit caput-
> que eius pilo circumtulit (9. 1; whence Pesc. Nig. 5. 8).

The context is almost entirely sound[168], and the sentence ought to come from the main source. Hence, unless there is an error (either by the HA or manuscript corruption in the source) this passage furnishes additional proof that the main source of the early v i t a e was not Marius Maximus[169]. In 193 Maximus marched south from the Danube with troops from Moesia and for three years prosecuted the siege of Byzantium[170]. A man so well placed for discovering the truth about Niger could hardly commit such an error. The postulated biographer perhaps could. The KG, therefore, took its information for the second and early third centuries from two identifiable sources: it was not, as HOHL opined, a virtual abridgement of Marius Maximus[171].

The unknown biographer finished in 217, Maximus in 222. Where did the compiler of the KG turn then? Even the most dedicated Q u e l l e n f o r s c h e r must now confess ignorance. For he can scarcely guess at what was available. There were Greek writers of history in the later third and early fourth centuries. But there is no positive sign that the KG used them, and a man writing the KG in Latin c. 337 was probably ill-equipped to do so[172]. As for Latin histories of any sort, what was there? Once the bogus authorities of the HA are set aside, the answer is simple—nothing[173].

---

[165] GCS XLVII. 205.

[166] Dio LXXV (LXXIV). 8. 3 (p. 332 BOISSEVAIN); Herodian III. 4. 6.

[167] SYME, o. c. 106.

[168] See J. HASEBROEK, Untersuchungen zur Geschichte des Kaisers Septimius Severus (1921), 50 ff. He, however, argues that Cyzicus comes from Victor or Eutropius (ib. 61).

[169] Above, p. 30, and the articles cited there.

[170] BARBIERI, Albo no. 1100; SYME, o. c. 89 f.

[171] Klio XXVII (1934), 156; Bursians Jahresber. CCLVI (1937), 144.

[172] On the cultural background, see E. LOMMATSCH, Zeitschr. für vergleichende Litteraturgeschichte, N. F. XV (1904), 177 ff.; E. MALCOVATI, Annali Cagliari XII (1942), 23 ff.; MOMIGLIANO, o. c. (1963), 79 ff.; SYME, o. c. 103 f.

[173] Cf. SYME, o. c. 88; 96; 200. If the genuine Asinius Quadratus is omitted from the reckoning, H. PETER, HRR II. 129 ff., lists the fragments of twenty four Latin writers of history between Marius Maximus and the emperor Constantine (who is said to have written memoirs): not one is attested as a historical writer outside the HA.

What then was the genesis of the KG? It is unlikely that it was merely the last of a long series of similar works produced at regular intervals, and equally unlikely that besides the discernible KG there existed in the fourth century a rich historical tradition which is completely unknown[174]. Otherwise, the writers of the later fourth century could not all display such abysmal ignorance of the third, or be so repetitious. The phenomena demand but one explanation: apart from the KG, which covered the whole of the first three centuries of the empire, there was no other source in Latin for the third century. Might the KG, therefore, be the result, at least in part, of genuine research in the 330's, possibly inspired by Constantine? Encouragement of historical work would not be out of character: according to the E p i t o m e.

> commodissimus . . . rebus multis fuit: . . . nutrire artes bonas, praecipue studia litterarum, legere ipse scribere meditari (41. 14)[175].

The hypothesis is adventurous, perhaps even wild—but will any other explain the facts as well? At all events, the role of Constantine in the revival of Latin letters in the fourth century requires elucidation.

* *
*

The consequences for 'the problem of the HA' are unmistakeable. In the long fight against DESSAU the KG has played a prominent role. DESSAU's demonstration that the HA utilised Aurelius Victor was countered by the claim that the HA's resemblances to Victor were always due to independent use of the KG[176]. It was assumed without proof that the HA could have used the KG in the reigns of Diocletian, Constantius and Constantine—the period at which it professes to be written. But such a defence of the ostensible date of the HA involves circular argument[177]. As ENMANN expressly stated, the HA itself

---

[174] As HARTKE, o. c. (1940), 17, believed: ‚es stand offenbar im 4. Jahrhundert ein reichhaltigeres Quellenmaterial zur Verfügung, als es der Zufall der Überlieferung uns bewahrt hat'. But how much richer? Since HARTKE held it to be considerably richer, he was forced to posit ‚eine Art Vor-Eutrop' between the abundant source-material (which he styled the KG, o. c. 17) and most of its derivatives. The necessity of the latter hypothesis renders the former otiose and baseless.

[175] Cf. Victor, Caes. 40. 12—14. Other relevant evidence is quoted by SCHANZ-HOSIUS, o. c. 7 ff.

[176] The first after DESSAU was E. KLEBS, Rh. Mus., N. F. XLV (1890), 436 ff.

[177] As MOMIGLIANO, o. c. (1960), 133 n. 43: 'It would, of course, be a different matter if we could prove that Aurelius Victor, or Eutropius, or any other writer of the late fourth century, did follow for post-Constantinian events one of the sources which the HA followed for pre-Diocletianic events. But, as far as I know, such a demonstration has not yet been provided (the

constitutes the only evidence that the KG was originally composed c. 300 rather than after the death of Constantine[178]. Hence the HA's use of the KG is no barrier to accepting its purported date, only if an independent proof is first provided of the Diocletianic or Constantinian date of the KG. Such a proof is impossible: in the only form for which there exists any evidence outside the HA, the KG postdates the death of Constantine[179]. This fundamental truth was seen and stated by SEECK in 1890[180]. It has subsequently been almost universally overlooked or ignored[181]. As a result, much of eighty years of bitter polemic has been beside the point. Scholars in both camps have supposed that the HA's use of the KG could afford an escape from the conclusions of DESSAU[182]. The truth is the exact opposite: DESSAU's conclusions are heavily reinforced. The KG provided the factual framework for some of the HA's biographies: therefore the HA was composed after 337.

*   *

*

By way of epilogue, a corollary of the analysis of the V i t a A l e x a n d r i offered above will briefly be stated. A recent writer has 'issue(d) a reminder—and a very necessary reminder—that the HA as we have it was not all written at the same time, and no theory which assumes that it was merits serious consideration'[183]. This is a confident claim: not merely is the view that the HA was planned and written by one man erroneous, it hardly deserves scholarly attention[184].

---

latest attempt was made by HARTKE in 1940); and there is a simple reason for this. As A. ENMANN saw . . ., even if we admit that a source K was used throughout both by the HA and (say) Eutropius, it does not follow that the HA and Eutropius used the same redaction of K. Eutropius may have used K "auctus" (K increased by the addition of an account of the post-Constantinian period).' It has been argued above (pp. 15 ff.) that the KG's account even of pre-Diocletianic events post-dates 337. MOMIGLIANO fails to state clearly enough that the HA (whose date he is discussing) is the only evidence to the contrary.

[178] o. c. 356 ff. And note his comment on Maxim. 33. 2; Gord. 2. 1; Max. et Balb. 15. 4—6; 16. 7; ,die ähnlichkeit ist so frappant, daß man annehmen müßte, Capitolinus habe geradezu den Aurelius Victor vor augen gehabt, wüßte man nicht, daß ersterer unter Constantin, letzterer erst unter Constantius I. geschrieben hat' (o. c. 339 f.).

[179] Above, pp. 15 ff.

[180] Jahrb. f. class. Phil. CXLI (1890), 638 (quoted above, n. 40).

[181] But note A. CHASTAGNOL, Rev. phil.³ XLI (1967), 89 f.

[182] Thus even E. HOHL, Neue Jahrb. XXXIII (1914), 704, and R. SYME, Ammianus and the Historia Augusta (1968), 104, have admitted the principle of an original KG and a later continuation.

[183] A. CAMERON, CR, N. S. XVIII (1968), 18.

[184] This is what I take CAMERON to be asserting—not the trivial truism that one man could not have written it in a day or even a week, or without revisions and untidy additions.

The claim has a double origin. First, it derives from a continuing reluctance to disbelieve the HA's professions about itself. The hypothesis of an original text revised by a 'Theodosian redactor' was invented by MOMMSEN: since most of DESSAU's arguments were undeniably valid, he needed this device in order to avoid their full consequences[185]. More recently, MOMIGLIANO has cited the statements of the various *scriptores* as p r i m a   f a c i e evidence for either redaction or a process of editing[186]. But here too the argument is circular: it is precisely the truth of the HA's statements about itself which has been in dispute since 1889. Secondly, proof is sought in the existence of different strata in several v i t a e. The A l e x a n d e r has always been the prime example: according to LEO and JARDÉ it contains numerous successive additions to the original text[187]. But JARDÉ's proof loses its cogency once the full extent of the fiction and the simplicity of the basic structure are realised[188]. As for LEO, MOMIGLIANO justly and acutely remarked that 'he could not prove that each layer is the work of a different author'[189]. That verdict applies to any similar attempt: no-one has yet shown that the different strata in any v i t a must come from more than one pen.

The A l e x a n d e r is fiction cast into a simple framework of fact. The fiction is messy and unsystematic, some subjects being treated twice or more[190]. It reads as if the writer's imagination flagged, and he later went through the standard biographical τόποι a second time[191]. Yet nothing indicates that the repetitions come from different hands. And once this is granted, an important undertaking becomes possible: the HA can be studied as a work of art, and set in its proper historical and literary context[192].

---

[185] Hermes XXV (1890), 228 ff. = Ges. Schr. VII (1909), 302 ff.

[186] o. c. 108 f.; 125 f.

[187] LEO, o. c. 280 ff.; JARDÉ, o. c. 95 ff., esp. 99 ff. CAMERON, o. c. 18, appeals to earlier pronouncements of his own: Hermes XCII (1964), 374; JRS LV (1965), 240 f. There appeal is again made to earlier pronouncements—those of LEO, JARDÉ and MOMIGLIANO just cited.

[188] As JARDÉ, o. c. 100, himself reveals: 'on a l'impression d'un travailleur qui, au cours de ses lectures, accroît sans cesse son bagage historique'. JARDÉ's view of the composition of the Alexander drove HOHL to the violent protest: ‚Ich fürchte, die von JARDÉ empfohlene Theorie treibt den Teufel mit Beelzebub aus' (Bursians Jahresber. CCLVI [1937], 149).

[189] o. c. 113 n. 10.

[190] Cf. HOENN, o. c. 1: the Alexander ‚bietet das Bild trostloser Zerrissenheit und Unordnung, eines Flickwerkes der rohesten und unzuverlässigsten Art'.

[191] Compare Avid. Cass. 9. 4—9. 5; 13. 7—13. 8; Pesc. Nig. 9. 4—9. 5; Clod. Alb. 13. 2—13. 3; Tac. 13 ff. In all or these the author has added untidily—but few today would claim that as proof of multiple authorship of these vitae.

[192] As R. SYME, Ammianus and the Historia Augusta (1968).

V

ULTIMUS ANTONINORUM

I. INTRODUCTION

M. Aurelius Antoninus has an evil reputation. Under his official style as emperor, he even runs some risk of failing to be recognised. For many centuries he has been known by the name of his God, Elagabalus or (in a more Hellenised form) Heliogabalus. Immediately after his murder (on 13 March 222) the sophist Aelian, in indignant and emphatic tones, recited his 'Denunciation of Gynnis'[1], and soon the historian Cassius Dio enshrined his vices, both real and imagined, in his history, thus stamping the dead youth's character with an impress with it has not yet lost. Dio refused to dignify the hateful boy with his official name: he was the False Antoninus, the Assyrian or a modern Sardanapallus (LXXX [LXXIX]. 1. 1 ff.).

Elagabalus' notoriety spread far and wide. An ancient papyrus contains the horoscope of a man born in the second year of 'Antoninus the catamite'[2]. The moderns concur: Elagabalus was 'a homosexual pervert of quite abnormal delinquency', 'a monster of lubricity', 'a remarkable example of psychopathia sexualis' who had the misfortune to live before the age of psychoanalysis[3]. And modern inventions supplement the ancient. A moral philosopher cites Elagabalus as a paradigm of vice and intellectual confusion: failing to distinguish the correct spheres of ethics and aesthetics, he had men slaughtered so that he could enjoy the sight of red blood on green grass. Further, with a logic more appropriate to metaphysics than to history, he affirms that since he cannot discover the source of the story he cannot therefore pronounce upon its truth or falsity[4]. An antiquarian, expounding the unfathomable mysteries of Roman re-

---

[1] Philostratus, Vit. soph. II. 31. 2. At the risk of some inconsistency, I shall throughout style the emperor Elagabalus and his biography in the HA either the Elagabalus or the Vita Elagabali.

[2] Unpublished, from Oxyrhynchus. Kindly brought to my attention by Dr. J. R. REA.

[3] J. B. BURY, Introduction to J. S. HAY, The Amazing Emperor Heliogabalus (1911), xxiii f.; xxvi.

[4] R. HARE, Freedom and Reason (1963), 161: 'The Nazis were like the emperor Heliogabalus, who, I have been told, . . .'.

ligion to the educated English public, uses Elagabalus to supply a comic touch: he perversely made mixed bathing compulsory[5]. Even the HA (the apparent source) was not so bold: scandal enough that the practice was permitted at all (Alex. 24. 2).

Elagabalus' own reputation has adversely affected that of the HA's account of his reign. Until very recently specialists dismissed the whole vita as a 'farrago of cheap pornography'[6]. Its historical value was equated with that of the Vita Alexandri and its fictional nature taken as axiomatic. One scholar, who found it 'singularly uninteresting' as a historical source, claimed to discern in it the hidden features of the Christian emperor Constantius[7]. Another detected an allusion to Constantine in what appears to be a factually accurate statement (Elag. 15. 7)[8]. To be sure, implicit faith in *Aelius Lampridius* persists in less expert quarters. Is he not one of the best witnesses to the decline of the empire of Rome[9]? The stories can be put to a wide variety of uses. If Roman women are in cause, who can resist the 'Parliament of Women' (Elag. 4. 2), which the HA also alleges that Aurelian resolved to revive (Aur. 49. 6)? A recent writer advances to the conjecture that this Senate of women might have met not only under Elagabalus and Aurelian, but also on other occasions[10]. The same scholar, contemplating ancient life and leisure, perforce includes Elagabalus' extravagant dinners, at which he sometimes released pet lions and leopards upon his unsuspecting guests (Elag. 20. 4 ff.)[11]. Pious topographers have chanced upon an item which may concern the relics of the apostle Peter: Elagabalus tore up tombs on the Vatican and set four *quadrigae* of elephants to career over the ground (Elag. 23. 1)[12]. And the HA even has something which pertains to contemporary problems of race and colour: for a prank Elagabalus would closet his friends for the night with elderly negresses (Elag. 32. 5)[13].

A third way exists, between outright rejection and undiscriminating acceptance. The excellence of part of the vita (13. 1—17. 7) is

---

[5] R. M. Ogilvie, The Romans and their Gods in the Age of Augustus (1969), 81.

[6] R. Syme, Bonner Historia-Augusta-Colloquium 1964/65 (1966), 258.

[7] N. H. Baynes, The Historia Augusta. Its Date and Purpose (1926), 101; 139.

[8] A. Chastagnol, Historia-Augusta-Colloquium Bonn 1963 (1964), 59; 64.

[9] H. Bardon, Le crépuscule des Césars. Scènes et visages de l'Histoire Auguste (1964), 24.

[10] J. P. V. D. Balsdon, Roman Women (1962), 160.

[11] J. P. V. D. Balsdon, Roman Life and Leisure (1969), 37; 49.

[12] B. M. Apollonj Ghetti — A. Ferrua — E. Josi — E. Kirschbaum, Esplorazioni sotto la Confessione di San Pietro in Vaticano I (1951), 13; M. Guarducci, La tomba di Pietro (1959), 38.

[13] Cited by F. M. Snowden, Blacks in Antiquity. Ethiopians in the Greco-Roman Experience (1970), 325.

beyond all dispute or cavil[14]. An explanation can be given which both provides a criterion for sifting fact from fiction in the rest of the Elagabalus and illuminates the composition of the whole HA. Two years ago I suggested that Marius Maximus was the source of the greater part of the first eighteen chapters of the Elagabalus[15]: I hope now to bring that hypothesis closer to proof.

II. THE BIOGRAPHIES OF MACRINUS, ELAGABALUS AND ALEXANDER

The Elagabalus contrasts sharply with the vitae which both precede and follow. A brief catalogue of four relevant and important types of divergence will suffice for demonstration.

1. Named historical characters.

Apart from gods and emperors, the Macrinus and its appendage the Diadumenus name only five historical characters: the Parthian king Artabanes (Macr. 8. 3); *Maesa sive Varia ex Emisena urbe, soror Iuliae uxoris Severi*, i.e. Julia Maesa (9. 1)[16]; Maesa's two daughters, *Symiamira* and Mamaea (9. 2); and the pretorian prefect Julianus (10. 1)[17]. Significantly, all occur in a single long passage which para-phrases Herodian (8. 3 ff. < Herodian IV. 15. 6 ff.).

The Alexander offers an equally meagre harvest. Emperors, illustrious men and usurpers of other periods are named, but the HA shows no awareness of certain pretenders during the reign who are obscurely attested elsewhere[18]. Genuine literary authors who lived in the third century naturally appear: Marius Maximus, Herodian and Dexippus (respectively, 5. 4 etc.; 52. 2, 57. 3; 49. 3). Otherwise, and although Alexander ruled for fully thirteen years, the HA can name only six historical personages active in the reign: the emperor's mother Mamaea (3. 1 etc.) and grandmother (1. 2); the jurists Paul and Ulpian (26. 5 f. etc.); the Persian monarch Ardashir who appears as Artaxerxes (55. 1; 56. 7); and the mysterious *quidam Macrianus* whose daughter Alexander married and who was proclaimed Caesar (49. 3, quoting Dexippus)[19]. Even here, however, all is not well. Paul is presented as a pretorian prefect (26. 5), Ulpian as the young emperor's constant counsellor in statecraft (15. 6 etc., esp. 51. 4, 67. 2).

---

[14] H. LAMBERTZ, P-W VIII A. 402 f.

[15] Bonner Historia-Augusta-Colloquium 1968/69 (1970), 30 f.

[16] The erroneous idea that Maesa bore the name Varia is peculiar to the HA (also at Elag. 10. 1; 12. 3; 31. 4; Alex. 1. 2).

[17] viz. Ulpius Julianus (Dio LXXIX (LXXVIII). 15. 1).

[18] For the evidence, G. BARBIERI, L'albo senatorio da Settimio Severo a Carino (1952), 401 f.

[19] She can be named as Seia Sallustia (PIR[1] S 252).

In fact, Paul's prefecture is unhistorical, and Ulpian was murdered before the end of 223 (Dio LXXX. 2. 2 ff., cf. CIL IX. 338; P. Ox. 2565)[20].

The Elagabalus is far superior. Besides *Symiamira* (2. 1 etc.), it names Protogenes and Gordius (6. 3), Hierocles and Zoticus (6. 5; 10. 2 ff.; 15. 2), the ignoble Claudius (12. 1), Antiochianus the pretorian prefect and a tribune Aristomachus (14. 8), Myrismus (15. 2), the consular Sabinus (16. 2), Ulpian and the rhetor Silvinus (16. 4). Further, there is an anonymous but accurate allusion to Valerius Comazon (12. 1).

2. Fictitious names.

The Macrinus has three. First, the invented biographer *Junius Cordus,* here given a full introduction (1. 3). Next, *Aurelius Victor, cui Pinio cognomen erat* (4. 2), who should owe his existence to the historian Aurelius Victor[21]. Third, Macrinus' alleged colleague as slave and freedman *Festus* (4. 4): his name may be inspired by Festus of Tridentum, whose breviarium (written in 369/70) was probably known to the author of the HA[22]. Be it noted, however, that Dio recorded an imperial freedman of this name commanding troops in 218 (LXXIX [LXXVIII]. 32. 4) and that Caracalla had a freedman Marcius Festus as *a cubiculo et a memoria* (ib.; Herodian IV. 8. 4; CIL XIV. 3638).

The Diadumenus provides several more bogus characters. First, Macrinus' wife *Nonia Celsa* (7. 5): the HA had already recorded a *Nonius Gracchus,* executed by Septimius Severus, who is probably genuine (Sev. 13. 3)[23], and invented a *Nonius Murcus* (Clod. Alb. 2. 3). Second, the African rhetor *Caelianus* who taught Diadumenianus (Diad. 8. 9). Third, *Arabianus et Tuscus et Gellius,* whom the youth denounces in a letter to his mother as secret traitors deserving to be crucified (9. 1). Finally, the alleged contemporary historian *Lollius Urbicus* (9. 2), whose name comes from an earlier vita (Pius 5. 4).

The Alexander has two long lists: of Alexander's teachers as a boy (3. 2 f.) and of the distinguished members of his *consilium* (68. 1)[24]. In addition, there appear a host of unhistorical characters, among them *Septimius Arabianus* (17. 3 f.), Alexander's wife *Memmia, Sulpicii consularis viri filia, Catuli neptis* (20. 3), who derives from Suetonius (Galba 3. 4)[25], *Verconius Turinus* who abused the emperor's trust in him (35. 5 ff., 67. 2), *Ovinius Camillus,* the scion of an ancient house

---

[20] See now R. SYME, Emperors and Biography (1971), 147 ff.
[21] R. SYME, Ammianus and the Historia Augusta (1968), 193.
[22] Class. Quart. XX (1970), 198 f.
[23] G. ALFÖLDY, Bonner Jahrbücher CLXVIII (1968), 148.
[24] In the latter, two names are undeniably genuine: Domitius Ulpianus and Julius Paulus. For the technique, compare the enrolment of another jurist Modestinus, among the teachers of the son of Maximin (Maxim. 27. 5).
[25] E. GROAG, P-W III. 1796 f.

who earned the emperor's gratitude, imperial regalia and the title *particeps imperii* by plotting armed rebellion (48. 1), and three victorious generals: *Furius Celsus* in Mauretania, *Varius Macrinus* in Illyricum, and *Junius Palmatus* in Armenia (58. 1).

In contrast, the Elagabalus contains no character whose name is either certainly or even probably an invention.

3. Other fabrications.

The following types of invention are absent from the Elagabalus[26]: A. Authors. *Junius Cordus* (Macr. 1. 3): *Lollius Urbicus* (Diad. 9. 2); *Aurelius Philippus, Acholius* and many others (Alex. 3. 2; 14. 6; 17. 1 etc.).

Letters. Macrinus and Diadumenianus to the Senate, technically an imperial *oratio* (Macr. 5. 9 ff.); Macrinus to his wife *Nonia Celsa* (Diad. 7. 5 ff.); Diadumenianus to his mother (Diad. 8. 5 ff.; 9. 1).

Speeches. *Aurelius Victor* in the Senate (Macr. 4. 2 ff.); Macrinus proclaiming his son an Antoninus (Diad. 1. 4 ff.); Severus Alexander in the Senate (Alex. 8. 1 ff.; 56. 2 ff.) and to the army (53. 5 ff.).

Official documents. Edict of Diadumenianus (Diad. 2. 10); *acta urbis* chronicling a speech of Severus Alexander shortly after his accession, dated to 6 March (Alex. 6. 2 ff.)[27]; *acta senatus* (Alex. 56. 2 ff.).

Acclamations. Of the soldiers (Diad. 1. 6 ff.); in the Senate (Alex. 6. 3 ff.).

Date by day and month. Alex. 6. 2; 56. 2.

B. Official posts and institutions. *Dux Armeniae et item legatus Asiae atque Arabiae* (Diad. 8. 4); *puellae Mamaeanae et pueri Mamaeani* (Alex. 57. 7); *sodales Alexandriani* (Alex. 63. 4).

Buildings. Alex. 25. 3 ff. (at least partly fiction)[28].

Statues. Six of Caracalla and two of Septimius Severus (Macr. 6. 8); many colossal statues erected in Rome (Alex. 25. 8; 28. 6).

C. Quotations from Virgil. Macr. 12. 9; Diad. 8. 7; Alex. 4. 6; 14. 5 (both *sortes Vergilianae*).

Omina imperii. Diad. 3. 4 ff.; Alex. 13. 1 ff.

---

[26] For the categories, cf. SYME, o.c. (1970), 61 f.

[27] Alexander was in fact proclaimed emperor by the soldiers on 13 March 222 and acclaimed by the Senate on 14 March (P. Dura 54, I. 23 ff.).

[28] Bonner Historia-Augusta-Colloquium 1968/69 (1970), 35. The topography and buildings registered in the HA have been investigated by several modern scholars, with insufficient attention either to source-criticism or to the patent differences between the various vitae: A. VON DOMASZEWSKI, Die Topographie Roms bei den S. H. A., Sb. Heidelberg, Phil.-hist. Kl. 1916, Abh. 7; H. G. RAMSAY, Ant. Class. IV (1935), 419 ff.; V (1936), 160 ff.; D. M. ROBATHAN, Trans. Amer. Phil. Ass. LXX (1939), 515 ff.; H. W. BENARIO, Latomus XX (1961), 281 ff.

Greek verses in translation. Macr. 11. 3 ff.; 14. 2 f.; Diad. 7. 3 f.; Alex. 38. 5 f.

Literary productivity. Macrinus replies to his detractors in both elegiac couplets and iambics (Macr. 11. 5 ff.; 14. 4); Alexander was eloquent in Greek and wrote polished poetry (Alex. 27. 5).

Litterati as friends of rulers. Macr. 13. 5; Alex. 3. 4 etc.

D. Parentage and relatives. *Nonia Celsa* the wife of Macrinus (Diad. 7. 5); *Varius* the father of Severus Alexander (Alex. 1. 2), his wife *Memmia* (20. 3) and *adfinis Varius Macrinus* (58. 1).

Physical appearance. Diad. 3. 2 f.; Alex. 4. 4.

Self-contradictory and vapid characterisations. Macr. 13. 4 f.; Alex. 3. 4 *(amavit litteratos homines vehementer, eos etiam reformidans).*

4. Greek sources.

The Macrinus paraphrases and summarises a long passage of Herodian (8. 3 ff. < Herodian IV. 15. 6 ff.)[29], and takes material from him on at least one other occasion (12. 6, cf. Herodian III. 9. 2 f.)[30]. The Diadumenus quotes Herodian once (2. 5, cf. Herodian V. 4. 12). The Alexander both quotes Herodian (52. 2; 57. 3), uses him (59. 7 f. < Herodian VI. 8. 2; 9. 4 ff.; 61. 8 < VII. 2. 1), and subjects him to anonymous polemic (25. 1 f., cf. Herodian VI. 1. 7; 9. 8). Further, it also adduces Dexippus (Alex. 49. 3). Again in contrast, the Elagabalus never names nor does it ever obviously copy Herodian.

III. TWO CHARIOTEERS

Aurigas Protogenen et Cordium primo in certamine curruli socios, post in omni vita et actu participes habuit (Elag. 6. 3).

The second name requires correction: not *Cordius*, but *Gordius*[31]. Graffiti provide the proof[32], and his name ought to indicate that Gordius derived from Anatolia[33]. As for Protogenes, the experts in prosopography appear to have unearthed no other evidence[34]. The gap can be supplied, albeit with conjectural argument.

A bell from the reins of a horse (found near Rome) bears the following words:

Εἰσαπέων Πρωτογένη νίκα.

---

[29] T. MOMMSEN, Ges. Schr. VII (1909), 343 ff.

[30] A. WIRTH, Quaestiones Severianae (1888), 27 f.

[31] H. SOLIN, Eranos LXI (1963), 65 ff.

[32] R. GARRUCI, Graffiti de Pompéi² (1856), 98; Planche XXX. 22 = L. CORRERA, Bull com. arch. 1893, 257 no. 152, cf. no. 160.

[33] Cf. SYME, o. c. 167. It may not be relevant that Gordius possessed a Carian slave (Dio LXXX (LXXIX) 15. 1).

[34] PIR¹ P 759; P-W XXIII. 980.

So the standard publication (IG XIV. 2409. 2)[35]. Better sense emerges when the words are divided differently:

εἷς ἀπ' ἐῶν(ος)· Πρωτογένη νίχα.

The acclamation εἷς ἀπ' αἰῶνος ('the best ever') can be abundantly documented for athletes, gladiators and other public performers in the Roman Empire—witness Nero (Dio LXII. 20. 5)[36]. This Protogenes is clearly a charioteer: why should he not be Elagabalus' favourite? His provenance may be revealed by a passage of Tertullian which has not yet received adequate elucidation. His Adversus Valentinianos describes the angelology of the Gnostic Valentinus, and explains how the primordial Bythos gave birth to Sige and how Sige produced Nus (also known as Monogenes) and Aletheia, thus forming the first Tetrad of Valentinus' Pleroma of Thirty Aeons. Tertullian took his matter from Irenaeus (Adv. Haer. I. 1. 1), but added sarcastic comments of his own:

hoc (sc. initium rerum) vice seminis in Sige sua velut in genitalibus vulvae locis collocat (sc. Bythos). suscipit illa statim et praegnans efficitur et parit, utique silentio, Sige. et quem parit? Nus est, simillimum patri et parem per omnia. denique solus hic capere sufficit immensam illam et incomprehensibilem magnitudinem patris. ita et ipse pater dicitur et initium omnium et proprie Monogenes. atquin non proprie, siquidem non solus agnascitur. nam cum illo processit et femina, cui Veritas nomen. Monogenes, quia prior genitus, quanto congruentius Protogenes vocaretur! ergo Bythos et Sige, Nus et Veritas prima quadriga defenditur Valentinianae factionis, matrix et origo cunctorum (Adv. Val. 7. 5 f.).

The only edition of the Adversus Valentinianos which has so far been published this century deletes the sentence beginning *Monogenes, quia . . .*[37]. It has recently been reinstated with purely philological arguments[38]. Rightly so. But what is the allusion? Tertullian's original audience clearly knew who Protogenes was, and the sentence which immediately follows contains the vital clue. If the Tetrad can be derided as the *prima quadriga Valentinianae factionis*, then Protogenes should be a charioteer. Furthermore, since Tertullian was writing in Carthage for the Christians of that city, Protogenes should be a figure known in Carthage—and therefore a charioteer in Carthage. He may consequently without difficulty be presumed identical with the later intimate of Elagabalus.

Protogenes occurs in no known historical writer except the HA. Prima facie, therefore, the author is drawing on a source of information which is both reliable and nearly contemporary.

---

[35] GARRUCCI reproduced a drawing (o. c. 41).

[36] L. ROBERT, Études épigraphiques et philologiques (1938), 108 ff.

[37] A. KROYMANN, Corp. Scr. Eccl. Lat. XLVII (1906), 185 = Corp. Chr., Ser. Lat. II (1954), 758.

[38] J.-C. FREDOUILLE, Vig. Chr. XX (1966), 58.

IV. HIEROCLES AND ZOTICUS

Aurelius Zoticus of Smyrna, nicknamed 'Mageiros' because his father was a cook, was both loved and hated by Elagabalus—and thus escaped death. The emperor sent spies to roam the empire and search out men with abnormally large genitals. They observed the handsome Zoticus performing in some games and despatched him to Rome, accompanied by a procession larger than those which escorted Abgar of Edessa to Septimius Severus or Tiridates to Nero. Already appointed *a cubiculo*[39] before the emperor ever saw him, Zoticus entered the imperial palace in truly royal style and saluted Elagabalus as his lord. Whereupon the latter kissed his neck and rebuked him: 'Call me not lord; for I am a lady'. At once the two bathed together and the spies' report was verified. Hierocles, however, fearful of losing his own influence over the emperor, slipped a potion into Zoticus' wine as he dined with the doting Elagabalus that very evening. The new favourite lost his virility: despite valiant efforts all night long he remained utterly impotent. In the morning his disgrace became obvious to all: he was deprived of his honours and banished from the palace, from Rome, and subsequently from Italy.

Thus Dio in epitome, for once amusing as well as salacious (LXXX [LXXIX]. 16. 1 ff.). The HA has something markedly different. It presents Zoticus as possessing great influence under Elagabalus, being treated as the emperor's husband by *omnes officiorum principes,* and amassing vast riches by corruption. Elagabalus formally married him (a bridesmaid in attendance) and exclaimed 'Go to work, cook', even though Zoticus was ill at the time (Elag. 10. 2 ff.).

The two stories have obvious points of contact: Zoticus' nickname *Magirus* and his indisposition on the 'wedding-night'. But they differ on Zoticus' political importance and how long he enjoyed the emperor's favour[40]. Prima facie, therefore, the HA is not dependent on Dio for its authentic information about Elagabalus.

V. RELIGIOUS REFORMS

The nature of the God Elagabalus requires a definition. For etymology appears flatly to contradict the unambiguous statements of ancient writers. The name should originally designate 'the god of the mountain'[41]. Yet Elagabalus is consistently described as a sun-god:

---

[39] For the equivalence of προκοιτος and *a cubiculo* note the evidence concerning Cleander: Dio LXXIII (LXXII). 12. 5; ILS 1737; AE 1952. 6; 1961. 280.

[40] He may have returned to Rome later, cf. CIL VI. 1094.

[41] F. Cumont, P-W V. 2219; K. Gross, Reallexicon für Ant. u. Christ. IV. 992.

Dio LXXIX (LXXVIII). 31. 1: τοῦ Ἡλίου, ὃν Ἐλεγάβαλον ἐπικαλοῦσι

Herodian V. 3. 4: θεῷ ἡλίῳ· τοῦτον γὰρ οἱ ἐπιχώριοι σέβουσι, τῇ Φοινίκων φωνῇ Ἐλαιαγάβαλον καλοῦντες

Victor, Caes. 23. 1: *solis . . ., quem Heliogabalum Syri vocant*

HA, Macr. 9. 2 (< Herodian V. 3. 4): *nam Heliogabalum Foenices vocant solem*

HA, Elag. 1. 5: *fuit autem Heliogabali vel Jovis vel Solis sacerdos*

HA, Elag. 17. 8: *Heliogabali dei, quem Solem alii, alii Jovem dicunt*

Epit. de Caes. 23. 2: *solis . . ., quem Phoenices, unde erat, Heliogabalum nominabant*

Avienus, Descriptio orbis terrae 1088 f.:
  denique flammicomo devoti pectora Soli
  vitam agitant (sc. the inhabitants of Emesa).

Coins and inscriptions are equally explicit:

Sanct(o) Deo Soli Elagabal(o) (BMC, R. Emp. V. 572; 574 f.)

Soli Alagabalo (ILS 4329: Rome, cf. 4330 f.)

sacerdos amplissimus invicti Solis Elagabali (ILS 473: Ferentium)

Deo Soli Alagabal(o) Ammudati (ILS 4332: Brigetio)[42]

θεῷ Ἡλίῳ Ἐλεγαβάλῳ ἡ βουλὴ καὶ ὁ σύνπας δῆμος (G. E. BEAN, Türk Tarih Belleten XXII (1958), 84 no. 112: Attaleia in Pamphylia)

Deo p[atrio] Soli Ela[gabalo] (A. RADNÓTI, Germania XXXIX [1961], 383).

Evidence of this quality cannot be gainsaid—nor can it provide any secure deductions about the relationship of the sources (e. g., that the Epitome derives from Herodian). Elagabalus accords with his Syrian and Arabian background, as both a sun-god and the local Baal of Emesa[43]. The black stone which was brought to Rome was a meteor fallen from the sky (Herodian V. 3. 5), and Mecca itself produces a precise parallel[44]. The HA is therefore entirely accurate when it describes the God as the equivalent of Jupiter or Sol (Elag. 1. 5; 17. 8). Further, an addition to the Vita Marci and the final appendage to the Caracalla carry an important notice: the emperor Elagabalus converted the temple of Diva Faustina at the foot of the Taurus mountains in Cilicia to the worship of his own God (Marcus 26. 9; Carac. 11. 7). The statement may well be authentic[45]. If so, one cannot avoid asking whence the HA knew so abstruse a fact.

---

[42] On the epithet, cf. TÜMPEL, P-W I. 1868 ff.

[43] J. H. MORDTMANN, Zeitschr. der deutschen morgenländischen Gesellschaft XXXI (1877), 91 ff. More recently, cf. F. ALTHEIM, Aus Spätantike und Christentum (1951), 26 ff.; Niedergang der antiken Welt II (1952), 218 ff.

[44] P. HITTI, A History of the Arabs⁹ (1960), 100.

[45] L. ROBERT (in collaboration with A. DUPONT-SOMMER), La déesse de Hiérapolis Castabala (Cilicie). Bibl. arch. et hist. de l'Inst. fr. d'arch. d'Istanbul XVI (1964), 81 f.

Herodian expatiates at some length on the religious antics of Elagabalus. He records the removal of the Palladium from the temple of Vesta, the 'marriage' of the God Elagabalus to Caelestis, whose statue was fetched from Carthage, and a temple and midsummer festival of the God in a suburb (V. 6. 3 ff.). But his ubiquitous distaste for facts leads him to concentrate on the emperor's unworthy behaviour rather than present a plethora of detail: the young Syrian would dress up in effeminate clothes, paint his face and manifest his religious mania in prolonged transvestite caperings.

The HA can offer a greater wealth of specific detail. Admittedly, there is no mention here of Caelestis, who elsewhere appears three times in fictitious or at least dubious contexts (Pert. 4. 2; Macr. 3. 1 ff.; Tyr. Trig. 29. 2)[46]. And some items could derive from Herodian: the theft of the Palladium (Elag. 3. 4; 6. 9), and the emperor's marriage to a Vestal virgin (Elag. 6. 5, cf. Herodian V. 6. 2). But the HA proffers several additional facts whose truth can be defended[47]. The temple of Elagabalus was built where that of Orcus formerly stood (Elag. 1. 6); the emperor had designs upon the sacred fire of Vesta and despoiled the cult of the Magna Mater (3. 4; 7. 1); among other grave delinquencies he entered and desecrated the *penus Vestae* (6. 7). Moreover, the HA appears to know the correct motive which underlay Elagabalus' innovations: he was attempting a fusion of all the traditional cults of the Greek and Roman world into a pantheon in which his God of Emesa would occupy the supreme place and others a subordinate rank (3. 4 f.; 7. 4). An ornamental capital found in the Roman forum ostensibly reflects this ideology[48], in conformity with which Elagabalus ordered his God to be named first in all public sacrifices (Herodian V. 5. 7). The author has sometimes added bogus details: for example, that Elagabalus frequently said that the worship of the Jews, Samaritans and Christians should also be transferred to Rome to participate in the grand syncretism (3. 5). But the extent of his reliable information on religious matters indicates his use of a source more detailed than Herodian.[49]

VI. CONJECTURAL ANALYSIS

Aelius Lampridius proclaims that he wrote the life of Elagabalus unwillingly and collected his material from both Greek and Latin

[46] JTS, N. S. XXI (1970), 96 ff.
[47] For detailed comment, below § VI.
[48] F. STUDNICZKA, Röm. Mitt. XVI (1901), 273 ff.
[49] Contrast T. OPTENDRENK, Die Religionspolitik des Kaisers Elagabal im Spiegel der H. A. (Diss. Bonn, 1968): the historical content of the vita is meagre (o. c. 103), its statements about Elagabalus' religious policy are either fiction or an elaboration of Herodian (o. c., esp. 21; 37). Not everyone will concede OPTENDRENK's basic assumption (derivative) that the HA is primarily a work of pagan propaganda, a 'Historia adversus Christianos' (o. c. 56; 104).

sources (Elag. 35. 1)[50]. However, since he adds that he did all this at the express command of Constantine, disbelief is both easy and entailed. To discover his real procedure a searching analysis will be necessary.

Disregarding brief or partial discussions[51], three full analyses of the Vita Elagabali have so far been published: by C. LÉCRIVAIN (1904)[52], by O. F. BUTLER (1910)[53], and by K. HÖNN (1911)[54]. All three exhibit fatal flaws. LÉCRIVAIN and HÖNN assimilated the Elagabalus too closely to the Alexander[55], the former even arguing that both vitae derived from the same source[56], while BUTLER postulated a multiplicity of both sources and authors, producing a schema of intolerable complication[57]. The analytical commentary which follows not only assumes but in part seeks to demonstrate two fundamental facts which these three scholars ignored. First, the manifold differences between the Elagabalus and the Alexander[58]. Second, despite his explicit claims, the author of the HA did not collate and compare a multitude of sources. As elsewhere when not romancing (e.g., in the lives of the emperors from Hadrian to Caracalla), he preferred for the most part to transcribe a single source, abridging, inserting, and appending additions in a manner which often verges on clumsiness[59].

---

[50] Accepted without question by H. PETER, Die Scriptores Historiae Agustae (1892), 121.

[51] I have not seen G. PASCIUCCO, Elagabalo. Contributo agli studi sugli S. H. A. (1905). BAYNES described it as a 'amateurish' (o. c. 12).

[52] C. LÉCRIVAIN, Études sur l'Histoire Auguste (1904), 201 ff.

[53] O. F. BUTLER, Studies in the Life of Heliogabalus. University of Michigan Studies, Humanistic Series IV (1910), 1 ff.

[54] K. HÖNN, Quellenuntersuchungen zu den Viten des Heliogabalus und des Severus Alexander im Corpus der S. H. A. (1911), 28 ff.

[55] LÉCRIVAIN, o. c. 235: ‹les deux vies d'Élagabal et d'Alexandre présentent la ressemblance la plus frappante qu'on puisse imaginer›; HÖNN, o. c. 33; 'die Art ihrer Komposition in vielem der Alexandervita gleicht'.

[56] LÉCRIVAIN, o. c. 208 ff.; 235 f.

[57] BUTLER first (and correctly) divided the vita into three sections: (a) dedication etc.: 1. 1—3; 2. 4; 34. 1—35. 7; (b) the history of the reign: 1. 4—2. 3; 3. 1—18. 3; (c) biographical section: 18. 4—33. 8 (o. c. 109). She then subdivided (b) into five parts: (1) 1. 4—2. 3: many sources; (2) 3. 1—4. 4: two sources, the KG and something of inferior worth; (3) 5. 1—12. 4: 'highly composite'; (4) 13. 1—17. 2: 'an extremely valuable bit of history'; (5) 17. 3—18. 3: composite, and serving as an appendix (o. c. 109; 149). She concluded that there were 'many indications of plurality of sources' and that it was 'impossible to think that the "Life" (i.e. her [b]) can be the work of any one author' (o. c. 149).

[58] Above, § II.

[59] For the early vitae, R. SYME, Emperors and Biography (1970), 30 ff. For the period 240—270 it may prove possible to demonstrate similar use of Dexippus, cf. F. ALTHEIM, Literatur und Gesellschaft im ausgehenden Altertum I (1948), 175 ff.

1. 1—3   Justification for writing the life of such an unworthy emperor. Ammianus put forward a similar plea when including a vignette of the worthy eunuch Eutherius: *Sed inter vepres rosae nascuntur, et inter feras non nullae mitescunt, itaque* ... (XVI. 7. 4). Clearly a commonplace; but the HA may have in mind a passage of Cicero (De natura deorum II. 99).

1. 4   Death of Macrinus and Diadumenianus: the latter took the name Antoninus (ILS 463 etc.) and, though at first a Caesar, was proclaimed joint emperor with his father at Apamea during the war against Elagabalus (Dio LXXIX [LXXVIII]. 34. 2; 37. 6). Herodian mentions Diadumenianus only as Caesar (V. 4. 12): the HA had earlier followed him though avowing that *plerique pari fuisse cum patris imperio tradiderunt* (Macr. 10. 4, cf. Eutropius, Brev. VIII. 21; Epit. de Caes. 22).

1. 5—7   The names of Elagabalus. Three points require emphasis or discussion. First, the temple of Elagabalus at Rome *in eo loco ..., in quo prius aedes Orci fuit,* which ought to be the famous Elagabalium on the Palatine close to the imperial palace (3. 4). No traces of a temple of Orcus have been discovered[60]; and if Elagabalus destroyed it totally, his temple may in its turn have been effaced by Severus Alexander's new temple of Juppiter Ultor (S. B. PLATNER-T. ASHBY, A Topographical Dictionary of Ancient Rome [1929], 307; 372). Second, Elagabalus was born Varius Avitus: he took the name Antoninus and passed himself off as a bastard son of Caracalla in order to seduce the troops of Macrinus (Dio LXXIX [LXXVIII]. 32. 1 ff.; Herodian V. 3. 11 ff.). Third, the stone which *e Suria secum advexit:* that is accurate and important (L. ROBERT, in collaboration with A. DUPONT-SOMMER, La déesse de Hiérapolis Castabala (Cilicie). Bibl. arch. et hist. de l'Inst. fr. d'arch. d'Istanbul XVI [1964], 80 f.).

2. 1   Elagabalus was devoted to his mother Julia Soaemias, who accompanied him everywhere: note, for instance, her presence at the decisive battle against Macrinus (Dio LXXIX [LXXVIII]. 38. 4). For *meretricio more vivens,* compare Dio's allegation of cohabitation with Gannys (LXXX [LXXIX]. 6. 2).

     The form *Symiamira* presents a puzzle: it was once conjectured that the HA originally wrote *Semiasura* and that

---

[60] H. J. ROSE conjectured *Hortae* for *Orci* (The Roman Questions of Plutarch (1924), 190).

this truthfully reflected contemporary slang (J. H. MORDT-
MANN, Zeitschr. der deutschen morgenländischen Gesellschaft XXXI [1877], 99)[61].

2. 2   Why Elagabalus was called Varius: one of the HA's phi-
logical fantasies.

2. 3   Elagabalus' retreat from the court to Emesa. The real
reason appears to be uncomplicated: his father died in 216
or early 217 and his mother returned with young Elagabalus to her home city (Dio LXXIX [LXXVIII]. 30. 2; ILS
478, cf. KLASS, P-W VIII A. 409 f.). Therefore, his flight
velut in asylum lest Macrinus murder him may derive
from Victor's *tamquam asylum insidiarum metu* (Caes.
23. 1)[62]. However, Victor has an error which the HA
avoids: '*in Solis sacerdotium ... confugerat*' (Caes. 23. 1).
Elagabalus was a hereditary priest (Herodian V. 3. 4; Epit.
de Caes. 23. 2)[63]. The HA more plausibly states *in templum
dei Heliogabali confugisse*.

2. 4   Address to Constantine.

3. 1—3 Dio confirms the letter (LXXX [LXXIX]. 2. 2), and Eutropius that Elagabalus came to Rome *ingenti militum e
senatus expectatione* (Brev. VIII. 22, repeated at Epit. de
Caes. 23. 3)[64].

The HA mentions the *ingens desiderium* for Caracalla
and the Antonine name also at Macr. 3. 9; Diad. 1. 5; 6. 10.
Perhaps from Victor on Diadumenianus: *eo quod ingens
amissi principis desiderium erat, adolescentem Antoni-
num vocavere* (Caes. 22. 2). But it could come direct from
Victor's ultimate source, i.e. Marius Maximus: the great
yearning was a historical fact (Dio LXXIX [LXXVIII].
32. 2) and the phrase *ingens desiderium* a natural expression (cf. Seneca, Ad Marciam 3. 1)[65].

3. 4/5   *sed ubi primum ingressus est urbem, omissis, quae in
provincia gerebantur, ...*
D. MAGIE translates 'as soon as he entered the city, however, neglecting all the affairs of the provinces, ...' (Loeb
Classical Library, The S. H. A. II [1924], 111). But elsewhere in the HA *omittere* never signifies 'neglect'. The
meaning of the words ought rather to be 'as soon as he

---

[61] Eutropius appears to have called her *Symiasera* (Brev. VIII. 22): for the
evidence, H. DROYSEN, Mon. Germ. Hist., Auct. Ant. II (1879), 148.
[62] *Asylum* is rare in Latin, cf. TLL. II. 990 f.
[63] A. VON DOMASZEWSKI, Abhandlungen zur römischen Religion (1909), 200.
[64] Note also the coin types: ROMA VICTRIX, FIDES PUBLICA, LAETI-
TIAE PUBLICAE, TEMPORUM FELICITAS, etc. (BMC, R. Emp. V. ccxxx f.).
[65] For further discussion, SYME, o. c. 85 ff.

entered the city—leaving out what was happening in the provinces—, . . .'. Is it fanciful to see in this sentence an instruction dictated by the author to a scribe to omit part of a source which he found too long for his purpose? There was no lack of material for Elagabalus' leisurely journey from Antioch to Rome: it lasted a full year and embraced a large number of plots and executions (Dio LXXX [LXXIX]. 3. 1 ff.). Four arguments in support of the hypothesis may be mustered. First, the HA's fatigue with lengthy stretches of fact is evident elsewhere (Hadr. 14. 7 f.; Sev. 17. 5). Second, on his own admittedly dubious assertion, the author employed dictation (Tyr. Trig. 33. 8). Third, the vita later goes back to the journey (5. 1). Fourth, the passage which immediately follows the clause under discussion, contains several clear doublets (3. 4^b ~ 6. 7 ff.) and a sentence of fiction (3. 5)[66].

4. 1/2   Cf. 12. 3; 15. 6 (Maesa); 18. 3 (prohibition on women entering the Senate). It is true that women had never taken part in meetings of the Senate before: so that Agrippina could listen to debates from behind a curtain, Nero convened the august body in the imperial palace (Tacitus, Ann. XIII. 5, cf. John of Antioch frag. 90 Müller). Dio records how Elagabalus adopted his cousin Alexander in the Senate, flanked by Julia Maesa and Julia Soaemias (LXXX [LXXIX]. 17. 2). Further, an ominous (though fragmentary) inscription was discovered in the curia (AE 1954. 28, cf. A. Bartoli, Atti della Pont. Acc. Rom. di Arch., Ser. III: Rendiconti XXVII [1951/52], 50 ff.)[67].

4. 3/4   Invention, and instructively to be compared with Jerome on the subject of women: J. Straub, Bonner Historia-Augusta-Colloquium 1964/65 (1966), 221 ff.

5. 1   Dio and Herodian confirm the winter at Nicomedia (Dio LXXX [LXXIX]. 6. 1; 7. 3; Herodian V. 5. 3), but Dio reports that Gannys tried to compel Elagabalus to live decently until he killed him for that very reason (LXXX [LXXIX]. 6. 3). The rest of this section presents a serious problem, since Alexander was created Caesar in June 221 (Dio LXXX [LXXIX]. 17. 2 ff.; Herodian V. 7. 1 ff.; CIL VI. 2001). The erroneous notion that the Senate saluted him Caesar immediately after the death of Macrinus in June 218 appears not only elsewhere in the HA (Macr. 4. 1;

---

[66] JRS LVIII (1968), 41 f.

[67] On the Severan ladies, H. W. Benario also adduced AE 1933. 281; 1956. 144 (Trans. Amer. Phil. Ass. XC [1959], 11 ff.). Illegitimately, cf. J. F. Gilliam, Class. Phil. LXVIII (1963), 26 ff.

Elag. 10. 1; Alex. 1. 2) but also in Victor (Caes. 23. 3). It might derive ultimately from Marius Maximus and be a deliberate, contemporary invention from the reign of Severus Alexander.

5. 2   Rhetorical question.

5. 3—12. 4   General account of Elagabalus in Rome.

5. 3   The *emissarii* existed, but Dio implies that they scoured the whole empire (LXXX [LXXIX]. 16. 2, cf. 13. 4).

5. 4   Dio has something almost identical (LXXX [LXXIX]. 13. 3 f.).

5. 5   According to Dio, the young emperor painted his eyes and had the hairs plucked out of his chin (LXXX [LXXIX]. 14. 4); Herodian has the painted eyes, rouge on his cheeks and cosmetics (V. 6. 10). The surviving busts show the normal face of a youth, at first hairless but later displaying adolescent whiskers (H. P. L'ORANGE, Symbolae Osloenses XX [1940], 152 ff.).

6. 1/2   For the charge of unworthy and outrageous appointments, cf. Dio LXXX (LXXIX). 4. 1 f. (Valerius Comazon); Herodian V. 7. 7. The HA's specific complaint that Elagabalus *in senatum legit sine discrimine aetatis, census, generis* can be illustrated from an anonymous career: *a studiis*, legionary legate, consul, *comes* and *amicus*, *praefectus annonae*, pretorian prefect (ILS 1329). Further, M. Aedinius Julianus seems to have proceded from being legate of Lugdunensis (in 220) to the prefecture of Egypt (CIL XIII. 3162; P. Flor. 382; P. Ox. 35)[68].

6. 3   Gordius taught Elagabalus to drive a chariot (Dio LXXX [LXXIX]. 15. 1)[69].

6. 4/5[a]   Hierocles can be adduced as a particular case of the generalisation (Dio LXXX [LXXIX]. 15. 1 f.), and Dio confirms Elagabalus' intense devotion to him (ib. 14. 1; 15. 1 ff.). The reference to the festival of the Floralia may be sheer invention (T. OPTENDRENK, Die Religionspolitik des Kaisers Elagabal im Spiegel der H.A. [Diss. Bonn, 1968], 25 ff.).

6. 5[b]   Elagabalus married the Vestal Virgin Aquilia Severa in 220 or 221 (Dio LXXX [LXXIX]. 9. 3): by Roman standards that was *incestum* and he wrote a letter to the Senate justifying his action (Herodian V. 6. 2, cf. Dio LXXX [LXXIX]. 9. 3 f.).

---

[68] H.-G. PFLAUM removed the anomaly by supposing that Julianus was in fact an imperial procurator acting as governor of Lugdunensis (Le marbre de Thorigny (1948), 35 ff.; Carrières procuratoriennes (1960/61), no. 257).

[69] See further above, § III.

6. 6   Explained in 6. 7 ff.
6. 7ᵃ   Elagabalus' desire to extinguish the *ignis perpetuus* of Vesta and to remove it to the Elagabalium (3. 4) are equivalent.
6. 7ᵇ   For the cult of the God Elagabalus outside Rome, ROBERT, o.c. 79 ff.
6. 7ᶜ   The parenthetical relative clause 'quod solae virgines solique pontifices adeunt' comes from the author of the HA and reveals a double misapprehension. As emperor, Elagabalus was naturally *pontifex maximus* (ILS 471 etc.)[70]. But no man (it seems) whatever—not even the *pontifex maximus*—was permitted to enter the *penus Vestae* (Ovid, Fasti IV. 450 f.; Lucan, Phars. I. 597 f.; IX. 993 f.; Plutarch, Camillus 20. 5; Lactantius, Div. Inst. III. 20. 4). In fairness to the HA, however, observe that Dionysius of Halicarnassus was of the same opinion: εἰσὶ δέ τινες οἵ φασιν ἔξω τοῦ πυρὸς ἀπόρρητα τοῖς πολλοῖς ἱερὰ κεῖσθαί τινα ἐν τῷ τεμένει τῆς θεᾶς, ὧν οἵ τε ἱεροφάνται τὴν γνῶσιν ἔχουσι καὶ αἱ πάρθενοι (Ant. Rom. II. 66. 3).
6. 8/9   Elagabalus removed the Palladium from the *penus Vestae* to the temple of his God on the Palatine (not to his own bedchamber as Herodian V. 6. 3 alleges). There it apparently remained in the fourth century when a *praepositus Palladii Palatini* is attested (ILS 1250), and gave the area its medieval name (R. VALENTINI-G. ZUCCHETTI, Codice topografico della città di Roma II [1942], 337 n. 2)[71].

            For the two earthenware jars, see Plutarch, Camillus 20. 6[72]. The HA appears to confuse these with the *ancilia*, of which there were many (cf. 3. 4).
7. 1/2   The verb *tauroboliari* is first attested c. 370 (AE 1945. 55)[73], but that need not prove that Elagabalus did not undergo all the rites of the Magna Mater, among them the taurobolium, or remove the *typus*, i.e. the famous black stone of Pessinus which arrived in Rome in 204 B.C.[74]. The

---

[70] W. HARTKE deduced that the HA must be writing some years after Gratian became the first emperor to renounce the title (Römische Kinderkaiser [1951], 300). The claim is hotly contested by A. CAMERON, JRS LVIII (1968), 100.

[71] Adduced by A. DEGRASSI, Scritti vari di antichità (1962), 457 f. OPTENDRENK, o. c. 14 ff., nowhere cites this important study 'Esistette sul Palatino un tempio di Vesta?', first published in Röm. Mitt. LXII (1955), 144 ff. For other modern discussions relevant to Elag. 6. 6 ff.; 7. 5 ff., see now T. PEKÁRY, Bonner Historia-Augusta-Colloquium 1968/69 (1970), 166 ff.

[72] Cf. further S. WEINSTOCK, P-W XIX. 442; 445.

[73] R. DUTHOY, The Taurobolium. Its Evolution and Terminology (1969), 85, lists its occurrences in inscriptions.

[74] G. WISSOWA, Religion und Kultus der Römer² (1912), 17 ff.

association with the Galli recurs in the Epitome de Caesaribus: *abscisisque genitalibus Matri se Magnae sacravit* (23. 3). Dio alleges circumcision, desire for castration and the wearing of the barbaric dress of Syrian priests (LXXX [LXXIX]. 11. 1 f.).

7. 3 Impossible to evaluate.

7. 4 In the HA the word *sane* must arouse suspicion (see the passages quoted by C. LESSING, S. H. A. Lexicon [1906], 575). Yet the motivation stated for Elagabalus' religious activities is both plausible and accurate[75].

7. 5 The *lapides qui divi dicuntur* are betyls like Elagabalus' own sacred stone from Emesa, and appear on the coins of various cities of the eastern empire (F. STUDNICZKA, Röm. Mitt. XVI [1901], 277; K. LATTE, P-W III A. 2302 ff.). For the Statue of Diana at Laodicea, cf. Pausanias III. 16. 8.

7. 6—10 Two excursus: Orestes' scattering of statues of Diana and his founding a city in Thrace (7. 6/7) and its refoundation by Hadrian (7. 8—10). The first seems to allude to the battle of Adrianople in 378 when the Goths defeated and killed the emperor Valens. The second (it would appear) misdates the refoundation. Hadrian's madness belongs to the last years of his life in Italy (134—138), his orders to kill senators to his very last months (cf. Hadr. 24. 4; 24. 9; 25. 8; Pius 2. 4): reconstituting the city was probably begun by Trajan (A. H. M. JONES, Cities of the Eastern Roman Provinces [1937], 380).

8. 1/2 The story of human sacrifices, if not true, was at least contemporary (Dio LXXX [LXXIX]. 11). Similar aspersions were cast on Didius Julianus (Dio LXXIV [LXXIII]. 16. 5—not in Herodian or the HA).

8. 3 Compare Herodian on Elagabalus' distribution of largesse at the summer festival of his God: ἐρρίπτει τοῖς ὄχλοις, ἁρπάζειν πᾶσιν ἐπιτρέπων, ἐκπώματά τε χρυσᾶ καὶ ἀργυρᾶ ἐσθῆτάς τε καὶ ὀθόνας παντοδαπάς, ζῷά τε πάντα, ὅσα ἥμερα, πλὴν χοίρων (V. 6. 9).

8. 4/5 In letters to the Senate, which Dio quotes, Elagabalus accused Macrinus of murdering Caracalla (LXXX [LXXIX]. 1. 2 ff.).

8. 6/7 On Elagabalus interest in large genitals, cf. 5. 3.

9. 1—3 Archaeological evidence (it has recently transpired) indicates German incursions on the frontier of Germania Superior c. 220 (T. BECHERT, Epigraphische Studien VIII

[75] Above, § V.

[1969], 53 ff.). And Domitius Antigonus, legate of the legion XXII Primigenia, dedicated an altar at Moguntiacum *pro salute et incolumitate d.n. imp. [Antonini] Aug. totiusq(ue) domus divinae eius* (AE 1965. 242 = [better] 1966. 262)[76]. But the Marcomanni menaced the Danube rather than the Rhine frontier. However, an inscription from Rome could be directly relevant: between June 221 and March 222 several officers in the tenth pretorian cohort *quod proficiscentes expeditionibus sacris voverant, regressi ... votum solverunt* (ILS 474).

10. 1   The ms. text is either corrupt or lacunose: *in Alexandrum omnes inclinantes, qui iam Caesar erat a senatu eo tempore † quo Macrinus † huius Antonini* ... HOHL follows SALMASIUS in simply emending *quo Macrinus* to *consobrinus*. The corruption may be deeper. F. RÜHL adduced Macr. 4. 1; Elag. 5. 1; Alex. 1. 2 and conjectured *qui iam Caesar erat ⟨appellatus⟩ a senatu eo tempore, quo Macrinus ⟨interemptus est, consobrinus⟩* etc. (Rhein. Mus. LXII [1907], 2). The grandmother of both Elagabalus and Alexander was Julia Maesa.

10. 2—5   Contrast Dio LXXX (LXXIX). 16. 1 ff.

10. 6/7   Neither Dio nor Herodian has anything precisely analogous.

11. 1   Herodian also reports that slaves and freedman became provincial governors (V. 7. 7).

11. 2—7   None of this can be verified. But it could be mainly contemporary slander, and there is no valid reason to disbelieve that *horum pleraque Marius Maximus dicit in vita ipsius Heliogabali* (11. 6).

12. 1   The dancer who became pretorian prefect (also anonymous in Herodian V. 7. 6) was Valerius Comazon (Dio LXXX [LXXIX]. 4. 1 f.); Gordius is elsewhere attested (and alluded to by Herodian V. 7. 7); Claudius is not (PIR² C 759). A lacuna may perhaps be suspected in the text. HOHL prints *Claudium tonsorem* where the mss. offer *Claudium censorem*. Herodian talks of some sort of censor: πάλιν δὲ ἕτερον ὁμοίως ἐκ τῆς σκηνῆς βαστάσας, παιδείας τῶν νέων καὶ εὐκοσμίας τῆς τε ὑποστάσεως τῶν ἐς τὴν σύγκλητον βουλὴν ἢ τὸ ἱππικὸν τάγμα κατατασσομένων προέστησεν (V. 7. 7).

12. 2   For the general charge, cf. 6. 1/2; 11. 1. The persons alluded to cannot be identified.

---

[76] On Antigonus' career, see further, G. ALFÖLDY, Bonner Jahrbücher CLXV (1965), 187 ff.; K. WACHTEL, Historia XV (1966), 243 ff.

12. 3   For Maesa und Soaemias in the Senate, cf. 4. 1.

12. 4   Confirmed by Dio, at least for the banquet which Elaga-
         balus gave to welcome Zoticus (LXXX [LXXIX]. 16. 5).

13. 1—17. 7 Attempts on Alexander's life and the murder of Elaga-
         balus. Detailed comment will not be needed to indicate
         the excellence of these chapters: the reader may be re-
         ferred to the successive studies of O. F. BUTLER, Studies
         in the Life of Elagabalus (1910), 140 ff.; K. HÖNN, Quellen-
         untersuchungen (1911), 28 ff.; A. JARDÉ, Études critiques
         sur la vie et le règne de Sévère Alexandre (1925), 9 ff.; R.
         SYME, Emperors and Biography (1971), 118 ff. In brief, the
         HA is demonstrably superior to the parallel accounts in
         Herodian (V. 8. 1 ff.) and Dio, admittedly preserved only
         in epitome (LXXX [LXXIX]. 19. 1 ff.).

13. 1   Elagabalus adopted Alexander in June 221 (CIL VI. 2001)
         and he received the title of *nobilissimus Caesar imperii
         et sacerdotis* (AE 1964. 269, cf. S. DUŠANIĆ, Historia XIII
         [1964], 487 ff.).

14. 8   The names are defended as authentic by E. BIRLEY, Bonner
         Historia-Augusta-Colloquium 1966/67 (1968), 47 ff.

15. 7   This section completes the episode begun in 15. 5: Elaga-
         balus refused to parade with his consular colleague
         Alexander on 1 January 222, Julia Maesa and Julia Soae-
         mias prevailed on him to enter the Senate, but two days
         later he refused to ascend the Capitol for the customary
         ceremony of *vota concipienda*. No reason therefore to
         imagine a covert allusion to Constantine (as A. CHASTA-
         GNOL, Historia-Augusta-Colloquium Bonn 1963 [1964],
         59; 64).

16. 1—4 For a defence, cf. R. SYME, Bonner Historia-Augusta-Col-
         loquium 1968/69 (1970), 320.

17. 1—7 Compare the practically identical description in the Epi-
         tome (23. 5 ff.).

         To elucidate the words *Tiberinus* and *Tractaticius*, J.
         GAGÉ adduced CIL VI. 1080 (Mélanges J. Carcopino [1966],
         403 ff.). Its style appears to brand it as a Renaissance
         forgery, cf. J. LE GALL, Le Tibre fleuve de Rome dans
         l'antiquité (1953), 269. Nonetheless, there could be some
         allusion to the lupus Tiberinus which frequented the
         impure waters *inter duos pontes* where the Cloaca Ma-
         xima disgorged into the Tiber (D'A. W. THOMPSON, A
         Glossary of Greek Fishes [1947], 141 f.).

17. 8/9   Three buildings are in question:
1. The Elagabalium on the Palatine *iuxta aedes impera-torias* (3. 4): PLATNER-ASHBY, o. c. 199; G. LUGLI, Roma antica (1946), 443 f.; 526 f.
2. The Colosseum, struck by lightning on 23 August 217 (Dio LXXIX [LXXVIII]. 25. 2), whose restoration was completed in 223 (BMC, R. Emp. VI. 54; 128 f.).
3. The Baths of Caracalla, *in vico Sulpicio*: PLATNER-ASHBY, o. c. 520 ff.; 578 f. The HA elsewhere chronicles both their original construction (Carac. 9. 4 f.; 9. 9) and Alexander's final completion (Alex. 25. 6).

18. 1—3   Epilogue: the end of the Antonine dynasty, author's apology for defiling the sacred name, death of Elagabalus' mother and dire penalties instituted for allowing women into the Senate. The emperor's name was in fact assiduously erased from public records everywhere[77].

18. 4—33. 8 Elagabalus' luxury
    The author knew (or else correctly surmised) that even contemporary authors, writing in the reign of Severus Alexander, had perpetrated deliberate inventions and slanders (30. 8). He consciously renounces pornography, cataloguing only those facts *quae ad luxuriam pertine-bant*: for Elagabalus himself professed to imitate Apicius, Nero, Otho and Vitellius (18. 4). The result is a long series of scholiastic jokes, grammarian's fantasies and a rich harvest for culinary lexicographers. There may (who can prove or disprove?) be some genuine items deriving from Marius Maximus. But the bulk of this long section reflects the HA's own age and interests. Note, for example, the use made of Suetonius:
    24. 4, cf. Vitellius 13. 1 ff.
    31. 5 < Nero 30. 3
    32. 9 < Caligula 11; Nero 26. 1 f.
    33. 1 < Tiberius 43. 1; Caligula 16. 1.
That is not a complete list of derivations. More significant, a long stretch of fiction in an earlier vita employs some of the very same passages in a similar fashion (Verus 4. 4 ff.)[78].

34. 1—35. 7 Address to Constantine, which includes an error about the Gordians (viz. that they numbered two, not three) which derives from the lost Kaisergeschichte (34. 6, cf. Victor, Caes. 26. 1 ff.; Eutropius, Brev. IX. 2. 1 f.).

---

[77] For the detail, G. FORNI, Archivio storico lodigiano² VII (1959), 13.
[78] JRS LVII (1967), 69.

VII. CONCLUSIONS

The problem posed at the outset was to segregate fact from fiction in the Elagabalus and to investigate the composition of the HA (§ I). The vita stands out from its context, in more ways than one (§ II): hence derivation from a contemporary or neary contemporary source was inferred (§ III), which both diverged from Cassius Dio (§ IV) and improved on Herodian (§ V). Next, the general accuracy of the first part of the Elagabalus (1. 4—18. 3) was illustrated by an analytical commentary (§ VI). By elimination, therefore, the source can be identified as Marius Maximus whom the author names once (Elag. 11. 6).

In itself, the hypothesis is not new. Both J. J. MÜLLER in 1870 and C. LÉCRIVAIN in 1904 came to the same conclusion. But the former assumed that Marius Maximus was the HA's main source for all the vitae as far as the Elagabalus, while the latter asserted that Marius Maximus was the source of both the Elagabalus and the Alexander[79]. In fact, for the 'main lives' from Hadrian to Caracalla another source must be postulated: to be styled, according to taste, 'an anonymous continuator of Suetonius' or more bluntly 'Ignotus'[80]. And the main source of the Alexander was the lost Kaisergeschichte[81]. In its correct form, however, the hypothesis here advocated will illuminate the HA's methods of working and open up fresh avenues for exploration. First, it will explain the shoddy quality of the Macrinus and its contrast to the Caracalla and Elagabalus. Second, the 'secondary lives' of princes and pretenders were written (it seems) after the Alexander—and therefore after the author had begun to employ Marius Maximus[82]. It follows that parts of them may carry authentic information from Maximus which does not appear in the 'main lives': for example, two citations of the autobiography of Septimius Severus (Pesc. Nig. 4. 7; Clod. Alb. 7. 1)[83]. Third, the sources of the Epitome de Caesaribus. For the emperors between Nerva and Elagabalus the witer may have used Marius Maximus directly: a passage of the Elagabalus is relevant (17. 1 f. ~ Epit. de Caes. 23. 5 ff.). Finally, the theme of the

---

[79] J. J. MÜLLER, Büdingers Untersuchungen zur römischen Kaisergeschichte III (1870), 111 ff.; C. LÉCRIVAIN, Études sur l'Histoire Auguste (1904), 208 ff.; 235 ff.

[80] LÉCRIVAIN, o. c. 191 f.; SYME, o. c. 30 ff.

[81] Bonner Historia-Augusta-Colloquium 1968/69 (1970), 30 ff.

[82] Ib. 31 f.; 35 f. For proof that the 'secondary lives' were written as a group and after those of the 'main series', R. SYME, Emperors and Biography (1970), 54 ff.

[83] MOMMSEN opined that all the material in these vitae was either drawn from the 'main lives' or invented (Ges. Schr. VII [1909], 319). He was incautiously followed by several scholars: e.g. T. D. BARNES, JRS LVII (1967), 65.

nomen Antoninorum: taken up and developed by the HA, it may originally have been the major theme of the imperial biographies of Marius Maximus[84].

VIII. ELAGABALUS' FAMILY AND MARRIAGES

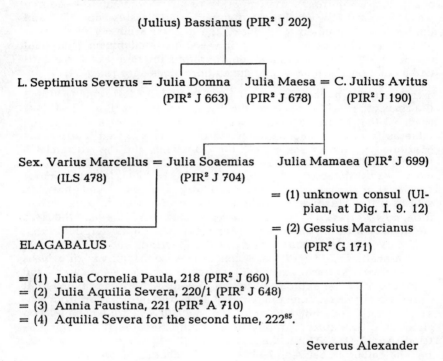

(Julius) Bassianus (PIR² J 202)

L. Septimius Severus = Julia Domna
(PIR² J 663)

Julia Maesa = C. Julius Avitus
(PIR² J 678)   (PIR² J 190)

Sex. Varius Marcellus = Julia Soaemias
(ILS 478)   (PIR² J 704)

Julia Mamaea (PIR² J 699)

= (1) unknown consul (Ulpian, at Dig. I. 9. 12)

= (2) Gessius Marcianus
(PIR² G 171)

ELAGABALUS

= (1) Julia Cornelia Paula, 218 (PIR² J 660)
= (2) Julia Aquilia Severa, 220/1 (PIR² J 648)
= (3) Annia Faustina, 221 (PIR² A 710)
= (4) Aquilia Severa for the second time, 222[85].

Severus Alexander

---

[84] On which, see now SYME, o. c. 85 ff.; 113 ff.
[85] For the chronology, J. VOGT, Die alexandrinischen Münzen I (1924), 176 f.; P. LEDERER, Num. Chr.⁶ III (1943), 94 ff.

VI

LACTANTIUS AND CONSTANTINE*

Flavius Valerius Constantius, the senior reigning emperor since Diocletian and Maximian had abdicated on 1 May 305, died at Eburacum on 25 July 306. At once his entourage and army proclaimed Augustus the son who stood beside his death-bed, and invested him with the purple. Constantine, however, with a subtlety beyond his years, contented himself with obtaining recognition as a Caesar from Galerius, who now, as the senior emperor, possessed the right of appointing new imperial colleagues. Constantine's modesty or foresight was soon repaid. On 28 October 306 the praetorian guard and people of Rome raised to power Maxentius, the son of Maximian. Severus, Augustus in the west since Constantius' death, marched on Rome to suppress the insurrection, but was forced to retreat by the desertion of his troops, besieged in Ravenna and inveigled into surrender by Maximian, who had emerged from retirement to aid his son.[1]

Such was the opening campaign (late winter or spring 307) in a series of civil wars during which Constantine became, by the end of 324, the sole ruler of a re-united Roman Empire. Hence a familiar historiographical problem, aggravated by a paucity of evidence for the nearly two decades which intervene between Constantine's first proclamation as emperor and his final victory. After this success, few who had witnessed what went before would wish or dare to publish an impartial narration. Stereotyped history better answered the needs and desires of contemporaries: the virtuous emperor triumphed over his wicked adversaries, he made war on his rivals in order to rescue their subjects from savage misrule.[2] Who could dispute or ask for further explanation? There was, moreover, an ideological issue which tended to dissuade later historians from rejecting this comfortable interpretation. Constantine viewed himself as God's champion, victorious by God's grace:[3] therefore, his enemies were also the foes of God. At least one contemporary historian duly responded by rewriting his work to remove inconvenient facts. When Licinius was an ally of Constantine, he was a paragon of virtue and piety. But when he turned against Constantine and his divine protector, his good deeds were excised from the historical record and he became a monster of depravity and lust.[4]

When truth has been distorted or concealed in this fashion, especially close attention must be paid to the genuinely contemporary evidence for the rise of Constantine. Official documents of all kinds (most notably coins,[5] inscriptions, calendars, and imperial laws and letters) have afforded invaluable aid in dispelling the cloud of uncertainty and falsehood. But to understand the moods and emotions of the

---

*The modern bibliography on Constantine is vast: for the literature before 1930, see N. H. Baynes, *Constantine the Great and the Christian Church* (1931), 30 ff. (the whole monograph is reprinted from *Proc. Brit. Acad.* xv (1929), 341 ff.); for subsequent work, see the surveys of A. Piganiol, *Historia* i (1950), 82 ff.; K. F. Stroheker, *Saeculum* iii (1952), 654 ff.; J. Vogt, *Mullus. Festschrift für T. Klauser* (1964), 364 ff.; A. Alföldi, *The Conversion of Constantine and Pagan Rome*[2] (1969), viii ff.; H. Chadwick's preface to the second edition of Baynes, o.c. (1972). No need, therefore, to encumber the following footnotes with excessive references to studies there catalogued and discussed.

I am grateful to Glen Bowersock, Leonard Boyle, Christopher Jones and Fergus Millar for their advice and help in improving an earlier, even more imperfect version of the present argument.

[1] Lactantius, *Mort. Pers.* 24, 8 ff., with evidence from other sources collected in the excellent commentary of J. Moreau, *Lactance De la Mort des Persécuteurs.* Sources chrétiennes xxxix (1954), 341 ff.
[2] Thus the pagan Praxagoras of Athens, according

to the summary of Photius, *Bibl.* lxii = *FGrH* 219 T 1. He was writing before 330, cf. F. Jacoby, *FGrH* ii D (1930), 632.

[3] As he is known to have stated himself as early as 314: 'ex quibus forsitan commoveri possit summa divinitas . . . etiam in me ipsum, cuius curae nutu suo caelesti terrena omnia moderanda commisit' (Optatus, App. III: *CSEL* xxvi, 206, 16-18); 'deus omnipotens in caeli specula residens tribuit, quod non merebar: certe iam neque dici neque enumerari possunt ea quae caelesti sua in me famulum suum benivolentia concessit' (Optatus, App. V: *CSEL* xxvi, 208, 28-31).

[4] Eusebius, *HE* x, 8, 11 ff., cf. ix, 11, 8. For the main manuscript variants, see E. Schwartz, *GCS* ix, 3 (1909), xlvii ff.

[5] Now collected in two scholarly and critical catalogues: C. H. V. Sutherland, *RIC* vi: *From Diocletian's Reform (A.D. 294) to the death of Maximinus (A.D. 313)* (1967); P. Bruun, *RIC* vii: *Constantine and Licinius A.D. 313-337* (1966). Too much modern scholarship has relied on erroneous dates and attributions, or sometimes even unverified types, in J. Maurice, *Numismatique constantinienne* i (1908); ii (1911); iii (1912).

30

time, and even to establish a reliable factual narrative, the more articulate testimony of the contemporary literary productions still extant is needed: principally five panegyrics delivered before Constantine (in the years 307, 310, 311, 313, 321),[6] and the subject of the present investigation. If Lactantius' *De Mortibus Persecutorum* can be dated accurately and precisely, it will serve as irrefragable evidence of attitudes voiced in a particular historical context, and perhaps also of facts later suppressed or embellished.

I. THE WORK

The *De Mortibus Persecutorum* addresses itself to the confessor Donatus, who had been tried and tortured nine times by three magistrates (the praetorian prefect Flaccinus, and Sossianus Hierocles and Priscillianus, successive governors of Bithynia),[7] and who had subsequently languished in prison in Nicomedia until the dying Galerius decreed an amnesty for all Christians (1, 1; 16, 3 ff.; 35, 2; 52, 5). The opening words appear to proclaim clearly the occasion of writing: God has heard Donatus' incessant prayers, the enemies are destroyed, a tranquil peace has returned to the world, the church so lately almost ruined is rising again. For God has raised up emperors to annul the wicked and cruel ordinances of the tyrants, and he has dried the tears of those who sorrowed by destroying the plots of the impious. Those who attacked God lie dead, and Lactantius proposes to relate the manner of their deaths, that both those who were afar off and future generations may know how God displayed his virtue and majesty in utterly destroying his foes (1, 1 ff.).

After a brief survey of the fate of earlier persecutors of the Christians (Nero, Domitian, Decius, Valerian and Aurelian: 2, 4–6, 3), Lactantius launches into a savage and detailed description of the persons, families and actions of Diocletian, Maximian and Galerius, with an account of the beginning of the persecution, of the abdication of Diocletian (1 May 305) and the nomination of two new Caesars, Severus and Maximinus Daia (7, 1 ff.).[8] There follows an equally severe and detailed account of Galerius' actions as Augustus (20, 1 ff.), which leads into the proclamation of Constantine as his father's successor—whose first action (so it is stated) was to restore to the Christians full freedom of worship (24, 9). From here Lactantius follows the tangled political events of the next four years:[9] Galerius' recognition of Constantine as Caesar, the proclamation of Maxentius, the death of Severus, Galerius' failure to reassert his authority in Italy, Maximian's attempt to dethrone Maxentius, the conference of Carnuntum at which Licinius was named Augustus, Maximian's final flight to Constantine and his subsequent death (25, 1 ff.).

Maximian was the first of the persecutors to die (30, 6). At once God turned his eyes to the other Maximian (i.e. Galerius), the instigator of persecution, who was already thinking about his *vicennalia* and extorting funds for their celebration (31, 1 ff.) In the course of his eighteenth year (310/11),[10] God struck him with an incurable disease (33, 1). Neither doctors nor Apollo and Asclepius could effect any improvement, and Galerius wasted away in great agony (33, 2 ff.). After a whole year, chastened by his misfortune, he was compelled to acknowledge God and proclaimed his intention of making restitution for his crimes (33, 11). Finally, as he was dying, he issued an edict (which Lactantius quotes) allowing his subjects once more to be Christians and build meeting-places, and requesting Christians to pray for himself and

[6] Respectively *Pan.Lat.* vii (vi); vi (vii); v (viii); xii (ix); iv (x). The best treatment of these speeches as a group remains that of R. Pichon, *Les derniers écrivains profanes* (1906), 36 ff.

[7] Flaccinus and Priscillianus seem to be otherwise unknown. Hierocles produced an anti-Christian polemic (Lactantius, *Div. Inst.* v, 2, 12 ff.; Eusebius, *Contra Hieroclem*) and later became prefect of Egypt (on his career, see *PLRE* i, 432).

[8] On the details, see Moreau, o.c. 231 ff. Lactantius' accuracy on specific facts has often had to

await very recent discoveries for decisive confirmation: e.g., that Diocletian's *dies imperii* was 20 November (17, 1, cf. *P. Beatty Panop.* 2, 162, etc.).

[9] For a significant omission, see p. 42.

[10] Galerius proposed to celebrate his *vicennalia* from 1 March 312 (*Mort. Pers.* 35, 4): therefore, his official *dies imperii* was 1 March 293. For the hypothesis that his actual investiture as Caesar occurred on 21 May 293, see W. Seston, *Dioclétien et la Tétrarchie* i (1946), 91 ff.

the state (34).[11] This edict was posted in Nicomedia on 30 April 311 (35, 1): the prisons were opened, but soon came news of Galerius' death (35, 4).

As soon as he heard, Maximinus occupied Asia Minor, made a treaty with Licinius on board ship in the straits between Europe and Asia, and proceeded to enforce in Asia Minor the policies he pursued in Syria and Egypt. Although Galerius had issued his edict of toleration in the name of all the emperors, Maximinus abolished it, ostensibly in response to petitions from his pagan subjects.[12] He instituted chief priests in every city, to sacrifice daily, to prevent Christians from either building or even meeting and to help in compelling them to sacrifice.[13] Further, he pretended to be merciful. Christians were not killed in the diocese of Oriens, only maimed: their eyes were put out, hands amputated, feet lopped off, and their ears or noses mutilated (36). Maximinus was preparing to institute the same régime in his new dominions, when he was deterred by a letter of Constantine (37, 1, cf. 36, 6). He therefore resorted to dissimulation, secretly drowning any Christian who fell into his hands (37, 1), and practising a wide variety of types of extortion and corruption on his subjects (37, 3 ff.).

With the death of Diocletian (42, 3), Maximinus was the only one of the foes of God left alive (43, 1). He entered into alliance with Maxentius, who was already at war with Constantine (43, 1 ff.). Soon Constantine defeated Maxentius, entered Rome in triumph and gave his sister in marriage to Licinius at Milan (44, 1 ff.). Maximinus attempted to surprise Licinius by an unexpected invasion of Europe but was defeated near Adrianople (45, 2 ff.).[14] Licinius, who had defeated him with God's aid (46, 3 ff.), advanced to Nicomedia, where on 13 June, in gratitude to God, he published a letter which he had sent to the governor of Bithynia: it gave everyone, including Christians, the right to follow whatever religion he pleased and restored to the Christians any property which had been seized from them (48, 1 ff.).[15] Licinius also, in a speech, encouraged churches to be restored, thus ending persecution after ten years and about four months (48, 13). He then pursued Maximinus, who killed himself at Tarsus when Licinius' army broke through the Cilician Gates (49, 1 ff.).

Three chapters of epilogue conclude the work. First, Licinius' execution of the sons of Galerius and Severus and the son and daughter of Maximinus, together with the suicide of Maximinus' widow (50). Then the capture of Galerius' wife Valeria after fifteen months, and her execution with her mother (51).[16] Finally, a claim to accuracy and a paean of gratitude to God for protecting his flock or people and extirpating the 'evil beasts', closing with a prayer that he guard his flourishing church in perpetual peace (52).

Lactantius was clearly writing in the immediate aftermath, or at least under the immediate impact, of persecution: 'nunc post atrae tempestatis violentos turbines placidus aer et optata lux refulsit' (1, 4). The publication of the *De Mortibus Persecutorum* should therefore follow very close on the death of Maximinus, the last of the persecutors, who perished in the summer of 313.[17] But a difficulty obtrudes. Lactantius includes later events. The chapters appended to the main narrative (50 f.) include not only the executions of Candidianus, the son of Galerius, in Nicomedia (perhaps as early as June 313), of the son of Severus, and of the family of Maximinus (in Antioch, therefore autumn 313), but also that of the widow and daughter of Diocletian, the latter after fifteen months of flight, i.e. no earlier than July or August

---

[11] Also reproduced, in Greek translation, by Eusebius, *HE* viii, 17, 3 ff.

[12] For these petitions, cf. *OGIS* 569; Eusebius, *HE* ix, 2, 1; 7, 12; 9 a, 4 ff.

[13] For the epigraphic attestation of one such priest, H. Grégoire, *Byzantion* viii (1933), 49 ff.

[14] On the site of the battle, see H. Grégoire, *Byzantion* xiii (1938), 585 f. Grégoire proposed to emend the 'campus Serenus' to 'Campus Ergenus' (*Mort. Pers.* 46, 9). Perhaps unnecessary, cf. P. Franchi de' Cavalieri, *Constantiniana. Studi e Testi* clxxi (1953), 78 f.

[15] Eusebius preserves substantially the same document with a different preamble (*HE* x, 5, 1 ff.).

[16] i.e. Prisca, the wife of Diocletian (*Mort. Pers.* 15, 1).

[17] The precise date would be worth knowing (*PLRE* i, 579, offers no opinion). It is usually held to be late summer, probably September (C. H. V. Sutherland, *RIC* vi, 35; P. Bruun, *RIC* vii, 76). But news of Maximinus' death had reached Karanis before 13 September 313 (*SB* 7675 = *P. Cair. Isid.* 103).

VI

32

314 (51, 1, cf. 50, 3).[18] What is the explanation? Can Lactantius have added these episodes, or at least the last of them, some months after the work was otherwise complete? Although the argument cannot rise above the purely subjective, at least some readers of Lactantius think they perceive a slight incoherence in these chapters indicative of addition or rewriting by the author.[19] For most practical purposes, however, it will make little difference whether Lactantius added to an already finished draft, began the work in 313 and only completed it during or after the autumn of the following year, or wrote the whole tract together (before or during winter 314/5).

If the text of the *De Mortibus Persecutorum* makes an early date (at latest 314/5) seem appropriate, why has a significantly later one (*c.* 318) so often been preferred? It was a necessary consequence of two erroneous dates: 3 December 316 for the death of Diocletian (42, 3), and 8 October 314 for the opening battle of the first war between Constantine and Licinius.

II. THE DEATH OF DIOCLETIAN

The ancient sources (it is commonly asserted) offer two dates for the death of Diocletian: 313 and 316.[20] Modern scholars have naturally not been unanimous in choosing either of the two, but the weightier names appear to prefer the later date.[21] And there is a further complication not always clearly perceived: the earliest and best evidence may indicate, not 313 rather than 316, but an even earlier date.

At first sight, the evidence adduced in favour of 316 is abundant and impressive. Closer inspection, however, should counsel strong doubts.[22] Much of the evidence can be discounted. First, John of Antioch as quoted, or rather abbreviated, in the excerpts copied out by Salmasius in the seventeenth century.[23] The twelve years, which John is alleged to give as the length of Diocletian's retirement, appear to result from a confusion with the length of the First Tetrarchy (293-305).[24] John is, therefore, irrelevant, and it is to be suspected that two later writers who state that Diocletian lived for twelve years as a private citizen are guilty of the same confusion.[25] Second, Zosimus, who specifies the date of Diocletian's death after a lengthy digression appended to his abdication:

Διοκλητιανὸς μὲν τελευτᾷ τρισὶν ἐνιαυτοῖς ὕστερον, ἤδη δὲ καταστάντες αὐτοκρά- τορες Κωνστάντιος καὶ Μαξιμιανὸς ὁ Γαλέριος ἀνέδειξαν Καίσαρας Σεβῆρον καὶ Μαξιμῖνον . . . (ii, 8, 1).

Three years later than the last date mentioned in the digression (the third consulate of Constantine and Licinius in 313) brings one to 316. But there are two difficulties. Zosimus has been employing inclusive reckoning.[26] Moreover, he should surely calculate from the point from which the digression started and to which the following clause returns: that is, the abdication of Diocletian and the proclamation of Severus

[18] That is, reckoning something over fourteen months from Licinius' entry into Nicomedia, a few days after 30 April 313 (*Mort. Pers.* 47, 5 ff.). The argument perforce operates on the assumption (inevitable though not provable) that the ms. 'quindecim' is what Lactantius wrote. Disproof would not surprise the present writer.

[19] K. Roller, *Die Kaisergeschichte in Laktanz 'de mortibus persecutorum'* (Diss. Giessen, 1927), 18 ff.; A. Alföldi, *The Conversion of Constantine and Pagan Rome* (1948), 45.

[20] 'Sur la date de la mort de Dioclétien il y a deux traditions: 316, que suit Zosime (cf. la corr. de Heyne) . . ., et 313, fondée sur Lact., *Mort.* 42, 3 . . .' (F. Paschoud, *Zosime* i (Budé, 1971), 192 f.) More erroneous still, 'his death is dated 313 by Lact., *Mort. Pers.* 42, 3' (R. T. Ridley, *Byz. Zeitschr.* lxv (1972), 288).

[21] E. Schwartz, *Nachr. Göttingen,* Phil.-hist. Kl. 1904, 536; O. Seeck, *Regesten der Kaiser und Päpste*

für die Jahre 311 bis 476 n. Chr. (1919), 165; W. Ensslin, P-W vii A, 2493; E. Stein, *Histoire du Bas-Empire* i² (1958), 93. Also, recently, *PLRE* i, 254.

[22] J. Moreau, *Lactance* (1954), 421 ff.

[23] J. A. Cramer, *Anecdota Graeca e codd. manuscriptis Bibliothecae Regiae Parisiensis* ii (1839), 398, whence John of Antioch, frag. 167, 2 (*FHG* iv, 602).

[24] Frag. 167, 2: Διοκλητιανὸς καὶ Μαξιμιανὸς . . . τὴν βασιλείαν κατέθεντο. καὶ Διοκλητιανὸς μὲν δώδεκα ἔτη πρωτεύσας ἀπέθανε· Μαξιμιανὸς δὲ βουληθεὶς πάλιν ἀναλαβέσθαι τὴν βασιλείαν καὶ ἀποτυχὼν ἀπήγξατο. W. Ensslin para- phrased 'Johannes Antiochenus . . . gibt dem D. zwölf Jahre als Privatmann' (P-W vii A, 2493).

[25] Cedrenus, p. 472 Bonn; [Leo the Grammarian], p. 82 Bonn.

[26] ii, 7, 2: 101 years between the *Ludi Saeculares* in 204 and Diocletian's ninth consulate (304), 110 between 204 and the third consulate of Constantine and Licinius (313).

and Maximinus as Caesars (1 May 305).[27] Third, the *Chronicle* of Jerome and two of its derivatives, Prosper Tiro and a Gallic chronicle of A.D. 511, both the latter offering 315, not 316.[28] Little reliance can be based on a chronicle which has so many erroneous dates in the near vicinity: for example, the deaths of Maximian, Galerius and Maximinus Daia in 308, 309 and 311 respectively (instead of 310, 311 and 313) and the war of Cibalae in 313 (316/7).[29] Now Jerome presumably took all these dates from Eusebius' *Chronicle*, which he used in an edition which went as far as the *vicennalia* of Constantine.[30] Accordingly, equally little reliance can be placed in the *Paschal Chronicle*, which also derives its date of 316 for the death of Diocletian from the same source.[31] Perhaps the date has been misplaced in transmission,[32] or Eusebius made a mistake. For one hypothesis or the other must be invoked to explain Eusebius' chronology for the reign of Diocletian, which seriously misdates events of his own lifetime.[33]

By itself stands a chronicle, apparently composed in Rome shortly after 330, which was later incorporated in the document known as the *Fasti* of Hydatius or, misleadingly, as the *Consularia Constantinopolitana*. This proffers a very precise date for Diocletian's decease: 3 December 316.[34] However, although the other contents of the document suggest that the original compiler possessed reliable information on day, month and year, any or all of these elements may have been distorted in transmission.[35]

The evidence against 316, on the other hand, cannot all be impugned or explained away.[36] One might waive the *Epitome de Caesaribus*, composed in or soon after 396, or Socrates, who was writing nearly another fifty years later.[37] But Lactantius can only be discounted either on an accusation of grave and deliberate falsification or through sheer forgetfulness.[38] He states unambiguously that Maximinus Daia, who died in the summer of 313, outlived Diocletian.[39] Further, the evidence of successive editions of Eusebius' *Ecclesiastical History*, though not entirely easy to interpret, unmistakeably implies that Diocletian died somewhat earlier than December 316.[40]

The *Epitome de Caesaribus* reports that Diocletian declined an invitation to attend the marriage of Licinius to Constantia, which was celebrated in Milan early in 313. Angry vituperation greeted the refusal and the retired emperor (so it was said) poisoned himself.[41] Socrates more vaguely dates his death after the marriage and Licinius' subsequent departure to the east.[42] The *Epitome* adds that Diocletian lived sixty-eight years, of which almost nine fell after his abdication, thus implying, on

[27] Hence 'τρισὶν ἐνιαυτοῖς' was emended to 'ὀκτώ' by C. G. Heyne, in J. F. Reitemeier, *Zosimi Historiae* (1784), 633. But note the *Souda* Δ 1156: Διοκλητιανὸς δὲ ἐν ἡσυχίᾳ κατεγήρα ἐν ἔτεσι τρισίν (ii, 104 Adler).
[28] *GCS* xlvi, 230; *Mon. Germ. Hist.*, Auct. Ant. ix, 448; 643 (the ninth year of Constantine, which corresponds to 315 on Jerome's reckoning).
[29] *GCS* xlvi, 229.
[30] *GCS* xlvi, 6 f.; 231.
[31] *Chron. Pasch.* p. 523 Bonn (Confusing him with Galerius), cf. pp. 526 f. (indicating use of Eusebius). The Armenian translation of Eusebius, which originally went to 325/6, breaks off at 301 (*GCS* xx, 227, cf. 34; 62).
[32] A common enough phenomenon in chronicles, cf. C. Courtois, *Byzantion* xxi (1951), 23 ff.
[33] The Armenian translation of The *Chronicle* (*GCS* xx, 227) gives Diocletian twenty years (he ruled from 20 November 284 to 1 May 305), dating the proclamation of Constantius and Galerius to his seventh year, i.e. 292/3 (it probably began in July 297, cf. T.C. Skeat, *Papyri from Panopolis* (1964), xii; *PLRE* i, 6; 263, Domitianus 6).
[34] *Mon. Germ. Hist.*, Auct. Ant. ix, 231. On the peculiar and diverse nature of the document, see T. Mommsen, ib. 199 ff. An apparent derivative exists in the fragment of a Greek chronicle, *P. Berol.* 13296, published by H. Lietzmann, *Quantulacumque. Studies*

presented to K. Lake (1937), 339 ff. = *Kl. Schr.* i (*Texte u. Unters.* lxvii, 1958), 420 ff.
[35] These *fasti* offer 1 April 305 for the abdication of Diocletian (ib. 231). Lactantius' date of 1 May (*Mort. Pers.* 19, 1) appears to be confirmed by the inscription recording a senator's taurobolium in Rome 'dd. nn. Constantio et Maximiano nobb. Caess. V. conss. xviii k. Mai.' (*ILS* 4145). More serious, the same *fasti* have 314 (not 316) for the battle of Cibalae (o.c. 231).
[36] J. Moreau, *Lactance* (1954), 421 ff.
[37] The *Epitome* closes with the burial of Theodosius in Constantinople on 8 November 395 (48, 20), Socrates' narrative extends to Theodosius' seventeenth consulate in 439 (*HE* vii, 47).
[38] O. Seeck averred that Lactantius deliberately moved the death from 316 to 310/11 in order to make his (invented) story of suicide more plausible (*Jahrb. für class. Phil.* cxxxix (1889), 628 f.); *PLRE* cites the *Epitome* as giving a date of 316 and Lactantius, *Mort. Pers.* 42, 3 as supporting 313 (i, 254).
[39] Lactantius, *Mort. Pers.* 42, 3 f.: 'ita viginti annorum felicissimus imperator ... in odium vitae deductus, postremo fame atque angore confectus est. Unus iam supererat de adversariis ille <Maximinus>: cuius nunc exitum ruinamque subnectam'.
[40] C. Habicht, *Hermes* lxxxvi (1958), 376 ff.
[41] *Epit. de Caes.* 39, 7.
[42] Socrates, *HE* i, 2, 10.

inclusive reckoning, that he died shortly before May 313. But before this date can be accepted a question arises. What were the immediate or ultimate sources of the *Epitome* and Socrates? The connection of Diocletian's death with the marriage alliance between Constantine and Licinius may be an imaginative guess or rationalisation not due to an immediate contemporary.[43] The primary witness still remains to be examined in detail.

Lactantius makes the death of Diocletian a direct consequence of the *damnatio memoriae* of Maximian. When Constantine ordered the statues and images of Maximian to be removed from their places of honour, those of Diocletian which accompanied them shared in the destruction. Diocletian then decided to die and self-starvation made his grief and anguish fatal (*Mort. Pers.* 42).[44] Unfortunately, Lactantius assigns the episode no precise date: he merely makes it comtemporaneous with the enormities which Maximinus Daia was perpetrating in the east after Galerius died in May 311 (42, 1). It has therefore been argued that the *damnatio memoriae* of Maximian was decreed by the Roman Senate after Constantine defeated Maxentius (i.e. in November or December 312), and hence that the date implied by Lactantius for the death of Diocletian accords with that stated by the *Epitome* and Socrates.[45] Two main considerations are advanced: Constantine's later rehabilitation of Maximian's memory would be easier if he had no direct part in its abolition;[46] and the Senate's role was preserved in a confused form by Gelasius of Caesarea (writing *c.* 395), who reported that, when Diocletian and Maximian made a joint attempt to resume their thrones, the Senate condemned both to death.[47] But the *a priori* argument will not convince those conversant with the techniques of propaganda in any age, and it is extremely unsound method to disbelieve Lactantius in order to accept much later evidence which must first be interpreted or rephrased in order to give the required sense. The legend that Diocletian and Maximian jointly attempted to resume imperial authority and were then killed together should simply be disbelieved. The true occasion of Constantine's destruction of Maximian's statues and images can easily be discovered.[48] It was, as Lactantius indicates (*Mort. Pers.* 42, 3 ff.), before he defeated Maxentius.

The memory of Maximian was not abolished immediately after his death. A panegyrist speaking in 310, who revealed the hitherto unsuspected fact that Constantine was related to Claudius (emperor 268-270) by an 'avita cognatio',[49] confessed himself uncertain how he should describe the dead conspirator and requested his godlike master's advice.[50] Hence he carefully eschewed any opprobrious epithets for Maximian, studiously referring to him by the bare demonstrative.[51] Of Constantine's subsequent attitude, there exists no precise testimony (except Lactantius) until after the death of Maxentius. In 313, however, another panegyrist of Constantine described the tyrant so justly killed. In accordance with the accepted canons of rhetoric, he gives a formal comparison of Constantine and Maxentius.[52] He could, therefore, quite naturally have observed that Maxentius' vices were largely inherited from the father who had ungratefully conspired against Constantine. But he chose instead to dissociate the two as far as possible: Maxentius was a supposititious son of Maximian, who tried to tear the purple from his ostensible son's shoulders and

---

[43] The sources of neither the *Epitome* nor Socrates for the fourth century are easy to discover, cf. Schanz-Hosius, *Gesch. d. röm. Litt.* iv, i² (1914), 76 f.: F. Winkelmann, *Sb. Berlin*, Klasse für Sprachen, Lit. u. Kunst 1965, Nr. 3, 25 ff.

[44] On the variant reports of how Diocletian died, see Moreau, o.c. 420. Eusebius believed that his death was caused by illness alone (*HE* viii, App. 3).

[45] So, recently, J.-R. Palanque, *Mél. Carcopino* (1966), 714.

[46] Moreau, o.c. 418: 'il semble que Constantin n'ait pas pris l'initiative de cette condamnation.'

[47] W. Ensslin, P-W xiv, 2515 f. For Gelasius, see Theophanes, a. 3796, p. 11 de Boor (with the name); Philippus of Side, frag. 3 (C. de Boor, *Texte u. Unters.* v, 2 (1888), 183) = G.C. Hansen, *Theodoros*

Anagnostes Kirchengeschichte (*GCS*, 1971), 158 §2. John of Nikiu alleged that the Senate exiled Diocletian after he was deposed (trans. Zotenberg, p. 418).

[48] C.H.V. Sutherland, *RIC* vi (1967), 33.

[49] *Pan. Lat.* vi (vii), 2, 1 ff.

[50] *Pan. Lat.* vi (vii), 14, 1: 'de quo ego quemadmodum dicam adhuc ferme dubito et de nutu numinis tui exspecto consilium.' Such a performer was not long baffled: he adopted the principle 'neminem hominum peccare nisi fato et ipsa scelera mortalium actus esse fortunae, contra autem deorum munera esse virtutes' (14, 3).

[51] *Pan. Lat.* vi (vii), 14, 5 ff.

[52] For the σύγκρισις standard in encomia, cf. L.B. Struthers, *Harv. Stud.* xxx (1919), 52; 83 ff.

realised that his own good furtune had passed to someone unworthy and disgraceful.[53] The way was open for Maximian's full rehabilitation: his statue appears on a relief on the arch which the Senate dedicated to Constantine in Rome in 315,[54] and in 317/8 the coinage of Constantine was styling him Divus Maximianus.[55] The *damnatio memoriae* must surely (even on this evidence alone) precede the Battle of the Milvian Bridge (28 October 312).

Maxentius' attitude to his father inevitably differed from that of Constantine. When the old man fled after attempting to depose him, silence was the best policy. But once dead he could safely be exploited for propaganda. Maxentius' coinage began to commemorate Divus Maximianus,[56] and he professed to be waging war on Constantine in order to avenge his murdered father (*Mort. Pers.* 43, 4). The *damnatio memoriae* was surely Constantine's *riposte* to this claim. Can the date be more closely determined? Lactantius places it some time after the death of Galerius (May 311). The next step is mere conjecture. The consuls recognized in Rome on 3 December 311 were C. Ceionius Rufius Volusianus and Aradius Rufinus.[57] Perhaps a chronographer has confused this pair ('Volusiano et Rufino') with the consuls of 316 ('Sabino et Rufino'), and thus entered the death of Diocletian under 316 when it really occurred on 3 December 311.[58] If this conjecture (it is no more) be admitted, then Constantine abolished the memory of Maximian in autumn 311, and Lactantius was correct in claiming, before he described the war of Constantine and Maxentius, that only one of the emperors who had persecuted Christians still survived (*Mort. Pers.* 43, 1).[59] Let it be proposed, therefore, that Diocletian died on 3 December 311. To be sure, more evidence could be marshalled in favour of 3 December 312, a date not incompatible with the *Epitome* and Socrates. However, on any view, some items of evidence must be discarded as untrustworthy,[60] and both the earliest witness (Lactantius) and external considerations (the political situation) point to late 311 or early 312.

---

[53] *Pan. Lat.* xii (ix), 4, 3: 'erat ille Maximiani suppositus, tu Constantii Pii filius'; 3, 4: 'ipse denique qui pater illius credebatur discissam ab umeris purpuram detrahere conatus senserat in illud dedecus sua fata transisse.'

[54] Constantine addresses the people of Rome in front of five columns with statues (of Jupiter and the four emperors), which were erected in the forum in 303 to commemorate the *vicennalia* of the Augusti and *decennalia* of the Caesars: A. Giuliano, *Arco di Costantino* (1955), plates 34; 40, cf. H. P. L'Orange, *Röm. Mitt.* liii (1938), 1 ff.

[55] The reverse legend proclaims 'requies optimorum meritorum', and the issues commemorate Claudius, Constantius and Maximian jointly: *RIC* vii, 180 (Trier); 252 (Arles); 310-312 (Rome: also with 'memoriae aeternae' as reverse legend); 394/5 (Aquileia); 429/30 (Siscia); 502/3 (Thessalonica). J. Maurice, *Numismatique constantinienne* i (1908), xciv; cxxvi, dated these coins to 314 and 324, regarding them as part of Constantine's preparations for the two wars against Licinius. The results were unfortunate for the understanding of Lactantius. For if Maximian was commemorated so honourably by Constantine in 314 and on the arch of 315, then it seemed that Lactantius must have written *De Mortibus Persecutorum* at a later date (W. Seston, *Dioclétien et la Tétrarchie* i (1946), 27; Moreau, o.c. 36 f.; A. Chastagnol, *Rev.num.*[6] iv (1962), 329).

[56] *RIC* vi, 381 ff. (Rome); 403 f. (Ostia). Probably late in 310, cf. C. H. V. Sutherland, ib. 347.

[57] *Mon. Germ. Hist.*, Auct. Ant. ix, 67 (reading 'Rufino et Eusebio' in apparent confusion with the consuls of 347, cf. T. Mommsen, ad loc.); 76; 231; *Liber Pontificalis* pp. 74; 168 Duchesne (all with 'Volusiano et Rufino' or 'Rufino et Volusiano'). For the identifications, see *PLRE* i, 775; 977. The consulate of Rufinus is not reported in A. Degrassi, *Fasti consolari* (1952), 78.

[58] The date of February 312 is stated, without

argument, by F. Corsaro, *Lactantiana* (1970), 40.

[59] Moreau, o.c. 419, argues that Lactantius' order is logical rather than chronological. The mention of Diocletian's death, but not that of Maximinus Daia, in Eusebius, *HE* viii, App. may also be significant.

[60] A law which bears the date of 313 poses special problems: 'Idem A. (i.e. Constantine) ad Eusebium v.p. praesidem Lyciae et Pamphyliae. Plebs urbana, sicut in orientalibus quoque provinciis observatur, minime in censibus pro capitatione sua conveniatur, sed iuxta hanc iussionem nostram immunis habeatur, sicuti etiam sub domino et parente nostro Diocletiano seniore Aug. eadem plebs urbana immunis fuerat. Dat. Kal. Iun. Constantino A. III et Licinio III conss.' (*C.Th.* xiii, 10, 2). Though the law appears to show Diocletian alive on 1 June 313 (Seston, o.c. 44 f.), something is clearly amiss with its attribution and date. In June 313 Constantine controlled neither Lycia and Pamphylia nor the diocese of Oriens. Accordingly, the law might be attributed to Licinius (H. Grégoire, *Byzantion* xiii (1938), 551 ff.). But, on 1 June 313, Licinius did not yet control the 'orientales provinciae', the law's reference to which surely designates Maximinus Daia as its promulgator (O. Seeck, *Zeitschr. für Social- und Wirtschaftsgesch.* iv (1890), 290 ff.; *Regesten* (1919), 52 f., cf. A. H. M. Jones, *The Later Roman Empire* i (1964), 63). What then is the date of the law? Hardly as late as 1 June 313, after Maximinus' invasion of Europe and defeat by Licinius. Possibly, therefore, 1 July 312 or 1 January 313, as proposed by A. Demandt, *Gnomon* xliv (1972), 693. Better, 1 June 311, which enables the law to be brought into connection with a measure recorded by Lactantius: after Galerius' death, Maximinus occupied Bithynia and 'cum magna omnium laetitia sustulit censum' (*Mort. Pers.* 35, 1). For a discussion, see H. Castritius, *Studien zu Maximinus Daia.* Frankfurter Althistorische Studien ii (1969), 9 ff.

III. FROM MILAN TO CIBALAE

Constantine fought two wars against Licinius. For the decisive battle in the latter, two chronological sources offer 324.[61] But both 323 and 324 had notable adherents, until a papyrus published forty years ago showed that Licinius was still recognized as emperor in Egypt as late as 3 September 324, thus confirming the explicit ancient testimony.[62] Matters stand otherwise, however, with the earlier war, the first battle of which (at Cibalae) the *Consularia Constantinopolitana* date to 8 October 314.[63] The correctness of this date was scarcely ever doubted until twenty years ago, and some were even bold enough to argue that, since Eusebius' *Vita Constantini* apparently puts the beginning of Constantine's discord with Licinius after his *decennalia* (celebrated for one year from 25 July 315), Eusebius could not be its author.[64] It was thus of the highest significance that a critical study of the coins minted by Constantine redated the war to 316.[65] The redating naturally provoked attempts at disproof (all ineffectual),[66] and some scholars, loath to give up old habits and sanctified dates, now posit wars in both 314 and 316.[67] But subsequent work has buttressed the new date, which receives confirmation not only from literary and legal sources,[68] but also from the coinage of Licinius.[69] Therefore, Constantine fought Licinius in 316/7 and 323/4. Nevertheless, knowledge of this signal advance in understanding the period and contemporary writers seems not yet to have percolated everywhere,[70] and ignorance of it has led a recent manual of reference to the remarkable deduction that Constantine (Augustus 337-340) was not the son of his father's lawful wife.[71] More than mere relevance to Lactantius, therefore, will justify a brief recapitulation of the decisive evidence.

Most explicit is Aurelius Victor:[72] Maximinus was defeated by Licinius and died at Tarsus after two years of rule as Augustus (i.e. two years from the death of Galerius):[73] the two remaining emperors, different in character though related by marriage, maintained an anxious peace for three years; the ensuing war ended with the proclamation of Crispus, the younger Constantine and Licinianus as Caesars (formally invested at Serdica on 1 March 317);[74] then, an eclipse of the sun portending a short peace,[75] hostilities were resumed after six years, and Licinius was finally overwhelmed. Victor's chronology can easily be inferred: three years of anxious peace from 313 to 316, the first war in 316/7, six years' respite from 317 to 323, the second war, 323/4, with the investiture of Constantius as Caesar (8 November 324) correctly stated to be contemporaneous with Licinius' final defeat (18 September 324).[76]

[61] viz. the *Consularia Constantinopolitana* and the *Chronicon Paschale* (Mon. Germ. Hist., Auct. Ant. ix, 232; the latter also p. 526 Bonn).

[62] For 323, T. Mommsen, *Codex Theodosianus* i, 1 (1904), ccxvii; i, 2 (1904), 350, on *CTh* vii, 20, 1; E. Schwartz, *Nachr. Göttingen*, Phil.-hist. Kl. 1904, 540 ff.; N. H. Baynes, *JRS* xviii (1928), 218 f. In disproof, *P. Osl.* ii, 44, cf. E. Stein, *Zeitschr. für d. neutest.* xxx (1931), 177 ff.

[63] *Mon. Germ. Hist.*, Auct. Ant. ix, 231.

[64] H. Grégoire, *Byzantion* xiii (1938), 561 ff.

[65] P. Bruun, *The Constantinian Coinage of Arelate.* Finska Fornminnesföreningens Tidskrift lii:2 (1953), 17 ff.

[66] J. P. C. Kent, *NC*⁶ xiv (1954), 225 f; xvii (1957), 30 f.; J. P. Callu, *Genio populi Romani* (1960), 87 ff.; D. Kienast, *Hamburger Beiträge zur Numismatik* v (1963), 687 f.

[67] W. Seston, *Relazioni del x Congresso Int. di Scienze Storiche* ii: *Storia di Antichità* (1955), 426; R. Andreotti, *Diz. Epig.* iv, 1002 ff.; *Latomus* xxiii (1964), 543 ff.

[68] C. Habicht, *Hermes* lxxxvi (1958), 360 ff.

[69] P. Bruun, *Studies in Constantinian Chronology.* Numismatic Notes and Monographs cxlvi (1961), 10 ff.

[70] The battle of Cibalae is still dated to 314, not only in unscholarly works, but also by A. H. M. Jones, *The Later Roman Empire* i (1964), 82; R. MacMullen, *Constantine* (1969), 97; 107; H. Dörries, *Constantine the Great* (trans. R. H. Bainton, 1972), 232. The old

date is also sometimes assumed by the editors of *PLRE* (e.g. i, 600, Mestrianus).

[71] *PLRE* i, 223: 'Born Feb. 317 . . . probably illegitimate since his brother Constantius II was born to Fausta on 317 Aug. 7 while no source refers to his descent from Maximianus.' In refutation, see P. Guthrie, *Phoenix* xx (1966), 330 f. Theophanes registers the relationship twice (pp. 5; 19 de Boor), an inscription explicitly describes Constantine as the son of Fausta (*CIL* xii, 688 = *AE* 1952, 107), and Julian states that Fausta was the daughter of one and mother of 'many emperors' (*Orat.* i, 9D). *PLRE* prints a stemma which shows Fausta as the mother of but two emperors (i, 1129), ascribes to Constans (220) an acephalous inscription perhaps better referred to Constantine (*ILS* 723: . . . nepoti M. Aureli Maximiani . . .), and has a separate entry for the invented mother (1040, Anonyma 25).

[72] *Caes.* 41, 1 ff., cf. Habicht, o.c. 362 f.

[73] Not from the date at which Maximinus began to style himself Augustus (towards the middle of 310), as supposed by R. Andreotti, *Latomus* xxiii (1964), 543 f.

[74] *Mon. Germ. Hist.*, Auct. Ant. ix, 231, cf. *Pan. Lat.* iv (x), 1, 1; 2, 2 ff.; 38, 2; *P. Osl.* 44, etc.

[75] Explicitly, but erroneously, dated to early 317 (41, 7). Victor must refer either to the eclipse on 6 July 316 or to that on 6 May 319 (F. Boll, P-W vi, 2362).

[76] For these two dates, see *CIL* i², p. 276; *Mon. Germ. Hist.*, Auct. Ant. ix, 232.

The other literary evidence exhibits confusion of various types, due not least to a tendency to conflate and confuse the two wars.[77] Further, even authors who can distinguish the two wars are unaware of a fact clearly implied by the coinage: before the formal joint proclamation of Caesars on 1 March 317, Constantine had already begun to style Crispus and the younger Constantine by that title.[78] Yet certain significant facts, very relevant to the date of the war, are preserved by various authors. Licinius' son was about twenty months old when proclaimed Caesar (1 March 317);[79] but he and his mother were at Sirmium at the time of the battle of Cibalae;[80] therefore, the battle occurred no earlier than summer 315.[81] Eusebius speaks allusively of plots which Licinius directed against Constantine after his *decennalia*,[82] while a normally well-informed writer supplies what seem to be the pertinent names and details: Licinius induced Senecio to persuade his brother, Bassianus, the husband of Constantine's sister Anastasia, to attempt to assassinate Constantine; Bassianus was caught in the attempt, convicted and executed; Licinius' refusal to surrender Senecio then led to war.[83] Such evidence is clearly incompatible with a date of autumn 314 for the war.

The movements of Constantine can partly be deduced from the *Codex Theodosianus*, which normally states the author, date and place of promulgation of each law. Unfortunately, on any view, some of the subscriptions contradict one another,[84] and the standard register of dates for the period bases itself on the assumption that in the autumn of 314 Constantine was campaigning in the Balkans.[85] However, let it be assumed that consular dates by private citizens are more reliable than dates given by imperial consulates—the normal working principle when seeking to harmonise dates in the law codes.[86] Then a clear picture emerges. In the autumn of 314 (consulate of C. Ceionius Rufius Volusianus for the second time, and Petronius Annianus),[87] Constantine remained in Trier.[88] During 315, the fourth consulate of both Constantine and Licinius, three laws appear to show the former in residence at Sirmium, Naissus and Thessalonica.[89] But there are some clear errors in this year, which offers one law purporting to be issued at Constantinople, and another issued by Constantine from Antioch.[90] On the other hand, one law dated to March 315 has the emperor at Cavillunum (Châlons-sur-Marne).[91] In 316 and 317, the consuls are again private citizens: in 316 Antonius Caecina Sabinus and Vettius Rufinus, in 317 Ovinius Gallicanus and Caesonius Bassus, who were recognised at Rome from 17 February[92]—an indication that Constantine and Licinius negotiated an agreement in January.[93] During these two years, if two obvious errors can be ignored,[94] the *Codex Theodosianus* shows Constantine residing in Gaul until August 316 (with a visit to Rome in 315), but at Serdica by 6 December.[95] Less ambiguous perhaps is a

[77] Habicht, o.c. 375 f.

[78] P. Bruun, *RIC* vii (1966), 66. Hence the younger Constantine cannot have been born as late as February 317, the date implied by Zosimus ii, 18, 1 ff.; *Epit. de Caes.* 41, 4—the only evidence cited by *PLRE* i, 223.

[79] *Epit. de Caes.* 41, 4; Zosimus ii, 20, 2.

[80] *Exc. Vales.* i, 17.

[81] A. Chastagnol, *Rev. num.*[6] iv (1962), 328.

[82] *Vita Const.* i, 48 ff. On which, see now F. Winkelmann, *Klio* xl (1962), 226 ff.

[83] *Exc. Vales.* i, 15.

[84] For the years 314-317, see T. Mommsen, *Codex Theodosianus* i, 1 (1904), ccx ff.

[85] O. Seeck, *Regesten* (1919), 162 ff.

[86] Seeck, ib. 65 f.; 154 f.

[87] *PLRE* i, 978; 68.

[88] *C.Th.* vi, 35, 1 (29 October); i, 2, 1 (30 December).

[89] *C.Th.* viii, 7, 1 (8 March); xi, 27, 1 (13 May); ii, 30, 1 (2 June). The third of these laws names no magistrate, so that its date is beyond the possibility of correction; but the first is addressed to a *consularis aquarum*, the second to Ablabius. They can accordingly be redated to 324 and 329, cf. *PLRE* i, 371; 3; 1048.

[90] *C.Th.* xi, 1, 1 (normally redated to 360, cf. *PLRE* i, 741, Procilianus 2); x, 14, 1 (of 346, cf. Seeck,

o.c. 38; *PLRE* i, 614).

[91] *C.Th.* ix, 40, 2.

[92] For the first pair, *PLRE* i, 793; 777; for the second, ib. 383; 154.

[93] Habicht, o.c. 365 f.

[94] *C.Th.* viii, 12, 2 (apparently issued on 20 April 316 at Serdica); viii, 12, 3 (allegedly issued at Rome on 1 May 316). Both laws are addressed to magistrates who cannot have held office at the time: Aco Catullinus as proconsul of Africa, and Cassius as *praefectus urbi*, cf. Seeck, o.c. 165; 173; *PLRE* i, 187; 733 f., Probianus 3 (proconsul of Africa from August 315 to August 316); 184 f.

[95] *C.Th.* i, 22, 1 (11 January 316, Trier); ii, 6, 1 (6 May, Vienne); xi, 30, 5 f. (13 August, Arelate); ix, 1, 1 (4 December, Serdica); ix, 10, 1 (17 April 317, Serdica); xi 30.7 (6 June, Sirmium). P. Bruun, *RIC* vii, 76, also adduces *Frag. Vat.* 290 as showing Constantine in Verona on 20 September 316, and *C.Th.* viii, 7, 1 and the non-existent *C.Th.* vi, 1, 4 as showing him in Thessalonica on 8 March and 27 June 317. But the date in *Frag. Vat.* 290 is no longer fully extant (Data iii Kal. Oct. Verona . . .), *C.Th.* viii, 7, 1 is dated 8 March 315 (n. 89) and *C.J.* vi, 1, 4 (the correct reference) belongs rather to 330, cf. Seeck, o.c. 180; *PLRE* i, 938, Valerianus 4.

communication of Petronius Annianus and Julianus (i.e. the pretorian prefects) to Domitius Celsus, *vicarius* of Africa.[96] The prefects inform Celsus that, after certain clerics came to Gaul to see Constantine on his orders, he instructed them to return home. Consequently, the prefects have provided free transport and lodging as far as the port of Arelate, where the clerics are to embark for Africa, and they apprise Celsus of the fact. The letter concludes with the note that the beneficiaries received the diploma on 28 April at Trier.[97] The year is not stated, but it can only be 315.[98] Therefore, Constantine was in Trier in April 315, not in northern Greece or the Balkan lands.

Finally, and clearest of all, the coinage of Constantine and Licinius.[99] In rapid succession (therefore in 316/7), most western mints dropped Licinius to coin in the name of Constantine alone, added Crispus and the younger Constantine, and then reinstated Licinius, now with Licinianus as Caesar.[100] A similar picture obtains for the mint of Siscia, which Constantine seized during the war.[101] Among the Licinian mints, the clearest evidence comes from Alexandria: the same issue includes obverses both of Valens, whom Licinius put up as emperor during the war, and of the two new Caesars, Crispus and Constantine.[102]

The historical outline which results from the new chronology should be clear. After their meeting in Milan (early 313), Licinius left to confront Maximinus, while Constantine proceeded to Gaul.[103] Licinius defeated Maximinus in Europe (30 April 313) and pursued him through Asia Minor, travelling at least as far as Antioch.[104] Licinius' further movements appear to be unknown.[105] Constantine resided in Gaul, dealing with Christians and barbarians, and visited Rome in 315 to celebrate his *decennalia*, entering the city on 18 or 21 July and departing on 27 September.[106] He travelled first to Mediolanum, but soon proceeded to Trier and remained in Gaul until the next summer.[107] The plot (real or alleged) which Licinius instigated against his life belongs to 316: in a letter apparently written in winter 315/6, Constantine states his intention of visiting Africa to put a decisive end to bickering between Christians.[108] Also to 316 belongs the birth of Fausta's first son, Constantine, whom she bore at Arelate:[109] probably during August, when Constantine is attested there.[110] Relations between Constantine and Licinius gradually soured, until there was open war (autumn 316). If the *De Mortibus Persecutorum* fails to mention the conflict, an easy explanation avails. Lactantius wrote before it occurred.

[96] Optatus, App. viii (*CSEL* xxvi, 212) = H. von Soden—H. von Campenhausen, *Urkunden zur Entstehungsgeschichte des Donatismus²*. Kleine Texte cxxii (1950), no. 22. For Petronius Annianus and Julius Julianus as colleagues in the pretorian prefecture, *ILS* 8938 (Tropaeum Traiani); *AE* 1938, 85 (Ephesus).

[97] *CSEL* xxvi, 212, 24 f.: 'Hilarius princeps obtulit iiii Kal. Maias Triberis.' Presumably Hilarius was *princeps officii* of the pretorian prefect at Trier (so *PLRE* i, 434).

[98] *PLRE* i, 195, Celsus 8. Seeck felt compelled to emend the date to 27 February, i.e. of 316, precisely because he believed that Constantine was not at Trier in April 315 (o.c. 142 f.; 164).

[99] Bruun, o.c. (1953), 17 ff.; o.c. (1961), 10 ff.

[100] *RIC* vii, 172 ff. (Trier); 240 ff. (Arles); 298 ff. (Rome); 366 ff. (Ticinum).

[101] *RIC* vii, 425 ff. (coinage in the name of Licinius alone, then of Constantine alone, before the Caesars appear); 498 ff.

[102] *RIC* vii, 706. There seem to exist only two undoubtedly genuine types of Valens (*RIC* vii, 644 no. 7 (Cyzicus); 706 no. 19), but very many forgeries, cf. R. A. G. Carson, *NC⁶* xviii (1958), 55 ff. It is therefore unfortunate that *PLRE* i, 931, Valens 13, cites only Cohen, whose 'inaccuracy or even negligence in even important details renders him useless for the purpose of modern numismatic research' (Bruun, o.c. (1953), 56).

[103] *Exc. Vales.* i, 13.

[104] Eusebius, *HE* ix, 11, 6.

[105] That is, once deductions from his alleged presence at Cibalae in October 314 are discarded (cf. O. Seeck, P-W xiii, 224 (F.).

[106] The Chronographer of 354 records 'advent(us) divi' on 18 and 21 July, and 29 October (*CIL* i², pp. 268; 274). Since the last entry refers to Constantine's entry into Rome in 312 (after the 'evictio tyranni', ib. 274), the others must refer to 315 and 326. It records 'profectio divi' on 27 September (ib. 272): almost certainly 315 rather than 326, cf. Seeck, *Regesten* (1919), 164; 177.

[107] Augustine, *Epp.* xliii, 7, 20; *Frag. Vat.* 273 (19 October 315, Mediolanum); *C.Th.* i, 22, 1 (11 January 316, Trier).

[108] Optatus, App. vii (*CSEL* xxvi, 211, 19 ff.).

[109] *Epit. de Caes.* 41, 4; Zosimus ii, 20, 2.

[110] *C.Th.* xi, 30, 5 f. (13 August 316). Polemius Silvius enters 'natalis Constantini minoris' under 7 August (*CIL* i², p. 271). Since Constantius was certainly born on 7 August (*CIL* i², p. 270; *C.Th.* vi, 4, 10), this is normally taken as an error. Yet the coincidence does not surpass belief, and August is approximately the correct month, as was seen long ago by E. Stein, *Zeitschr. für d. neutest. Wiss.* xxx (1931), 183 f.; J.-R. Palanque, *Rev. ét. anc.* xl (1938), 249 f. Polemius Silvius, the only direct testimony to the exact day of his birth, is nowhere adduced in the articles on the younger Constantine by J. Moreau, *JAC* ii (1959), 160 f.; *PLRE* i, 223.

IV. DATE, AUTHOR AND AUDIENCE

The *De Mortibus Persecutorum* combines three features which long seemed to contradict one another. Lactantius writes as if persecution has very recently ceased, he records the death of Diocletian, and he betrays no hint of conflict between Constantine and Licinius. The date of composition consequently presented a vexing problem, with no universally agreed solution. If the work was written close to the events which it describes, then one of three implausible hypotheses seemed to be imposed.[111] Either its completion fell within the brief (or non-existent) interval between Lactantius' learning of the capture and execution of Valeria (hardly earlier than September 314) and the outbreak of war (before the end of the same month),[112] or Lactantius wrote 'restituta per orbem tranquillitate' and 'pax iucunda et serena' (*Mort. Pers.* 1, 2 f.) during the war,[113] or else the passages which refer to events of 314 (either chapter 51 alone, or both 50 and 51) had to be deleted as interpolations.[114] Then came wide acceptance of the notion that Diocletian died on 3 December 316.[115] That entailed a date for the *De Mortibus Persecutorum* which solved or alleviated the existing difficulty: Lactantius was writing between 317 and 321. Such was the opinion which prevailed in recent times,[116] with the corollary (not always clearly enunciated) that Lactantius indulged in a deliberate artifice: whether or not he has displaced the death of Diocletian, he omitted the war and he purported to be writing from four to seven years earlier than the genuine time of composition.[117] Correct chronology redeems Lactantius' candour and accuracy.[118] No longer does either the death of Diocletian (certainly no later than 312/3 and possibly as early as 3 December 311)[119] or the war (316/7) present any problem. The implications of the text may now be accepted: the author completed the *De Mortibus Persecutorum* in autumn 314 or (at the very latest) during the following winter.

Jerome records that Lactantius composed one book 'de persecutione'.[120] This has not been preserved with his other extant works, but appears to correspond to a work preserved in a manuscript of the ninth century: 'Lucii C(a)ecilii liber ad Donatum confessorem de mortibus persecutorum'.[121] The ascription to 'L. Caecilius' is no argument against identification. On the contrary: the manuscripts of the *Divinae Institutiones*, the *Epitome*, *De Opificio Dei* and *De Ira Dei* present the author's name in a wide variety of forms, most fully as 'L. Caelius Firmianus Lactantius' or 'L. C(a)ecilius Firmianus Lactantius', and the latter form of the *nomen* has perhaps the better claim to be regarded as correct.[122] However, the *De Mortibus Persecutorum* was not discovered until 1677,[123] after a picture of Constantine based on Eusebius had established itself.[124] In consequence, many were inclined to dispute Lactantius' authorship of the newly discovered evidence, and controversy ensued for more than

[111] P. Monceaux, *Histoire littéraire de l'Afrique chrétienne* iii (1905), 305 f.; Schanz-Hosius, *Gesch. d. röm. Litt.* iii³ (1922), 431.

[112] F. Görres, *Philologus* xxxvii (1877), 596 ff.

[113] S. Brandt, *Sb. Wien* cxxv, 6 (1892), 107 f.

[114] A. Ebert, *Ber. Leipzig* xxii (1870), 124; A. Harnack, *Chronologie der altchristlichen Litteratur bis Eusebius* ii (1904), 422 f.

[115] O. Seeck gave the lead, mainly through the first volume of his *Geschichte* (first edition, 1895).

[116] e.g., J. Quasten, *Patrology* ii (1953), 400; J. Moreau, *Lactance* (1954), 34 ff.; W. Seston, *RAC* iii (1957), 1037; M. F. McDonald, *Lactantius, The Minor Works*. Fathers of the Church liv (1965), 127; J. Stevenson, *OCD²* (1970), 576. It has even been asserted that Lactantius' narrative continues to c. 318 (J. Vogt, *Der Niedergang Roms* (1965), 178).

[117] Moreau claimed that the opening sentences are little more than a rhetorical commonplace, and that Lactantius was simply copying Cyprian, *Laps.* 1 and possibly also Curtius Rufus x, 9, 1 ff. (o.c. 190 f.).

[118] J.-R. Palanque, *Mél. Carcopino* (1966), 711 ff.

[119] p. 35.

[120] Jerome, *De vir. ill.* 80, also reporting other works now lost (for the fragments, *CSEL* xxvii, 155 ff.).

[121] Paris, Bibliothèque Nationale, Ms. lat. 2627, ff. 1ʳ–16ʳ. The ms. is ascribed to the eleventh century by S. Brandt, *CSEL* xxvii, ix; Quasten, o.c. 401; Moreau, o.c. 73; to the ninth by Schanz-Hosius, o.c. 431; P. de Labriolle, *Histoire de la littérature latine chrétienne* i³ (1947), 275. Professor L. E. Boyle advises me that the earlier date is palaeographically preferable.

[122] For attestations of 'Caecilius', see S. Brandt's critical notes (*CSEL* xix, 94; 580; xxvii, 64; 132). It is held to be the correct form of Lactantius' *nomen* in Schanz-Hosius, o.c. 414, adducing *CIL* viii, 7241 (Cirta): D. M. L. Caecilius Firmianus v.a. xxv h.s.e. 'Perhaps an ancestor', according to *PLRE* i, 338.

[123] First edited by S. Baluzius, *Miscellaneorum Liber Secundus* (Paris, 1679), 1 ff.

[124] Observe the recent verdict that Baronius' *Annales*, published in Rome between 1588 and 1605, 'remained till the nineteenth century the standard text of Catholic ecclesiastical history' (H. Jedin, *Handbook of Church History* i (1965); 25).

two hundred years.[125] The decisive arguments in favour were formulated at the beginning of the present century: the historical accuracy and detail of *De Mortibus Persecutorum* prove a date within Lactantius' lifetime; the differences of style from Lactantius' undisputed works derive from differences of genre, of audience and in the author's state of mind, while pervasive similarities of thought indicate the same author.[126] Few have subsequently doubted Lactantius' authorship.[127]

Lactantius' movements help to identify the audience which his work envisages. He was in Nicomedia when the 'Great Persecution' began (early 303) and implies that he remained there for at least two years.[128] Hence a strong temptation to infer that his vivid narrative of later events in Nicomedia represents the report of an eyewitness. Lactantius (it is commonly and perhaps correctly supposed) was there, not only when Diocletian abdicated on 1 May 305 (*Mort. Pers.* 35), but also when Galerius' edict of toleration was posted there on 30 April 311 (35, 1) and when Licinius ordered the publication of a letter on 13 June 313 (48, 1).[129] However, the validity of the inference may awake doubt or scepticism when it is applied to events outside Nicomedia. From the *De Mortibus Persecutorum* alone, it has been deduced that Lactantius may have been also in Gaul in 310 (29, 3 ff.),[130] and in Serdica in 311 and perhaps early 313 (33; 45 ff.).[131] With equal plausibility, he might be supposed to have accompanied Constantine in Italy in 312 (43 f.).[132] Not all of these deductions are likely to be valid, and the vividness of the narrative may come from Lactantius' rhetorical skill rather than autopsy.[133] Since he could discover and question eye-witnesses of most of the events which he describes, the narrative need not reveal anything about his movements.

Lactantius left Bithynia not long after 305, and wrote at least part of his *Divinae Institutiones* elsewhere.[134] Neither the date nor the place can be specified exactly, but a reference to persecution should indicate that he was writing before April 311, perhaps in the territory of Constantine.[135] In 311 Lactantius may have returned to Bithynia, since he reproduces the texts of the edict of Galerius and letter of Licinius which were published in Nicomedia (*Mort. Pers.* 35; 48). Yet he could have acquired copies from friends there, or even from the recipient of the work: the only evidence outside the *De Mortibus Persecutorum* shows him still (or again) in the west a little later, as the tutor to Crispus Caesar.[136]

The *De Mortibus Persecutorum* addresses itself to the confessor Donatus, who had been imprisoned in Nicomedia from 305 to 311 (1, 1, etc., esp. 35, 2). It must therefore be supposed either that Lactantius was writing in Nicomedia or that he sent there at least one copy of his tract. But what was the wider audience which he

[125] For the details, F. Corsaro, *Lactantiana* (1970), 6 ff.

[126] R. Pichon, *Lactance. Étude sur le mouvement philosophique et religieux sous le règne de Constantin* (1901), 337 ff. In a review, S. Brandt conceded the case (*Berl. phil. Wochenschr.* xxiii (1903), 1257).

[127] Note the half-hearted attempt at disproof by J. W. P. Borleffs, *Mnemosyne*, N.S. lviii (1930), 223 ff. Most of the facts there adduced favour authenticity rather than the reverse, cf. J. Moreau, *Lactance* (1954), 25 ff.

[128] *Div. Inst.* v, 2, 2; 11, 15.

[129] Harnack, o.c. 417; Schanz-Hosius, o.c. 428. B. Altaner—A. Stuiber, *Patrologie*[7] (1966), 185 state that he remained there continuously until c. 317.

[130] Pichon, o.c. 359.

[131] H. J. Lawlor, *Eusebiana* (1912), 242.

[132] So Pichon playfully suggested (o.c. 358 f.). Lawlor advanced the same hypothesis seriously (o.c. 241), and a written source was invoked by K. Roller, *Die Kaisergeschichte in Laktanz 'de mortibus persecutorum'* (Diss. Giessen, 1927), 12 ff.

[133] Even the apparently explicit claim 'vidimus' need not always prove autopsy, cf. *Tertullian* (1971), 245 f.

[134] *Div. Inst.* v, 2, 2: 'ego cum in Bithynia oratorias litteras accitus docerem ..., duo extiterunt ibidem ...'

[135] *Div. Inst.* vi, 17, 6: 'spectatae sunt enim semper spectanturque adhuc per orbem poenae cultorum dei.' A serious problem is posed by passages not included in all mss., particularly two long invocations of Constantine (i, 1, 13 ff.; vii, 26, 11 ff.). Three, and only three, solutions can be devised. Either the passages are interpolations (S. Brandt, *Sb. Wien* cxviii, 8 (1889); cxix, 1 (1889)—retracted in *Berl. Phil. Wochenschr.* xxiii (1903), 1225), or they belong to a second edition of the work by Lactantius himself (A. Piganiol, *Rev. d'hist. et de phil. rel.* xii (1932), 368 f., dated i, 1, 13 ff. to 322 or 323, vii, 26, 11 ff. to the period between Licinius' defeat and his execution), or they originally stood in the sole edition which Lactantius published and were expunged by another hand (Pichon, o.c. 4 ff.).

[136] Jerome, *Chronicle*, under A.D. 317 (*GCS* xlvii, 230), *De Vir. Ill.* 80. Since Jerome merely appends the notice to Crispus' investiture as Caesar in 317, his date has no authority. Pichon argued that Lactantius left Nicomedia for Gaul, never to return, between 306 and 308 (o.c. 356 ff.).

envisaged? He states that he writes so that all who were afar off and all who shall come after may know how God showed his excellence and majesty in destroying the enemies of his name (1, 7). Moreover, he was writing primarily, if not exclusively, for Christians: contrary to the practice of his apologetical writings, he uses specifically Christian terminology.[137] A double purpose may thus be detected. Lactantius had contacts enough to be able to inform himself about contemporary happenings in both East and West. Since few were in such a position, his work probably contained something new for Christians everywhere. It is thus misleading to view Lactantius either as intent on informing Christians in the Western Empire of Licinius' virtues or as circulating Constantine's version of events among the subjects of Licinius. Lactantius was writing at a time when he could attempt to portray Constantine and Licinius with relative accuracy for an audience which embraced the subjects of both.[138] On the correct chronology, it becomes possible to consider him more as an impartial witness to the policies of the later rivals than as a propagandist for either.

V. CONSTANTINIAN PROPAGANDA

Lactantius' relationship to Constantine has often been misunderstood. If the *De Mortibus Persecutorum* were written *c.* 318-320, then Lactantius was surely disseminating an official version of events acceptable in Constantinian circles at that time,[139] he omitted the war between Constantine and Licinius at the emperor's express command,[140] and some of his information came from Constantine in person.[141] An earlier date for the work will clearly require such hypotheses to be either reformulated or discarded.[142] Lactantius' treatment of Maximian and Maxentius discountenances the idea that he was closely following changes in official attitudes.

Constantine had (in 307) allied himself with Maxentius and Maximian: he married Fausta, the daughter of the latter (*Mort. Pers.* 27, 1), and was invested by him as Augustus.[143] Later, after the Conference of Carnuntum had finally forced him to retire (November 308), Maximian attempted to seize power from Constantine by occupying Massilia, failed and was allowed (or compelled) to commit suicide (early 310).[144] The explanation which found immediate official favour represented the episode as a family tragedy: the ungrateful Maximian sinned by fate or fortune, then perceived that he did not deserve to live and met an entirely voluntary death.[145] Soon, however, Maxentius was waging war on Constantine as if to avenge his father (*Mort. Pers.* 43, 4). Constantine therefore ordered the condemnation of Maximian's memory (311 or 312) and a second plot was revealed. After failure at Massilia and pardon, Maximian had tried to murder his son-in-law with his own hand: forewarned of the impending attempt by Fausta, whom her father urged to betrayal, Constantine placed a eunuch in his bed and apprehended Maximian after he killed the substitute. The old man was allowed to choose how to die and hanged himself (*Mort. Pers.* 30, 1 ff.). This

---

[137] e.g. 'oratio', in the sense of 'prayer', in the very first sentence (1, 1), which Lactantius avoids in his other works (Borleffs, o.c. 262). Hence the 'candidati ministri' seen by the blinded Maximinus (49, 5) are probably not angels, but elders or 'those to whom judgement was committed' (Rev. 4, 4; 20, 4).

[138] For the extent of knowledge of Latin in the East, see the works cited by W. Christ–W. Schmid–O. Stählin, *Gesch. d. griech. Litt.* ii⁶ (1924), 945 f.; 960 f.; E. Stein, *Historie du Bas-empire* i² (1958), 500 f. Observe that the town of Orcistus, on the borders of Galatia and Phrygia, petitioned Constantine in Latin (*MAMA* vii, 305).

[139] A. Piganiol, *L'empereur Constantin* (1932), 48; J. Moreau, *Scripta minora* (1964), 115.

[140] H. Grégoire, *Byzantion* xiii (1938), 566.

[141] J. Moreau, *Lactance* (1954), 44.

[142] On the possibility of reformulation, note J.-R. Palanque, *Mél. Carcopino* (1966), 715 f.

[143] The precise date diverges widely in modern treatments: *PLRE* dates the marriage to March (i, 325) and seems to express no opinion on Constantine's becoming Augustus (i, 223 f.); C. H. V. Sutherland dates the marriage to April and the investiture to the autumn (*RIC* vi, 12 ff.); J. Lafaurie both to precisely 25 December (*CRAI* 1965, 201 ff.; *Mél. Piganiol* ii (1966), 799 ff.). December is probably too late, but the late summer or autumn of the year appears certain. The marriage and the investiture were contemporaneous (*Pan. Lat.* vi (vi), esp. 1, 1; 5, 3; 8, 1), and Constantine was still only Caesar on 25 July 307 (R. Strauss, *Rev. Num.*⁵ xvi (1954), 26 ff.; *RIC* vi, 213, nos. 744-747).

[144] Moreau, o.c. (1954), 367; Sutherland, o.c. 14 f.

[145] *Pan. Lat.* vi (vii), 14, 3 ff.; 20, 3 ff. The speech was delivered in 310, on the 'natalis dies' of Trier (22, 4).

story shows clear signs of being invented during Constantine's war against Maxentius.[146] Subsequently, it was officially ignored: Maximian soon became Divus Maximianus and the grandfather of Constantine's sons.[147]

Lactantius could not avoid being affected by some of this propaganda and was deceived by the story of Maximian's two plots. But the falsehoods were the invention of others.[148] Lactantius, to be sure, omits Maximian's investiture of Constantine as Augustus and Constantine's refusal to acknowledge the decisions taken at Carnuntum, by which he was demoted again to Caesar and thus regarded as junior in rank to Maximinus.[149] Instead, he ascribes Galerius' eventual recognition of both as Augusti to the contumacy of Maximinus alone (*Mort. Pers.* 32, 1 ff.), for he considers Constantine an Augustus from the day of his father's death (24, 9; 25, 5).[150] But his picture of Maximian hardly corresponds to Constantinian propaganda at the time of writing (313-315). Lactantius' Maximian possesses many of the traits of the typical tyrant: as ruler of Italy, Africa and Spain, for example, he continually executed the wealthiest senators on false charges of treason,[151] practised sodomy, and raped the virgin daughters of leading citizens wherever he journeyed (8, 4 ff.). It thus comes as no surprise to learn that he was expelled from Rome (in April 308) like a second Tarquinius Superbus (28, 4). Further, Lactantius' views on the Diocletianic Tetrarchy diverged from those of Constantine and the Roman Senate:

> ubi sunt modo magnifica illa et clara per gentes Ioviorum et Herculiorum cognomina, quae primum a Dioclete et Maximiano insolenter adsumpta et postmodum ad successores eorum translata viguerunt (52, 3)?

The coinage of Constantine continued for some years more to present Licinius, and occasionally himself, as being under the protection of Jupiter,[152] and the Senate (in 315) portrayed Constantine in stone as the legitimate successor of the Tetrarchy.[153] One whom Constantine had taken into his confidence or who habitually moved in court circles would surely have written with greater tact or avoided the topic.[154] Hence, if Lactantius reflects official attitudes towards Maximian, they are not the attitudes of the time of writing but of Constantine's war against Maximian's son (i.e. 311/2).[155]

Maxentius fares better than his father at the hands of Lactantius. Admittedly, he was of an evil disposition and so arrogant and resentful that he did not prostrate himself in adoration before his father or father-in-law (Galerius), who both therefore hated him (18, 9). But that is hardly a severe condemnation. Moreover, Lactantius entirely avoids vituperation. According to other contemporaries Maxentius committed crimes still more abominable than Lactantius attributes to his father (8, 4) or to Maximinus (37, 3 ff.): he indulged in every form of sexual debauchery, he robbed temples and butchered the Senate, he distributed other men's wives and the lives and property of the innocent to his followers to secure their loyalty, and he even slaughtered pregnant women and new-born babies for magical purposes.[156] Constantine naturally welcomed (if he did not inspire) such allegations, since they

[146] No ancient writer other than Lactantius has both plots (Moreau, o.c. 373 ff.).

[147] p. 35. For a slightly different hypothesis of two successive stories, cf. A. Maddalena, *Atti Ist. Veneto* xciv, 2 (1934/5), 575.

[148] An important distinction, cf. Moreau, o.c. 44 ff.

[149] For Galerius' view of the settlement of Carnuntum, note esp. *ILS* 658 f.; *RIC* vi, 514 (Thessalonica). Constantine (an important fact not made clear by *PLRE* i, 1043) refused, both in 309 and later, to recognise the consulate which Galerius gave him for that year: *P. Cairo Isid.* 47; 90; 91, cf. *Mon. Germ. Hist.*, Auct. Ant. ix, 60; 76; 231 (post cons. x et septimum). Further, in the territory of Galerius and Maximinus, the *dies imperii* of Constantine was not 25 July 306, but the day (subsequent to 29 August) on which Galerius formally appointed him (*P. Cairo Isid.* 41, etc., confirming *Mort. Pers.* 25, 2 ff.).

[150] Which was, presumably, the legal basis of

Constantine's claim, ratified by the Senate in November 312, to be the senior emperor (*Mort. Pers.* 44, 11).

[151] Maximian's relations with the Roman Senate are not discussed in M. T. W. Arnheim. *The Senatorial Aristocracy in the Later Roman Empire* (1972).

[152] *RIC* vii, 246 ff.; 305 ff.; 371 ff.; 393 (all Licinius or his son); 498 ff. (Constantine: Thessalonica, after it passed into Constantine's control in 316/7).

[153] Above, n. 54.

[154] Impossible, therefore, to suppose that 'un des objectifs de Lactance . . . était de justifier l'attitude de Constantin a l'égard de Maximien' (Moreau, o.c. 366).

[155] p. 34 f.

[156] *Pan. Lat.* xii (ix), 3, 6; 4, 3 ff.; Eusebius, *HE* viii, 14, 2 ff. On the conventional nature of the charges, cf. J. Ziegler, *Zur religiösen Haltung der Gegenkaiser im 4 Jh. n. Chr.* Frankfurter Alt-historische Studien iv (1970), 9 ff.; 35 ff.

supported his claim to be liberating Rome and Italy from tyranny.[157] But his wife was the daughter of Maximian and thus a sister of Maxentius.[158] The unpleasant fact was removed (or at least palliated) by the expedient of denying the tyrant's paternity: an orator addressing Constantine in 313 boldly asserted that he was not really Maximian's son at all, and a story was circulated that Eutropia had conceived him in adultery with a Syrian.[159]

The argument can be reduced to a schematic form. Constantinian propaganda treated the memory of Maximian favourably except for a brief period (in 311 and 312), but consistently vilified the dead Maxentius. Lactantius treats Maxentius dispassionately but vilifies Maximian.[160] The contrast both confirms an early date for *De Mortibus Persecutorum* and proves that the author was not simply purveying the contemporary official version of events accepted at the court of Constantine.

VI CONSTANTINE AND THE CHRISTIANS

suscepto imperio Constantinus Augustus nihil egit prius quam Christianos cultui ac deo suo reddere. haec fuit prima eius sanctio sanctae religionis restitutae (*Mort. Pers.* 24, 9);

opus nunc nominis tui auspicio inchoamus, Constantine imperator maxime, qui primus Romanorum principum repudiatis erroribus maiestatem dei singularis ac veri et cognovisti et honorasti. nam cum dies ille felicissimus orbi terrarum inluxisset, quo te deus summus ad beatum imperii columen evexit, salutarem universis et optabilem principatum praeclaro initio auspicatus es, cum eversam sublatamque iustitiam reducens taeterrimum aliorum facinus expiasti. (*Div. Inst.* i, 1, 13).

Lactantius presents a clear and almost unambiguous account of how the persecuting edicts of Diocletian were enforced by different emperors, and how the Christians gained freedom from molestation in one part of the empire after another. Galerius was the moving force and cowed the senile Diocletian into executing his wishes (*Mort. Pers.* 10, 6 ff.).[161] Letters were sent to Maximian and Constantius bidding them take similar action: in Italy Maximian gladly obeyed, but in Gaul Constantius frustrated the intentions of his colleagues by allowing churches to be destroyed but preserving unharmed God's true temple in men's hearts (15, 6 f.). When Diocletian abdicated, Galerius was then able to practise on all the savage tortures he had learnt to apply to Christians (22, 1). But God's judgement was drawing near, and Galerius' position began to be threatened when Constantius died (24, 1). On his death, Constantine was proclaimed Augustus, and immediately allowed the Christians to worship God—a step which Lactantius clearly regards as something more than a mere continuation or reaffirmation of his father's policy (24, 8-f.).[163]

In the subsequent narrative, Lactantius marks several more steps in the deliverance of the Christians. The dying Galerius issued an edict of toleration in the name of all the emperors (i.e. himself, Maximinus, Constantine and Licinius), which was published in Nicomedia on 30 April 311 (33, 11 ff.; 36, 3) and in the other cities of the east.[164] But Maximinus, who had been harrying Christians in Syria and

[157] *ILS* 687 ff.; *RIC* vi, 387 nos. 303/4: LIBERATORI URBIS SUAE.

[158] In fact, a full sister (*Epit. de Caes.* 40, 12).

[159] *Pan. Lat.* xii (ix), 3, 4; 4, 3; *Exc. Vales.* i, 12. Eutropia was a Syrian herself (*Epit. de Caes.* 40, 12).

[160] Note the allegations that Maximian intended to kill Galerius at Carnuntum (*Mort. Pers.* 29, 1) and to exterminate all the emperors except Diocletian, who was to be his sole colleague (43, 6).

[161] For discussion of the real role of Galerius, see N. H. Baynes, *CQ* xviii (1924), 192 f.; M. Gelzer, *Vom Wesen und Wandel der Kirche. Festschrift E. Vischer* (1935), 35 ff. = *Kl. Schr.* ii (1963), 378 ff.; G. E. M. de Ste. Croix, *HTR* xlvii (1954), 108 f.

[162] On the enforcement of the various edicts (four

in number) in different areas, see de Ste. Croix, o.c. 75 ff. This fundamental study appears to be unknown to a recent writer on the subject (J. Molthagen, *Der römische Staat und die Christen im zweiten und dritten Jahrhundert*, Hypomnemata xxviii (1970), 101 ff.)

[163] H. Kraft, *Kaiser Konstantins religiose Entwicklung* (1955), 7.

[164] For a Greek translation, with the names and titles of the emperors (except Maximinus), see Eusebius, *HE* viii, 17, 3 ff. It is not a necessary deduction from Eusebius' ἠπλωτο κατὰ πόλεις βασιλικὰ διατάγματα' (ib. 2) that the edict was published in the territory of either Maxentius or Constantine.

Egypt, at once occupied Asia Minor and introduced the same policies there, though later compelled by a letter of Constantine to resort to subterfuge (36, 1 ff.). Two years later, however, when Licinius defeated Maximinus, he guaranteed religious liberty to all his subjects and restored the Church in Asia and later (a fact only implied by Lactantius) in Syria and Egypt (48, 1 ff.).[165]

On Lactantius' showing, the Christians gained freedom in several distinct stages: first, in Gaul and Britain (306), then in the Balkan lands (311), and finally throughout the East (313). The only uncertainty left by Lactantius concerns Italy and Africa, which were ruled by Maxentius until 312,[166] and Spain, about whose allegiance in these years there seems to exist no explicit evidence.[167] The explanation for this apparent uncertainty can easily be discerned. Lactantius, who makes no statement whatever about Maxentius' attitude toward the Christians, has deliberately omitted his actions in their favour. Maxentius (it is known) put an end to persecution in Africa (perhaps as early as 307),[168] and ordered the Prefect of the City of Rome to aid the Christians in recovering what had been taken from them during the persecution.[169]

Lactantius' picture is reproduced in very few modern accounts of the period, and some lengthy books on Constantine disdain to mention what Lactantius asserts to be his first act as emperor.[170] Instead, the edict of Galerius is presented as the first occasion on which the illegality of being a Christian was 'explicitly revoked' by 'direct imperial enactment'.[171] Alternatively, 'the very famous "Edict of Milan" . . . marks the decisive turning point in the history of the relations between the Church and the State'.[172] And even those who perceive that Lactantius' account not only fails to mention an 'Edict of Milan',[173] but also renders it impossible to suppose that Constantine and Licinius needed to promulgate any edict ordaining toleration in their own territories as late as 313, incline to keep the term for its symbolic value.[174] But on what basis has Lactantius' express testimony been discarded? It will be wise to review the arguments advanced with some care.

Two statements of Lactantius are at issue: that Constantine restored religious liberty in 306 (*Mort. Pers.* 24, 9), and that he wrote to Maximinus in 311 discouraging him from persecution (37, 1). Lactantius (it is argued or assumed) has antedated the letter: he refers in fact to a letter which Constantine wrote to Maximinus after the battle of the Milvian Bridge (cf. 44, 11),[175] or to the 'most perfect law' which Constantine and Licinius communicated to Maximinus at the same time,[176] and which should accordingly be identical with the letter.[177] Apparent disproof of Constantine's earlier action comes from Africa: the Donatist bishops (it is contended) were totally

---

[165] Eusebius presents substantially the same document with a different preamble (*HE* x, 5, 1 ff.), presumably reproducing the version which Licinius dispatched to Palestine and which was published there. For modern discussion of the two versions, cf. J. Moreau, *Scripta Minora* (1964), 99 ff.

[166] For Africa, *Pan. Lat.* xii (ix), 16, 1; 25, 2 f.

[167] R. Grosse, *Fontes Hispaniae Antiquae* viii: *Las fuentas desde César hasta el siglo v d. de J. C.* (1959), 55 f., cites only alleged coins of Tarraco, which were in fact minted at Ticinum (C. H. V. Sutherland, *RIC* vi, 6 f.; 266 ff). It thus becomes possible to draw the obvious deduction from the absence of any mention of Spain in *Pan. Lat.* xii (ix): Constantine ruled the peninsula from 306 in succession to his father (cf. E. Stein, *Histoire du Bas-Empire* i² (1958), 435 f.).

[168] Optatus, i, 18. Usually dated to 311, as by H. von Schoenebeck, *Beiträge zur Religionspolitik des Maxentius und Constantin. Klio*, Beiheft xliii (1938), 4 ff. But Eusebius states explicitly that Maxentius began by pretending to be a Christian (*HE* viii, 14, 1, cf. *Mart. Pal.* 13, 12).

[169] Augustine, *Brev. coll.* iii, 18, 34; *Contra partem Donati post gesta* 13, 17 (*CSEL* liii, 84; 113 f.).

[170] e.g. H. Dörries, *Das Selbstzeugnis Kaiser Konstantins. Abh. Göttingen*, Phil.-hist. Kl.³ xxxiv

(1954). Nor is there any discussion of *Mort. Pers.* 24, 9 in the article 'Constantinus der Grosse', by J. Vogt, *RAC* iii (1957), 306-379.

[171] N. H. Baynes, *CAH* xii (1939), 671.

[172] F. Lot, *The End of the Ancient World* (trans. P. and M. Leon, 1931), 28.

[173] The term is conventionally applied to *Mort. Pers.* 48, 2 ff.–which, as O. Seeck pertinently remarked, is not an edict, was not published in Milan and was not issued by Constantine (*Zeitschr. für Kirchengesch.* xii (1891), 381 ff.).

[174] 'The Edict of Milan may be a fiction, but the fact for which the term stood remains untouched' (N. H. Baynes, *Constantine the Great* (1931), 11). For bibliography on the 'Edict' see M. V. Anastos, *Rev. ét. byz.* xxv (1967), 13 ff. That writer essays 'a defence of its traditional authorship and designation' and professes respect for contemporary evidence as his 'cardinal principle' (ib. 15), yet seems nowhere to mention *Mort. Pers.* 24, 9.

[175] N. H. Baynes, *CAH* xii (1939), 685 f.

[176] J. Moreau, *Lactance* (1954), 404 ff.

[177] Eusebius, *HE* ix, 9, 12; 9a, 12. In favour of identifying the letter implied by *Mort. Pers.* 44, 11 and the 'νόμος τελεώτατος', N. H. Baynes, *CQ* xviii (1924), 193 f.

unaware of it when they appealed to Constantine, and in 314 the legal basis of the Christians' position in Africa was the edict of Galerius, not the alleged enactment of Constantine.[178] However, the first argument rests on the false premiss that Lactantius consistently echoes Constantinian propaganda. If he wrote *c.* 314, then the alleged anachronism could only be a deliberate and implausible distortion. For, on Lactantius's showing, Maximinus was preparing to introduce open persecution of Christians into his newly conquered domains in Asia Minor, when he was deterred by the letter of Constantine and therefore resorted to subterfuge (36, 6; 37, 1). Further, the letter precedes the account of Maximinus' crimes (37, 1 ff.). The narrative thus unambiguously implies a date in summer or autumn 311. The second argument (it may be maintained) relies upon evidence which should be otherwise interpreted.

First, the Donatist petition to Constantine, from which Optatus quotes:

rogamus te, Constantine optime imperator-quoniam de genere iusto es, cuius pater inter ceteros imperatores persecutionem non exercuit, et ab hoc facinore immunis est Gallia, nam in Africa inter nos et ceteros episcopos contentiones sunt—petimus, ut de Gallia nobis iudices dari praecipiat pietas tua. datae a Luciano, Digno, Nasutio, Capitone, Fidentio *et ceteris episcopis partis Donati* (i, 22).[179]

Since the Donatist bishops mention only Constantius' favourable behaviour to the Christians, then it might seem that Constantine himself has so far done nothing comparable.[180] Such an argument, however, assumes that Optatus quotes the petition in full,[181] and that 'hoc facinore' refers to persecution. Neither assumption is correct. For the crucial clause means 'and Gaul is immune from this crime', and thus refers to a present (not a past) occurrence:[182] hence the crime should be dissension among Christians, and the demonstrative refers back to an earlier clause which Optatus does not quote. In order to interpret the crime as being persecution, the wording of the petition has not always been properly respected: one English translation blandly transposes the order of the clauses,[183] another takes 'nam' as lacking any reference whatever to what precedes ('whereas there are disputes . . ., we pray . . .'),[184] while a third omits the embarassing 'nam' and renders the present tense 'immunis est' by the past 'remained free'.[185] If Optatus is not quoting the full text of the petition, then the Donatists' words can be allowed their natural meaning, and cease to prove that Constantine had so far done nothing to benefit the Christians. The conclusion ought not to surprise. For in his reply Constantine angrily objected to the appeal: 'You seek judgement from me on earth, when I myself expect the judgement of Christ.'[186] He had already, therefore, begun openly to declare himself a Christian.[187]

The second argument arises from a passage in the *Acta purgationis Felicis*:

Aelianus proconsul dixit: <Constantinus> Maximus semper Augustus et Licinius Caesar<es> ita pietatem Christianis exhibere dignantur, ut disciplinam corrumpi nolint, sed potius observari religionem istam et coli velint. noli itaque tibi blandiri, quod cum mihi dicas dei cultorem te esse [ac] propterea non possis torqueri. torqueris, ne mentiaris, quod alienum Christianis esse videtur. et ideo dic simpliciter, ne torquearis. Ingentius dixit: iam confessus sum sine tormento (Optatus, App. ii).[188]

[178] J. Moreau, *Scripta minora* (1964), 121 f.
[179] *CSEL* xxvi, 25 f. The words 'et ceteris episcopis partis Donati' are Optatus' summary of an originally longer list, cf. L. Duchesne, *Mél. d'arch. et d'hist.* x (1890), 608 f.
[180] H. Grégoire, *Byzantion* vii (1932), 650.
[181] As Duchesne unequivocally asserted (o.c. 598; 608).
[182] So it is apparently taken by A. Piganiol, *L'empereur Constantin* (1932), 101.
[183] O. R. Vassall-Phillips, *The Work of St. Optatus* (1917), 43: 'we beseech . . . that we be granted judges from Gaul; for between us and other Bishops in Africa disputes have arisen'.
[184] A. H. M. Jones, *Constantine and the Conversion of Europe* (1948), 104. 'Nam' is a coordinating, not a subordinating conjunction, cf.

Leumann – Hofmann – Szantyr, *Lateinische Grammatik* ii (1965), 504 ff.
[185] W. H. C. Frend, *The Donatist Church* (1952), 147. Similarly, Grégoire has 'la Gaule est restée indemne', with 'donc' for 'nam' (o.c. 650).
[186] Optatus i, 23 (*CSEL* xxvi, 26): 'quibus (i.e. the petition) lectis Constantinus pleno livore respondit. in qua responsione et eorum preces prodidit dum ait: petitis a me in saeculo iudicium, cum ego ipse Christi iudicium expectem.'
[187] The document quoted by Optatus can be identified as one of the two *libelli* which the proconsul of Africa forwarded to Constantine on 15 April 313 (Augustine, *Epp.* lxxxviii, 2).
[188] M. J. Routh, *Reliquiae Sacrae*[2] iv (1846), 293; *CSEL* xxvi, 203. 5 ff.

The apparent allusion to a phrase in Galerius' edict (*Mort. Pers.* 34, 4: 'denuo sint Christiani . . . ita ut ne quid contra disciplinam agant') has been judged to show that in 314 in Africa this edict was the only legal basis of the Christians' position.[189] The deduction does not follow from the evidence. Respect for 'disciplina' is a principle so rooted in Roman law and Roman attitudes that no specific reference to Galerius' edict need be supposed.[190] Moreover, the proconsul is not telling Ingentius the law as it concerns Christians, but stating imperial policy on the use of torture. Although Constantine and Licinius (he explains) show respect for Christians, they do not intend Christians to be absolved from observing either normal proprieties or the moral standards expected of Christians. Thus it is reasonable for Ingentius to be tortured, since he is suspected of perjury. No cause or justification, therefore, for inferring from Aelianus' words either that Galerius' edict was in force,[191] or that it had been superseded,[192] or that it had ever been promulgated in Africa. For, in Africa, persecution had been formally ended by Maxentius, who also ordered restitution of church property.[193] Constantine needed to reiterate the latter ordinance, since its terms had not been completely fulfilled.[194] But he did not need to re-enact freedom of worship for the Christians of Africa. Only those acts of Maxentius were rescinded which offended the canons of justice: the rest simply continued in force, or were perhaps confirmed if challenged.[195]

The case against Lactantius thus lapses. He was writing between 313 and 315 about the deaths of those who persecuted Christians during the preceding decade. It hardly seems possible that he has misstated, either deliberately or by mistake, a fact of such central relevance to his theme as the identity of the first emperor to restore full freedom of worship to the Christians. Although Lactantius fails to state explicitly the precise nature of Constantine's action at his accession, he nevertheless represents Constantine as adopting a policy more favourable to the Christians than his father Constantius. He thus implies, even if he does not state, that Constantine allowed the rebuilding of the churches which Constantius destroyed (*Mort. Pers.* 15, 6). Constantine's subsequent conduct amply reveals his ability to draw political support from men of almost every religious persuasion. His protection of Christianity was originally a purely political act, which proclaimed that the new ruler would emphasise those policies of his father which most set him apart from the other emperors. It thus preceded by several years his personal adhesion to the religion, which Constantine first publicly declared (*Mort. Pers.* 44, 5 f.) when about to do battle with a rival who was not an enemy, but another friend of the Christians. It is not the least of Lactantius' merits that his *De Mortibus Persecutorum* contains such a favourable account of Maxentius.

The preceding study appropriately appears with articles by other pupils of Sir Ronald Syme which aptly 'attest the variety of his inclinations' in the field of Roman History. Its object, its method, and the choice of subject were inspired by his writings and by the advice which he has so freely given to a young scholar. Ever since I began to study under his guidance (in 1964), he has steadily encouraged me to investigate areas and authors not normally the central concern of an ancient historian or student of Latin literature—in other words, to become, like himself, 'unus ex curiosis'.

University College, Toronto

[189] E. Caspar, *Geschichte des Papsttums* i (1930), 581: H. Grégoire, *Byzantion* vii (1932), 648 f. Against this view, see also J.-R. Palanque, *Byzantion* x (1935), 607 ff.; M. V. Anastos, *Rev. ét. byz.* xxv (1967), 36 f.

[190] See O. Mauch, *Der lateinische Begriff DISCIPLINA. Eine Wortuntersuchung* (Diss. Freiburg in der Schweiz, 1941), 52 ff.; 66 ff.

[191] J. Moreau, *Lactance* (1954), 405, assumes that Galerius' edict automatically replaced Maxentius' legislation relating to Christians.

[192] i.e. by the 'Edict of Milan', as argued by P. Batiffol, *La paix constantinienne et le catholicisme* (1914), 240.

[193] p. 44.

[194] Note the emphasis on speed in the letter to Anullinus: Eusebius, *HE* x, 5, 15 ff.

[195] Constantine enunciated the principle clearly: 'tyranni et iudicum eius gestis infirmatis nemo per calumniam velit quod sponte ipse fecit evertere nec quod legitime gestum est' (*CTh* xv, 14, 2); 'quae tyrannus contra ius rescripsit non valere praecipimus, legitimis eius rescriptis minime impugnandis' (*CTh* xv, 14, 3). These two laws bear the dates 12 February 325 and 8 July 326, but the latter should be redated to 6 January 313, and thus refers to Maxentius (O. Seeck, *Regesten* (1919), 64 f.; 160).

VII

WHO WERE THE NOBILITY OF THE ROMAN EMPIRE?

In 1912 MATTHIAS GELZER proved that the contemporaries of Cicero reserved the term *nobilis* to denote strictly and solely consular rank and descent from a consul, and this demonstration has provided the basis for most subsequent study of the social structure of the Roman Republic.[1] Three years later, Gelzer attempted a similar definition for the imperial period, which was far less conducive to understanding and, unfortunately, almost as influential.[2] As recently as 1969, when both studies were published in an English version, the translator was bold enough to assert that, despite minor difficulties, "as long as there is no unquestionable instance where *nobilitas* is ascribed to a man descended from a consular of the triumviral period or later, it seems better to accept Gelzer's view," viz., that under the Roman Empire the term *nobilis* was restricted to the descendants of Republican consuls.[3]

A single passage, overlooked by Gelzer and his translator, provides conclusive refutation.[4] Tacitus makes the freedmen of Claudius describe C. Silius, the lover of Messalina, as *iuvenem nobilem* (*Ann.* 11.28.3). The first consul in the family was P. Silius Nerva, *cos. ord.* 20 B.C., and the unfortunate C. Silius (consul designate when he died in 48) appears to be his grandson in the direct line.[5] Moreover, on the most natural interpretation, other passages in Tacitus and other writers of the early imperial period clearly state or imply that *nobilitas* could still be created or acquired both under Augustus and under his successors.[6] The present brief

---

[1] *Die Nobilität der römischen Republik* (Berlin 1912). On the significance of the thesis, R. Syme, *Roman Revolution* (Oxford 1939) 10 ff.

[2] "Die Nobilität der Kaiserzeit," *Hermes* 50 (1915) 395–415. Both studies are reprinted in Gelzer's *Kleine Schriften* 1 (Wiesbaden 1962) 17–153. For subsequent discussion, cf. R. Syme, *Tacitus* (Oxford 1958) 654. Imperial *nobiles* were defined as the descendants of Republican senators (not consuls) by E. Groag, *Bulićev Zbornik/Strena Buliciana* (Zagreb/Split 1924) 254; G. Barbieri, *L'Albo Senatorio da Settimio Severo a Carino (193–285)* (Rome 1952) 474.

[3] R. Seager, in his introduction to M. Gelzer, *The Roman Nobility* (trans. R. Seager, Oxford 1969) xiv.

[4] The sociological implications of Gelzer's definition are also impossible: it becomes necessary to believe that by A.D. 200 there existed no senatorial nobility of any sort, that under the empire "new fortunes were hardly ever amassed" (*Kleine Schriften* 1 [1962] 150; 152–153 = *Roman Nobility* [1969] 157; 159–160), and that "Die Kaiserzeit hat keine neue Nobilität gebildet" (H. Strasburger, *RE* 17 [1936] 790).

[5] *PIR*[1] S 505 ff., with stemma on p. 246. C. Silius' mother, Sosia Galla (S 563), appears to descend from C. Sosius, *cos. suff.* 33 B.C. (556).

[6] For full references and discussion, see H. Hill, "Nobilitas in the Imperial Period," *Historia* 18 (1969) 230–250. He described Gelzer's thesis as "clearly indefensible on the evidence of the *Annals* alone" (232).

THE NOBILITY OF THE ROMAN EMPIRE   445

note is mainly lexicographical, and concerns itself with a later period than that considered by Gelzer and most of those who have discussed his definition.[7]

In the fourth century the *nobilitas* still formed a special group within the senatorial order, even though the word was sometimes used to designate the Senate as a body (Ammianus 16.10.13; 21.12.24). Symmachus clearly viewed the nobility as a category within the Senate which enjoyed a marked predominance over newcomers. Speaking on behalf of Synesius, whose father was a senator and had probably already served as both *magister memoriae* and proconsul of Africa,[8] he remarked that *propago generis, quanto longius recedit a novis, tanto altius tendit ad nobiles* (*Orat.* 7.4). Whether the observation is general or specific ("a family tree" or "his extraction"), Symmachus reveals that Synesius could advance no claim to nobility simply because his father was a senator.

Ammianus Marcellinus makes the same distinction. Memmius Vitrasius Orfitus, who was less cultured than befitted a *nobilis* (14.6.1), is lauded on inscriptions as being pre-eminent for both nobility of birth and personal distinction (*CIL* 6.1739–42):[9] although no immediate forebears are attested, his pedigree was presumably believed to derive from consular families of the second century.[10] Alypius, a *nobilis adulescens* (28.1.16), is Faltonius Probus Alypius, whose father had been Prefect of the City and whose mother was related to the great Petronius Probus.[11] Aginatius, whom Ammianus describes as *iam inde a priscis maioribus nobilem* (28.1.30), appears to belong to the family of the Anicii, whose first consul was a general of Septimius Severus.[12] By contrast, and in the same context, Ammianus names four men as being *clarissimi*: Tarracius

[7]M. T. W. Arnheim, *The Senatorial Aristocracy in the Later Roman Empire* (Oxford 1972) 8, alleges that in the fourth century "writers such as Symmachus and Ammianus" use the word *nobilis* "to refer to someone of senatorial birth or senatorial origin," and this definition is accepted by A. Chastagnol, *RevPhil*³ 47 (1973), 375. For summary disproof, *Phoenix* 27 (1973) 306–307.

[8]*PLRE* 1.479–480 Julianus 37: attested as *magister memoriae* in 367, proconsul of Africa from 371 to 373, *praefectus urbis Romae* in 387 or 388. Symmachus' speech cannot be independently dated.

[9]A. Chastagnol nevertheless argued that "il semble bien avoir été lui-même l'artisan de sa propre *nobilitas*" (*Les Fastes de la Préfecture de Rome au Bas-Empire* [Paris 1962] 140).

[10]As possible consular ancestors, observe T. Pomponius Proculus Vitrasius Pollio, *cos. II ord.* 176, Scipiones Orfiti as *cos. ord.* 110, 149, 172, 178, and C. Memmius Fidus Julius Albius, *cos. des.* on 18 September 191 (*ILS* 9082). Discussing the Orfitus of the fourth century, Arnheim alleges that "Vitrasius is a rare name, only one other holder of it being known", viz., Vitrasius Praetextatus from *ILS* 4844 ([above, note 7] 127).

[11]*PLRE* 1.49; 192–193; 732.

[12]Viz., Q. Anicius Faustus (*PIR*² A 595). Aginatius' connexion with the Anicii was postulated by O. Seeck, *RE* 1 (1894) 809–810.

Bassus, his brother Camenius, Marcianus, and one Eusafius (28.1.27). Even though the brothers may be related to the noble Ceionii,[13] the choice of a different word implies the existence of a social distinction.

A precise definition can be offered. In the fourth century, or at least after Constantine, a senator was a *nobilis* if he or a forebear had been either ordinary consul or Prefect of the City or a pretorian prefect. Two passages seem explicit enough for proof. First, Ammianus on the maternal uncles of Gallus Caesar, Vulcacius Rufinus (*cos.* 347) and Naeratius Cerealis (*cos.* 358)—*quos trabeae consulares nobilitarunt et praefecturae* (14.11.27). Rufinus was several times a pretorian prefect (ca 345, 347–352, 354, 364–368) but never *praefectus urbis Romae*, while Cerealis was Prefect of the City in 352/3 but never (so far as can be ascertained) a pretorian prefect.[14] Second, when lauding the virgin martyr Sotheris, Ambrose twice implies a formal equation between *nobilitas* and "consulates and prefectures":

habemus enim nos sacerdotes nostram nobilitatem praefecturis et consulatibus praeferendam;

nobilis virgo maiorum prosapia, consulatus et praefecturas parentum sacra posthabuit fide.
(*Exhortatio Virginitatis* 12.82; *PL* 16.376)

Ambrose need not have possessed any precise or authentic evidence about Sotheris' extraction. Indeed, the less he knew, the more valuable will be his testimony for the meaning of the word *nobilis* in the late fourth century.[15]

A third passage, however, seems at first to imply a somewhat wider definition. In his hymn on the martyr, Prudentius narrates at some length how the death of St. Laurentius affected the Roman aristocracy (*Peristephanon* 2.489 ff.). The luminaries of the Roman Senate, who once held pagan priesthoods, have been converted to Christianity, and families of the highest rank now dedicate their children to God:

> *videmus inlustres domos,*
> *sexu ex utroque nobiles,*
> *offerre votis pignera*
> *clarissimorum liberum.*　　　　　　　　　　　(521–524)

Since the language is almost technical (the son of a *vir illustris* was by birth a *clarissimus puer*),[16] Prudentius appears to equate the rank of *illustris* with nobility. Hence (so it might be deduced) the ordinary consulate and the high prefectures were not the only offices to confer

---

[13]As is assumed by Chastagnol (above, note 9) 195–196; *PLRE* 1.158; 177.

[14]For the evidence, see respectively *PLRE* 1.782–783; 197–198.

[15]The true significance of Ambrose's words has unfortunately escaped W. Eck, *Chiron* 1 (1971) 388–389.

[16]A. H. M. Jones, *The Later Roman Empire* (Oxford 1964) 2.529; 3.151–152.

nobility. When Prudentius was writing (ca 400), the rank of *illustris* was possessed not only by consuls, *praefecti urbis*, and pretorian prefects, but also by *patricii* (a higher title than any other), by *magistri officiorum*, *comites sacrarum largitionum* and *comites rerum privatarum*.[17] But Prudentius may in fact be employing the same definition as Ammianus and Ambrose. For he elsewhere makes the martyr Romanus explain how Christian *nobilitas* differs from the pagan variety:

> *absit, ut me nobilem*
> *sanguis parentum praestet aut lex curiae;*
> *generosa Christi secta nobilitat viros.*   (10.123–125)

On the contrary, Christian nobility consists in obedience to God, with martyrdom the *honos novus et splendor ingens* which comes like a magistracy (126–135). The martyr wins an everlasting crown but earthly glory soon fades:

> *incumbe membris, tortor, ut sim nobilis!*
> *his ampliatus si fruar successibus,*
> *genus patris matrisque flocci fecero.*
> *haec ipsa vestra dignitatum culmina*
> *quid esse censes? nonne cursim transeunt*
> *fasces secures sella praetextae togae*[18]
> *lictor tribunal et trecenta insignia,*
> *quibus tumetis maxque detumescitis?*   (138–145)

The high dignities to which Prudentius alludes are precisely the consulate (*fasces, secures, sella, praetextae*),[19] the urban prefecture (*togae*),[20] and the pretorian prefecture (*lictor, tribunal*),[21] and he clearly associates them with the acquisition of nobility.

Furthermore, the narrower definition accords better with the usage of other authors writing in the fourth century,[22] and can also be illustrated from the fifth century. The clearest case is perhaps Sidonius Apollinaris on Avitus:

[17]A. Berger, *RE* 9 (1916) 1070–1085, s.v. *illustris*.

[18]As some MSS and most editions (e.g., M. Lavarenne, Paris: Budé[3], 1963, 124). M. P. Cunningham prints Heinsius' emendation *praetexta et toga* (*CCL* 126 [1966] 335).

[19]Cf. 146: *cum consulatum initis.*

[20]The toga was the distinctive garb of the *praefectus urbi*, cf. A. Chastagnol, *La Préfecture urbaine à Rome sous le Bas-Empire* (Paris 1960) 197. Note Rutilius Namatianus' reference to his own tenure of the office as *iura meae togae* (*De Reditu* 1.468).

[21]Romanus is being tried by a pretorian prefect at Antioch (41 ff.), and these are the judge's normal appurtenances (*Perist.* 3.64–65).

[22]E.g., Firmicus Maternus *Math.* 1.7.5 (*consularium fascium nobilitas*); Ausonius *Epp.* 16.1 (*nobilitas tua* of Petronius Probus when pretorian prefect); *Grat. Actio* 7.32 (on the consulate of Fronto); Claudian *Cons. Prob. et Olyb.* 13 ff. (consulates in every generation renew the nobility of the Anicii); Gregory of Nazianzus *Orat.* 42.24 (*PG* 36.488).

> *sed portio quanta est*
> *haec laudum, laudare patres, quos quippe curules*
> *et praefecturas constat debere nepoti?*
> *sint alii per quos se postuma iactet origo,*
> *et priscum titulis nureret genus alter: Avite,*
> *nobilitas tu solus avos.* (*Carm.* 7.157-162)

Once more, nobility is implicitly equated with "consulates and prefectures."[23]

The evidence from the late Empire confirms the view that the Roman nobility, even of the early Empire, was an open, not a closed class. For it indicates that *nobilitas* was conferred (as it had been earlier) by tenure of the highest office or offices in the Roman state.[24] Under the late Republic and early Empire, the term *nobilis* (in its strictest sense) was reserved for consuls and their descendants, whether their consulate had been ordinary or suffect. By the later fourth century, the suffect consulate no longer counted, but nobility could be acquired not only through an ordinary consulate but by becoming pretorian prefect or Prefect of the City (either at Rome or at Constantinople).[25] It is thus the qualification for *nobilitas* rather than the meaning of *nobilis* which undergoes significant alteration.

These linguistic phenomena are clearly the result of historical changes, whose nature may not be entirely beyond rational conjecture. A deliberate reform has been inferred, and dated to the early years of the fourth century, whereby the standing of both the ordinary consulate and pretorian prefecture was elevated, while that of the suffect consulate was degraded.[26] But the change may be partly the product of a gradual evolution. For the status of the pretorian prefecture had begun to rise significantly much earlier. When the imperial *consilium* met on 6 July 177, former consuls took precedence over the pretorian prefects;[27] a generation later, other *amici* of the emperor were preceded by the prefects.[28] Further, the order in which the town of Canusium listed its patrons in 223 may be relevant: the first name appears to be that of the Prefect of the City (Ap. Claudius Julianus, *cos.* II 224);[29] there follow two pairs of pretorian

---

[23]W. B. Anderson mistranslates *curules* as "curule rank" (Loeb ed., 1 [1936] 131).

[24]For the second century, note Fronto *Ad amicos* 1.27, p. 178 van den Hout. In Apuleius *Flor.* 8.1, all modern editors add the words *pauci consulares ex*, following a suggestion of J. F. Gronovius (see the edition of F. Oudendorp and G. F. Hildebrand [Leipzig 1842] 2.31). On the correct definition of *nobilis*, the addition may not be needed.

[25]The Theodosian Code consistently assumes that the urban prefecture of Constantinople had the same status as that of Rome (*CTh* 1.6; 6.4.12; 6.6; 6.7).

[26]A. Chastagnol, *RHist* 219 (1958) 224 ff.; (above, note 20) 398–399.

[27]*CRAI* 1971. 472.

[28]*Syria* 23 (1942–43) 178 (216); *CJ* 9.51.1 (Caracalla), cf. Dio 77 (76). 17.3–4.

[29]*PIR*[2] C 901: attested as *praefectus urbi* under Severus Alexander (*Dig.* 31.87.3).

prefects;[30] only then come consuls, probably ranked in the chronological order of their consulates, whether ordinary or suffect (*CIL* 9.338).[31] It is normal to deduce that the four pretorian prefects must have acquired consular rank either by the grant of *ornamenta consularia* or by adlection *inter consulares*, or from holding suffect consulates.[32] If the order of names can be taken to reflect the enhanced prestige of the prefecture, then none of these hypotheses may in fact be necessary.

UNIVERSITY COLLEGE, TORONTO

[30]Viz., T. Lorenius Celsus (*PIR*[2] L 343), M. Aedinius Julianus (A 113); L. Didius Marinus (D 71: add *AE* 1954, 171), L. Domitius Honoratus (D 151). For discussion, see now R. Syme, *Emperors and Biography* (Oxford 1971) 151 ff.

[31]M. Statius Longinus, *cos. suff.* before 217 (*Albo* no. 486) precedes C. Bruttius Praesens, *cos. ord.* 217 (*PIR*[2] B 166).

[32]A. Chastagnol, *Recherches sur l'Histoire Auguste* (Bonn 1970) 47–48.

[33]I am grateful to Professor P. S. Derow for his help in greatly clarifying an earlier version of the argument presented here.

VIII

THE BEGINNINGS OF DONATISM

THE earliest years of Donatism will never be more than imperfectly known. For the polemic which still survives reveals that both later Donatists and their opponents were almost as ignorant of its beginnings as any modern investigator. The statements of Optatus and Augustine, no less than the arguments of both Catholics and Donatists at the conference of Carthage in 411, all appear to be based on a single dossier, composed late in the reign of Constantine, which contained documents particularly relevant to the issues of whether Felix, bishop of Abthungi, had validly ordained Caecilanus as bishop of Carthage, and whether Felix or the Donatist bishops had compromised themselves in the Great Persecution.[1] The dossier still survives, at least in part, appended to Optatus' work against the Donatists, as the *Gesta apud Zenophilum* (320) and the *Acta purgationis Felicis* (315). Both documents are preserved by a single manuscript, and both are defective, the former at the end, the latter at the beginning (p. 197 Ziwsa).[2] Also appended to Optatus in the same manuscript are six letters of Constantine, a letter from the Council of Arles (314), and a warrant from the pretorian prefects giving Donatist representatives free transport from the imperial court at Trier to Africa (28 April 315).[3]

None of these last eight documents appears to be quoted or alluded to by any subsequent writer of antiquity, and their value as evidence has sometimes been severely impugned.[4] But their authenticity is now completely vindicated, and scholarly treatment of Donatism has of late tended to concentrate on broader questions than the genuineness of these

[1] L. Duchesne, 'Le dossier de Donatisme', *Mélanges d'archéologie et d'histoire,* x (1890), pp. 589–650.

[2] Optatus and the appended documents are quoted from the edition of K. Ziwsa, *C.S.E.L.* xxvi (1893). The edition is variously defective (see C. H. Turner, *J.T.S.* xxvii (1926), pp. 287 ff.), but I believe that my arguments nowhere depend upon questionable readings.

[3] Optatus, *App.* iii–x (pp. 204–16 Ziwsa).

[4] For the controversy before 1930, see N. H. Baynes, *Constantine the Great and the Christian Church* (1931), pp. 75 ff. The genuineness of some items in the appendix has more recently been questioned by W. H. C. Frend, *The Donatist Church* (1952), pp. 152–3 (App. v only); H. Kraft, *Kaiser Konstantins religiöse Entwicklung, Beiträge zur historischen Theologie,* xx (1955), pp. 172 ff. In refutation, see respectively H. Chadwick, *J.E.H.* v (1954), p. 104; H. U. Instinsky, *Gnomon* xxx (1958), pp. 130 ff.

14

documents.[1] At the same time, however, a questionable assumption tends to be made—that if the documents are genuine, they require no further scrutiny, and can be used without hesitation as valid evidence for the history of Donatism. Yet authenticity does not necessarily entail veracity.

Four apparently minor questions of fact are crucial to understanding or interpreting Donatism as a historical phenomenon. Were the Numidian bishops who denounced Felix as a *traditor* themselves self-confessed *traditores*? Was the Donatus who gave his name to the dissident party a Numidian? What was the date and precise historical context of the eruption of schism? What was the precise purport of the Donatist appeal to Constantine? On these questions a wide uniformity of opinion seems to prevail. The Numidian bishops (it is held) were *traditores* and therefore insincere; Donatus was either a Numidian by birth or bishop of a Numidian see; the dispute began no earlier than 311 or 312; the appeal marks 'one of the decisive moments in the history of the early Church', when 'appeal had been made to the State' and 'for the first time schism or unorthodoxy could become an offence punishable by law'.[2] In all four cases, the present enquiry seeks to disprove, or at least to challenge, these interpretations of the available evidence.

NUNDINARIUS

Nundinarius was a deacon of the church of Cirta during or shortly after the 'Great Persecution'. Later, after the sub-deacon Silvanus became bishop of Cirta, he quarrelled with him. Unable to prevail inside the local community, the deacon was stoned and sought support from other churches, whose bishops (among them Purpurius of Limata) he persuaded to write on his behalf both to Silvanus and to the clergy and *seniores* at Cirta (pp. 189–92). But when the differences proved irreconcilable, Nundinarius resorted to threats as well as pleading, and began to side with the Catholics against the now firmly Donatist Silvanus. He is next discovered on 13 December 320 at Cirta, actively assisting Domitius Zenophilus, *consularis* of Numidia, in a judicial investigation of Silvanus' conduct during the 'Great Persecution' (p. 185. 4 ff.). The full record of these interesting proceedings originally contained the reading of a document which Nundinarius himself produced: the account of a council of Numidian bishops, held at Cirta shortly after persecution ceased, with

---

[1] Note esp. various articles and reviews by P. Brown collected in *Religion and Society in the Age of Saint Augustine* (1972), pp. 237–338.

[2] So, among many others, W. H. C. Frend, *The Donatist Church* (1952), pp. 11 ff., 147.

Secundus, bishop of Tigisis, presiding.[1] At this council (so it was revealed), all those present confessed to being *traditores*, while some admitted having burnt incense and Purpurius of Limata even conceded that he had murdered the sons of his sister.

This remarkable document was gratefully exploited by Optatus and Augustine: it proved that those who accused Felix of Abthungi of *traditio* and who argued that his *traditio* rendered his subsequent ordination of Caecilianus as bishop of Carthage invalid were themselves guilty of the same offence.[2] More surprisingly perhaps, modern historians continue to credit the accounts in Optatus and Augustine, and to exploit them as crucial evidence on the nature of the Donatist schism. For the 'cynical confessions at Cirta reveal the other face of Donatism', disprove its moral integrity, and encourage the assumption that the issue of *traditio* was in no sense the cause of the Donatist schism, but merely its 'superficial occasion'.[3] Almost the only note of scepticism was sounded by A. H. M. Jones, who invited the reader to 'judge for himself whether the minutes of so incriminating a meeting are likely to have been taken or preserved'.[4] Such doubts can be considerably strengthened.

All extant reports of the council of Cirta derive from the document produced by Nundinarius, whom his change of side and role in investigating Silvanus indicate as less than impartial. Nundinarius had already given proof of his skill in using documents: on his own showing, it was a *libellus rei gestae* or *libellus in quo omnia sunt conscripta* which induced other bishops to write to Cirta after he quarrelled with Silvanus (p. 189. 16; 190. 2–3). Now, having fallen out completely with the

[1] Optatus, i. 14, p. 16. 9–16: 'hi et ceteri ... in domum Urbani Carisi consederunt die iii. Iduum Maiarum, sicut scripta Nundinarii tunc diaconi testantur et vetustas membranarum testimonium perhibet, quas dubitantibus proferre poterimus. harum namque plenitudinem rerum in novissima parte istorum libellorum ad implendam fidem adiunximus'; Augustine, *Epp.* liii. 2. 4: 'recita illi gesta apud Zenophilum consularem, ubi Nundinarius quidam diaconus iratus Silvano, quod ab eo fuerit excommunicatus, haec omnia iudiciis prodidit, quae certis documentis et responsionibus testium et recitatione gestorum et multarum epistularum luce clarius constiterunt.'
[2] Optatus, i. 14 ff.; Augustine, *C. litt. Petil.* i. 21.23 (*C.S.E.L.* lii, p. 18); *c. Cresc.* iii. 27. 30 (*C.S.E.L.* lii, pp. 435 ff.); *De unico bapt.* 17. 31 (*C.S.E.L.* liii, p. 32); *C. Gaud.* i. 16. 17; 37. 47 (*C.S.E.L.* liii, pp. 212, 246).
[3] P. Monceaux, *Histoire littéraire de l'Afrique chrétienne*, iv (1912), p. 14; J. Daniélou and H. I. Marrou, *The Christian Centuries*, i (trans. V. Cronin, 1964), p. 244; K. Baus, *Handbook of Church History*, i (1965), p. 418.
[4] A. H. M. Jones, *Constantine and the Conversion of Europe* (1949), p. 123. The 'Acts of the Council of Cirta in Numidia, 4 March 305' are included, with no word of doubt or caution, in J. Stevenson, *A New Eusebius. Documents illustrative of the history of the Church to A.D. 337* (1957), pp. 308–10, no. 266.

16

Donatist party, he turned on them and produced proof that their leaders had committed the crime which they made the basis of their case against Caecilianus. But if they really were all guilty of *traditio* themselves, why did they make the *traditio* of Felix the central issue of the dispute? They could have chosen to take their stand on some other aspect of the case. Moreover, the Cirtan council was not necessarily a provinical synod of all Numidian bishops. It was rather a small informal gathering in a private house of about a dozen bishops.[1] The meeting presumably occurred and those named presumably attended. But for our knowledge of what they did and said, we ultimately seem to depend on Nundinarius' word alone. There is, therefore, even at the lowest count, a distinct possibility of deliberate fraud or malicious invention.

'DONATUS OF CASAE NIGRAE'

In the fourth century there seems to have been no doubt about the identity of the Donatus who was involved in the origins of the schism which bears his name: he was 'Donatus of Carthage', sectarian bishop of the city in succession to Maiorinus, and the predecessor of Parmenianus. In the early fifth century, however, there appears a 'Donatus of Casae Nigrae', who became prominent at the conference of 411 when both Catholics and Donatists stated that it was he whom a Council at Rome condemned in October 313, not Donatus of Carthage. The distinction was bogus:[2] since 'Donatus of Casae Nigrae' disappears as soon as Donatus of Carthage appears, the two descriptions clearly belong to one individual.[3] But why 'from Casae Nigrae'? Perhaps Donatus was a bishop of Casae Nigrae, deposed before moving to Carthage.[4] Better, he was a native of Casae Nigrae, and thus by origin a Numidian.[5] It has consequently been conjectured that he 'led some sort of rigorist campaign' and exhibited schismatic tendencies in Numidia, before he ever went to Carthage.[6] Both explanations assume that whoever first stated that Donatus was of Casae Nigrae discovered an authentic item of information. Doubts should be entertained.

---

[1] Augustine, *C. partem Donati post gesta* 14. 18 (*C.S.E.L.* liii, p. 115): vix undecim vel duodecim episcopi fuerunt.

[2] This important fact is obscured by Ziwsa, whose index purports to distinguish the two (pp. 230–1).

[3] J. Chapman, *Revue bénédictine*, xxvi (1909), pp. 13 ff.; P. Monceaux, *Histoire littéraire*, v (1920), pp. 100 ff.

[4] Ibid., iv (1912), p. 16.

[5] Chapman, op. cit., p. 13.

[6] Frend, *Donatist Church*, p. 14.

The evidence for 'Donatus of Casae Nigrae' needs closer and more accurate attention than it has sometimes received.[1] There are only two items. First, Augustine's *Contra Cresconium*, written *c.* 406:

per Donatum non tantum Carthaginis, qui hanc haeresem maxime roborasse perhibetur, sed etiam maiorem Donatum a Casis Nigris, qui altare contra altare in eadem civitate primus erexit, magnum scandalum factum est (ii. 1. 2).[2]

Second, the conference of 411. For the relevant part of the debate, the full minutes are lost. The proceedings must thus be hazardously reconstructed from the chapter-headings which introduce the minutes and Augustine's brief popular account. The distinction between the two Donati was perhaps introduced by a Catholic, but was certainly accepted by the Donatists with eagerness.[3] Both the reports, however, reveal clearly the evidence on which the distinction was based:

Prosecutio Donatistarum, qui dicunt alium Casae non fuisse Donatum.
Catholicorum ad ista responsio, quod in actis Miltiadis Donatus Casensis evidenter expressus sit.
Ubi Petilianus episcopus partis Donati impedimento raucedinis agere se non posse testatur.
Ubi Catholici testantur, ideo se Petilianum excusationi subtrahere voluisse, quod ei Donatus Casensis ex gestis evidenter ostensus est (*Capitula gestorum Coll. Carth.* iii. 539–42);[4]
legi coepit etiam episcopale iudicium Miltiadis . . . ubi etiam Donatus a Casis Nigris in praesenti convictus est adhuc diacono Caeciliano schisma fecisse Carthagine (*Brev. Coll.* iii. 12. 24);
cum et de Donati nomine contendissent quod non Carthaginiensis, sed Casensis Donatus in iudicio Miltiadis adversus Caecilianum adstitisset, quod et catholici concedebant, aliquando transitum est (*Brev. Coll.* iii. 20. 38).[5]

All the evidence that Donatus had any connection with Casae Nigrae clearly derives from the acts of the Roman council of 313. More specifically, it comes from the occurrence there of the words *Donatus Casensis*. It is possible that 'Carthaginiensis' or an abbreviated form of the word was misread as 'Casaenigrensis' or 'Casensis'.[6] That would explain the late appearance of 'Donatus of Casae Nigrae' in the history of the schism—and remove all the evidence which connects him with Numidia.

[1] Chapman asserted that the distinction never appeared before 411 (op cit., p. 13), while Frend alters the order of the minutes of the conference (*Donatist Church*, p. 287).   [2] *C.S.E.L.* lii, p. 362.
[3] Chapman, op. cit., p. 19.
[4] J. D. Mansi, *Sacrorum conciliorum nova et amplissima collectio*, iv (1769), col. 49 = *P.L.* xi, col. 1256.
[5] *C.S.E.L.* liii, pp. 72, 88.
[6] For the two forms, *Thes. Ling. Lat.*, Onom. ii, col. 223.

CHRONOLOGY

No precise date is known in the early history of Donatism between the meeting of Numidian bishops in Cirta (305)[1] and the letter which the proconsul Anullinus wrote to Constantine, when he forwarded a petition from the Donatists together with one from their opponents (April 313).[2] Nevertheless, most modern accounts assume the same definite chronology, and assign the disputed election from which the schism arose to 311 or 312.[3] Optatus provides the sole evidence: correctly interpreted, he indicates a significantly earlier date.

Optatus states explicitly that the Numidian bishops began the schism by ordaining Maiorinus not long after the council at Cirta (i. 15, p. 17. 9: 'non post longum tempus').[4] He then describes how the rich Lucilla fomented trouble when the church was still at peace, before the storm of persecution (i. 16). Next (p. 19. 3: 'isdem temporibus'), the deacon Felix was arraigned for writing a scurrilous letter 'de tyranno imperatore' (p. 19. 4), and Mensurius, then bishop of Carthage, concealed him, and publicly refused to surrender the fugitive. The governor reported to the emperor, and Mensurius was summoned to the imperial palace. After making provision for his church's property, he set out and appeared in court, but died before he could return to Carthage (i. 17). Then persecution ended. Freedom was restored to the Christians when Maxentius granted toleration. Caecilianus was elected bishop of Carthage and ordained by Felix of Abthungi in the absence of the Numidian bishops (i. 18). When they arrived, they deposed Caecilianus and ordained Maiorinus (i. 19).

By *tyrannus imperator* (it has been assumed), Optatus intended to designate the usurper Maxentius.[5] Now this identification would indeed follow from Optatus' words if *tyrannus* invariably meant 'usurper' in writers of the late fourth and early fifth centuries. But, though this is

---

[1] Augustine, *Brev. Coll.* iii. 17. 32 (*C.S.E.L.* liii, p. 81). Observe, however, that *c.* 406 Augustine had quoted the proceedings with a consular date of 303 (*C. Cresc.* iii. 27. 30), and that the Donatists in 411 disputed the authenticity of the whole document and especially that of the date (*Brev. Coll.* iii. 15. 27).

[2] Augustine, *Epp.* lxxxviii. 2.

[3] W. Jülicher, *RE* iii (1899), col. 1173, s.v. Caecilianus 9; P. Monceaux, *Histoire littéraire*, iv (1912), pp. 16 f.; E. Groag, *R.E.* xiv (1930), col. 2464, s.v. Maxentius; H. Schoenebeck, *Beiträge zur Religionspolitik des Maxentius und Constantin. Klio*, Beiheft xlii (1939), p. 14; Frend, *Donatist Church*, pp. 15 f.; A. Chastagnol, *Les Fastes de la Préfecture de Rome au Bas-Empire* (1962), p. 55.

[4] *P.L.R.E.* states that Maiorinus was elected bishop of Cirta (i, p. 517, Lucilla).

[5] Optatus' words are actually translated as 'the usurping emperor [sc. Maxentius]' in J. Stevenson, *A New Eusebius* (1957), p. 314.

the most common meaning, and perhaps the only meaning which the word bears in political contexts,[1] Christian writers often use it in a quite different sense, to signify 'persecutor'.[2] Optatus must clearly be using *tyrannus* in the latter sense, as he does elsewhere (vii. 1, p. 167. 26: 'tyrannus Antiochus'). Otherwise the phrase *tyrannus imperator* contradicts itself. Moreover, Optatus refers to Maxentius by name in the next chapter as acting at God's behest (p. 19. 18: 'iubente deo indulgentiam mittente Maxentio'), and Maxentius never persecuted the Christians.[3] Accordingly, the 'persecuting emperor' must be another. Only three possibilities are available: the Augustus Maximianus, who abdicated on 1 May 305; Severus, who was created Caesar on 1 May 305 and who controlled Africa for the next year and a half; and Domitius Alexander, who rebelled against Maxentius and ruled in Africa for two years (308–10).[4] But there is no evidence that any of the persecuting edicts was enforced in Africa after Maximianus abdicated.[5] Almost certainly, therefore, the emperor who summoned Mensurius was Maximianus.

The chronology of the early years of the Donatism schism must be constructed on this basis,[6] and the following dates should be approximately correct:

304	Felix accused of insulting Maximianus
305	Mensurius dies
November 306	Africa recognises Maxentius

[1] e.g. Prudentius, *C. Symm.* i. 22, 410 (Maximus and Eugenius), 463, 482 (Maxentius). Prudentius also designates Alaric as *Geticus tyrannus* (*C. Symm.* ii. 696).

[2] Note particularly the practice of Prudentius, who uses *tyrannus* almost as a generic term for all enemies of God, of the Jews, of Jesus, and of the Christians. Hence the word is applied, not only to usurpers, but also to (1) the Devil: *Hamart.* 175, 500, 721; *C. Symm.* ii. 876; (2) the Egyptian Pharaoh: *Cath.* xii. 150; Nebuchadnezzar: *Cath.* iv. 43; *Apoth.* 129; *Perist.* vi. 111; King Antiochus: *Perist.* v. 534; x. 766; (3) King Herod: *Cath.* xii.93; (4) a persecuting emperor: *Perist.* x. 1115 (Galerius); or, most common of all, the magistrate who tries and executes a martyr: *Perist.* iii. 127; v. 168, 429; x. 76, 520, 676; xiii. 65; xiv. 21.

[3] A secure inference from the silence of Lactantius, cf. *J.R.S.* liii (1973), pp. 43 ff.

[4] For the allegiance of Africa in 306–7, see C. H. V. Sutherland, *Roman Imperial Coinage*, vi (1967), p. 417; on the chronology of Alexander, Chastagnol, op. cit., pp. 55 f.

[5] Nor was the fourth and most severe edict ever enforced there, though it was issued *c.* February 304, cf. G. E. M. de Ste. Croix, *H.T.R.* xlvii (1954), pp. 84 ff.

[6] O. Seeck, *Geschichte des Untergangs des antiken Welt*, iii[2] (1921), pp. 323, 509 (also adducing Augustine, *Epp.* xciii. 10. 43); E. Stein, *Geschichte des spätromischen Reiches*, i (1928), pp. 128, 152 = *Histoire du Bas-Empire*, i (trans. and revised by J. R. Palanque, 1959), pp. 84, 100.

20

? November 306	Maxentius restores freedom to the Christians of Africa
Early 307	Caecilianus elected bishop of Carthage
307	Carthaginian council installs Maiorinus in his stead.

THE APPEAL TO CONSTANTINE

'rogamus te, Constantine optime imperator—quoniam de genere iusto es, cuius pater inter ceteros imperatores persecutionem non exercuit, et ab hoc facinore immunis est Gallia, nam in Africa inter nos et ceteros episcopos contentiones sunt—petimus ut de Gallia nobis iudices dari praecipiat pietas tua. datae a Luciano, Digno, Nasutio, Capitone, Fidentio' et ceteris episcopis partis Donati (Optatus, i. 22).[1]

'We ask you, Constantine the best of emperors—because you are of a just race, whose father did not enforce persecution with the other emperors, and Gaul is immune from this crime, for in Africa there are disputes between us and the other bishops—we beg that your piety may order arbitrators to be given us from Gaul. Submitted by Lucianus, Dignus, Nasutius, Capito, Fidentius' and the other bishops of the party of Donatus.

This famous document has not always been interpreted or translated with due attention or respect for the text. O. R. Vassall-Phillips surreptitiously changed the order of clauses and translated: 'We beseech . . . that we be granted judges from Gaul; for between us and other Bishops in Africa disputes have arisen.'[2] H. Grégoire rendered *nam* into French as 'donc', A. H. M. Jones into English as 'whereas', and W. H. C. Frend simply omitted it altogether from his rendering.[3] But *nam* is a coordinating conjunction and the implied logical connection between the clauses which it joins ought not to be reversed or concealed. Further, the tense of the verb in the phrase *immunis est* has sometimes been disregarded, it means neither 'est restée indemne', nor 'was immune', nor 'remained free', but 'is free' in the present.[4]

Such misrepresentation of the document is not deliberate, but the consequence of interpreting it in the light of two probable misconceptions:

---

[1] The last five words are Optatus' (or another's) summary of an originally longer list, cf. L. Duchesne, *Mélanges*, x (1890), pp. 608 f.

[2] *The Work of St. Optatus* (1917), p. 43. The transposition of clauses is retained in J. Stevenson, *A New Eusebius* (1957), p. 317, no. 271.

[3] H. Grégoire, *Byzantion*, vii (1932), p. 650; Jones, *Constantine* (1949), p. 104; Frend, *Donatist Church*, p. 147.

[4] *J.R.S.* liii (1973), p. 45.

first, that Optatus has quoted the petition in its entirety;[1] second, that the *facinus* mentioned is persecution.[2] In fact, *nam* surely implies that the *facinus* is not persecution, but schism or quarrelling among Christians, and this interpretation in turn permits *immunis est* to be taken as referring to the present. The Donatists give two reasons for asking Constantine to send *iudices* from Gaul: first, the emperor's justice or righteousness; second, the fact that Gaul is free from dissensions of the type which the *iudices* are to adjudicate. But, if this is the sense of *ab hoc facinore*, then the phrase refers back to something which Optatus either does not or could not quote.[3]

The consequences are important. If the petition is incomplete, then it cannot be adduced to prove that the Donatists had not yet heard of any action by Constantine in favour of the Christians.[4] On the contrary, if this is one of the two documents which Anullinus forwarded in April 313, they already knew that Constantine had instructed Anullinus to hasten the restoration of property to 'the Catholic Church of the Christians' (Eusebius, *H.E.* x. 5. 15–17), and Constantine's reply contains the firm assertion, 'I myself await the judgement of Christ' (i. 23).

What sort of *iudices* did the Donatists request? It is sometimes assumed that they are Roman officials or magistrates with judicial powers, and hence that the Donatists invoked 'the secular arm' against the Catholics.[5] But the logical structure of the petition surely implies that the Donatists were thinking specifically of Gallic bishops as arbitrators.[6] Constantine, at least, seems to have construed their request in this sense.[7] As *iudices* he appointed Maternus of Cologne, Reticius of Autun, and Marinus of Arles, who were to judge the case with Miltiades, the bishop of Rome, and one other, who might conceivably be Merocles the bishop of Milan.[8]

---

[1] Duchesne so stated, emphatically (op. cit., pp. 598, 608).

[2] Hence Frend translates *ab hoc facinore* as 'from that crime' (*Donatist Church*, p. 147).

[3] Optatus' knowledge of the petition may derive entirely from the emperor's reply, cf. i. 23 (p. 26.6 ff.): 'quibus (i.e. the petition) lectis Constantinus pleno livore respondit. in qua responsione et eorum preces prodidit, dum ait: petitis a me in saeculo iudicium, cum ego ipse Christi iudicium expectem.'

[4] As argued by H. Grégoire, *Byzantion*, vii (1932), p. 650; J. Moreau, *Scripta minora* (1964), p. 120.

[5] Frend, *Donatist Church*, p. 147.

[6] H. U. Instinsky alleged that all previous interpreters had assumed that the Donatists were asking for bishops—and himself argued the contrary thesis, *Bischofstuhl und Kaiserthron* (1955), p. 70.

[7] Similarly Augustine, *Epp.* liii. 2.5: 'preces Donatistarum ad Constantinum, ut propter ipsam causam inter Afros episcopos dirimendam iudices ex Gallia episcopos mitteret.'

[8] The MSS. of Eusebius call him Μάρκῳ (*H.E.* x. 5. 18), O. Seeck proposed the

Conclusion

It has not been the aim of these pages to write a history of the early years of Donatism, or to set the known events and documents in their full context. They have merely challenged some traditional interpretations in the hope that this history may some day be rewritten on a sounder basis. The Donatist leaders were not necessarily the scoundrels and hypocrites whom Nundinarius depicted; Donatus himself may have had no connection with Numidia; the schism probably began in the immediate aftermath of persecution; and neither the fact nor the known contents of the Donatist petition to Constantine manifest a radically new attitude of Christians to the Roman state.[1]

emendation Μερόκλη (*Zeitschr. f. Kirchengesch.* x (1889), p. 512). In defence of the transmitted text, however, see H. Kraft, *Kaiser Konstantins religiöse Entwicklung* (1955), pp. 168 f.

[1] Note Eusebius, *H.E.* vii. 30. 19 (an appeal to the pagan Aurelian). On the circumstances and significance of the earlier appeal, see F. Millar, *J.R.S.* lxi (1971), pp. 14 ff.

IX

TWO SENATORS UNDER CONSTANTINE *

A handbook of astrology seems an improbable source of information about Constantine's dealings with the Roman Senate. Yet if the work were contemporary, and if both author and addressee were senators, then a few passages might betray a hint of transactions either not otherwise attested or not elsewhere documented in any detail. Such is in fact the case with the *Mathesis* of Julius Firmicus Maternus Junior v.c., of which one passage in particular can be made to disclose specific facts of some historical importance. Maternus discusses the horoscope of a man, whose father was exiled after twice being ordinary consul, and whose own career advanced from exile to the urban prefecture of Rome. Neither is named; they were familiar to both the author and the addressee of his work.[1]

Maternus was writing in the last years, probably in the very last months, of the reign of Constantine. He refers to an eclipse of the sun during the consulate of Optatus and Paulinus, which occurred on 17 July 334 (*Math.* i, 4, 10).[2] On the other hand, news of the death of Constantine (22 May 337) had not yet reached Maternus. For the reigning emperor is styled ' dominus atque imperator noster Constantinus Augustus ' (i, pr. 7), and ' divi Constantii filius ' (where the manuscripts have ' Constantini ', but the context imposes emendation),[3] and Maternus beseeches the gods to protect and preserve ' Constantinum maximum principem et huius invictissimos liberos, dominos et Caesares nostros ' (i, 10, 14).

Apart from his own references to activity in the law courts (iv, pr. 1 f.), no official career is known for Firmicus Maternus.[4] For the addressee, however, inscriptions supplement what his friend or client discloses.[5] Maternus first promised to compose a treatise on astrology, when Fl. Lollianus Mavortius was *consularis* of Campania (i, pr. 2): when Lollianus became *comes Orientis*, he continued to ask for what had been promised, and Maternus finally dedicated the work to him as ' proconsuli ... et ordinario consuli designato ' (i, pr. 7/8). The proconsulate was that of Africa, and all these posts fall after 328, when Lollianus is attested as *curator* of the water supply and the Via Minucia.[6] But the ordinary consulate was not in fact bestowed for many years. Lollianus was Prefect of the City in 342, but not consul for another thirteen years (355), after which he served Constantius as pretorian prefect in Illyricum. It is an easy hypothesis that Lollianus had received formal designation to an ordinary consulate (for 338) before the death of Constantine interrupted his career.[7] Hence Maternus should be writing precisely in the spring of 337.[8]

I. THE HOROSCOPE

Quantum autem antisciorum vis valeat et quantum antisciorum ratio operetur, ex hac genitura discere poteris, quam subicere curabimus. Is, in cuius genitura Sol fuit in Piscibus, Luna in Cancro,

* The substance of the present paper was delivered in a colloquium at Harvard University on 21 February 1974, and I learnt much from the discussion on that occasion. The subsequent written version has been read and greatly improved by Professors G. W. Bowersock and C. P. Jones, Dr. F. G. B. Millar, Dr. J. F. Matthews and Mr. E. J. Champlin. I am also extremely grateful to Professor G. J. Toomer for his advice on astrological questions.

[1] *Math.* ii, 29, 20: ' cuius haec genitura sit, Lolliane decus nostrum, optime nosti '. The horoscope received no discussion in L. Thorndike, ' A Roman Astrologer as a Historical Source: Julius Firmicus Maternus ', *CP* viii (1913), 415–35.

[2] F. Boll, *RE* vi (1909), 2362.

[3] *Math.* i, 10, 13: ' dominus et Augustus noster ac totius orbis imperator pius felix providus princeps, Constantinus scilicet maximus divi Constantii filius augustae ac venerandae memoriae principis, qui ...

apud Naissum genitus a primo aetatis gradu imperii gubernacula retinens, quae prosperis nanctus fuerat auspiciis, Romanum orbem ad perennis felicitatis augmentum salubri gubernationis moderatione sustentat '. For the necessity of emendation, cf. F. Boll, *RE* vi, 2366. The fact that W. Kroll and F. Skutsch printed ' divi Constantini ' occasionally misleads scholars (Teubner ed., i (1897), 37, cf. ii (1913), 547).

[4] He was from Syracuse (*Math.* vi, 30, 26, as emended by Skutsch) and lived in Sicily (i, pr. 4).

[5] *PLRE* i, 512–14. But *ILS* 3425 might belong to another Lollianus, cf. *Phoenix* xxvii (1973), 145.

[6] *ILS* 8943.

[7] But not that ' possibly Lollianus fell from imperial favour owing to the dedication to him of this work on astrology ' (*PLRE* i, 513).

[8] T. Friedrich, *In Iulii Firmici Materni de Errore profanarum religionum libellum quaestiones* (Diss. Giessen, 1903; pub. Bonn, 1905), 53.

Saturnus in Virgine, Iuppiter in Piscibus in eadem parte in qua Sol, Mars in Aquario, Venus in Tauro, Mercurius in Aquario isdem cum Marte partibus, horoscopus in Scorpione; eius geniturae pater post geminum ordinarium consulatum in exilium datus est, sed et ipse ob adulterii crimen in exilium datus et de exilio raptus in administrationem Campaniae primum destinatus est, deinde Achaiae proconsulatum, post vero ad Asiae proconsulatum et praefecturam urbi Romae.

(*Math.* ii, 29, 10)

Firmicus Maternus devotes a lengthy chapter of his *Mathesis* to the doctrine of *antiscia*, first expounding how *antiscia* are computed (ii, 29, 1–9), then illustrating the application of the doctrine from a single horoscope, which he quotes (ii, 29, 10) and then expounds in great detail (ii, 29, 11–20). Once the true adept in astrology has calculated the *antiscia* of a particular horoscope, he can easily discover ' omnia quae in fatis hominum quaeruntur ',[9] and if he has carefully ascertained the *vis antisciorum*, then ' numquam eum tractantem fata hominum coniecturae fallit intentio ' (20). The horoscope adduced is discussed for its relevance to the careers and vicissitudes of both its possessor (' ipse ') and his father (' eius geniturae pater '), and the discussion discloses information which Maternus does not include in the initial presentation (10).

The father, who was exiled after twice holding an ordinary consulate (10), had suffered ' adsiduae insidiae ' (11). The exile was the work of his enemies whom Jupiter, transmitting his influence from Pisces to Libra, made superior to him (12), and it was decreed by a vote of the Roman Senate (13). Further, Sol and Jupiter together, transmitting their influence to Libra and to the *cacodaemon*, show that the father's extraction was ignoble (12).

The son was exiled for adultery, then snatched from exile to govern Campania, and advanced to the proconsulates of Achaea and Asia, and finally to the prefecture of the city of Rome (10). Before his exile, he had been oppressed by many illnesses (14; 16). His exile, like his father's, was the work of enemies who overcame him (12), but he was tried and sentenced by the emperor (18). Nor was adultery (14; 17) the only charge: he was also accused of being ' absconsarum litterarum scius ' (18), that is, presumably, of acquaintance with magic or the occult.[10] Subsequently, however, he was liberated from exile (16) and advanced to the highest honours (19), while Saturn in Virgo and Mercury in Aquarius (in the original horoscope) decreed such learning and literary skill that his oratory and style were compared to those of ancient authors (20).

So far Maternus' explicit testimony. The date of the horoscope which he describes and expounds can be calculated with some precision. In 1931, in an astrological journal, W. Koch determined the time at which the subject was born as approximately eleven p.m. on 14 March 303,[11] and in 1953, in one of the more prominent classical periodicals, O. Neugebauer calculated the hour of birth as 9 p.m. on the same day.[12] G. J. Toomer advises me that the year and the month are absolutely certain (no others fit the stated configuration), but that the day may be 15 March 303 :[13] all the other specifications will fit both days, but the full moon which occurred ' tertio die ' (*Math.* ii, 29, 16) belongs to the night of 19–20 March,[14] so that Maternus has made a mistake in his reckoning, either of two days (counting exclusively from 14 March) or of one (counting from 15 March).

II. IDENTIFICATION

The subject of the horoscope was born on 14 or 15 March 303 and became *praefectus urbi* before the death of Constantine, and his father was twice ordinary consul. Since the

[9] On ' antiscium ' as an astrological term, cf. A. Bouché-Leclerq, *L'astrologie grecque* (1899), 161 f. *TLL* registers no other occurrence of the word in Latin literature (ii, 184).

[10] Compare *Math.* iii, 12, 6 : ' absconsarum litterarum facient peritos, magos philosophos et caelestia saepe tractantes '; iv, 12, 4: ' absconsarum aut inlicitarum litterarum actibus inhaerescunt '.

[11] W. Koch, ' Ceionius Rufius Albinus,' *Astrologische Rundschau* xxiii (1931), 177–83. The article is not registered by K. Ziegler in the ' Addenda Addendis ' to the reprinted second volume of the Teubner edition of the *Mathesis* (ii (1968), 559 f.).

I am grateful to Professor G. P. Goold for procuring me a photographic copy from the library of the Warburg Institute, London.

[12] O. Neugebauer, ' The Horoscope of Ceionius Rufius Albinus ', *AJP* lxxiv (1953), 418–20, cf. O. Neugebauer and H. B. van Hoesen, *Greek Horoscopes*. Memoirs of the American Philosophical Society xlviii (1959), 161, n. 5.

[13] Private letter, 12 April 1974.

[14] H. H. Goldstine, *New and Full Moons 1001 B.C. to A.D. 1650* (1973), 109 ; at the longitude of Babylon, the full moon occurred at precisely 0.35 a.m. on 20 March 303.

ordinary consuls of every year are known from several calendars and chronicles,[15] and since there is extant a complete list of prefects of the city for the early fourth century,[16] both men must be identical with attested persons, and their identification ought not to pose insoluble problems. Yet modern scholarship has often gone sadly astray.

Progress was long prevented by the lack of a critical edition of Firmicus Maternus' work. The *editio princeps*, published at Venice in 1497, was at once eclipsed by the Aldine edition (1499) and the two editions which Nicholas Pruckner based on it and published in Basle (1533 and 1551).[17] No new edition was undertaken until the late nineteenth century, when the publishing house of Teubner decided to include the *Mathesis* in their series of Latin texts. K. Sittl produced the first volume of his edition in 1894: it was denounced at once for gross incompetence,[18] and no more ever appeared. Instead, Teubner transferred the commission to W. Kroll and F. Skutsch, whose edition was published in two volumes, the first in 1898 and the second in 1913 (after the death of Skutsch, and with the assistance of K. Ziegler).

Although only the last really deserves to be styled a critical edition, it was Sittl who took the decisive step which permitted identification of the horoscope. The Aldine and Pruckner's editions are based on badly interpolated manuscripts and print the horoscope under the heading ' Lolliani genitura ',[19] thus deceiving scholars for more than three centuries.[20] The *editio princeps* lacks the misleading gloss, and Sittl rightly ejected it from the text.[21] T. Mommsen immediately produced an identification: if the argument proceeds from the iterated ordinary consulate, the father must be C. Ceionius Rufius Volusianus, consul in 311 and 314, the son Ceionius Rufius Albinus, Prefect of the City of Rome from 30 December 335 to 10 March 337.[22]

The identification was long accepted as certain,[23] but in recent decades it has come to be discarded by practitioners of prosopography and students of the fourth century. E. Groag, who had formerly accepted the prevailing identification,[24] gave the lead. He adduced two grounds for rejection: first, that the *geniturae pater* was of low birth, whereas Volusianus was of a noble lineage ; and second that it was inconceivable that the son's consulate (in 335) should be omitted.[25] But what other candidates are there? Groag rejected T. Fl. Postumius Titianus (*cos.* II 301)[26] and Sex. Anicius Paulinus (*cos.* 325)[27] since neither was twice *consul ordinarius* and neither was of low birth. Hence, since no more iterated consulates are attested in·the early fourth century, except for emperors, Groag was compelled to postulate one: he conflated the two Vettii Rufini who were consuls in 316 and 323 to produce the father, and identified the son as C. Vettius Cossinius Rufinus (*praefectus urbi* from 20 August 315 to 4 August 316).[28] This bold hypothesis entails at least one other improbable corollary, which Groag explicitly drew: the father's exile was presumably related in some way to Constantine's execution of his son Crispus (326), whereas the son must have been exiled more than twenty years earlier, by Diocletian or one of his imperial colleagues.[29] Nevertheless, A. Alföldi and A. Chastagnol accepted the

[15] See the conspectus (44 B.C.–A.D. 613) provided by T. Mommsen, *MGH*, Auct. Ant. xiii (1898), 499 f.

[16] *MGH*, Auct. Ant. ix, 66 f. (certainly complete from 291 to 354).

[17] For precise bibliographical details, see *Br. Mus. Cat. of Printed Books*, lxxiii (1961), 432.

[18] W. Kroll and F. Skutsch, ' In Firmicum Sittelianum emendationum centuriae duae primae ', *Hermes* xxix (1894), 517–29. T. Mommsen was brief in the extreme, but still more devastating (ib. 618–19).

[19] Pruckner's edition (1533, 1551), p. 42.

[20] Including B. Borghesi, *Oeuvres complètes* iv (1865), 521, and, less excusably, R. MacMullen, *Ancient Society* ii (1971), 106.

[21] It finds no mention in his edition, not even in the apparatus criticus (i (1894), 71 f.). Sittl, however, continued to adhere to the false identification, and printed the words ' Achaiae ... Romae ' in italics as ' vestigia editionis alterius a. 354 confectae ' (ib. 72, cf. *Archiv für lat. Lexicographie* iv (1887), 610).

[22] *Hermes* xxix (1894), 471 f. = *Ges. Schr.* vii (1909), 449 f.

[23] C. H. Moore, *Julius Firmicus Maternus, der Heide und der Christ* (Diss. Munich, 1897), 3 f.; Bouché-Leclercq, o.c. (n. 9), 164 f.; Friedrich, o.c. (n. 8), 53 ; F. Boll, *RE* vi (1909), 2366 ; Schanz-Hosius, *Gesch. d. röm. Litt.* iv, 1² (1914), 131. There is no mention, however, in O. Seeck's treatment of the Ceionii, *RE* iii (1899), 1858 f.

[24] *Wiener Studien* xlv (1926–7), 108.

[25] *Die Reichsbeamten von Achaia in spätrömischer Zeit*. Diss. Pann., Ser. i, 14 (1946), 16 f.

[26] Certified as a second consulate by contemporary evidence: *CIL* vi, 2143 ; *IGRR* iii, 1268 ; *P. Flor.* 3 ; *PSI* 1037.

[27] Registered as a second consulate by A. Degrassi, *Fasti Consolari* (1952), 79. But contemporary documents bearing the consular date of 325 record no iteration: *ICUR* i, 35 ; *P. Oxy.* 52 ; 1626 ; *P. Lond.* 977 ; Thead. 7 ; 35 ; *Sammelbuch* 8019 ; 8020.

[28] Groag, o.c. (n. 25), 18.

[29] ibid. 20.

identification,[30] and A. H. M. Jones, though he made no acknowledgement to Groag, took it for indubitable.[31]

A third identification has recently been propounded. The first volume of the *Prosopography of the Later Roman Empire* enters both father and son as persons whose name is not certainly known,[32] but argues with some degree of confidence that the son is the poet Publilius Optatianus Porfyrius (Prefect of the City in 329 and 333), the father C. Junius Tiberianus (*cos.* 281, 291).[33] The career of the horoscope (it is urged) corresponds closely to Optatianus' career, but not to that of any other contemporary. Hence, since no *bis consules* of the preceding generation have similar nomenclature, it must be supposed that Optatianus did not use his father's names. Once that has been granted, the way lies open to identify the father as Junius Tiberianus, and the identities are held to be confirmed by the fact that Tiberianus was probably born *c.* 240, Optatianus between 260 and 270.[34]

Such speculations are ruined by the date which the horoscope bears. Its subject was born on 14 or 15 March 303 : the calculation is technical and precise, and far outweighs vaguer arguments derived from history or prosopography. It will not do to dismiss the astrological date as ' specious mathematical reasoning '.[35] A date of birth as late as 303 decisively disproves two of the three proposed identifications.[36] C. Vettius Cossinius Rufinus was *corrector* of Campania under Maxentius (306–312), before which he had already held several official posts in Italy.[37] Publilius Optatianus Porfyrius wrote poems from exile in 324 referring to his earlier enjoyment of imperial favour—which is also not at all plausible for a man born in 303.[38] Moreover, the other evidence for his career, though neither plentiful nor all easy to interpret, seems to indicate that he was in fact born *c.* 260/70.[39]

Rufius Volusianus and Ceionus Rufius Albinus remain as the father and son to whom Firmicus Maternus alludes. No private citizen of the late third or early fourth centuries was twice *consul ordinarius* except Volusianus and C. Junius Tiberianus (*cos.* 281, 291). But for Volusianus alone can a son be produced who possesses the requisite qualifications. Ceionius Rufius Albinus was *praefectus urbi* from December 335 to March 337, he was honoured at Rome as both a philosopher and as Volusianus' son,[40] and his birth can coincide with the date indicated in the horoscope (14 or 15 March 303).

III. THE FAMILY OF VOLUSIANUS

Meministi dixisse nos, quod Pisces antiscium in Libram mittant et Libra rursus in Pisces. Sol itaque et Iuppiter in Piscibus pariter constituti, in Libram mittentes antiscium, in hoc signo, in quo humiliatur atque deicitur,[41] et in XII loco geniturae id est in cacodaemone, paternum genus ostendit ignobile et ipsi ⟨et⟩ patri famosum decernit exilium ; [42] Iuppiter vero, cuius vim ac potestatem antiscii radius ex signo Piscium ad Librae transtulit signum, in XII loco id est in cacodaemone per

[30] A. Alföldi, *The Conversion of Constantine and Pagan Rome* (1948), 74, n. 2 ; A. Chastagnol, *Les Fastes de la Préfecture de Rome au Bas-Empire*. Études prosopographiques ii (1962), 65–8.
[31] *The Later Roman Empire* iii (1964), 17, n. 64. B. Malcus, *Opuscula Atheniensia* vii (1967), 98 f., rejected Groag's identification, but offered a list of proconsuls of Asia under Constantine which fails to register anyone else who can be the proconsul of the horoscope (ib. 141).
[32] *PLRE* i, 1004, Anonymus 1 ; 1006–1008, Anonymus 12. The entry for Ceionius Rufius Albinus makes no reference at all to the horoscope (i, 37).
[33] *PLRE* i, 1008: ' Optatianus is the most probable subject of the horoscope '.
[34] *PLRE* i, 1004: ' Paternus [i.e. Nonius Paternus, *cos.* II 269] and Tiberianus are thus left by elimination ; dates make Tiberianus more likely ; a consul of 281 without patrician ancestry should have been born about 240 ; a *Praefectus Urbi* of 329 . . . would have been born between 260 and 270.'
[35] As does Chastagnol, o.c. (n. 30), 95 : ' Nous

avons vu que Groag pense plutôt—avec raison, nous semble-t-il—à Vettius Rufinus, préfet en 315–16, et à son père homonyme. Dès lors tombe entièrement le raisonnement mathématique spécieux de O. Neugebauer.'
[36] *Phoenix* xxvii (1973), 307.
[37] *ILS* 1217.
[38] Porfyrius, *Carm.* i, 1 f.
[39] On the chronology of Porfyrius' political and literary career, see now *AJP* (forthcoming).
[40] *ILS* 1222. For writers named Albinus, who might be identical with Ceionius Rufius Albinus, see W. S. Teuffel, *Gesch. d. röm. Litt.* iii⁶ (1913), 231, § 407. 5 ; *PLRE* i, 33 f.
[41] Kroll and Skutsch note : ' sc. Sol de quo etiam sequentia solo dicuntur ' (edn. i (1897), 82).
[42] The addition of ' et ' is due to E. Badian (verbally, on 21 February 1974). Elsewhere in his discussion, Maternus consistently uses ' ipse ' to distinguish the son from the father : ' eius geniturae pater . . . , sed et ipse ' (10), ' patrem . . . de ipso ' (11), ' et ipsi et patri eius exicitavit inimicos ' (12), ' ipsum vero ' (14).

44

antiscium [fuisset] constitutus plurimos et ipsi et patri eius excitavit inimicos et eos superiores esse perfecit.

(*Math.* ii, 29, 12)

Investigation of the family connections of C. Ceionius Rufius Volusianus has been hampered by the preconception that he was of noble birth,[43] which also provided the main motive for denying his identity with the *bis consul* to whom Firmicus Maternus alludes.[44] Although no father is attested by explicit evidence, a putative ancestor has been discovered in the Nummius Ceionius Albinus whom works of reference register as *praefectus urbi* in 256 and 261–63 and consul for the second time in 263 ; [45] and Volusianus is sometimes supposed to descend from the consular Nummii Albini of the Severan age, or even perhaps from earlier Ceionii and Republican patrician families.[46]

This reconstruction of his pedigree, however, relies excessively on dubious evidence. It is the *Historia Augusta* alone which indicates an alliance between Ceionii and Nummii Albini before the later third century. According to this source, the pretender Clodius Albinus descended from the Roman families of the Postumii and Albini and Ceionii: his father was one ' Ceionius Postumus ' and his career was aided by his relative ' Ceionius Postumianus '.[47] Further, after Septimius Severus defeated Albinus, he executed ' Ceionius Albinus ' together with many other nobles.[48] At a later stage, the *Historia Augusta* produces another ' Ceionius Albinus ' as *praefectus urbi*, to whom the emperor Aurelian writes a bogus letter.[49] Since all these allegations are either fraudulent or (at the very least) suspect of being invented, the *Historia Augusta* provides no warrant either for accepting the existence of these persons or even for turning Nummius Albinus (*cos.* II 263) into ' Nummius Ceionius Albinus '.[50] Since a Nummius Albinus is not a plausible father for C. Ceionius Rufius Volusianus, better evidence is required to establish the latter's alleged noble birth.

Nor need Rufius Volusianus descend from the noble Ceionii of the early empire. This family rose to prominence with L. Ceionius Commodus (*cos. ord.* 78), who subsequently governed Syria.[51] His son was consul a generation later (*cos. ord.* 106), and likewise his son in turn (*cos. ord.* 136).[52] The latter, better known to posterity as Aelius Caesar, did not long survive his adoption as Hadrian's imperial heir. But he fathered three known children: his son became emperor as Lucius Verus and married a daughter of Marcus Aurelius, but had no discoverable male issue, while two daughters married respectable senators.[53] Thus, although descendants of L. Ceionius Commodus (*cos. ord.* 78) still existed in the Severan age,[54] the line bearing his name had disappeared, unless it was represented by unattested descendants of M. Ceionius Silvanus (*cos. ord.* 156), who was presumably a relative.[55]

During the early third century, only a single Ceionius of any note is on authentic record: L. Ceion[ius. . . .] Alienus, an imperial procurator and governor of Sardinia under either Caracalla (211–17) or Elagabalus (218–22).[56] Towards the close of the century, there appear two Ceionii of some prominence, whom it may be possible to link to Volusianus and to each other: Ceionius Varus, attested only as *praefectus urbi* on 1 January 284 and

[43] Hence the mistaken attempt to force the sense of ' paternum genus ostendit ignobile ' in *Phoenix* xxvii (1973), 306 f.

[44] E. Groag, *Reichsbeamten* (1946), 17 ; A. Chastagnol, *Fastes* (1962), 66 ; *PLRE* i, 1004.

[45] E. Groag, *RE* xvii (1937), 1409–11 ; G. Barbieri, *L'Albo senatorio da Settimio Severo a Carino (193–285)* (1952), 298, no. 1674 ; *PLRE* i, 35, Albinus 9. H. Dessau was more cautious (*PIR*[1] N 180 ; 185).

[46] J. Morris, *Bonner Jahrbücher* clv (1965), 91 f. ; *PLRE* i, 978 ; M. T. W. Arnheim, *The Senatorial Aristocracy in the Later Roman Empire* (1972), 130 f. Morris prints a stemma (o.c., Beilage) which makes Rufius Volusianus the grandson of the *cos* II ord. 263 and the latter a direct descendant of L. Ceionius Commodus, *cos. ord.* 106.

[47] *HA*, *Clod. Alb.* 4, 1 f ; 6, 1. For a probable Ceionius Postumianus in the late fourth century, see *PLRE* i, 718–9, Postumianus 3.

[48] *HA*, *Sev.* 13, 3.

[49] *HA*, *Aurel.* 9, 2.

[50] R. Syme, *Ammianus and the Historia Augusta* (1968), 154 f.

[51] *PIR*[2] C 603.

[52] *PIR*[2] C 604 ; 605.

[53] *PIR*[2] C 606 ; 612 ; 614. Ceionia Fabia married Plautius Quintillus (*cos. ord.* 159), Ceionia Plautia Q. Servilius Pudens (*cos. ord.* 166).

[54] A daughter of Lucius and Lucilla was at least betrothed to Claudius Pompeianus Quintianus (Dio lxxiii (lxxii), 4. 4. p. 285 Boissevain). L. Ti. Claudius Aurelius Quintianus, *cos. ord.* 235, appears to be a descendant of the pair (*PIR*[2] C 992, cf. 975).

[55] *PIR*[2] C 610. The consul of 157 (*PIR*[2] C 602) is now known to have borne the names M. Vettulenus Civica Barbarus (*AE* 1957, 18).

[56] *PIR*[2] C 601, known only from *AE* 1910, 33 (Caralis).

285, and [Ce]ionius Proculus, consul suffect on 1 March 289.[57] If Volusianus' full name were taken to indicate that his mother was a Ceionia, then Ceionius Varus could be his maternal uncle, and Ceionius Proculus a cousin or brother.

As for Volusianus' father, two arguments can be combined and exploited. If his mother was a Ceionia, then his father was surely a C. Rufius, who may or may not have possessed the *cognomen* Volusianus. The horoscope in Firmicus Maternus reveals that its subject's paternal pedigree was ignoble (*Math.* ii, 29, 12): therefore, the father of Volusianus came from a family which had not yet attained consular rank.[58] Taken together, the two inferences permit a precise conjecture. Volusianus is surely one of the Rufii of Etruscan Volsinii, a family whose fortunes can be plotted in some detail, from the Severan age to the fifth century.[59] Their rise begins with C. Rufius Festus, a *primipilaris* of the late second or early third century, who became procurator of Dalmatia and Histria.[60] His children possessed senatorial rank (C. Rufius Festus Laelius Firmus v.c. and Rufia Procula c.f.), and two grandsons are attested as *clarissimi viri*, viz. Rufius Marcellinus and Rufius Proculus.[61] Rufius Volusianus was presumably born in the fifth decade of the third century (240–50),[62] and could, on the evidence available, be the son of the attested Rufius Proculus.

IV. CONJECTURAL STEMMA

The hypotheses adumbrated in the preceding discussion can be exhibited most clearly in a stemma.[63] But it must be emphasized that most of the relationships depicted result from combinations and conjectures of varying degrees of uncertainty.

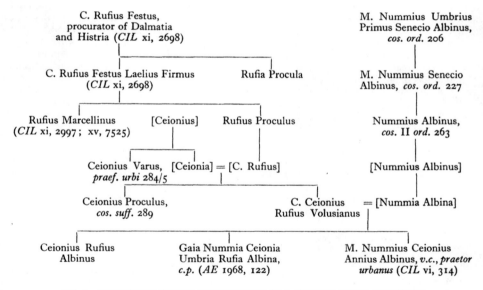

FIG. 1. CONJECTURAL STEMMA OF THE FAMILY OF C. CEIONIUS RUFIUS VOLUSIANUS

[57] *PIR²* C 611 (only the Chronographer of the year 354); 609 (from the Fasti Caleni, *CIL* x, 4631 = *Inscr. It.* xiii. 1, p. 269).

[58] On the meaning of 'nobilis' in the imperial period, see *Phoenix* xxviii (1974), 444 f.

[59] On whom, see J. F. Matthews, 'Continuity in a Roman Family; the Rufii Festi of Volsinii', *Historia* xvi (1967), 484–509.

[60] *CIL* xi, 2698, cf. H. G. Pflaum *Carrières*

procuratoriennes i (1960), no. 215.

[61] *CIL* xi, 2698; 2997; xv, 7525, cf. *Albo*, nos. 840–2; 2094.

[62] He ought to have held a consulate before becoming *corrector Italiae c.* 282 (p. 46).

[63] Which differs considerably from those offered or assumed by O. Seeck, *RE* iii (1899), 1861 f.; E. Groag, *RE* xvii (1937), 1410; Morris, o.c. (n. 46), Beilage; Arnheim, o.c. (n. 46), 248; *PLRE* i, 1138.

46

If this reconstruction is well founded, several additional facts enhance its attractiveness. First, Ceionius Varus was appointed *praefectus urbi* during the course of 283, either by Carus or in the joint reign of his sons, Carinus and Numerian: [64] Volusianus, presented here as his nephew, was almost certainly appointed *corrector Italiae* under the same régime. Second, a fragmentary list of priests and philosophers begins with the names of Rufius Volusianus and Rufius Festus, both *viri clarissimi* and both *quindecimviri sacris faciundis*: the conjunction is all the more appropriate if the pair were cousins.[65] Third, as *praetor urbanus*, M. Nummius Ceionius Annius Albinus made a dedication to Hercules in Rome, and Gaia Nummia Ceionia Umbria Rufia Albina is attested as a *sacerdos publica* at Beneventum.[66] The latter activity would be eminently suitable for the child of a prominent supporter of Maxentius.

V. THE CAREER OF VOLUSIANUS

C. Ceionius Rufius Volusianus was not a noble who inherited a lofty position in Roman imperial society. He came rather from a family whose fortunes were rising, but which had not yet acquired a title to nobility. He rose high through his own exertions and political astuteness, made a good marriage into an established family (presumably not his first),[67] and founded a noble lineage which continued to hold high office in every generation for two centuries.[68]

The earliest attested post for Volusianus is as *corrector Italiae* for eight years.[69] Since the second year of this tenure probably fell in the reign of Carinus and Numerianus (i.e. between July 283 and autumn 284), he was *corrector* from *c.* 282 to *c.* 290.[70] Volusianus' continuous tenure encourages speculation about what role he may have played in the civil war in which Diocletian defeated Carinus (spring or summer 285). When the two armies met at the river Margus, the outcome was decided by an assassination. Carinus was killed by a military tribune, who, whatever his private motives, need not have been acting alone.[71] T. Cl. Aurelius Aristobulus was Carinus' consular colleague in 285 and his pretorian prefect: Diocletian maintained him in both offices.[72] It is an easy surmise that both Aristobulus and Volusianus had performed useful services in the transference of the imperial power.

Volusianus continued to prosper, both during the reign of Diocletian and for a decade after Diocletian abdicated the imperial power (1 May 305). He was probably proconsul of Africa, in 305/6.[73] Maxentius entrusted him with the delicate task of suppressing a usurper, whose seizure of Africa was threatening the corn-supply of Rome and thereby the stability of his régime.[74] As a reward for success, Volusianus became *praefectus urbi* (28 October 310 to 28 October 311) and *consul ordinarius* in September 311, when he and Aradius Rufinus were proclaimed consuls for the year in the domains of Maxentius.[75] Nor did the death of Maxentius impair Volusianus' position. He soon became a *comes* of Constantine, who preserved his former rank and standing by appointing him *praefectus urbi* (from 8 December 313) and *consul ordinarius* (314).[76]

[64] From 254 to 287, the Chronographer of 354 records the *praefectus urbi* in office on each 1 January, cf. G. Barbieri, *Akte des IV. Internationalen Kongresses für griechische und lateinische Epigraphik* (1964), 48.

[65] *CIL* vi, 2153 (Rome, St. John Lateran), cf. Matthews, o.c. (n. 59), 492 f.

[66] *CIL* vi, 314; *AE* 1968, 122. Both inscriptions must be dated from nomenclature, rather than the reverse, cf. G. Barbieri, *Albo* (1952), no. 1675; P. Cavuoto, *Epigraphica* xxx (1968), 133 f.

[67] Volusianus was born c. 245, while the postulated marriage to Nummia Albina should be dated c. 295.

[68] For possible descendants in the late fifth century, see A. Chastagnol, *Le Sénat romain sous le regne d'Odoacre* (1966), 79 f.

[69] *ILS* 1213. Volusianus' jurisdiction appears to have embraced most of peninsular Italy, but to have excluded the Po valley, cf. A. Chastagnol, *Historia* xii (1963), 349 f.

[70] *CIL* x, 1655 (Puteoli), cf. A. Chastagnol, *Fastes* (1962), 53; *PLRE* i, 977.

[71] Victor, *Caes.* 39, 11; Eutropius, *Brev.* ix, 20, 2; *Epit. de Caes.* 38, 8; Zosimus i, 73, 3 = John of Antioch, frag. 163. On the role of the high command in the deaths of earlier emperors, cf. R. Syme, *Emperors and Biography* (1971), 210 (Gallienus); 242 f. (Aurelian).

[72] For his full career, *PIR²* C 806; Chastagnol, o.c. (n. 30), 21 f.

[73] *ILS* 1213. Possibly also *Inscr. lat. d'Afrique* 365 (Carthage); *AE* 1949, 59 (Mactar). On the date, cf. L. Poinssot, *Mém. soc. nat. ant. France* lxxvi (1924), 333 f.

[74] Victor, *Caes.* 40, 18; Zosimus ii, 14, 2 f. The suppression is assigned to 311 by C. H. V. Sutherland *RIC* vi (1967), 33; 419; 432. In favour of an earlier date, Chastagnol, o.c. (n. 30), 54 f.

[75] *Mon. Germ. Hist.*, Auc. Ant. ix, 67; 76; 231.

[76] *ILS* 1213, etc.

Volusianus remained Prefect of the City until 20 August 315.[77] But his political position was becoming less tenable. Firmicus Maternus discloses pertinent details. His enemies began to attack him, and they eventually overcame him (*Math.* ii, 29, 11/12); he was tried in the Senate and exiled by senatorial decree (13).[78] The occasion is perhaps not beyond the reach of conjecture.[79] Constantine visited Rome during 315 to celebrate his *decennalia*, arriving on 18 or 21 July and departing on 27 September.[80] In the course of this visit, it seems, the Roman Senate dedicated an arch to Constantine to commemorate his liberation of the city three years earlier, and praised him for rescuing the state at one time from both the tyrant and all his faction.[81] When Volusianus departed from office on 20 August 315, his disgrace and exile may have been immediate.

The fallen prefect died in exile, or at least without redeeming his disgrace and returning to office and imperial favour. That seems a legitimate, or rather a necessary, deduction from Maternus' discussion of the horoscope, which must otherwise have proceeded in a different fashion. Had Volusianus been restored to high office, then Maternus would surely have included his restoration among the facts which the true expert in astrology could predict from the stars. For, since he seeks to demonstrate how knowledge of the *antiscia* reveals all the vicissitudes of a man's life (*Math.* ii, 29, 9), he could not silently omit a second reversal of Volusianus' fortune without damage to the argument.

A law dated ' Crispo et Constantino CC. Conss.' is addressed ' ad Volusianum ', with no title appended.[82] The date intended is either 321 or 324, and the content of the law (the privileges of doctors and teachers) is more appropriate to a pretorian or urban prefect than to any other magistrate.[83] Hence, so it has sometimes been deduced, Ceionius Rufius Volusianus was pretorian prefect for a second time.[84] That is not possible. Alternatively, the date of the law has been emended to 354, and its recipient identified as a later Volusianus holding the pretorian prefecture of Illyricum in that year.[85] It might be better to let the transmitted date stand.[86] A Volusianus receiving a law in 321 could be a son of the fallen Volusianus (by a presumed earlier marriage)—and father of C. Ceionius Rufius Volusianus (*praefectus urbi* in 365).[87]

VI. THE CAREER OF ALBINUS

The details which Firmicus Maternus has vouchsafed can be combined with more explicit evidence to reveal a highly abnormal career for Ceionius Rufius Albinus. Both tribulation and supreme office came to him in his youth. He was born on 14 or 15 March 303, and became ordinary consul on 1 January and *praefectus urbi* on 30 December 335. In the intervening years, however, he had undergone the vicissitudes to which Maternus alludes. Albinus succumbed to the attack of his enemies and was exiled (*Math.* ii, 29, 12; 14); he was condemned by the emperor in person (18) on a charge of adultery (14; 17) and magic (18), and he might have met an untimely and violent death in exile, had the stars not ordained otherwise (16). Subsequently, Albinus was released from exile (16) and entrusted with administrative office, first in Campania, then as proconsul of Achaea and Asia (10).

[77] *Mon. Germ. Hist.*, Auct. Ant. ix, 67.
[78] This passage alone suffices to invalidate recent assumptions that the Roman Senate of the fourth century never acted as a court or witnessed the activities of mutually hostile factions (A. H. M. Jones, *The Later Roman Empire* i (1964), 332; 506 f.; Arnheim, o.c. (n. 46), 17).
[79] *Phoenix* xxxvii (1973), 308.
[80] O. Seeck, *Regesten der Kaiser und Päpste für die Jahre 311 bis 476 n. Chr.* (1919), 163 f.; T. D. Barnes, *JRS* lxiii (1973), 38.
[81] *ILS* 694.
[82] *CTh* xiii, 3, 1.
[83] T. Mommsen considered redating the law to Volusianus' urban prefecture, i.e. 313-15 (*Codex Theodosianus* i. 1 (1904), ccxvi).
[84] O. Seeck, *RE* iii (1899), 1859; A. Alföldi, o c.

(n. 30), 73; Chastagnol, o.c. (n. 30), 57. Observe that *CJ* iv, 35, 21 ' ad Volusianum pp.' lacks a date: although Seeck adduced it to support Volusianus' second pretorian prefecture in 321 (*Regesten* (1919), 61; 124; 171), an error for ' ad Volusianum pu.' is equally probable, cf. *CJ* xii, 1, 2.
[85] *PLRE* i, 979. A separate entry would have been advisable.
[86] So Arnheim, o.c. (n. 46), 196, without, however, perceiving the relevance of the horoscope, to which he alludes only when discussing Vettii (ib. 61).
[87] Who is normally presumed the son of Ceionius Rufius Albinus, cf. recently Chastagnol, o.c. (n. 30), 293: *PLRE* i, 1138; Arnheim, o.c. (n. 46), 248. If the arguments presented here are valid, the progeny of Volusianus' two marriages can perhaps be distinguished for several generations.

From Maternus' presentation, it is not necessary to deduce that Albinus came to grief at the same time as his father. On the contrary, the father was banished by senatorial decree, while the son was accused and tried before the emperor. Given the complete absence of evidence, speculation about the occasion and circumstances appears hazardous. Nevertheless, a hypothesis may be ventured, which, if true, would cast some light on a notoriously obscure episode. Albinus' exile should fall in the third decade of the fourth century: he could not have been plausibly accused of adultery many years before 320, and his recall must fall early enough to allow time for three governorships before his consulate and prefecture (335).[88] It might, therefore, stand in some relationship to the execution of Crispus (326).[89] The Caesar was presumably not murdered out of hand, but executed either after a formal trial and condemnation or at least after some sort of formal enquiry.[90] As for the charge or reason alleged, the penalty ought to indicate some form of treason. Albinus, who was convicted of adultery and magic, may have been implicated in some way. If that could be granted, the same hypothesis will serve to explain his subsequent sudden restoration (*Math.* ii, 29, 10: ' de exilio raptus '). Crispus (it is clear) died as the result of a dynastic intrigue which benefited the sons of his step-mother Fausta.[91] But the empress herself was put to death not long after, apparently on a charge of adultery, which was always treasonable for the wife of an emperor.[92] If Albinus had been exiled on the earlier occasion, he would without doubt have been recalled on the later.

Albinus became ordinary consul at the age of thirty-one, and *praefectus urbi* at the age of thirty-two. Both were remarkable distinctions for one so young: at this period an ordinary consulate or the urban prefecture was normally the culmination of a man's career and held by men many years his senior.[93] But the possibility of such an early elevation certainly existed:

In parte XIII Scorpionis quicumque habuerint horoscopum, Luna in aliquo cardine constituta, erunt iudices famosa reportantes insignia dignitatis, de aliorum iudicum sententiis iudicantes, habentes vitae necisque maximam potestatem. sed haec illis potestas decernitur ab anno XXX vel XXXV.

(*Math.* viii, 26, 4/5)

Maternus is not alluding to Albinus' own horoscope.[94] But the magistrates envisaged are clearly the urban prefect and the pretorian prefects: both types of prefect received appeals from the verdicts of other magistrates,[95] and both types of prefecture conferred nobility on their holders.[96]

The age of Albinus has a modest relevance to a problematical inscription of Rome, known only by manuscript report, which commemorated the erection of a statue:

Ceinonium rufium albinum uc. cons. filo
sophum. rufi volusiani bis ordinarii cons
finium. senatus ex consulto suo quod eius liberis
post caesariana tempora id est post annos.
CCCLXXX. et ·I· auctoritatem decreverit
Fl. magnus ienuarius. uc. cur statuarum

(*Sylloge Einsidlensis* 40 (*CIL* vi, p. xii)).[97]

It seems obvious that at least one reading is erroneous (' finium ' for ' filium ' in line 3), that the division between lines is faulty, and that the copy represents only part (the left

---

[88] None of the three is on independent attestation.
[89] Probably late spring 326, cf. *MGH*, Auct. Ant. ix, 232. The circumstances remain obscure. A recent writer asserts that ' the significant fact is that Crispus was illegitimate ' (P. Guthrie, *Phoenix* xx (1966), 325). But the earliest allusion to his mother (in 307) uses the word ' matrimonium ' (*Pan. Lat.* vii (vi), 4, 1).
[90] He was put to death near Pola (Ammianus xiv, 11, 20): therefore while Constantine was travelling to Rome from the East.
[91] Guthrie, o.c. (n. 89), 327 f.
[92] Philostorgius, *HE* ii, 4.

[93] A. Chastagnol, *La Préfecture urbaine à Rome sous le Bas-Empire* (1960), 405 f., assuming that Albinus became prefect at the age of forty-eight (ib. 413).
[94] Professor G. J. Toomer kindly investigated the possibility of an allusion to Albinus, and pronounces against it (letter of 12 April 1974).
[95] A. H. M. Jones, *The Later Roman Empire* i (1964), 481.
[96] *Phoenix* xxviii (1974), 445 f.
[97] Also *Sylloge Poggiana* 28 (*CIL* vi, p. xxxii), from a manuscript closely related to the extant Codex Einsidlensis, cf. ib., pp. ix; xxviii.

side) of the original inscription.[98] Whatever the purport of the last three lines (the precise figure points to a reckoning from 46 or 45 B.C.), the children of Albinus must have been too young for public life in 336: as was urged long ago on different grounds, ' liberis ' (line 3) should probably be emended to ' litteris '.[99]

VII. THE POLITICAL CONTEXT

The reconstruction of the families and careers of individuals is a necessary preliminary to any worthwhile social or political history, especially in a period as badly documented as the Constantinian age. The present prosopographical study is intended primarily to reconstruct the careers and family ties of two prominent individuals. But it ought to conclude with an indication, however brief, of the historical background against which the vicissitudes of Rufius Volusianus and his son must be set.

On 28 October 312, Constantine defeated Maxentius before the walls of Rome. The next day he entered the city in triumph, and soon he addressed the Senate in the Curia in a conciliatory fashion, steadfastly refusing to allow any revenge whatever for crimes committed under the ' tyranny ' of Maxentius.[100] Both emperor and Senate (it will be supposed) had assessed the political consequences of Maxentius' death and saw the necessity of cooperation for mutual advantage. Constantine received validation of his claim to be the senior ruling emperor,[101] while the first three *praefecti urbi* of Constantine had earlier been prefects of Maxentius—Annius Anullinus, Aradius Rufinus, and C. Ceionius Rufius Volusianus.[102]

As for the career of Ceionius Rufius Albinus, the influence of dynastic intrigues appears to preponderate. His exile and restoration (it has been argued above) can be correlated with the executions of Crispus (326) and Fausta, and his consular colleague was Julius Constantius, the half-brother of Constantine and another former exile.[103] Constantius lost his life in 337, together with other actual and potential rivals to the sons of Constantine.[104] Albinus disappears from the historical record on vacating the urban prefecture (10 March 337), and the patron of Firmicus Maternus was denied the ordinary consulate to which he had been designated (*Math.* i, pr. 8). The three things may have a connection : at least one of the consuls who displaced Lollianus may be conjectured to be a general who played some part in disturbing Constantine's plans for the imperial succession.[105]

University of Toronto

---

[98] O. Seeck, *Hermes* xix (1884), 186 f., criticizing the text of W. Henzen (*CIL* vi, 1708). Seeck's bold restoration (producing an allusion to the reintroduction of senatorial elections) was accepted and printed in *CIL* vi, 31906 (C. Hülsen), but not by H. Dessau, *ILS* 1222.

[99] Seeck, o.c. 196.

[100] *Pan. Lat.* xii (ix), esp. 20, 4, addressing Rome : ' gladios ne in eorum quidem sanguinem distringi passus est quos ad supplicia poscebas ', cf. 4, 4 : ' conservati usque homicidarum sanguinis gratulatio.'

[101] Lactantius, *Mort. Pers.* 44, 11.

[102] A. Chastagnol, *Fastes* (1962), 63. On the identity of Anullinus, cf. *Phoenix* xxvii (1973), 139.

[103] *PLRE* i 226.

[104] Julian, *Ep. ad. Ath.* 270 c, etc.

[105] viz. Fl. Ursus, cf. *Phoenix* xxviii (1974), 226 f. About his colleague, Fl. Polemius, nothing whatever appears to stand on record before 338 (*PLRE* i, 710).

X

PUBLILIUS OPTATIANUS PORFYRIUS

The poems of Publilius Optatianus Porfyrius, and his exchange of letters with Constantine, are a contemporary witness for the emperor's reign and for his attitude to literature,[1] whose value is enhanced by the vicissitudes of Porfyrius' career: he was exiled, and later advanced to a double tenure of the prefecture of the city of Rome. But the poems and the letters can be related to their author's career, only if some degree of chronological precision is attained. The present article has three specific aims: first, to review the sparse evidence for Porfyrius' career; second, to argue that he composed a cycle of twenty poems for presentation to Constantine in 324 (viz. I – XVI, XVIII – XX, with XIIIa and XIIIb counting as two poems); and third, to propose that the poet's exchange of letters with Constantine be dated to November/December 312, immediately after Constantine became master of Rome.

If little claim to complete originality can be advanced, a fresh treatment of Publilius Optatianus Porfyrius can easily be justified. Although his life and career have been discussed several times in the present century, the results have been divergent, and the twenty poems have sometimes been distributed over a period of fully thirteen years (319 to 332).[2] Moreover, the

---

[1] Three critical editions have been published: L. Müller (Leipzig: Teubner 1877); E. Kluge (Leipzig: Teubner 1926); G. (I.) Polara (Turin: Paravia 1973)—I. *Textus adiecto indice verborum;* II. *Commentarium criticum et exegeticum.* Where these scholars are named without an explicit reference being given, a reference should be understood (1) to Müller's introduction, pp. vii-x, (2) to Kluge's discussion of the dates of the individual poems on pp. 336-48 of the article cited in note 2, or (3) to Polara's commentary on the passage under consideration.

[2] See especially O. Seeck, 'Das Leben des Dichters Porphyrius', *RhM,* N.F. 63 (1908) 267-82; E. Kluge, 'Studien zu Publilius Optatianus Porfyrius', *Münchener Museum* 4 (1924) 323-48; E. Groag, 'Der Dichter Porfyrius in einer stadtrömischen Inschrift', *WS* 45 (1926/27) 102-9; R. Helm *RE* 23 (1959) cols. 1928-1936, s.v. Publilius 29; A. Chastagnol, *Les Fastes de la Préfecture de Rome au Bas-Empire* (1962) 80-82; E. Castorina, *Questioni neoteriche* (1968) 275-95.

174

Prosopography of the Later Roman Empire has done a grave disservice to scholarship by proposing to identify Porfyrius as the anonymous prefect of the city of Rome whose horoscope Firmicus Maternus discusses (*Math.* 2.29.10-20).[3] The identification has already been uncritically accepted and employed in the largest and fullest commentary on Porfyrius' works yet to be published.[4] The *Prosopography*, however, neglected to mention the cardinal fact that the subject of the horoscope was born in March 303.[5] He must, therefore, be Ceionius Rufius Albinus, *praefectus urbi* from 30 December 335 to 10 March 337, and the horoscope has a relevance to Porfyrius of a type which has not always been perceived.[6] The *geniturae pater*, that is, on the correct identification, C. Ceionius Rufius Volusianus, was exiled by senatorial decree after twice holding an ordinary consulate and appears never to have returned to high office — which may be very pertinent to the date of Porfyrius' own exile.

I. *The Chronology of Porfyrius' Career*

Apart from his poems and the two letters, there are only four items of explicit evidence for the career of Porfyrius, heterogeneous in nature and disparate in the testimony which they provide. It will be necessary to proceed from the certain to the conjectural, and at least partly in reverse chronological order. The Chronographer of 354 registers Publilius Optatianus as *praefectus urbi* twice, from 7 September to 8 October 329 and from 7 April to 10 May 333 (*Chr. min.* I, p. 68). The double tenure, and the brevity of each term, are abnormal, but the

---

[3] *P.L.R.E.* I (1971) 649, Optatianus 3; 1006-8, Anonymus 12, cf. p. 1004: "the career fits best that of Publilius Optatianus Porphyrius (*sic*) 3 (*Praefectus urbi* 329 and 333), and no other contemporary".

[4] Polara includes Maternus' discussion of the horoscope as 'Testimonia de Optatiano' no. 3 (II, pp. 1-3). For the consequences, see his commentary on I. 13-18; II.32, etc. Nor is that the only peculiarity in Polara's treatment of Porfyrius. He denies the authenticity of poems XXII and XXIV and of the exchange of letters with Constantine (I, pp. xxix-xxxii). The arguments advanced are very far from being persuasive, and the following pages will assume that all four pieces are genuine.

[5] W. Koch, *Astrologische Rundschau* 23 (1931) 177-83; O. Neugebauer, *AJP* 74 (1953) 418-20.

[6] For a full discussion of the horoscope, see *JRS* 65 (1975) 40ff.

source of the information is beyond reproach. Next, Jerome records 'Porphyrius misso ad Constantinum insigni volumine exilio liberatur', under the twenty-third year of Constantine (*Chronicle* p. 232ᵉ Helm). The year intended is presumably A.D. 328/9, but Jerome's precise date has no authority,[7] and involves the implausibility that Porfyrius would have been plucked from exile and almost immediately invested with the urban prefecture. A decent interval between recall and prefecture can safely be postulated, and the *vicennalia* of Constantine would be a more appropriate occasion than any other.[8]

The other two pieces of evidence are inscriptions. One, from Sparta, reveals that Publilius Optatianus was proconsul of Achaea: the city honoured him as a benefactor and saviour, and the expense of the statue was defrayed by M. Aurelius Stephanus, twice high priest of the Augusti (*SEG* XI, 810 = *AE* 1931,6). The discoverer of the inscription contemplated a date of 330 or 334.[9] But no man is likely to have been proconsul of Achaea after an urban prefecture. Publilius Optatianus Porfyrius must have been proconsul either before his exile or between his restoration and first prefecture.[10] The later date tends to be preferred.[11] But a date before 324 cannot be excluded,[12] and two very different possibilities are open: either after 316/7, when Constantine gained control of Greece in the War of Cibalae,[13] or else a decade or more earlier, before Maxentius began to rule Rome and Italy. Although an equestrian *praeses provinciae Achaiae* is attested between 293 and 305 (*Corinth*

---

[7] R. Helm, *Philologus*, Supp. 21.2 (1929) 89.

[8] For amnesty on the occasion of an imperial anniversary, observe Eusebius, *Hist. Eccl.* 8.6.10; *Mart.Pal.*, praef. 2 (the *vicennalia* of Diocletian).

[9] A. M. Woodward, *BSA* 29 (1930) 36.

[10] E. Groag also admitted (implausibly) the interval between the two prefectures, *Die Reichsbeamten von Achaia in spätrömischer Zeit* (1946) 26.

[11] A. Chastagnol, *Fastes*, 82; *P.L.R.E.* 1, pp. 649; 1077.

[12] For the high priesthood of the Augusti at Sparta, see K. M. T. Chrimes/Atkinson, *Ancient Sparta* (1949) 202ff. It cannot be deduced from the title of the high priest that *SEG* XI, 810 must belong to a date when there was more than one Augustus, i.e. before 324.

[13] M. T. W. Arnheim, *The Senatorial Aristocracy in the Later Roman Empire* (1972) 50, 63, assumes that Constantine did not gain control of Achaea until 324.

VIII, 2, nos. 23-25), there is also evidence for senatorial proconsuls in the same period: Eunapius speaks of a well-educated Roman as proconsul, apparently c. 300 (*VS* 9.2.3ff., p. 483f.), and C. Vettius Cossinius Rufinus, *praefectus urbi* in 315/6, had earlier in his career been allotted the proconsulate of Achaea by sortition (*ILS* 1217).[14]

The second inscription which bears Porfyrius' name is a fragment found at Rome, in the Piazza Colonna, which contains nothing but seven names, all incomplete:[15]

TURRANIU	
CREPEREIUS	RO
PUBLILIUS	OPTATIAN
CEIONIUS RUFIUS	VOLUSI
N. ANICIUS	P
CILIUS	
PR	

For the date, two quite distinct possibilities are open. The fourth name is universally identified as Ceionius Rufius Volusianus, consul in 311 and 314, a powerful supporter of Maxentius who maintained his standing under Constantine, at least initially.[16] If so, the inscription should be earlier than his fall and exile, probably in or shortly after 315 (Firmicus Maternus, *Math.* 2.29.10-12), and may without difficulty be assigned to the very early fourth century. On this dating, Turraniu[s] will be L. Turranius Gratianus, *praefectus urbi* in 290/1, and the fifth man may be Anicius Faustus, consul for the second time in 298, whose full name has been conjectured to be M. Junius Caesonius Nicomachus Anicius Faustus Paulinus.[17] On the

---

[14] For these governors, see now, respectively, *P.L.R.E.* I, p. 685, Paulus 11; p. 1013, Anonymus 45; p. 777, Rufinus 15, arguing that the proconsulate should be dated 306 or earlier.

[15] I print a conflation of the two reports, *Notizie degli Scavi* (1917) 22 and *Bull. Comm.* 45 (1917) 225. The first element of the fifth name has been read both as '[I]VN' (F. Fornari, *Notizie degli Scavi* [1917] 22) and as '[AM]N' (A. Chastagnol, *Fastes*, 92).

[16] For discussion of his family and career, see now *JRS* 65 (1975) 1ff.

[17] He is so entered in *PIR*², A 601; G. Barbieri, *L'Albo senatorio da Settimio Severo a Carino (193-285)* [1952] no. 1802; A. Chastagnol, *Fastes*, 31-33. But

other hand, a date of c. 320 is sometimes adopted,[18] and can perhaps be rendered strictly irrefutable by the easy (and probable) hypothesis that the great Volusianus had a homonymous son, father of C. Ceionius Rufius Volusianus, *praefectus urbi* in 365, and that it is he, not his father, who appears on the inscription.[19] Turraniu[s] will then be the prefect's son,[20] and Anicius P[aulinus] can be the man with those names who was *praefectus urbi* in 334/5.[21]

The earlier date, though not demonstrable, is clearly preferable, and E. Groag very attractively identified the names as belonging to members of a priestly college whom Maxentius induced (or compelled) to contribute to the building of a temple.[22] If that is correct, then Porfyrius had entered the college earlier than a man who was born in the fifth decade of the third century,[23] and his own birth can hardly be assigned to a date later than c. 260/270. However, even on the other view, there would still be a chance, perhaps even a probability, that he was proconsul of Achaea before 306 — and therefore born before c.275.

II. *Historical Allusions in the Poems*

Long ago L. Müller printed poems I – XX under the title 'Panegyricus Constantini' (a title which appears in the manuscripts, but is not there confined to these poems alone), and poems XXI — XXVIII as 'Carmina reliqua'. (Poem XVII is

Barbieri later corrected the entry to read 'Anicius Faustus' (p. 640), and *P.L.R.E.* I, p. 329 registers him under these two names alone. The second, sixth and seventh names are of no aid in dating, cf. *P.L.R.E.* I, p. 767, Rogatus 2; p. 10, Acilius 1; p. 1001, s.v. PR.

[18] A. Chastagnol, *Fastes*, 16; 57; 81; 92. But Chastagnol denied the relevance of the horoscope of March 303, which he attributed to a Vettius Rufinus (ibid. 65ff.).

[19] This Volusianus may already be attested by *Cod. Theod.* 13.3.1 (dated 321 or 324). Clearly not the consul of 311 and 314 as 'préfet du prétoire II en 321' (A. Chastagnol, *Fastes*, 58).

[20] *P.L.R.E.* I, pp. 402; 925.

[21] A. Chastagnol, *Fastes*, 92.

[22] E. Groag (note 2, above) 102ff.

[23] Volusianus was *corrector Italiae* from c. 282 to c. 290 (*ILS* 1213; *CIL* X, 1655).

correctly rejected by Müller, Kluge and Polara as inauthentic: it is a metrical explanation of XVIII composed by a much later hand.) Moreover, Müller expressly asserted that the 'panegyric' was written in exile and dedicated to Constantine at his *vicennalia*, in July 325. Similarly O. Seeck, in his study of Porfyrius' career, though preferring 326.[24] But E. Kluge, followed by most subsequent scholars, assigned three poems to dates somewhat removed from 325/6, viz. VI to 322/3, X to 319, XVIII to 332. Since the *Prosopography of the Later Roman Empire* confuses the issue by referring to "panegyrics on the occasion" of Porfyrius' recall,[25] the evidence for the date of each poem must be reviewed individually. The essential and undisputed points of reference are as follows: (1) Crispus and the younger Constantine had been officially invested as Caesars on 1 March 317; (2) Licinius was defeated in the summer of 324, in battles at Hadrianople on 3 July and at Chrysopolis on 18 September; (3) Constantius was proclaimed Caesar on 8 November 324; (4) Constantine's *vicennalia* were celebrated at Nicomedia for a month beginning on 25 July 325 and again in Rome in the following summer, (5) Crispus was executed in the spring or early summer of 326, while the court was traveling to Rome.[26]

I is clearly introductory and written in exile, but contains no datable historical allusion.

II seems to allude to the defeat of Licinius (25-28: 'armis civilibus ultor, . . . per te pax, optime ductor,/et bellis secura quies').

III implies that Constantine rules the whole world (12/13: 'aurea iam toto, victor, tua saecula pollent,/Constantine polo').

[24] O. Seeck (note 2, above) 275ff. For the arrangement of the poems in the various manuscripts, see the table provided by G. Polara, I, p. xix.

[25] *P.L.R.E.* I, p. 649.

[26] For these dates, O. Seeck, *Regesten der Kaiser und Päpste für die Jahre 311 bis 476 n. Chr.* (1919) 165; 173ff. There are several errors in E. Kluge's discussion, 'Beiträge zur Chronologie der Chronologie Constantins des Grossen', *Historisches Jahrbuch*, XLII (1922) 89-102, some of which reappear in Polara's commentary (e.g. II, p. 77: 'Constantini victoriam ex Licinio a. 323 partam').

IV introduces V and refers twice to 'vicennia' (1; 7). One couplet is of some historical importance:

> hos (i.e. Crispus and the younger Constantine) rupes Cirrhaea sonet
> videatque coruscos
> Ponti nobilitas, altera Roma, duces (5-6)

L. Müller identified the second Rome as Nicomedia, E. Kluge as Constantinople. The latter is surely correct, but Porfyrius ought to be writing before he discovered that on 8 November 324 Constantine had both formally founded the city and proclaimed his son Constantius Caesar.[27] For he speaks of two Caesars only (cf. XVI, 36). The poem, therefore, appears to indicate that Constantine already intended to establish a 'second Rome' on the Bosporus in 324.[28]

V celebrates Constantine's conquest of Licinius (3: 'Oriente recepto', etc.), to which it conjoins his *vicennalia:* the pattern reads 'AUG XX CAES X'.

VI alludes to a victory over Sarmatians (15) and to battles at Campona (18ff.), on the River Margus (22ff.), and at Bononia on the Danube (26ff.). The poem is normally dated 322/3 and used as evidence for Porfyrius' career.[29] Two passages are argued to prove that the poet accompanied Constantine, presumably as *comes*, on his Sarmatian campaign:

> factorum gnarum tam grandia dicere vatem
> iam totiens, Auguste, licet (16-17)

>> quaecumque parat (sc. Musa) sub lege sonare,
> scruposis innexa modis, perfecta Camenis
> vult resonare meis, et testis nota tropaea

[27] For the *dies imperii* of Constantius, see Amanianus 14.5.1;*CIL* I^2,p.276 = *Inscr. Ital.* XIII.2, p. 259; *Chr. min.* I, p. 232; *Notizie degli Scavi* (1936) 96/7 = *AE* 1937, 119 (with plain 'idibus Nob.' in error). The coincidence of the two events is expressly stated by Themistius: βασιλεῖ δὲ εἰκότως συναυξάνεται πόλις ἡ τῆς βασιλείας ἡλικιῶτις · πυνθάνομαι γὰρ ὡς καὶ ἡμφίασεν ὁμοῦ ὁ γεννήτωρ τό τε ἄστυ τῷ κύκλῳ καὶ τὸν υἱέα τῇ ἁλουργίδι (*Orat.* 4.58b).

[28] Porfyrius tends to be overlooked in discussions of the foundation of Constantinople: e.g. A. Alföldi, *JRS* 47 (1947) 10ff.; R. Janin, *Constantinople byzantine*^{2} (1964) 21ff.

[29] G. Polara rejects the date for the poem but retains the inference: 'Optatianus aperte palamque dixit se bello interfuisse' (on VI, 17).

depictis signare metris, cum munere sacro
mentis devotae placarint fata procellas   (31-35)

Neither passage necessarily entails that Porfyrius was an eye-witness of Constantine's battles, only that he is a contemporary who knows about them (16). On the contrary, the second passage implies rather that the poet's exile prevents him from being an eye-witness: his Muse wishes to depict the victories as such, when 'the fates soothe the storms of her devoted mind by a sacred gift'. Since the 'sacred gift' must be an imperial pardon, the poem need not show that Porfyrius was exiled after the Sarmatian campaign. It may, nonetheless, have been written immediately after it, in 322 or 323 (the year is uncertain).[30]

VII also refers to the Sarmatian campaign (32: 'victor Sarmatiae totiens'), and hence, despite the mention of 'toto victoria in orbe' (29), was probably written before the defeat of Licinius. If so, one passage has some historical significance:

indomitos reges seu pacis lubrica victor
aut bello sternens aut mitis foedere, nutu
esse tuos facis agrosque exercere tuorum   (20-22)

Porfyrius seems to be saying that Constantine has defeated Sarmatian kings and made a treaty with them, by which they work the fields of his subjects.

VIII refers to the sons of Constantine (6ff.) and their military achievements (33). G. Polara dates the poem to 320/1 and detects an allusion to the *quinquennalia* of the Caesars (6ff.), but E. Kluge had already observed that a date c. 325 is also tenable.

IX alludes to the defeat of Licinius (2ff.), names Crispus (24) and ends with the wish for a successful celebration of the emperor's *vicennalia* and his sons' *decennalia* (35/36).

X is commonly dated to 319, on the strength of a reference to Crispus and the Franci:

paras nunc omine Crispi
Oceani intactas oras, quibus eruta Franci
dat regio procul ecce deum, cui devia latis
tota patent campis.   (25-28)

---

[30] For the date of 322, most are content to appeal to O. Seeck, *Regesten*, 172. But Seeck adduced only Porfyrius and Zosimus 2.21, neither of whom actually states a date.

E. Kluge claimed that the poem was written to celebrate Crispus' victory over the Franci (which she dated to 319).[31] But Porfyrius' main emphasis is surely on a future campaign by Constantine himself: with Crispus' earlier success as a good omen, he will reach the untouched shores of the Ocean. A phrase such as 'concordi saeclo' (21) and the line 'aspice! pacato parta est lux laeta sub orbe' (35) suggest that the poem was written after Licinius' defeat.

The words of the pattern, which include the phrase 'pater imperas, avus imperes', have commended a date in 322 to G. Polara, who puts the poem before Constantine's Sarmatian campaign, at a time when the wife of Crispus was known to be pregnant. However, since the child in question is attested only by a single allusion (*CTh* IX, 38, 1, of 30 October 322), she probably died in infancy, and the subjunctive of 'avus imperes' could have been equally apt in 324.

XI expressly celebrates the defeat of Licinius.

XII is normally also held to celebrate the defeat of Licinius, and the description of Constantine as 'mundi gloria, consul' (1) is often held to refer to his consulate in 326: hence O. Seeck dated the poem to that year, while E. Groag argued that Porfyrius used the term in autumn 325 in anticipation of Constantine's consulate on the following 1 January.[32] But G. Polara has correctly observed that the future tenses (e.g. 3/4: 'mox carus Eois/tot populis pia iura feres') and the plea to Constantine to rescue the world (15-18) show that Porfyrius is writing before the defeat of Licinius (which Polara mistakenly here dates to 323). But what of 'consul'? Constantine was not in fact consul between 320 and 326. E. Kluge proposed to take the word as a synonym for 'consiliarius' or 'consultor',[33] and Polara alleges that it is 'generatim positum'. A better hypothesis is that Porfyrius, writing in the summar of 324, expected Constantine, after his impending victory, to become consul for the next year. It must surely have come as a surprise to many when one of the consuls of 325 was Licinius' pretorian prefect.[34]

---

[31] P. Bruun, *RIC* 7 (1966) 76, prefers 318.

[32] O. Seeck (note 2, above) 275; E. Groag (note 2, above) 104.

[33] E. Kluge (note 26, above) 92f.

[34] viz. Julius Julianus (*P.L.R.E.* I, pp. 478/9).

XIIIa, XIIIb and XIV again celebrate the defeat of Licinius. XIIIa and XIIIb should be regarded as two poems, since they would have been written separately, presumably as a sort of diptych.

XV seems to contain no precise historical allusion.

XVI is normally dated after the defeat of Licinius, but G. Polara has observed that the poem speaks rather of a Constantine who rules Italy, Africa and the horrid north (10ff.) but not yet the whole world:

> undique pakatis salvator maxima rebus
> gaudia praestabis, dabis otia victor in orbe;
> virtutum meritis vicennia praecipe vota. (33-35)

Although Polara dates the poem to 322, a date early in 324 cannot be excluded.

XVIII is commonly dated to 332, on the strength of the mention of Getae (11ff.), taken as an allusion to a Gothic war in that year (*Exc. Vales.* I, 31; *Chr. min.* I, p. 234). But the alleged allusion should be otherwise interpreted:

> vincere florenti Latiales Sarmata ductu
> rex tibi posse Getas viso dat limite, ultor.
> vidit te, summum columen, qua velifer aestu
> serus in Oceani pressit iuga Nysia pontus,
> atque rudis radii scit lux exorta tropaea (11-15)

The first two lines (as G. Polara sees) allude to the Sarmatian victory of 322 or 323, the last three to Constantine's conquest of the east in 324. Moreover, civil war has recently ended and the emperor is styled consul:

> Alme, tuas laurus aetas sustollet in astra.
> luce tua signes fastus sine limite consul!
> Marte serenus habes reiecto munia Graium
> et Medi praestas in censum sceptra redire. (1-4)

Again (as in XII, 1), an allusion may be detected to a consulate which Constantine was expected to assume on 1 January 325.

XIX alludes to the *vicennalia* (12; 30ff.) and its pattern contains the letters 'VOT. XX'. Further, the pattern (of a ship) appears to allude to Crispus' naval victory at Chrysopolis (36: [sc. pagina] 'Augustae subolis memorans insignia fata').

X

XXa and XXb are a single poem. For all the twenty-six lines in XXa have eighteen letters, while the twenty-six in XXb ascend one by one from twenty-five to fifty letters: set on their sides, with 'Augusto victore iuvat rata reddere vota' between them, the two halves of the poem depict an organ (described in XXb). The poem refers to the celebration in Rome of recent victories of the emperor and the Caesars (XXa. 1ff.)[35] — and to the poet's enforced and unwilling absence.

Poems XXI – XXVIII differ considerably, both from the preceding poems and from one another. None is addressed to Constantine, there is no common theme or group of themes, and while one is a hymn to Christ (XXIV), another depicts a pagan altar (XXVI, esp. 1: 'vides, ut ara stem dicata Pythio'), and a third invokes pagan deities (XXVII). Only two of these poems contain anything indicating a date: XXI attributes its existence to one Bassus (14/15: 'Bassus nunc prodere carmen/imperat'), while XXII refers to the consulate of its unnamed addressee (33). O. Seeck identified the addressee of XXII with Bassus, and both with the Bassus consul in 317.[36] The identification, if correct, would indicate that at least two of these poems were written some years before those which Porfyrius addressed to Constantine.[37]

Poem XXIII deserves to be brought to the attention of students of late imperial prosopography. Porfyrius warns a Greek friend from Phrygia of his wife's adultery. The *versus intextus* reads

Μάρκε τέην ἄλοχον, τὴν Ὑμνίδα, Νεῖλος ἐλαύνει.

The poet claims to be giving the real names (XXIII, 9): two senators with the *cognomen* Nilus are known from the middle of the fourth century.[38]

---

[35] Not necessarily the *vicennalia*, as appears to be universally assumed.

[36] O. Seeck (note 2, above) 270f. Now known to be Caesonius Bassus (*P.L.R.E.* I, p. 154).

[37] Identity with Junius Bassus, consul in 331, is hesitantly preferred by A. Chastagnol, *Fastes*, 81; *P.L.R.E.* I, p. 155.

[38] *P.L.R.E.* I, p. 632.

III. *Porfyrius and Constantine*

From the facts set out so far, it is a legitimate inference (though not a necessary one) that Porfyrius composed a cycle of twenty poems (viz. I – XIIIa, XIIIb – XVI, XVIII – XX), which he intended to be presented to Constantine in support of his plea to be restored from exile. Most of the poems were written after Constantine defeated Licinius, and several passages refer to the emperor's *vicennalia* (325/6) and to the *decennalia* of the Caesars (326/7). Can a precise date be deduced? O. Seeck argued for the early months of 326,[39] while E. Kluge and others date many (though not all) of the poems to Constantine to the preceding year. But Porfyrius speaks of two Caesars alone (XVI.36), and never alludes to the Caesar proclaimed on 8 November 324. Accordingly, a slightly earlier date seems preferable: let it be proposed that Porfyrius finished and dispatched his cycle of poems pleading for mercy in the autumn of 324, and was recalled from exile shortly thereafter.[40]

The extant poems to Constantine were not the first which Optatianus addressed to the emperor. He had presented expensively decorated manuscripts before his exile:

Quae quondam sueras pulchro decorata libello
    carmen in Augusti ferre, Thalia, manus,
ostro tota nitens, argento auroque coruscis
    scripta notis, picto limite dicta notans,
scriptoris bene compta manu meritoque renidens
    gratificum, domini visibus apta sacris,
pallida nunc, . . .
hinc trepido pede tecta petis venerabilis aulae   (I.1-9)

Some of these poems may have been bucolic, for Porfyrius describes himself as 'ruris vates' (XV.15). It is accordingly of some interest that Porfyrius seems to reveal that he was African by origin (XVI.16ff.).[41] In Africa at least, Latin culture and literature maintained an existence through the dark days of the

---

[39] O. Seeck (note 2, above) 267ff.

[40] Similarly, but not quite accurately, *P.L.R.E.* I, p. 649: "presumably composed in 324 and early 325, since no mention is made of Constantius Caesar".

[41] O. Seeck (note 2, above) 268ff.

third century, and Nemesianus of Carthage wrote pastoral ec-
logues and didactic poetry c. 280.[42]

The exchange of letters between Porfyrius and Constantine
belongs to this earlier period, before the poet's exile. The imperial titles probably indicate a date before 324: 'domino Constantino maximo pio invicto et venerabili semper Augusto' and
'Invictus Constantinus Maximus Augustus'.[43] There is no allusion to the poet's exile or restoration, and the correspondence
appears to proceed on the assumption that its occasion is Porfyrius' first (or possibly second) presentation of poems to the
emperor.[44] A precise date can be divined. In autumn 312, Constantine defeated Maxentius and gained control of Italy and
Africa, the Roman Senate rapidly came to terms with their new
master and declared him to be the senior ruling Augustus.[45] If
Optatianus speaks of 'clementia tua' (*Ep. Porfyrii* 1;9), of 'tuae
manus victrices' (2) and Constantine's legislation (6), and refers
to his position as the first of the emperors (6: 'et invictus semper
et primus es'), that may suggest that the letter was written in
November/December 312 by one who had supported the de-
funct régime.

If this conjecture (it is no more) can be admitted, then
Constantine's reply takes on a greater significance. For it be-
comes a sort of cultural manifesto, issued by the new ruler of
Italy and Africa:

> saeculo meo scribentes dicentesque non aliter benignus
> auditus quam lenis aura prosequitur; denique etiam
> studiis meritum a me testimonium non negatur (*Ep. Constantini* 6/7)

IV. *The Life of Porfyrius*

The occasion of the poet's exile can now be discussed. E.

---

[42] Nemesianus, *Cynegetica* 64 alludes to 'divi fortissima pignora Cari', which
entails a date of 283/4. On the cultural context, cf. *Tertullian. A Historical and
Literary Study* (1971) 187ff.

[43] For the forms of Constantine's official titulature, *Diz. ep.* I, pp. 645ff. After
324 one would expect the inclusion of 'victor' or 'triumphator'.

[44] Many of the correct arguments were used by L. Müller, in his preface, p.
ix.

[45] Lactantius, *Mort. Pers.* 44.11.

Groag once proposed that Porfyrius' exile (which he dated after 322) should be connected with the fall of Ceionius Rufius Volusianus, whom he also conjectured to be a relative.[46] That hypothesis can stand, in a modified form. The poem from which Groag deduced that Porfyrius was still in favour at court in 322 will not bear that interpretation (VI), and Volusianus, who was exiled when his enemies combined to overcome him in the Roman Senate (Firmicus Maternus, *Math.* 2.29.11-12), probably fell in or shortly after 315. There is no obstacle to supposing that Publilius Optatianus Porfyrius was exiled as a result of the same political conflict.

For clarity, and ease of verification (or disproof), the various hypotheses argued above can be stated schematically:—
Publilius Optatianus Porfyrius

> born c. 260/270
> proconsul of Achaea before 306
> *Epistula ad Constantinum* November/December 312
> exiled in or shortly after 315
> presented poems I – XX to Constantine in autumn 324
> recalled from exile early in 325
> *praefectus urbi* 7 September-8 October 329 and again 7 April-10 May 333.

Only the prefecture of the city of Rome (it must be emphasized) is firmly dated by reliable evidence: the rest depends strictly and solely on hypothesis and conjecture.[47]

University College, Toronto

---

[46] E. Groag (note 2, above) 107f.

[47] E. Castorina arrived at a similar general chronology, though by a slightly different route: "Tutto ciò, in definitiva, fa ritenere quanto mai probabile che già ai primi anni del IV secolo, e forse anche agli ultimi del III, Porfirio abbia poetato da *neotericus*" (note 2, above) 278.

I am grateful to my colleague Richard Tarrant for much helpful advice on the interpretation of Porfyrius' poems.

The Chronology of Plotinus' Life

THE PRECISE CHRONOLOGY of the life of Plotinus is known only from a single ancient source, the *Vita Plotini*, which Porphyry wrote more than thirty years after his master's death and which dates several important events to specific years of Roman emperors. Plotinus was born in the thirteenth year of Septimius Severus and died at the age of sixty-five towards the end of the second year of Claudius (*Vita* 2.29–37)[1]; Amelius came to Rome during the third year of Plotinus' residence there in the third year of Philip and stayed for twenty-four years until the first year of Claudius (3.38–42). Porphyry himself came to Rome shortly before the end of Gallienus' tenth year, when Plotinus was in his fifty-ninth year, and stayed until approximately the end of Gallienus' fifteenth year, when he went to Sicily (4.1–8, 4.67–68; 5.1–5, 6.1–3). After ten years in Rome during which he wrote nothing (3.31–35), Plotinus began to write in the first year of Gallienus (4.9–11). Moreover, Porphyry lists separately the twenty-one treatises which Plotinus wrote before his own arrival in the tenth year of Gallienus (4.11–68), the twenty-four which he wrote while Porphyry was in Rome (5.1–64), and the nine which he wrote after Porphyry had departed for Sicily, divided into the five treatises which Plotinus sent him during Claudius' first year (6.1–16) and the four sent at the beginning of Claudius' second (6.16–25).

The problem at once arises, how should these dates be translated into Julian calendar years? Serious discussion began when Hermann Dessau suggested (privately to F. Heinemann) that Porphyry was using either Egyptian regnal years or the Syro-Macedonian year,[2] and there have been three substantial and detailed treatments of the problem in the last fifty years—by H. Oppermann in 1929, by M. J. Boyd in 1937, and by J. Igal in 1972.[3] Unfortunately, however, it was

---

[1] *Vita* 2.29–30: ἔτη γεγονώς, ὡς ὁ Εὐστόχιος ἔλεγεν, ἕξ τε καὶ ἑξήκοντα. Porphyry consistently uses inclusive reckoning (*cf. Vita* 3.20, 3.23–24, 3.38–42, 4.6–8 + 4.67–68, where ἦν . . . ἀμφὶ τὰ πεντήκοντα ἔτη καὶ ἐννέα means the same as πεντηκοστὸν καὶ ἔννατον ἔτος ἦγε τότε).

[2] F. Heinemann, *Plotin* (Leipzig 1921) 240.

[3] H. Oppermann *Plotins Leben: Untersuchungen zur Biographie Plotins* (*Orient und Antike* 7, Heidelberg 1929) 29–57; M. J. Boyd, "The Chronology in Porphyry's *Vita Plotini*," *CP* 32

not until 1972 that the publication of a group of papyri from Oxyrhynchus finally put the chronology of the reign of Claudius on a firm
and indisputable basis.[4] Since Roman imperial chronology in the
middle of the third century has long been a matter of dispute among
ancient historians and papyrologists,[5] Boyd and Igal have some excuse
for deducing the wrong date for Plotinus' death from a chronology of
Claudius' reign which has now been disproved. It was widely believed
that Gallienus died *ca* March 268, and that Claudius became emperor
ca March 268 and died *ca* March 270:[6] accordingly both Boyd and Igal
argued that Plotinus' death, towards the end of Claudius' second year,
occurred *ca* February 270.[7] It is now established that Claudius came to
the throne *ca* September 268 and died *ca* August 270—which entails
that Plotinus died in summer 270. That date, to be sure, was advocated by Oppermann but only by means of illegitimate arguments.[8]
Both clarity and correct method, therefore, demand that the dates of
the *Vita Plotini* be deduced afresh from the correct imperial chronology—and without assuming *a priori* that Porphyry used one system
of reckoning rather than another.

Egyptian regnal years ran from 29 August (30 August in the Julian
year preceding a leap year) to 28 August, and an emperor's first
regnal year was the period between his *dies imperii* and the immediately following 1 Thoth (=29 [or 30] August), however short
that period might be. For the Egyptian regnal years of Gallienus and
Claudius, the contemporary papyri present the following picture:

        15 Gallienus= 267/8
        16 Gallienus= 268/9 = 1 Claudius
                    269/70= 2 Claudius
  1 Aurelian (4) Vaballathus= 270/1 = 3 Claudius

(1937) 241–57; J. Igal, *La cronología de la Vida de Plotino de Porfirio* (Publ. Univ. Deusto I,
Bilbão 1972).

   [4] P.Oxy. XL 2892–2940, ed. J. R. Rea (1972).

   [5] See A. Stein, *ArchPap* 7 (1924) 30–51; H. Mattingly, *NC*[5]4 (1924) 119; P. Schnabel, *Klio*
20 (1926) 363–68; A. Stein, *Klio* 21 (1927) 78–82; A. Stein, *ArchPap* 8 (1927) 11–13; H. Mattingly, *JEA* 13 (1927) 14–18; A. Stein, H. Mattingly and J. G. Milne, *JEA* 14 (1928) 16–21; G.
Walser and T. Pekáry, *Die Krise des römischen Reiches: Bericht über die Forschung zur Geschichte
des 3. Jahrhunderts (193–284 n. Chr.) von 1939 bis 1959* (Berlin 1962) 28–54.

   [6] *e.g.*, recently, *PLRE* 1.384, 209. That volume gives the span of Plotinus' life as "203/4—
269/270" (707).

   [7] Boyd, *op.cit. (supra* n.3) 251; Igal, *op.cit. (supra* n.3) 126.

   [8] Oppermann, *op.cit. (supra* n.3) 34ff, assumed that Claudius became emperor *ca* March
268, but argued that 1 Claudius was the Egyptian regnal year 29 August 268–28 August 269
—a manifestly impossible combination.

$$2 \text{ Aurelian } 5 \text{ Vaballathus} = 271/2 = 3 \text{ Aurelian}$$
$$272/3 = 4 \text{ Aurelian}[9]$$

From these dates, all attested by several contemporary documents, a series of deductions can be drawn. First, the *dies imperii* of Claudius falls after 28 August 268. Second, news of Claudius' death had not reached Egypt before 28 August 270: besides papyri, there are Alexandrian coins of his third year.[10] Third, the *dies imperii* of Aurelian was redated in 272 from a date on or after 29 August 270 to a date on or before 28 August 270, and this redating implies three historical consequences: that Claudius died on or shortly before 28 August 270, that Aurelian was proclaimed emperor on or shortly after 29 August 270, and that Aurelian later claimed to have been emperor from the moment of Claudius' death.[11]

The dates in the *Vita Plotini* can now be considered. Tabulated below are the Julian equivalents of the years in the *Vita Plotini* on four methods of conversion:

(A) if the year is always reckoned from the *dies imperii*;
(B) Egyptian regnal years, which begin on 29 August;
(C) Seleucid regnal years beginning 1 October;[12]
(D) regnal years beginning 1 January.

	A	B	C	D
13 Severus	9 Apr. 205–	29 Aug. 204–	1 Oct. 204–	205
	8 Apr. 206[13]	28 Aug. 205	30 Sept. 205	
3 Philip	Feb./Mar. 246–	29 Aug. 245–	1 Oct. 245–	246
	Feb./Mar. 247[14]	28 Aug. 246	30 Sept. 246	
10 Gallienus	Sept. 262–	29 Aug. 262–	1 Oct. 261–	262
	Sept. 263[15]	29 Aug. 263	30 Sept. 262	

[9] Rea, *op.cit.* (*supra* n.4) 24. The equation 1 Gallienus=253/4 is rendered certain by *P.Oxy.* IX 1201; XII 1476, 1563 (three horoscopes with dates by Egyptian regnal years); XLI 2951 (which has both regnal year and consular date); the equation 7 Aurelian=275/6 by *P.Oxy.* XXXI 2557; *PSI* VII 764 (two horoscopes with dates by regnal years).

[10] J. Vogt, *Die alexandrinischen Münzen* II (Stuttgart 1924) 159–60.

[11] Rea, *op.cit.* (*supra* n.4) 23–25; T. D. Barnes, *Phoenix* 26 (1972) 179–81.

[12] On the Seleucid era and new year, see E. J. Bickermann, *Chronology of the Ancient World* (London 1968) 70ff; A. E. Samuel, *Greek and Roman Chronology* (Munich 1972) 139ff.

[13] The *dies imperii* of Septimius Severus was 9 April 193, *cf.* P. Dur. 54 (*Feriale Duranum*) col. ii line 3.

[14] The accession of Philip can be dated only approximately, *cf.* PIR[2] J 461.

[15] The accession of Valerian and Gallienus cannot fall long after 29 August 253, *cf.* ILS 531 (21 October 253: Gemellae, in southern Numidia).

15 Gallienus	Sept. 267–	30 Aug. 267–	1 Oct. 266–	267
	Sept. 268	28 Aug. 268	30 Sept. 267	
1 Claudius	Sept. 268–	Sept. 268–	Sept. 268	268
	Sept. 269	28 Aug. 269		
2 Claudius	Sept. 269–	29 Aug. 269–	1 Oct. 268–	269
	Aug. 270	Aug. 270	30 Sept. 269	

The last two computations can be rejected outright: (C), which should be what Dessau meant by the Syro-Macedonian year, is clearly incompatible with Porphyry's assumption that 1 Claudius followed immediately after 15 Gallienus (6.1ff), while (D) fails to allow "sixty-six years" for Plotinus' life (2.29–30) on any method of reckoning.[16] A decision between (A) and (B) is more difficult since they yield virtually identical results for all events in Plotinus' life after his departure from Alexandria in 243. The correct chronology for the reign of Claudius seems to allow (A) without necessitating the desperate expedient of rejecting Porphyry's statement that Plotinus was born in the thirteenth year of Severus as a sheer error.[17] Nevertheless, (B) is a neater, more elegant and less arbitrary computation than (A), and it should probably be inferred that Porphyry used Egyptian regnal years, or at least regnal years calculated from *ca* 1 September (which will differ from those of computation (B) by only a few days in each case). Hence the following chronology for the *Vita Plotini* can be deduced:

Plotinus born in 13 Severus (2.37).	September 204–August 205
He begins to study philosophy in his 28th year (3.6ff).	September 231–August 232
He becomes a pupil of Ammonius.	September 232–August 233
He joins Gordian's expedition in his 39th year (3.18ff). (3.20: ἔνδεκα ὅλων ἐτῶν= 10 years)	?Spring 243
He comes to Rome (3.22ff). (3.23–24: τεσσαράκοντα γεγονὼς ἔτη= 39)	Summer 244
He spends ὅλων δέκα ἐτῶν, i.e. nine years, in Rome without writing (3.34–35).	Summer 244–late summer 253

[16] The year of the emperors' *tribunicia potestas* (10 December–9 December) would give the same inadmissible result.

[17] So Igal, *op.cit.* (*supra* n.3) 124: "Plotino nace (*últimos meses de 203—primeros de 204*), dentro del año 11.° de reinado de Severo."

Amelius comes when Plotinus is in his third year at Rome, in 3 Philip (3.38ff). Amelius stays ἔτη ὅλα ... εἴκοσι καὶ τέσσαρα until 1 Claudius, i.e. (with allowance made for Porphyry's use of inclusive reckoning) for 23 years until summer 269.	Summer 246
Plotinus begins writing from 1 Gallienus (4.9ff).	ca September 253
Porphyry comes to Rome in 10 Gallienus (4.1ff) shortly before the emperor's tenth anniversary (5.1ff).[18]	July or August 263
Porphyry in Rome with Plotinus for the rest of 10 Gallienus and 11–15 Gallienus (5.1ff; 5.59ff).	July or August 263–August 268
Porphyry goes to Siciliy at the end of 15 Gallienus (6.1ff).	August 268
Plotinus dies towards the end of 2 Claudius (2.29ff).	July or August 270

The chronology which the *Vita Plotini* predicates for its hero is wholly consistent with itself. But does Porphyry give—and did he know—the correct date for Plotinus' birth? Plotinus refused to talk about his family, parents or home-town (*Vita* 1.2–4), and he kept secret the day and month of his birth, revealing his age only as he lay dying, to the doctor who attended him (2.29ff). Hence Porphyry's only evidence was the doctor's report (he, the doctor and two others then calculated the year of Plotinus' birth); and if Plotinus never celebrated his birthday, he may have been mistaken in his belief about his own age. Scepticism is therefore in place: if Porphyry's date for his birth is deduced solely from Plotinus' own words as he lay dying, it would be imprudent to accept it with confidence.[19] Matters are fortunately different with Plotinus' later career. Porphyry's dates are precise and credible: they come from his own recollection, from

[18] The word δεκαετία does not signify Gallienus' *decennalia*—which should have been celebrated at both the beginning and the end of his tenth year.

[19] Oppermann, *op.cit.* (*supra* n.3) 55–56; J. M. Rist, *Plotinus: The Road to Reality* (Cambridge 1967) 3.

Amelius, who came to Rome in 246, from the pagan Origen, who was a student with Plotinus in Alexandria—and from Plotinus himself.[20]

UNIVERSITY OF TORONTO
August, 1975

---

[20] Porphyry explicitly cites Plotinus as his authority for his subject's life as far as 243 (*Vita* 3.1–17).

I am grateful to Professor John Rist for drawing my attention to the problem discussed here and for scrutinising the solution offered.

XII

IMPERIAL CAMPAIGNS, A.D. 285–311

THE NARRATIVE SOURCES for most of the reign of Diocletian are notoriously exiguous, confused, and unreliable. The fullest narrative of the whole reign which survives in Greek is that of Zonaras in the twelfth century, who drew on much earlier writers, either directly or indirectly, but commits some gross and obvious blunders.[1] The extant Latin accounts, though far closer in time to the events, are all variously defective or unhelpful. Lactantius must have known the essential facts, but the central narrative of his *De Mortibus Persecutorum* only commences in earnest near the end of the reign, and it concentrates on political events and civil wars to the almost complete exclusion of campaigns against external enemies.[2] The Latin epitomators of the later fourth century appear to depend very largely on a historical work composed ca 337, which itself already enshrined some serious errors.[3] Thus Aurelius Victor, Eutropius, and Jerome all make the proclamation of Constantius and Galerius as Caesars the result of a military emergency caused by the Persian War and the revolt of Achilleus in Egypt (Victor *Caes.* 39.22 ff.; Eutropius *Brev.* 9.22.1; Jerome *Chronicle* p. 225ᵍ Helm), whereas the Caesars were in fact appointed in 293, while the Persian War began in 296, the Egyptian revolt in 297.

In these circumstances, an investigation of the military history of the late third and early fourth centuries must be sceptical and cautious, loath to trust demonstrably unreliable authors, even where nothing else offers.[4] Instead, though not disdaining individual items from any ancient source, it should rely primarily on the more oblique, but less dangerous, testimony of contemporary documents and writers. The point of departure can only be the full imperial titles recording the victories over

---

[1] E.g., the African tribal confederation called the Quinquegentani become "the five Gentiani" and Carausius is "Crassus" in Theophanes, p. 8.1–4 de Boor and Zonaras 12.31. The former error derives ultimately from a fourth-century translation of Eutropius *Brev.* 9.22 (*Mon.Germ.Hist.*, Auc.Ant. 2.163).

[2] The work was probably written between 313 and 315, cf. *JRS* 63 (1973) 29 ff.

[3] Viz., the lost "Kaisergeschichte" postulated by A. Enmann in 1883, on which see recently R. Syme, *Ammianus and the Historia Augusta* (Oxford 1968) 105 f.; *Emperors and Biography* (Oxford 1971) 221 ff.; T. D. Barnes, *Bonner Historia Augusta Colloquium 1968/69* (Bonn 1970) 13 ff.

[4] An obvious and important principle of method, whose neglect vitiates almost all modern accounts of the period: they will accordingly be cited but rarely in the following pages.

external enemies which were officially acknowledged in an edict of late 301, on a military diploma of 7 January 306, and in an edict of April 311.

THE IMPERIAL TITLES IN 301

The imperatorial salutations of early Roman emperors are often an important guide for military chronology.[5] But Diocletian and his colleagues automatically renewed the title of *imperator* on each anniversary of their accession, so that these salutations have lost their relevance to actual victories or warfare. The function of advertising victories passed exclusively to another element in the emperors' titulature: where emperors in the second century had taken both an imperatorial salutation and the title "Parthicus" in honour of a single event,[6] the Tetrarchs took only the descriptive sobriquet, which they renewed for a subsequent victory over the same enemy. Hence the full form of Diocletian's name and titles when he issued the edict on maximum prices: "Imp. Caesar C. Aurelius Valerius Diocletianus Pius Felix Invictus Augustus pontifex maximus Germanicus maximus VI Sarmaticus maximus IIII Persicus maximus II Brittanicus maximus Carpicus maximus Armenicus maximus Medicus maximus Adiabenicus maximus tribunicia potestate XVIII consul VII imperator XVIII, pater patriae, proconsul." The date can be determined very precisely: Diocletian became *imperator* XVIII on 20 November 301, and his eighteenth *tribunicia potestas* expired on 9 December of the same year.[7]

Fragments of the *Edictum de pretiis rerum venalium* and an edict on currency reform from the same year allow the full titles of all the emperors to be reconstructed.[8] Since the iterations are important, the numbers may be tabulated (Table 1). It should be noted that a small fragment recently published by K. T. Erim and J. Reynolds (*JRS* 63 [1973] 100, with Plate X) reads "Sarm. m. III" for Maximian where "Sarm(aticus) [max(imus) IV]" is conventionally restored.[9]

The victories celebrated should all pertain to campaigns which the

[5]E.g., in the later years of Augustus, cf. *JRS* 64 (1974) 23 ff.

[6]Thus Marcus Aurelius and Lucius Verus took the titles Armeniacus, Medicus, and Parthicus maximus for the campaigns which produced their second, third, and fourth imperatorial salutations (see esp. *BMC*, R. Emp. 4, cii ff.).

[7]The computation was first clearly explained by H. Dessau, *Eph.Ep.* 7 (1892) 429–435.

[8]For the two edicts, see S. Lauffer, *Diocletians Preisedikt* (Berlin 1970) 90 ff.; K. T. Erim, J. Reynolds, and M. Crawford, "Diocletian's Currency Reform; a new inscription," *JRS* 61 (1971) 171–177. Two fragments from Aphrodisias, long regarded as part of the price-edict, are now known to belong to the edict about currency (*CIL* 3, p. 824: Aphrodisias I, V).

[9]T. Mommsen restored "IIII" from *ILS* 641 (*CIL* 3, pp. 802–3). No one dissented.

TABLE 1: IMPERIAL VICTORY TITLES IN A.D. 301

	Number of times title taken			
	Diocletian	Maximian	Constantius	Galerius
Germanicus maximus	6	5	2	2
Sarmaticus maximus	4	3	2	[2]
Persicus maximus	2	[2]	2	[2]
Brittanicus maximus	1	[1]	1	[1]
Carpicus maximus	1	[1]	1	[1]
Armenicus maximus	1	[1]	1	[1]
Medicus maximus	1	[1]	1	[1]
Adiabenicus maximus	1	[1]	1	[1]

Evidence: *CIL* 3, pp. 802–803 (20 November–9 December 301); *JRS* 63 (1973), Plate X.

emperors waged in person against foreign enemies (not in civil wars or suppressing internal rebellions), and the titles occur in the order in which Diocletian at least took them for the first time.[10] Thus it follows (for example) that the first Persian victory preceded the reconquest of Britain (during 296) and that a campaign against the Carpi followed it. The latter can thus be dated to late 296 or early 297, since an orator speaking on 1 March 297 alludes to *proxima illa ruina Carporum* (*Pan.Lat.* 8[5].5.2). Moreover, the principle of collegiality obviously operates. Hence the victories celebrated in the titles of all four emperors must fall after 1 March 293, which was the official *dies imperii* of Constantius and Galerius;[11] the victories reflected in the titles of both the Augusti, but not in those of the Caesars, must be earlier than 1 March 293 and subsequent to Maximian's *dies imperii*, which was almost certainly 1 March 286 in the official computation employed in the edict;[12] and victories reflected in Diocletian's titles alone can be dated between his proclamation as emperor on 20 November 284 (*PBeattyPanopolis* 2.162 etc.; Lactantius *Mort.Pers.* 17.1) and that date. A chronological table may accordingly be offered (Table 2).

DIOCLETIAN AND MAXIMIAN, 285–293

Diocletian was proclaimed emperor near Nicomedia on 20 November 284, but did not become master of the whole Roman Empire until he defeated

[10]A. Arnaldi, *Rendiconti dell'Istituto Lombardo*, Classe di Lettere e Scienzi Morali e Storiche 106 (1972) 28 ff. For the criteria of inclusion, compare Mamertinus on Maximian's defeat of the Bagaudae: *video enim te, qua pietate es, oblivionem illius victoriae malle quam gloriam* (*Pan.Lat.* 10 [2].4.4).

[11]For the papyri which establish the year, A. Chastagnol, *Rev.num.*⁶ 9 (1967) 71 ff.; for the day, *Pan.Lat.* 8[5].3.1; Lactantius *Mort.Pers.* 35.4.

[12]R. E. Smith, *Latomus* 31 (1972) 1058 ff.

TABLE 2: IMPERIAL VICTORIES, 284–301

Area of victory or name of enemy	Number of victories celebrated		
	20.11.284–28.2.286	1.3.286–28.2.293	1.3.293–11.301
Germans	1	3	2
Sarmatians	1	1	2
Persians			2
Britain			1
Carpi			1
Armenia			1
Media			1
Adiabene			1

Carinus by the River Margus in the following year.[13] He immediately confronted the problem of how to extend his effective control to the western provinces of Gaul, Spain, and Britain. The chosen instrument was Maximian, whom he invested as Caesar, probably on 21 July 285, sent to Gaul, and elevated to the rank of Augustus the following spring.[14] By good fortune, two panegyrics which Mamertinus delivered in Gaul before Maximian, on 21 April 289 and 22 December 291, allude to the military activities of both emperors in some detail.[15]

The four victories between 286 and 293 reflected in the imperial titulature can be readily identified. Since the later speech records a Sarmatian victory of Diocletian which occurred before December 290 (*Pan.Lat.* 11[3].5.4; 7.1), but about which the earlier speech says nothing, the emperors both took the title "Sarmaticus maximus" after a campaign which Diocletian conducted in 289 or 290: the earlier date is probably preferable,[16] and an allusion in a speech delivered in 297 implies that

[13]For the evidence, *PIR*² A 1473.

[14]Maximian appears as Augustus and as Diocletian's colleague on Egyptian documents from the spring of 286 onwards (*BGU* 1090 [31 March] etc.). But Eutropius records that he was made Caesar before becoming Augustus (*Brev.* 9.20.3), and the *Acta Marcelli* of 298 record a *dies festus imperatoris/imperii vestri* on 21 July. These two items are here accepted and combined.

[15]The earlier speech, *Pan.Lat.* 10[2], was recited on the *natalis Romae dies* (1.4), i.e., 21 April: the content (esp. 6.2; 12.3) indicates that the year is 289. The later speech, *Pan.Lat.* 11[3], commemorates Maximian's birthday, which he shared with Diocletian (2.2; 19.3), and it was delivered shortly after he had completed five years of rule (1.1 ff.). Since Diocletian's birthday is now attested as 22 December (*P Beatty Panopolis* 2.164; 173; 181–182; 193–194; 262: not noted in *PLRE* 1.253–254, Diocletianus 2), and the speech alludes to a conference of the Augusti in December 290 or January 291 (2.4; 4.1 ff.; 8.1 ff.), the date should be 22 December 291.

[16]In 289, Diocletian's movements are unknown; in 290, he left the Danube before 27 February and perhaps returned no earlier than July, cf. T. Mommsen, *Ges.Schr.* 2 (Berlin 1905) 270 f.

Diocletian was defending the new Dacia south of the Danube (*Pan.Lat.* 8[5].3.3). Diocletian was also responsible for one of the three German victories, when he invaded *illam quae Raetiae est obiecta Germaniam* and advanced the Roman frontier, probably in 288 (*Pan.Lat.* 10.[2].9.1, cf. 11[3].5.4; 7.1). By elimination, therefore, the other two German victories are Maximian's defeat of the Chaibones and Heruli in 286 (*Pan.Lat.* 10[2].5.1 ff; 11[3].7.2) and his expedition across the Rhine in 287 (*Pan.Lat.* 10[2].7.1 ff.; 11[3].5.3; 7.2).

These campaigns, however, are not the only ones to which Mamertinus alludes. Recounting the exploits of Diocletian and Maximian which gave each other joy and encouraged them to confer in Milan in the winter of 290/1, he adds two more victories:

Laurea illa de victis accolentibus Syriam nationibus et illa Raetica et illa Sarmatica te, Maximiane, fecerunt pio gaudio triumphare; itidemque hic gens Chaibonum Erulorumque deleta et Transrhenana victoria et domitis oppressa Francis bella piratica Diocletianum votorum compotem reddiderunt (Pan.Lat. 11[3].7.1/2).

The "tribes bordering on Syria" are the Saraceni (cf. 5.4): since Diocletian is attested in Syria on 10 May 290 (*CJ* 9.41.9), Mamertinus should be referring to operations of spring or early summer 290 which did not receive commemoration in the imperial titulature. A triumph over Franci in 288/9 is noted in the speech of 289, which also reveals why the emperors failed to take a victory-title: Maximian himself was not in command (*Pan.Lat.* 10[2].11.4 ff., esp. 5: *a vobis proficiscitur etiam quod per alios administratur*).

The two victories reflected in Diocletian's titles, but not in those of Maximian, remain to be identified. The German victory is presumably an episode which Mamertinus had good reason to omit. After defeating the Bagaudae (*Pan.Lat.* 10[2].4.2 ff.), Maximian conducted naval operations against Franci and Saxones who were infesting the seas, with Carausius in command of the fleet (Victor *Caes.* 39.20; Eutropius *Brev.* 9.21). An orator surveying Maximian's past successes and looking forward to his suppression of *ille pirata* (*Pan.Lat.* 10[2].12.1 ff.) was well advised to pass silently over an episode in which Carausius held a high command and which led to his rebellion against Maximian (Victor *Caes.* 39.21; Eutropius *Brev.* 9.21). As for the Sarmatian victory, the hypothesis that Diocletian conducted an otherwise unattested campaign on the Danube ought to occasion no disquiet. The chronology can be deduced from three facts. Maximian assumed the purple as Caesar on 21 July 285, the German victory precedes the Sarmatian in the imperial titulature, and Diocletian was in Nicomedia by January 286 (*CJ* 4.21.6). Both victories, therefore, belong to the last months of 285.

MAXIMIAN AND CONSTANTIUS, 293–301

The panegyric to Constantius delivered on 1 March 297 (*Pan.Lat.* 8[5]), supplemented by two speeches recited in the presence of Constantine, constitutes the fullest evidence for the campaigns of Constantius as Caesar. In 293, very shortly after his proclamation as Caesar, he captured Gesoriacum and expelled the troops of Carausius from Gaul (*Pan.Lat.* 8[5].6–7). He then defeated barbarians who were overrunning Roman territory near the mouth of the Rhine and forced many of them into agricultural service (*Pan.Lat.* 8[5].8–9; 21.1; 7[6].4.2; 6[7].5.3). Next, Constantius recovered Britain and restored it to the Roman Empire (*Pan.Lat.* 8[5].11–19), and the evidence of coins and literary sources converges to establish the date as 296.[17] Subsequently, Constantius won four victories which an orator in 310 distinguishes: a defeat of *intimae Franciae nationes*; a *Lingonica victoria*, which ought to designate a battle near the source of the River Marne; the plains of Vindonissa covered with the bones of fallen foes; and the defeat of an immense horde of various German peoples who crossed the Rhine when it was frozen(*Pan.Lat.* 6[7].6.2–4). Since Constantius was "Germanicus maximus II" in late 301, and "Germanicus maximus V" on 7 January 306 (*AE* 1961.240), the first of the victories to which the panegyrist of 310 alludes occurred between 297 and 301, the other three between late 301 and late 305.

For Maximian too, three speeches provide the fullest evidence: the panegryic to Constantius, the speech which Eumenius gave at Augustodunum before the provincial governor in the summer or autumn of 298 (*Pan.Lat.* 9[4]), and the speech which celebrates the marriage of Constantine to Fausta, the daughter of Maximian, ca September 307 (*Pan. Lat.* 7[6]).[18] But the subscriptions preserved to four laws add some precise facts: they certify Maximian's presence in Milan on 21 March and 21 December 295 (*Consultatio* 4.7; *Frag.Vat.* 292), in Aquileia on 31 March 296 (*Frag.Vat.* 313), and at Carthage on 10 March 298 (*Frag.Vat.* 41). Apart from these laws, there seems to be no certain testimony for Maximian's activities between 293 and 296, when he advanced north to defend the Rhine during Constantius' invasion of Britain (*Pan.Lat.* 8[5].13.3). From there he marched across Gaul, fought in Spain, and then crossed to Africa to deal with a serious revolt of the Moorish tribes: the orator who spoke on 1 March 297 described the present situation as *Mauris inmissa vastatio* (*Pan.Lat.* 8[5].5.2), thus dating the beginning of Maximian's

[17]R. A. G. Carson, *Journal of the British Archaeological Association*³ 22 (1959) 33–40, arguing principally from Victor *Caes.* 39.40; Eutropius *Brev.* 9.22.2; Orosius *Hist.adv.pag.* 7.25.6; *RIC* 5.2.516–523, cf. *Rev.Arch.* 3 (1846/7) 532.

[18]For the two dates, see, respectively, below p. 185 and *JRS* 63 (1973) 41 n. 143.

African campaigns to spring 297. Since the emperor was in Carthage on 10 March 298 (*Frag.Vat.* 41), it is sometimes assumed that Africa had been pacified by that date.[19] That cannot be, for Eumenius implies that fighting was still continuing in the summer of 298: *te, Maximiane invicte, perculsa Maurorum agmina fulminantem* (*Pan.Lat.* 9[4].21.2). Subsequently, Maximian returned to Rome to celebrate a triumph either late in 298 or in 299 (*Pan.Lat.* 7[6].8.7), and afterwards (it may safely be presumed) proceeded to one of his normal residences in north Italy (Milan and Aquileia).[20]

THE THREE IMPERIAL VISITS TO EGYPT

Three imperial visits to Egypt must be very carefully distinguished, whose dates are 293/4, 297/8, and 301/2. Unfortunately, the first two visits have often been confused and the third denied, with disastrous consequences for modern understanding of the military and political history of the period.[21] Nor was the full range of evidence now known available to T. Mommsen and G. Costa who first began to apprehend the truth.[22]

Eusebius distinguished two revolts in his *Chronicle*, separated in the extant versions by four years: in the first, Busiris and Coptos rebelled and were destroyed (Jerome *Chronicle*, p. 226[a] Helm), while in the second Alexandria with all Egypt rebelled under the leadership of Achilleus and Diocletian captured the city after a siege (p. 226[e] Helm). Although the precise dates in the Armenian translation and in Jerome's version have no authority,[23] the separate entries clearly designate and describe two distinct episodes. The distinction is also apparent in the Gallic orators. When alluding briefly to the triumphs of Constantius' colleagues since 293, the speech of 1 March 297 refers to *trophaea Niliaca sub quibus Aethiops et Indus intremuit* (*Pan.Lat.* 8[5].5.2), while Eumenius in the summer of 298 invokes *sub tua, Diocletiane Auguste, clementia Aegyptum furore posito quiescentem* (*Pan.Lat.* 9[4].21.2). In its context, the former passage clearly implies that an emperor went to Egypt, but such words could scarcely be used to refer to Diocletian's capture of Alexandria. Moreover, a papyrus lends support. A document from Oxyrhynchus, dated to February 295, appears to imply an imperial expedition to the south of Egypt: supplies are furnished to men who are described as

---

[19]P. Romanelli, *Storia delle provincie romane dell'Africa* (Rome 1959) 504; C. H. V. Sutherland, *RIC* 6 (1967) 23.

[20]W. Ensslin, *RE* 14 (1930) 2506 f.

[21]E.g., W. Seston, *Dioclétien et la Tétrarchie* 1 (Paris 1946) 142 ff. (rejecting the separation of the first two revolts); *PLRE* 1.474: "the evidence for a visit in 302 is unsound."

[22]T. Mommsen, *Collectio Librorum Juris Antejustiniani* 3 (Berlin 1890) 188–189; G. Costa, *Diz.ep.* 2.1810 ff.

[23]*JRS* 63 (1973) 33.

protector of the emperor(s) and *optio* of the *comites* of the emperor(s), and there are references to the legions IV Flavia, VII Claudia, and XI Claudia (*POxy* 43). As these are legions from Moesia, and a *praepositus* of IV Flavia and VII Claudia and other *praepositi* appear, it has long been recognized that the papyrus attests the presence in Egypt of an expeditionary force comprising detachments of several legions.[24] The papyrus also implies the presence of an emperor (whose identity remains to be established) and should be relevant to the orator's "trophies on the Nile." Nor is there any obvious difficulty in assigning the destruction of Busiris and Coptos to the same expedition.

The revolt in which Achilleus was prominent began in July or August 297, and Alexandria was captured in the following spring or summer.[25] Diocletian then, as Eumenius implies, remained in Egypt for some time: in September 298 preparations were being made for his impending visit to Upper Egypt (*PBeattyPanopolis* 1). He next proceeded to Syria, where his presence in Antioch on 5 February 299 is implied by one law (*CJ* 8.53[54].24, as emended by Mommsen), and certified by laws of February, March, and June 300 (*CJ* 9.21.1; 3.3.3; 7.22.2: the dates of the first two are not quite certain) and July 301 (*CJ* 3.28.25). Diocletian was in Egypt again in 302: the visit is recorded in two sources which preserve Alexandrian local traditions, viz. the so-called "Barbarus Scaligeri" (*Chr.min.* 1.290) and the Paschal Chronicle (p. 514.16-17 Bonn),[26] and Diocletian issued a rescript concerning the Manichees from Alexandria on 31 March (*Mos. et Rom. legum collatio* 15.3) in a year which can only be 302.[27]

It remains to identify the emperor who visited Egypt in 293 or shortly thereafter. He cannot be Diocletian, who spent the whole of 293 and 294 in the Balkans or near the shores of the Propontis, only travelling to Syria in spring 295.[28] He must, therefore, be Galerius. Now Eusebius includes the titles "Aegyptiacus maximus, Thebaicus maximus" in his report of Galerius' titulature in April 311 (*HE* 8.17.3). It is customary to reject them on summary verdict.[29] The preceding discussion removes the

[24]For comment on the document, E. Ritterling, *RE* 12 (1925) 1359 ff.; W. Ensslin, *Aegyptus* 32 (1952) 163 ff.; W. Seston, *Historia* 4 (1955) 292 ff.

[25]For the evidence, *PLRE* 1.263, Domitianus 6; for discussion of the date, A. C. Johnson, *CP* 45 (1950) 15 ff.; T. C. Skeat, *Papyri from Panopolis* (London 1964) x–xiii; A. K. Bowman, *Akten des XIII. Internationalen Papyrologenkongresses* (Munich 1973) 50 f.

[26]On which, see respectively A. Bauer, *Texte und Untersuchungen* 29.1 (Leipzig 1905) 162 ff.; E. Schwartz, *RE* 3 (1899) 2460 ff.

[27]L. Poinssot, *Mémoires de la Société Nationale des Antiquaires de France* 76 (1924) 313 ff. Most recent scholars have adopted the impossible date of 31 March 297 proposed by W. Seston, *Mélanges Ernout* (Paris 1940) 345 ff.

[28]Below, p. 186.

[29]E. Schwartz, *GCS* 9.2.792: "die Beinamen *Aegyptiacus maximus Thebaicus maximus*

obstacle to acceptance. Galerius went to Egypt in or soon after 293, the fighting involved the destruction of two Egyptian cities, and Diocletian did not celebrate the victory officially as a victory over external enemies. When senior emperor (i.e., after 25 July 306), Galerius took the titles, which appear in the appropriate chronological place—between "Germanicus maximus" and "Sarmaticus maximus." It follows that the victories were won in late 293 or early 294.[30]

THE PERSIAN WAR

The Persian War falls into three distinct phases. First, the Persian King Narses attacked the province of Syria and a Roman army was defeated between Carrhae and Callinicum. Second, Galerius collected a new army from the Danube, marched through Armenia, captured the Persian harem, and invaded Mesopotamia. Third, Diocletian and Galerius negotiated an advantageous peace which added new territory to the Roman Empire. The bare outline is clear from a variety of sources.[31] The chronology and even essential details are more obscure, and have so far eluded modern enquiry. The reason is only partly the recent publication (in 1964) of a papyrus which shows that Diocletian was in Egypt in September 298 (*PBeattyPanopolis* 1). A papyrus published in 1902 (*PArgent* 480) contains fragments of a contemporary epic poem on the war, which establishes two crucial facts: that the Roman defeat belongs to 296, and that it was incurred, not by Galerius alone, but in a campaign which he and Diocletian waged together. This evidence has never been properly exploited: W. Ensslin appears to have overlooked it completely,[32] while those who have offered historical comments on the poem (including the editor of what is now the standard edition) wrongly assign it to the second and successful campaign.[33] For clarity, the three phases of the war will be discussed separately.

sind von Seeck mit Recht als unerhört bezeichnet;" W. Ensslin, *RE* 14 (1930) 2525–2526: "die von Eusebios fälschlich eingeführten Siegertitel."

[30]It may be relevant that a city named Maximianopolis is attested in Egypt, cf. R. Kees, *RE* 14 (1930) 2484 f.

[31]See the evidence collected by J. W. Eadie, *The Breviarium of Festus* (London 1967) 146 ff. Add the arch of Galerius, only accessible at the time of writing in the inadequate publication by K. F. Kinch, *L'Arc de Triomphe de Salonique* (Paris 1890).

[32]The omission invalidates the central section of his otherwise valuable paper, "Zur Ostpolitik des Kaisers Diocletian," *SBMünchen*, Phil.-hist. Abt., 1942, Nr. 1.

[33]R. Reitzenstein, *Zwei religionsgeschichtliche Fragen nach ungedruckten griechischen Texten der Strassburger Bibliothek* (Strassburg 1901) 48–51; F. Cumont, *REA* 4 (1902) 36–40; G. Costa, *Diz. ep.* 2.1816; E. Kornemann, *Weltgeschichte des Mittelmeerraumes* 2 (Munich 1949) 265–266; E. Heitsch, *Die griechischen Dichterfragmente der römischen Kaiserzeit* 1². *Abh. Göttingen*, Phil.-hist. Kl.³, 49 (1963) 79–81, no. XXII.

The first campaign

Fragments survive of an epic poem, clearly written by a contemporary, which describe two episodes from the Persian War (Heitsch, *Dichterfragmente* XXII).[34] Only two connected passages can be recovered, separated by about thirty lines. In the first, after what appears to be the very last word of a speech, the Persians array themselves in a vast throng from all over the east (1 recto 1–14), and news of the impending attack reaches the Roman Empire (15: οὐδὲ καὶ 'Ελλὰς ἄπυσ[τος]). The second passage commences as follows:

. . . . . . τ[η]λεθάοντα κατηώρησε κορύμβω[ν.
τοῖν δὲ κ]εν 'Ιταλίηθεν ἐπερρώοντο καὶ ἄλλοι
κοίρανοι, εἰ μὴ τὸν μὲν ['I]βηρικὸς εἴρυεν "Αρης,
τῷ δὲ μόθος νήσοιο Β[ρ]εταννίδος ἀμφιδεδήει.
5 οἷα] δ' ὁ μὲν Κρήτηθεν, ὁ δ' εἰναλίης ἀπὸ Δήλου
εἶσι, Ζεὺς ὑπὲρ "Οθρυν, ὁ [δ'] ἐς Πάγγαιον 'Απόλλων,
τοῖν δὲ κορυσσομένοιν ὅμαδος πέφρικε Γιγάντω[ν,
τοῖος ἄναξ πρέσβιστος [ἄ]γων στρατὸν Αὐσονιήων
ἀντολίην ἀφίκανε σὺ[ν ὁ]πλοτέρῳ βασιλῆι.
10 καὶ γὰρ ἔσ[αν μακάρεσσιν ὁ]μοίιοι, ὃς μὲν ἐοικὼς
αἰθερίῳ [Διὶ κάρτος, ὁ δ'] 'Απόλλωνι κομήτῃ.

(1 verso 1–11).[35]

The names are easily supplied. The western emperors could not come from Italy because Maximian was detained by a war in Spain, while Constantius was fighting in Britain (2–4), but Diocletian and Galerius were together, like Zeus and Apollo (5–11). The references to Britain and Spain fix the date, even though no other source records fighting in Spain: Constantius recovered the island in 296 while Maximian defended the Upper Rhine, and by 1 March 297 Constantius was in Gaul, Maximian in Africa (*Pan.Lat.* 8[5], esp. 5.2; 13.3). If the poet's chronology is consistent, the dramatic date is no later than the autumn of 296, so that he must be describing the first campaign.

The Invasion of Mesopotamia

Although much will always remain obscure about the second campaign, it can be rendered probable that a Roman army advanced as far as

[34]Also D. L. Page, *Select Papyri* 3 (Loeb Classical Library 1941) 542–545, no. 135.

[35]The restorations are those of R. Reitzenstein, except in line 2, where I have substituted τοῖν for τῷ. Line 1 is obscure: Reitzenstein and Heitsch saw an allusion to a victory in Egypt (which is now unlikely), while Page translates "hung blooming (garlands) from the sterns of ships."

184

Ctesiphon. The route of Galerius' advance is both stated by literary sources and reflected in the imperial titles: he marched through Armenia, and through the territory lying immediately north of the Tigris, where his successes merited the titles of Armenicus, Medicus, and Adiabenicus.[36] The advance to Ctesiphon needs to be established by argument. There are two early items of explicit evidence. The first is the *Historia Augusta*, whose author pretends to be writing close to the event. Many assert (so he alleges) that fate will not allow a Roman emperor to go beyond Ctesiphon and that Carus was struck down by a thunderbolt for wishing to cross the boundaries laid down by fate (*Carus* 9.1). This opinion the writer controverts:

licet plane ac licebit (per sacratissimum Caesarem Maximianum constitit) Persas vincere atque ultra eos [sc. fines] progredi, et futurum reor, si a nostris non deseratur promissus numinum favor. (9.3)

An allusion to Julian in 363 appears probable,[37] with the possible imputation that Christians caused his failure: hence the writer should be appealing to a fact which he believes to be true, viz. that the pagan Galerius reached Ctesiphon. The second item of evidence is indirect, but derives from autopsy:

τοιγάρτοι καρπὸν ἤραντο τὸν προσήκοντα τῇ τοιαύτῃ θρησκείᾳ Μέμφις καὶ Βαβυλὼν, ἐρημωθεῖσαι καὶ ἀοίκητοι καταλειφθεῖσαι μετὰ τῶν πατρῴων θεῶν. καὶ ταῦτα οὐκ ἐξ ἀκοῆς λέγω, ἀλλ᾽ αὐτός τε παρὼν καὶ ἱστορήσας ἐπόπτης τε γενόμενος τῆς οἰκτρᾶς τῶν πόλεων τύχης

(Constantine *Oratio ad sanctorum coetum* 16, p. 177.1–4 Heikel)

The ruins of Babylon, or what passed for such, were still visible in the fourth century (Eusebius *In.Is.* 13.19 [*PG* 24.189]), but how could Constantine have seen them? The statement has been disbelieved and even used to prove that Constantine did not compose the speech.[38] The emperor, however, had been a tribune in the Roman army (*Pan.Lat.* 7[6].5.3; 6[7].3.3; Lactantius *Mort.Pers.* 18.10), and served under Diocletian and Galerius "in Asia" (*Exc. Vales.* 1.2). All the evidence falls into place if he accompanied Galerius on his march to Ctesiphon.

As for the chronology of the campaign, the *Consularia Constantino-*

---

[36]Note Victor *Caes.* 39.34: *per Armeniam in hostes contendit*; Eutropius *Brev.* 9.25.1: *cum Narseo Hormisdae et Saporis avo in Armenia maiore pugnavit*; Festus *Brev.* 25: *in Armenia maiore ipse imperator cum duobus equitibus exploravit hostes.* The army appears to have returned along the Euphrates, cf. Ammianus 24.1.10.

[37]N. H. Baynes, *The Historia Augusta: its date and purpose* (Oxford 1926) 62, 103.

[38]So, recently, R. P. C. Hanson, *JTS* n.s. 24 (1973) 506: "it is highly improbable that he could in fact have visited either of these ruins."

politana and the Paschal Chronicle date the Persian defeat to 297 (*Chr. min.* 1.230; p. 512.18–19; 513.19), while Joshua the Stylite dates the Roman capture of Nisibis to year 609 of the Seleucid era (*Chronicle*, trans. W. Wright [Cambridge 1882] p. 6), i.e., between October 297 and October 298. There is also the weighty evidence of a contemporary, who gives a correlation between the activities of the four emperors:

[*sc.* men contemplate] *aut sub tua, Diocletiane Auguste, clementia Aegyptum furore posito quiescentem aut te, Maximiane invicte, perculsa Maurorum agmina fulminantem aut sub dextera tua, domine Constanti, Bataviam Britanniamque squalidum caput silvis et fluctibus exserentem aut te, Maximiane Caesar, Persicos arcus pharetrasque calcantem.*
(*Pan.Lat.* 9[4].21.2)

The date must be summer or autumn 298: the Persian war is still in progress, and the omission of specific details implies that Eumenius had not yet heard of Galerius' capture of the Persian harem or his advance to Ctesiphon.

The peace negotiations

The political implications of the preceding reconstruction are serious. On the normal view, Galerius was defeated when he fought alone, while Diocletian and Galerius jointly supervised the successful campaign. The truth is the exact opposite: the Persians defeated Diocletian and Galerius, but Galerius won his Persian victories while Diocletian was in Egypt (from autumn 297 until at least September 298). Moreover, when the emperors returned to Antioch after their defeat, Diocletian rode in a carriage with the Caesar, dressed in the purple, preceding him on foot (Eutropius *Brev.* 9.24; Festus *Brev.* 25; Ammianus 14.11.10).[39] Contemporaries construed this as a humiliation for Galerius, and Diocletian successfully laid the blame for the Roman defeat on the Caesar alone. Galerius was a proud man (Lactantius *Mort. Pers.* 9.1 ff.), and it was not to be expected that he would easily allow Diocletian to arrogate the credit for the subsequent victories which he won unaided.

It is against this background that there occurred the negotiations, of which the *Excerpta de legationibus* preserve at least a partial description: the excerpts are taken from Petrus Patricius, who wrote in the sixth century and must therefore have derived his information from a much earlier writer (probably Eunapius).[40] The first of the two fragments shows Aphpharban going to Galerius and receiving the promise of a reply later

---

[39]The episode was dismissed as an invention by H. M. D. Parker, *A History of the Roman World A.D. 138 to 337* (London 1935) 233; W. Seston, *REA* 42 (1940) 515–519.
[40]For another probable example of Petrus' dependence on Eunapius, cf. *CP* 71 (1976) 267.

(frag. 13), whereas the second commences with Diocletian and Galerius meeting at Nisibis and sending Sicorius Probus to negotiate with the Persians (frag. 14).[41] The date cannot be either 297 or early 298 (as commonly supposed),[42] but must be the winter of 298/9 or the spring of 299.

THE DANUBIAN FRONTIER, 293–301

When Galerius assumed the purple in the spring of 293, he began to share the defence of the eastern provinces with Diocletian. The preceding section has reconstructed the movements of the two emperors from late 296 to early 299: the other eastern victories reflected in the imperial titulature of 301 (over Sarmatians twice, a Persian victory distinct from the Persian War of 296–299, and against the Carpi) can now be apportioned and dated. The argument proceeds from the numerous laws which establish Diocletian's presence at a particular place. The following is a summary of the chronological tables which T. Mommsen drew up, from the subscriptions in the *Codex Justinianus*:[43]

293	Sirmium (January–February) to Byzantium (April), with return to Sirmium (September–December)
294	Sirmium (January–August), then to Nicomedia (November–December)
295	Nicomedia (18 March), Damascus (1 May)[44]
296–298	no certain eastern laws
299	Antioch (5 February)[45]
300	Antioch (12 February–25 June)[46]
301	Antioch (4 July).[47]

It will at once be apparent that Diocletian cannot have visited Egypt between 1 March 293 and the summer of 295: therefore, Galerius was the emperor whose presence in Egypt is implied by two items of evidence (*POxy* 43; *Pan.Lat.* 8[5].5.2).[48] But what of the Persian victory earlier than 296? It is tempting to connect it with Diocletian's journey to Syria in 295, especially since a reorganisation of the Syrian and Arabian frontier

---

[41]For a recent discussion, G. S. R. Thomas, *Latomus* 28 (1969) 658 ff.

[42]As recently by T. D. Barnes, *Phoenix* 27 (1973) 140, 141.

[43]T. Mommsen, *AbhBerlin* 1860.421 ff. = *Ges.Schr.* 2 (Berlin 1905) 267 ff.

[44]*CJ* 5.72.3 (18 March); 5.4.17 = *Collatio* 6.4 (1 May).

[45]*CJ* 8.53(54).24. The date is corrupt in the MSS.

[46]*CJ* 9.21.1 (12 February); 3.3.3 (26 March); 7.22.2 (25 June).

[47]*CJ* 3.28.25.

[48]Above, pp. 181–182.

at about this time has long been recognized.[49] Yet an inscription which bears the date of 294 styles Diocletian and Maximian "[Ger. max.,] Sar. max., Pers. max." (*ILS* 640: near Vitidurum, in Switzerland). That should imply a date of 294 and a consequent attribution to Galerius.

All modern accounts assume that in 293 Galerius was entrusted with the defence of the Danubian frontier.[50] In fact, the evidence upon which they rely, though early and explicit,[51] is valid only for the period after the Persian War (i.e., from 299). In 293 and 294, Galerius was active in the East, campaigning in Egypt and then on the Syrian frontier, while Diocletian defended the Danube. Nor did the Augustus and the Caesar exchange their stations in 295. For the defeat of the Carpi in 296, which modern scholars have ascribed to Galerius or even to Maximian,[52] must be restored to the senior emperor: *Carporum, quos antiquis excitos sedibus Diocletianus transtulit in Pannoniam* (Ammianus 28.1.5).

There remain two Sarmatian victories. One must correspond to the *Sarmaticae expeditiones quibus illa gens prope omnis extincta est* to which the orator of 297 alludes (*Pan.Lat.* 8[5].5.1); and a chronicle notes *castra facta in Sarmatia* under the year 294 (*Chr.min.* 1.230). The other should derive from a campaign which Galerius waged in or after 299. Now an inscription, which styles all the Tetrarchs "Germanici maximi V Sarmat. max. IIII Persici max. II Brittanici maximi" (*ILS* 641: Bucarest, cf. *AE* 1936.10; 1966.357),[53] implies that Diocletian celebrated a fourth Sarmatian victory before the sixth German victory; and the same chronicle reports that the Marcomanni were defeated in 299 (*Chr.min.* 1.230). If the date is correct, then the sixth German victory, won by Constantius against Franci, presumably belongs to 300 or 301.

---

[49] R. E. Brünnow and A. von Domaszewski, *Die Provincia Arabia* 3 (Strassburg 1909) 271 ff.; F. M. Abel, *Géographie de la Palestine* 2³ (Paris 1967) 169.

[50] E.g., A. H. M. Jones, *The Later Roman Empire* 3 (Oxford 1964) 3: "The division of the empire in 293 is described by Aur. Victor, *Caes.* xxxix. 30 and Praxagoras (*FHG* IV, p. 2)." To the best of my knowledge, no modern scholar has ever contested the point.

[51] Lactantius *Mort.Pers.* 18.6 (referring to Galerius): *iam fluxisse annos quindecim (quibus) in Illyricum id est ad ripam Danuvii relegatus cum gentibus barbaris luctaretur;* Praxagoras, *FGrH* 219 T 1: ὁ δὲ ἕτερος Μαξιμῖνος (sic) τῆς τε Ἑλλάδος καὶ Μακεδονίας καὶ τῆς κάτω Ἀσίας καὶ Θράκης, Διοκλητιανὸς δὲ ὁ καὶ ἄλλων πρεσβύτατος τῆς τε Βιθυνίας ἦρχε καὶ τῆς Ἀραβίας καὶ τῆς Λιβύης καὶ τῆς Αἰγύπτου; Victor *Caes.* 39.30: *Illyrici ora adusque Ponti fretum Galerio* [*sc. commissa*].

[52] H. Schiller, *Geschichte der römischen Kaiserzeit* 2 (Gotha 1887) 137; H. Mattingly, *CAH* 12 (1939) 334 (Galerius); A. Stein, *RE* 3 (1899) 1610; O. Seeck, *Geschichte des Untergangs der antiken Welt* 1⁵ (Berlin 1921) 27, 452; E. Stein, *Geschichte des spätrömischen Reiches* 1 (Vienna 1928) 116 = *Histoire du Bas-Empire* 1² (Bruges and Paris 1959) 78, 447 (Maximian).

[53] On these inscriptions, see J. Kolendo, *Eirene* 5 (1966) 139 ff. They establish the equivalence of the titles "Carpicus" and "Gothicus."

THE IMPERIAL VICTORIES REFLECTED IN
DIOCLETIAN'S TITLES OF NOVEMBER/DECEMBER 301

Germanicus maximus	285, Maximian (p. 178)
Sarmaticus maximus	285, Diocletian (p. 178)
Germanicus maximus II	286, Maximian (p. 178)
Germanicus maximus III	287, Maximian (p. 178)
Germanicus maximus IV	288, Diocletian (p. 178)
Sarmaticus maximus II	289, Diocletian (p. 177)
Germanicus maximus V	293, Constantius (p. 179)
Sarmaticus maximus III	294, Diocletian (p. 187)
Persicus maximus	294, Galerius (pp. 186–187)
Brittanicus maximus	296, Constantius (p. 179)
Carpicus maximus	296, Diocletian (pp. 176, 187)
Armenicus maximus ⎫	
Medicus Maximus ⎬	298, Galerius (p. 185)
Adiabenicus maximus ⎪	
Persicus maximus II ⎭	
Sarmaticus maximus IV	?299 Galerius (p. 187)
Germanicus maximus VI	?300 or 301 Constantius (pp. 179, 187)

THE TITLES OF GALERIUS

Towards the end of 301, Diocletian boasted that the tranquil world lay in the lap of deep quiet and that imperial exertions had replaced barbarian invasion with an eternal peace (*Edictum de pretiis*, praef. 5), and on 31 March 302 he denounced the Manichees for disturbing the leisure of mankind (*Mos. et Rom. legum collatio* 15.3). The emperor's protestations have been eagerly credited in the recent age,[54] and it is widely believed that "during the last years of his reign Diocletian was occupied with his struggle with Christianity."[55] But was the peace which Diocletian lauded a lasting phenomenon or merely a brief respite? The official titulature of Galerius unambiguously indicates the continuance of warfare.[56]

Four items of evidence are available. First, two military diplomas. The

[54]E.g., W. Seston, *Dioclétien et la Tétrarchie* 1 (1946) 10: "Dès les premières années du IVe siècle s'ouvre une crise qui risque de remettre en question l'oeuvre entière de Dioclétien. Crise toute intérieure, car la paix que gagna Dioclétien par ses victoires et celles de ses collègues, et par les réformes militaires qu'il fit, fut assurée pour plus d'une génération."

[55]A. H. M. Jones, *The Later Roman Empire* 1 (1964) 40. He argues that, because "we hear of no more rebellions or foreign wars" after 298, therefore Rome's "external foes had been for the time being quelled" (39).

[56]J. Kolendo, *Hommages à Marcel Renard* 2 (Brussels 1969) 378 ff.

one, probably to be dated 7 January 305, is very fragmentary (*CIL* 16.157 = *AE* 1958.190),[57] but the other is well preserved and gives the full victory titles of Constantius and Galerius on 7 January 306 (*AE* 1961.240: found near Grosseto).[58] The other two items also cohere closely in date. One is a letter which Galerius issued in 310 or early 311, known only from a single nineteenth century copy (*EphEp* 4.44 = *CIL* 3.6979 = *ILS* 660:Sinope). As reported, two lines preserve a relevant part of the emperor's titles:

> quint., Persic. max. tert., Brett.
> Med. max., Adiab. max., trib. pot.

The word before "quint." can only be "Sarmaticus": hence there had been three Sarmatian victories since 301, as well as Galerius' third commemoration of a Persian victory.

The final item is an imperial edict preserved in a literary source. In late April 311, Galerius issued an edict ending the persecution of Christians in his domains in the name of himself and his three acknowledged imperial colleagues (Lactantius *Mort.Pers.* 33.11–35.1; 36.3). Eusebius included a Greek version in his *Ecclesiastical History*, which commences with the full official titles of Galerius (*HE* 8.17.3 ff.). Apart from the omission of "Pius Felix" (perhaps by Eusebius himself), the manuscripts appear to have corrupted their pristine form very little:

Αὐτοκράτωρ Καῖσαρ Γαλέριος Οὐαλέριος Μαξιμιανὸς ἀνίκητος Σεβαστός, ἀρχιερεὺς μέγιστος, Γερμανικὸς μέγιστος ⟨ἑπτάκις⟩ Αἰγυπτιακὸς μέγιστος, Θηβαικὸς μέγιστος, Σαρματικὸς μέγιστος πεντάκις, Περσῶν μέγιστος ⟨τρίς, Βρεττανῶν μέγιστος⟩ δίς, Κάρπων μέγιστος ἑξάκις, Ἀρμενίων μέγιστος, Μήδων μέγιστος, Ἀδιαβηνῶν μέγιστος, δημαρχικῆς ἐξουσίας τὸ εἰκοστόν, αὐτοκράτωρ τὸ ἐννεακαιδέκατον, ὕπατος τὸ ὄγδοον, πατὴρ πατρίδος, ἀνθύπατος.[59]

A number has clearly fallen out after "Γερμανικὸς μέγιστος." Since the diploma of 7 January 306 has "Germ. m. V," and Constantine's official titulature reflects two German victories which he won between 25 July 306 and 311 (*ILS* 696; *AE* 1934.158), Galerius must have been "Germanicus maximus VII" in April 311. Hence "ἑπτάκις" can be supplied with confidence. Moreover, comparison with the preceding document shows that three words are missing between "Περσῶν μέγιστος" and "δίς": mechanical loss is perhaps more probable than deliberate omission.[60]

---

[57]Discussed most fully by G. Forni, *Bollettino dell'Istituto di Diritto Romano* 62 (1959) 247 ff. (assuming that the date is 7 January 304).

[58]Published and discussed by M. Bizzarri and G. Forni, *NSc* 1959.58 ff.; *Athenaeum* N.S. 38 (1960) 3 ff., with Tavole I–IV.

[59]For the readings of the MSS, see E. Schwartz, *GCS* 9.2 (1908) 790–792.

[60]Despite Rufinus *HE* 8.17.3: *Persicus bis Carpicus sexies.*

Finally, it may be observed that the figures "tribunicia potestate XX imperator XIX" are correct on the hypothesis that Galerius had taken an additional renewal of each title on 1 May 305, when he was promoted from Caesar to Augustus.[61]

Taken in pairs, and compared with the edict of 301, the four documents permit some precise deductions (Tables 3, 4).

TABLE 3: THE VICTORY TITLES OF GALERIUS, 301–311

	Number of times title taken		
Title	1. November/December 301	2. 7 Jan. 306	3. April 311
Germanicus maximus	2	5	[7]
Aegyptiacus maximus	omitted	omitted	1
Thebaicus maximus			1
Sarmaticus maximus	2	3	5
Persicus maximus	2	2	3
Brittanicus maximus	1	2	2
Carpicus maximus	1	5	6
Armenicus maximus	1	1	1
Medicus maximus	1	1	1
Adiabenicus maximus	1	1	1

Evidence: 1. *Edictum de pretiis* (Table 1).
2. *AE* 1961.240, cf. *CIL* 16.157 (? 7 January 305)
3. Eusebius, *HE* 8.17.3, cf. *ILS* 660 (310/1). "Germanicus maximus VII" is deduced from *ILS* 696; *AE* 1934.158.

TABLE 4: VICTORIES OVER EXTERNAL ENEMIES, 301–311

Area of victory or name of enemy	Number of victories celebrated	
	ca 1 December 301–7 Jan. 306	7 Jan. 306–April 311
Germans	3	2
Sarmatians	1	2
Persians	0	1
Britain	1	0
Carpi	4	1

[61]Additional renewals must also be postulated for Maximian in 293 (*ILS* 640; *Edictum de pretiis*, praef. 1) and for Constantine before 311 (*FIRA*² 1.93; *AE* 1934.158). Failure to see this crucial fact has led a recent writer to date the edict to December 311 and to attribute it to Maximinus (R. M. Grant, *Studia Patristica* 12 [*Texte und Untersuchungen* 119 (1975)], 417).

WARFARE, 302–305

Of the nine imperial victories attested between late 301 and January 306, only those won by Constantius can readily be dated and identified. The British victory belongs to Constantius' campaign against the Picts, in which Constantine participated (*Pan.Lat.* 6[7].7.1 ff.; *Exc. Vales.* 1.4). The diploma of 306 establishes the date as 305—and thus incidentally disproves the story that Constantine fled from Nicomedia in summer 306 and found his father on his death-bed.[62] The three German victories must be the three victories to which the orator of 310 alludes: among the Lingones, near Vindonissa, and on the Rhine (*Pan.Lat.* 6[7].6.2–4). An inscription styling Diocletian "[German] ico max. VII" in 302 dates the first to that year (*CIL* 10.3343: Puteoli). Presumably, therefore, if Constantius crossed to Britain in 305, the other two German victories belong to 303 and 304.

No evidence so specific avails to date the five victories on the Danube in these years. Yet two allusions in Lactantius appear to imply victories over Sarmatians and Carpi in autumn 302 and over Carpi in autumn 303 (*Mort.Pers.* 13.2; 38.6).[63] It may also be relevant that Diocletian travelled up the course of the Danube in 303 on the way from Nicomedia to Rome, and in the following year, on the return journey, made a circuit of the *ripa Thracia* (*CJ* 5.73.4 [8 June 302: Durostorum]; Lactantius *Mort. Pers.* 17.4).[64]

IMPERIAL CAMPAIGNS AGAINST EXTERNAL ENEMIES, 306–311

The existence of ancient accounts of the persecution of the Christians between 303 and 313 and of the civil wars between 306 and 313 has tended to overshadow the foreign warfare which followed the abdication of Diocletian (1 May 305). To be sure, the full details are irretrievably lost. But the titles of Galerius in 311 reflect several victories subsequent to 7 January 306, whose dates can be deduced from the titulature of Constantine and Licinius.[65] Besides the German victories, for which Constantine took the title "Germanicus maximus" twice, there are two Sarmatian victories, one Persian, and one over Carpi (Table 4).

The *dies imperii* of Constantine was 25 July 306, and he gained his first German victory before ca September 307 (*Pan.Lat.* 7[6].4.2; 6[7].

---

[62]Lactantius *Mort.Pers.* 24.4 ff.; Eusebius *Vita Const.* 1.21; Victor *Caes.* 40.2 ff.; *Epit. de Caes.* 41.2 f.; Zosimus 2.8.2 ff.

[63]But see below, p. 192.

[64]The MS has "strige": on the problem of the correct reading, cf. J. Moreau, *Lactance: De la Mort des Persécuteurs (Sources chrétiennes* 39 [1954]) 305 f.

[65]On the victory titles of Constantine, see now *ZPE* 20 (1976) 149 ff.

10.2 ff.; 4[10].16.5). Hence, when an inscription of 315 has the order "Sarmatico max., Germ. max., Got. max." (*ILS* 695: Sitifis, cf. *CIL* 2.481: Emerita), two conclusions follow: one of the Sarmatian victories should belong to late 306 or to early 307, the victory over Carpi to 307 or later. The other Sarmatian victory appears to be dated explicitly to 27 June 310 (*ILS* 664: from Noricum). Since Galerius became gravely ill in spring 310 (Lactantius *Mort.Pers.* 33.1 ff.), Licinius will have been in command. Further, since Licinius, whose *dies imperii* was 11 November 308 (*Chr.min.* 1.231), is styled "Sarmatico max., Germanico max." on an inscription of late 317 (*ILS* 679: Bisica Lucana, in Africa), Constantine's second German victory (*Pan.Lat.* 6[7].12.1; 4[10].18.1 ff.) occurred before 11 November 308.

As for the victory over the Carpi, a date of 308 seems at first sight probable, since it leaves no trace in the titulature of Licinius.[66] However, the attested examples of Licinius' victory titles (*CIL* 8.1357 = *ILS* 679; *CIL* 8.22119, 22176, 22259; 9.6061; 10.6966) come from territory subject to Constantine—whose own titulature often omits titles pertaining to campaigns of Galerius.[67] The date of 309, therefore, cannot be wholly excluded.

The Persian victory can be dated from an African milestone of winter 312/3 (*ILAlg* 1.3956: between Theveste and Thelepte). In this text, Constantine has the titles "Germanicus," "Sarmaticus," and "Persicus": if victories won by Galerius are excluded (Constantine lacks the title "Gothicus"), then the Persian victory will be later than Licinius' Sarmatian victory of 27 June 310. Further, the order of Maximinus' titles on the same inscription (viz., "Sarmaticus," "Germanicus," "Persicus," with no "Gothicus") could be held to imply that the victory for which Galerius took the title "Sarmaticus maximus III" was won by the Caesar Severus between Maximinus' *dies imperii* (1 May 305) and Constantine's (25 July 306).[68]

THE IMPERIAL VICTORIES REFLECTED IN GALERIUS' TITLES OF APRIL 311

Germanicus maximus	293, Constantius (p. 179)
Aegyptiacus maximus ⎱	293/4, Galerius (pp. 180–182)
Thebaicus maximus ⎰	

[66]Galerius was occupied with Maxentius in the summer and autumn of 307 (Lactantius *Mort.Pers.* 27.1 ff.).

[67]E.g., *ILS* 8942 (315); 696 (318); 6091 (331); 705 (ca 334); *AE* 1934.158 (337).

[68]This possibility was overlooked in *ZPE* 20 (1976) 155. However, it is not certain that in 305/6 Severus ruled more than Italy and Africa, cf. *Exc.Val.* 1.5 (assigning Galerius all of "Illyricum"); 9 (the only evidence that Severus received "Pannoniae").

I am extremely grateful to Professor J. F. Gilliam who contributed much to the improvement of an earlier draft of the present paper.

Sarmaticus maximus	294, Diocletian (p. 187)
Persicus maximus	294, Galerius (pp. 186–187)
Brittanicus maximus	296, Constantius (p.179)
Carpicus maximus	296, Diocletian (pp. 176, 187)
Armenicus maximus ⎫	
Medicus maximus ⎪	
Adiabenicus maximus ⎬	298, Galerius (p. 185)
Persicus maximus II ⎭	
Sarmaticus maximus II	?299, Galerius (p. 187)
Germanicus maximus II	?300 or 301, Constantius (p. 179, 187)
Germanicus maximus III–V	302, 303, 304, Constantius (p. 191)
Carpicus maximus II–V	?302, 303, 304, 305 (p. 191)
Sarmaticus maximus III	?late 302, Galerius (p. 191)
	(possibly 305/6, Severus [p. 192])
Britannicus maximus II	305, Constantius (p. 191)
Sarmaticus maximus IV	306/7, Galerius (p. 192)
Germanicus maximus VI	306/7, Constantine (p. 191)
Germanicus maximus VII	308, Constantine (p. 192)
Carpicus maximus VI	308 (or 309), Galerius (p. 192)
Sarmaticus maximus V	27 June 310, Licinius (p. 192)
Persicus maximus III	310, Maximinus (p. 192).

UNIVERSITY OF TORONTO

XIII

THE *EPITOME DE CAESARIBUS* AND ITS SOURCES*

The Latin epitomators of the fourth century have begun to benefit from increased scholarly interest in the later Roman Empire and its literature. But much remains to be done. A need exists for a proper elucidation of Aurelius Victor: the *Caesares* survives in only two manuscripts, neither older than the fifteenth century, and the text contains many passages which are either corrupt or extremely hard to understand.[1] Moreover, good intentions never guarantee expertise, and some recent work has been of poor quality—a commentary on Festus which passes over some of the most interesting passages in silence and avoids many of the real problems in the text;[2] a study of Florus, Victor, Festus, and the *Epitome de Caesaribus* which makes some strange misstatements of both fact and opinion;[3] and an edition of the anonymous *De viris illustribus* which ranks as a paradigm of incompetence and ineptitude.[4] Everyone, therefore, should welcome most warmly the appearance of Jörg Schlumberger's full study of the *Epitome*, for it is careful, thoughtful, and usually accurate. Until its publication, the only systematic treatments of the sources of the *Epitome* were parts of two articles, admittedly both extremely long, by Theodor Opitz (1872) and Ernst Hohl (1911),[5] and A. Cohn's dissertation on the first eleven chapters (1884).[6]

Schlumberger's book meets an obvious need, and meets it well. The bulk of his treatment comprises a discussion of the work's contents chapter by chapter, and he proceeds with exemplary clarity and fair-mindedness. To be sure, there are some minor errors and misjudgments which do not affect the main argument. That is virtually inevitable, and they are here deliberately ignored. For, if Schlumberger's central conclusion must be pronounced inadmissible, that is the result of three principal causes: the problems which the *Epitome* poses are both difficult and intricate; the conclusions of any inquiry are partly circumscribed by the initial assumptions; and Schlumberger has taken on trust some erroneous opinions about the historical and literary background. Hence the ample proportions of the present

---

* *Die "Epitome de Caesaribus": Untersuchungen zur heidnischen Geschichtsschreibung des 4. Jahrhunderts n. Chr.* By JÖRG SCHLUMBERGER. Vestigia: Beiträge zur alten Geschichte, vol. 18. Munich: Verlag C. H. Beck, 1974. Pp. xv + 275 + 1. DM 44.

1. The recent Budé edition, with translation and lengthy commentary, by P. Dufraigne (Paris, 1975), is variously unsatisfactory.

2. J. W. Eadie, *The "Breviarium" of Festus: A Critical Edition with Historical Commentary* (London, 1967). For some specific defects, see T. D. Barnes, *JRS* 57 (1967): 263–65; A. Cameron, *CR* n.s. 19 (1969): 305–7.

3. W. den Boer, *Some Minor Roman Historians* (Leyden, 1972). In Den Boer's hands, Gallienus' wife Cornelia Salonina Chrysogone becomes "Julia Cornelia Salonina Pipa" (p. 80), and Festus of Tridentum "Festinus" (pp. 178 ff.). Not all reviewers seem to have noticed.

4. W. K. Sherwin (ed.), *Deeds of Famous Men* ("De Viris Illustribus") (Norman, Okla., 1973). For restrained comment, see G. V. Sumner, *Phoenix* 27 (1973): 209 f.

5. T. Opitz, "Quaestionum de Sex. Aurelio Victore capita tria," *Acta Societatis philologae Lipsiensis* 2.2 (1872): 208–269; E. Hohl, "Vopiscus und die Biographie des Kaisers Tacitus," *Klio* 11 (1911): 192–229. This section of Hohl's study of the *HA*'s *Vita Taciti* bears the title "Beiträge zur Restituierung der Enmannschen 'Kaisergeschichte.'"

6. A. Cohn, *Quibus ex fontibus S. Aurelii Victoris et "Libri de Caesaribus" et "Epitomes" undecim capita priora fluxerint* (Diss. Leipzig; Berlin, 1884).

critique: the high quality of Schlumberger's treatment of most details encourages a reconsideration of the basic problems—especially since he has caused me to revise some statements which I made about the *Epitome* some years ago.[7]

The identification of the sources of the *Epitome* involves not so much a single problem, or even a single complex of interrelated problems, as a series of very different problems. For the work falls into four parts, which differ from one another in their affiliations (viz., 1–11, 12–23, 24–38, and 39–46). Each part, therefore, will be discussed separately (sections II–V) and apart from general questions which concern the work as a whole (sections I and VI). Further, for the sake of clarity, I shall include in sections II–V tables which depict schematically the two views of the literary relationships of the *Epitome* which are being contrasted in each case. The function of these tables is merely to aid the reader to visualize the particular problem under review: they do not show the full relationship among all the sources, and in each case Schlumberger's implied stemma is shown on the left, whether or not it is argued to be preferable to the stemma on the right.

I

Schlumberger commences with an introduction (pp. 1–16), which has three main sections. He reviews the textual transmission of the *Epitome*, which indicates that the work originally had no connection with Aurelius Victor. That needed to be said, for there are still scholars who cite the *Epitome* as the work of Victor.[8] The common designation "Pseudo-Victor" is equally inappropriate, because it suggests that the anonymous author intended to pass himself off as Victor. Schlumberger then summarizes previous research into the *Epitome*, and states the nature of his own inquiry.

One very important preliminary question must be faced at the outset. Schlumberger accepts the existence of the lost "Kaisergeschichte" (henceforward KG) which Alexander Enmann postulated in 1883,[9] and consistently employs the postulate in his analysis of the *Epitome* (p. 9, etc.). He also accepts my own argument for 337 as the probable terminal date of the KG (pp. 56, 93, 193, 200, 202).[10] Predictably, I welcome an approach which coincides with my own. But it might have been advisable to buttress the argument in more detail.

Since the author of the KG has recently been derided (albeit inaccurately) as a historian "manufactured in 1874,"[11] a brief restatement may be apposite. Schlumberger accepts the KG for essentially the right reason: the resemblances between Victor and Eutropius for the period 235–284 are of such a nature that a common source must be invoked, which can probably also—at a lower level of cogency—be detected in their accounts of the first and second centuries (p. 9). But Enmann's original formulation was fallacious, since it assumed that the *Historia Augusta* was written under Diocletian and Constantine, and Hermann Dessau deserves explicit

7. T. D. Barnes, "The Lost Kaisergeschichte and the Latin Historical Tradition," *Bonner Historia-Augusta-Colloquium 1968/69* (1970), pp. 22–23.

8. Thus *PLRE*, vol. 1 (Cambridge, 1971), p. xii, etc.

9. A. Enmann, "Eine verlorene Geschichte der römischen Kaiser . . .," *Philologus*, suppl. 4 (1884): 335–501. Although the *Supplementband* as a whole bears the date 1884, *Heft* 3, which includes Enmann's article, was published in June, 1883 (*Deutsche Literaturzeitung* 4 [1883]: 861).

10. Barnes, "The Lost Kaisergeschichte," pp. 18–20.

11. Den Boer, *Some Minor Roman Historians*, p. 21.

credit for expressing the argument in its valid form: the close coincidence in their selection of facts, the large number of common factual errors, and the frequent parallelism in formulation compel the conclusion that Victor and Eutropius independently used a lost source of comparatively brief compass.[12] It may be added that a common source must also be posited to explain the accounts which Victor and Eutropius give of the reign of Diocletian: Eutropius has not copied the far more individualistic Victor, and it seems impossible that two writers should independently make the appointment of the Caesars in 293 the result of a war which began in 296 and a revolt which broke out in 297 (*Caes.* 39. 22 ff.; *Brev.* 9. 22). In brief, the KG should be defined as the common source of Victor and Eutropius, since its existence is (and must be) deduced primarily from their resemblances. By a second series of arguments, it can then be identified as a source for other writers too (including the author of the *Epitome*).[13]

Another question also requires preliminary discussion. Given that the source of a passage has been securely identified, how can it be established whether it is the immediate or only the ultimate source, whether the derivation is direct or indirect? When the *Epitome* repeats a phrase, clause, or sentence from an earlier author, it does not necessarily follow that the writer has himself read, consulted, or copied the earlier author. The possibility of an intermediate source arises and needs to be examined. For example, a passage in the chapter on Nerva (which Schlumberger surprisingly fails to discuss) repeats a letter of Pliny:

hic ne accessu malivolorum terreretur, Iunii Maurici, constantis viri, dicto ita admonetur: qui convivio familiari adhibitus cum Veientonem consulari honore functum quidem apud Domitianum, tamen multos occultis criminationibus persecutum adesse vidisset, inter colloquia mentione Catulli facta, calumniatoris praecipui, dicente Nerva: "quid nunc faceret, si Domitiano supervixisset?" "Nobiscum" inquit Mauricus "cenaret." [*Epit.* 12. 5]

cenabat Nerva cum paucis; Veiento proximus atque etiam in sinu recumbebat: dixi omnia cum hominem nominavi. incidit sermo de Catullo Messalino, qui luminibus orbatus ingenio saevo mala caecitatis addiderat: non verebatur, non erubescebat, non miserebatur; quo saepius a Domitiano non secus ac tela, quae et ipsa caeca et improvida feruntur, in optimum quemque contorquebatur. de huius nequitia sanguinariisque sententiis in commune omnes super cenam loquebantur, cum ipse imperator: "Quid putamus passurum fuisse si viveret?" et Mauricus: "Nobiscum cenaret." [Pliny *Epp.* 4. 22. 4–6]

The comparison might seem to prove that the author of the *Epitome* had read Pliny.[14] But can direct derivation be demonstrated? Schlumberger's careful chapter on "Arbeitsweise und literarisches Ziel der Epitome" (pp. 63–77) shows that the author tended to follow a small number of sources very closely. Moreover,

12. H. Dessau, "Über Zeit und Persönlichkeit der *SHA*," *Hermes* 24 (1889): 361–62.

13. For Festus, see Eadie, *The "Breviarium" of Festus*, pp. 70 ff.; for Jerome, R. Helm, "Hieronymus und Eutrop," *RhM* n.s. 76 (1927): 138 ff., 254 ff.; for the *HA*, R. Syme, *Emperors and Biography: Studies in the "Historia Augusta"* (Oxford, 1971), p. 45, etc. Den Boer, *Some Minor Roman Historians*, p. 117, attributes to Helm a view diametrically opposed to the one he in fact affirmed.

14. The passage is, however, not discussed in A. Cameron, "The Fate of Pliny's *Letters* in the Late Empire," *CQ* n.s. 15 (1965): 289–98, with addendum in *CQ* n.s. 17 (1967): 421–22.

the rank of Veiento (cos. III ?83) must come from elsewhere than Pliny. It is far more probable that the story of the dinner party has reached the *Epitome* through the medium of Marius Maximus than that the author sought it out for himself.[15]

Since a letter-writer like Pliny could not be one of the main sources of the *Epitome*, the decision is relatively easy. With Suetonius, the problem becomes more difficult.

II

The first eleven chapters of the *Epitome* (see Table 1) describe Roman emperors from Augustus to Domitian, and they alone can be compared with two indubitable sources. The *Epitome* frequently repeats ideas, phrases, and sentences from Aurelius Victor, and there can be little doubt that the author had a text of Victor before him as he wrote this section (Schlumberger, pp. 65-66). The *Epitome* also exhibits some close similarities to Suetonius (the closest being *Epit.* 10. 4 and Suet. *Titus* 6. 2) and clearly reproduces much material which derives from Suetonius (Schlumberger, pp. 17-62). Both Cohn[16] and Schlumberger deny direct derivation from Suetonius, and with good cause. On a careful reading of both the text and of Schlumberger's discussion, I can see no passage where direct consultation of Suetonius by the *Epitome* must be inferred. Hence, since there is authentic material which does not derive from either Suetonius' imperial biographies or Victor (e.g., in 1. 6, 9, 16, 20, 24, 27, 28), either the *Epitome* has combined a multiplicity of sources for the first century or it has employed a source or sources which combined both Suetonian and non-Suetonian material. The character of the work, so Schlumberger judges (rightly in my view), renders the second alternative preferable to the first.

Can the source or sources be identified? The KG meets some of the requirements and can be equated with a source which Cohn in 1884 described as "Suetonius auctus"—by which Cohn meant a lost writer who abbreviated Suetonius while

TABLE 1

"Epitome" 1–11

Schlumberger   **Cohn**

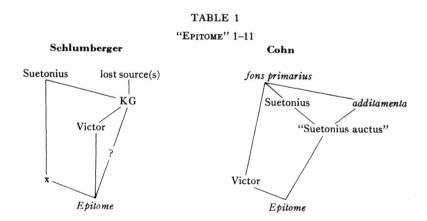

15. Similarly, Maximus probably played a role in transmitting the much-discussed passage with the phrase *quinquennium Neronis* (Victor *Caes.* 5. 2; *Epit.* 5. 2).
16. Cohn, *Quibus ex fontibus . . .* , pp. 21, 36–37. For the meaning of "Suetonius auctus," note the description "ille qui Suetonium excerpserit et ornaverit" (p. 48).

working in additional material. But Schlumberger denies that the KG alone can explain all the additional material, and posits another lost source, which will allow him (if necessary) to dispense with use of the KG in these chapters (p. 61). For myself, I think that a confident decision on this question is probably not justified.

The resemblances of the *Epitome* to Aurelius Victor suddenly cease with the accession of Nerva (12. 1). Subsequently, only a very few passages exhibit any close similarity to Victor (the most conspicuous being *Epit.* 34. 3 and *Caes.* 34. 5; *Epit.* 41. 2–3 and *Caes.* 40. 2–4). Instead, the *Epitome* begins to show close resemblances to Eutropius and the *Historia Augusta* (whose lives of Nerva and Trajan are regrettably lost).

III

Schlumberger's discussion of *Epitome* 12–23 (see Table 2) does not confine itself to this work: the titles of his two chapters aptly describe their contents, viz., "Epitome und Historia Augusta bis Elagabal" (pp. 78–123), and "Marius Maximus, Nicht Ignotus" (pp. 124–33); and Schlumberger often seems more concerned with the sources of the *HA* than with those of the *Epitome*. Since I am named as one of the two "Hauptverfechter" of a theory about the *HA* which Schlumberger describes as a "wenig überzeugende Hypothese" (p. 104) and "nicht notwendig und in die Irre führend" (p. 131), I shall digress to controvert him.[17]

The postulate of an unknown biographer (for convenience styled "Ignotus") as the main source of the *HA* as far as Caracalla is derived from the *HA* alone, and it rests solely upon a central proposition about the *HA*: that to identify Marius Maximus as the main source, as well as the source of those passages which the *HA* attributes to him by name and those which the specific content indicates as deriving from him, creates more difficulties in understanding the *HA* than it

TABLE 2

"Epitome" 12–23

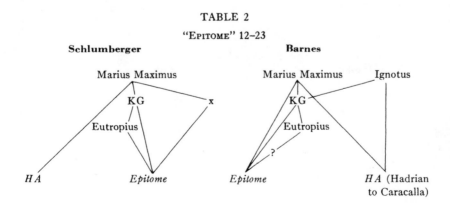

17. The hypothesis of Ignotus is set forth and (in my view) demonstrated by R. Syme in the following publications: *Ammianus and the "Historia Augusta"* (Oxford, 1968), pp. 92–93; "Ignotus, the Good Biographer," *Bonner Historia-Augusta-Colloquium 1966/67* (1968), pp. 131–53 = *Emperors and Biography*, pp. 30–53; "Not Marius Maximus," *Hermes* 96 (1968): 494–500; *Emperors and Biography*, pp. 113–34; "Marius Maximus Once Again," *Bonner Historia-Augusta-Colloquium 1970* (1972), pp. 287–302. For my adherence to Syme's conclusion, see "Hadrian and Lucius Verus," *JRS* 57 (1967): 66, 74; "The Lost Kaisergeschichte," pp. 30, 39–40; "*Ultimus Antoninorum*," *Bonner Historia-Augusta-Colloquium 1970* (1972), p. 73.

solves.[18] This is not the place to restate a full case in favor of Ignotus; it will suffice to observe that nothing in Schlumberger's discussion of the *Epitome* counts seriously against the thesis. The reason is simple. Granted that the *Epitome* derives much of its material from Marius Maximus, then similarities between the *Epitome* and the *HA* will only prove that the main source of the *HA* was Maximus, if they occur in passages which the hypothesis of Ignotus requires to be attributed to Ignotus rather than to Maximus. If they occur in passages which the hypothesis of Ignotus allows to be attributed to Maximus, then they do not impair the hypothesis. The latter is in fact the case: the closest similarities occur in passages of the *HA* which are either obvious or probable additions to the main source (e.g., *Epit.* 14. 2[a] and *HA Hadr.* 1. 5; *Epit.* 14. 2[b] and *HA Hadr.* 14. 9; *Epit.* 18. 1 and *HA Pert.* 15. 8; *Epit.* 18. 6 and *HA Comm.* 18. 1 ff.)—except in the *Vita Heliogabali*, whose main source (for 1–18. 3) I have already argued to be Marius Maximus.[19] On the other side, there are some passages of the *Epitome* which purvey accurate and important information not in the *HA* (esp. *Epit.* 15. 4 [embassies to Antoninus Pius]; 15. 9 [Pius stoned in a food-riot]; 20. 6 [four friends of Septimius Severus]). That seems more easily explicable on the hypothesis that Marius Maximus was not the *HA*'s main source.

For the period A.D. 96–222, the *Epitome* shows itself far superior to Victor and Eutropius as a historical source, and no one will seriously quarrel with Schlumberger's explanation: it reproduces material from Marius Maximus which has escaped the earlier authors. But there is room for difference of opinion on two further questions. First, the relationship of the *Epitome* to Eutropius: Schlumberger argues for frequent recourse to Eutropius, supplemented by less frequent use of the KG (pp. 67–69, 124 ff.). But if Eutropius (as is often supposed) followed the KG faithfully, then it may be that, in some or all of those passages where the *Epitome* appears to copy Eutropius, it has in fact copied Eutropius' source, the KG. Now Schlumberger rates Eutropius' originality more highly than I would be inclined to do (p. 67), and on his estimate his conclusion does indeed follow. On my estimate of Eutropius, however, there are no criteria to permit a confident decision. Secondly, does the *Epitome* draw on Maximus directly? Schlumberger consistently denies it. But since the exact wording of the lost source is *ex hypothesi* unknown, the question cannot be decided conclusively.

In contrast to Schlumberger, I believe that the evidence available allows us to identify Maximus and the KG as the main sources of the *Epitome* for the second and early third centuries, and I am not willing to postulate additional sources until the necessity becomes evident. A good case can perhaps be made for Eutropius, but not (in my judgment) for an intermediate source intervening between the *Epitome* and Maximus.

IV

Schlumberger's discussion of the chapters of the *Epitome* which describe the period A.D. 222–285 (see Table 3) represents his most significant contribution to the subject (pp. 134–82). He has succeeded in emancipating himself from Hohl's refutation of F. Graebner,[20] where many (myself included) had followed with

18. Z. Rubin, rev. of Birley, *JRS* 64 (1974): 233.
19. T. D. Barnes, *"Ultimus Antoninorum,"* pp. 53–74.
20. Hohl, "Vopiscus und die Biographie des Kaisers Tacitus," pp. 192–229.

TABLE 3

"Epitome" 24–38

Schlumberger   **Hohl**

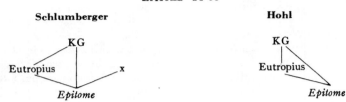

excessive docility. Graebner's theory, it is true, was untenable as formulated; for he derived not only the *Epitome*, but also Victor, Eutropius, and the KG, exclusively from Greek sources.[21] Hohl reacted too violently and, in effect, denied that the *Epitome* owed anything to Greek sources. As a result, he was driven to assert that, in cases where the *Epitome* has the truth while Victor and Eutropius are in error (e.g., two Gordians instead of three), it is the former which represents the KG, not the latter. But if the KG is defined strictly as the common source of Victor and Eutropius, that explanation of the facts must be disallowed. Schlumberger steers a middle course between Graebner and Hohl (pp. 134–35), and establishes that the *Epitome* shows derivation (direct or indirect) from a Greek writer or writers. The following are perhaps the clearest cases:

24. 2 The usurper Taurinus, who threw himself into the Euphrates, should be identical with one or more of the rebels to whom Greek writers allude (Dio 80. 4. 1–2; Herodian 6. 4. 7; Zosimus 1. 12; Syncellus, pp. 674–75 Bonn). He is elsewhere named only by Polemius Silvius (*Chr. min.* 1. 521).

27. 1 Gordian III was indeed *nepos Gordiani ex filia* (Dessau, *ILS* 498, 500; Herodian 7. 10. 7).

27. 2 The *Epitome* agrees with Herodian (8. 8. 8) on the young Gordian's age.

29. 2 Decius died *gurgite paludis submersus,* cf. Zosimus 1. 23. 3; Zonaras 12. 20.

31. 2 Only the *Epitome* and Zonaras 12. 21 have the African origin of Aemilianus.

32. 1 That Valerian was *cognomento Colobius* is nowhere else attested, and, as Schlumberger confesses, "Die Forschung weiss nichts damit anzufangen" (pp. 145–46). The occurrence of Colobius as a *cognomen* is no help (*CIL* 14. 1630: unique according to *TLL*, *Onom.* 2. 534). But some later writers use *colobium* to designate a sleeveless tunic (*TLL* 3. 1693–94). Two explanations of the text can be advanced. "Colobius" may be an opprobrious nickname alluding to Valerian's status in Persian captivity. Alternatively, the *Epitome* may have attributed to Valerian a nickname which in reality adhered to Gallienus and charged him with neglect of his imperial duties: the whole sentence appears more appropriate to Gallienus than to his father (e.g., *imperavit annos quindecim*). In any event, however, the word is originally Greek (LSJ[9], 972, s.v. κολόβιον).

35. 2 Aurelian's battles in Italy in 270–71, at Placentia, by the River Metaurus, and near Ticinum. These precise details should derive from a Greek source: cf. *FGrH* 100 F 6 (Dexippus); Zosimus 1. 49. 1; Petrus Patricius, *Excerpta Vaticana* 175.

35. 3 Septimius is named elsewhere only by Zosimus 1. 49. 2.

21. F. Graebner, "Eine Zosimosquelle," *ByzZ* 14 (1905): 87–159, esp. 154 (stemma).

For the rest, this section of the *Epitome* (24–38) stands in the same relationship to Eutropius as the preceding twelve chapters (12–23). One passage, however, resembles Victor and appears to provide incontrovertible proof that the KG has been used:

Claudius vero cum ex fatalibus libris, quos inspici praeceperat, cognovisset sententiae in senatu dicendae primi morte remedium desiderari, Pomponio Basso, qui tunc erat, se offerente ipse vitam suam haud passus responsa frustrari dono reipublicae dedit, praefatus neminem tanti ordinis primas habere, quam imperatorem. [*Epit.* 34. 3]	proditum ex libris Sibyllinis est primum ordinis amplissimi victoriae vovendum. cumque is, qui esse videbatur, semet obtulisset, sibi potius id muneris competere ostendit, qui revera senatus atque omnium princeps erat. ita nullo exercitus detrimento fusi barbari summotique, postquam imperator vitam reipublicae dono dedit. [Victor *Caes.* 34. 3–5]

The wording runs closely parallel, but only the *Epitome* supplies the name of Pomponius Bassus (cos. ord. 259, 271, and *praefectus urbi*).[22] The content and the observable techniques of the *Epitome* render derivation from Victor improbable (Schlumberger, p. 155). The KG, therefore, has been employed. Hence, as before, use of Eutropius, even if probable, becomes difficult to demonstrate conclusively

V

For the reign of Theodosius (*Epit.* 48, except 48. 3–4 which relate to the affair of Theodorus in 371), speculation about the sources of the *Epitome* is pointless: there is no comparable historical account, and no systematic written source needs to be invoked. But the account of the emperors from Diocletian to Valens (see Table 4) deserves, and receives, a full comparison with Zosimus and Ammianus (Schlumberger, pp. 183–232). Franz Pichlmayr noted two coincidences with Ammianus in his edition (*Epit.* 42. 14 = Amm. Marc. 16. 12. 63; *Epit.* 45. 2 = Amm. Marc. 30. 7. 2), but the similarities to Zosimus are more frequent and equally striking (e.g., *Epit.* 40. 20 and Zosimus 2. 13. 3 [Domitius Alexander]; *Epit.* 41. 6 and Zosimus 2. 25. 2 [Martinianus]; *Epit.* 41. 11–12 and Zosimus 2. 29. 2 [the deaths of Crispus and Fausta]; *Epit.* 42. 7 and Zosimus 2. 54. 1 [Magnentius]; *Epit.* 45. 10 and Zosimus 4. 19. 1 [the proclamation of young Valentinian in 375]). What is the explanation? Zosimus, it will generally be conceded, reproduces

TABLE 4

"EPITOME" 39–46

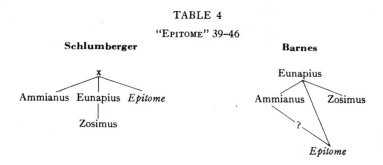

22. On whom see now *PLRE*, 1:155–56, Bassus 17.

266

Eunapius. Opitz accordingly invoked Ammianus and a continuator of Ammianus as the source of Eunapius and (indirectly) of the *Epitome*.²³ Schlumberger prefers a common source which Ammianus, Eunapius, and the *Epitome* all shared. I wish to propound a still simpler hypothesis: that Ammianus and the *Epitome* both used Eunapius as a source, whether or not the *Epitome* also shows occasional derivation from Ammianus.²⁴ Schlumberger has shown (I believe) that the resemblances among the three writers indicate a close literary relationship. Conventional chronology then compels the conclusion that at least Eunapius and the *Epitome* employed a common source. For the *Epitome* was clearly composed not long after the burial of Theodosius at Constantinople on 8 November 395 (*Epit.* 48. 20), while it is normally supposed that Eunapius carried the first edition of his *History* down to 395.²⁵ I wish to propose 378 as its terminal date.

Eunapius' *Vitae philosophorum* was written in 396 or slightly later (7. 3. 4, p. 476), and it refers to the first edition of his *History* in a number of passages.²⁶ The latest certain references are to the reign of Valens: Eunapius alludes to Musonius, apparently as *vicarius Asiae* in 367–68 (10. 7. 13, p. 493), and to the execution of Maximus of Ephesus, soon after 371 (7. 6. 5, p. 480).²⁷ Admittedly, there are two passages which are conventionally interpreted as referring to later events. In both cases, however, I believe that Eunapius has been misunderstood. The first can be construed as implying that the *History* described the destruction of the Serapeum in Alexandria in 391 (6. 11. 7, p. 472)—or as implying that it described the general behavior of monks. The second passage might appear to say specifically that the *History* narrated Alaric's invasion of Greece in 395 (7. 3. 4, p. 476). But there is an anacolouthon in the traditional text (as the Loeb translator, W. C. Wright, notes), and the latest editor prints a text which implies rather that Eunapius hopes to describe Alaric's invasion at some future date.²⁸ Moreover, a fragment of the second edition of the *History* states that the author mentioned, but was ignorant of, the habits of the Huns when he composed the first edition (frag. 41).²⁹ That should imply a date not too long after 376. I conclude, therefore, that Eunapius' own references indicate that the first edition of his *History* went no further than the battle of Adrianople or its immediate aftermath.

If this is conceded, then it becomes chronologically possible for both Ammianus and the author of the *Epitome* to have read and used Eunapius. Furthermore, the *Epitome* not only exhibits verbal coincidences with Zosimus; its portrayal of

23. Opitz, "Quaestiones de Sex. Aurelio Victore," pp. 260 ff.

24. I once argued that *Epit.* 34. 3 might owe the name of Bassus to the lost books of Ammianus ("The Lost Kaisergeschichte," pp. 22–23). That is not the best explanation of the phenomena (above, p. 265). But some passages in the last part of the *Epitome* show verbal similarities to Ammianus which are hard to explain as independent copying of the same Greek source (e.g., *Epit.* 45. 6; cf. Amm. Marc. 30. 9. 4).

25. C. Müller, *FHG*, vol. 4 (Paris, 1852), p. 8. I know of no dissentient.

26. Listed by W. Chalmers, "The νέα ἔκδοσις of Eunapius' *Histories*," *CQ* n.s. 3 (1953): 169–70.

27. For the dates, *PLRE*, 1:613, Musonius 2; 1:583–84, Maximus 21.

28. G. Giangrande (ed.), *Eunapii Vitae Sophistarum* (Rome, 1956), p. 46: καὶ οὐκ εἰς μακρὰν πολλῶν καὶ ἀδιηγήτων ἐπικλυσθέντων κακῶν, ὧν τὰ μὲν ἐν τοῖς διεξοδικοῖς τῆς ἱστορίας εἴρηται, τὰ δέ, ἐὰν ἐπιτρέπῃ τὸ Θεῖον, λελέξεται, ὁ [τε] Ἀλλάριχος ἔχων τοὺς βαρβάρους διὰ τῶν Πυλῶν παρῆλθεν.

29. On the interpretation of this fragment, see Chalmers, "The νέα ἔκδοσις of Eunapius' *Histories*," pp. 168–69.

Constantine contains other passages whose content may betray the influence of Eunapius.

39. 7   The version of the death of Diocletian, with its implied date of early 313, finds its only analogue in Socrates *HE* 1. 2. 10.[30] It is probable that Socrates here depends on a source (viz., Gelasius of Caesarea) who knew Eunapius.[31]

41. 4   The passage runs closely parallel to Zosimus 2. 22. 2. The erroneous description of Minervina as a concubine (she was Constantine's first wife; cf. *Pan. Lat.* 7[6]. 4. 1 ff.) should come from a writer who emphasized sexual misdemeanors at Constantine's court (cf. Zosimus 2. 29. 1, 39.1).

41.7   The death of Licinius is presented as murder after a promise of safety (*pacta salute*), without the excuses or justification which Christian writers offer—and which some modern students of Constantine believe (e.g., *PLRE*, 1:509: "executed in 325 after plotting to renew the war").

41. 13 Constantine's *bon mot* about Trajan recurs in Petrus Patricius, *Excerpta Vaticana* 191, who probably derived at least some material from Eunapius, either directly or indirectly.

41. 16 The division of Constantine's reign into three decades as *praestantissimus*, then *latro*, and finally *pupillus ob profusiones immodicas* clearly reflects the judgment of an eastern pagan, for whom Constantine's wars against Licinius (316–17 and 324) marked significant points in his reign.[32] It was in fact immediately after the defeat of Maxentius (28 October 312) that Constantine began to grant money and privileges to the Christian church in the West (Eusebius *VC* 1. 39 ff.).

VI

So far I have deliberately suppressed the identity of Schlumberger's source *x*, for his proposed identification is the weakest and most vulnerable part of his study. He believes that the unknown source in all four sections of the *Epitome* is the *Annales* of Nicomachus Flavianus (pp. 233–48; cf. 60–61, 157, 182, 209–213). Some scholars (I fear) may be tempted to judge the issue on form: a theory whose main proponents have been A. von Domaszewski, W. Hartke, and F. Paschoud is not likely to be correct.[33] More serious, Schlumberger nowhere confronts the most obvious weakness of the theory: can Eunapius really be imagined as transcribing a Latin historian into Greek? Further, his actual arguments rest upon a series of chronological errors.

Schlumberger appears to assume the standard date of circa 395 for Eunapius' first edition of his *History*, and accepts Hartke's date of 382–83 for Flavianus' *Annales* (p. 241). But Eunapius (I have argued above) probably wrote circa 380, and the sole precise fact known about Flavianus' *Annales* is that he dedicated it to Theodosius: "quos consecrari sibi a quaestore et praefecto suo voluit" (Dessau, *ILS* 2948). That should mean that Flavianus dedicated the work when he was pretorian prefect, i.e., no earlier than 390. Admittedly, a law which bears the date

---

30. On the various versions, see T. D. Barnes, "Lactantius and Constantine," *JRS* 63 (1973): 32 ff.

31. On the obscure question of Socrates' sources, see esp. L. Jeep, "Quellenuntersuchungen zu den griechischen Kirchenhistorikern," *Jahrb. f. class. Philol.*, suppl. 14 (1885): 105 ff.; F. Winkelmann, *Sb. Berlin*, Klasse für Sprachen, Lit., und Kunst 1965, no. 3, pp. 25 ff.

32. Schlumberger unfortunately dates the first war to 314 instead of 316–17 (pp. 189, 197).

33. A. von Domaszewski, "Die Personennamen bei den *Scriptores Historiae Augustae*," *Sb. Heidelberg*, Phil.-hist. Kl. 1918, Abh. 13, pp. 23, 110; W. Hartke, *Geschichte und Politik im spätantiken Rom*, Klio, Beiheft 45 (Leipzig, 1940), pp. 18 ff.; idem, *Römische Kinderkaiser* (Berlin, 1951), pp. 329 ff.; F. Paschoud (ed.), *Zosime*, vol. 1 (Paris, 1971), p. lv.

268

18 August 382 is addressed *Flaviano p.po. Illyrici et Ital.* (*CTh* 9. 40. 13). But it has long been recognized that the year is an error for 390, and that Flavianus probably did not become *quaestor sacri palatii* before 389.[34] Hence, whatever the source or sources of the *Epitome* may have been, it is chronologically impossible for the *Annales* of Nicomachus Flavianus to be a source for Eunapius (or perhaps even for Ammianus).[35]

No less serious are two other difficulties in Schlumberger's theory. He assumes without argument that Flavianus wrote about Roman emperors, although the evidence for the literary tastes of Theodosius (*Epit.* 48. 12) ought to suggest rather that the *Annales* were devoted to the history of the Roman Republic.[36] And he has failed to demonstrate that the *Epitome* uses a single lost source throughout. For, if the observable affiliations of the four main sections (1–11, 12–23, 24–38, 39–46) vary, then it cannot be assumed that all four are indebted to the same lost source. Schlumberger, admittedly, is aware of this objection, and advances positive arguments to show that the characteristics of the lost source remain constant in all four sections (pp. 235–46, summarizing points made throughout the book). The argument, however, assumes that the *Epitome* not only reproduces specific passages of the lost source, but also its general tenor. The assumption is unverifiable and dubious: where it has used him, the *Epitome* has hardly preserved the overall tenor of Aurelius Victor. The sad truth appears to be that the available evidence does not permit a complete identification of the sources of the *Epitome de Caesaribus.*

University of Toronto

34. On his career, see O. Seeck, *Regesten der Kaiser und Päpste für die Jahre 311 bis 476 n. Chr.* (Stuttgart, 1919), pp. 93, 278; E. Stein, *Geschichte des spätrömischen Reiches,* vol. 1 (Vienna, 1927), p. 310 = *Histoire du Bas-Empire,* vol. 1² (Paris–Bruges, 1959), p. 524; J.-R. Palanque, *Essai sur la préfecture du prétoire au Bas-Empire* (Paris, 1933), p. 68; H. L. Levy, *The Invective "In Rufinum" of Claudius Claudianus* (Geneva, N.Y., 1935), pp. 27 ff. = *Claudian's "In Rufinum": An Exegetical Commentary,* APA Monographs, 30 (Cleveland, 1971), pp. 245 ff.; *PLRE,* 1:347–49, Flavianus 15.
35. On the date at which Ammianus completed his history, see now A. Cameron, rev. of Syme, *JRS* 61 (1971): 259 ff.
36. J. Matthews, *Western Aristocracies and Imperial Court A.D. 364–425* (Oxford, 1975), p. 231, n. 3.

Reprinted from Classical Philology *vol. 71 (1976), 258-68,*
by permission of The University of Chicago Press.
ⓒ *1976 by The University of Chicago*

XIV

Tertullian the Antiquarian

The culture of the Roman Empire, whether Greek or Latin, was highly traditional. Both the schoolboy and the mature man nourished their minds on contemplation of the past, and in particular on contemplation of a remote past which still retained a power to influence actions and ideas. A satirist might mock a Hannibal destined to become a stock debating theme.[1] He could not predict that a century later the emperor Caracalla would erect statues and pictures of Rome's enemy and construct a marble monument over his grave on the shores of the Propontis.[2] Caracalla regarded great generals of the past as worthy of emulation: Sulla received honours equal to those of Hannibal, the name of Alexander was forever on his lips and, when a favourite freedman died at Troy, Caracalla placed his body on a pyre and performed the last rites as if he were Achilles mourning Patroclus.[3] Further, the organization of his army owed something to the war of the ancient Greeks against Xerxes: beside the Macedonian phalanx in honour of Alexander (with arms and armour of the correct period) there marched a Spartan contingent including a 'company from Pitane' such as fought seven hundred years before at Plataea.[4] The influence of the ancients was powerful and enduring. When barbarians raided Greece, its inhabitants emulated (or surpassed) Leonidas at Thermopylae.[5] When the Heruli occupied and sacked Athens (c. 267), the historian Dexippus organised resistance in Attica and employed an overtly Thucydidean oration exhorting his soldiers to show that the spirit of Athens remained unbroken.[6] When Byzantine historians of the sixth and later centuries wrote accounts of their own age, they deliberately modelled their language, composition and categories of historical analysis on classical models, above all Herodotus and Thucydides.[7]

---

[1] Juvenal X. 166f.

[2] Herodian IV. 8. 5; Tzetzes, Chil. I. 799ff.

[3] Dio LXXVIII (LXXVII). 13. 7; Herodian IV. 8. 3ff.; HA, Carac. 2.2.

[4] Dio LXXVIII (LXXVII). 7.1; 18.1; Herodian IV. 8.2f., cf. Herodotus IX. 53.

[5] IG II/III². 13172. For the date (probably 170) and circumstances, A. von Premerstein, Klio XII (1912), 139ff.

[6] FGrH 100 F 28 — set in its full context by F. Millar, JRS LIX (1969), 12ff.

[7] For a discussion of one specific case, Averil Cameron, Agathias (1970), 53ff.

4

In the west as well as the east, men thought in terms of the past. Was praise needed for the tranquil reign of Antoninus Pius? Pompilius Numa, the successor of Romulus, provided the inevitable comparison.[1] Did an orator wish to instruct and entertain an audience in Carthage? His technique could be exhibited to advantage in a series of panegyrics on ancient Greek philosophers and poets.[2] Were the Carthaginians to be reminded of the beneficial results of living under the rule of Septimius Severus? Tertullian saw that they would not take amiss reference to the legendary wealth of Midas and the idyllic charms of Homer's Phaeacia (*Pall.* 2.7).

Facts such as these illustrate an important facet of the society in which Christian writers of the second and third centuries found themselves. If they desired to communicate with those outside their faith, they could hardly do so except in terms of the common cultural traditions of Greek and Roman civilisation. Moreover, at a deeper level, they could hardly avoid retaining some of those traditions themselves, even if they consciously set out on the path of utter rejection. Hence the interesting (and much studied) problems of the relationship between Christianity and classical culture.[3] The early Christians were not, and could not be, isolated from pagan society and pagan ideas. Tertullian perhaps exemplifies their predicament most clearly: despite an explicit claim that Athens and Jerusalem, the Academy and the Church have nothing in common (*Praescr. Haer.* 7.10), he reveals a wider and deeper knowledge of pagan antiquity and literature than any other Christian who wrote in Latin.

By both birth and education, Tertullian belonged to intellectual circles in Carthage. In three unduly neglected passages he reveals all that is necessary for defining his precise milieu. The *De Praescriptione Haereticorum* explains how even heretics are able to claim the support of scripture for

---

[1] Fronto, Princ.hist. 10; De Feriis Als. 6 (pp. 196; 215 Hout); HA, Pius 2.2; 13. 4.

[2] Apuleius, Flor. 3 (Hyagnis); 4 (Antigenidas), etc.

[3] To name only the major books of a mere three decades: A. H. Armstrong-R. A. Markus, Christian Faith and Greek Philosophy (1960); H. Chadwick, Early Christian Thought and the Classical Tradition (1966); C. N. Cochrane, Christianity and Classical Culture (1940); G. L. Ellspermann, The Attitude of Early Christian Latin Writers toward Pagan Literature and Learning. Catholic University of America, Patristic Studies LXXXII (1949); O. Gigon, Die antike Kultur und das Christentum (1966); H. Hagendahl, Latin Fathers and the Classics. Studia Graeca et Latina Gothoburgensia VI (1958); St. Augustine and the Classics. Ib. XX (1967); W. Jaeger, Early Christianity and Greek Paideia (1962); W. Krause, Die Stellung der frühchristlichen Autoren zur heidnischen Literatur (1958); M. L. W. Laistner, Christianity and Pagan Culture in the Later Roman Empire (1951); H.-I. Marrou, St. Augustin et la fin de la culture antique² (1949); J. H. Waszink and others, Het oudste Christendom en de antieke Cultuur (1951); A. Wifstrand, Fornkyrkan och den grekiska Bildningen (1957), translated as L'église ancienne et la culture grecque (1962). For further guidance on the vast bibliography, G. Glockmann, Homer in der frühchristlichen Literatur bis Justinus. Texte u. Unters. CV (1968), 11ff.

their odious beliefs. Any literary text can easily be adapted to a new purpose, any author can be pillaged for choice phrases which, torn from their original context, acquire a meaning other than the author intended. Tertullian quotes three examples:

vides hodie ex Virgilio fabulam in totum aliam componi, materia secundum versus et versibus secundum materiam concinnatis. denique Hosidius Geta Medeam tragoediam ex Virgilio plenissime exsuxit. meus quidam propinquus ex eodem poeta inter cetera stili sui otia Pinacem Cebetis explicuit. Homerocentones etiam vocari solent qui de carminibus Homeri propria opera more centonario ex multis hinc inde compositis in unum sarciunt corpus. et utique fecundior divina litteratura ad facultatem cuiusque materiae (*Praescr. Haer.* 39.3ff.).

The product of Hosidius Geta may still be extant: a manuscript written c. 700 contains an anonymous Virgilian cento in the form of a play about Medea (Paris, Bib. Nat., Lat. 10318, pp. 26–43).[1] More important, Tertullian appears to locate a relative in the upper échelons of Carthaginian society.[2]

If he could number a fashionable littérateur among his relatives, Tertullian was also familiar with the rhetorical schools of the African metropolis. Ridiculing the Thirty Aeons of Valentinus, he catalogued their names and described Valentinus' celestial cosmogony (*Val.* 7.3ff., closely based on Irenaeus, *Adv. Haer.* I. 1.1ff.). The first four Aeons were Bythos and Sige, Veritas and Nus, who was also styled Monogenes. How inappropriate! Since Veritas was his sister, Monogenes ought to have been called Protogenes, like the popular charioteer,[3] and Valentinus' primitive tetrad is really the 'prima quadriga Valentinianae factionis'. Then the incestuous procreation of Sermo and Vita, Homo and Ecclesia produced an ogdoad. Finally, Sermo and Vita founded a 'decuria Aeonum', while Homo and Ecclesia produced a further dozen, thus forming the full Pleroma of Thirty Aeons. At this point Tertullian felt impelled to recall a derisive analogy:

cogor hic, quid ista nomina desiderent, proferre de pari exemplo. in scholis Karthaginiensibus fuit quidam frigidissimus rhetor Latinus, Phosphorus nomine. cum virum fortem peroraret: 'venio' inquit 'ad vos, optimi cives, de proelio cum vic-

---

[1] A. Riese, Anthologia Latina I. 1 (1869), 49ff.; E. Baehrens, Poetae Latin Minores IV (1882), 219ff. Tertullian should imply that Geta lived in Carthage: therefore, probably neither a descendant of the Cn. Hosidius Geta proscribed by Triumvirs (Dio XLVII. 10. 6) nor 'ex Histonio quod est patria Hosidiorum Getarum ortus' (PIR² H 214). Rather, another item of indirect evidence that Cn. Hosidius Geta, cos. suff. 44 (see now Ann. épig. 1968, 5 c), may have been proconsul of Africa (cf. Ann. épig. 1947, 74, cited in PIR² H 216).

[2] L. Herrmann has recently identified the relative with the jurist Sex. Pomponius (on whom see W. Kunkel, Herkunft und soziale Stellung der römischen Juristen (1952), 170f.) and both with the Pomponius recorded by Isidore of Seville (Orig. I. 39.26), who composed a Virgilian cento entitled 'Tityrus' in honour of Christ (Latomus XXX (1971), 151). His argument appears to fall far short of either proof or probability.

[3] Arguably the later favourite of Elagabalus (HA, Elag. 6. 3), cf. Bonner Historia-Augusta-Colloquium 1970/71 (1972), 59.

toria mea, cum felicitate vestra, ampliatus, gloriosus, fortunatus, maximus trium-
phalis'. et scholastici statim familiae Phosphori φεῦ acclamant. audisti Fortunatam
et Hedonen et Acinetum et Theletum: acclama familiae Ptolemaei φεῦ. hoc erit
Pleroma illud arcanum, dignitatis tricenariae plenitudo (*Val.* 8.2ff.).

The occasion was a declamation in the schools on a historical or counter-
historical theme, Phosphorus speaking in the person of a 'vir fortis' from
Greek or Roman history. His pupils jeered when his attempt at grandeur
descended to laughable bathos.[1] The observation is surely that of an eye-
witness — who perhaps joined in applauding the proud rhetor. Tertullian
himself will have been no mean performer on similar occasions.

The *Adversus Valentinianos*, moreover, enunciates a valuable statement
of its author's literary, moral and religious aspirations:

nec utique dicemur ipsi nobis finxisse materias quas tot iam viri sanctitate et prae-
stantia insignes, nec solum nostri antecessores sed ipsorum haeresiarcharum con-
temporales, instructissimis voluminibus et prodiderunt et retuderunt, ut Justinus,
philosophus et martyr, ut Miltiades, ecclesiarum sophista, ut Irenaeus, omnium
doctrinarum curiosissimus explorator, ut Proculus noster, virginis senectae et
Christianae eloquentiae dignitas, quos in omni opere fidei, quemadmodum in isto,
optaverim adsequi (*Val.* 5.1).

The Montanist Proculus (hence 'noster') combines the subject-matter and
technique of a large part of Tertullian's later writings: Christian eloquence
obsessed with virginity. But at the start of his literary career the works
of Miltiades (now lost) were probably an important influence.[2] The sobriquet
'sophist of the churches' will not only describe Tertullian most aptly but
will also relate him to his Carthaginian background. In the late second
and early third centuries the word 'sophist' had a very precise connotation.

Tertullian's general debt to ancient rhetoric has long been acknowledged
and partly documented in detail.[3] In particular, Tertullian modelled the
form, arrangement, and structure of his tracts on accepted canons of rhetorical theory, which often determined the nature and content of his ar-
gumentation.[4] However, although rhetorical theory and precept remained
remarkably constant through the centuries, practice perceptibly changed
and developed.

A younger contemporary of Tertullian (c. 230) wrote 'Lives of the Sophists', in which he proclaimed two highly significant doctrines. First,

---

[1] On the interpretation of this passage (which I have misinterpreted in print),
see F. J. Dölger, Antike und Christentum V (1936), 272ff.

[2] For this conjecture, Tertullian. A Historical and Literary Study (1971), 104.

[3] The classic study remains that of R. Heinze, 'Tertullians Apologeticum', Bericht
über die Verhandlungen der könig. sächs. Gesellschaft der Wissenschaften zu Leipzig,
Phil.-hist. Klasse LXII (1910), 281ff. Among subsequent studies, note especially
H. Pétré, L'exemplum chez Tertullien (1940).

[4] R. D. Sider, Ancient Rhetoric and the Art of Tertullian (Oxford Theological
Monographs, 1971).

the ancient and respectable sophistic art should be regarded as philosophical rhetoric. Second, this art was succeeded by another, more historically orientated, which was originally founded by Aeschines (the enemy
of Demosthenes), but then languished in long decay until its rescue by
Nicetes of Smyrna under the Flavian emperors. And on this latter art – or
rather movement – Philostratus bestowed the name which it retains for
ever: the Second Sophistic.[1] This was no idle literary fashion, but assumed
the aspect of a political, social and economic phenomenon. Whatever
modern taste may think of their oratory (its verdict tends to universal
damnation), the sophists of the second and third centuries were powerful
figures in Roman provincial (and sometimes imperial) society. They could
on occasion humble a mere proconsul, at any time their professional skill
might win recognition and reward from the emperor, and a city's prosperity
and reputation depended in no small measure on its ability to produce or
attract practitioners of the sophistic art.[2] Nor did the Greek sophists of
the Antonine age lack pupils and imitators in the Western Empire. The
wealthy Apuleius of Madauros studied in Carthage, but completed his
education at Athens.[3] Early in the reign of Marcus Aurelius he can be
discovered in the African capital, in all externals apart from language a
typical representative of the Second Sophistic movement. Both epideictic
orator and public figure, he recalls such sophists of Asia Minor as Scopelian
of Smyrna or the precocious T. Flavius Hermocrates of Phocaea, who
died before he was thirty. Scopelian was himself high-priest of Asia – and
so were all his ancestors, inheriting the office from father to son. As for
Hermocrates, the emperor Septimius Severus once heard him declaim
and adjudged him the equal of his great-grandfather, the illustrious Polemo. He invited him to ask for presents. Hermocrates observed that he
had inherited from Polemo crowns, immunities from taxation, meals at
public expense, a senator's toga with its purple stripe and the high-priest-
hood of Asia. He therefore contented himself with requesting fifty talents
of frankincense to fulfil a vow to Asclepius. The emperor gladly granted
the request, blushing for shame at so trivial a gift.[4] Apuleius came of a less
resplendent family which had not risen above municipal honours.[5] But he
became high-priest of the provincial council of Africa and was honoured
by statues in the city of Carthage.[6] He delivered speeches before proconsuls,
at least one of whom deemed it worthwhile (or perhaps necessary) to solicit

---

[1] Philostratus, Vit. soph. pp. 480; 507; 511; 481.

[2] G. W. Bowersock, Greek Sophists in the Roman Empire (1969), esp. 17ff.

[3] Apuleius, Flor. pp. 35; 40 Helm. For his travels in the rest of Greece and Asia
Minor, Apol. 23; 55; De Mundo 17.

[4] Philostratus, Vit. soph. pp. 515; 611.

[5] Apuleius, Apol. 24: in qua colonia patrem habui loco principis IIviralem cunctis
honoribus perfunctum.

[6] Apuleius, Flor. pp. 23, 29 Helm; Augustine, Epp. CXXXVIIII. 19.

his friendship before he sailed out from Rome to the province. As he observed himself, Apuleius had no need to seek praise or boast of the feigned amity of the powerful: men knew his 'mores et studia' even in the imperial city.[1]

The *Florida* (a collection of excerpted purple passages) parallel contemporary public eloquence in the East, and their content and style have strong affinities with contemporary Greek practice.[2] Philostratus justified the effort expended by Dio of Prusa in his 'Encomium of a parrot' by asserting that the subject was well worthy of a sophist.[3] Apuleius clearly agreed, for he entertained a Carthaginian audience by describing the same animal in ornate Latin.[4] But if Apuleius may be depicted as the African equivalent of a Scopelian or Hermocrates, then Tertullian should be regarded as the Christian equivalent of the pagan Apuleius. Although it cannot be proved that Tertullian either heard Apuleius speak or read any of his surviving works, he cannot have escaped all knowledge of him, least of all his reputation. Both lived in the same city at the distance of a single generation, and within little more than a century Apuleius had passed into African folklore as a powerful magician, the peer of Apollonius of Tyana.[5] The two men display several features in common which were characteristic of the oratory of their time: for example, frequent allusion to or quotation of Plato, interest in the lives of ancient philosophers, and the prominence of philosophical themes and subjects. Since the Second Sophistic had married the long estranged disciplines of philosophy and rhetoric, aspiring orators resorted to special tutors for instruction in the doctrines of Plato.[6] As for virtuosity, the supreme accolade has been awarded to Apuleius.[7] But Tertullian was his equal or even superior in incisiveness. The *Scorpiace* opens with a formal vituperation:

magnum de modico malum scorpio terra suppurat. tot venena quot et genera, tot pernicies quot et species, tot dolores quot et colores, Nicander scribit et pingit. et tamen unus omnium violentiae gestus de cauda nocere . . . (*Scorp*. 1. 1).

By comparison, Apuleius on the parrot seems flabby and verbose. And despite the other's frequent and ostentatious display of learning, Tertullian

---

[1] Apuleius, Flor. p. 31 Helm: . . . ut non minus vobis amicitia mea capessenda sit quam mihi vestra concupiscenda. The proconsul was Ser. Cornelius Scipio Salvidienus Orfitus, cos. ord. 149 (PIR² C 1447).

[2] E. Norden rightly stressed Apuleius' debt to contemporary Greek oratory, but failed properly to document his programmatic pronouncements (Antike Kunstprosa² (1909), 604f.). Later research on this aspect of Apuleius' style has tended to concentrate on the Metamorphoses: P. Médan, La Latinité d'Apulée dans les Métamorphoses (1926), 136f.; M. Bernhard, Der Stil des Apuleius von Madaura (1927), 143ff.

[3] Philostratus, Vit. soph. p. 487.

[4] Apuleius, Flor. 12: psittacus avis Indiae avis est . . .

[5] Lactantius, Div. Inst. v. 3. 7.

[6] Philostratus, Vit.soph. p. 565 (Herodes Atticus).

[7] 'Der virtuoseste Wortjongleur, den es gegeben hat' (E. Norden, o. c. 600).

does not deserve to be considered inferior on the score of erudition. As Jerome observed, 'Tertulliano quid eruditius? quid acutius?'[1]

Tertullian had read widely both in Latin and in Greek. The *Apologeticum*, being designed for perusal by educated pagans, appeals to more than thirty pagan authorities. Nor can Tertullian's knowledge all be dismissed as second-hand or derivative. On the contrary, its more than occasional inaccuracy should be ascribed to excessive reliance on a fallible memory. Tertullian can quote, summarise or paraphrase Plato (e. g. *Apol.* 24.3; *An.* 18.1f.), adduce apt parallels from Herodotus (*An.* 46.4; 49.2; 57.10), allude to Pindar (*Apol.* 14.5), and even produce a story which happens to be extant nowhere else: when the half-barbarous Macedonians heard the tragedy 'Oedipus' for the first time they laughed at the hero for taking incest so seriously and shouted 'ἔλαυνε εἰς τὴν μητέρα' (*Nat.* 1.16.5; *Apol.*9.16). As for Latin literature, Tertullian exhibits a more than casual knowledge of Tacitus, Pliny the Younger and Juvenal – three authors who seem not to have been at all widely read until long after his death.[2]

One area of Tertullian's learning will repay especial attention. That is, Roman Republican antiquities, whose relevance to his own concerns Tertullian perceived very clearly. Since he wished to move from defence of Christianity to an attack on paganism (*Apol.* 4.1: nec tantum refutabo quae nobis obiciuntur, sed etiam in ipsos retorquebo qui obiciunt), he needed facts which pagans acknowledged to provide a basis for argument:

conversus ad litteras vestras, quibus informamini ad prudentiam et liberalia officia, quanta invenio ludibria! (*Apol.* 14.2)

Even for pure apologetics, however, knowledge of history was needed to refute two exceptionally dangerous beliefs: that Rome's greatness depended on her traditional religion (*Apol.* 25.13 etc.), and that Christians were the cause of natural calamities (*Apol.* 40.2 etc.). With good reason Tertullian steeped himself in the antiquarian researches of Varro (*Nat.* II. 1.8 etc.), and made himself able to quote Ennius (*Val.* 7.1; *An.* 33.8; *Res. Mort.* 1.5).[3] An annotated list will perhaps best illustrate the wealth of historical and religious material from the Roman Republican past which Tertullian decided to employ in the *Apologeticum*:

5.1   vetus erat decretum, ne qui deus ab imperatore consecraretur, nisi a senatu probatus. scit M. Aemilius de deo suo Alburno. Elsewhere Tertullian names the *imperator* as Metellus (*Marc.* I. 18.4: the name occurs in a lacuna at *Nat.* I. 10.14). Now the consuls of 115 B.C. were M. Aemilius Scaurus and M. Metellus,

---

[1] Jerome, Epp. LXX. 2.
[2] For fuller details, Tertullian (1971), 196ff.
[3] On the last two passages, see J. H. Waszink, Tertulliani De Anima (1947), 398f.

so that the variation can be held to tie down the allusion.[1] Tertullian alone has preserved a valuable item of ancient lore for any constitutional historian of Rome.[2] Further, he has wilfully confused a prohibition on dedicating altars or shrines without permission (e. g. Cicero, *De domo sua* 128; 136; Livy IX. 46) with the consecration of a god. The earlier *Ad Nationes* is more accurate but less effective: 'mentior, si nunquam censuerant, ne qui imperator fanum, quod in ⟨bell⟩o vovisset, prius dedicasset quam senatus probasset, ut contigit [. . .]ilio, qui voverat Alburno deo' (I. 10.14).

6.4 In the reign of Romulus, Metennius killed his wife with impunity for touching wine.
Perhaps from the elder Pliny (*Nat.Hist.* XIV. 89). However, as Pliny reveals, the case was well known 'inter exempla' (cf. Valerius Maximus VI. 3.9).[3]

6.7 The Senate expelled the cult of Liber Pater from Italy (in 186 B.C.). A full narration in Livy (XXXIX. 8.1ff.). The consuls were instructed to eradicate the cult from Italy 'extra quam si qua ibi vetusta ara aut signum consecratum esset' (ib. 18.7, cf. ILS 23).

6.8 The consuls Piso and Gabinius (58 B. C.) suppressed the cult of Serapis, Isis, Harpocrates and Anubis from the Capitol.
Quoted from Varro in *Ad Nationes* (I. 10.17).

9.9 Catiline's conspiracy sealed with blood.
Sallust, *Cat.* 22.1.

10.6ff. Saturn originally a man; his reception in Italy 'ab Iano, vel Iane, ut Salii volunt'.
Tertullian here adduces as authorities Diodorus Siculus, Thallus, Cassius Severus (wrongly, in place of Cassius Hemina)[4] and Cornelius Nepos; the *Ad Nationes* had added Tacitus (II. 12.26).

11.8 Lucullus' introduction of the cherry into Italy from Pontus.
Presumably from Pliny, *Nat. Hist.*XV. 102.

11.16 quis ex illis deis vestris gravior et sapientior Catone? iustior et militatior Scipione? quis sublimior Pompeio, felicior Sulla, copiosior Crasso, eloquentior Tullio?
As elsewhere in imperial oratory (e. g. in Pliny's panegyric to Trajan) the normal examples of human excellence are predominantly or even exclusively Republican.

14.9 Varro's three hundred headless Joves or Jupiters.

---

[1] G. Wissowa, P—W I. 1338, following Pamelius. The deity Alburnus is not now attested independently of Tertullian.
[2] T. Mommsen, Römisches Staatsrecht II³ (1887), 619.
[3] For other ancient allusions, T. Mommsen, Römisches Strafrecht (1899), 19.
[4] H. Peter, Historicorum Romanorum Reliquiae I² (1914), cclxxi; 98.

15.1   The mimes of Lentulus and Hostilius, with subjects such as 'The Reading of Jupiter's Will'.

21. 23   The ascension of Jesus into heaven is better attested than an ascension like that of Romulus on the authority of Proculus. 'Julius Proculus' can hardly even be a historical character.[1]

21. 29   Pompilius Numa 'Romanos operosissimis superstitionibus oneravit'. Numa recurs as the originator of 'curiositas superstitiosa' (25. 12). For Numa as founder of Roman law and religion, cf. Cicero, *De Rep.* II. 26f.; V. 3; Livy I. 21; Tacitus, *Ann.* III. 26.

22.10   The ambiguous oracle given to Pyrrhus.
Quoted from Ennius by Cicero (*De Divin.* II. 116) and Quintilian (*Inst. Orat.* VII. 9.6): 'aio te, Aeacida, Romanos vincere posse.'[2]

24. 8   The local deities of Italian municipalities: Delventinus of Casinum, Visidianus of Narnia, Ancharia of Asculum, Nortia of Vulsinii, Valentia of Ocriculum, Hostia of Sutrium and Curris of Falisci. Again from Varro (*Nat.* II. 8.6): no extant ancient writer apart from Tertullian so much as mentions Visidianus.

25. 3   The native Roman Gods *par excellence* are the vile Sterculus, Mutunus and the prostitute Larentina (cf. 25.10).[3]

25. 4ff.   Contempt for Rome shown by Cybele ('nostra etiam aetate', i. e. in A.D. 180), by Jupiter and Juno.

25. 12ff. Rome's greatness antedates her religion: the latter cannot therefore be the cause of the former.

26. 2   Comparative newness of Rome's priestly colleges: *pontifices, quindecimviri, salii, luperci*, Vestal virgins.

26. 3   Rome was once an ally of Judaea and showed respect to her god. I Maccabees 8.17ff.; Josephus, *Ant. Jud.* XII. 414ff.[4] Tacitus glossed over the treaty between Rome and Judaea with the phrase 'Romani procul erant' (*Hist.* V. 8.3).

33. 4   A victorious general is reminded of his mortality even during his triumph: someone behind him (in fact, a slave) observes 'look behind you! remember you are a man!'
Tertullian furnishes perhaps the clearest literary evidence for this custom,[5] but must also (it appears) receive some blame for misleading modern scholars on the problem of its origin and motivation.[6]

---

[1] F. Münzer, P–W X. 112f.

[3] Ennius, Ann. fr. 179 Vahlen.

[8] On these deities, see respectively E. Marbach, P–W III A. 2412; K. Vahlert, P–W XVI. 979ff.; G. Wissowa, Religion und Kultus der Römer[2] (1912), 233f.

[4] For the historical context, E. Badian, Foreign Clientelae (1958), 108.

[5] J. Marquardt, Römische Staatsverwaltung II (1876), 568f.; W. Ehlers, P–W VII A. 506f. For a pictorial representation (with the triumphant emperor Tiberius), H. Kähler, Rom und seine Welt (1960), Tafel 145.

[6] L. Bonfante Warren, JRS LX (1970), 61. For a more than full discussion, see

39.12f. Cato the censor acted like a pimp in lending his wife to a friend. Tertullian confuses Cato of Utica with his forbear a century earlier. It was the former who divorced Marcia so that she could marry Hortensius and remarried her after Hortensius' death (Plutarch, *Cato minor* 25.1ff.; 52.3f.), thus providing a theme for declamation in the schools: 'Cato Marciam honestene tradiderit Hortensio' (Quintilian, *Inst. Orat.* X. 5.13).

40.8 Disasters which long antedate Christianity: the destruction of Vulsinii by a thunderbolt (92 B.C.: Julius Obsequens 112); Hannibal's crushing victory at Cannae (216 B.C.); the Gallic Senones occupying the Capitol (traditionally 390).
Tertullian could have taken the disaster at Vulsinii from Pliny (*Nat.Hist.* II. 139).

40.14 The rites of the 'nudipedalia'.
Among extant authors, Tertullian provides the most explicit evidence for the ceremony (also *Jej.* 16.5), only described elsewhere in any detail by Petronius (*Sat.* 44.13).[1]

50.4ff. Traditional examples of fortitude, including Mucius who sacrificed his right hand before Lars Porsenna, the suicide of Dido to avoid a second marriage, and Regulus who declined to trade his life for the lives of many enemies.
It mattered nothing to Tertullian and his contemporaries that the stories of Mucius and Dido are legendary, or that the patriotic tale of the return of Regulus to death at Carthage is probably sheer invention.[2]

Twenty four passages have been adduced, of varying significance. Some of the knowledge displayed was trite: who had not heard of Cannae, of Mucius and Regulus? Some of the more abstruse facts derive from Varro, and the *Apologeticum* tends to conceal what the *Ad Nationes* explicitly confessed. But in one item at least Tertullian surpassed both himself and others (*Apol.* 40.8). Patriotic legend asserted that when the Gauls captured Rome they were unable to take the Capitol, which pertinaciously held out till Camillus freed the rest of the city.[3] The legend lived on in an annual festival commemorating the sacred geese whose quacking alerted the defenders when the Gauls

---

now H. S. Versnel, Triumphus. An Inquiry into the Origin, Development and Meaning of the Roman Triumph (1970).

[1] E. Marbach, P—W XVII. 1239 ff.; K. Latte, Römische Religionsgeschichte (1960), 79.

[2] E. Klebs declared in 1896 that modern scholarship had banished the ghost of the saintly Regulus to the realm of shadows (P—W II. 2092). He still occasionally returns to the domain of history: e. g. M. Cary, A History of Rome² (1954), 150, with appeal to T. Frank, Class. Phil. XXV (1926), 311 ff.

[3] Livy V. 39. 9ff.

had almost ascended the Capitol by stealth.[1] And it imposed itself on Augustine and Orosius.[2] Tertullian was more alert. He followed a version of the story less flattering to Rome which occasionally appears in Latin poets (Ennius, Lucan, Silius Italicus): in reality (it was conceded) the Senones captured both city and Capitol.[3]

The contemporary milieu and Tertullian's erudition provide a key to interpreting the briefest and most enigmatic of all his works, one which proves (if proof were needed) that Tertullian as a Christian lost none of his expertise in the art of epideictic oratory. The *De Pallio* recalls Apuleius' *Florida* and deliberately exhibits an extravagant, almost rococco style, full of Graecisms,[4] rare or archaic words,[5] and historical,[6] literary[7] or mythical allusions[8], compressed almost beyond the bounds of intelligibility. It is perhaps the most difficult work ever written in Latin.[9] Consequently, the way lies open for *a priori* and tendentious interpretation. The *De Pallio* sometimes becomes a mere personal apologia: having shed his toga and donned the cloak of a philosopher, Tertullian justified his conduct before his fellow-citizens.[10] Alternatively, Tertullian wrote because he needed to silence

---

[1] Aelian, Nat. Anim. XII. 33, cf. Livy V. 47. 2ff.

[2] Augustine, De civ. Dei II. 22; Orosius II. 19. 6ff. Even a recent scholar can succumb, with hesitation but without adducing Tertullian: R. M. Ogilvie, A Commentary on Livy Books 1–5 (1965), 720.

[3] Ennius, Ann. 164 Vahlen; Lucan, frag. 12 Morel; Silius Italicus I. 525f.; IV. 150f.; VI. 555f. On the interpretation of these passages, see O. Skutsch, JRS XLIII (1953), 77f.; H. J. McGann, Class. Quart. VII (1957), 126ff. Relevance to Tertullian was diagnosed by G. W. Clarke, Class.Rev. XVII (1967), 138. His knowledge could derive from Ennius (Tertullian (1971), 204).

[4] E. g., 'Romanum praecoca' = ἄωρος τὸ ῾Ρωμαῖον (Pall. 1. 2); 'multa dicendum fuit' = πολλὰ εἰρητέον ἦν (3. 4). Editors have tried to amend some Graecisms away (e. g., the accusative absolute 'expeditum' (1. 1)).

[5] E. g., 'blatire' (2. 1: attested only in Plautus, once perhaps in Aulus Gellius, and in the glossographers), 'flustra' (2. 2: once in Naevius, and in glossographers); 'decimanus' (2. 2: very rare with the meaning here ('large'), cf. TLL V. 1.170); 'emissicius' (3. 3: only Plautus, Aulularia 41, and one gloss).

[6] E. g., the sandstorm which destroyed part of Cambyses' army (2. 4, cf. Herodotus III. 26. 3); the eruption of Vesuvius in A.D. 79 (2. 4); 'impuriorem Physcone et molliorem Sardanapallo Caesarem' (4. 5).

[7] E. g. to a Sibylline oracle (2. 3, cf. Orac. Sib. III. 363); Hercules as 'ille scytalosagittipelliger' (4. 3: source not identifiable, and perhaps Tertullian's own invention); to Menander, frag. 683 Körte (4. 8). The last allusion is referred to an unknown Latin writer by O. Ribbeck, Comicorum Romanorum Fragmenta³ (1898), 133; V. Bulhart, CSEL LXXVI. 118.

[8] E. g., to Mercury, Minerva and Arachne (3. 4), to Achilles disguised as a girl (4. 2: 'Larissaeus heros'). Note also the list of areas which produce fine sheep: 'nec de ovilibus dico Milesis et Selgicis et Altinis aut quis Tarentum vel Baetica cluet' (3. 6).

[9] So Norden opined (o. c. 615).

[10] B. Altaner-A. Stuiber. Patrologie⁷ (1966), 159: 'eine persönliche Verteidigungsschrift'.

critics who alleged that Christianity had blunted his rhetorical powers[1] — or welcomed the opportunity to indulge in exhibitionism.[2] Any relevance to Christianity is often denied. The *De Pallio* was 'not written in a specifically Christian spirit', but 'in the tones of a pagan humanist', and its subject is 'trifling'.[3] If Tertullian had a serious purpose, it was to decry the Carthaginians' abandonment of Punic dress and customs in favour of Roman.[4] And it was once solemnly asserted that he did little more than plagiarise a menippean satire by Varro.[5] Even when the Christian overtones of *De Pallio* are perceived, however, agreement does not ensue. The pamphlet may announce Tertullian's conversion either to Christianity, or to Montanism, or to asceticism.[6] Or perhaps the *De Pallio* is both a 'jeu d'esprit' and a 'profession de foi', addressed not so much to pagans as to Christians, who alone could penetrate the deeper meaning hidden in Tertullian's words.[7] But the toga can denote a man's possession of the Roman citizenship. In the *De Pallio*, therefore, Tertullian writes a manifesto against Rome and renounces his status as a 'civis Romanus'[8] or (still better) his putative membership of the local Senate of Carthage.[9] Contemporary fashion can even adduce the *De Pallio* to picture Tertullian as comparable to modern hairy and unkempt exponents of the 'counter-culture'.[10]

Comparison with Apuleius (ostentatious oratory combined with political and social importance) ought to have produced a more objective exegesis.[11] For the ostensible theme, 'a toga ad pallium', sets the *De Pallio* in the context of the Second Sophistic movement. Philostratus wrote epistles dissuad-

---

[1] G. Boissier, La fin du paganisme I (1891), 302: 'sous ces reproches, sa vanité d'homme de lettres se cabra et bondit'.

[2] J. M. Vis, Tertullianus' De Pallio tegen de Achtergrond van zijn overige Werken (Diss. Nijmegen, 1949), 136ff., esp. 146: 'cette tendance à se montrer supérieur à ses détracteurs et à se glorifier lui-même . . .'.

[3] E. A. Isichei, Political Thinking and Social Experience. Some Christian Interpretations of the Roman Empire from Tertullian to Salvian (1964), 28; 36.

[4] W. H. C. Frend, Martyrdom and Persecution in the Early Church (1965), 332.

[5] J. Geffcken, Kynika und Verwandtes (1909), 80ff.

[6] E. g., respectively, H. Kellner, Theol. Quartalschr. LII (1870), 547ff.; E. Noeldechen, Tertullian (1890), 261ff.; A. Zappalà, Richerche religiose I (1925), 132ff.; 327ff.

[7] P. Monceaux, Histoire littéraire de l'Afrique chrétienne I (1901), 407; 411.

[8] D. van Berchem, Mus. Helv. I (1944), 109.

[9] G. Säflund, De Pallio und die stilistische Entwicklung Tertullians (1955), 27ff.

[10] D. E. Groh, Church History XL (1971), 14. This writer's interpretation appears in part to depend on his assertion (at second hand) that Tertullian's works have survived 'almost complete'. In fact, while thirty one survive, no less than sixteen (including his longest work, seven books De Ecstasi, and three treatises in Greek) are lost (listed at CCL I. v. f.).

[11] Tertullian (1971), 229ff. For criticism of some of the above interpretations, R. Klein, Tertullian und das römische Reich (1968), 89ff.

ing a friend from wearing shoes of any sort.[1] Tertullian has transformed
just such an exercise into something far nobler and profoundly serious. For
a Roman the pallium had always symbolised things Greek and especially
Greek cultural pursuits. At Puteoli once, Augustus distributed togas and
pallia, insisting that Romans use Greek dress and speech and the Greeks
Roman.[2] Hence, by an easy association of ideas, the pallium represented
philosophy (a primarily Greek pursuit) or even, more generally, a preference
for intellectual or spiritual over material values: Marcus Aurelius dedicated
himself to philosophy by assuming the pallium when he was twelve,[3] and
the frugal table of the emperor Julian seemed to contemporaries to portend
a retirement 'velut ad pallium'.[4] Some, it is true, like Apuleius, disapproved
of 'beggars clad in the pallium' whose intellect did not match their style of
dress.[5] Tertullian was, on one level, answering such opinions.

The exordium opens with a compliment and a *captatio benevolentiae* which
find two close analogies in Apuleius:

principes semper Africae viri Carthaginienses, vetustate nobiles, novitate felices,
gaudeo vos tam prosperos temporum, cum ita vacat ac iuvat habitus denotare:
pacis hoc et annonae et oti: ab imperio et a caelo bene est (*Pall.* 1.1);
priusquam vobis occipiam, principes Africae viri, gratias agere ob statuam . . . (*Flor.*
16, p. 23 Helm);
is etiam laudator mihi apud principes Africae viros quodam modo astitit (*Flor.* p.
28 Helm).

Tertullian was not directly imitating Apuleius, whose 'principes Africae
viri' are the members of the provincial council gathered in Carthage from
every town of Africa.[6] He echoed what must have been a commonplace for
any public speaker in the African metropolis. Next, a brief and sarcastic
review of Carthaginian history (with allusions to Utica and Hadrumetum)
proves the pallium to be the traditional dress of African cities (1. 1–1. 3).[7]
The audience ought not to feel shame at something Punic (2. 1), even though

---

[1] Philostratus, Epp. XVIII; XXXVI.

[2] Suetonius, Div. Aug. 98.3.

[3] HA, Marcus 2.6.

[4] Ammianus XXV. 4.4.: in pace victus eius mensarumque tenuitas erat recte
noscentibus admiranda, velut ad pallium mox reversuri.

[5] Apuleius, Flor. pp. 9; 11 Helm.

[6] Säflund assumed, without argument or justification, that both Apuleius and
Tertullian were addressing the decurions of Carthage (o. c. 29). But Apuleius
appears clearly to distinguish between 'in curia Carthaginiensium' (Flor. p. 28 line 19
Helm) and 'apud principes Africae viros' (p. 28 line 22).

[7] Observe that Tertullian's proof depends on equating the Carthaginian tunic
with the Greek pallium: 'tamen et vobis habitus aliter olim, tunicae fuere etc.'
(1.1). There was a Roman proverb distinguishing the two 'tunica propior pallio
est' (Plautus, Trinummus 1154). It should not therefore be assumed without further
evidence that Tertullian's original audience would instinctively identify the pallium as something inherently Punic (as does Frend, o. c. 332).

'Romanitas' be everybody's aim in life (4. 1).[1] To change one's dress is in accordance with nature (2.1–4.8), to wear the pallium (a convenient garment) makes a man better and releases him from the cares of public life (5.1–5.4), and those who wear it are the only guardians of morality (5. 5–6. 1) and monopolise the liberal arts (6. 2–6. 3). Tertullian has thus justified and commended wearing of the pallium in terms of the popular philosophies of the Stoics, Epicureans and Cynics. He could claim, as Seneca once did, that he was exhorting men

> cum Epicuro quiescere, hominis naturam cum Stoicis
> vincere, cum Cynicis excedere (*De Brev. Vitae* 14.2).[2]

But the humble pallium has now been ennobled by the divine philosophy of the Christians (6. 4). As elsewhere (for example, in *De Fuga in Persecutione*)[3] Tertullian postpones his main point until the very end. On the basis even of his own presuppositions about life and morality, any decent pagan ought to adopt the pallium – and become a Christian. Tertullian is thus transforming the traditional and highly respectable appeal for conversion to philosophy into an appeal for conversion to Christianity.[4]

In form, the *De Pallio* is a *suasoria* on the theme 'a toga ad pallium' (5. 1; 6. 3; cf. 4. 10: suadeo, reverere habitum), with many elements of the Cynic diatribe (esp. 4. 9–4. 10, on the dress of prostitutes). But Tertullian has carefully inserted passages to display his techniques of virtuosity on familiar set-themes. Thus the ἐκφράσεις, or brief encomia, on the pallium itself (1. 1), on the chamaeleon (3. 3) and on the peacock:

> mutant et bestiae pro veste formam;
> quamquam et pavo pluma vestis, et quidem de cataclystis,
> immo omni conchylio pressior
> qua colla florent,
> et omni patagio inauratior
> qua terga fulgent,
> et omni syrmate solutior
> qua caudae iacent,
> multicolor
> et discolor
> et versicolor,
> numquam ipsa,

---

[1] A recent critic, castigating 'the wide range and poor quality' of another's scholarship, pronounces the word 'Romanitas' to be 'not Latin' (A. S. Gratwick, Class. Rev. XX (1970), 334). It is registered in Lewis and Short, A Latin Dictionary (1955), 1599.

[2] For Seneca's explicit coupling of Stoic and Epicurean, cf. De Const. Sap. 15. 4; De Vita Beata 13. 1; 18. 1. Further, what is highly relevant to Tertullian, he denies any radical difference between the political precepts of Epicurus and Zeno: 'alter otium ex proposito petit, alter ex causa' (De Otio 3. 2).

[3] Tertullian (1971), 178; 183.

[4] For the very real attractions of the former, A. D. Nock, Conversion (1933), 164ff.

semper alia,
etsi semper ipsa
quando alia,
   totiens denique mutanda
   quotiens movenda (3. 1).

And there occurs a motif borrowed from the patriotic oratory of the Severan age, perhaps not entirely lacking undertones of parody:

sed vanum iam antiquitas, quando curricula nostra coram.
quantum reformavit orbis saeculum istud!
quantum urbium
   aut produxit
   aut auxit
   aut reddidit
praesentis imperii triplex virtus!
Deo tot Augustis in unum favente
quot census transcripti,
quot populi repurgati,
quot ordines illustrati,
quot barbari exclusi!
revera orbis cultissimum huius imperii rus est,
      eradicato omni aconito hostilitatis
      et cacto et rubo subdolae familiaritatis,
      concultus et amoenus super Alcinoi pometum
                  et Midae rosetum.
      laudans igitur orbem mutantem quid denotas hominem? (2.7)

Septimius Severus had defeated his rivals for the throne in civil war (193/4, 195/6), campaigned twice against Rome's external enemies in the East (194/5, 197–199), created a new province of Mesopotamia, and journeyed through both the eastern provinces and Africa bestowing favours upon cities and individuals. The world seemed more prosperous than ever before, and in 204 were celebrated Ludi Saeculares, heralding a new (and golden) age.[1] The following January the powerful pretorian prefect Fulvius Plautianus, whose daughter Severus' elder son had married, abruptly fell from grace and was put to death. In the official version of events, he was plotting to assassinate the emperor, truly 'subdola familiaritas'.[2] God cherished the trinity of emperors, Septimius Severus and his two sons, Caracalla and Geta. Geta, it is true, was not yet formally an Augustus, but no harm could come from anticipating his joyful and inevitable elevation.[3] Who could

---

[1] J. B. Pighi, De ludis saecularibus populi Romani Quiritium libri sex (1941) 95ff. For the ideology of the occasion, cf. Horace, Carm. Saec. 66ff.; (Apollo) remque Romanam Latiumque felix/alterum in lustrum meliusque semper/prorogat aevum. The Carmen Saeculare of 204 is preserved only in meagre fragments: see most conveniently C. Hülsen, Rhein. Mus. N. F. LXXXI (1932), 379f.

[2] See, most recently, A. R. Birley, Septimius Severus the African Emperor (1971), 231ff.

[3] The date of De Pallio is argued to be 204 in Tertullian (1971), 35ff.

predict that once their father was dead Caracalla would murder his brother?
But some inhabitants of Carthage might recall sinister happenings of seven
years earlier: an imperial procurator arrived to supervise confiscations in
Africa from those who had chosen the wrong side in the civil wars.[1] Tertullian's *Apologeticum* alluded to the terror which struck the city of Carthage
(*Apol.* 35. 11). The bland phrases of the *De Pallio* could have been uttered
by an official panegyrist.[2]

Throughout *De Pallio* Tertullian prosecuted an undertaking far more
serious than simply commending the pallium or personal apologetics. He
intended to annex pagan culture for Christianity. Was evidence desired of
climatic change? The Bible could furnish it: 'aspice ad Palaestinam . . .'
(2. 4). Pagan history, 'superiorum profanitas' or 'aevi historiae', began with
the Assyrians and asserted that Ninus (the eponymous hero of Niniveh) was
the first monarch in the world:[3] the readers of God's history 'ab ipsis mundi
natalibus compotes sumus' (2. 5). And who wears the toga, who the pallium?
The toga is worn by tomb-robbers, pimps, gladiators, torturers and degene-
rate reprobates of every sort (4. 8; 5. 5–5. 7; 6. 3). In contrast the wearers of
pallium can boast of all the cultured and educated:

> viderit nunc philosophia, quid prosit;
> nec enim sola mecum est:
> habeo et alias artes
> in publico utiles:
>   de meo vestiuntur et primus informator litterarum
>   et primus enodator vocis
>   et primus numerorum harenarius
>   et grammaticus
>   et rhetor
>   et sophista
>   et medicus
>   et poeta
>   et qui musicam pulsat
>   et qui stellarem coniectat
>   et qui volaticam spectat;
> omnis liberalitas studiorum quattuor meis angulis tegitur (6. 2).

It is a holy, venerable garb, worn by the truly wise who have renounced
empty superstitions (4. 10). The fusion of Christianity and classical culture

---

[1] ILS 1421 (Ephesus): a man appointed '[pro]c. Aug. ad bona cogenda in Africa'.

[2] For the general theme of the passage, compare a coin of Cius with the legend
ΣΕΥΗΡΟΥ ΒΑΣΙΛΕΥΟΝΤΟΣ Ο ΚΟΣΜΟΣ ΕΥΤΥΧΕΙ ΜΑΚΑΡΙΟΙ ΚΙΑΝΟΙ (Br.
Mus. Cat., Pontus 133 no. 36).

[3] Ninus became known to the Greek (and hence the Roman) world through
Ctesias of Cnidus (FGrH 688 F 1a), whom Tertullian cites elsewhere (Nat. I. 16. 4;
Apol. 9. 16). Ctesias' account of Ninus appears to be deliberately modelled on Herodotus' account of the Egyptian Sesostris (II. 102ff.), cf. F. Jacoby, P–W XI.
2051f.; A. Momigliano, Quarto contributo alla storia degli studi classici e del mondo
antico (1969), 192f.

was no distant dream when a man could imply the possibility of Christian astrology and Christian divination.[1] All Carthage knew that a sophist of overwhelming force and outstanding virtuosity was a declared Christian. In his own person, Tertullian demonstrated the intellectual respectability of the new faith. He could pass under review the most disreputable figures of Roman society:

> taceo Nerones et Apicios, Rufos; dabo catharticum impuritati
> Scauri et aleae Curii et vinulentiae Antonii (5.7).

The emperor Nero and Apicius were indeed paradigms of the glutton and the gourmand, and Antony's tract *De ebrietate sua* (written shortly before the battle of Actium) enjoyed a lasting notoriety.[2] But who were Rufus, Curius and Scaurus? The first is presumably the Sempronius Rufus who, according to the learned Porphyrio, was once the target of Horace:

> tutus erat rhombus tutoque ciconia nido,
> donec vos auctor docuit praetorius (Serm. II. 2. 49f.).

Rufus began the habit of eating the young of the stork.[3] The second will be the quaestorian Curius attacked by Cicero in the lost oration 'de toga candida' and characterised by the contemporary Calvus as 'talos pereruditus'.[4] The last is Mam. Aemilius Scaurus, consul probably in A.D. 21.[5] Tertullian could easily find his impurity in Seneca, who denounced Scaurus as 'palam obscoenus', a man who importuned fellow senators, and the depths of whose depravity must (even in this broad-minded age) be described in the decent obscurity of a learned language.[6] In his attitude towards Scaurus, as on other matters, Tertullian found an ally in Seneca, whom he could justifiably claim as 'saepe noster' (*An.* 20. 1).[7] He was thus, albeit unconsciously, preparing the way for those in the fourth century who would depict Seneca as an admirer and correspondent of St. Paul.[8]

Tertullian's interest in the Roman past cannot be denied and must not be underestimated. Antiquarian knowledge formed part of the equipment of any contemporary orator, and Tertullian can hardly be understood without

---

[1] Contrast Idol. 9. 1 ff. On Christian attitudes to astrology, cf. L. Koep, Mullus. Festschrift Theodor Klauser (1964), 199 ff.

[2] Pliny, Nat. Hist. XIV. 147.

[3] A. Holder – O. Keller, Scholia antiqua in Q. Horatium Flaccum I (1894), 293.

[4] Asconius p. 72 Stangl = p. 93 Clark. He was 'flagitiis atque facinoribus coopertus' in the opinion of Sallust (Cat. 23. 1).

[5] PIR² A 404; E. Badian, Studies in Greek and Roman History (1964), 105 ff.

[6] Seneca, De Beneficiis IV. 31. 3: 'ignorabas ancillarum illum suarum menstruum ore hiante exceptare?'

[7] Quoting De Beneficiis IV. 6. 6.

[8] The forged letters 'Pauli ad Senecam et Senecae ad Paulum' were widely accepted as genuine by 392 (Jerome, De vir.ill. 12).

reference to the Second Sophistic movement, whose most famous practitioner in Latin literature was Apuleius of Madauros, himself active in the same city as Tertullian. It will not be paradoxical to assert that his antiquarian enquiries both rendered his own oratory more effective and helped later Christians who knew his writings to annex so much of pagan culture for the newer creed. Tertullian's own position in at least one literary genre can be neatly defined within the Roman tradition:[1] he stands half way between the pagan satirist Juvenal and the Christian satirist Jerome.

---

[1] Cf. G. Quispel, Nederlands Theologisch Tijdschrift II (1948), 280ff.; D. S. Wiesen, St. Jerome as a Satirist (1964), 12ff.

XV

THE FRAGMENTS OF TACITUS' *HISTORIES*

O F THE original twelve books of Tacitus' *Histories*, only the first four and part of the fifth have survived the hazards of textual transmission, and that by the thread of a single manuscript. The continuous text thus breaks off in the course of the year 70 (5. 26). Eight fragments are also printed in the standard modern editions, viz., the Teubner of C. Halm (4th ed., Leipzig, 1912), C. Fisher's Oxford text (Oxford, 1910), and E. Koestermann's Teubner (2d ed., Leipzig, 1969).[1] But the editors dispense with an apparatus criticus and conceal the principles according to which these *fragmenta "Historiarum"* are included. To be sure, Fisher states, "Vide Bernays, de chronicis Sulpicii Severi, p. 53," in annotation on the first two fragments. Yet he (like other editors) prints as Tacitus' own several words and phrases which Bernays expressly denied that Tacitus either wrote or could have written. More surprising still is the editors' treatment of Orosius. They print five passages from his *Historiae adversum paganos* (frags. 3–7). But other passages too were long ago signaled as deriving from Tacitus' *Histories*, not only in the standard edition of Orosius (by C. Zangemeister, *CSEL*, vol. 5 [Vienna, 1882]), but also in a dissertation of 1888, which still appears to be the only systematic treatment of the knowledge of Tacitus in late antiquity.[2]

The standard "fragments" of the *Histories* clearly need a reconsideration which proceeds from what is known about the habits and sources of the two historians from whom they are mainly culled: Sulpicius Severus and Orosius. First, however, two allusions to Tacitus may be considered which it is hard to describe as fragments, even on the broadest possible definition of the term.

1. FRAGMENTS 7 AND 8

The last fragment in the standard collections (frag. 8) appears unproblematical. Commenting on Virgil *Aen.* 3. 399 ("hic et Narycii posuerunt moenia Locri"), Servius Auctus states:

> [*sc.* Locri] qui autem Libyam delati sunt Nasamones appellantur, ut Cornelius Tacitus refert, oriundi a Naryciis, quod ibi invenies ubi ait [11. 265] *Libycone habitantes litore Locros.*

The present paper was originally composed for a departmental seminar in Toronto on 8 January 1976: I am most grateful to those of my colleagues who attended for their comments, particularly Graham Sumner and Christopher Jones.

1. Also in the editions of C. Giarratano (Rome, 1939) and R. Till (Heidelberger Texte, 33 [Heidelberg, 1963]).

2. E. Cornelius, *Quomodo Tacitus, historiarum scriptor, in hominum memoria versatus sit usque ad renascentes litteras saeculis XIV. et XV.* (Diss. Marburg, 1888), pp. 28 ff.

Tacitus, therefore, recorded the identification of the Nasamones as emigrant Locrians: the historical context must be the campaign which Cn. Suellius Flaccus waged against the Nasamones in about 87.[3]

The preceding fragment (frag. 7) comes from a passage which ought to be quoted in full:

> [*sc.* Theodosius] omnem fiduciam sui ad opem Christi conferens maximas illas Scythicas gentes formidatasque cunctis maioribus, Alexandro quoque illi Magno, sicut Pompeius Corneliusque testati sunt, evitatas, nunc autem extincto Romano exercitu Romanis equis armisque instructissimas, hoc est Alanos Hunos et Gothos, incunctanter adgressus magnis multisque proeliis vicit. [*Hist. adv. pag.* 7. 34. 5]

Editors of Tacitus mangle the passage by excising the words "omnem . . . conferens" and "nunc autem . . . instructissimas." The collocation of Alans, Huns, and Goths smacks of the later fourth century, and Tacitus could never have written thus.[4] When the passage is read in full, Orosius' reference to the destruction of a Roman army at the battle of Adrianople (9 August 378) becomes clear. Orosius does not ascribe knowledge of the Huns to Tacitus; he identifies the contemporary Alans, Huns, and Goths with the *Scythicae gentes* mentioned in Tacitus and in Justin's epitome of Pompeius Trogus. What he specifically attributes to Trogus and Tacitus is the statement that Alexander avoided the *Scythicae gentes*.

To what lost part of Tacitus is Orosius alluding? If the allusion stood alone, one might perhaps think of a passage, presumably in *Annals* 18, where Tacitus described Nero's preparations for the war against the Albani, for which troops had already in March 68 been dispatched to the Caspian Gates (*Hist.* 1. 6). But an earlier passage of Orosius is also relevant:

> modo autem Getae illi qui et nunc Gothi, quos Alexander evitandos pronuntiavit, Pyrrhus exhorruit, Caesar etiam declinavit . . . [*Hist. adv. pag.* 1. 16. 2]

Pompeius Trogus included in the thirty-second book of his *Historiae Philippicae* a digression on the origins of the Pannonii and the rise of the Daci (*Prologus libri XXXII*), in which he identified the Daci as *suboles Getarum* (Justin 32. 3. 16). By analogy, therefore, Orosius should be alluding to an excursus with which Tacitus prefaced his treatment of the Dacian wars in the reign of Domitian.

2. SULPICIUS SEVERUS

Sulpicius Severus composed his *Chronica* in A.D. 400 (though he appears to have added at least one passage later and to have published the two books no earlier than 403).[5] The work is largely derivative: if Severus never names

3. For the evidence, B. E. Thomasson, *Die Statthalter der römischen Provinzen Nordafrikas von Augustus bis Diocletianus*, vol. 2 (Lund, 1960), pp. 158 f.

4. E. Täubler, "Zur Geschichte der Alanen," *Klio* 9(1909): 14, n. 2; B. Bachrach, *A History of the Alans in the West* (Minneapolis, 1973), p. 124.

5. Severus reckons dates from Stilicho's consulate (*Chron.* 2. 9. 2, 2. 27. 5), but incorporates material from a letter of Paulinus of Nola which (it appears) must be dated to 403; cf. P. Fabre, *Essai sur la chronologie de l'oeuvre de Saint Paulin de Nole* (Paris, 1948), pp. 34, 40.

226

an authority, most of his sources are extant and easily identifiable.[6] The first book is based almost entirely on the Old Testament, with occasional use of Eusebius' *Chronicle*, presumably in Jerome's Latin version (1. 36. 6, 42. 1, 46. 5). The second book is more varied, for it begins with Daniel, Ezra, and Apocryphal books of the Old Testament (Judith and Maccabees), but culminates in an account of Priscillian and his followers which has long been recognized as a valuable piece of contemporary history (2. 46–51).[7] Between these extremes, the matter displays equal variety: Severus uses the New Testament, Rufinus' translation of Eusebius' *Ecclesiastical History*, Jerome's *Chronicle* again (2. 5. 7, 6. 1), a letter of Paulinus of Nola (2. 33–34 < Paulinus *Epp.* 31),[8] a collection of documents on the Arian controversy compiled by Hilary of Poitiers[9]—and Tacitus.[10]

The Roman historian is used to supply the background of the martyrdoms of Peter and Paul: Severus summarizes Tacitus' portrayal of Nero's moral turpitude (2. 28. 2 < *Ann.* 15. 37; 2. 28. 3 < *Ann.* 14. 62), and his account of the fire at Rome in 64 and its aftermath, the burning alive of Christians (2. 29. 1–2 < *Ann.* 15. 40–44). In each case, the technique is the same: a rapid summary which nevertheless preserves Tacitean phrases, even whole clauses, virtually unchanged (e.g., 2. 28. 2: "cuncta denique, quae vel in feminis non sine verecundia conspiciuntur, spectata" < *Ann.* 15. 37. 5: "cuncta denique spectata quae etiam in femina nox operit"; 2. 29. 2: "quin ab eo iussum putaretur" < *Ann.* 15. 44. 3: "quin iussum incendium crederetur").

Severus' next chapter (2. 30) also uses Tacitus, in two ways. First, there is a brief summary of the events of A.D. 69 (2. 30. 1–3ᵃ) which appears to be based on the first four books of the *Histories*. Then there is a fuller account of the capture of Jerusalem in 70 (2. 30. 3ᵇ–7) which draws indirectly on Josephus, but differs from the Jewish historian's account of the same episode on a matter of crucial importance: whereas in Josephus the temple is destroyed by accident, against the wishes of Titus (*BJ* 6. 429 ff.), Sulpicius Severus makes Titus himself (as well as some of his advisers) adopt a deliberate policy of destruction. The contradiction poses two questions: Which version is true? And what was Severus' source? Both admit of easy answers. Josephus was writing for a Jewish audience (he originally wrote his *Jewish War* in Aramaic for Jews of Babylonia),[11] and he set out to depict the

---

6. The most perceptive discussion of most aspects of the work remains that of J. Bernays, *Über die Chronik des Sulpicius Severus: Ein Beitrag zur Geschichte der classischen und biblischen Studien* (Berlin, 1861), reprinted in his *Gesammelte Abhandlungen*, vol. 2 (Berlin, 1885), pp. 81–195. What follows here is closely based on Bernays: references will be given sparingly, and then to the pages of the original publication.

7. On this episode, see now J. Matthews, *Western Aristocracies and Imperial Court A.D. 364–425* (Oxford, 1975), pp. 160 ff.

8. Severus adapts Paulinus, slightly but deliberately; cf. P. Fabre, *Saint Paulin de Nole et l'amitié chrétienne* (Paris, 1949), p. 328, n. 1.

9. *Chron.* 2. 35. 3 = *CSEL*, 65:149. 11–13 (Arius' teaching), and the names of bishops in 2. 38. 3 come from the synodical letter of the Council of Serdica (*CSEL*, 65:119. 5 ff.).

10. Bernays, *Chronik*, pp. 53 ff.

11. Josephus *BJ* 1. 3; cf. 1. 6.

Roman authorities in a favorable light: the Flavian poet Valerius Flaccus had
no inhibitions about praising Titus for willing the deliberate destruction of
the temple (*Argonautica* 1. 13–14: Domitian describes in verse "Solymo
nigrantem pulvere fratrem, / spargentemque faces et in omni turre furen-
tem"). That is surely correct.[12] As for Severus' source (in 2. 30. 6), at least
three considerations point strongly to the lost portion of Tacitus *Histories* 5:
Severus has already employed Tacitus in the immediately preceding chapter;
Orosius has something very similar (*Hist. adv. pag.* 7. 9. 4–6), which may
also most naturally be supposed to come from Tacitus; and Severus reproduces Tacitean vocabulary.[13]

Severus' differences from Orosius, however, suggest a somber inference:

fertur Titus adhibito consilio prius delibe-
rasse, an templum tanti operis everteret.
etenim nonnullis videbatur, aedem sacra-
tam ultra omnia mortalia illustrem non
oportere deleri, quae servata modestiae Romanae testimonium, diruta perennem cru-
delitatis notam praeberet. at contra alii et
Titus ipse evertendum in primis templum
censebant, quo plenius Iudaeorum et Christianorum religio tolleretur: quippe has religiones, licet contrarias sibi, isdem tamen
ab auctoribus profectas; Christianos ex Iudaeis extitisse: radice sublata stirpem facile
peritura. [Sulpicius Severus *Chron.* 2.
30. 6–7 = frag. 2]

quod tamen postquam in potestatem redac-
tum opere atque antiquitate suspexit, diu
deliberavit utrum tamquam incitamentum
hostium incenderet an in testimonium victoriae reservaret. sed Ecclesia Dei iam per
totum orbem uberrime germinante, hoc
tamquam effetum ac vacuum nullique usui
bono commodo arbitrio Dei auferendum
fuit. itaque Titus, imperator ab exercitu
pronuntiatus, templum in Hierosolymis in-
cendit ac diruit. [Orosius *Hist. adv. pag.*
7. 9. 5–6]

If both passages quoted derive from the same passage or passages of Tacitus,
then the original text cannot be reconstructed with any confidence.

So far Severus on the destruction of the temple. The beginning of his
account of the siege may also be claimed as deriving from Tacitus:

Iudaei obsidione clausi, quia nulla neque pacis neque deditionis copia dabatur, ad extremum fame interibant, passimque viae oppleri cadaveribus coepere, victo iam officio
humandi: quin omnia nefanda esca super ausi ne humanis quidem corporibus peper-
cerunt, nisi quae eiusmodi alimentis tabes praeripuerat. [*Chron.* 2. 30. 3 = frag. 1]

Again Severus diverges from Josephus, who presents Titus as eager for a
negotiated surrender up to the end (*BJ* 5. 356, 6. 93 ff., 6. 323 ff.), and the
Sallustian echo in "omnia nefanda esca super ausi" points to Tacitus as the
source.[14]

12. For further arguments, E. Schürer, *A History of the Jewish People in the Age of Jesus Christ*,
revised by G. Vermes and F. Millar, vol. 1 (Edinburgh, 1973), pp. 506–7, n. 115.

13. Most obviously *at contra*: cf. *Ann.* 4. 28. 3: *at contra reus* . . .

14. J. Bernays, "Zu Sallustius und Sulpicius Severus," *RhM*, ser. 3, 16 (1861): 319–20 = *Gesammelte Abhandlungen*, 2 : 204–5. The manuscripts of Priscian (who quotes the relevant fragment) have
"multa nefanda casu super ausi": Maurenbrecher accepts Bernays' emendation, based on Severus,
esca super (Sallust *Hist.* 3. 86).

Sulpicius Severus, therefore, read and used a lost portion of Tacitus' *Histories*. The proof was first formulated by Jacob Bernays in 1861, and the only attempt to gainsay it must be pronounced a hopeless failure.[15] But, as Bernays stated very clearly, the passage of Severus describing Titus' council of war contains phrases (e.g., Christianity described as a *religio*) which Tacitus cannot have written.[16] Hence it is misleading to print (as editors do) the unchanged text of Sulpicius Severus as if it were authentic Tacitus. Where Severus' habits can be verified, as in his use of the *Annals*, he has abbreviated so drastically and introduced so many small changes that the original continuous text could not be reconstructed from his report alone. His treatment of Tacitus' account of the siege of Jerusalem and Titus' deliberations was clearly similar, as a comparison with Orosius implies. Hence, although Tacitus' actual words cannot be recovered, part of the substance of what he wrote can be inferred with some confidence.

An important substantive problem remains. Sulpicius Severus presents Christianity as a crucial factor in Titus' calculations, and Orosius mentions the Christian church at precisely the same juncture. That is not likely to be an accurate analysis of Titus' actual motivation.[17] But it might seem to follow from the preceding arguments that Tacitus mentioned Christianity when reporting (or inventing) Titus' deliberations. The inference is not imperative. Tacitus introduces Christianity in his *Annals* (15. 44) as if he had not mentioned it before in his writings.[18] And the differences between Severus and Orosius are such as to permit the hypothesis that each has independently introduced a reference to Christianity. Tacitus' *Histories* (it may still be held) eschewed all mention of the new religion.

A passage which stands between the material which Sulpicius Severus took from *Annals* 15 and that which he took from the *Histories* deserves attention. Severus states that Nero died "incertum an ipse sibi mortem consciverit" (2. 29. 5). No reader of Suetonius would be left in any uncertainty: Nero cut his own throat with the aid of the freedman Epaphroditus (*Nero* 49. 3). Moreover, Severus employs a common Tacitean device (*incertum an* appended to the main verb of the sentence)[19] and a turn of phrase which Tacitus used of the suicide of L. Junius Silanus in 49 (*Ann.* 12. 8. 1: "die nuptiarum Silanus mortem sibi conscivit"). It may be suggested, therefore, that Severus is perhaps drawing on Tacitus' account of Nero's death in the lost *Annals* 18—a book which some recent scholars have denied that Tacitus ever lived to compose.[20]

15. H. Montefiore, "Sulpicius Severus and Titus' Council of War," *Historia* 11 (1962): 156–70. He argues that Severus' source for the council is the Antonius Julianus who wrote *de Iudaeis* (Minucius Felix *Oct.* 33. 4). That is totally implausible; cf. A. Momigliano, "Jacob Bernays," *Mededelingen der koninklijke Nederlandse Akademie van Wetenschappen*, Afd. Letterkunde, n.s. 32, no. 5 (1969): 167.

16. Bernays, *Chronik*, p. 57.

17. Montefiore, "Sulpicius Severus and Titus' Council of War," pp. 167 f.

18. Hence the bizarre theory that the sentence "auctor nominis eius . . . confluunt celebranturque" (*Ann.* 15. 44. 3) originally stood in Tacitus' *Histories* (C. Saumagne, "Tacite et Saint Paul," *RH* 232 [1964]: 67 ff.).

19. A. Gerber and A. Greef, *Lexicon Taciteum* (Leipzig, 1903), p. 614.

20. E. Koestermann, in his commentary, vol. 4 (Heidelberg, 1968), p. 410, argues that Tacitus died before he could write beyond 16. 35 (where the manuscripts break off).

3. OROSIUS

Orosius' *Historiae adversum paganos* are less a history than a polemical tract: their purpose is to absolve Christianity of blame for Alaric's sack of Rome in 410 by showing that the Roman state encountered many disasters before Christ was born and that Christians had nothing to do with recent disasters (the pious Stilicho is conveniently supposed a secret pagan).[21] There are seven books, with the birth of Christ deliberately and symbolically placed at the very end of the sixth (6. 22. 5 ff.), so that Book 7 covers more than four hundred years, down to A.D. 417 (7. 43. 19). Orosius uses comparatively few sources: the bulk of his material can easily be identified as deriving from the Old and New Testaments, Caesar's *Gallic Wars* (including the eighth book which A. Hirtius added), Virgil, Livy (probably in epitome), Suetonius, Florus, Justin, Eutropius, Jerome's *Chronicle*, Rufinus' *Ecclesiastical History*, and the early books of Augustine's *De civitate Dei*.[22]

Tacitus is also employed, but only (so it appears) the *Histories*. One section, in particular, was important for Orosius, who provides the only direct quotation to be found among the standard fragments:

> deinde, ut verbis Corneli Taciti loquar, sene Augusto Ianus patefactus, dum apud extremos terrarum terminos novae gentes saepe ex usu et aliquando cum damno quaeruntur, usque ad Vespasiani duravit imperium. hucusque Cornelius. [*Hist. adv. pag.* 7. 3. 7 = frag. 4]

The context was clearly a digression on the temple of Janus and its closures and openings, which Tacitus appended to his description of Vespasian's closure in 71.[23] Orosius later notes that Tacitus reported Vespasian's reopening of the temple after a year (*Hist. adv. pag.* 7. 19. 4 = frag. 5), but he had probably already drawn on the passage to prove that when Christ was born the world was at peace:

> itaque anno ab Urbe condita DCCLII Caesar Augustus ab oriente in occidentem, a septentrione in meridiem ac per totum Oceani circulum cunctis gentibus una pace compositis, Iani portas tertio ipse tunc clausit. quas ex eo per duodecim fere annos quietissimo semper obseratas otio ipsa etiam robigo signavit, nec prius unquam nisi sub extrema senectute Augusti pulsatae Atheniensium seditione et Dacorum commotione patuerunt. [6. 22. 1–2]

The chronology is fraudulent, for it was in about 2 B.C. that the temple of Janus, probably closed since 8, was reopened.[24] The rebellion of the Athenians presumably comes from Jerome's *Chronicle* (p. 170[h] Helm), from which Orosius has probably also deduced the twelve years of closure. Nevertheless,

---

21. Similarly Claudian, the panegyrist of Stilicho, is damned as *paganus pervicacissimus* (7. 35. 21). On the difficult problem of discovering his real religious beliefs, see A. Cameron, *Claudian: Poetry and Propaganda at the Court of Honorius* (Oxford, 1970), pp. 189 ff.

22. See Zangemeister's "Index scriptorum quibus Orosius usus est," *CSEL*, 5:684–700.

23. The date, nowhere directly attested, is secure; cf. P. Weynand, s.v. "Flavius (206)," *RE* 6 (1909): 2644 ff.

24. R. Syme, *Danubian Papers* (Bucharest, 1971), pp. 38–39.

Tacitus may have ascribed the reopening to a *Dacorum commotio*, whose true date was about 2 B.C.[25]

Orosius uses the *Histories* more extensively for the geography of Palestine (1. 5. 1–14 quotes *Hist.* 5. 7; 1. 10. 3–4 quotes *Hist.* 5. 3) and in his account of the reigns of Vespasian, Titus, and Domitian. The following brief analysis notes all of Orosius' sources in this section, but quotes and discusses only the material which is probably Tacitean:

7.	8.	9	Perhaps a summary of *Hist.* 4. 1
	9.	1	Orosius' own
	9.	2	? Rufinus *HE* 2. 26. 1; then Suetonius *Vesp.* 5 and 4
	9.	3	A complex paragraph. The first sentence is taken from Suetonius *Vesp.* 4. The second appears to combine Jerome *Chronicle* p. 187ª Helm and Suetonius *Vesp.* 5 with a brief summary of events narrated in Tacitus' *Histories:* the details that Vespasian took power "hortatu plurimorum regum et ducum" and that he "cognita interfectione Vitelli paulisper Alexandriae substitit" reproduce the substance of *Hist.* 2. 74 ff., 3. 48, 4. 81 ff.
	9.	4–6	The siege and sack of Jerusalem: probably based exclusively on Tacitus, but summarized and rephrased by Orosius himself.
	9.	7	Orosius quotes Tacitus and Suetonius as giving the Jewish casualties in the rebellion as 600,000 killed, in contrast to Josephus' figures of 1,100,000 killed and 97,000 taken captive (*BJ* 6. 420). (Orosius quotes Josephus from Jerome *Chronicle* p. 187ª Helm.) But there is no figure in Suetonius, and Tacitus gives 600,000 as the number besieged in Jerusalem (*Hist.* 5. 13). It is surely to this extant passage which Orosius alludes: the "fragment" should accordingly be discarded.
	9.	8–9	The triumph of Vespasian and Titus and the closure of the temple of Janus clearly come from Tacitus: hence the precise detail that theirs was the first triumph out of three hundred and twenty celebrated by a father and son together.[26] It may also be noted that Tacitus disallowed (and presumably omitted) Nero's well-attested closure of the temple of Janus in 66 (Suetonius *Nero* 13; cf. *B.M. Coins, Rom. Emp.*, 1:215, 229 ff., 238 f., 243 f., 263, 267, 273, 398 f.).
	9.	10–12	The rest of the reign of Vespasian (from Jerome *Chronicle* p. 188 Helm).
	9.	13–15	Titus (from Jerome *Chronicle* p. 189 Helm, and Eutropius *Brev.* 7. 21–22).
	10.	1–2	Domitian's domestic policies (from Jerome *Chronicle* pp. 189–91 Helm; Eutropius *Brev.* 7. 23; and Suetonius *Dom.* 22).
	10.	3–4	Orosius refers to Tacitus' account of Roman disasters at the hands of the Dacians, and preserves some precise details: that Fuscus fought against Diurpaneus, *rex Dacorum;* that Tacitus justified his omission of casualty figures with appeal to Sallust; and that Domitian "pravissima elatus iactantia, sub nomine superatorum hostium de extinctis legionibus triumphavit" (cf. Tacitus *Agr.* 39. 1; Dio 67. 9. 6). Editors print the first two of these items as fragment 6; but Orosius is surely also drawing on Tacitus in what immediately precedes and follows.[27]

25. In favor of this date (but not invoking Tacitus), Syme, ibid., p. 39.

26. That Orosius is here adapting Tacitus is allowed by S. Borszák, s.v. "P. Cornelius Tacitus," *RE*, suppl. 11 (1968): 445–46.

27. R. Syme, *Tacitus* (Oxford, 1958), p. 215, n. 4. Koestermann's latest edition (Leipzig, 1969) appends to frag. 6 the observation that "insequentia quoque Orosii verba *Domitianus . . . triumphavit* fortasse quodam modo ad Tacitum referenda sunt."

10. 5–6 Domitian's persecution of the Christians and seeking out the descendants of
          David (from Jerome *Chronicle* p. 192 Helm).
10. 7   The death of Domitian (from Eutropius *Brev.* 7. 23 and Suetonius *Dom.* 17).

4. CONCLUSION

A firm distinction must always be drawn between fragments which preserve
the actual words of a lost work, reports of its contents, and traces of it
surviving in later writers. When this distinction is applied to Tacitus'
Histories, the standard collection of eight *fragmenta "Historiarum"* shrinks
to a single fragment in the narrow sense.

Of the standard eight "fragments," only one (frag. 4) preserves Tacitus'
original text unchanged. At the other extreme, one (frag. 3) appears to derive
from an extant passage. The remaining six adapt Tacitus or reproduce only
the substance of what he wrote. But there are other passages, too, which
probably preserve Tacitean material from the lost portion of the *Histories*
in exactly the same way, viz., Orosius *Hist. adv. pag.* 6. 22. 1–2, 7. 9. 8–9,
and the rest of 7. 10. 3–4.[28] Editors of Tacitus who wish to print *fragmenta
"Historiarum"* have a clear duty to do justice to the true complexity of the
facts.

University of Toronto

---

28. The name Diurpaneus (Orosius *Hist. adv. pag.* 7. 10. 4) recurs (perhaps in a corrupt form) in
Jordanes *Get.* 76–78. This passage has been printed as a fragment of Dio of Prusa's lost *Getica* by
H. F. A. von Arnim, in his edition of Dio, vol. 2 (Berlin, 1896), p. ix, and by F. Jacoby, *FGrHist* 707,
Anhang F 5. There is an outside chance that it, too, might ultimately derive, if only in part, from
Tacitus.

Reprinted from Classical Philology *vol. 72 (1977), 224-31,
by permission of The University of Chicago Press.*
© *1977 by The University of Chicago*

XVI

Two Speeches by Eusebius

SOME MANUSCRIPTS of Eusebius' *Life of Constantine* contain not only the four books of the *Life* and Constantine's *Speech to the Assembly of the Saints* but also two speeches which are conventionally known by a single title as *Laus Constantini, Laudes Constantini, De laudibus Constantini*, or the "Tricennial Oration," and which all editors of Eusebius so far have published as a single work.[1] That the two speeches are in fact separate compositions ought to be clear, and some obvious differences between the first ten chapters in the traditional numeration and the last eight were stated long ago.[2] Nevertheless, some scholars still continue to treat the whole as a single speech,[3] so that it will be necessary to preface a discussion of the dates of the two speeches by restating the decisive arguments for dividing the text into two halves.

Both external attestation and internal criteria point to two separate and distinct works. First, all three primary manuscripts have traces of a break between chapters 10 and 11, and the most reliable of them explicitly marks the two parts as bearing distinct titles (*viz.*, "τριακονταετηρικός" and "βασιλικός" respectively).[4] Second, each part constitutes a logical and stylistic unity, which differs from the other in tone and purpose.[5] The first ten chapters are a panegyric addressed to Constantine in his presence (1.1), with a formal preface and an easily recognisable conclusion (10.7).[6] The last eight chapters, in contrast, read like a sermon on a solemn occasion: they justify Constantine's building of churches, particularly his building of the Church of

---

[1] The most recent edition is that of I. A. Heikel, *Eusebius Werke* 1 (*GCS* 7, 1902) 195–259. Although he prints a continuous text, not even marking a lacuna between 10 and 11, he argues in his introduction that "eine neue Schrift" begins with ch.11 (*ibid.* civ–cvi).

[2] P. Wendland, *BPW* 22 (1902) 232f (reviewing Heikel); E. Schwartz, *RE* 6 (1909) 1428f.

[3] So, recently, S. Calderone, *Le Culte des souverains dans l'empire romain* (*Entretiens Hardt* 19, 1973) 220.

[4] Heikel, *op.cit.* (*supra* n.1), on 223.22, 259.29, *cf.* on 196.14.

[5] H. A. Drake, *In Praise of Constantine: A Historical Study and New Translation of Eusebius' Tricennial Orations* (*University of California Publications*, Classical Studies 15, 1976) 31ff.

[6] Eusebius looks forward to Constantine's reception into heaven—a Christian version of the traditional closing prayer for an emperor's longevity, *cf. AJP* 96 (1975) 444.

the Holy Sepulchre, repeat many well-worn apologetical arguments
in favour of Christianity, and advance an interpretation of human
history as culminating in the Christian Empire (11–18). Thirdly, the
two parts present themselves as delivered in different places: the
panegyric was delivered in the imperial palace (*praef.* 4), with Constantine and the Caesar Constantius present (1.1; 3.4, *cf.* VC 4.49), while
the eleventh chapter, despite its invocations of Constantine in the
second person (11.1; 11.7; *cf.* 18.1), refers to Jerusalem as πόλεως τῆςδε
(11.2)—which implies that Eusebius was speaking in that city. Moreover, a passage towards the end of the whole refers back to a sentence
in chapter 11 as occurring "at the start of the speech" (16.9, *cf.* 11.4).
The traditional designation, therefore, embraces two quite separate
works: the preface and chapters 1–10 are a panegyric on Constantine,
chapters 11–18 a treatise on the Church of the Holy Sepulchre.

Both panegyric and treatise can be dated precisely by reference to
external events. Constantine celebrated his *tricennalia* for a full year,
with the principal festivities occurring on 25 July 335 and 25 July 336
(*Chr.min.* 1.235). The extant panegyric genuinely deserves the title
Laudes Constantini or "Tricennial Oration," for it is the speech in
honour of Constantine's *tricennalia* which Eusebius promised to
append to his *Life* (VC 4.46). Although some scholars have dated it to
25 July 335,[7] or even to early September 335,[8] Eusebius alludes to the
Caesar Dalmatius, who was raised to the purple on 18 September 335
(3.4, *cf.* *Chr.min.* 1.235). Since, moreover, Eusebius delivered the
speech on an occasion when Constantine was also praised by other
panegyrists (*praef.*), and in Constantinople (1.1; VC 4.46), the correct
date must be 25 July 336.[9] The treatise, however, was composed for
the dedication of the Church of the Holy Sepulchre in Jerusalem,
which was solemnly inaugurated by a council of bishops on 13 September 335.[10] Hence it is chronologically impossible to argue (as
several scholars have done)[11] that Eusebius composed the treatise

---

[7] A. Harnack, *Chronologie der altchristlichen Litteratur bis Eusebius* II (Leipzig 1904) 117;
J. Quasten, *Patrology* III (Utrecht and Westminster [Md.] 1960) 326; B. Altaner and A.
Stuiber, *Patrologie*[7] (Freiburg 1966) 220.

[8] A. Piganiol, *L'Empire chrétien* (Paris 1947) 82 n.62; Calderone, *op.cit.* (*supra* n.3) 220 n.1.

[9] H. A. Drake, *Historia* 24 (1975) 345ff.

[10] For the very varied evidence attesting the date, see A. Bludau, *Die Pilgerreise der
Aetheria* (*Studien zur Geschichte und Kultur des Altertums* 15.1–2, 1927) 185ff; P. Peeters,
Bulletin de l'Académie royale de Belgique, Classe des Lettres 30 (1944) 167 n.1.

[11] Thus Calderone, *op.cit.* (*supra* n.3) 220 n.1.

for the ceremonies in Jerusalem in September 335 and later combined it with the already written panegyric to form a single speech which he delivered in Constantinople in the late autumn of that year. If the panegyric belongs to 336, then the treatise is not only a separate work, but earlier in date.

The hypothesis that chapters 11–18 of the *Laudes Constantini* were delivered twice represents an attempt to solve a dilemma which Eusebius' own references to orations about the Church of the Holy Sepulchre appear to impose. The *Life of Constantine* mentions a speech or speeches which its author composed on this church in three passages. In the first, Eusebius states that he delivered a speech "about the monument of our salvation" in the imperial palace and that Constantine insisted on standing throughout its delivery (4.33). Second, a passage which is partly corrupt in the manuscripts alludes to a speech which Eusebius gave in Jerusalem when the Church of the Holy Sepulchre was dedicated in September 335 (4.45.3). As printed by the most recent and most careful editor, it reads as follows:

> ἔνθα δὴ καὶ ἡμεῖς τῶν ὑπὲρ ἡμᾶς ἀγαθῶν ἠξιωμένοι ποικίλαις ταῖς εἰς τὸ κοινὸν διαλέξεσι τὴν ἑορτὴν ἐτιμῶμεν, τοτὲ μὲν τῶν βασιλεῖ πεφιλοσοφημένων τὰς ἐκφράσεις ποιούμενοι, τοτὲ δὲ καιρίους καὶ τοῖς προκειμένοις συμβόλοις τὰς προφητικὰς ἑρμηνεύοντες θεωρίας.[12]

The third passage (4.46.1) immediately follows that quoted, and in it Eusebius describes briefly a speech which he intends to append to the *Life* in the appropriate place:

> οἷος δ' ὁ τοῦ σωτῆρος νεώς, οἷον τὸ σωτήριον ἄντρον, οἷαί τε αἱ βασιλέως φιλοκαλίαι ἀναθημάτων τε πλήθη ἐν χρυσῷ τε καὶ ἀργύρῳ καὶ λίθοις τιμίοις πεποιημένων, κατὰ δύναμιν ἐν οἰκείῳ συγγράμματι παραδόντες αὐτῷ βασιλεῖ προσεφωνήσαμεν.

It has been assumed that all three passages allude to the same speech: hence it seems natural to combine the second and third passages, which are almost consecutive, and to deduce from them that Eusebius presented the speech of September 335 a second time, before the

[12] F. Winkelmann, *Eusebius Werke* I.1² (GCS, 1975) 139. The main textual variants are these: (1) Winkelmann, following Heikel, deletes διὰ γράμματος after τοτὲ μέν; (2) πεφιλοσοφημένων V πεφιλοκαλημένων J N A B; (3) ποιούμενοι and ἑρμηνεύοντες have been transposed—an emendation whose necessity Valesius had detected.

emperor, when he came to Constantinople in November of that year.[13] Yet the contents of the speech which Eusebius states that he delivered before Constantine do not match the extant speech, since this lacks any physical description of the site or buildings. From the contradiction one of two unwelcome corollaries appears inevitably to follow. Either identity of the two orations must be sustained by the hypothesis that Eusebius removed the description when he gave the speech a second time,[14] or the speech to which Eusebius alludes must be different from the speech which survives.[15] But Eusebius does not explicitly say that the speech which he delivered in Constantinople was the same as he had spoken in Jerusalem, and the juxtaposition of the two references need not imply identity. If the speeches of September and November 335 were in fact different, then all the evidence falls neatly into place.

The speech which Constantine heard standing is clearly the speech of November 335, since the panegyric of 25 July 336 was only the second occasion on which Eusebius glorified God in the imperial palace (*VC* 4.46). But the speech of September differed in content from the one which he delivered before the emperor: it did not describe the site, the building or the emperor's dedications in gold, silver and precious stones, but dealt with the philosophical assumptions from which Constantine's actions proceeded and their theological explanation. Now the content of the extant speech corresponds, not to the speech which Eusebius delivered before the emperor and which he promises to append to the *Life*, but to the one which he affirms that he delivered in Jerusalem. Moreover, the extant speech was in fact delivered in Jerusalem (11.2), and its invocations of Constantine in the second person need not imply that it was ever spoken in his presence.[16]

On the available evidence, it should thus be concluded that the

---

[13] So, recently, F. Millar, *The Emperor in the Roman World* (31 B.C.–A.D. 337) (London 1977) 607.

[14] Drake, *op.cit.* (*supra* n.5) 44f. The phrase φέρε δή at the very beginning of 11 does not (as Drake urges) suffice to prove that something has been omitted: for apparently resumptive beginnings to speeches, *cf.* Euseb. *C.Hier.* 1; Themist. *Or.* 24.1 (ἀλλὰ καί); 25.1 (ἀλλ' εἰ); Julian. *Or.* 8 (ἀλλά); Liban. *Or.* 25.1 (τὼ δὲ ὀνόματε τούτω).

[15] I. A. Heikel, *Kritische Beiträge zu den Constantin-Schriften des Eusebius* (*Eusebius Werke* I) (*Texte u. Untersuchungen* 36.4, 1911) 81ff.

[16] For similar invocations of an absent emperor, note *Pan.Lat.* 4 (10) 3.1; Themist. *Or.* 13, *cf.* HSCP 79 (1975) 329; Liban. *Or.* 19; 20, *cf.* A. F. Norman, *Libanius' Autobiography* (*Oration I*) (London 1965) 222.

speech which survives is the speech which Eusebius delivered in September 335. Why this has been preserved, and not the speech promised in the *Life*, can readily be explained. Eusebius died with his *Life of Constantine* unfinished.[17] The man who added the chapter-headings and published it knew Eusebius' intentions and attempted to put them into effect. But Eusebius had left two speeches on the Church of the Holy Sepulchre, and his literary executor unfortunately appended the wrong one.

UNIVERSITY OF TORONTO
October, 1977

---

[17] G. Pasquali, *Hermes* 45 (1910) 386; Winkelmann, *op.cit.* (*supra* n.12) lvii.

A Correspondent of Iamblichus

THE CORRESPONDENCE of the emperor Julian, as transmitted in various manuscripts, includes six letters addressed to the philosopher Iamblichus (*Epp.* 181, 183–187 Bidez–Cumont).[1] Since Iamblichus died before Julian was born, it is impossible that the emperor could ever have written to the philosopher. On the other hand, the letters do not read like the productions of a deliberate forger, nor do they simulate an emperor's authorship. On internal criteria, one would naturally interpret them as letters from an absent pupil to his former teacher. Accordingly, Franz Cumont argued that these six letters, together with another two (*Epp.* 180, 182) and possibly another ten (*Epp.* 188–197), are genuine letters, which were mistakenly attributed to the emperor Julian because their real author was Julianus of Caesarea, otherwise known as a sophist active in Athens in the early fourth century.[2] Joseph Bidez subsequently amplified Cumont's arguments into a study of Iamblichus and his circle which remains, after more than fifty years, the standard account of the philosopher's life.[3]

The central thesis of Cumont and Bidez seems as secure as the nature of the case admits, but their deductions from it need some important modifications. First, as Bidez and Cumont later realised, a sophist from Caesarea in Cappadocia (*Suda I* 435) cannot be supposed to have written these letters,[4] for one of the letters to Iamblichus states that writer and recipient share the same fatherland (*Ep.* 183, 448B): that must mean at least that both are Syrians. On the available evidence, therefore, the correspondent of Iamblichus should be left

---

[1] J. Bidez and F. Cumont, *Iuliani Imperatoris Epistulae et Leges* (Paris and London 1922) 238–55 [hereafter, BIDEZ AND CUMONT]. In W. C. Wright's Loeb edition, these six letters bear the numbers 76–78, 75, 74, 79.

[2] F. Cumont, *Sur l'authenticité de quelques lettres de Julien* (Université de Gand *Travaux* 3, 1889) 12ff.

[3] J. Bidez, "Le philosophe Jamblique et son école," *REG* 32 (1919) 29–40.

[4] Bidez and Cumont 228.

100 A CORRESPONDENT OF IAMBLICHUS

anonymous.[5] Second, and more serious, Bidez and Cumont misinterpreted the one historical allusion in these letters which can be identified and dated with confidence (*Ep.* 181, 449A). As a result, they located the correspondent of Iamblichus at the wrong imperial court: on their interpretation he was with Constantine,[6] whereas in reality he was with Licinius when this emperor fought against Constantine. Similarly, and on the basis of the interpretation and chronology of Bidez and Cumont, a recent account of the career of Sopater uses *Epp.* 184 and 185 as alluding to Constantine in Nicomedia and Constantinople.[7] It will be salutary to examine closely what the letters really disclose about Iamblichus and his former pupil.

I

In *Ep.* 181 (448D–50A), Iamblichus' friend reports his escape from a series of dangers. The worst which he has suffered is the long separation from Iamblichus, even though he has endured καὶ πολέμων θορύβους καὶ πολιορκίας ἀνάγκην καὶ φυγῆς πλάνην καὶ φόβους παντοίους, ἔτι δὲ καὶ χειμώνων ὑπερβολὰς καὶ νόσων κινδύνους καὶ τὰς ἐκ Παννονίας τῆς ἄνω μέχρι τοῦ κατὰ τὸν Καλχηδόνιον πορθμὸν διάπλου μυρίας δὴ καὶ πολυτρόπους συμφοράς...

Cumont and Bidez proposed to connect these adventures with the Sarmatian invasion of A.D. 323, while W. C. Wright argued that the writer accompanied Constantine in his campaign against Licinius in the following year.[8] Neither proposal will fit the indications of the text. If the writer complains of enduring "the necessity of a siege and the wandering of flight," that implies that he was besieged himself

---

[5] The letters may have been ascribed to the emperor Julian because of his known interest in Iamblichus, cf. J. and J. C. Balty, *Dialogues d'histoire ancienne* I (*Annales littéraires de l'Université de Besançon* 166, 1974) 288.

[6] Bidez and Cumont 228. In his article of 1919, however, Bidez had argued that Iamblichus sent Sopater to the court of Licinius to intervene in support of 'Hellenism' (*op.cit.* [*supra* n.3] 35, citing *Epp.* 184, 192).

[7] *PLRE* I (1971) 846 "Sopater" 1: "He visited Constantine's court Eun. *V.Soph.* 6.2.1, probably at Nicomedia Ps.-Iul. *Ep.* 184 (*c.a.* 327) and in Constantinople Ps.-Iul. *Ep.* 185 (?*a.* 327/8)." The entry for Iamblichus himself, with predictable inconsistency, dates his death *ca* 325 (*PLRE* I 450–51).

[8] Cumont, *op.cit.* (*supra* n.2) 24; J. Bidez, *L'Empereur Julien: Oeuvres complètes* I.2: *Lettres et fragments* (Budé, Paris 1924; repr. 1960) 235; W. C. Wright, *The Works of the Emperor Julian* III (LCL, London/New York 1923) 244 n.1; 254 n.1. In their joint edition Bidez and Cumont (228) appear to accept the later date, for they state that the writer came with Constantine from Pannonia to Chalcedon.

and then fled from a beleaguered or captured city, not that he was the camp-follower of a victorious army which besieged and captured others. Moreover, Constantine began the campaign of 324 from Thessalonica,[9] and there was no fighting in or near Upper Pannonia, which lay far to the west of the boundary between his and Licinius' territory. Nor would the Sarmatian invasion of 323 have compelled anyone to flee from Upper Pannonia to Asia Minor. On the contrary, since the invaders crossed the lower Danube (while Constantine sallied forth to meet them from Thessalonica and fought at Campona, Margus and Bononia),[10] such a journey would in fact have been more difficult in 323 than at almost any other time in the early fourth century.

One occasion, and one only, appears to provide all that the text demands: battles, a siege, flight, bad weather and a journey from Upper Pannonia to the Straits of Chalcedon. That is the first war between Constantine and Licinius in 316/7.[11] The first battle was fought at Cibalae on 8 October 316. The defeated Licinius fled to Sirmium and thence to Hadrianople. After negotiations failed, battle was joined again at the Campus Ardiensis. Again defeated, Licinius withdrew, not in the obvious direction towards Byzantium but obliquely towards Beroea. Constantine advanced incautiously, found his lines of communication broken and was compelled to agree to a negotiated peace, apparently in late January 317. These events provide a background against which the allusions in the letter make perfect sense. Iamblichus' friend was in Upper Pannonia when war broke out, and he attempted to escape to the East. On the way he was overtaken by Constantine's army and besieged for a time, perhaps in Sirmium or Serdica, but he gained safety when he reached the Bosporus and crossed into Asia Minor.

A letter written more than two years later (*Ep.* 184, 416D–17B) describes the occasion of the writing of the earlier letter as well as Iamblichus' reaction to the news of his friend's escape: Ἦλθον ἐκ Παννονίας ἤδη τρίτον ἔτος τουτί, μόλις ἀφ᾽ ὧν οἶσθα κινδύνων καὶ πόνων ϲωθείϲ. ὑπερβὰϲ δὲ τὸν Καλχηδόνιον πορθμὸν καὶ ἐπιϲτὰϲ τῇ Νικομήδους

[9] Zos. 2.22.1–3, cf. *Cod.Theod.* 13.5.4 (8 March 324); 2.17.1 (9 April 324, cf. O. Seeck, *Regesten der Kaiser und Päpste für die Jahre 311 bis 476 n. Chr.* [Stuttgart 1919] 61, 173).

[10] Zos. 2.21; *Origo Constantini Imperatoris* 21 (*vastata Thracia et Moesia*); Publilius Optatianus Porfyrius, *Carm.* 6.18ff, cf. *ZPE* 20 (1976) 152.

[11] On the date (not 314), *JRS* 63 (1973) 36ff. The summary of the course of the war is based on *Origo* 15–19.

πόλει, coì πρώτῳ καθάπερ πατρίῳ θεῷ τὰ πρωτόλεια τῶν ἐμαυτοῦ cώcτρων
ἀπέδωκα, cύμβολον τῆc ἀφίξεωc τῆc ἐμῆc οἷον ἀντ' ἀναθήματοc ἱεροῦ τὴν
εἰc cὲ πρόcρηcιν ἐκπέμπων. καὶ ἦν ὁ κομίζων τὰ γράμματα τῶν βαcιλείων
ὑπαcπιcτῶν εἷc, Ἰουλιανὸc ὄνομα, Βακχύλου παῖc, Ἀπαμεὺc τὸ γένοc, ᾧ
διὰ τοῦτο μάλιcτα τὴν ἐπιcτολὴν ἐνεχείριζον, ὅτι καὶ πρὸc ὑμᾶc ἥξειν καὶ
cε ἀκριβῶc εἰδέναι καθυπιcχνεῖτο. If a member of the emperor's body-
guard took that letter from Nicomedia to Syria, then at least two
deductions seem permissible: first, that the war of 316/7 had ended
and hence that the letter was written no earlier than February 317;
second, that the emperor Licinius had already begun to reside in
Nicomedia, which is attested as his residence from ca 318,[12] as early as
the spring of 317. The two letters, therefore, may be dated to spring
317 (181) and to 319 (184).

II

Bidez and Cumont argued that *Ep.* 181 must be the earliest of the
extant letters to Iamblichus, and hence they dated *Ep.* 185 later than
Ep. 184 because *Ep.* 184 complains of Iamblichus' failure to write
more than a single, reproachful letter since the time he congratulated
his friend on his arrival in Nicomedia more than two years before
(417c–18b).[13] It then followed from their dating of *Ep.* 181 to 323 or
324 that Iamblichus was still alive in or after 325.[14] If correct, the date
would be significant, for Eunapius reports that it was only after
Iamblichus' death that his favourite pupil Sopater betook himself to
the court of Constantine (*Vit.phil.* 6.2.1, p.462). But there is no internal
reason for dating *Epp.* 185 later than 184: the letters themselves
prove only that it cannot have been written between *Ep.* 181 and 184.
Moreover, the chronology of Cumont and Bidez entails a contradiction in the evidence: they argued that *Ep.* 185 shows Sopater at the
court of Constantine in Iamblichus' lifetime, whereas Eunapius states
categorically that he went there after his teacher died.

Now Sopater was with the correspondent of Iamblichus in Thrace
(*Ep.* 185, 439c). But his references to Thrace will suit residence at the
court of Licinius at least as well as they will support the allusion detected by Bidez and Cumont. The writer commences the letter with

[11] Socr. HE 1.6.33; Soz. HE 4.16.6.
[13] Bidez and Cumont 237: "haec epistula...manifesto prima est earum quas Iamblicho
se misisse refert (sc. scriptor)." In support, they cite only the passage of *Ep.* 184 quoted
above. Similarly, Bidez in the Budé edition (*supra* n.8) 236.
[14] Bidez, *op.cit.* (*supra* n.3) 32, deduced that Iamblichus died ca 325/6.

a complaint (*Ep.* 185, 438D–39A): ᾿Ω Ζεῦ, πῶς ἔχει καλῶς ἡμᾶς μὲν ἐν
Θρᾴκῃ διάγειν μέςῃ καὶ τοῖς ἐνταῦθα ςιροῖς ἐγχειμάζειν, παρ᾿ Ἰαμβλίχου
δὲ τοῦ καλοῦ καθάπερ ἑῴου τινὸς ἔαρος ἡμῖν τὰς ἐπιστολὰς ἀντὶ χελιδόνων
πέμπεςθαι, καὶ μήτε ἡμῖν εἶναι μηδέπω παρ᾿ αὐτὸν ἐλθεῖν, μήτ᾿ αὐτῷ παρ᾿
ἡμᾶς ἥκειν ἐξεῖναι; τίς ἂν ἑκὼν εἶναι ταῦτα δέξαιτο, ἐὰν μὴ Θρᾷξ τις ᾖ
καὶ Τηρέως ἀντάξιος; The words "in the middle of Thrace" surely
imply that the noun is here used in a wide, generic sense, not to
denote the small contemporary Roman province of Thracia (in which
Byzantium lay). They are entirely appropriate for a man writing
from the court of Licinius between 308 and 316: at this period the
emperor resided principally on or near the Danube, at Sirmium and
elsewhere.[15] An imperial palace has recently been discovered near
the ancient Naissus which apparently belonged to a pagan emperor of
the early fourth century and was suddenly abandoned: either that or
Serdica could be described as lying "in the middle of Thrace."[16]

III

Epp. 186 and 187 are connected to each other, for the second alludes
to extravagant compliments which Iamblichus has bestowed on his
friend (405C τῶν γε μὴν παλαιῶν καὶ coφῶν ἀνδρῶν, οἷς ἡμᾶς ἐγκρίνειν
ἐθέλεις παίζων), and these can readily be construed as comments on
the speech which accompanied the first letter (421C προςοῦ δὴ καὶ
αὐτὸς τὸν λόγον εὐμενεῖ νεύματι).[17] Moreover, the whole tenor of the
first letter indicates that this speech should be the first which
Iamblichus' friend has composed since he left him (esp. 420D–21A:
ἡμᾶς δὲ ἔδει μέν, ὡς ἔφην, εἴςω τῶν οἰκείων ὅρων ἑςτάναι καὶ τῆς ὑπὸ coῦ
μουςικῆς ἐμφορουμένους ἠρεμεῖν, ὥςπερ οἳ τὴν Ἀπόλλωνος μαντείαν ἐξ
ἀδύτων ἱερῶν προϊούςαν ἡςυχῇ δέχονται).

The date and occasion are hard to deduce from the description
given: πρῶτόν coι τῶν λόγων, οὓς βαςιλεῖ κελεύςαντι πρὸς τὴν ἀοίδιμον τοῦ
πορθμοῦ ζεῦξιν ἔναγχος ἐξειργαςάμεθα, ἐπειδὴ τοῦτό ἐςτι τὸ δοκοῦν,
ἀπαρξώμεθα. Bidez and Cumont conjectured τοῦ ποταμοῦ and detected
an allusion to the bridge which Constantine built over the Danube in
328.[18] More convincingly perhaps, Wright identified the speeches as

---

[15] For Sirmium, *Origo* 8, 16–17; *CIL* III 10107.
[16] *Illustrated London News*, October 1975, 97–99.
[17] Bidez, *op.cit.* (*supra* n.8) 238f.
[18] Bidez and Cumont on 252.2. For the bridge, *RIC* 7.331, Rome 298; Victor, *Caes.* 41.18;
Epit. de Caes. 41.14; *Chr.Pasch.* 525 Bonn (=*Chr.min.* 1.233).

ones "on the stock theme of Xerxes and the Hellespont."[19] If that is correct, then the speech might have been delivered when or shortly after Licinius crossed from Asia Minor into Europe. Since Licinius was in Antioch in autumn 313 (Euseb. *HE* 9.11.6) and appears to have returned to the Danubian frontier before the end of 315,[20] the writer might have attached himself to Licinius' court when he was in Syria in 313 or 314 and accompanied him westwards.

IV

The chronological conclusions argued so far can easily be summarised: the earliest of the six letters to Iamblichus are *Epp.* 186 and 187, which can be dated to 314/5 by a very speculative argument; *Ep.* 185 is later than 186 and 187, but was written before October 316; *Ep.* 181 was written *ca* March 317 and *Ep.* 184 more than two years later, in 319. The historical implications of this chronology are important, for the letters to Iamblichus become contemporary evidence for the ethos of Licinius' court and can shed new light on the obscure career of the philosopher.

Iamblichus was born before 250, since he had a son who was already married by 300 (Porph. *V.Plot.* 9.3–5).[21] His death was traditionally placed *ca* 330 for two reasons: the *Suda* states that he flourished in the reign of Constantine (*I* 27), while Eunapius reports that Sopater went to the court of Constantine and attained influence there only after Iamblichus died.[22] When Bidez rejected the traditional date of *ca* 330 in favour of *ca* 325, he argued from his own chronology of the letters, according to which *Ep.* 187 implies that Iamblichus was already far advanced in age *ca* 325 (407AB).[23] If the arguments advanced above are valid, the letter which refers to Iamblichus' extreme old age need be no later than 314/5, and the latest datable evidence that the philosopher was still among the living belongs to 319 (*Ep.* 184).

[19] Wright, *op.cit.* (*supra* n.8) 238 n.2.

[20] *ILS* 8938 indirectly attests his presence at Tropaeum Traiani between 314 and 316, and a Danubian campaign in 314 or 315 may be deduced from *ILS* 8942 and 696, *cf. ZPE* 20 (1976) 154.

[21] A. Cameron, "The Date of Iamblichus' Birth," *Hermes* 96 (1968) 374–76.

[22] G. Mau, *RE* 9 (1916) 645.

[23] Bidez, *op.cit.* (*supra* n.3) 32. His date for Iamblichus' death is accepted by A. C. Lloyd, *Cambridge History of Later Greek and Early Medieval Philosophy* (London 1967) 295 ("about 326"); E. R. Dodds, *OCD*[2] (1970) 538; *PLRE* I 450–51; B. D. Larsen, *Jamblique de Chalcis. Exégète et philosophe* (Aarhus 1972) 34 (*ca* 325).

The letters show that Iamblichus was teaching in Apamea (esp. *Ep.* 184, 418A), and Libanius later refers to his activity there (*Orat.* 52.31; cf. *Ep.* 1447 Wolff = 1389 Foerster). But Malalas states that he taught in Antioch under Galerius (312.11–12 Bonn): ἐπὶ δὲ τῆς αὐτοῦ βασιλείας Ἰάμβλιχος ὁ φιλόσοφος ἐδίδασκεν, οἰκῶν ἐν Δάφνῃ ἕως τῆς τελευτῆς αὐτοῦ. Bidez did not consider this notice worthy of attention, and it is definitely untrue that Iamblichus lived at Daphne until his death. But Malalas is often well-informed on local matters concerning Antioch,[24] and neither the letters nor any other evidence excludes the possibility that Iamblichus taught in Antioch between 293 and 311—or that he lived there until the death of Galerius in 311 or of Maximinus in 313. Iamblichus had previously studied with Porphyry (Eunap. *Vit.phil.* 5.1.3, p.458), presumably in Rome, but it is not known when he left Porphyry and returned to the East.[25] It is quite possible, therefore, that Iamblichus taught in Antioch in the 290's.[26] It is also possible that he deliberately withdrew to the philosophical centre of Apamea about the time that persecution of the Christians commenced[27]— perhaps in order to avoid any direct political involvement.[28]

From Apamea Iamblichus sent his friends and pupils to a pagan court. His anonymous correspondent seems to have resided at the court of Licinius both before and after the war of 316/7, and Iamblichus

[24] A. Schenk von Stauffenberg, *Die römische Kaisergeschichte bei Malalas* (Stuttgart 1931) 407, argues that the notice derives from the 'Stadtannalen' of Antioch: he is followed by G. Downey, *A History of Antioch in Syria* (Princeton 1961) 332.

[25] On the relationship between Iamblichus and Porphyry, see H. D. Saffrey, "Abamon, pseudonyme de Jamblique," in *Philomathes. Studies and Essays in the Humanities in memory of P. Merlan* (The Hague 1971) 227–39. On one important point, Saffrey's conclusions are incompatible with those argued here. On his showing (p.231), Iamblichus resided in Apamea before he taught in Antioch. But Iamblichus was still in Apamea when *Ep.* 184 was written: if the date is 319 (as argued above), that would entail the improbable corollary that he started to teach in Antioch at the age of seventy.

[26] Cameron, *op.cit.* (*supra* n.21) 375, states, without documentation, that Iamblichus left Rome "after Porphyry's death *ca* 303." For indications in his writings that Iamblichus left Porphyry long before the latter's death and was in Syria in the 290's, see J. Dillon, *Iamblichi Chalcidensis in Platonis Dialogos Commentariorum Fragmenta* (*Philosophia Antiqua* 23, 1973) 9ff. It has been proposed that, between leaving Porphyry and establishing himself in Syria, Iamblichus spent more than a decade in Alexandria: B. D. Larsen, "La place de Jamblique dans la philosophie antique tardive," in *Entretiens Hardt* 21 (Vandœuvres-Genève 1975) 4.

[27] For philosophy at Apamea, see Saffrey, *op.cit.* (*supra* n.25) 231; J. Dillon, *The Middle Platonists. A Study of Platonism 80 B.C. to A.D. 220* (London 1977) 361.

[28] At Nicomedia in 303 a philosopher "who dined better at home than in the imperial palace" recited an anti-Christian pamphlet (Lact. *Div.Inst.* 5.2.2ff). It is tempting to see in him another pupil of Iamblichus—if not the author of the extant letters.

sent Sopater both to Thrace before October 316 and to Nicomedia *ca* 318 (*Epp.* 185, 439BC; 184, 417D). The later prominence of Sopater at the court in Constantinople (Eunap. *Vit.phil.* 6.2.2, 10; Zos. 2.40.3) accordingly gains in significance: despite his Christian policies, Constantine took some care to conciliate, even to cultivate, the pagan intellectuals over whom he ruled. It may be suggested that the quietism of Iamblichus (in contrast to the polemic of Porphyry) permitted his favourite pupil to gain influence at the Christian court and his own ideas to circulate freely in an officially Christian society. But Iamblichus himself did not live (as is still sometimes loosely asserted) "under Constantine."[29] Although his life overlapped Constantine's by almost fifty years, he was probably never his subject. When Constantine became emperor of the eastern provinces of the Roman Empire in 324, Iamblichus was probably already dead: if so, he lived, taught, wrote and died under pagan emperors.[30]

UNIVERSITY OF TORONTO
January, 1978

[29] R. E. Witt, "Iamblichus as a Forerunner of Julian," in *Entretiens Hardt* 21 (Vandœuvres-Genève 1975) 41.

[30] I am grateful to Professor G. W. Bowersock for comment and advice on an earlier version of the present article.

XVIII

EMPEROR AND BISHOPS, A.D. 324–344: SOME PROBLEMS*

The extant ecclesiastical historians of the fifth century present a picture of the reigns of Constantine and his successors which is obviously unrealistic in many details, and sometimes legendary or even fictitious.[1] The principal cause of their ignorance and misapprehensions has been convincingly diagnosed: although each of them adds material from his own knowledge, Rufinus, Socrates, Sozomenus, Theodoretus and Gelasius of Cyzicus all derive their general interpretation and their main narrative from the lost ecclesiastical history of Gelasius of Caesarea.[2] Now Gelasius composed his continuation of Eusebius' *Ecclesiastical History* in the reign of Theodosius,[3] and he wrote from a partisan viewpoint, to justify the triumph of the orthodox party to which he belonged, and perhaps also to controvert the pagan thesis that Christianity had ruined the Roman Empire.[4] Gelasius, therefore, was two generations removed from Constantine, so that the truth often already lay beyond his reach, even had he desired to produce an accurate and dispassionate account of the reign of the first Christian emperor. Moreover, Philostorgius, who stands apart from the dominant tradition of ecclesiastical history and presented a significantly different version of the fourth century, from an Arian perspective, survives only in an epitome and fragments, which, though extremely valuable, are perhaps least helpful for the reign of Constantine himself.[5]

Any attempt to reconstruct either Constantine's ecclesiastical policies or ecclesiastical politics in general during the years in which Constantine ruled the East (324–337) must accordingly discard the narrative of the ecclesiastical historians, and with it the chronology which it implies, and utilise instead evidence which, though it can legitimately be employed, rarely provides a full and unbiassed account of consecutive episodes. The most important category of valid evidence comprises contemporary documents of various types quoted by the ecclesiastical historians themselves and by writers of the fourth century, or preserved in ancient collections of documents.[6] Admittedly, the authenticity of almost all the official documents (imperial pronouncements, letters of officials, bishops, priests and councils) has at some time been impugned.[7] But the challenges have often provoked a cogent defence of genuineness, and virtually all the documents quoted by writers of the fourth and fifth centuries deserve to be accepted as authentic,[8] subject only to the proviso that their precise wording may sometimes have been altered deliberately or corrupted in transmission.[9] Next in value come the surviving polemical and tendentious writings of contemporaries—principally Eusebius' *Life of Constantine* and Athanasius' letters and apologetical works, the most important of which were written about twenty years after Constantine died. Among the other sources of information available may be noted papyri which illuminate the events of 334 and 335 (*P. Lond.* 1913; 1914),[10] and the introduction and headings which a scholarly hand has added to the collected Easter letters written yearly from 329 onwards by Athanasius to the churches of the Egyptian provinces.[11]

The utmost discrimination is needed in assessing the ecclesiastical historians. Although their common narrative of Constantine's reign should be rejected, each of them (with the possible exception of Rufinus) had access to genuine documents and to controversial writings of the fourth century which have not survived. Their reports of such primary evidence can never be neglected, and their knowledge of lost documents and lost works sometimes makes their testimony about specific episodes very valuable.[12]

The lack of a satisfactory ancient narrative account of Constantine's later years renders it difficult in the extreme to produce a historical reconstruction which will win general acceptance from modern scholars, and the present article does not attempt to do so.[13] It seeks rather to lay the foundations for a reconstruction, by applying a realistic evaluation of the sources to some important problems in ecclesiastical history between Constantine's conquest of the East in 324 and the Council of Serdica, whose date is disputed. The task was begun some seventy-five years ago by Eduard Schwartz in his nine papers, 'Zur Geschichte des Athanasius',[14] to which the present article may be regarded as a supplement: the problems discussed are ones which Schwartz either did not discuss explicitly or failed to solve adequately, or where his views require correction. The treatment will inevitably be discursive, even piecemeal: the subject has suffered from too many premature syntheses.

I. Constantine in 324/5

After Constantine defeated and deposed Licinius in September 324, he was confronted with the theological controversies raging in the East. He first attempted to solve the quarrel between Alexander and Arius by sending Ossius of Corduba to Alexandria on a mission of reconciliation (Eusebius, *VC* 2.63):[15] the letter which Ossius carried survives in full (Eusebius, *VC* 2.64-72 = *Urkunden* 17). Ossius predictably failed to reconcile the adversaries (Eusebius, *VC* 2.73): it is known that Ossius then presided over a council of bishops at Alexandria which demoted a certain Colluthus from bishop to priest and declared his ordinations of priests invalid (Athanasius, *Apol. sec.* 74.3-4; 76.3), and it may be inferred that this council also took some action concerning Arius and his followers. Ossius returned from Alexandria to the imperial court by way of Antioch, where he presided over a council, whose synodical letter survives in Syriac (*Urkunden* 18).[16] Ossius' mission and Constantine's letter (*VC* 2.64-72) are conventionally dated to October 324.[17] That date is probably too early. Constantine's letter to Alexander and Arius contains an allusion which, interpreted in conjunction with other evidence, can be argued to prove that the emperor wrote it after visiting Antioch:

πρώην ἐπιστὰς τῇ Νικομηδέων πόλει παραχρῆμα πρὸς τὴν ἑῴαν ἠπειγόμην τῇ γνώμῃ. σπεύδοντι δή μοι ἤδη πρὸς ὑμᾶς καὶ τῷ πλείονι μέρει σὺν ὑμῖν ὄντι ἡ τοῦδε τοῦ πράγματος ἀγγελία πρὸς τὸ

ἔμπαλιν τὸν λογισμὸν ἀνεχαίτισεν, ἵνα μὴ τοῖς ὀφθαλμοῖς ὁρᾶν
ἀναγκασθείην, ἃ μηδὲ ταῖς ἀκοαῖς προσέσθαι δυνατὸν ἡγούμην.
ἀνοίξατε δή μοι λοιπὸν ἐν τῇ καθ᾽ ὑμᾶς ὁμονοίᾳ τῆς ἑῴας τὴν ὁδόν,
ἣν ταῖς πρὸς ἀλλήλους φιλονεικίαις ἀπεκλείσατε.

The passage has been translated in two very different ways:

> Not long since I had visited Nicomedia, and intended forthwith to
> proceed from that city to the East. It was while I was hastening towards
> you, and had already accomplished the greater part of the distance, that
> the news of this matter reversed my plan, that I might not be compelled to
> see with my own eyes that which I felt myself scarcely able even to hear.
> Open then for me henceforward by your unity of judgement that road to
> the regions of the East which your dissensions have closed against me.[18]

> Yesterday when I set foot in Nicomedia, I was pressing immediately to
> the East in my imagination. But as I hastened to you and was all but with
> you, the news of this trouble reined back my purpose, that I might not be
> compelled to see with my eyes what I felt I could not bear to hear with my
> ears. Open to me by your agreement the road to the East, which you have
> closed by your mutual discord.[19]

The second rendering entails that Constantine wrote the letter in Nicomedia,
even when the correct 'recently' is substituted for the mistaken 'yesterday'. But
the first implies that Constantine set out from Nicomedia towards Alexandria,
and accomplished much of the journey before he changed his mind and wrote
the letter. Which version better represents what Constantine originally wrote,
presumably in Latin? External evidence is relevant.

Malalas, whose testimony on such local matters often merits credence,[20]
states that Constantine visited Antioch, apparently implying a date not long
after September 324 (pp. 318/9 Bonn). Now an issue of coins at Antioch,
which must be dated to 324/5 on numismatic grounds, bears the legend
ADVENTVS AVGVSTI N (RIC 7.685, Antioch 48), and two Egyptian papyri
reveal that preparations were being made for an impending imperial visit in
January and in May 325 (P. Oxy. 1261; 1626). Constantine in fact never visited
Egypt, but the expectation of a visit indirectly confirms the statement of
Malalas and the implication of the coins that he visited Antioch in 324/5.[21] It
may also be relevant that the poet Publilius Optatianus Porfyrius, probably
writing in the autumn of 324, appears to allude to Constantine's reception of
Persian ambassadors (Carm. 14.25-27).[22]

The letter to Alexander and Arius surely alludes to this journey: Constantine set out towards Egypt, reached Antioch, and then turned back. Hence the
date of the letter can be deduced from its attested or probable relation to other
events which can be independently dated. Constantine first set foot in
Nicomedia, the capital of his defeated rival Licinius, in late September 324
(Chr. min. 1.232; CIL 1², p. 272; Origo Const. Imp. 27; Socrates, HE 1.4.2;

Zosimus 2.26-28), and it is most improbable that he travelled further east before 8 November, when he founded his new city of Constantinople on the shores of the Bosporus (Themistius, *Orat.* 4,63d; *Chr. min.* 1.232; *CIL* 1², p. 276). The next precise evidence for Constantine's presence in a specific place on a specific day is a law in the *Theodosian Code,* issued, according to the manuscripts, at Nicomedia on 25 February 325 (*CTh* 1.15.1). Unfortunately, the recipient of the law is otherwise unknown and the consular date has certainly been emended, at least in form, so that the subscription cannot be used with complete confidence to show that Constantine was in Nicomedia on that day.[23] The subscription may nevertheless be accepted as consistent with the other ascertainable facts. After Constantine turned back from Antioch, Ossius went to Alexandria, conducted a council of bishops there, returned to Bithynia by way of Antioch, where he convened and presided over another council of bishops from Syria and neighbouring provinces (*Urkunden* 18)—all before the Council of Nicaea opened, probably *c.* 1 June 325.[24] Since Philogonius, the bishop of Antioch, died on 20 December 324,[25] while Ossius convened the council of Antioch precisely to put an end to disorders which followed his decease (*Urkunden* 18.3), it may reasonably be conjectured that Constantine was in Antioch when Philogonius died, and that it was perhaps precisely his death which forced the dispute between Alexander and Arius on his attention. If that is so, Constantine will have written his letter to Alexander and Arius after he left Antioch to return to Nicomedia.

The following approximate chronology may accordingly be proposed:

324	Nov. 8	Constantine founds Constantinople
	Nov.	Constantine travels across Asia Minor
	Dec.	Constantine in Antioch
	Dec. 20	Death of Philogonius
	late Dec.	Constantine leaves Antioch for Bithynia
325	Jan.	Ossius sent to Alexandria
	Feb. 25	Constantine in Nicomedia
	Feb. or March	Ossius presides over a council at Alexandria
	March or April	Ossius in Antioch
	c. June 1	Council of Nicaea begins

II. Constantine at the Council of Nicaea

Many modern writers assume that Constantine automatically presided at the Council of Nicaea, just as he did when conducting routine imperial business.[26] From this initial assumption serious corollaries have sometimes been drawn. Schwartz, for example, boldly asserted that the debates at Nicaea had the form of a dispute in civil law decided by the emperor.[27] Similarly, a recent study with the title 'Emperor's Court and Bishops' Court' argues that the bishops at Nicaea acted as the emperor's *consilium*: Constantine formally presided over the council as he did in his *consilium,* so that the decisions of the Council had the same status as advice given in the *consilium,* which the emperor was free to accept or reject as he pleased.[28] Moreover, if this legal definition were correct, then Constantine was insincere when he repeatedly asserted that decisions of church councils were of divine origin, given by God and as binding as God's laws.[29] The ancient evidence, however, does not sustain the modern assumption. Once the formal opening ceremony is distinguished from the substantive debates, the notion that Constantine presided over the council while it conducted its business becomes completely untenable.

The Council of Nicaea gathered in the audience-hall of the imperial palace, the emperor entered, a small stool was produced and Constantine seated himself, after first requesting permission from the bishops. The bishops then seated themselves and Eusebius of Nicomedia delivered a panegyric to the emperor.[30] Constantine replied briefly, in Latin, with an interpreter translating into Greek, and then gave the floor 'to the leaders of the council' (Eusebius, *VC* 3.10-13.1).

In the actual debates, Ossius presided.[31] That is adequately attested by Athanasius and by the signatures to the Creed. In the lists of subscriptions to the Creed, Ossius' name always stands first, sometimes with the sentence 'I believe as it is written'.[32] And Athanasius asserts both generally that Ossius presided at every council which he attended (*Apol. de Fuga* 5.2) and specifically that he 'put forward the Creed at Nicaea' (*Historia Arianorum* 42.3). Against the background of ancient rules of debate, these facts are decisive. In the Roman Senate and other similar deliberative bodies, proposals from the floor could only be put to the meeting if they were first adopted by the presiding officer and included in his motion. To be sure, the views of an emperor carried very great weight, whatever the technical definition of his standing. But, if Ossius proposed the Creed and signed first, he presided over the debate which preceded its approval.[33]

At Nicaea, not only did Constantine not preside, he was not even technically a member of the council. The decisions were taken by the assembled bishops 'in the presence of the most pious emperor Constantine' (*Urkunden* 23.2). When Constantine asserted that he was at Nicaea with the bishops 'just as if I were one of you', he was writing to congregations of laymen (*Urkunden* 25.2; 26.1): he was present at the Council and participated in the debates (*Urkunden* 27.13; 32.2), but his contribution was to sit in a humble position trying to cool the temperature of debate (*Urkunden* 27.13; Eusebius, *VC* 3.13). His standing at Nicaea, therefore, corresponds to that attested earlier for priests, deacons and laymen at the Council of Iliberris.[34] Nor was Nicaea (it may be noted) the first council of bishops which Constantine attended: Eusebius describes how he attended church councils and sat 'in the middle as if he were one of the crowd'—in a context which must refer primarily to the Council of Arles in 314 (*VC* 1.44.2).[35]

III. Eustathius on the Council of Nicaea

The ecclesiastical historian Theodoretus quotes a passage of Eustathius, in which the bishop of Antioch describes the Council of Nicaea and its aftermath in colorful and difficult language:[36]

(1) From here I shall now turn to what was done. Well then, when because of this a very great synod arrived at Nicaea, with perhaps two hundred and seventy in number having gathered together (I cannot write down the exact figure because of the enormous throng, since I did not at all enquire after it carefully), and when the definition of the faith was being sought, the document was brought forward as manifest proof of the blasphemy of Eusebius.[37] (2) Read in the presence of all, it immediately caused immeasurable offence to those who heard it because of its divergence from the truth, and gave irremediable shame to the writer. (3) When the gang around Eusebius was clearly exposed, the lawless document having been torn up in the sight of all together, certain persons as a result of an intrigue, putting forward the name of peace, reduced to silence all those who normally spoke best. And the Arian madmen, fearing that they might after all perhaps be ostracised, since such a great synod had been gathered in the same place, leapt forward and anathematised the forbidden doctrine, subscribing agreed upon documents with their own hands. (4) And having gained their position as bishops[38] by the utmost dishonesty, although they deserve to be kneeling among the penitents, they advocate the rejected beliefs, sometimes secretly, sometimes openly, plotting against their outstanding critics.[39] So, wishing to make the crops of tares take firm root, they fear men of good sense, corrupt the secular rulers[40] and thus go to war with the heralds of piety. (5) But we do not believe that impious men can ever thus overcome divine power. For even *if they become strong again, they will be defeated again*, as the grave prophet Isaiah says (Is. 8.9) (Theodoretus, *HE* 1.8.1-5 = Eustathius, frag. 32).

Theodoretus does not describe the context of this fragment, except to state that Eustathius was commenting on the Arian proof-text, Proverbs 8.22, 'The Lord created me the beginning of his ways', on which he composed a whole treatise.[41] Although scholars have discussed the passage at some length,[42] the historical allusions which it contains remain problematical and obscure.

Eustathius makes three distinct allusions: to the reading at Nicaea of a document written by Eusebius and its immediate effect (1-2), to the subsequent debate and the acceptance of the Nicene creed by the Arians (3), and to the activities of the Arians after the council (4). To which Eusebius, the bishop of Caesarea or the bishop of Nicomedia, does Eustathius refer? The bishop of Caesarea (it is known) arrived at Nicaea under a provisional ban of excommunication (*Urkunden* 18.14 f.), and he rehabilitated himself by submitting a statement of his beliefs, which Constantine endorsed, provided that Eusebius would also admit that the Son was 'of one substance' with the father (*Urkunden* 22.2 ff.).[43] Eusebius' orthodoxy, therefore, should have been discussed and determined before the council began to seek 'the definition of the faith'. On the other hand, a letter of Eusebius of Nicomedia was certainly read out at the Council (Ambrose, *De Fide* 3.15.125 = *Urkunden* 21). Hence it seems natural to identify Eustathius' target as the bishop of Nicomedia, especially since the phrase 'the gang around Eusebius' seems better suited to the politically more important and more influential Eusebius of Nicomedia.[44]

The allusion to events after 325, however, suggests a doubt. Eustathius was deposed from his see in 327, by a council of bishops over which Eusebius of Caesarea presided, while the bishop of Nicomedia was in exile. The tone and contents of the passage which Theodoretus quotes imply that Eustathius was writing before his deposition: his enemies appear to have accused him before the secular authorities (4), but he is confident that the council of bishops summoned to consider the charges will vindicate him (5). If that is so, then the active Eusebius of Caesarea would be a more appropriate target for Eustathius' invective than his exiled homonym. Moreover, the bishop of Caesarea had given a suspicious exegesis of Proverbs 8.22 on probably more than one occasion (*DE* 5.1.21 ff., cf. *Urkunden* 8.4-6 = Theodoretus, *HE* 1.6.4-6). Hence it is a tenable hypothesis that Eustathius may here allude to the debate over whether Eusebius of Caesarea and others should be excluded from the council as heretics, with which the council must have begun its substantive business. Eusebius himself describes how his orthodoxy was vindicated:

> When this creed was produced by me, there was no occasion for contradiction, but our most pious emperor himself was the first to declare that its contents were most correct. He confessed that he too believed the same, and he encouraged all to agree with it and to subscribe to these very doctrines, with the addition of only the word *homoousios* . . . (*Urkunden* 22.7).

If Eustathius and Eusebius in fact refer to the same episode, it follows that Eustathius must include among those who 'reduced to silence all those who normally spoke best' the emperor who intervened to protect Eusebius.[45]

Neither identification can be conclusively proved. Whichever is correct, however, Eustathius provides valuable evidence for the theological composition of the council. He distinguishes three groups: the Eusebian gang or Arian madmen, the right-minded, and those who 'put forward the name of peace'. That is not necessarily a complete enumeration, for it may exclude a large number of bishops taking a passive part in the Council. According to Athanasius long afterwards, the vast majority of bishops at Nicaea were orthodox, those who sympathized with Arius' views a small, disreputable and ultimately inconstant group of dissidents (*De decretis Nicaenae synodi* 19/20; *Ep. ad Afros* 5/6). The allusions of Eustathius, and the whole course of ecclesiastical politics under Constantine, imply that the majority of eastern bishops in 325, while prepared to condemn some of Arius' opinions, did not regard him as irredeemably heterodox.

IV. Two Councils at Antioch

Eustathius of Antioch was deposed from his see by a council which met at Antioch (Socrates, *HE* 1.24.1 ff.; Sozomenus, *HE* 2.19.1 ff.; Theodoretus, *HE* 1.21.3 ff.). Subsequently, a synod at Antioch invited Eusebius of Caesarea

60

to become bishop of the city (*VC* 3.59-62, with index). Moreover, the canons and subscriptions survive in Latin and Syriac of a council held at Antioch: although the Syriac manuscripts and some of the Latin attribute the canons to the 'dedication-council' of 341,[46] it has long been recognized that so many of the names of the bishops coincide with the Nicene subscriptions that the date must be much closer to 325.[47] There are, therefore, at least three problems: was there one council or two? if two, to which do the canons and subscriptions belong? and what are the absolute dates?

The first of these questions can easily be answered. The letter of Constantine to the council which had offered the see of Antioch to Eusebius invites the bishops to elect Euphronius from Cappadocian Caesarea or George from Laodicea or any other equally worthy person (Eusebius, *VC* 3.62.2-3). Euphronius was duly elected and served as bishop for one year and some months before he died and was succeeded by Flaccillus (Theodoretus, *HE* 1.22.1). But Euphronius was not the immediate successor of Eustathius: there intervened Paulinus of Tyre, for six months, and then Eulalius (Eusebius, *C. Marc.* 1.4.2; Philostorgius, *HE* 3.15; Theodoretus, *HE* 1.22.1). There were, therefore, two councils at Antioch, separated by at least a year.

The other two problems have essentially been solved by H. Chadwick, whose solution requires only a minor modification in detail.[48] Chadwick drew attention to three facts: that Asclepas of Gaza was deposed by a council at Antioch over which Eusebius of Caesarea presided (*CSEL* 65.118.3-6 = Athanasius, *Apol. Sec.* 45.2), that the letter of the eastern bishops at Serdica states that Asclepas 'ante decem et septem annos episcopatus honore discinctus est' (*CSEL* 65.56.19-20), and that one of the charges against Eustathius was of offensive behavior to Helena (Athanasius, *Historia Arianorum* 4.1). Chadwick, therefore, assuming that the Council of Serdica met in 342, attributed the deposition of both Eustathius and Asclepas to a council which met in autumn 326, and he argued that it was this council which issued the extant canons: for the name of Aetius of Lydda, who certainly attended the second council (Eusebius, *VC* 3.62.1), is lacking from the subscriptions (*EOMIA* 2.312-315; Schwartz, *Ges. Schr.* 3.219-221). This reconstruction is convincing, except in one detail: since the Council of Serdica met in the winter of 343/4, the date of the first council should be 327.[49] It may be added that this council probably also deposed other bishops of Syria, Phoenicia and Palestine whom Athanasius names as ejected from their sees—Euphrantion of Balaneae, Cymatius of Paltos, Cymatius of Gabala, Carterius of Antarados and Cyrus of Beroea (Athanasius, *Apol. de Fuga* 3.3; *Hist. Ar.* 5.2).[50]

V. The Council of Nicomedia (327/8)

Eusebius of Nicomedia and Theognis of Nicaea, who had been deposed and exiled in autumn 325 for failing to comply with the Nicene resolutions (*Urkunden* 27, esp. 16), were restored to their sees after they submitted an apology and recantation to a council of bishops (*Urkunden* 31). Hence (so Schwartz and others have argued) a second council met at Nicaea late in 327.[51] Admittedly, this conclusion has sometimes been rejected or pronounced fragile.[52] But it is illegitimate to pronounce the recantation of Eusebius and Theognis spurious merely because it contradicts the narrative sources. The document deserves to be accepted as genuine,[53] and, since the two bishops speak of 'your holy council', it attests a council to which they addressed their petition: the only problem which remains is to establish the date and place of the council.

A series of arguments converges to situate the council at Nicomedia during the winter of 327/8. First, Constantine attended the council in person (*VC* 3.23): his presence is attested at Nicomedia on 30 July 327 and 1 March 328 (*CTh* 12.5.1 Seeck; 14.24.1) and he may well have resided there continuously from summer 327 to spring 328. Second, Constantine summoned Arius to court on 27 November of an unspecified year (*Urkunden* 29), while the council which Eusebius and Theognis address had already rehabilitated Arius (*Urkunden* 31.4). Third, Philostorgius reported that Eusebius and Theognis were restored 'after three years' and in the same context recorded a council at Nicomedia which two hundred and fifty bishops attended (*HE* 2.7; 7ª). Fourth, a problematical passage of Athanasius states that the Melitians were quiescent for less than five months, during which Alexander of Alexandria died (*Apol. sec.* 59.3).[54] Now Alexander died on 17 April 328, and Athanasius was elected bishop on 8 June 328 (Festal Index, preface; *Chr. min.* 1.292; *Historia acephala* 17) in opposition to the Melitians (*Apol. sec.* 6.4-5; 59.3), who elected a counter-bishop of their own (Epiphanius, *Pan.* 68.7.3). On the basis of this evidence, it may reasonably be inferred that the council which rehabilitated Arius, Eusebius and Theognis met in Nicomedia during December 327 or January 328.

VI. Dalmatius the *Censor*

When Athanasius was accused of murder, Constantine wrote to Dalmatius the *censor*, who was then residing in Antioch, instructing him to investigate the charge, and the *censor* then wrote to the bishop of Alexandria (Athanasius, *Apol. sec.* 65.1-2; Socrates, *HE* 1.27.19-21). The letters of Constantine and Dalmatius are regrettably known only by report, but the fact that they styled Dalmatius *censor* helps to date them. A papyrus dated 9 April 333 (*P. Oxy.* 1716) gives the names of the consuls as follows:

ὑπατείας Φλαουίου Δαλματίου ἀ[δ]ελφ[ο]ῦ τοῦ δεσπότου ἡμῶν Κωνσταντίνου Α<ὐγ>ούστου καὶ Δομιτίου Ζηνοφίλου τῶν λαμπροτάτων Φαρμοῦθι ιδ᾽

The description of Dalmatius as Constantine's brother, but not as *censor*, implies that he has not yet acquired the title *censor*.[55] Hence either Athanasius is mistaken in styling Dalmatius *censor* or the letters which he reports were written no earlier than *c*. February 333.[56] Of the two possibilities, the former can be excluded, since Athanasius received a letter from Dalmatius, which he presumably kept for future reference. The title *censor*, though otherwise unknown at this period, is plausible and readily explicable: like the revived title of *patricius* conferred on the consuls of 334 and 335 (Zosimus 2.40.2), it enabled Constantine to confer abnormally high status on his half-brother without admitting him to the imperial college. Constantine's letter to Dalmatius, therefore, cannot belong to 332, as Schwartz believed.[57] The title of *censor* implies a date in 333 or 334.

An apparent discrepancy between Athanasius and the ecclesiastical historians can now be exploited. In his account of his career, Athanasius nowhere mentions explicitly the council of bishops which Constantine summoned to meet at Caesarea in the summer of 334 (Sozomenus, *HE* 2.25.1; Theodoretus, *HE* 1.28, cf. *P. Lond.* 1913). On the other hand, Athanasius speaks of 'the court of the *censor*' in a context conventionally construed as attesting a council at Antioch which is unknown to the ecclesiastical historians (*Apol. sec.* 65.4).[58] The hypothesis may be advanced that Athanasius' 'court of the *censor*' is identical with the attested council of Caesarea. This hypothesis painlessly removes the strange and complementary silences of the different accounts of Athanasius' career, and the misrepresentation has an exact parallel. Athanasius and his allies state categorically that the imperial *comes* Dionysius presided at the Council of Tyre in 335 (*Apol. sec.* 8.3 (a synodical letter of 338); 86.1)—a charge which still takes in the unwary and inaccurate.[59] In this case, however, Athanasius also quotes letters written to and by Dionysius which convict him of lying (*Apol. sec.* 78; 79; 81).

The story of Arsenius now makes perfect sense (*Apol. sec.* 65-69). Athanasius was accused of murdering Arsenius late in 333 or early in 334. The accusation reached Constantine, who instructed Dalmatius to investigate. Dalmatius wrote to Athanasius, who could not at once disprove the charge. Hence Constantine convened the Council of Caesarea, instructing Dalmatius to supervise its conduct. Eusebius of Nicomedia and other bishops from far afield came to Caesarea to condemn and depose their enemy. Before the council convened, however, Athanasius and his allies succeeded in finding Arsenius alive. The bishop of Alexandria informed Constantine, who dissolved the Council ('the court of the *censor*') and bade the bishops to return to their sees.

VII. The First Exile of Athanasius

The index to Athanasius' Festal Letters states that Constantine despatched Athanasius from Constantinople to Gaul on 10 Athyr, i.e. 7 November 335 (Festal Index 8). More than a century ago, G.R. Sievers emended the date to 10 Mechir, i.e. 5 February 336—an emendation which has been widely accepted.[60] In two articles published in 1944 and 1945, however, P. Peeters defended the transmitted date, basing on it a brilliant elucidation of the events preceding Athanasius' departure for Gaul.[61] Unfortunately, these articles are often ignored, as in recent studies of the Council of Tyre and of the activities of Eusebius of Caesarea in 335/6, which advocate theories which Peeters'

analysis of the evidence disproves.[62] His main conclusions, therefore, deserve
to be rescued from an unmerited oblivion.

The index to Athanasius' Festal Letters provides precise and precious
information about Athanasius' movements in the late summer and autumn of
335 (Festal Index 8): he left Alexandria to attend the Council of Tyre on 17
Epeiphi (11 July), he fled from Tyre in an open boat and arrived in Constantinople on 2 Athyr (30 October), was unable to see Constantine until the eighth
day (i.e. 9 Athyr, or 6 November), and departed for exile in Gaul on 10 Athyr (7
November 335). The detail about the open boat or raft (which Schwartz
regrettably failed to understand) is vital: it indicates that Athanasius fled
secretly, using a raft or open boat to escape the probably blockaded harbour of
Tyre.[63] When Athanasius arrived in Constantinople, the emperor chanced to be
absent: a law attests his presence at Nicopolis a week earlier, on 23 October 335
(CJ 1.40.4).[64] Athanasius accosted him in the street as soon as he returned to
the capital (Gelasius of Cyzicus, HE 3.18.4).[65]

The index implicitly distinguishes two audiences with Constantine, on
successive days (6 and 7 November). The first occurred when Athanasius
hailed the emperor as he rode through Constantinople, after which he wrote to
the bishops who had taken part in the Council of Tyre (Athanasius, Apol. sec.
86.2-12 (partially abbreviated) = Gelasius of Cyzicus, HE 3.18.1-13). At the
second audience Athanasius was confronted by a group of six bishops who had
already arrived from Tyre: Athanasius names them as Eusebius of Nicomedia,
Theognis, Patrophilus, Eusebius of Caesarea, Ursacius and Valens, and specifically asserts that only they came, while the rest remained in Palestine (Apol.
sec. 87.1-2). Athanasius' enemies promptly accused him of treason: he lost his
temper with the emperor, who despatched him to Gaul (Athanasius, Apol. sec.
9.1-4; Epiphanius, Pan. 68.9.4-6). To call this 'exile' in the normal sense is
perhaps misleading. For Athanasius was not deposed from his see: he was not
even tried, but sent to Gaul without either condemnation or trial.[66] Hence, when
Constantine died, the Caesar Constantinus was able plausibly to claim that his
father had sent Athanasius to Gaul to save him from his enemies, intending to
restore him to his former position as soon as possible (Apol. sec. 87.4-7).

This reconstruction both does full justice to the primary evidence and
explains why the narrative sources all err in making Athanasius' exile consequent upon his condemnation by the Council of Tyre (Rufinus, HE 10.17-18;
Socrates, HE 1.28-35; Sozomenus, HE 2.25-28; Theodoretus, HE 1.29-31;
Gelasius, HE 3.17-18). Constantine did indeed summon the bishops who took
part in the Council of Tyre to come to Constantinople, and the ecclesiastical
historians knew Athanasius' version of his letter to this effect, though without
realising that the letter implicitly annuls the decisions of the council.[67] But the
summons was overtaken by the course of events: the day after it was written,
Athanasius' enemies accused him of treason before the emperor and secured his
removal, if not from his see, at least from active exercise of his episcopal
functions—and his abrupt departure removed the need for the bishops from
Tyre to reconvene in Constantinople.

VIII. The Deposition of Marcellus

The ecclesiastical historian Socrates dates the deposition of Marcellus of Ancyra to late 335 or early 336 (*HE* 1.35-36). Although Socrates' date has traditionally been accepted, it rests upon the assumption that the council which Constantine summoned on 6 November 335 (Athanasius, *Apol. sec.* 86.2-12 = Gelasius of Cyzicus, *HE* 3.18.1-13) met in Constantinople shortly thereafter.[68] But Constantine's summons proved abortive and the council never met: therefore, the inferred date is invalid.

Can the correct date be established from other evidence? Schwartz discarded the traditional date long ago, on the different but still cogent grounds that Socrates' opinion carries no weight, unless supported by documents: at first he proposed to date Marcellus' deposition to 328, but later pronounced the evidence inconclusive.[69] Similarly, W. Schneemelcher, though regarding 330/1 and 334 as possible, declared the problem almost hopeless.[70] G. Bardy inferred a precise date, but by *a priori* reasoning from a false premiss: he associated the exile of Marcellus with that of Eustathius and dated both to 330.[71] The correct date is summer 336. It can be deduced confidently from a neglected passage in the most obvious of all sources.

Marcellus was deposed from his see by a council held in Constantinople which Constantine attended in person (*CSEL* 65.50-51), and the charges against him included his behaviour during the Councils of Tyre and Jerusalem in late summer 335 (Sozomenus, *HE* 2.33.2).[72] Eusebius of Caesarea took part in the council, and afterwards produced a denunciation of Marcellus in two books. The conclusion of the work alludes to the Council and employs a significant phrase when describing how Constantine convened it (2.4.29):

εἰκότως ἄρα ταῦτα βασιλέα τὸν ὡς ἀληθῶς θεοφιλῆ καὶ τρισμακάριον κατὰ τοῦ ἀνδρὸς ἐκίνει.

The date of writing cannot be 336 (as is normally assumed):[73] the epithets applied to Constantine entail that he was already dead when the *Contra Marcellum* was written:[74] in Eusebius' usage (and Constantine's), the words τρισμακάριος and μακάριος are always used of the dead, never of the living.[75] It follows that Eusebius wrote, or at least completed, the *Contra Marcellum* after he received news of Constantine's death on 22 May 337.

The circumstances of 337 now afford a secure inference from the date of the *Contra Marcellum* to the date of the council. Eusebius was urged to compose the work by his conciliar colleagues and he wished to persuade those who thought that Marcellus had been wronged (2.4.29-30). He was surely writing, therefore, after Constantine's sons had decreed that all exiled bishops should return to their sees (Athanasius, *Hist. Ar.* 8.1), but perhaps before Marcellus had resumed effective possession of his bishopric. The request from the bishops who took part in the council and the stated need to justify their decision imply a very recent date for the council: hence it will have met in the summer of 336, when Constantine celebrated his *tricennalia* in Constantinople, with Eusebius delivering a panegyric on 25 July in his presence.[76] The council at Constantinople, which deposed Marcellus of Ancyra, will have met shortly before 25 July 336.[77]

IX. Athanasius and Constantius

In his *Apologia ad Constantium*, Athanasius recalls that he met the emperor for the first time in Viminacium, for the second at Caesarea in Cappadocia, and for the third in Antioch (5). The third meeting occurred some time after the Council of Serdica, when Nestorius was prefect of Egypt, and shortly before Athanasius returned to Alexandria from his second exile (*Apol. sec.* 54.1, cf. 51.1; 57.1). Since Athanasius entered Alexandria on 24 Phaophi, i.e. 21 October 346 (Festal Index 18), the interview at Antioch presumably occurred in the summer of that year. The first two meetings should precede Athanasius' second sojourn in the West (339–346). But do they both (as Seeck and Baynes thought)[78] precede his restoration? And, given that Athanasius entered Alexandria on 27 Athyr, i.e. 23 November (Festal Index 10), was the year of his return 337 or 338? These questions can only be answered when the full range of available evidence is taken into account.

For the date of Athanasius' return, the decisive fact (neglected by both Seeck and Baynes, and not stressed sufficiently even by Schwartz) is the visit of the monk Antonius to Alexandria. He came in the month of Mesore, which corresponds to parts of July and August (Festal Index 10), and when he departed, Athanasius escorted him to the city-gate (*Vita Antonii* 71). Now Athanasius was expelled from his see on 18 March 339 (Festal Index 11): therefore, unless he has lied outright about his meeting Antonius, it follows that he had returned to Alexandria on 23 November 337.[79] The meeting at Viminacium, therefore, belongs to the summer or early autumn of 337. In June 337, Athanasius was still in Trier (*Apol. sec.* 87.4-7: 17 June), while Constantius was in Constantinople (Eusebius, *VC* 4.70; Libanius, *Orat.* 59.74; *Chr. min.* 1.236). Constantius subsequently conferred with his brothers in Pannonia (Julian, *Orat.* 1,19A, cf. Libanius, *Orat.* 59.75), and all three were proclaimed Augusti on 9 September (*Chr. min.* 1.236), it is uncertain whether before, during or after the conference. Constantius' attested presence on the Danube in 337 thus provides the occasion for his first interview with Athanasius.

The meeting at Caesarea can hardly belong to the same year, especially since an inscription from Troesmis appears to show that Constantius and Constans waged a campaign against the Sarmatians in 337 (*ILS* 724).[80] But it will fit perfectly into the secular history of 338, when Constantius went to Cappadocia to instal Arsaces on the throne of Armenia (Julian, *Orat.* 1,20-21).[81] The occasion of the interview can perhaps be identified precisely. In the winter of 337/8 bishops opposed to Athanasius met at Antioch, presumably as a formally constituted council, and submitted to Constantius a document which accused Athanasius of murder and probably of treason (*Apol. sec.* 3.5-7).

Athanasius (it may be deduced) was immediately summoned to appear before the emperor to answer these secular charges, for he penned his Easter Letter of 338 far from the city of Alexandria (Festal Letter 10.1 ff.).[82]

X. The First Exile of Paul of Constantinople

The date of Athanasius' first return from exile is highly relevant to the chronology of the first bishops of Constantinople.[83] For Athanasius was present when Macedonius accused Paul before the latter was deposed and exiled for the first time by Constantius (*Hist. Ar.* 7.1-3). Paul, therefore, occupied the see of Constantinople in the late summer or early autumn of 337. The dates at which this first tenure began and ended can be established within narrow limits.

The first bishop of Constantinople was Alexander, who served for twenty-three years (Socrates, *HE* 2.6.1). Confusion has been caused by the fact that Paul attended the Council of Tyre in 335 and signed the deposition of Athanasius (*CSEL* 65.57.20/21). Schwartz hastily inferred that Paul was certainly bishop in 335, and had acceded to the see as early as 332.[84] That cannot be: Paul must have acted as Alexander's representative at Tyre, while still a priest,[85] since Alexander was alive in 336 when Constantine attempted to make him admit Arius into communion, only to be frustrated by Arius' sudden death (Athanasius, *Ep. ad Serapionem/De Morte Arii* 2/3).[86] Hence there is no positive reason to disbelieve Socrates (*HE* 2.6) and Sozomenus (*HE* 3.3), both presumably following Gelasius of Caesarea, when they place Alexander's death later than that of Constantine, i.e. after 22 May 337. The date of Paul's deposition can be deduced from the *Contra Marcellum*, where Eusebius of Caesarea states that 'very many distinguished provinces and cities' have laid claim to the services of Eusebius of Nicomedia as their bishop (*C. Marc.* 1.4.20). Since Eusebius, who replaced Paul, was only ever bishop of three cities (Berytus, Nicomedia and Constantinople), that implies that he had already been translated from Nicomedia to Constantinople before Eusebius of Caesarea wrote. Hence, since the *Contra Marcellum* appears to belong to 337, Eusebius became bishop of Constantinople in 337.

The evidence so far discussed can be combined with the narrative of an ecclesiastical historian to establish a still more precise date. Socrates reports that the emperor Constantius arrived in Constantinople shortly after Paul's election as bishop, convened the council which deposed him, installed Eusebius as his successor, and then proceeded to Antioch (*HE* 2.7). From this sequence of events, it seems clear that Paul became bishop while Constantius was in the Balkans in the summer of 337 and was deposed on his return. Moreover, Socrates' account implies that Constantius returned to Syria for the winter of 337/8—a fact apparently otherwise unattested.

The dates of the first three bishops of Constantinople are thus as follows:

Alexander	314–*c*. July 337
Paul	*c*. July–*c*. October 337
Eusebius	*c*. October 337–autumn 341.

XI. The Date of the Council of Serdica

The letter of the eastern bishops at the Council of Serdica states that Asclepas of Gaza was deposed from his see seventeen years before (*CSEL* 65.56.19-21), which presumably means sixteen years on the conventional modern method of computing temporal intervals.[87] Hence the date of the Council of Serdica has a clear relevance to the chronology of ecclesiastical politics under Constantine. It is also highly controversial.

Both Socrates (*HE* 2.20.4) and Sozomenus (*HE* 3.12.7) give the consular date of 347 for the council. But it has long been recognized that it cannot have met earlier than autumn 342 or later than winter 343/4.[88] The date of Socrates and Sozomenus is disproved by better evidence: the *Historia Acephala* dates Athanasius' restoration from exile to 21 October 346 (*EOMIA* 1.663), and the index and headings to Athanasius' Easter Letters record three Easters between the council and Athanasius' return to Egypt (viz. 344, 345, 346). On the other side, the council was convened after negotiations between Constantius and Constans which began when Athanasius had already been in exile for more than three full years (*Apol. ad Constantium* 4). Since Athanasius was expelled from the bishop's palace in Alexandria on 18 March 339 (Festal Index 11), the negotiations cannot have begun before spring 342. But to decide whether the Council of Serdica assembled in autumn 342 or autumn 343 is not entirely easy.

The index to Athanasius' Easter Letters puts the council in the consular year 343, and this date was accepted by all scholars of the late nineteenth century. Schwartz, however, argued for 342, and reiterated this opinion when E. Loofs and O. Seeck challenged his initial arguments and restated a case for the previously accepted date of 343.[89] Both dates have subsequently found advocates.[90] Moreover, even though V.C. De Clercq carefully marshalled the general historical arguments in favour of 343,[91] a recent study of Paschal cycles by M. Richard advanced some novel arguments for 342,[92] which W. Schneemelcher has hailed as the definitive proof of the earlier date.[93] It is necessary, therefore, to restate the main arguments in favour of 343, which have lost none of their cogency.[94]

Athanasius states that, before the Council of Serdica met, the emperor Constans summoned him to court twice, first in Milan and later to Trier, whence he travelled with Ossius to Serdica (*Apol. ad Constantium* 4). The first imperial summons came in Athanasius' fourth year of exile, and hence can be no earlier than spring 342.[95] Although Constans had already written to Constantius proposing a council, time must be allowed for Constantius' reply and the journeys of Athanasius before the council actually convened.[96] After the council, the western bishops sent a delegation to Constantius, with a letter from Constans, to ask him to restore the banished bishops. The delegation arrived in Antioch shortly before Easter, and some time later Constantius wrote to Alexandria—less than ten months before the Arian bishop Gregorius died (Athanasius, *Hist. Ar.* 20-21). Since Gregorius died on 26 June 345,[97] the Easter in question must be that of 344, and the bishops will have seen Constantius in the spring of 344. Hence a date of 342 for the Council of Serdica entails two serious difficulties which a date of 343 avoids. First, the movements of Constans in 342 become incredible: after defeating the Franks (*Chr. min.* 1.236; Socrates, *HE* 2.13.4), he must rush to Milan, and then return abruptly to Trier—all before autumn, and that in a year when a law purports to be issued from Milan on 4 December (*CTh* 9.7.3). Second, an interval of more than a year must be postulated between the council and the arrival in Antioch of a delegation asking Constantius to enforce its decisions. Admittedly, Richard accepts this corollary of the earlier date, and urges that the absence of Constans in Britain for several months in 343 accounts for at least part of the delay.[98] But Constans had returned to Gaul by 30 June 343 (*CTh* 12.1.36), so that an unexplained delay of several months still remains.

A second argument, equally powerful, concerns the date of Easter. The subject was discussed at Serdica and the western council adopted a table covering fifty years to ensure that the churches of Rome and Alexandria henceforth celebrated Easter on the same day (Festal Index 15). But in 343 Rome celebrated Easter on 3 April (*Chr. min.* 1.63), Alexandria on 1 Pharmouthi, i.e. 27 March (Festal Index 15). Admittedly, Schwartz retained 342 as the date of the council by attributing the divergence to the fact that Athanasius was unable to notify the Alexandrian church of the correct date.[99] But it is precisely the index to Athanasius' Easter Letters which attests the date of 27 March, and this document should surely give the date at which Athanasius instructed the church of Alexandria to celebrate Easter—whether or not his instructions were observed in Egypt. And if the index shows that Athanasius proposed to celebrate Easter in 343 at a date contrary to the decisions at Serdica, then either Athanasius disregarded the decisions of the council (which is impossible) or the council had not yet met.

The Council of Serdica, therefore, assembled in the autumn of 343, and the following approximate chronology for the movements of emperors Constantius and Constans and for ecclesiastical history should be adopted:

342	spring or summer	Constans finishes his campaign against the Franci	*Chr. min.* 1.236; Socrates, *HE* 2.13.4
	summer or autumn	Constans writes to Constantius proposing a council and summons Athanasius to Milan	Athanasius, *Apol. ad Constantium* 4
	December 4	Constans still in Milan	*CTh* 9.7.3
343	January 25	Constans at Bononia	*CTh* 11.16.5; cf. *CJ* 3.26.6
	February	Constans crosses to Britain	Firmicus Maternus, *De errore profanarum religionum* 28.6;[100]

		Libanius, *Orat*. 59.139; Ammianus 20.1.1
June 30	Constans at Trier	*CTh* 12.1.36
summer/autumn	Constans summons Athanasius and Ossius to Trier and sends them to Serdica	Athanasius, *Apol. ad Constantium* 4
autumn	Constantius defeats the Persians in battle	Athanasius, *Hist. Ar.* 16.2
c. Nov.	The Council of Serdica convenes	
	The Council receives a letter from Constantius announcing a triumph over the Persians	Athanasius, *Hist. Ar.* 16.2
344 *c*. Jan.	The opposing parties leave Serdica	
April	The embassy of the western bishops reaches Antioch	Athanasius, *Hist. Ar.* 20.2
April 15	Athanasius celebrates Easter at Naissus	Festal Index 16

XII. Conclusion

The ecclesiastical policy of Constantine has frequently been studied and analysed in general terms. Yet most writers on the subject appear to have been more interested in speculation about the personality and religious beliefs of Constantine himself than in the pedestrian and often difficult task of reconstructing the course of events from evidence which is often unsatisfactory or insufficient. As a result, no one has yet produced a detailed and convincing narrative of Constantine's dealings with the Christian Church after 324 which does full justice to the primary evidence. The present article has investigated precise dates and disputed facts: if its solutions to a series of discrete problems are valid, then a synthesis may become possible. But any general conclusions about Constantine's policy and relations with the Christian church must await the combination of the separately established details into a coherent whole.

University of Toronto

NOTES

*A first draft of the present article was composed during a year's sabbatical leave in 1976/7, which I spent at the Institute for Advanced Study in Princeton as the recipient of a Leave Fellowship from the American Council of Learned Societies. That draft has been read and greatly improved by Harold Drake and John Rist; and it was Melissa Hardy who first suggested to me the reconstructions argued in Sections VI and X.

The following special abbreviations are used:

> EOMIA   C.H. Turner, *Ecclesiae Occidentalis Monumenta Iuris Antiquissima* (1899–1939)

> Festal Index Introduction to Athanasius' Easter Letters, preserved only in Syriac, which I cannot read. For translations into German, Latin and English, see F. Larsow, *Die Fest-Briefe des Heiligen Athanasius Bischofs von Alexandria* (1852) 25-46; *PG* 26, 1351-1360; J. Payne Smith, in A. Robertson, *Select writings and letters of Athanasius, Bishop of Alexandria* (*Nicene and Post-Nicene Fathers*[2] 4 (1892)) 503-506. A retroversion into Greek of much of the text is given in an unsystematic fashion by E. Schwartz, *Ges. Schr.* 3 (1959), esp. 5-26; 257

> Urkunden   H.-G. Opitz, *Urkunden zur Geschichte des arianischen Streites* (*Athanasius Werke* 3.1 (1934))

1.   See the list of thirteen 'legends and uncertain stories' in Rufinus drawn up by H.M. Gwatkin, *Studies of Arianism*[2] (1900) 97 ff.

2.   F. Winkelmann, *Forschungen und Fortschritte* 38 (1964) 311 ff.; *Untersuchungen zur Kirchengeschichte des Gelasios von Kaisareia* (*Sb. Berlin, Klasse für Sprachen, Literatur und Kunst* 1965, Nr. 3); *Byzantinoslavica* 27 (1966) 104 ff.; *Polychordia. Festschrift F. Dölger zum 75. Geburtstag* 1 (*ByzF* 1 (1966)) 346 ff.

3.   The preface, which may have been written last, alluded to the death of Cyril of Jerusalem (Theodore Lector p. 158.1-3 Hansen; Photius, *Bibliotheca* 89), which occurred on 18 March 386, or possibly 387 (Jerome, *De Viris Illustribus* 112, cf. P. Nautin, *RHE* 56 (1961) 35). On the other side, by spring 395 Gelasius himself was dead, since Johannes is attested as bishop of Caesarea (Marcus, *Vita Porphyrii* 14 ff.), and also in 395 Ambrose of Milan appears to show knowledge of his history when he alludes to Helena's discovery of the true cross (*De obitu Theodosii* 41 ff., cf. Rufinus, *HE* 10.7; Socrates, *HE* 1.17.1 ff.; Sozomenus, *HE* 2.1.2 ff.; Theodoretus, *HE* 1.18).

4.   On Gelasius' intentions, see F. Winkelmann, *ByzF* 1 (1966) 356 ff.; T.D. Barnes, *AJP* 97 (1976) 384 f.; *The sources of the Historia Augusta* (Collection Latomus 155 (1978)) 117.

5.   Superbly edited by J. Bidez (*GCS* 21 (1913); second edition revised, and with additions, by F. Winkelmann, 1972).

6.   H.-G. Opitz, *Urkunden* (1934), collected and edited thirty-four documents (down to 327/8, with two of 333). My researches have been greatly aided by the kindness of Professor W. Schneemelcher, who has most generously supplied me with a numbered list of the Constantinian documents which he will include in his forthcoming continuation of Opitz's work.

7.   Athanasius was accused of systematic forgery by O. Seeck, *ZKG* 30 (1909) 399 ff.; for a survey of attempts to impugn the documents in Eusebius' *Life of Constantine*, see F. Winkelmann, *Klio* 40 (1962) 197 ff.

8. As Constantine's letters are in H. Dörries, *Das Selbstzeugnis Kaiser Konstantins (Abh. Göttingen*, Phil.-hist. Klasse³ 34 (1954)) 55 ff. One certainly fabricated document is the dialogue between a philosopher named Phaedo and the bishops at Nicaea reproduced by Gelasius of Cyzicus, *HE* 2.14-24, cf. M. Jugie, *Échos d'Orient* 24 (1925) 403 ff.

9. For examples, see N.H. Baynes, *JEA* 11 (1925) 61 ff.; F. Scheidweiler, *ByzZ* 47 (1954) 90 ff.

10. H.I. Bell, *Jews and Christians in Egypt* (1924) 47 ff. Not all subsequent scholars or works of reference have noted the perceptive discussion of these two letters by K. Holl, *Sb. Berlin*, Phil.-hist. Kl. 1925, 18 ff., reprinted in his *Gesammelte Aufsätze zur Kirchengeschichte* 2 (1928) 283 ff.

11. The introduction and headings name consuls and governors of Egypt, offer precise dates and record some otherwise unattested events: on the provenance of this material, see E. Schwartz, *Ges. Schr.* 3.4 ff.; 4 (1960) 9 ff.

12. Thus Sozomenus alludes to and summarizes the official proceedings of the Council of Tyre in 335 (*HE* 2.25, esp. 11; 16/17). Sozomenus' immediate source is normally identified as a lost collection of documents compiled by the Arian Sabinus c. 375, cf. P. Batiffol, *ByzZ* 7 (1898) 265 ff. W.-D. Hauschild, *VChr* 24 (1970) 117, challenges this view, but proposes no alternative explanation of Sozomenus' knowledge.

13. The most helpful and acute recent discussion is by F. Millar, *The Emperor in the Roman world (31 B.C.–A.D. 337)* (1977) 590 ff.

14. Originally published in *Gott. Nach.*, Phil.-hist. Kl. 1904–1911, and largely reprinted in his *Ges. Schr.* 3 (1959): the one paper completely omitted there is included in H. Kraft (ed.), *Konstantin der Grosse* (Wege der Forschung 131 (1974)) 109 ff.

15. Socrates, *HE* 1.7.1; Sozomenus, *HE* 1.16.5 provide the name which corresponds to Eusebius' periphrasis.

16. For proof that Ossius presided, H. Chadwick, *JTS*, N.S. 9 (1958) 292 ff. The authenticity of this synodical letter continues to be called into question by some scholars unwilling to abandon the traditional picture of Nicaea which it disproves: I. Ortiz de Urbina, *Histoire des conciles oecuméniques* I: *Nicée et Constantinople* (1963) 43; D.H. Holland, *ZKG* 81 (1970) 163 ff.

17. To the best of my knowledge, no one has challenged the date for the letter argued by O. Seeck, *ZKG* 17 (1896) 328 ff.; *Regesten der Kaiser und Päpste für die Jahre 311 bis 476 n. Chr.* (1919) 152; 174 (late September or early October); H.-G. Opitz, *Athanasius Werke* 3.1 (1934) 32; 76 (October); *ZNTW* 33 (1934) 151 (last quarter of 324). Nothing (it seems) can be built on the statement of Gelasius of Cyzicus that Constantine summoned the Council of Nicaea after reigning fifteen years and six months, i.e., c. January 322 (*HE* 2.5.1; 37.28).

18. E.C. Richardson, *Eusebius: Church history, life of Constantine the Great and oration in praise of Constantine* (Nicene and Post-Nicene Fathers² 1 (1890)) 518.

19. A.H.M. Jones, *Constantine and the conversion of Europe* (1949) 145 f.

20. The visit of Constantine is, however, dismissed as fictitious by G. Downey, *A history of Antioch in Syria* (1961) 651.

21. P. Bruun, *RIC* 7 (1966) 77; 664; T.D. Barnes, *Phoenix* 28 (1974) 230. Strictly, the legend *Adventus Augusti n.* proves only that whoever authorised the minting of such coins expected Constantine soon to visit Antioch.

22. For the date, *AJP* 96 (1975) 182; 184.

23. As transmitted, the law is addressed *ad Silvium Paulum mag' Italiae* and the subscription reads *dat. V K. Mart. Nicom(ediae) Paulino et Iuliano consul.* But until c. 1 May 325 the ordinary consuls were (?Valerius) Proculus and Sex. Anicius Paulinus

72

(P. Oxy. 3125; CTh 2.25.1 = CJ 3.38.11; Chr. min. 3.380, cf. P. Oxy. 889 as conjecturally restored in ZPE 21 (1976) 280). In April or May, Proculus suffered *damnatio memoriae* and was replaced as consul by Julius Julianus (P. Strasbourg 137, 138 = Sammelbuch 8019, 8020).

24.   The erroneous date of 20 May often given (e.g. Seeck, Regesten (1919) 175) is deduced from a passage where Socrates (HE 1.13.13) has clearly misreported the day on which the creed was adopted ('a.d. XIII Kal. Iul.') as 'a.d. XIII Kal. Iun'. (Schwartz, Ges. Schr. 3.81).

25.   John Chrysostom, De beato Philogonio (PG 47.747-756), cf. Theodoretus, HE 1.7.10.

26.   E.g., recently, R.M. Grant, JR 54 (1974) 5; W. Ullmann, JEH 27 (1976) 10 ff.

27.   E. Schwartz, Kaiser Constantin und die christliche Kirche² (1936) 127.

28.   K.M. Girardet, Kaisergericht und Bischofsgericht. Studien zu den Anfängen des Donatistenstreites (313–315) und zum Prozess des Athanasius von Alexandrien (328–346) (Antiquitas 1.21 (1975)), esp. 43 ff.

29.   Optatus, App. 5, p. 209.23-25 Ziwsa (314); Rufinus, HE 10.5, p. 965.6-9 Mommsen = Gelasius, HE 2.27.10 (325).

30.   The text describes the speaker as ὁ τοῦ δεξίου τάγματος πρωτεύων, and the index and chapter-headings name him as 'Eusebius the bishop' (VC 3.11). The description and the fact that Eusebius of Caesarea had been excommunicated by the council at Antioch in spring 325 (Urkunden 18.14) establish his identity as Eusebius of Nicomedia. Sozomenus mistakenly identifies the speaker as Eusebius of Caesarea (HE 1.19.2). Theodoretus as Eustathius of Antioch (HE 1.7.10)—presumably confusing the opening ceremony with the subsequent debate, in which Eustathius played a prominent part (Athanasius, Hist. Arian. 4.1; Theodoretus, Epp. 151 (PG 83.1440); Facundus of Hermiane, Pro defensione trium capitulorum 8.1; 11.1 (PL 67.711; 795)).

31.   P. Batiffol, La paix constantinienne et le catholicisme (1914) 331 ff.

32.   H. Gelzer, H. Hilgenfeld and O. Cuntz, Patrum Nicaenorum nomina (1898) li f.; lx.

33.   For a more detailed proof, see P. Batiffol, Études de liturgie et d'archéologie chrétienne (1919) 84 ff. The analysis offered by F. Dvornik, DOP 6 (1951) 3 ff., proceeds from the strange premiss that the emperor was not a member of the Roman Senate.

34.   M.J. Routh, Reliquiae Sacrae IV² (1846) 259: 'residentibus etiam et sex presbyteris, adstantibus diaconibus et omni plebe, episcopi dixerunt. . . .'

35.   O. Seeck, ZKG 10 (1889) 507 ff.; S. Calderone, Costantino ed il cattolicesimo 1 (1962) 293.

36.   I offer my own translation of L. Parmentier's text (GCS 19 (1911), revised by F. Scheidweiler, GCS 44 (1954)), annotating only a few of the most problematical phrases.

37.   I take προύβαλλετο (but not the rest of the clause) in the same sense as Cassiodorus-Epiphanius, Historia ecclesiastica tripartita 2.6.2: 'aperta quidem inpudentia Eusebii scripturam protulit blasphemiae.'

38.   τῶν προεδριῶν κρατήσαντες: which might mean 'having retained their episcopal sees' (so B. Jackson, Nicene and Post-Nicene Fathers² 3 (1892) 44).

39.   διαφόροις ἐπιβουλεύοντες τοῖς ἐλέγχοις: I take ἔλεγχος here in the sense ὁ ἐλέγξας for which LSJ, Supp. 52 cites a metrical epitaph from Olympus in Lycia (TAM 2.3.991).

40.   ἐκκλίνουσι τοὺς ἐφόρους—an exceedingly difficult phrase. I cannot see how, in the context, the verb can have the more normal sense of 'avoid'.

41.   Theodoretus quotes Eustathius several times in his *Eranistes* ἐκ τοῦ λόγου εἰς τό· κύριος ἔκτισέ με ἀρχὴν ὁδῶν αὐτοῦ: whence fragments 18-31 in the collection of M. Spanneut, *Recherches sur les écrits d'Eustathe d'Antioche* (1948) 101, ff.

42.   Most fully, R.V. Sellers, *Eustathius of Antioch* (1928) 24 ff.; J.N.D. Kelly, *Early Christian creeds*[3] (1972) 211 ff.; G.C. Stead, *JTS*, N.S. 24 (1973) 92 ff.

43.   On the interpretation of Eusebius' letter to the church of Caesarea, see esp. Kelly, o.c. 220 ff. The creed adopted officially at Nicaea was not (as has often been held) based on the document produced by Eusebius. Cf. H. Lietzmann, *ZNTW* 24 (1925) 196 ff.; Kelly, o.c. 217 ff.

44.   A. Lichtenstein, *Eusebius von Nikomedien* (1903) 27 ff.; Stead, o.c. 100, identifying the document as his extant letter to Paulinus (*Urkunden* 8).

45.   A.H.M. Jones, *Constantine and the conversion of Europe* (1949) 159.

46.   For the texts, F. Schulthess, *Die syrischen Kanones der Synoden von Nicaea bis Chalcedon* (*Abh. Göttingen*, Phil.-hist. Klasse N.F. 10.2 (1908)) 66-85; *EOMIA* 2.216-320.

47.   P. and H. Ballerini, *Leonis Opera* 3 (Venice, 1757) XXV ff., reprinted in *PL* 56.35 ff.; Schwartz, *Ges. Schr.* 3.216 ff.

48.   H. Chadwick, *JTS* 49 (1948) 27 ff.

49.   On the date of Serdica, see Section XI. The narrative sources again discredit themselves by placing the deposition of Eustathius after the restoration of Eusebius of Nicomedia and Theognis of Nicaea (winter 327/8) or even asserting that they attended the council which deposed him (Socrates, *HE* 1.24-25; Sozomenus, *HE* 2.16-19; Theodoretus, *HE* 1.21; Gelasius, *HE* 3.16).

50.   E. Honigmann, *Patristic studies* (*Studi e Testi* 173 (1953)) 366 f.

51.   O. Seeck. *Geschichte des Untergangs der antiken Welt* 3 (1909) 560; Schwartz, *Ges. Schr.* 3.205 ff.; G. Loeschke, *RhM* N.F. 61 (1905) 47 f.; H.-G. Opitz, *ZNTW* 33 (1934) 155 f.; A. Piganiol, *L'empire chrétien* (1947) 41; F. Winkelmann, in his edition of Eusebius, *Vita Constantini* (1975), p. 94.

52.   G. Bardy, *RSR* 8 (1928) 522 ff.; J.-M. Szymasiuk, *Athanase d'Alexandrie* (*Sources chrétiennes* 56 (1958)) 169 ff. . For arguments that *Urkunden* 31 is inauthentic, see Rogala, *Die Anfänge des arianischen Streites* (*Forschungen zur christlichen Literatur- und Dogmengeschichte* 7 (1907)) 77 ff.; G. Bardy, *Recherches de Science religieuse* 23 (1933) 430 ff.

53.   As demonstrated definitively by K. Müller, *ZNTW* 25 (1925) 290 ff.

54.   As transmitted, the text reads as follows: ἀλλ' ἐν τῇ συνόδῳ τῇ κατὰ Νικαίαν ἡ μὲν αἵρεσις ἀνεθεματίσθη καὶ οἱ Ἀρειανοὶ ἐξεβλήθησαν, οἱ δὲ Μελιτιανοὶ ὁπωσδήποτε ἐδέχθησαν· οὐ γὰρ ἀναγκαῖον νῦν τὴν αἰτίαν ὀνομάζειν. οὔπω γὰρ πέντε μῆνες παρῆλθον, καὶ ὁ μὲν μακαρίτης Ἀλέξανδρος τετελεύτηκεν, οἱ δὲ Μελιτιανοὶ πάλιν τὰς ἐκκλησίας ἐτάραττον. Either there is a lacuna or Athanasius has deliberately conflated two distinct episodes, which belong, respectively, to summer 325 and winter 327/8.

55.   Contrast similar documents of 335, e.g. *P. Oxy.* 1206: ὑπατείας Ἰουλίου Κωνσταντίου πατρικίου ἀδελφοῦ τοῦ δεσπότου ἡμῶν Κωνσταντίνου Αὐγούστου καὶ Ῥουφίου Ἀλβίνου τῶν λαμπροτάτων.

56.   Millar, *Emperor* (1977) 602 n. 71, appears by implication to doubt the title.

57.   Schwartz, *Ges. Schr.* 3.197 ff. He argued that Constantine summoned the Council of Caesarea, after the abortive 'Council of Antioch', as early as February or March 333 (ib. 200 n. 1).

58.   H.G. Opitz, *Athanasius Werke* 2 (1935) 144 f.

59.   Thus, recently, W.H.C. Frend. *JRS* 67 (1977) 206: 'Athanasius was tried before the emperor's representative, Count Dionysius, and condemned.'

60. G.R. Sievers, *Zeitschrift für historische Theologie* 38 (1868) 98—whence, recently, F. Millar, *Emperor* (1977) 603: 'he set out for Trier probably on 5 February 336.'

61. P. Peeters, *BAB* s.5, 30 (1944) 131 ff.; *AB* 63 (1945) 131 ff.

62. K.M. Girardet, *Kaisergericht und Bischofsgericht* (1975) 66 f.; H.A. Drake, *Historia* 24 (1975) 345 ff.

63. Peeters, o.c. (1944) 156 ff. That Athanasius fled under cover of darkness could be inferred, even were it not attested by Epiphanius, *Pan.* 68.9.4.

64. Observe, however, that the governor who received the law is otherwise unknown, and that P. Krüger, ad loc., emended 'd(ata) X k. Nov.' to 'p(roposita) X k. Nov.', thus removing the implication that Constantine was at Nicopolis.

65. Gelasius has often been accused of adding those phrases in this letter of Constantine which are absent from the version quoted by Athanasius, *Apol. sec.* 86.2-12 (e.g., by H.G. Opitz, *Athanasius Werke* 2 (1935) 164). It is much more likely that Athanasius has removed those parts of the letter which depict most vividly his pitiable and desperate condition in 335, cf. N.H. Baynes, *JEA* 11 (1925) 61 ff.—and Gelasius alone has the transliteration of a Latin technical term for an imperial progress (*HE* 3.18.4: εἰσιόντι μοι ἀπὸ προκέσσου).

66. Note *Apol. sec.* 87.2: ἀντὶ τῆς ἀκροάσεως εἰς τὰς Γαλλίας ἡμᾶς ἀπέστειλεν. It is totally impossible to construe Athanasius' exile as 'die Vollstreckung des tyrischen Urteils' (Girardet, o.c. 73).

67. Constantine tells the bishops that they must show him that their decisions were not motivated by any favour or enmity, that their decision is pure and uncorrupt (Athanasius, *Apol. sec.* 86.3,10 = Gelasius, *HE* 3.18.3, 9).

68. See Drake, o.c. 348 ff. (and the writers cited there).

69. E. Schwartz, *RE* 6 (1909) 1421 (this part of the volume was published in 1907); *Ges. Schr.* 3.237 (originally published in 1911).

70. W. Schneemelcher, *TLZ* 79 (1954) 397 ff.

71. G. Bardy, *Histoire de l'Église*, ed. A. Fliche and V. Martin, 3 (1936) 101 ff.

72. Schwartz, *Ges. Schr.* 3.234 ff., declined the inference, arguing that Sozomenus here deserts his documentary source.

73. J. Quasten, *Patrology* 3 (1960) 341.

74. As appears to be realised by G. Bardy, *RSR* 2 (1922) 35.

75. See esp. *VC* 1.11.2; 4.48. Observe that, while in the *Life of Constantine* both epithets are freely applied to Constantine (F. Winkelmann's index registers more than twenty occurrences), neither is ever applied to him in the panegyric of 336 (*Triac.* 1-10).

76. On the date, see Drake, o.c. 345 ff.

77. A date early in 336 is excluded by the fact that Constantine went to Thessalonica (*RIC* 7.527 no. 203) and conducted a campaign north of the Danube (Festus, *Brev.* 26; Julian, *Caes.* 329 B-D; *AE* 1934.158, cf. *ZPE* 20 (1976) 152).

78. Seeck, *Regesten* (1919) 186; N.H. Baynes, *JEA* 11 (1925) 65 ff. Both date Athanasius' arrival in Alexandria to 338, but Seeck dates both meetings with Constantius to 338, while Baynes dates the first to 337.

79. Schwartz, *Ges. Schr.* 3.286 f.

80. *ZPE* 20 (1976) 154.

81. On this episode, see P. Peeters, *BAB* s.5, 17 (1931) 10 ff.

82. Athanasius' appearance before Constantius at Caesarea unfortunately appears to receive no discussion in K.M. Girardet, *Kaisergericht und Bischofsgericht* (1975).

83. Among earlier discussions, note F. Fischer, *Commentationes philologae Jenenses* 3 (1894) 313 ff.; G. Dagron, *Naissance d'une capitale. Constantinople et ses institutions de 330 à 451* (1974) 419 ff.

84. Schwartz, *Ges. Schr.* 3.274. That Alexander died in August 335 has subsequently been argued by W. Telfer, *HTR* 43 (1950) 52 ff.; A. Cameron, *JTS*, n.s. 27 (1976) 128 f.

85. Compare the two priests who represented the bishop of Rome at the Council of Nicaea (H. Gelzer, H. Hilgenfeld and O. Cuntz, *Patrum Nicaenorum nomina* (1898), li f.; lx).

86. The date is deduced from two facts: Arius had only been readmitted after his second exile by the Council of Jerusalem in September 335, and Constantine was present in Constantinople when he died (Athanasius, *Ep. ad Serapionem* 2.1/2).

87. See discussion in Section IV.

88. C.J. Hefele and H. Leclercq, *Histoire des conciles* 1 (1907) 737 ff.

89. Schwartz, *Ges. Schr.* 3.11; 325 ff.; E. Loofs, *Sb. Berlin* 1908, 1013 ff.; *Theologische Studien und Kritiken* 82 (1909) 292 ff.; O. Seeck, *ZKG* 30 (1909) 404 f.; *Geschichte* 4 (1911) 416 f.

90. In favour of 342, note H.-G. Opitz, *Athanasius Werke* 2 (1935) 193; H. Chadwick, *JTS* 49 (1948) 34; W. Telfer, *HTR* 43 (1950) 91 f.; Girardet, o.c. 106 ff.; of 343, J. Zeiller, *Les origines chrétiennes dans les provinces danubiennes* (1918) 228 ff.; G. Bardy, *Histoire de l'Église* 3 (1936) 123; H. Hess, *The canons of the Council of Sardica A.D. 343* (1958) 140 ff.

91. V.C. De Clercq, *Ossius of Cordova. A contribution to the history of the Constantinian period* (1954) 313 ff.

92. M. Richard, *Le Muséon* 87 (1974) 307 ff.

93. W. Schneemelcher, *Bonner Festgabe Johannes Straub* (1977) 330 n. 42: 'Das immer wieder umstrittene Datum der Synode von Serdika ist jetzt wohl endgültig auf 342 festgestellt.'

94. For the first argument deployed here, cf. G.R. Sievers, *Zeitschrift für historische Theologie* 38 (1868) 106 ff.; Seeck, *Regesten* (1919) 190 ff.; for the second, Loofs, o.c. (1909) 295 f.

95. Girardet, o.c. 108, with appeal to Opitz's annotation on *Apol. ad Constantium* 4 (as yet unpublished), makes Athanasius' three years begin, not with his deposition or arrival in Rome in 339, but with Athanasius' letter to Constans from Alexandria in 338: hence he dates his meeting with Constans in Milan to April or May 341.

96. For what it is worth, Socrates, *HE* 2.20.6, records an interval of eighteen months between the announcement and the meeting of the council.

97. Festal Index 17 (day); Athanasius, *Apol. sec.* 51.1 ff.; *Historia Arianorum* 21.2 (year).

98. Richard, o.c. 320 ff. Athanasius asserts that the council sent the delegation on its own initiative (*Historia Arianorum* 21), but Theodoretus involves Constans in the decision (*HE* 2.8.54).

99. E. Schwartz, *Christliche und jüdische Ostertafeln* (*Abh. Göttingen,* Phil.-hist. Klasse, N.F. 8.6 (1905)) 51; 123.

100. On the chronology adopted here, it becomes possible to date Firmicus Maternus' pamphlet *De errore profanarum religionum* to 343 precisely, before Constantius could yet claim a positive victory over the Persians (29.3: *Persica vota conlapsa sunt,* cf. Athanasius, *Hist. Ar.* 16.2).

METHODIUS, MAXIMUS, AND VALENTINUS

IT is a notorious fact that a passage of more than two hundred lines appears, in identical or largely identical form, in three different works ascribed to three different authors:

(1) in Eusebius' *Praeparatio Evangelica* (vii. 22), where it is quoted as from Maximus, *On Matter*—a writer whom Eusebius elsewhere dates to the reign of Septimius Severus (*HE* v. 27.1);

(2) in the dialogue conventionally entitled 'On right belief in God' (*De recta in deum fide*), whose main interlocutor is named Adamantius and which was ascribed to Origen from the fourth century onwards (pp. 146.15–162.3);[1]

(3) in Methodius, *On Free Will* (5.1–12.8).[2]

The close similarities between the dialogue and Methodius continue beyond the point where Eusebius' quotation stops, and in both writers the passage quoted by Eusebius is preceded by another virtually identical passage of almost one hundred lines (pp. 135.25 ff. = *On Free Will* 3.1–4.5). In addition, the dialogue contains a number of very substantial similarities to Methodius' dialogue *On the Resurrection*, sometimes extending over several pages.[3]

What is the relationship between the three writers? At first sight, it might seem that Maximus should be the source of the other two.[4] But a close comparison of Eusebius' quotation with the dialogue and with Methodius shows that, whatever Eusebius intended to do, he has in fact quoted Methodius, from whom there is hardly a single significant or substantial divergence in wording over more than two hundred lines.[5]

---

[1] All references are given to the (admittedly unsatisfactory) edition of W. H. van de Sande Bakhuyzen, *G.C.S.* iv (1901). The new edition in the same series promised by V. Buchheit (*Byzantinische Zeitschrift*, li (1958), p. 314) has not yet been published. Buchheit has, however, produced a separate edition, with commentary, of Rufinus' translation alone (*Studia et Testimonia Antiqua*, i, 1966).

[2] Edited by G. N. Bonwetsch, *G.C.S.* xxvii (1917), p. 157.6–178.9.

[3] Listed by van de Sande Bakhuyzen, op. cit., pp. xxxviii f.; Bonwetsch, op. cit., p. ix.

[4] E. Salmon, *Dictionary of Christian Biography*, iii (1882), pp. 884 f. This view appears to be reasserted by K. Mras, in his edition of the *Praeparatio Evangelica*: he holds that Eusebius quotes Maximus, whom Methodius copied (*G.C.S.* xliii.1 (1954), p. 405).

[5] J. A. Robinson, *The Philocalia of Origen* (1893), pp. xl ff.; 212 ff.—though he does not adequately distinguish between the separate questions of what Eusebius quotes and how Methodius and the dialogue are related.

48

An explanation of how and why Eusebius does this must await an elucidation of the relationship between the dialogue and Methodius, but of
the fact there can be no serious doubt. Eusebius, therefore, may be disregarded in a discussion of the relationship between the other two passages. The prevailing view of this relationship derives from an article
published in 1888, in which Theodor Zahn argued that the dialogue
copies Methodius, from which he deduced the inevitable corollary that
the dialogue was written no earlier than c. 300.[1] Zahn's conclusion has
subsequently been adopted by editors, translators and commentators,
and in standard works of reference.[2] To the best of my knowledge, no
scholar has contested Zahn's arguments or his main conclusion in order
to argue that Methodius copied the dialogue. This latter view I hope, if
not to prove conclusively, at least to render more plausible and more
probable than the conventional one.

I

The dialogue *De recta in deum fide* is preserved both by several Greek
manuscripts, of which only one is earlier than the fourteenth century,[3]
and in a Latin translation made by Rufinus in 399, which survives in a
single manuscript of the twelfth century.[4] This fact is very relevant to
the date, the original title and the authorship of the dialogue.

The form of the work is a series of linked but separate conversations
in which Adamantius refutes the dualistic theories of five interlocutors.
The Greek text consistently and clearly identifies the type of heresy
which each espouses: Megethius and Marcus are Marcionites (pp. 16;
60; 96; 114; 200), Marinus is a follower of Bardesanes (p. 114), and
Droserius and Valens are Valentinians (pp. 136; 152; 154). Rufinus

[1] T. Zahn, 'Die Dialoge des "Adamantius" mit den Gnostikern', *Zeitschrift
für Kirchengeschichte*, ix (1888), pp. 193–239.

[2] Van de Sande Bakhuyzen, op. cit., p. xvi; A. Harnack, *Chronologie der
altchristlichen Litteratur bis Eusebius*, ii (1904), pp. 149 ff.; Bonwetsch, op. cit.,
p. ix; J. Farges, *Méthode d'Olympe: Du libre arbitre* (1929), p. 6; A. Vaillant,
Patrologia Orientalis, xxii (1930), p. 637; F. X. Murphy, *Rufinus of Aquileia
(345–411). His Life and Works* (1945), p. 124; J. Quasten, *Patrology*, ii (1953),
pp. 146 f.; H. Musurillo, *St. Methodius, The Symposium: A Treatise on Chastity
(Ancient Christian Writers*, xxvii, 1958), p. 3; G. Schroeder, *Eusèbe de Césarée:
La Préparation Évangelique, Livre VII (Sources chrétiennes*, cxv, 1975), p. 119;
E. Junod, *Origène, Philocalie 21–27: Sur le libre arbitre (Sources chrétiennes*,
ccxxvi, 1976), p. 67.

[3] viz. Venetus Graecus 496, probably of the twelfth century, from which all
the other manuscripts appear to derive, cf. P. Koetschau, *Theologische Literaturzeitung*, xxvi (1901), cols. 475 ff.

[4] Discovered and published by C. P. Caspari, *Kirchenhistorische Anecdota*,
i (1883), pp. 1–219, it is printed *en face* with the Greek text by van de Sande
Bakhuyzen, *G.C.S.* iv, pp. 1–243—to which references are here given.

translates accurately all except one of the passages which establish these identifications, but he also makes three additions, or glosses, external to the text of the actual dialogue, which have no parallel in the Greek: Megethius is twice described as a Manichee (pp. 3; 5) and Marcus as *Marcionis schismaticus, ut sunt Manichaei* (p. 61), where the Greek has merely Μαρκιωνιστής (p. 60). Zahn explained the contrast by the hypothesis that the Greek version, reworked under Constantine, omits the original references to Manichaeism.[1] That will not do. The whole dialogue is devoted to a problem as central to Mani as to Marcion, Valentinus, and Bardesanes: how many uncreated First Principles are there, one or more? Yet the heterodox ideas attacked are not those of Mani and his followers, but ones advanced by thinkers of the second century. The natural inference from that fact is that the dialogue was composed before Mani's ideas became familiar to the inhabitants of the Roman Empire, i.e. before the end of the third century.[2] In the three places where Rufinus refers to Manichees, he has surely glossed the original in an anachronistic fashion, precisely because he missed an allusion which he expeced the text to contain.

The relation of the Greek and Latin versions to the original appears to be different in a passage which refers to persecution. The Greek text describes persecution as a thing of the past, and expressly states that 'now the emperor is a worshipper of God' (p. 40.20)—which entails a date after 313. Rufinus' version, however, represents persecution as a contemporary phenomenon:

Meg(ethius) d(ixit): Vel ex eo quod in persecutionibus sumus semper, manifestum debet esse quod alterius dei sumus, contrarii huius qui fecit mundum et odit nos cum suo mundo. Denique sic scriptum est, quia *cor regis in manu dei est* (Proverbs 21.1), huius scilicet qui praeest huic regno et habet in manu sua cor regis et inclinat illud ad persequendum nos.

Ad(amantius) d(ixit): . . .Secundum etenim hanc rationem quam dicis omnes reges, quippe quorum cor in manu eius dei sit qui adversatur boni dei famulis et favet his qui sui sunt, deberent omnes omnino persequi Christianos, nec unquam aliud agere posteriorem liceret quam egit prior. Nunc autem videmus quod alios oderat ille qui prior fuit, et alios deligit qui nunc est . . ... Sed nec nos soli persecutionem patimur. Et prophetae eadem passi sunt . . ... Similiter autem et Christi discipuli, exempla prophetarum sequentes, persecutionum saevitiam tolerant (i. 21, p. 41.12–43.2).

Zahn argued that Rufinus here preserves the sense of the Greek original, which a reviser changed to meet the changed circumstances of

---

[1] Zahn, op. cit., pp. 213 ff.

[2] Eusebius dates the entry of Mani's ideas into the Roman Empire *c.* 280 (*Chronicle*, p. 227 Karst; *H.E.* vii. 31; Jerome, *Chronicle* 223[1] Helm).

50

Constantine's reign and a Christian emperor.[1] On the other side, V. Buchheit has contended that Rufinus, whom he brands as a notorious mistranslator, has perverted the original, whose composition must accordingly fall later than 324.[2] This latter opinion is implausible. First, it postulates a writer under Constantine who ignores all the theological issues of the late third and early fourth century in order to refute antiquated heresies which flourished in the second and third centuries. Second, it appeals to an estimate of Rufinus' capacities and honesty as a translator which has been vigorously challenged in the case of other works.[3] And third (though this is not so strong an argument), a motive for falsification of the passage is lacking, unless Rufinus be supposed deliberately to have altered the dramatic date of the original dialogue. Zahn's view of the relationship between the two passages remains by far the more probable.[4] But, if it is correct, then Zahn's date of c. 300 is too late. The passage quoted presupposes a single Roman emperor and virtually continuous persecution: that should exclude composition during the persecution which began in 303, when there were four emperors and when different emperors adopted divergent policies towards the Christians. On the natural interpretation of Rufinus' version, the allusions to the different religious policies of successive emperors suit the middle of the third century—and no other period, either earlier or later. Specifically, the successive emperors who loved and hated the Christians (apparently in that order) should be either Severus Alexander and Maximinus, or Philip and Decius.[5] Admittedly, the date of composition may be significantly later than the dramatic date of the dialogue, in which Adamantius is presumably intended to be Origen, who probably died in 253/4.[6] Nevertheless, no Christian writing much after 260 could plausibly represent persecution as a frequent contemporary phenomenon.[7]

Both its philosophical and its historical content, therefore, indicate

---

[1] Zahn, op. cit., pp. 205 ff.

[2] V. Buchheit, 'Rufinus von Aquileja als Fälscher des Adamantiosdialogs', *Byzantinische Zeitschrift*, li (1958), pp. 314–28, and in his edition (1966), pp. xxxv ff.

[3] J. M. Rist, 'The Greek and Latin texts of the discussion on free-will in *De Principiis*, Book III', *Origeniana* (*Quaderni di 'Vetera Christianorum'*, xii, 1975), pp. 97–111; H. Crouzel, 'Comparaisons précises entre les fragments du *Peri Archon* selon la *Philocalie* et la traduction du Rufin', ibid., pp. 113–121.

[4] Van de Sande Bakhuyzen conveniently prints the words which have probably been altered in smaller type (p. 40).

[5] For the changes in imperial attitude in 235 and 249, see Eusebius, *H.E.* vi. 28; 39.1; 41.9 (a letter of Dionysius of Alexandria).

[6] Eusebius, *H.E.* vi. 14.10 ('Ἀδαμάντιος (καὶ τοῦτο γὰρ ἦν τῷ Ὠριγένει ὄνομα)); vii.1 (death).

[7] Eusebius, *H.E.* vii. 13 ff.; Lactantius, *Mort. Pers.* 4–6.

that the dialogue ought to be dated long before the end of the third century.[1] Its author's name was known neither to Basil and Gregory nor to Rufinus, and it leaves no trace in the Greek manuscripts. The prologue which precedes the work in the manuscripts describes it as 'Dialogue of Adamantius, also called Origen, about right belief in God, with Megethius and Marcus, Droserius, Valens and Marinus the heretics', while an editorial note in the *Philocalia* observes that 'this passage is found word for word in Origen's dialogue with Marcionites and other heretics, where Eutropius adjudicates and Megethius opposes',[2] and Rufinus describes the work in similar words as *libri Adamantii Origenis adversus haereticos numero quinque*. The author, therefore, remains to be identified.[3] Nor does the late evidence of the manuscripts prove that the original title was 'On right belief in God'. Neither Basil and Gregory nor Rufinus seems to know what the dialogue was originally entitled: on the available evidence, the original title could have been 'Adamantius'— or even 'On Matter'.

II

The chronology of Methodius' career and works is obscure. Four facts, however, stand out. First, Methodius was alive early in the fourth century: in a work written in 310, Eusebius complained that he had recently turned against Origen, despite having praised him in the past.[4] Second, Jerome's report that Methodius was martyred 'at the end of the last persecution' should indicate that he died in 312 or 313.[5] Third, the long work *On the Resurrection*, which is overtly hostile to Origen, is later than the *Symposium*, which propounds some ideas which resemble Origen's and perhaps even derive from him.[6] Fourth, the *Symposium* belongs to a period when Christians were not being actively persecuted, and was therefore written between *c.* 260 and *c.* 300.[7]

---

[1] It may be relevant that it puts the word 'ὁμοούσιος' into Adamantius' mouth (p. 4.12): it was condemned by the council of bishops at Antioch which deposed Paul of Samosata in 268 (Athanasius, *De Synodis*, 43.1; 45.4; Hilary, *De Synodis* 81–2; Basil, *Epp.* 52.1).

[2] van de Sande Bakhuyzen, op. cit., pp. xxiii; xi.

[3] Hence the theory that the dialogue was published anonymously or pseudonymously by a disciple of Methodius (A. Vaillant, *Patrologia Orientalis*, xxii (1930), pp. 646 ff.).

[4] Jerome, *Contra Rufinum*, i. 11 (*P.L.* xxiii, col. 423): 'Eusebius . . ., in sexto libro Ἀπολογίας Origenis, hoc idem obiicit Methodio episcopo et martyri, quod tu in meis laudibus criminaris, et dicit: Quomodo ausus est Methodius nunc contra Origenem scribere, qui haec et haec de Origenis locutus est dogmatibus?'

[5] Jerome, *De Viris Illustribus*, 83.

[6] Methodius, *De cibis* 1.1 (p. 427.10 ff.), expressly states that the *Symposium* has been completed, but that he is still working at *On the Resurrection*. For discussions of Methodius' 'Origenism', see H. J. Musurillo, *St. Methodius, The Symposium* (1958), p. 180.　　　　[7] Musurillo, ibid., pp. 11 ff.; 175 f.

52

These facts suffice to render the hypothesis that the dialogue used Methodius highly improbable. First, Methodius appears, on the independent evidence, to be the later writer: in particular, the anti-Origenist *On the Resurrection* should have been completed towards the end of Methodius' life—therefore, hardly much earlier than *c.* 300. Second, it is implausible, on philosophical grounds, to suppose that the writer of the dialogue, for whom Origen is a figure of authority and deserving respect, closely copied a work devoted to attacking Origen's ideas. However, if it is Methodius' work *On the Resurrection* which copies the dialogue (not vice versa), that implies most strongly that the resemblances between the dialogue and Methodius' *On Free Will* also result from imitation by (not of) Methodius.

III

When Zahn argued that the dialogue copies Methodius, he did not undertake a close comparison of the two texts with an open mind. He argued rather from the general literary and artistic inferiority of the dialogue, and specifically that the introduction of Valentinus' doctrines in the dialogue reflects Methodius' dialogue-form in an inappropriate context.[1] A general argument of this nature should not be regarded as decisive, since some authors are capable of improving on models whom they imitate closely. Moreover, the specific comparison adduced by Zahn tends to support the opposite conclusion.

In the dialogue, a document is read (pp. 136–142), which is described as ὁ ὅρος τοῦ Οὐαλεντίνου and τὸ δόγμα Οὐαλεντίνου and designated as a quotation from Valentinus' own writings (ὀρθότατον δόγμα καὶ ὅρος ἀκλινὴς ἐκτιθεὶς ὑπὸ τοῦ σοφοῦ Οὐαλεντίνου). It begins as follows:

Οὑτωσὶ δέ πως εὖ διατεθεῖσθαι νομίζων ἐπὶ τὴν οἰκίαν ἀνεχώρουν τὴν ἐμήν· τῇ δὲ ἐπιούσῃ, τουτέστι σήμερον, ἐλθὼν ἑώρων δύο τινάς, ὁμογενεῖς ἀνθρώπους λέγω δή, διαπληκτιζομένους καὶ λοιδορουμένους ἀλλήλοις, ἕτερον πρὸς τὸν ἕτερον, τὸν δ' αὖ πάλιν ἀφιματῶσαι πειρώμενον τὸν πλησίον.   (pp. 136.25–138.4).

From the two men and their behaviour, the writer infers the existence of two gods, hostile to each other. Can this be an authentic quotation from Valentinus? Modern students of Gnosticism silently imply a negative answer by steadfastly ignoring the passage. It shows, nevertheless, a marked affinity of thought to something which Hippolytus reports: Valentinus said he saw a new-born baby which told him it was the Logos, then he added a tragic myth and thence derived his heretical

[1] Zahn, op. cit., pp. 221 ff.

ideas.[1] Similarly, the document quoted in the dialogue appeals to Greek
mythology in the course of its exposition. As for the opening words of
the quotation, they do not (as Zahn supposed) necessarily indicate derivation from a dialogue: they could come from a letter, and Valentinus
(it is known) propounded his theories in letters which, artifice or not,
read like genuine letters.[2]

In Methodius' dialogue *On Free Will*, the same passage is put into the
mouth of one of the interlocutors, whose name may be Valentinus and
who may be intended to be the heresiarch himself (3.5).[3] It occurs in
a continuous passage, but what precedes does not perhaps perfectly
explain why the speaker should have been in a good humour on the
preceding day (2.1–9). Comparison of the passages, therefore, does not
suggest that their relationship differs from that which chronological and
philosophical arguments indicate: it is Methodius who imitates the dialogue, not the dialogue which copies Methodius.

It should be observed that this conclusion does not depend on the
assumption that the quoted document is a genuine letter of Valentinus.
It requires only the hypothesis that the author of the dialogue regarded
it as such. However, if the dialogue does preserve a genuine, though
unnoticed, fragment of Valentinus, then Methodius must be the
imitator. Clearly the authenticity of the quotation merits a most careful
examination by students of Gnosticism.

IV

If the preceding arguments are valid, the dialogue conventionally known
as *De recta in deum fide* was written long before A.D. 300, probably close
to the middle of the third century. Can its author be identified? There
are three possibilities—Maximus, Methodius, and unknown author—of
which none can be completely excluded. The dialogue could conceivably be an early work of Methodius, which he later plundered when
composing *On Free Will* and *On the Resurrection*, even though it differs
greatly in style from Methodius' known writings. Alternatively, the
author may be otherwise unknown. But the third possibility is the most
attractive: that Eusebius has preserved the writer's name, even though
he misdates him by fifty years. For if *De recta in deum fide* is indeed
identical with Maximus' *On Matter*, then the cause of all the confusion

---

[1] Hippolytus, *Refutatio* vi. 42.2 = Valentinus, frag. 7 Völker.

[2] Clement, *Strom.* ii. 36.2; ii. 114.6; iii. 59.3 = frags. 1–3 Völker.

[3] The manuscripts style the speakers 'Οὐαλ.' (or 'Οὐα.' or 'Οὐ.') and ''Ορθόδ
(οξος)' (pp. 147.21; 156.14; 162 ff.). Bonwetsch expanded the contraction as
'Οὐαλεντινιανός' (in the index, p. 540). But the parallel of 'Thecla' in the
Symposium suggests that the speaker may be Valentinus himself.

54

can be elucidated. When composing the *Preparatio Evangelica*, Eusebius employed assistants to insert the quotations into the text which he dictated:[1] in this case, the assistant mistakenly inserted the passage of Methodius which so closely resembles the passage which Eusebius intended to quote—from Maximus' surviving dialogue on matter and the origin of evil.

Although it is dangerous to build hypothesis on hypothesis, this reconstruction will perhaps explain a divergence of traditions about Methodius' date and milieu which existed at least as early as 392:

Methodius, Olympi Lyciae et postea Tyri episcopus . . ... Ad extremum novissimae persecutionis, sive ut alii adfirmant, sub Decio et Valeriano, in Chalcide Graeciae martyrio coronatus est (Jerome, *De Viris Illustribus* 83).

The problem of deciding which episcopal see or sees Methodius occupied is notoriously difficult: Greek traditions independent of Jerome have Olympus and also Patara, while Tyre is often repeated from Jerome, and various items of late evidence state that Methodius was bishop of Side in Pamphylia, Myra in Lycia and Philippi in Macedonia.[2] It seems, however, that Tyre must be an error (perhaps Jerome misheard or misunderstood),[3] whereas for a bishop to move from the small town of Olympus to the important city of Patara is extremely plausible. Moreover, the setting of Methodius' dialogues, the *Symposium* and *On the Resurrection*, confirms a Lycian milieu. It may be proposed, therefore, albeit with diffidence, that Methodius was bishop of Olympus and then of Patara, and that he was executed at Patara on 20 June 312[4]—perhaps after a trial by the emperor Maximinus who may well have visited Patara during the summer of that year.[5]

The divergent tradition known to Jerome, which assigns Methodius to Greece and to the middle of the third century, may derive precisely from a confusion of Methodius with Maximus. Much commends the hypothesis that it was Maximus, the writer of the extant dialogue on

[1] K. Mras, *G.C.S.* xliii. 1 (1954), p. lviii.

[2] On the evidence and its evaluation, see especially F. Diekamp, 'Über den Bischofssitz des hl. Märtyrers und Kirchenvaters Methodius', *Theologische Quartalschrift*, cix (1928), pp. 285–308; Musurillo, op. cit., pp. 170 ff.

[3] Tyrannion was bishop for several years until his martyrdom *c.* 312 (Eusebius, *H.E.* viii. 13.3): there is, therefore, no niche for Methodius at Tyre at the appropriate time, cf. T. Zahn, *Zeitschrift für Kirchengeschichte*, viii (1886), pp. 18 ff.

[4] For the day, *Synaxarium Eccl. Cpl.*, cols. 757–8, cf. *Propylaeum ad Acta Sanctorum Decembris* (1940), p. 404.

[5] Maximinus resided in Nicomedia from summer 311 to spring 312, and was at Antioch in July or August 312 (Eusebius, *H.E.* ix. 9a.4; 6.3; 3; Malalas, p. 311 Bonn), apparently after visiting Stratonicea in Caria (*Sylloge*[3] 900).

matter and the origin of evil, who was martyred in Greece under Decius
or Valerian. His work deserves to be restored to a historical and intellectual context, from which both Eusebius and modern scholarship have
displaced it.[1]

---

[1] I am extremely grateful to my colleague John Rist for discussion of the
problems which surround Methodius and for his careful scrutiny of this attempt
to solve some of them.

XX

The Editions of Eusebius'
Ecclesiastical History

E USEBIUS PUBLISHED several editions of his *Ecclesiastical History*, and it is clearly of the highest importance for understanding the age of Constantine to establish the approximate date at which he first composed the work. Did the original design include the contemporary persecution of the Christian church which Eusebius witnessed and recorded? Or had he already completed the first edition before February 303, when Diocletian issued the first edict directed against the Christians? Most modern historians, whether of ideas, of the Roman Empire, or of Christianity, have adopted the former view: hence they present Eusebius' *Ecclesiastical History* as a manifestation of the *Zeitgeist* of the Constantinian period.[1] The present article seeks to demonstrate that Eusebius probably completed the first edition a full decade before Constantine was proclaimed emperor.

The problem of disentangling the various editions of the *Ecclesiastical History* is extremely intricate. Fortunately, the successive efforts of A. Harnack, E. Schwartz, H. J. Lawlor, and R. Laqueur have performed much valuable clarification, without which the present exposition would hardly be possible.[2] But these scholars were hampered by a secular chronology which precluded a correct dating of two of the editions of the *History*—and which reversed their order. For they dated the first war between Constantine and

[1] *E.g.*, H. Lietzmann, *Geschichte der alten Kirche* III (Berlin 1938) 154ff; C. N. Cochrane, *Christianity and Classical Culture*[2] (Oxford 1944) 183ff. Similarly, in a survey of history-writing between Constantine and Theodosius, A. Momigliano, *The Conflict between Paganism and Christianity in the Fourth Century* (Oxford 1963) 79ff, assumes that the *History* "probably appeared in a first edition about 312" (80).

[2] A. Harnack, *Chronologie der altchristlichen Litteratur bis Eusebius* II (Leipzig 1904) 111ff; E. Schwartz, *Eusebius Werke* II.3 (*GCS* IX.3, 1909) xlvii ff; H. J. Lawlor, *Eusebiana* (Oxford 1912) 243ff; H. J. Lawlor and J. E. L. Oulton, *Eusebius: The Ecclesiastical History* II (London 1928) 2ff; R. Laqueur, *Eusebius als Historiker seiner Zeit* (Leipzig 1929); *cf.* D. S. Wallace-Hadrill, *Eusebius of Caesarea* (London 1960) 39ff. The last-named dates Books One to Seven "before 303" (57), but also asserts that "Eusebius' scheme took the narrative to 303 in seven books, and in this form the work was first published" (41).

Licinius to autumn 314 and (with the exception of Harnack) the death of Diocletian to 3 December 316—from which it followed that the speech on the rebuilt basilica at Tyre, which comprises the greater part of Book Ten (10.4), was composed before October 314, while the so-called Appendix to Book Eight (8 App.), which refers to the death of Diocletian, cannot have been written before 317. But it is now clear that Diocletian died no later than 313, and in fact probably earlier (in 311/12, perhaps precisely on 3 December 311), and that the war of Cibalae must be dated to 316/7.[3] Hence, so far as concerns these historical references, the Appendix to Book Eight could have been written before the original form of Book Ten and as early as 313, while Book Ten could have been written as late at 316. Now the correct date for the war of Cibalae was first propounded by P. Bruun in 1953,[4] and five years later C. Habicht, when strengthening Bruun's arguments, adumbrated the consequences for Eusebius' *Ecclesiastical History*, though he declined to essay a complete unravelling of its various editions.[5] The present article attempts to separate and date the various editions of the *History* by combining arguments drawn from Harnack, Schwartz, Lawlor, and Laqueur (in the interests of brevity, not always acknowledged fully or in detail) with a well-founded secular chronology, in order to arrive at a better conclusion. The exposition must begin, however, by considering other works of Eusebius to which the *History* either refers or is closely related.

I

Eusebius published two editions of the *Chronicle*.[6] The second terminated with the *vicennalia* of Constantine, which were celebrated from 25 July 325 to 25 July 326 (p.34.2f, 62.3ff Karst; Jerome, *Chr.* 6.17–7.3 and 231[e,f] Helm), while the first preceded both the first edition of the *Ecclesiastical History* (*HE* 1.1.6) and the *General Elementary Introduction* (*Ecl. Proph.* 1.1, Migne, *PG* 22.1024a), and was therefore completed more than twenty years

---

[3] *JRS* 63 (1973) 32ff.

[4] P. Bruun, *The Constantinian Coinage of Arelate* (Finska Fornminnesföreningens Tidskrift 52.2 [1953]) 17ff; *Studies in Constantinian Chronology* (Numismatic Notes and Monographs 146 [1961]) 10ff.

[5] C. Habicht, *Hermes* 86 (1958) 360–78, esp. 376–78.

[6] A third edition "completed after 303 and before 311" has been imagined by D. S. Wallace-Hadrill, *JThS* n.s. 6 (1955) 250ff.

earlier. It has traditionally been held that Eusebius completed the first edition of the *Chronicle* in 303.[7] That date has no valid foundation. On the contrary, R. Helm suggested in 1923 that the elaborate synchronism of various local eras which the *Chronicle* enters under the second year of Probus (277/8), which is also the first year of the eighty-sixth Jewish Jubilee (223[h,k] Helm), marked the end of the first edition[8]—which would appear to imply composition before 303. It is unfortunate that even those who cite Helm's paper have taken scant notice of this observation. Jerome's statement that Eusebius wrote *On the Place-names in Holy Scripture* after the *Chronicle* and *Ecclesiastical History* also indicates a date earlier than 303: for, if Eusebius was engaged in compiling the gazetteer *ca* 295 (as appears probable), Jerome may be held to imply that he had completed the *Chronicle* by that date.[9] In the present context, however, it is not necessary to establish the validity of these inferences. It will suffice to observe that, since the traditional date of the first edition of the *Chronicle* is vulnerable, the fact that the *History* alludes to and presupposes the *Chronicle* need not entail that Eusebius completed the *History* after 303 rather than before.

II

Eusebius' *Martyrs of Palestine* survives in two distinct recensions, which are normally and aptly described as 'the long recension (or version)' and 'the short recension (or version)'. The two versions have suffered very different fates. The long recension is fully extant only in a Syriac translation, although some fragments of the original Greek can be disinterred from Greek hagiographical sources.[10] The short recension is preserved by four of the principal

---

[7] Harnack (*supra* n.2) 112ff; Wallace-Hadrill (*supra* n.2) 43. The last-named again gives "before 303" in the tabulation of his conclusions (57): E. Schwartz sets at least the collection of material before 303 (*RE* 6 [1907] 1376).

[8] R. Helm, *AbhBerlin* 1923.4, 42.

[9] *Onom.* p.3.1ff Klostermann; cf. *JThS* n.s. 26 (1975) 412–15.

[10] Published, respectively, by W. Cureton, *History of the Martyrs of Palestine by Eusebius, discovered in a very ancient Syriac manuscript* (London 1861), and H. Delehaye, *AnalBoll* 16 (1897) 113ff. I have used the English translation by H. J. Lawlor and J. E. L. Oulton, *Eusebius* I (London 1927) 327–400, which incorporates fragments translated from another Syriac version originally published by S. E. Assemani, *Acta Martyrum Orientalium et Occidentalium* II (Rome 1748) 169ff. B. Violet, *Die Palästinischen Märtyrer des Eusebius von Cäsarea. Ihre ausführlichere Fassung und deren Verhältnis zur Kürzeren*

Greek manuscripts of the *Ecclesiastical History*, two of which insert it between Books Eight and Nine.[11] Their textual transmissions, therefore, imply that the long recension is an independent work, while the short is intimately related to the *History*, perhaps even at some stage part of it.[12] Inspection of the contents of each version confirms the inference.

The long recension is a complete and self-sufficient work in itself, which begins with a formal preface and ends with a proper conclusion (13.11), and internal criteria indicate that Eusebius was writing in 311 precisely. For the narrative ends with martyrs of the eighth year of persecution, *i.e.*, 310/1,[13] and yet the work claims explicitly to describe "the entire time of the persecution among the people of Palestine."[14] Eusebius clearly wrote this passage in the interval between Galerius' edict of toleration, which will have become known in Palestine in May or June 311, and Maximinus' resumption of persecution in the following November.[15] Eusebius was thus writing while Maximinus still reigned, and at least one passage in the long recension refrains from insulting the emperor where the corresponding passage of the short calls him a 'tyrant' (4.8). In the long recension of the *Martyrs of Palestine*, Eusebius assumed that the persecution which had begun in 303 was at an end and he set out to record the martyrdoms of Christians in Palestine whom he knew personally (praef. 8).

Admittedly, the long recension contains some passages which, in their present form, can hardly have been written before the summer of 313, since they denounce Maximinus as an impious tyrant, "a terrible serpent and cruel tyrant" (4.1; 6.1f; 6.7; 7.7), and allude to his defeat and death (3.6f) and perhaps to the en-

---

(Texte und Untersuchungen 14.4 [1896]), prints in parallel German translations of Cureton's text and of the principal variants from Assemani and Latin and Greek fragments from printed sources.

[11] Edited by E. Schwartz, *GCS* IX.2 907ff (printing in parallel the Greek fragments of the long recension from Delehaye's edition). All four manuscripts, including two where the *Martyrs* follows Book Ten, have a note explaining that the work belongs in or after Book Eight (*GCS* IX.2 907; IX.3 xlix).

[12] J. Viteau, *De Eusebii Caesariensis duplici opusculo Περὶ τῶν ἐν Παλαιστίνῃ μαρτυρησάντων* (Diss. Paris 1893) 40ff.

[13] 13.4–10, *cf.* p.107.4–5 Violet = p.328.20–21 Lawlor and Oulton. The "years of persecution" in the *Martyrs* run from shortly before one Easter to shortly before the next Easter, beginning with Easter 303 (see G. W. Richardson, *CQ* 19 [1925] 96–100).

[14] 13.11. The Greek original presumably had ἔθνος, *i.e.*, in Eusebius' usage, "the province of Palestine."

[15] See Lawlor (*supra* n.2) 279ff.

suing purge of his supporters (7.8). But such passages are merely the result of a superficial revision. For a general contrast between the two recensions strongly confirms the inference that the longer was written in 311, while Maximinus still ruled Palestine. The short recension makes the emperor far more prominent as an active persecutor in contexts where the long recension focuses attention on and attributes responsibility to the successive governors of Palestine, particularly Urbanus, whom Maximinus executed in early 308 (*e.g.*, 8.3, 8.13, 13.10). Moreover, the following pair of variants in the long recension may document author's revision (6.5):

> when Maximin arrived at the exhibition described above, as though to reward the prowess of Urban, he increased his power to do evil (p.356.15–17 Lawlor and Oulton);
> the impious Maximin was more rabid in his wickedness than the evil Urban (p.356 app.crit. 7–8).

The long recension of the *Martyrs of Palestine*, therefore, was written by Eusebius between May and November 311, and retouched in 313 or later.[16]

The short recension of the *Martyrs of Palestine*, in contrast, does not claim to report "the entire time of the persecution," only "the martyrdoms accomplished in Palestine in eight entire years" (13.11), and it is, at least as extant in the manuscripts, incomplete at both beginning and end. It begins abruptly (praef. 1):

> It was the nineteenth year of the reign of Diocletian, the month Xanthicus, or April as the Romans would call it, in which, as the festival of the Saviour's Passion was approaching, while Flavianus was governor of the province of Palestine, a letter was all at once everywhere promulgated, ordering the razing of the churches to the ground.

No introduction, no explanation, no setting, just the start of a narrative. Similarly, at the end, after describing the end of persecution in 311 (13.11f), Eusebius introduces the edict which Galerius issued in April and promises to quote it: "The recantation also must be placed on record" (13.14). But the text breaks off with these words and thus fails to reproduce the promised document.

---

[16] If correct, this date completely undermines the attempt by T. Christensen to discredit Eusebius' picture of Maximinus as a mere repetition of the abuse normally heaped on a fallen tyrant: C. *Galerius Valerius Maximinus. Studier over Politik og Religion i Romerriget 305–313* (Copenhagen 1974) 43ff.

The peculiarities can be explained when the short recension of the *Martyrs of Palestine* is considered, not in isolation, but together with the eighth book of the *Ecclesiastical History*. The passage with which it begins (partly quoted above) and a passage in the first chapter also stand in the eighth book of the *History* with wording unchanged (praef. 1–2 = *HE* 8.2.4–5; 1.3–5 = *HE* 8.3.1–4), while the substance (though this time not the precise words) of a passage just before the end also recurs in the *History* (13.13, *cf. HE* 8.13.10–11). Moreover, the document promised in the *Martyrs* is quoted in the *History* (*HE* 8.17.3ff), and a passage in the body of the text of the *Martyrs* refers back to a passage which stands in the introduction to Book Eight of the *History* with the words "as I stated at the beginning" (12, *cf. HE* 8.2.2f).[17] It seems an inescapable inference that at some stage Eusebius intended the short recension of the *Martyrs of Palestine* to stand between the passages which now constitute the beginning and the end of Book Eight of the *Ecclesiastical History*.[18]

III

The existence of several editions of the *Ecclesiastical History* is demonstrated by variant readings and historical allusions in the text. Schwartz and H. Emonds have set out the evidence in full and discussed it thoroughly:[19] hence, for present purposes, a brief summary of the principal variants in Books Eight to Ten will suffice:

8.16.2–3. The manuscripts **A T E R** add a clause and a sentence which describe Galerius as responsible for "the whole persecution."

8.17.5. **A T E R** include the names and titles of Licinius together with the address "greetings to their provincials" in the heading to Galerius'

---

[17] Laqueur (*supra* n.2) 7ff, *cf.* Lawlor and Oulton, *Eusebius* I 395; II 9, 335. Schwartz noted the parallel but argued that Eusebius was referring to a lost prologue of the short recension of the *Martyrs* (*GCS* IX.3 l, IX.2 947).

[18] One pair of passages appears impossible to reconcile with the inference drawn here. In the *History* Eusebius appears to refer to the *Life* of Pamphilus as not yet written: Πάμφιλος ... οὗ τῶν ἀνδραγαθημάτων τὴν ἀρετὴν κατὰ τὸν δέοντα καιρὸν ἀναγράψομεν (*HE* 8.13.6). But the short recension of the *Martyrs* describes the *Life* as already completed (11.3). The difficulty can be met, either by accepting the aorist ἀνεγράψαμεν (in two manuscripts) or by the hypothesis that Eusebius refers to the account of Pamphilus in the *Martyrs*, destined to follow Book Eight as a sort of illustrative appendix (Lawlor and Oulton, *Eusebius* II 279).

[19] E. Schwartz, *GCS* IX.3 xlvii f; H. Emonds *Zweite Auflage im Altertum* (Klassisch-philologische Studien 14 [1941]) 25ff.

edict of toleration; B D M, Rufinus, and the Syriac translation omit both elements.

8.App. A E R have a passage of more than thirty lines on the deaths of Diocletian and his colleagues, which is an obvious doublet of *HE* 8.13.13–14.

9.1.1. All the manuscripts have an obvious doublet: Maximinus' instructions to governors are described twice in separate sentences in almost identical language.

9.3.1–6. Only A T E R quote the letter of Maximinus' praetorian prefect.

9.9.1. The text preserved in A T E R makes Constantine and Licinius jointly responsible for defeating "the two most impious tyrants," that attested by B D M and the Syriac translation Constantine alone.

9.9.12. Only A T E R call Licinius emperor.

9.9a.12. Only A T E R state the names of "the champions of peace and piety" as Constantine and Licinius.

9.10.3. A T E R insert Λικινίῳ, which is a clear doublet of the τῷ τότε κρατοῦντι which stands in all the manuscripts.

9.11.8 + 10.1.1. The doxology ends Book Nine in B D, where Rufinus also found it, begins Book Ten in A T E R M, and stands in both places in the Syriac translation. Further, the manuscripts which omit it in Book Nine have instead a passage which names both Constantine and Licinius as champions of the Christians.

10 Index and chapter-headings. Variants reflect the omission of 10.5–7 in some manuscripts.

10.5–7. These five imperial letters are found only in A T E R M.

10.9.4,6. The Syriac translation lacks the references to Crispus' role in the war of 324 which all the Greek manuscripts contain: it refers instead to Constantine's sons (in the plural).

How many editions are implied by these variants? And how closely can they be dated? The exposition may proceed in reverse chronological order.

The Syriac translation alone attests the deletion of any reference to the Caesar Crispus. The deletion presupposes Crispus' disgrace and execution in the spring of 326, and was presumably made by Eusebius himself. The *Life of Constantine*, for example, contains no allusion whatever to Crispus, and frequently, by implication, denies his very existence.[20] It may be excessive to regard the alteration of two passages as a new edition, but the removal of Crispus'

---

[20] E.g., *VC* 4.40.1; 51.1ff (on Constantine's three sons). The allusion in 1.48.1 is not to Crispus and Fausta, but to Maximian (Habicht [*supra* n.5] 374).

name implies that Eusebius was careful to remain up-to-date in his political opinions.

The final two chapters of Book Ten, which describe the defeat of Licinius, must have been written after the war of 324, which deposed Licinius, and before the execution of Crispus in spring 326. In the edition for which these chapters were composed, which may for convenience be designated the edition of 325, Eusebius systematically expunged the name of Licinius in Books Eight and Nine, especially from passages which presented Licinius and Constantine as joint champions of the Christian church. Hence the manuscript variants in 8.16, 8.17, 9.9–11, where the manuscripts A T E R reproduce passages in the form in which they stood before 324. It may be inferred also that, because the imperial letters in 10.5–7, described in 10.5.1 as ordinances of Constantine and Licinius, appear only in one manuscript besides A T E R, they too were removed from the edition of 325.

There was, therefore, an edition of the *History* earlier than 324 which apparently ended with the imperial documents quoted in 10.5–7, the latest of which was issued by Constantine no later than the spring of 314.[21] Now these documents are preceded by Eusebius' speech on the basilica at Tyre, rebuilt after the persecution, which alludes to plural emperors as acting in harmony to destroy the persecutors (10.4.16, 60). The speech was clearly delivered some time after Maximinus' defeat (because rebuilding has progressed far), but before Constantine and Licinius went to war in the autumn of 316. It follows that Eusebius published an edition of the *History* in ten books between 314 and 316, with the tenth book comprising his own oration at Tyre and the imperial letters contained in some, but not all, manuscripts. For convenience this edition may be styled the edition of 315.

The edition of 315 was not the only edition before that of 325. For the so-called Appendix to Book Eight, which is found in only three manuscripts, can hardly have been composed for the same edition of the *History* as Book Eight proper, since it contains a passage on the death of Constantius which reproduces a passage in Book Eight word for word (8 App. 4 = 8.13.13–14). But that the Appendix was once part of the *History* is shown by the fact that it seems to refer back to a passage in Book Eight with the words "as I have shown before" (8 App. 2, *cf.* 8.13.11). More-

---

[21] Viz., *HE* 10.5.21ff, which summons the bishop of Syracuse to the Council of Arles, due to convene on 1 August 314.

over, the alternative positions of the doxology at the end of Book Nine and the beginning of Book Ten should reflect the existence of at least two editions earlier than 324, one of which ended where the present Book Nine ends, with the doxology.

IV

Harnack, Schwartz, and Lawlor, followed by the vast majority of subsequent scholars who have written about Eusebius, believed that the first edition of the *Ecclesiastical History* comprised eight books and was not completed before 311.[22] Laqueur, however, argued for a first edition in seven books and hence for composition before 303.[23] The latter view is commended by at least five converging considerations. First, if analogy may be trusted, the opening words of Book Seven (*HE* 7 praef., Τὸν ἕβδομον τῆς ἐκκλησιαστικῆς ἱστορίας αὖθις ... Διονύσιος ἰδίαις φώναις συνεκπονήσει) imply that the seventh is the last book.[24] Second, Jerome implies that Eusebius completed the *History* before *On the Place-names in Holy Scripture*, a work which Eusebius apears to have been engaged in compiling *ca* 295.[25] Third, the narrative of the internal history of the church comes to an end *ca* 280—a fact which is completely comprehensible if Eusebius was writing in the 290s, but hard to explain if Book Seven were written *ca* 310. Fourth, the last chapter of Book Seven states that Gaius in Rome and Cyrillus in Antioch were bishops "in our day," then that they were succeeded by Marcellinus and Tyrannus, in whose tenures the persecution began (*HE* 7.32.1–4). Up to this point Eusebius has conscientiously recorded all the bishops of Rome and Antioch as part of the chronological framework of the *History* (*cf.* 1.1.3), but after this passage they are ignored.[26] It is an attractive in-

[22] Harnack (*supra* n.2) 114f; E. Schwartz, GCS IX.3 xlvii ff; Lawlor (*supra* n.2) 243ff.

[23] Laqueur (*supra* n.2) 210ff. Laqueur was prevented from solving the problems of Eusebius' later revisions by two fundamental misconceptions—that the short recension of the *Martyrs* preceded the long (26ff), and that Eusebius indulged in wholesale invention of history (97ff).

[24] R. Laqueur, *Hermes* 46 (1911) 189ff.

[25] See *supra* n.9.

[26] E. Schwartz, GCS IX.3 6ff. Miltiades, the bishop of Rome, is mentioned, but only in imperial letters quoted for another purpose (*HE* 10.5.18, 22). Observe also that Eusebius fails to correlate the accession of Theonas as bishop of Alexandria *ca* 282 with the regnal year of an emperor (*HE* 7.32.30).

ference that Book Seven was originally written while Gaius was bishop of Rome, *i.e.*, between December 282 or 283 and April 295 or 296 (*Chr.min.* 1.75), and that Eusebius later added the references to Marcellinus and Tyrannus. Finally, if Eusebius wrote the first edition before 303, then the composition of two recensions of the *Martyrs of Palestine* can easily be explained: Eusebius penned the long recension in 311 before he decided to continue his *History* to include the "Great Persecution," the short recension in 313/4 as part of that continuation. J. Viteau demonstrated long ago that the so-called Appendix to Book Eight of the *History* ought, on internal criteria, to belong to the lost ending of the short recension of the *Martyrs*.[27]

A hypothesis can now be propounded which will explain the phenomena. It cannot be proved conclusively, but it may be claimed to explain better than any alternative not only why Eusebius produced several editions of the *Ecclesiastical History*, but also why he produced two versions of the *Martyrs of Palestine*. This hypothesis may be expounded most clearly in six main steps, as follows:

(1) Eusebius composed the first edition of the *Ecclesiastical History* in the 290s, in seven books, ending almost exactly where the first edition of the *Chronicle* ended.

(2) Between May and November 311 he wrote the *Martyrs of Palestine* as an entirely independent work, whose only connexion with the *History* was psychological: Eusebius considered that as a historian of the church he had a duty to record the heroism which he had witnessed.

(3) The resumption of persecution by Maximinus in the winter of 311/2 rendered the *Martyrs*, in this form, out-of-date.

(4) When persecution ceased again in 313, Eusebius set out to integrate into a single work the existing *History*, partially revised, a shorter version of the *Martyrs* rewritten for the purpose, and an account of the last two years of Maximinus, from his failure to enforce Galerius' edict of toleration to his death (*i.e.*, Book Nine).

(5) Soon, however, Eusebius realised that the *Martyrs of Palestine*, with its personal emphasis and provincial focus, was, even in its rewritten form, unsuitable as a general account of the persecution between 303 and 311. Accordingly, he replaced it with the

---

[27] J. Viteau, *Compte rendu du Troisième Congrès Scientifique International des Catholiques*, sect. v^e (Brussels 1895) 151ff.

present Book Eight, at the same time as he added the first version of Book Ten. The date of this edition is *ca* 315.

(6) When Licinius was defeated in 324, Eusebius retouched the last three books in order to deny him any credit as a benefactor of the Christians.

The hypothesis can also be stated more schematically:

FIRST EDITION (*ca* 295). Books One to Seven, as they stand now except for the end of Seven and passages added or retouched throughout, such as (1) the reference to contemporary persecution in the preface (1.1.2); (2) the references to Pamphilus' and Eusebius' *Defence of Origen* composed in 308–310 (6.23.4, 33.4, 36.4) and to Eusebius' *Life of Pamphilus* (6.32.3); (3) the allusion to Porphyry's *Against the Christians* (6.19.2ff).[28]

SECOND EDITION (*ca* 313/4). Books One to Seven revised, plus the introduction to Book Eight, plus the short recension of the *Martyrs of Palestine*, plus Galerius' edict (8.17) followed by the Appendix to Book Eight, plus Book Nine—perhaps all arranged in eight books.[29]

THIRD EDITION (*ca* 315). Ten books, ending with the documents quoted in 10.5–7.

FOURTH EDITION (325). The present ten books, with the passages which refer to Licinius deleted or altered, and the documents in 10.5–7 removed.[30]

UNIVERSITY OF TORONTO
January, 1980

---

[28] Also 1.2.27; 1.9.3f; 1.11.9; 7.18f; 7.30, index and chapter-heading; 7.30.22; 7.32.1ff.

[29] Laqueur (*supra* n.2) 190.

[30] A version of the present paper was presented to the Eighth International Conference on Patristic Studies at Oxford in September 1979, and I am grateful to the audience on that occasion for helpful advice and comment. The implications of the chronology argued here are fully explored in *Constantine and Eusebius* (forthcoming), chapters VIII, IX, and XI.

INDEX